PLAY

74-116

animals 74-83

hevol 89-91

rituals 91-97

relg° 109-16

RELIGION IN HUMAN EVOLUTION

Religion in Human Evolution

From the Paleolithic to the Axial Age

Robert N. Bellah

THE BELKNAP PRESS OF
HARVARD UNIVERSITY PRESS

Cambridge, Massachusetts
London, England
2011

Library of Congress Cataloging-in-Publication Data

Bellah, Robert Neelly, 1927–
   Religion in human evolution : from the Paleolithic to the Axial Age / Robert N. Bellah.
      p.   cm.
   Includes bibliographical references and index.
   ISBN 978-0-674-06143-9 (alk. paper)
   1. Religion.   2. Human evolution—Religious aspects.   3. Theological anthropology.
4. Ethnology—Religious aspects.   5. Religions.   I. Title.   II. Title: From the Paleolithic
to the Axial Age.
   BL256.B435   2011
   200.89'009—dc22   2010054585

*In memory of Melanie Bellah
and for our grandchildren,
and theirs . . .*

Contents

Preface

Very deep is the well of the past.

THOMAS MANN, *Joseph and His Brothers*

Those moments which the spirit appears to have outgrown still
belong to it in the depths of its present. Just as it has passed
through all its moments in history, so also must it pass through
them again in the present.

HEGEL, *Reason in History*

When one reads the poems and the writings of the ancients,
how could it be right not to know something about them as
men? Hence one should try to understand the age in which they
have lived. This can be described as "looking for friends in
history."

MENCIUS 5B:8

This is a large book about a large subject. It is therefore incumbent on me to
give the reader an explanation of why it is so long (it could be many times longer), a road map, and a response to certain objections that may leap to the
mind of some readers. I will begin by using the three epigraphs above to give
an idea of what I am trying to do.

Mann's metaphor of the past as a well, in the opening sentence of his book,
is complemented immediately by his second sentence: "Should we not call it
bottomless?" It becomes clear in the long prologue that starts with these sentences that Mann is afraid, as he embarks on a story that reaches back into the
second millennium BCE, that he will fall ever further into the past, lose his

grip on each ledge that he reaches for in order to try to stop his fall, and instead plummet ever deeper into what appears to be bottomless. Among other things he shudders at the thought of falling below the human altogether into the deep crevasses of biological evolution. Toward the end of the prologue he becomes preoccupied with another fear: that the past is dead and that to fall into the past is to die. But just as he completes the prologue he comes to the truth that guides his enterprise: he thinks about time. "The past of life, the dead-and-gone world" is death, yet death, because it is the eternally present, is life. Thus of the past he writes, "For it *is*, always *is*, however much we may say It was."[1] Girded with the thought that the past *is*, and therefore though apparently dead is also alive, he is ready to embark on his sixteen-year project of writing a book that even in the one-volume edition is over 1,200 pages long.

Hegel, we might say, picks up Mann's metaphor of the well and uses it in a way that Mann doesn't: the well as a source that gives us living water, without which we would die. Hegel is our modern Aristotle who took the effort to think about everything and put it into time, development, and history. For Hegel, we cannot know objective spirit, what we would call culture in the deepest sense, without knowing its history, even though we may think, wrongly, that we have outgrown it. Unless we pass through all the moments of the spirit's history in our present, we will not know who we are, will not be conscious of subjective spirit—that is, of our present cultural possibilities.

Finally, Mencius suggests that in history we can find friends who, if we make the effort to understand them, can help us on our way.[2] The passage in the epigraph is preceded by the thought that a "Gentleman"—the English term used to translate the ancient Chinese term *junzi* for a man of superior social status, which Confucius had transformed into a term for a man of superior ethical quality—would seek to befriend other Gentlemen in his own village and state, and even the whole empire, but also in history itself. Mencius is reminding us that we can find friends from whom we can learn all the way into the deep past.

Eric Hobsbawm has suggested that the acceleration of cultural change in our most recent past has threatened to cut us loose from history altogether, "snapping the links between generations, that is to say, between past and present."[3] That would threaten the entire project to which I have just shown Mann, Hegel, and Mencius contributing, and call into question who we are as humans or where we want to go. No past, no future: it's that simple. One might also say, no present either. Cultural vacuum. Not likely, but even a threat of such a thing has to be taken seriously and has been countered of late by the call for deep or big history. David Christian's *Maps of Time: An Intro-duction to Big History* and Daniel Lord Smail's *On Deep History and the Brain* may be taken as signs of the time.[4] What Christian and Smail do is link us back to our history as a species, one species among many, all of which are our relatives, right back to the unicellular organisms of 3.5 billion years ago. And Christian goes even further than that, starting with the big bang of 13.5 bil-lion years ago and ending with a universe that will have decayed into a state of "featureless equilibrium" billions of years hence. Both Christian and Smail are historians, and both recognize that they are breaking rather strong taboos in their profession, rejecting the established view that history begins with texts and so is only about 5,000 years old, and that anything before that is to be left to biologists and anthropologists. I follow them, rather modestly confining my concern to one subject area, religion, though in premodern societies that is quite an inclusive category, and to our own species, with only a glance into our biological ancestry, and ending, not with the present, but with the first millennium BCE, for reasons I will explain later.

One thing that both Smail and Christian take for granted, with which I very much agree, is that history goes all the way back and any distinction be-tween history and prehistory is arbitrary. That means that biological history—that is, evolution—is part of the human story all the way through, though quite a long time ago it gave rise to culture and has coevolved with it ever since.[5] That will inevitably raise questions that I can deal with at length only in Chapter 2, which is devoted to religion in the context of human evolution, but that I must address briefly right from the start. Mann in his Prologue to *Joseph and His Brothers* was especially frightened of falling in the "bottom-less" well into the prehuman vortex of evolution. He need not have been. Even though he wrote that book from 1926 to 1942, before the great ad-vances in evolutionary theory that have occurred since the mid-twentieth century, there was still enough available for him, if he had had the time, to find that he had many friends among nonhuman organisms. It was known then, for example, that the atmosphere of the earth, with its plentiful sup-ply of oxygen, was not present in the early years of our solar system, and that it developed only because unicellular organisms in the primeval sea had discovered how to use photosynthesis to feed themselves, thus produc-ing a surplus of oxygen that, over the course of a billion years or so, created an atmosphere in which multicellular life—plants, animals, and others—could begin to inhabit the land masses that had previously been barren rocks. A little vote of thanks to these tiny microscopic creatures, without whom nothing presently existing on dry land would be here, might have been fearlessly offered.

Most worrisome to many who fear the merging of evolution and history is the belief that they are based on two incompatible methodologies: evolution is natural science, rigidly deterministic and reductionist, allowing no freedom or creativity, whereas history is a humanistic study in which human freedom is at the center, in both its marvelous creativity and its terrifying violence. Grim determinism is not missing in some forms of neo-Darwinism, might I say the fundamentalist forms, in which the subject of evolution is genes, selfish genes at that, and organisms are only vehicles at the mercy of the blind forces of selection through which genes relentlessly propagate themselves. Richard Dawkins, particularly in his widely known book *The Selfish Gene,* is the best-known proponent of this view. In that book he writes, "We are survival machines—robot vehicles blindly programmed to preserve the selfish molecules known as genes. I shall argue that a predominant quality to be expected in a successful gene is ruthless selfishness. This gene selfishness will usually give rise to selfishness in individual behavior."[6] Dawkins's views attracted widespread attention after the publication of *The Selfish Gene,* but since then other, competing views have gained ground.[7]

Most students of evolution continue to believe, contrary to Dawkins, that it is the organism that evolves, not just the genes.[8] Mary Jane West-Eberhard emphasizes the role of the organism (phenotype) in its own evolution: "I consider genes followers, not leaders, in adaptive evolution."[9] Marc Kirschner and John Gerhart, in their important book *The Plausibility of Life,* develop a conception of the organismic control of variation: "On the side of generating phenotypic variation, we believe the organism indeed participates in its own evolution, and does so with a bias related to its long history of variation and selection."[10] Of particular importance are the behavioral and symbolic aspects of evolution, which build on genetic capacities but are themselves not genetically controlled, as it is there that we will probably find most of the resources for religion—cultural developments from biological beginnings.[11] The evolutionary linguist Derek Bickerton suggests just how far back we must go to find these beginnings. Speaking of language but implicitly of culture, he writes: "The trouble with almost all previous attempts to look at origins is that they do not go back far enough. If we were to understand thoroughly all that language involved, we would probably have to go back to the birth of the lowliest animate creatures, for language depends crucially on a matrix of volition and primitive consciousness which must have begun to be laid down hundreds of millions of years ago."[12]

A very suggestive elaboration of the degree to which organisms participate in their own evolution, an important kind of behavioral evolution, has been offered by John Odling-Smee and his colleagues in their book *Niche Construction: The Neglected Process in Evolution.* Odling-Smee et al. argue that we cannot understand evolution unless we see how actively organisms create the conditions for their own evolution. Natural selection is indeed blind, yet paradoxically it leads to purposive action: "If natural selection is *blind,* yet niche construction is *semantically informed* and *goal-directed,* then evolution must comprise an entirely *purposeless* process, namely, natural selection, selecting for *purposive* organisms, namely niche-constructing organisms. This must be true at least insofar as the niche-constructing organisms that are selected by natural selection function *so as to* survive and reproduce."[13] Therefore Dawkins's argument that the unit of biological selection is the gene and that the organism is a "throwaway survival machine" is fundamentally mistaken. If the organism can learn, and that learning can change its environment and thus the survival chances of its offspring, then it is the organism, though to be sure it includes the genes (Odling-Smee et al. call it the phenogenotype), that is "the central unit" of evolution.[14]

There are a number of continuities between humans and nonhuman mammals and birds, some closely related genetically and some fairly distant, that I will discuss further in Chapter 2, but among them are empathy, including occasional empathy with members of other species, a sense of justice, and the capacity for many forms of cooperation.[15] Play, found only in mammals and birds, with perhaps a few exceptions, is a particularly significant evolutionary heritage, as we will see. All is not rosy: aggression and violence also evolve, with the particularly nasty result that humans and our nearest primate relative, the chimpanzees, deliberately kill other members of their own species.

What evolution as a whole means gets us into large issues, which almost inevitably become issues of ultimate meaning that overlap with religion. Some scientists have expressed "awe" at the immense process of evolution extending over billions of years. Whether awe moves us into another realm than science is something we will have to consider later. Even when evolution is declared meaningless, as when Dawkins writes, "The universe we observe has precisely the properties we should expect if there is, at bottom, no design, no purpose, no evil and no good, nothing but blind pitiless indifference,"[16] that is a kind of religious position: the ultimate meaning of life is that there is no meaning. Perhaps Dawkins too has moved into another sphere.

I have been trying to suggest that evolution is considerably more complex than what some biologists and many humanists think, that there is a place within it for meaning and purpose, and that indeed meaning and purpose evolve. My particular interest in evolution is in the evolution of capacities, which has been a remarkable part of the story: the capacity for creating oxygen; the capacity for forming large complex organisms after a couple of billion years when only unicellular organisms had been around; the capacity for endothermy—the ability of birds and mammals to maintain a constant body temperature that allows them to survive in quite extreme hot or cold temperatures; the capacity to spend days or weeks, in the case of many mammals and birds, or years, in the case of chimpanzees and other apes, or decades, in the case of humans, in raising helpless infants and children unable to survive on their own; the capacity to make atomic bombs. Evolution gives us no guarantee that we will use these new capacities wisely or well. Such capacities can help us or they can destroy us, depending on what we do with them.

I hope this gives some idea of what I mean by evolution and why I think it is important if we are to understand who we are and where we might want to go. But what do I mean by religion, and what is the evolution of religion? Religion is a complex phenomenon, not easily defined, though I will spend much of the first two chapters trying to define it. Just to get things started I will draw on Clifford Geertz's well-known definition.[17] Paraphrasing him, religion is a system of symbols that, when enacted by human beings, establishes powerful, pervasive, and long-lasting moods and motivations that make sense in terms of an idea of a general order of existence.[18] It is interesting to note what Geertz left out. There is no mention of "belief in supernatural beings" or "belief in gods (God)," which many current definitions take for granted as essential. It is not that Geertz or I think such beliefs are absent in religion, though in some cases they may be, just that they are not the defining aspect.

I agree with Geertz that symbols are basic to religion (as they are to many spheres of human action, including science); that is to say, religion becomes possible only with the emergence of language.[19] The idea of a prelinguistic religion, as in the notion of "chimpanzee spirituality," seems implausible to me, though there are developments among some nonhuman animals that provide resources that could contribute to what would become religion among human beings. There is even the possibility that something like religion might have developed in earlier species of the genus *Homo, Homo erectus* in particular, who might have had some kind of protolanguage, but not full modern syntactical language.

In his essay "Religion as a Cultural System," Geertz was trying to specify what religion is in relation to a number of other spheres that are organized by other systems of symbols. Following Alfred Schutz, he contrasts these several cultural spheres to the world of daily life, which Schutz took to be the "paramount reality" of life. As Geertz puts it:

> The everyday world of common-sense objects and practical acts is, as Schutz says, the paramount reality of human experience—paramount in the sense that it is the world in which we are most solidly rooted, whose inherent actuality we can hardly question (however much we may question certain portions of it), and from whose pressures and requirements we can least escape.[20]
>
> What distinguishes common sense as a mode of "seeing" is, as Schutz has pointed out, a simple acceptance of the world, its objects, and its processes as being just what they seem to be—what is sometimes called naïve realism—and the pragmatic motive, the wish to act upon that world so as to bend it to one's practical purposes, to master it, or so far as that proves impossible, to adjust to it.[21]

For Schutz the world of daily life is characterized by striving, by working, by anxiety. It is the premier world of functioning, of adapting, of surviving. It is what some biologists and some historians think is all there is. Among language-using humans, however, the world of daily life is never all there is, and the other realities that human culture gives rise to cannot fail but overlap with the world of daily life, whose relentless utilitarianism can never be absolute.

There are two more things that we can say now, saving for later a fuller discussion of the world of daily life. In spite of its "apparent actuality," the world of daily life is a culturally, symbolically constructed world, not the world as it actually is. As such it varies in terms of time and space, with much in common across the historical and cultural landscape, but with occasional sharp differences. Yet because the world of daily life appears "natural," it involves the suspension of disbelief in the world as it appears. In what Schutz calls "the natural attitude" one "puts in brackets the doubt that the world and its objects might be otherwise than it appears."[22]

What is significant here is that in the various other worlds—cultural spheres, symbolic systems—in which Geertz was interested throughout his life, the brackets that the commonsense world of daily life puts on the idea that anything could be other than it appears have come off. In these other worlds, taken-for-granted assumptions no longer rule. In "Religion as a Cultural System" Geertz compares the religious perspective to two other perspectives besides the commonsensical one in terms of which the world may be construed: the scientific and the aesthetic.[23] In the scientific perspective, he says, the givenness of daily life disappears: "Deliberate doubt and systematic inquiry, the suspension of the pragmatic motive in favor of disinterested observation, the attempt to analyze the world in terms of formal concepts whose relationships to the informal conceptions of common sense become increasingly problematic—here are the hallmarks of the attempt to grasp the world scientifically."[24] Rather than pursue Geertz's to me somewhat eccentric view of the aesthetic perspective, I will return to its distinctive features briefly toward the end of this Preface.

It is with his discussion of ritual that Geertz shows us most directly what is characteristic of religion as a cultural system and what makes it different from other spheres, for ritual is not just religious beliefs but religious action. Geertz sums up ritual in a way I could not improve on: "In ritual, the world as lived and the world as imagined, fused under the agency of a single set of symbolic forms, turn out to be the same world, producing thus that idiosyncratic transformation in one's sense of reality to which Santayana refers in my epigraph . . . [It is] out of the context of concrete acts of religious observance that religious conviction emerges on the human plane . . . In these plastic dramas men attain their faith as they portray it."[25] The part of his epigraph to which he refers is this: "The vistas [that a religion] opens and the mysteries it propounds are another world to live in; and another world to live in—whether we expect ever to pass wholly over into it or no—is what we mean by having a religion" (George Santayana, *Reason in Religion*).

To illustrate his point, Geertz, as he always did, gave examples of how rituals create worlds. His most extensive example is from Bali—the ritual combat between Rangda, the queen of the witches, evil, terrifying, Fear itself, and Barong, a kind of farcical sheepdog dragon, who attempts to defend the villagers against Rangda, in a ritual that ends inevitably in a draw. In the course of his discussion, Geertz describes the many ways in which the combat between Rangda and Barong sums up central concerns of Balinese culture, but he concludes:

> It is in the direct encounter with the two figures in the context of the actual performance that the villager comes to know them as, so far as he is concerned, genuine realities. They are, then, not representations of anything, but presences. And when the villagers go into trance they become—*nadi*—themselves part of the realm in which those presences

exist. To ask, as I once did, a man who has *been* Rangda whether he thinks she is real is to leave oneself open to the suspicion of idiocy.[26]

But then Geertz reminds us that however real the world of religious symbols may be to those who participate in it, no one, not even a saint, lives in the world of religious symbols all the time, and most of us live there only at moments. The ritual is over and fields have to be tended and children fed. The world of daily life returns with its brackets perhaps dented, but not entirely missing. Yet when enough people have entered that other world, then the world of daily life to which they return is never quite the same again. As Geertz says, "religion is sociologically interesting not because it describes the social order but because it shapes it."[27]

How religion creates those other worlds and how those worlds interact with the world of daily life is the subject of this book. Like Geertz, I cannot imagine making an argument about symbolic forms and their enactment without illustrating them. If all that is necessary is the argument, this Preface might suffice, or come close to it. But if one wants to understand religious symbol systems in their variety and in their development, there will have to be extensive illustrations. Even in my first two general chapters there are many brief illustrations, but beginning with Chapter 3, on tribal religion, I will offer more extensive descriptions that will become progressively longer as I deal with religion in the chiefly archaic and axial societies. Even so, the long chapters on the four axial-age cases are hardly scratching the surface, as are the earlier ones as well. They tell just enough, I hope, to help the reader, if only for a moment, actually experience what living in those worlds might be like.

I can imagine that there will be readers who will like the cases and throw away the argument, and that is fine with me. I have even thought that might be the way Cliff Geertz would have read my book. But I cannot make the argument I want to make without the illustrations, and so the book is rather long. On the other hand it is not long enough: it leaves out the last 2,000 years. But if I tried to give the major religious developments of the last 2,000 years the same degree of attention that I gave to earlier religions, inadequate though that is, the detail I would have to master would overwhelm me. I would need another lifetime or a phalanx of collaborators. At most I can hope to write another book of modest size that will try to show some of the linkages from the axial age to the modern era, dipping only occasionally into deep detail. We will see.

I have given some idea, however preliminary and inadequate, of what I take evolution to be and what I take religion to be. Now, perhaps even more cryptically, I will try briefly to say how they come together. I agree with the opening sentence of Geertz's epigraph from Santayana: "Any attempt to speak without speaking any particular language is not more hopeless than the attempt to have a religion that shall be no religion in particular." My attempts to describe carefully a variety of religions in all their particularity should give evidence of my agreement, but I also believe that there are types of religion and that these types can be put in an evolutionary order, not in terms of better or worse, but in terms of the capacities upon which they draw.

In trying to describe such an evolutionary order, I have found Merlin Donald's scheme of the evolution of culture particularly convincing. Donald shows how, in the coevolution of biology and culture, three stages of human culture—mimetic, mythic, and theoretic—developed over the last 1 or 2 million years.[28] The evolutionary process starts from the baseline of episodic culture, which we share with other higher mammals—that is, the capacity to recognize what episode the individual is in and what happened before in similar episodes that might give a clue as to how to act now, even though lacking what is called autobiographical memory in which the episodes are strung together in a larger story. We then proceed to mimetic culture, possibly as long as 2 million years ago with such species as *Homo erectus,* in which we use our bodies to enact past and future events as well as gesture for communication. Mimetic culture, though primarily gestural, was by no means silent, and in all likelihood involved music as well as some beginnings of linguistic capacity, though very simple ones. Dance may be one of the earliest forms of such mimetic culture, and dance is basic to ritual in almost all tribal societies, so, though we can only imagine what it was like, some kind of religion may well begin in those early days. What is important to remember about Donald's scheme is that though he speaks of stages, earlier stages are not lost, but only reorganized under new conditions. Thus even in our highly verbal and, to a degree, abstract culture, gestural communication remains basic, not only, obviously, in intimate life, but in public, in our grand spectacles of sport or politics.

Sometime between 250,000 and 100,000 years ago, full grammatical language developed, making complex narratives possible. Perhaps fully developed autobiographical memory depends on grammatical language and narrative and so emerged only then, or perhaps it was already foreshadowed in the mimetic stage. Donald calls the new stage mythic. Myth greatly extends the capacities of mimetic ritual in terms of what it can enact, but it does not replace it. All cultures that we know of have narrative culture intertwined with mimetic culture. I have tried to illustrate religions that are primarily mimetic and mythic under the rubric of tribal religion, being fully aware of how treacherous the word "tribe" is. But even when religions move to include a theoretic dimension, mimetic and mythic culture in reformulated ways continue to be central; humans cannot function without them.

As society became more complex, religions followed suit, explicating, in their own way, the enormous differences between social strata that replaced the basic egalitarianism of forager tribes. Chiefdoms and then archaic kingships require new forms of symbolization and enactment to make sense of the increasing hierarchical division of social classes in terms of wealth and power. In the first millennium BCE, theoretic culture emerges in several places in the old world, questioning the old narratives as it reorganizes them and their mimetic bases, rejecting ritual and myth as it creates new rituals and myths, and calling all the old hierarchies into question in the name of ethical and spiritual universalism. The cultural effervescence of this period led to new developments in religion and ethics but also in the understanding of the natural world, the origins of science. For these reasons we call this period axial.[29]

This brief picture of the evolution of religious symbol systems, which it will take the whole book to flesh out, provides one consolation about stopping where I do. I end with the axial age, the emergence of theoretic culture and the reorganization of the relation between mimetic, mythic, and theoretic elements that that requires. The last 2,000 years have seen an enormous development of all the resources from which religion draws. It is also the story of how the theoretic becomes—partially, never totally—disembedded from the mimetic and mythic. Though I cannot tell that story nor consider the achievements and predicaments to which it has led, I will at least have given an idea of all the dimensions in play. Some have suggested that we are in the midst of a second axial age, but if we are, there should be a new cultural form emerging. Maybe I am blind, but I don't see it. What I think we have is a crisis of incoherence and a need to integrate in new ways the dimensions we have had since the axial age. I will return to this issue in the Conclusion.

It is out of the series of evolutionary developments leading to the emergence of theoretic culture that the various worlds, the "cultural systems" of which Geertz speaks, became more clearly defined. But following his logic we can ask, what was the relation of these new developments, these new capacities, to the world of daily life? If we see the world of daily life as the world of Darwinian survival—as to some extent we must—how, we might ask, could humans "afford" the luxury of spending time on alternative worlds, on dance and myth, even on theory, when there was hunger and danger all around them and the necessity to procreate if their lineages were to survive?

Just to suggest the kind of luxury I am referring to, how can people have created the aesthetic sphere, the nonutilitarian sphere par excellence? Let me take a passage from the poet and critic Mark Strand to illustrate the point:

> Something beyond knowledge compels our interest and our ability to be moved by a poem . . . The poem is bound by a schema that is no less true for standing apart from what science tells us is true . . . A poem is a place where the conditions of beyondness and withinness are made palpable, where to imagine is to feel what it is like to be. It allows us to have the life we are denied because we are too busy living. Even more paradoxically, a poem permits us to live in ourselves as if we were just out of reach of ourselves.[30]

Because we are too busy living? Exactly. How is it possible for us to have that life? It seems that there are a variety of ways in which evolution has allowed living creatures to outwit Darwinian pressures and "have a life" after all. Or maybe. As we will see, every attempt to avoid Darwinian selection can be co-opted; every effort to avoid function and adaptation, if it is at all successful, will be recaptured by what it was trying to escape, if I can speak anthropomorphically about large evolutionary tendencies. But maybe not entirely. It may even turn out that it is "functional" to have spheres of life that are not functional.

While reading a number of recent publications by biologists at work on things of interest to me, I have been interested to find them using the computer language of "online" and "offline." Online is the world of daily life, of what is immediately before us, of Darwinian pressures with a vengeance. Online is the world of foraging, fighting, fleeing, procreating, and the other things that all creatures must do to survive. Offline is when those pressures are off and there are other things at work. I have often found that articles or books about offline things such as sleep or play begin with qualifying statements such as "Sleep is not well understood," or "Play is not well understood, some people even argue it doesn't exist." No one begins a discussion of foraging techniques with such a disclaimer. Of course, when it comes to particular subjects, even in the world of grim survival, saying that something is not well understood is, to me reassuringly, common. But when applied to whole fields, it is mainly the offline fields that are so described.

Take sleep, for example. It seems to be close to universal among all organisms. In organisms without brains we cannot scan for brain waves that indicate sleep, but we can observe quiet withdrawal. So we all seem to need it. It is apparently necessary for survival: I have read that rats who are continuously kept awake die in about two weeks. But exactly what is going on isn't clear. And sleeping is expensive. Sleeping animals are more vulnerable to predators than wide-awake animals. We can't do any foraging or child care or procreating when we're asleep. Yet we need it and we do it.

Then there is the further problem of REM (rapid eye movement) sleep, only discovered in the 1950s, which seems to be the part of sleep in which dreams occur. Human babies need a lot of it. About 80 percent of their sleep is REM sleep, whereas for human adults it is only about 20 percent. But what are dreams about? There is no agreement that I have found, even though in a variety of cultures dreams have been taken very seriously and have influenced daily life, sometimes significantly. REM sleep seems to have to do with learning; with consolidating memories, sorting out important memories, and removing evanescent ones; or with creativity. So there are functions, yes, but exactly what functions is not so clear. Sleep is a luxury that turns out to be a necessity even if we still don't understand it too well.

What about play? Play is the luxury of luxuries. No daily-life concerns allowed. You can play-fight, but if you bite too hard, the game is over. You can play at sexual intercourse (with your own or the other sex), but if you really try to do it, the game is over. Play is not universal; it is especially well developed among mammals and birds, particularly among intelligent and social mammals and birds, though it is also found among fish and some reptiles, and even insects have something that might be considered play. Play is largely, but not exclusively, an activity of the young. It is commonest in species that continue child care for a long time so that the young of the species are not directly involved in the quest for survival: they are fed and protected and have the energy for just having a good time, or so it seems to us.

Play is, of course, expensive. It makes playing animals vulnerable to predators and keeps them from helping to forage. So we have many theories of the functions of play—it is exercising the muscles, it is learning to be social, it is learning to outwit the other players, and so on—yet few observers doubt that it includes an element of sheer joy that is seldom seen in other things animals do. Johan Huizinga wrote a famous book, *Homo Ludens,* "The Playing Human," that still has a lot to teach us.[31] He even saw play as involved in the origin of culture.

One final example. Derek Bickerton, the evolutionary linguist, has argued that the origin of language occurred offline.[32] The cries of other primates are not words; they are commanding vocal gestures, which we can translate as "Danger! Predator!" or "Come here! Food!" but there are no words for danger, or predator, or food. There is no semantic content other than a terrified scream, on the one hand, or a joyous one, on the other, no words that could then be used to discuss the possibility of predators or food when there is no predator approaching nor any new discovery of food at hand, offline, so to speak. How did we ever get offline enough to invent language, which is talk *about* things, not an immediate intervention in the world, or not necessarily so? Bickerton has his own answer, but for now, just the idea that something as "functional," as "adaptive," as language originated offline, so to speak, boggles the mind.

What I am suggesting is that the capacity to go offline in a number of ways, which is present even in simple organisms but much more extensive in complex ones and especially so among humans, may be one of our greatest capacities of all, and that religion, along with science and art, may be the result of that capacity to go offline. I'm not denying function and adaptation. The ethologist Gordon Burghardt has a theory that there is primary play, which is just play, and then there is secondary play, which in a variety of ways has become adaptive.[33] Maybe some such distinction could be made in other spheres.

What all this means for religion, is that in this book the search is not to find the ways in which religion is adaptive, and thus a good thing, or maladaptive, and thus a bad thing, or even something that developed in a spandrel, a kind of empty evolutionary space, and is neutral with respect to adaptation. I want to understand what religion is and what religion does and then worry about its consequences for the world of daily life. The consequences are enormously important, and the question of whether they are adaptive or not cannot finally be avoided. But adaptations can be found for almost any phenomenon—biologists call them just-so stories. They are not the place to start; the reality of life in the religious mode is where I will begin.

There is one more point that, though I touched on it earlier, I need to emphasize in concluding: religious evolution does not mean a progression from worse to better. We have not gone from "primitive religion" that tribal peoples have had to "higher religions" that people like us have. I think it is that problem that worried Cliff Geertz when I talked about religious evolution, because the idea of religious evolution had in earlier days so often been couched in those terms.[34] Religious evolution does add new capacities, but it tells us nothing about how those capacities will be used. It is worth remembering, as Stephen J. Gould pointed out, that complexity is not the only good.[35] Simplicity has its charms. Some relatively simple organisms have survived in more or less the same form for hundreds of millions of years. The more complex the species, the briefer its life. In some cases this is because species have changed into even more complex forms, yet extinctions have been massive. There have been several species of the genus *Homo;* now there is one. The one remaining species may be partly responsible for the extinction of its last remaining relative, the Neanderthals. The more complex, the more fragile. Complexity goes against the second law of thermodynamics, that all complex entities tend to fall apart, and it takes more and more energy for complex systems to function. I will have more to say about all that in Chapter 2.

Genetic change is slow; cultural change is fast, at least in biological time. By now it is obvious that cultural change can be fast in any kind of time. Once the offline achievements of science get translated into technology, then, as they say, all hell breaks loose. Technology takes the possibilities of science and brings them to bear on the world of daily life, with dramatic consequences both for human beings and for the biosphere. For one thing, the sudden growth of the world's population, itself only possible because of technology, has, in my own lifetime, almost outstripped the population growth in all previous history, from the hypothetical "bottleneck" population of perhaps 10,000 humans at the end of the last ice age to well over 6 billion now and 12 billion before we hardly know it. The enormous need for energy, so long available apparently endlessly directly from the sun through photosynthesis, has driven us to tap the enormous but finite and nonrenewable resources of the sun stored in fossil fuels, all to maintain our ever-increasing complexity.

We have proven to be enormously successful at adapting. We are now adapting so fast that we can hardly adapt to our own adaptations. Our technological progress is geometric. It would be hard to argue that our moral progress is even arithmetic. As one who has lived through one horrifying decade after another for eighty years, I confess that I cannot see much in the way of moral advance. There is an irony here, as moral sensitivity has grown steadily in the last hundred years. We are far more sensitive to the needs of whole categories of people that were previously despised and repressed. Yet our growing moral sensitivity seems to have occurred in a world of widespread and undiminished moral horror. Yes, there are the bad guys to blame, and Hitler, Stalin, Mao, and so on were very bad. But it was not they who invented and used the atomic bomb to kill hundreds of thousands of civilians, most of them women and children. No one's hands are clean if we look at the recent history of the world with any seriousness.

Religion is part of this whole picture, a very complex part, leading sometimes to great moral advances and sometimes to deep moral failures. But that religious evolution is simply the rise, onward and upward, of ever more compassionate, more righteous, more enlightened religions could hardly be farther from the truth. No serious reader of this book can think it is a paean to any kind of religious triumphalism. Or any other triumphalism. Technological advance at high speed combined with moral blindness about what we are doing to the world's societies and to the biosphere is a recipe for rapid extinction. The burden of proof lies on anyone who would say it is not so. We can hope for and work for new directions that could change our course, but self-satisfied we cannot be.

This book asks what our deep past can tell us about the kind of life human beings have imagined was worth living. It is an effort to live again those moments that belong to us in the depths of our present, to draw living water from the well of the past, to find friends in history who can help us understand where we are. It is not a book about modernity. But surely, as Leszek Kolakowski has eloquently put it, modernity is on trial.[36] I cannot in this book give an account of that trial. All I can do is call up some very important witnesses.

Acknowledgments

I want to thank my wife, Melanie, who has been the first reader and editor of everything I have ever written, including, of course, this book, which she finished not long before she died. I also want to thank the coauthors of *Habits of the Heart*—Richard Madsen, William Sullivan, Ann Swidler, and Steven Tipton—for, year by year, chapter by chapter, at our annual meeting, reading and commenting on this book. William Sullivan has been particularly helpful with this book and with all my work for many years, as has Eli Sagan; lively discussions with both of them have deepened my work in many ways, even when I did not do exactly what they suggested. There have been others who have read all or some of the chapters and have helped me: Renée Fox, Hans Joas, Shmuel Eisenstadt, Steven Smith, Arvind Rajagopal, Harlan Stelmach, Yang Xiao, John Maguire, Samuel Porter, Mohammad Nafissi, Matteo Bortolini, Wade Kenny, and perhaps others I am overlooking. To all of them I owe a special debt of gratitude.

I could not have written this book without the expert scholarship of scholars in the many fields the book deals with. In some cases they have helped me with detailed criticisms of my drafts of particular chapters, which have been much improved by their help. They will be mentioned by name in the relevant chapters. Among those who have had a pervasive influence on the book as a whole, I must give special mention to Merlin Donald for his theory of cultural evolution, and Gordon Burghardt for his work on animal play and its evolutionary implications.

I must thank two extraordinary editors without whom this book would never have been completed: Douglas Mitchell at the University of Chicago Press, who believed in the book when it was only a dream in my head, and Lindsay Waters at Harvard University Press, who saw the book through to completion in its final form.

I also want to thank the John Templeton Foundation for supporting my work on this book since 2004. Their generous grants helped me in many ways and prevented a long process from becoming even longer. Among their staff I am particularly grateful to Paul Wason and Drew Rick-Miller. I am also grateful to the Foundation for funding a conference in 2008 at the Max Weber Center at the University of Erfurt, under the chairmanship of Hans Joas, on "The Axial Age and Its Consequences," in preparation for which the participants received the four chapters on the axial age in this book. I thank the Committee on Research of the University of California, Berkeley, for modest research grants from the very beginning of this project. I have depended greatly on the wonderful library of the University of California, Berkeley, supplemented by the excellent holdings of the Graduate Theological Union Library. It has been a rare moment when neither of these libraries could supply what I needed.

These are my debts to the living. Probably my debts to the dead are even greater. I owe a great deal to Émile Durkheim and Max Weber. That will be more obvious in the case of Durkheim, because I am closer to him in my sense of calling as a sociologist and an intellectual. Almost every line, however, displays a hidden debt to Weber, whose work was much closer as a model for me than Durkheim's. I have decided not to mention every idea I have borrowed from Weber, or the instances, many fewer, where I disagree with him—that would virtually be a book in itself. Much as I admire Weber, I do not share his cultural pessimism *(Kulturpessimismus),* though I respect it and am often tempted by it. I don't agree with the idea that we should forget our founders (I have been impressed by the many biologists who never fail to remember Charles Darwin), but I do agree with Clifford Geertz when he argued at several points that we social scientists have much to learn from historians, philosophers, theologians, and natural scientists and that merely adding footnotes to the founders will not get us far.

I must mention the three great teachers who taught me face-to-face but who are no longer living: Talcott Parsons, Wilfred Smith, and Paul Tillich. Parsons handed on to me the great sociological tradition, because he lived it and practiced it. Wilfred Smith taught me, paradoxically, that the religion of each person, group, or tradition is unique and can never be captured adequately with general terms such as "Christianity" or "Confucianism," right up to the term "religion" itself, while at the same time teaching me that religion is one because every expression of religion is historically related, somehow, to every other. And Tillich taught me to see the "dimension of depth" in every cultural expression and that Christianity is not "belief in the unbe-lievable" at a time when I thought it was. I could mention my friends Clif-ford Geertz, Kenneth Burke, Edward Shils, and legions of others who were present in my life and from whom I learned much. Books, many of them at least, never fail to fascinate and surprise me, but it was the spirit of my teach-ers that taught me to hear the authors speak, not just watch them lie quietly on the page.

It perhaps goes without saying, but I will say it anyway, that I owe much to the friends in history that Mencius talked about, not least to Mencius himself, but to all the creators of the great traditions that I deal with in the later chap-ters of this book, as well as to the reciters of myth and the dancers of ritual in the tribal and archaic traditions, who must remain anonymous, but who have been, not merely my examples, but my teachers in this enterprise.

lovely

RELIGION IN HUMAN EVOLUTION

1

Religion and Reality

Many scholars ask whether the very word "religion" is too culture-bound to be used in historical and cross-cultural comparison today. I cannot avoid the question, but for practical purposes I will use the term, because for the philosophical and sociological traditions upon which this book draws, the idea of religion has been central. The justification for its use will depend more on the persuasiveness of the argument of the book as a whole than on a definition; nonetheless definitions help to get things started. In the Preface I offered a simplified version of Geertz's definition; here I will begin again with a simplified Durkheimian definition, not incompatible with Geertz's but opening up somewhat different dimensions: Religion is a system of beliefs and practices relative to the sacred that unite those who adhere to them in a moral community.[1] Even this simple definition raises immediately a second definitional issue: What is the sacred?

Durkheim defined the sacred as something set apart or forbidden. Durkheim's definition might be widened to define the sacred as a realm of non-ordinary reality. The notion of non-ordinary reality, though widely held among a variety of peoples, might appear to be ruled out for modern consciousness. Do we not believe that there is no non-ordinary reality, that ordinary reality is all there is? If so, then cannot both the sacred and religion be relegated to the historic past, to the mistaken beliefs of earlier cultures? But we can draw on Alfred Schutz's analysis of multiple realities, developing more fully what was sketched in the Preface, to indicate that today we operate all the time in a series of non-ordinary realities as well as in ordinary reality.[2]

Multiple Realities

Schutz argues that, methodologically speaking, the paramount reality in which we live is the world of daily life, what Max Weber called the every-day.[3] We assume that the world of daily life is natural. Schutz characterizes the world of daily life as the world of *wide awake, grown up* men. We face the world of daily life with a *practical* or *pragmatic* interest. In the world of daily life, the primary activity is to "bring about [a] projected state of affairs by bodily movements," which Schutz calls *working*. The world of working is governed by the means/ends schema: we could also define it as a world of *striving*. The world of daily life operates in *standard time* and *standard space*.

Further, according to Schutz, the world of daily life is based on a *fundamental anxiety*, ultimately, though not necessarily consciously, arising from the knowledge and fear of death. Finally, according to Schutz, the world of daily life involves what he calls the epoché of the natural attitude—the suspension of disbelief in the world as it appears. In the natural attitude, one "puts in brackets the doubt that the world and its objects might be otherwise than it appears to him."[4]

At this point we have a clear contrast between the world of daily life and the world of religion, where doubt about the world as it appears is often fundamental. For example, the Daoist teacher Zhuangzi (Chuang Tzu), speaking of himself, wrote:

> Once Chuang Chou dreamt he was a butterfly, a butterfly flitting and fluttering around, happy with himself and doing as he pleased. He didn't know he was Chuang Chou. Suddenly he woke up and there he was, solid and unmistakable Chuang Chou. But he didn't know if he was Chuang Chou who had dreamt he was a butterfly, or a butterfly dreaming he was Chuang Chou.[5]

But we do not have to become so fanciful to see that even in the modern world we do not spend all our time in the world of daily life.

For example, most of us spend up to a third or more of our life asleep. Not only does sleep rather dramatically suspend our involvement in the world of daily life, but it is also the time when we dream, and dreams clearly do not follow the logic of daily life.[6] Dreams, for example, do not operate in standard time and space: they can bring together persons from different times and places in a single interaction.

We are often involved in activities that deliberately alter the conditions of the world of daily life, sometimes in a way that emphasizes some features of it while ignoring others. Games such as football artificially create a separate reality. Football operates not with standard time and space but with the bounded time and space of the game. Football events occur only on the football field. If, for example, a pass is caught out of bounds, it doesn't count as a catch, for it did not occur in game space. Game time is one hour, but it is suspended for a variety of reasons and usually lasts about three hours of standard time. Most centrally, football plays with the anxieties of the world of working, the striving for pragmatic advantage. Unlike the world of daily life, one hour of game time produces a clear result: someone wins and someone loses, or occasionally there is a tie. We may borrow a metaphor from football in daily life when we speak in an economic or political context of a "game plan" or a "winning quarterback." Indeed, for highly paid professional football players the world of the game *is* the world of daily life. But for the rest of us it is "only a metaphor."

What is true of football is true of many other common experiences. When we watch television, or a movie, or a play, or listen to music, we become absorbed in the activities we are watching or listening to. We are diverted from the world of daily life, and that is a major reason we spend so much time at these activities. However, in our society these activities tend to be viewed as "less real" than the world of daily life, as fictional, and ultimately as less important than the world of working. They can be switched off like a TV set and we will be back in the "real world," the world of daily life. Yet one of the first things to be noticed about the world of daily life is that *nobody can stand to live in it all the time.* Some people can't stand to live in it at all—they used to be sent to mental institutions, but today in the United States they can be found wandering in the city streets. All of us leave the world of daily life with considerable frequency—not only when we are sleeping and dreaming (the structure of dreams is almost completely antithetical to the structure of the world of working), but when we daydream, travel, go to a concert, turn on the television. We do these things often for the sheer pleasure of getting out of the world of daily life. Even so we may feel guilty that we are shirking our responsibilities to the real world.

However, if we follow the analysis of Alfred Schutz, the notion that the world of daily life is uniquely real is itself a fiction that is maintained only with effort. The world of daily life, like all the other multiple realities, is socially constructed. Each culture, each era, constructs its own world of daily life, never entirely identical with any other. Even the meaning of "standard" time and space differs subtly between cultures, and fundamental conceptions of person, family, and nation are all culturally variable. By this I do not mean that the world of daily life even in its cultural variability is not real—it is real enough. But it lacks the unique ontological reality, the claim to be perfectly natural, that it seeks to secure when it puts in brackets the doubt that it could be other. It is one of the functions of other realities to remind us that that bracketing is finally insecure and unwarranted. Occasionally a work of art will break its bounds, will deeply unsettle us, will even issue us the command "Change your life"—that is, it will claim not a subordinate reality but a higher reality than the world of daily life.

The world of daily life is challenged by another reality much more sober than art, namely science. However closely science may seem to approximate the features of the world of daily life, there is one fundamental difference: science does not accept the world of daily life as it appears; science is premised on a permanent lifting of the epoché of the natural attitude. As William James pointed out in his original discussion of multiple realities, the physicist understands heat in terms not of "felt warmth" but of the "molecular vibrations" that cause that bodily warmth and are the truth of its appearance.[7]

It is religion, however, that traditionally directed the most frontal assault on the world of working. As Zhuangzi put it:

> He who dreams of drinking wine may weep when morning comes; he who dreams of weeping may in the morning go to hunt. While he is dreaming he does not know it is a dream, and in this dream he may even try to interpret a dream. Only after he wakes does he know it was a dream. And someday there will be a great awakening when we know that this is all a great dream. Yet the stupid believe they are awake, busily and brightly assuming they understand things, calling this man ruler, that one herdsman—how dense![8]

The Buddha proclaimed that the world is a lie, a burning house from which we must escape. Early Christians believed that the world was in the grip of sin and death and would soon come to an end to be replaced by a new heaven and a new earth. Zhuangzi's metaphor of awakening, as though the world of daily life is really a dream, can be found in many traditions, including Buddhism and Christianity.

Religious Reality

How can we characterize the religious reality that calls the world of daily life into question? Certainly religious worlds are as variable as the worlds of daily life, and we will have occasion to comment on that variability throughout this book, but as an initial effort to characterize the religious experience of reality I will borrow from the psychologist Abraham Maslow. Maslow in his *Toward a Psychology of Being* and other works has distinguished between what he calls Being cognition (or B-cognition) and Deficiency cognition (or D-cognition).[9] His characterization of D-cognition is remarkably parallel to Schutz's notion of the world of daily life, for D-cognition is the recognition of what is lacking and what must be made up for through striving. D-cognition is motivated by a fundamental anxiety that propels us toward practical and pragmatic action in the world of working. When we are controlled by Deficiency motives, we operate under the means/ends schema, we have a clear sense of difference between subject and object, and our attitude toward objects (even human objects) is manipulative. We concentrate on partial aspects of reality that are most germane to our needs and ignore the rest, both of ourselves and of the world, but we operate with scrupulous attention to the constraints of standard time and space.

Being cognition is defined in sharpest contrast to Deficiency cognition on every dimension. When we are propelled by B-motives, we relate to the world by participation, not manipulation; we experience a union of subject and object, a wholeness that overcomes all partiality. The B-cognition is an end in itself, not a means to anything else, and it tends to transcend our ordinary experience of time and space. Maslow does not identify B-experiences exclusively with religion—they may occur in nature, in relation to art, in intense interpersonal relations, even in sports.[10] But because B-experiences are so frequently reported in religious literature, they may provide an initial mode of entry into the particular way that people experience the world religiously, even though it is certainly not the only way and we will have to broaden our phenomenological description of religious worlds as we encounter particular religions in more detail.

Herbert Richardson, drawing on such writers as Charles Peirce and Friedrich Schleiermacher, describes something similar to Maslow's B-cognition when he points out the cognitive aspect of feeling. Feeling, he says, "perceives by participation. Just as feeling is a perception of a whole, so a whole is that which is perceived through participation."[11] According to Richardson, aesthetic and some other kinds of knowing involve a feeling of a finite whole, whereas religious knowing involves the feeling of an infinite Whole. He gives as examples of our "affectual communion" with a finite whole the feeling of "the immensity of the ocean," or "the presence of another." Jonathan Edwards, as quoted by Richardson, describes the feeling of an infinite Whole:

> There came into my soul, and was, as it were, diffused through it, a sense of the glory of the Divine Being; a new sense, quite different from anything I ever experienced before . . . I thought with myself, how excellent a Being that was, and how happy I should be if I might enjoy that God, and be rapt up to him in heaven, and be as it were swallowed up in him forever![12]

Edwards's feeling of union with the infinite Whole, which he experienced as participation in the life of God, was accompanied by two other feelings that both Richardson and Maslow argue often accompany such experiences: the general rightness of all things, and personal well-being.

Václav Havel in his letters written from prison describes such an experience in entirely nontheistic terms:

> Again, I call to mind that distant moment in [the prison at] Hermanice when on a hot, cloudless summer day, I sat on a pile of rusty iron and gazed into the crown of an enormous tree that stretched, with dignified repose, up and over all the fences, wires, bars and watchtowers that separated me from it. As I watched the imperceptible trembling of its leaves against an endless sky, I was overcome by a sensation that is difficult to describe: all at once, I seemed to rise above all the coordinates of my momentary existence in the world into a kind of state outside time in which all the beautiful things I had ever seen and experienced existed in a total "co-present"; I felt a sense of reconciliation, indeed of an almost gentle consent to the inevitable course of things as revealed to me now, and this combined with a carefree determination to face what had to be faced. A profound amazement at the sovereignty of Being became a dizzying sensation of tumbling endlessly into the abyss of its mystery; an unbounded joy at being alive, at having been given the chance to live through all I have lived through, and at the fact that everything has a deep and obvious meaning—this joy formed a strange alliance in me with a vague horror at the inapprehensibility and unattainability of everything I was so close to in that moment, standing at the very "edge

of the finite"; I was flooded with a sense of ultimate happiness and harmony with the world and with myself, with that moment, with all the moments I could call up, and with everything invisible that lies behind it and has meaning. I would even say that I was somehow "struck by love," though I don't know precisely for whom or what.[13]

Here we find experiences of participation, of the rightness of things, and of personal well-being, similar to those we found in Edwards. Wallace Stevens has put such experiences in poetic form on several occasions. The following resonates particularly with Havel, though it brings in the idea of awakening, common in religious writing, but not explicit in either Edwards or Havel:

> Perhaps
> The truth depends on a walk around a lake,
>
> A composing as the body tires, a stop
> To see hepatica, a stop to watch
> A definition growing certain and
>
> A wait within that certainty, a rest
> In the swags of pine-trees bordering the lake.
> Perhaps there are times of inherent excellence,
>
> As when the cock crows on the left and all
> Is well, incalculable balances,
> At which a kind of Swiss perfection comes
>
> And a familiar music of the machine
> Sets up its Schwärmerei, not balances
> That we achieve but balances that happen,
>
> As a man and woman meet and love forthwith.
> Perhaps there are moments of awakening,
> Extreme, fortuitous, personal, in which
>
> We more than awaken, sit on the edge of sleep,
> As on an elevation and behold
> The academies like structures in a mist.[14]

In the ecstatic language of poetry, Stevens evokes the sense of participation instead of describing it as Edwards and Havel attempt to do. In any case, the elements of the rightness of things and of personal well-being are particularly evident.

Overlapping Realities

So far I have treated the multiple realities as largely serial: so much time for sleep, so much for work, so much for television, for socializing, for contemplation, and so forth. But we can also see the various realms of reality as going on at the same time, and occasionally cutting into one another. Objects in the world of daily life may carry more than one meaning, and we may not be conscious of all the meanings. We may relate to our boss in the world of working, perhaps unconsciously, as if he were our father. As psychotherapists know, such a meaning can distort our behavior to the extent that it disrupts our ability to function in the work situation. Many objects that we encounter in the world of everyday have, at least potentially, religious meanings. The tree shimmering in the sunlight that Havel observed could have been hardly noticed as the background of the daily walk in the prison yard, but, for whatever reason, it served at that particular moment to break through the everyday: it was the world-tree that concentrated the whole meaning of the cosmos in its shimmering presence.

In other words, it is always possible that an object, a person, or an event in the world of daily life may have a meaning in another reality that transcends the world of working. If so we may call it a symbol, following Alfred Schutz's usage with respect to that term.[15] We will have much more to say about symbols, but here we may only note that we are surrounded by symbols, or potential symbols, all the time. A tree, water, the sun are all multivalent symbols, but a room is a symbol, a door is a symbol, a book is a symbol, a teacher is a symbol, a student is a symbol. Most of the time in daily life we are operating with a narrowly pragmatic consciousness, with what Maslow calls D-cognition, and we don't see symbols, or at least we don't consciously see them. At times, however, even in the midst of daily life, we may experience a B-cognition when something ordinary becomes extraordinary, becomes symbolic.

Abraham Maslow once in my presence told of such a B-cognition. He was serving as chair of the Department of Psychology at Brandeis and was expected to attend the graduation ceremony in full academic regalia. He had avoided such events previously, considering them silly rituals. But, he said, as the procession began to move he suddenly "saw" it as an endless procession. Far, far, ahead, at the very beginning of the procession, was Socrates. Quite a way back but still well ahead of Maslow was Spinoza. Then just ahead of him was Freud followed by his own teachers and himself. Behind him stretching endlessly were his students and his students' students, generation after generation as yet unborn. Maslow assured us that what he experienced was not a hallucination: rather it was a particular kind of insight, an example of B-cognition. It was also, I would suggest, the apprehension of the academic procession as a symbol, standing for the true university as a sacred community of learning, transcending time and space. He was in a sense apprehending the "real" basis of any actual university. One could say that if we can no longer glimpse that sacred foundation, the actual university would collapse. For the real university is neither a wholesale knowledge outlet for the consumer society nor an instrument in the class struggle, though the actual university is a bit of both. But if the university does not have a fundamental symbolic reference point that transcends the pragmatic considerations of the world of working and is in tension with those considerations, then it has lost its raison d'être.

Without the capacity for symbolic transcendence, for seeing the realm of daily life *in terms of* a realm beyond it, without the capacity for "beyonding," as Kenneth Burke put it, one would be trapped in a world of what has been called dreadful immanence.[16] For the world of daily life seen solely as a world of rational response to anxiety and need is a world of mechanical necessity, not radical autonomy. It is through pointing to other realities, through beyonding, that religion and poetry, and science too in its own way, break the dreadful fatalities of this world of appearances.

We can begin to see why taking the world of daily life as the paramount reality is dangerous if it is anything more than a methodological assumption. We have noted that no one can stand to live in the world of daily life all the time. Its governing anxiety derives from two of its features: the fact that it is a world of lack, of Deficiency motives that must be made up; and the fact that the manipulations in which it is engaged have no guaranteed success—they might fail in the attempt to overcome some deficiency. The world of daily life must then be punctuated with periods that are more inherently gratifying: with sleep, with common meals, with activities that are not means to any ends. Alasdair MacIntyre has used the term "practices" to apply to activities whose goods are internal to them.[17] The kind of B-cognition that we have used to characterize religious experience is not a practice, because, to paraphrase Stevens, it is not something we achieve but something that happens. Ritual, however, is a form of practice that is broader than religion but of which religion provides important examples. Regularly recurring activities, such as meals, sports, concerts, can take on the quality of ritual. The notion of the Sabbath, the day of rest, is intimately connected with ritual, because traditionally it has involved participation in religious ritual, in worship. In any case the notion that the Sabbath is different from the other six days of the week implies that it is time, in part at least, set aside from the world of daily life, time in which the anxieties of the world of daily life are temporarily allayed, time out of time. If today many people allay those anxieties with sports or other recreation instead of or in addition to worship, this does not change the significance of time that breaks with the rhythm of the world of daily life.

However, the fact that the world of daily life cannot consume the whole of our lives is not the only reason why we may hesitate to characterize it as the paramount reality. In its own citadel it is not always sovereign. The world of working as the world of the manipulation of objects in order to satisfy needs is inadequate to the understanding even of the world of working. The world of working as a world of the satisfaction of marginal utility is devoid of culturally specific subjective meaning. Weber, in describing instrumental rationality (*Zweckrationalität*), which he did indeed take to be a kind of paramount reality, felt that it could be read off by the observer from purely objective observations. Given the external situation of need, the meaning of the instrumentally rational action would be obvious. There would be no necessity for the interpretation (*Verstehen*) of subjective meaning.

Yet, I believe, there is a pull, even in the very center of the world of working, toward the understanding of work as practice, as intrinsically meaningful and valuable, rather than as means to an end. The psychologist Mihaly Csikszentmihalyi has described the phenomenon of what he calls flow, a kind of optimal experience of full engagement with the world and full realization of one's own potentialities, as frequently occurring among ordinary Americans at work.[18] The anthropologist Victor Turner has used the notion of flow to understand ritual, and it is perhaps not stretching things too much to suggest that it is when work becomes (in the positive sense) ritual that it approximates flow.[19]

We may take, for example, the Zen Buddhist notion of practice, which in its primary sense means meditation, preferably in the lotus posture for definite periods in a meditation hall with other Zen devotees. The notion of Zen practice is then extrapolated to all activities, so that sweeping becomes practice, doing the dishes becomes practice, and so would any kind of work. What makes work into practice from the Zen point of view would be the attitude of mindfulness, a particular form of religious attention. Mindfulness does not mean concern for outcome but openness to the reality of what is actually happening, a kind of B-cognition. Perhaps I can suggest that ritual, in the extended meaning I have given to it, may rival the world of daily life as the paramount reality. Such an assertion bears on the widely shared religious idea that the world of daily life is a world of illusion.

Modes of Religious Representation

Religious reality is a realm of experience, to be sure, but it is also a realm of representation. In fact, experience and representation belong inexorably together. George Lindbeck has described the current major alternative theories of religion in ways that will be helpful to our exposition.[20] The first theory of religion he describes is what he calls propositional. It sees religion as consisting of a series of propositional truth claims, stated conceptually. I will have more to say about concepts below, as they are of great importance in religious discourse, but I believe that Lindbeck is right in arguing that the propositional theory of religion is inadequate as a major approach to religion and largely abandoned by scholars today. To identify religion with a set of propositions whose truth can be argued would be to make it into what more accurately should be called philosophy. Religion and philosophy are intimately related, as we will explore in later chapters, but they are not identical.

Lindbeck's second theory of religion is the widely influential experiential-expressive approach. This view assumes that there is a general human capacity for religious experience that is actualized differently in different religious traditions. The experiential-expressive view in its modern form Lindbeck traces to Friedrich Schleiermacher, and in recent times it was widely propagated by Paul Tillich. The emphasis on B-cognition and the felt-whole in the discussion so far largely belongs in the category of the experiential-expressive theory of religion. In one understanding the deep structure of religious experience exists generically in the human psyche. Particular religions are the surface manifestations of this deep panhuman experiential potentiality.

Lindbeck, however, opts for a third theory as most promising, what he calls the cultural-linguistic theory. The cultural-linguistic theory, which derives from cultural anthropology, particularly from Clifford Geertz, takes symbolic forms as primary, seeing them not so much as expressions of underlying religious emotions, but as themselves shaping religious experiences and emotions. I would agree that the cultural-linguistic approach is a valuable corrective to the experiential-expressive approach, but I don't think we have to choose between them. It seems to me that we can view them as coordinate approaches and that we need to move back and forth between them to understand the phenomenon of religion. Thus when I characterize widely different expressions as examples of Being cognition, I am not arguing that there is a subsistent reality of Being experience that simply comes out in different forms on different occasions. Rather, I am recognizing that there are some common human experiential potentialities that have recognizable similarities, but are inchoate until given shape by symbolic form. Once so shaped, their similarities are always qualified: the differences may be crucial. I am also fully in agreement with Lindbeck that cultural traditions not only shape, they even call forth, emotional experiences. In short, we cannot disentangle raw experience from cultural form. Nevertheless we can see them as equally essential, like the Aristotelian notions of matter and form, and do not have to choose one approach as primary.

As an example of why we need both theoretical approaches, we may consider the experience of the felt-whole. It is true that many who have had such an experience speak of it in terms of ineffability, of the inability of words to express the experience, and so forth. The experience of the felt-whole, a radical form of Maslow's Being cognition, provides a valuable point of entry (by no means the only one) into the realm of religious reality, but it is problematic with respect to an analysis of religious representations, a central concern of the cultural-linguistic approach. For what we can perhaps best call unitive experience, all representation must be inadequate. Representation implies a duality between the representative form and the reality it represents, but it is just this duality that the unitive experience transcends. Perhaps it is even dangerous to speak of unitive *experience,* because in terms of modern Western cultural categories, experience implies subjectivity or innerness as opposed to objectivity, again imposing a false dualism. With this consideration in mind it might be well to speak of unitive events as well as unitive experiences.

Without ourselves experiencing them, we would not know anything about unitive events except through representations. The unitive event, then, is a kind of ground zero with respect to religious representations. It transcends them yet it requires them if it is to be communicable at all. Christian negative theology and the Buddhist teaching of emptiness *(sunyata)* attempt to express this paradoxically by speaking of nothingness, the void, silence, or emptiness. Yet the very negative terms themselves are symbolic forms, are representations, and therefore introduce an element of dualism into the unitive event even when they are trying to overcome the dualism of representation. This is not a paradox to be solved but one to be pointed to as we survey a variety of expressions of the unitive event in the world's religions.

So in developing a typology of religious representations, we must start with the null category of unitive representation—that is, representations that attempt to point to the unitive event or experience. As I develop the typology in the following sections, I will ground the modes of experience and representation in their earliest forms in children and in the modes of apprehension of reality that are more general than religion, but from which religious modes of representation draw. My interest in grounding the modes of representation in the earliest experiences of reality is not only psychological. I don't want to reduce such modes to childhood levels. They may involve, however, what psychoanalysts call "regression in the service of the ego." If so, they also involve regression in the service of the world, in its earliest apprehensions.

Because I will be locating the modes of religious representation in stages of the cognitive development of the child, it is worth pointing out that there is a certain affinity between unitive experience and what Piaget, borrowing from J. M. Baldwin, calls the "adualism" of the child. Piaget says that in this adualism of the early months of life "there does not yet exist any consciousness of self; that is, any boundary between the internal or experienced world and the world of external realities. Freud talked about narcissism but did not sufficiently stress the fact that this was narcissism without a Narcissus."[21] I do not mean to imply that unitive experiences are in any simple sense a "return" to early infantile experience, but it may be that possibilities existing then, as in other kinds of early experiences, are never lost but can be reappropriated in much more complex form later on. The view that "nothing is ever lost" can, as we shall see, also be brought to bear on religious history.

The second mode of religious representation is what I shall call enactive representation, adapting from what Jerome Bruner sees as the earliest form of true representation in the child.[22] Religious enactive representation is the bodily acting out of religious meaning, as in bowing, kneeling, eating, dancing. That the modes are not watertight categories but constantly cross each other is indicated by the fact that the unitive event is very much enactive. It is an event in which the whole body participates, along with mind and spirit, again without a sense of bifurcation. Yet the enactive mode does not have to have the same radical quality as the unitive event. It may be a simple gesture, almost unconscious, like crossing oneself for those for whom that gesture has become second nature. Such a gesture may put one in tune with religious reality only slightly and peripherally and may entirely lack any radical implications. Yet even so it also raises the question of the adequacy of such terms as representation or meaning. The gesture *is* the meaning—it enacts it—it doesn't, or doesn't necessarily, point to anything else. The enactive mode therefore partakes of the unitive even in its partiality.

The word "symbol" is at least as dangerous as the words "meaning" and "representation," not the least because of its numerous, often contradictory usages, yet it is unavoidable in speaking of modes of religious representation. Symbols, in the sense of material or verbal representations, more obviously "stand for" something else than do unitive events or bodily gestures, though unitive events and bodily gestures can be both symbolic and symbolized. Symbols can be, consciously or unconsciously, perceived as such in the very midst of the stream of consciousness of the world of daily life, as we have already seen in the examples of the tree, or water, or a door. But symbols can also be consciously created in drawings, statues, even buildings, in sounds and, of course, in words. When symbols are primarily visual in their appeal, we can speak of iconic symbolization; when they involve sound, they are or verge upon musical symbolization; when they involve words, we can speak of poetic symbolization. A critically important mode of verbal symbolization is narrative, the story or myth (we should remember that *mythos* is simply the Greek for "story"), which is important in almost all kinds of religion. To show again how the various modes of representation overlap, we can point to dramatic representation where narratives are bodily enacted, often with the accompaniment of visual symbols, such as masks, and of music, vocal and/or instrumental.

Finally we can speak of the conceptual mode of representation, a form of abstract verbal reflection and argument that follows on and criticizes primary religious actions and representations. Conceptual reflection is present in all religions to some degree but becomes particularly significant in the axial religions, where theory, though still related to ritual and narrative, has to some degree become disembedded. In that there is a cognitive moment, a knowing, in the very heart of the unitive event, we can say that conceptual representation is incipiently present even there, and all symbolic representation gives food for conceptual reflection. But even though conceptual representation is an indelible element in religious reality, it does not, as we have argued, define it.

Unitive Representation

Although unitive representation in the pure sense is a null category, the unitive event is of such importance in religion that we need to inquire further how, with the help of actions and symbols, it is represented. The instances we have discussed so far—the accounts of Edwards, Stevens, and Havel—are all from the modern West and may carry excessive experiential-expressive baggage. I want to consider several quite different examples where the element of subjectivity is either absent or much less prominent than we moderns would normally expect.

Cicero's *Somnium Scipionis,* "The Dream of Scipio," is a doubly removed account of a unitive event.[23] Cicero does not claim to have had the experience himself, and Scipio, to whom Cicero attributes it, recounts it as having occurred in a dream. Nonetheless the "Dream" has suggestive attributes common to many such accounts. Scipio says that in his dream he met his father and grandfather in the highest heaven where they now dwell:

> When I gazed in every direction from that point, all else appeared wonderfully beautiful. There were stars which we never see from the earth, and they were all larger than we have ever imagined . . . The starry spheres were much larger than the earth; indeed the earth itself seemed to me so small that I was scornful of our empire, which covers only a single point, as it were, upon its surface. (6.16)

Scipio's vision relativizes the empire, for which, in real life, he bore a heavy political and military responsibility. In the dream he asks his father if he might immediately join him in this beautiful heavenly realm, but his father tells him that the only way to get there is to carry out his earthly duties, but to do so with the vision of the heavens in his mind so that he never forgets the relative significance of things. Among the other things Scipio sees: "almost midway in the distance is the Sun, the lord, chief, and ruler of the other lights, the mind and guiding principle of the universe, of such magnitude that he reveals and fills all things with his light" (6.17). But Scipio does not just see; he hears a "loud and agreeable sound," which, his father assures him, is the music of the spheres (6.18).

Cicero's overwhelming emphasis is on the majesty of the eternal and the relative insignificance of the transient, even though he does not lose sight of the relation between moral action on the earth and one's eternal fate. Scipio's subjective reactions are of marginal importance. His sense of the beauty of the heavenly spheres and his scorn for the insignificance of the earth, and even more the empire, are intended to communicate to us the power of the vision, a vision that puts reality in true perspective, rather than anything important about Scipio's feelings as such. Feeling is not absent, but it is vision more than feeling that represents the unitive event. It is hardly necessary to point out the symbols of the heavens, the sun, and light that "fills all things," which occur so often in such accounts.

My next account is also indirect. It tells of three witnesses to a unitive event that they themselves experience as a unitive event. Even if we may presume that the account derives from one or more of the witnesses, it is given in the third person. This is the story of the transfiguration of Christ, found in all three synoptic Gospels (Matthew 17:1–8; Mark 9:2–8; Luke 9:28–36). In Matthew's account, Jesus led Peter, James, and John "up a high mountain apart." There Jesus "was transfigured before them, and his face shone like the sun, and his garments became white as light." The disciples see Jesus speaking to Moses and Elijah, and then "a bright cloud overshadowed them, and a voice from the cloud said, 'This is my beloved Son, with whom I am well pleased; listen to him.'" The disciples fell on their faces, filled with awe, but Jesus said to them, "Rise and have no fear," and then they saw no one but Jesus.

To the symbols of the sun and light we can now add height, in this case a high mountain, not the actual heavens as with Scipio or an elevation as Stevens puts it, but a variation on the same theme. I want to emphasize the bare objectivity of the account. The only feeling mentioned is the sense of awe experienced by the disciples. What is most striking is that the Gospels have no interest at all in Jesus's subjective experience in this remarkable moment. Today we would very much like to know how Jesus felt. One can imagine the television interviewer asking him, "What went through your mind up there on the mountain?" But what the Gospels are concerned with is the truth revealed in the unitive event, not what anyone felt about it.

In my next example, the issue of subjectivity has become consciously thematized. Ishida Baigan, an eighteenth-century Japanese religious teacher, practiced meditation under the guidance of a Zen monk for a long time. When he was about 40, while nursing his mother, "he opened a door and suddenly the doubts of former years scattered . . . Fish swim in the water and birds fly in the sky. The Way is clear above and below. Knowing the nature to be the parent of heaven and earth and of all things he greatly rejoiced." Baigan went to his teacher to recount his experience, but the teacher was not entirely satisfied. He recognized that Baigan had seen something real: "What you have seen is what can be known of how things ought to be." But there is still a further stage: "The eye with which you saw our nature as the parent of heaven and earth and all things remains. There must be the nature but without the eye. Now you must lose the eye."

Baigan returned to the practice of meditation night and day for over a year:

> Late one night, he lay down exhausted, and was unaware of the break of day. He heard the cry of a sparrow in the woods behind where he was lying. Then within his body it was like the serenity of a great sea or a cloudless sky. He felt the cry of that sparrow like a cormorant dividing and entering the water, in the serenity of a great sea. After that he abandoned the conscious observation of his own nature.[24]

The symbolic repertory here introduces a number of elements that are related to, but somewhat different from, what we have seen up to this point: the cloudless sky, the great sea, the cormorant. Here the experiences of opening a door or hearing the cry of a sparrow touch off a unitive event. But what is particularly interesting is that this account, though much fuller of subjective experience than that of Cicero or the Gospels, is specifically concerned to get the self out of the experience, to "lose the eye," as Baigan's teacher puts it. So once again it is the objective reality, not the subjective "meaning," that is at the forefront, even though we are in a world much more sensitive to subjectivity than in the other two accounts in this section.

Finally I would like to consider a quite different kind of unitive event. Up to this point our examples have all focused on single individuals. Only in the transfiguration story have we had a group, and even there the focus is as much or more on Jesus as on the three disciples. But there is no reason why the unitive event cannot occur in a group, cannot be a group experience. According to Émile Durkheim such events were primarily and originally collective. He speaks of "collective effervescence," as that condition in which people experience a different and deeper reality. Durkheim describes the rituals of the Australian Aborigines: "Commencing at nightfall, all sorts of processions, dances and songs had taken place by torchlight; the general effervescence was constantly increasing." After describing the ritual events, he gives the following analysis:

> One can readily see how, when arrived at this state of exaltation, a man does not recognize himself any longer. Feeling himself dominated and carried away by some sort of an external power which makes him think and act differently than in normal times, he naturally has the impression of being himself no longer [later Durkheim describes the experience of

being literally ecstatic, from the etymological sense of (Greek) *ekstasis,* "being out of oneself"]. It seems to him that he has become a new being: the decorations he puts on and the masks that cover his face figure materially in this interior transformation, and to a still greater extent, they aid in determining its nature. And as at the same time all his companions feel themselves transformed in the same way and express this sentiment by their cries, their gestures and their general attitude, everything is just as though he really were transported into a special world, entirely different from the one where he ordinarily lives, and into an environment filled with exceptionally intense forces that take hold of him and metamorphose him.[25]

Durkheim's point is that the world of the ritual is quite different from the one "where his daily life drags wearily along." It is the world of the sacred in contrast to the profane everyday. And, for Durkheim, it is the profound creative and transformative power of society itself that is the reality apprehended in the ritual. We do not at the moment need to give Durkheim's theory, his conceptual interpretation of religious reality, more than provisional recognition. We will return to it. What is important here is Durkheim's quite valid insistence that what I am calling unitive events can be and often are collective.

Enactive Representation

Jerome Bruner in his *Studies in Cognitive Growth* has developed a typology of modes of representation in the cognitive development of young children from which, as I have already indicated, I have drawn to develop my own typology. Bruner has no unitive representation; rather his first mode is what he calls enactive representation. Bruner argues that although the child is born with a capacity for visual perception and "the initial form of action is 'looking at,'" it is "the actions of grasping, mouthing, holding, and the like [that] further 'objectify' and 'correlate' the environment."[26] Children first understand objects as extensions of their own bodies. A pencil or a ball is understood in terms of how it can be bodily manipulated. In this early stage of learning, things are "lived rather than thought," as Bruner quotes Piaget as saying.[27] It is only gradually, as Piaget notes, that the child can "hold an object in mind" without holding it in hand. Bruner argues that the idea of enactive *representation* (rather than simply action) derives from the existence of enactive habits that the child can use to move beyond simple reflex in organizing action. Indeed, as he puts it, "the principle use to which enactive representation can be put [is] the guidance of action itself."[28]

Bruner points out that representations can be thought of in two ways: as representations *of* something, or as representations *for* something.[29] In modern Western culture we tend to think of representations—symbols in the broadest sense—as something we have in our heads, as something like pictures *of* external things. But representations as recipes for action, as representations *for,* may be fundamental even in the case of language. Bruner cites Luria's emphasis on the "pragmatic function" of speech, as when a child says, "A hole is to dig."[30] Something of this "representation for" quality of enactive representations characterizes all the modes of representation and is perhaps related to the fact that enactive representation is at least subliminally present also in symbolic and conceptual forms of representation. As Bruner says, "The degree to which the child, even after action-free imagery is well developed, continues to depend on some forms of enactive representation is striking."[31] The separation of imagery from the world of action is never complete.[32]

The idea of enactive representation as a recipe for action can be illustrated by knot tying or bicycle riding. One can be instructed verbally or by diagrams as to how to tie a knot, but one doesn't *know how* to tie a knot until one has practiced the knot, until one's body, one's sensorimotor system, has *learned,* the knot. This is even more obvious with bicycle riding, where verbal or diagrammatic instructions are almost useless. Literally one learns to ride a bicycle by riding a bicycle; but the sensorimotor habit of tying the knot or riding the bicycle then becomes a representation of sorts, a recipe for a certain kind of action when that action is called for.

In the very young child a number of such habits—sucking, grasping, and such—are innate or learned even before a sense of the child as a self separate from the mother–child (or parent–child) totality has yet developed. Seeing and hearing, which later specialize for iconic, linguistic, and other modes of representation, are still embedded in a total sensory matrix in which touching, tasting, biting, urinating, defecating, and crying are all significant. The child's capacity to recognize a schematic face is linked to the holding, feeding, warming, comforting activities that usually accompany the face. As I have said, this total bodily relation to reality is never lost. Other modes—symbolic, conceptual—develop later, which for certain purposes take precedence over the enactive. But because human beings remain corporeal, the product of any form of representation is in part a changed bodily state, a gesture. Significant abstractions have *tangible* consequences. Enactive representation can become symbolic through what George Herbert Mead called the conversation of gestures.[33] The body itself becomes an image and a symbol, and this opens up new representational possibilities.

Although in most situations enactive representation is combined with other modes of representation in complex ways, I would like for the moment to concentrate specifically on the enactive. Religion by and large has been deeply involved with the body; ritual is always significantly embodied, in ways we will need to consider. In religions of a wide variety of types there is a close relation to curing. Health is a central religious preoccupation and a metaphor for salvation. Birth and death are recurrent religious preoccupations, and the phenomenon of religious rebirth, symbolized by the Australian Aborigines by the ritual passage of adolescent boys through the legs of grown men, is a widespread phenomenon. Eating and drinking, feasting and fasting, are frequent elements in religious ritual.

Bodily gestures of a wide variety of forms are intrinsic features of ritual. In some forms of Christian liturgy there is sequential movement involving kneeling, sitting, standing, and going to the altar to receive communion. Muslim prayer and Buddhist ritual, among others, involve forms of prostration. Bodily gestures become elaborated in dance, a frequent element in ritual, one that is common to many traditions. Fundamental to dance is rhythmic movement, and rhythm is related to physiological regularities such as heartbeat and breathing. Breathing itself has become focal in Buddhist meditation: a one-pointed attention to breathing, which unites the inner and the outer, can become a unitive experience. The posture of meditation, the lotus posture of the Buddha, was seen by the Japanese Zen master Dogen as enlightenment. Those who sit in Zen meditation are enlightened already; there is nothing more to expect.[34]

R. R. Marett said of tribal religion that "it is something not so much thought out as danced out."[35] But it is not only for "primitives" that the enactive is primary. William Butler Yeats wrote, six days before his death: "I know for certain that my time will not be long . . . I am happy and I think full of an energy I had despaired of. It seems to me that I have found what I wanted. When I try to put all into a phrase I say 'Man can embody truth but he cannot know it.' I must embody it in the completion of my life."[36] We will see that truth is a problematic idea and that not everyone would agree with Yeats that it must be embodied. Yet one of the historic religions rests its claim to truth on the incarnation.

Symbolic Representation

We may begin the consideration of the complex subject of symbolism by attending to the phenomenon of play, inasmuch as Piaget links the beginnings of symbol formation in the child to what he calls "symbolic play." For Piaget, symbols "assimilate" reality to the needs, wishes, desires of the child.[37] As an example of the assimilative function of symbolic play Piaget writes: "A little girl who while on vacation had asked various questions about the mechanics of the bells observed on an old village church steeple, now stood stiff as a ramrod beside her father's desk, making a deafening noise. 'You're bothering me, you know. Can't you see I'm working?' 'Don't talk to me,' replied the little girl. 'I'm a church.'" The little girl, one is tempted to say, was also "working," making sense of a perhaps intimidating experience. In this case we can see how close the symbolic is to the enactive. The child enacts the steeple, but it is only her visual and audible, not her motor, experience of the steeple that allows her to do so. Insofar as there is some image of the church, more is involved than in what Piaget calls "exercise play," which is the child's first, purely sensorimotor, form of play.[38] Here the symbol makes possible the integration of inner and outer, experience and feeling, self and world.

In the young child, Piaget tells us, perception is "egocentric," but what he means is that self and world are as yet undifferentiated parts of a whole. Somewhere Piaget tells of a boy who, on a sunny day, gets into a car in Geneva for a trip to Basel. On arriving, the child gets out, looks up, and says, "Oh, the sun came with us." We could say that the child has not yet located himself and the sun in what Schutz called standard time and space. There is a dynamic quality to the child's world that leads Piaget to speak of the "animism" of the child.[39]

Piaget's examples of symbolic play are largely solitary, as when a little girl "works through" with her dolls an unpleasant scene at lunch where she had refused to finish her soup. In the reenacted scene the little girl shows more understanding of the doll's distaste for the soup than her mother had shown in fact.[40] Bruner gives an example of symbolic play that intrinsically requires an adult as well as a child. This is the common game of peekaboo, whose "deep structure" is "the controlled disappearance and reappearance of an object or person," but whose surface structure can be varied almost infinitely in terms of who or what disappears (a doll, a teddy bear, the mother's face, even the child's face), of what screens the object that has disappeared, of the length of time of the disappearance, and so forth.[41] What is interesting is how fascinated the children Bruner studied were with this game, which began in the preverbal early months of the first year and continued long past early language learning. Several things are interesting here. If a stranger attempts to play this game with a very young child, the result will almost certainly be tears. If the mother plays, the result is often laughter. Peekaboo is playing with one of the child's deepest anxieties, the fear of being left by the mother or caregiver. It would seem to be an instance of what Bruner elsewhere calls "bring[ing] the young to the edge of terror," a normal part of parental play with children.[42] The child takes what we might almost call a ritualistic delight in the endless repetition of a game that arouses anxiety and dispels it. Peekaboo may perhaps be seen as coping with the elemental problem of what Freud in "Mourning and Melancholia" called the lost object.[43]

Before going on to consider more closely the various subtypes of symbolic representation, I would like to turn to Paul Ricoeur for a splendid explanation of why it is worth looking at the psychic origins of religious symbolism in the life of children:

> To manifest the "sacred" *on* the "cosmos" and to manifest it *in* the "psyche" are the same thing.
>
> Perhaps we ought even to refuse to choose between the interpretation that makes these symbols the disguised expression of the infantile and instinctual part of the psychism and the interpretation that finds in them the anticipation of our possibilities of evolution and maturation. Later we shall have to explore an interpretation according to which "regression" is a roundabout way of "progression" and of the exploration of our potentialities . . . Re-immersion in *our* archaism is no doubt the roundabout way by which we immerse ourselves in the archaism of humanity, and this double "regression" is possibly, in its turn, the way to a discovery, a prospection, and a prophecy concerning ourselves.
>
> It is this function of symbols as surveyor's staff and guide for "becoming oneself" that must be united with and not opposed to the "cosmic" function of symbols as it is expressed in the hierophanies described by the phenomenology of religion. Cosmos and Psyche are the two poles of the same "expressivity"; I express myself in expressing the world; I explore my own sacrality in deciphering that of the world.[44]

Iconic Symbolization

As in the case of the little girl who was a church, the relation between iconic and enactive representation is a close one. I. A. Richards told Bruner that images are "full of muscles."[45] Indeed, the first thing 2-year-old children create when they discover what they can do with a crayon is the scribble, something still primarily enactive.[46] The crayon is an extension of the child's body; the pleasure is in the movement. The child is not "making a picture," certainly not making a picture *of* something. The child *is* the picture. As with every element of the child's expression, we can quickly think of sophisticated adult versions. It is not just the look of Jackson Pollock's paintings that comes to mind but the fact that he called them action paintings, capturing something close to Bruner's notion of enactive representation.

Not long after scribbling begins, the child discovers shape. The earliest shapes are swirls, not too different from random scribbles, but beginning to look like something round.[47] Of course, the child is incapable of anything approaching a perfect circle, but vaguely circular shapes begin to appear. Between ages 3 and 4, shape develops into outline, which may be circular or four-sided.[48] The child appears to be playing with form. But form of what? Adults with their strong sense of difference between self and world want the form to be a form *of* something. But what the child is doing with the circles and squares and the cross marks dividing them and the spokes coming out of them is as much expressing the child's own sense of bounded form in an emerging self as anything in the world. And yet it is probably not only to please adults that the child will call a circle with spokes coming out of it the sun or a flower, for the child is making sense of the world as well as the self and seeing balanced form in both. Kellogg and O'Dell in their wonderful book on the psychology of children's art are probably not overinterpreting when they see mandalas in the crossed circles and similar forms that emerge in profusion in children's paintings between ages 3 and 5.[49] The mandala (the term is Buddhist) is a centered design, sometimes of great complexity and remarkable sophistication, that is to be found not only in India, Southeast Asia, and East Asia but in Navajo sandpaintings, medieval European rose windows, modern sculptures, and so forth. Whatever else it is, the mandala is an expression of ordered coherence, a fundamental human concern, and so it is not surprising that it appears spontaneously in the paintings of young children as well as in a variety of high cultural expressions.

Amid the transformations of design, around the ages of 4 and 5, children produce forms that are identifiably, if "abstractly," people. A round form with spokes, a "sun," gets a stem and becomes a "flower," and then gets a face and becomes perhaps not just a person, but "me." Children's art is close to Piaget's symbolic play, but perhaps symbolic play is an element in all art. Though humor is common in children's art, we must not forget that psychologists also speak of "serious play," a term that might be applied to high art and ritual alike, as we shall see in later chapters.

Musical Symbolization

If images are "full of muscles," music is even more obviously kinesthetic. In considering enactive representation we have already had occasion to notice that rhythm is characteristic of bodily life and that early on it gets expressed musically and in the dance. Music, if we may say so, reaches right into the body. Indeed, music without some bodily response is hard to imagine: I am always amazed at the stillness of impassive audiences listening to Bach or Vivaldi, with only a very occasional head moving. If one looks at the musicians who are not at the moment playing, one usually can pick up slight bodily movements or silent foot tapping. I remember being unnerved, when on one occasion as an adolescent I was by chance sitting next to Otto Klemperer at a Bach concert, by the fact that he kept meticulous time to the music with his finger on his knee throughout the entire concert. At concerts of classical music the conductor (Stokowski, Bernstein) is the only one permitted to "dance" to the music, though we can vicariously (and at home with the hi-fi not so vicariously) enjoy it. Singing is also inevitably enactive. In some forms of Protestant worship, singing is the only moment in the service when bodily action, the full-throated use of the vocal chords, is appropriate, and even then one must keep rather still while singing.

I am not saying that music divorced from bodily movement (at least for the hearer—never for the performer) cannot communicate; obviously it can. If it were not so, we could not speak of musical symbolism as something beyond enactive representation. Yet there is something mysterious about musical symbolism compared to iconic or poetic symbolism. What does musical symbolism symbolize? The commonest modern answer, and an adequate one as far as it goes, is that music symbolizes feeling. Susanne K. Langer gives a sophisticated version of this view:

> The imagination that responds to music is personal and associative and logical, tinged with affect, tinged with bodily rhythm, tinged with dream, but *concerned* with a wealth of formulations for its wealth of wordless knowledge, its whole knowledge of emotional and organic experience, of vital impulse, balance, conflict, the *ways* of living and dying and feeling . . . The lasting effect is, like the first effect of speech

on the development of the mind, to *make things conceivable* rather than to store up propositions. Not communication but insight is the gift of music; in a very naive phrase, a knowledge of "how feelings go."[50]

Alfred Schutz, while agreeing with Langer that musical meaning cannot be paraphrased verbally or conceptually, differs from her in seeing music as quintessentially communicative:

> We have therefore the following situation: two series of events in inner time, one belonging to the stream of consciousness of the composer, the other to the stream of consciousness of the beholder, are lived through in simultaneity, which simultaneity is created by the ongoing flux of the musical process. It is the thesis of the present paper that this sharing of the other's flux of experience in inner time, this living through a vivid present in common, constitutes what we called . . . the mutual tuning-in relationship, the experience of the "We," which is at the foundation of all possible communication. The peculiarity of the musical process of communication consists in the essentially polythetic character of the communicated content, that is to say, in the fact that the flux of the musical events and the activities by which they are communicated, belong to the dimension of inner time.[51]

Although Schutz emphasizes communication as strongly as possible, what is being communicated is the "flux of experience in inner time," first of the composer, but through the performance becoming one with the performers and the hearers. As Schutz puts it, in a musical performance composer, performers, and audience "grow old together"—that is, share inner time together (even though the composer, and in a recording, the performers as well, may be dead at the time of hearing).[52]

What modern interpreters largely ignore is what premoderns in many traditions assume: that music is related not only to inner reality but to cosmic and social reality as well. In the passage from Cicero's "Dream of Scipio," already cited, Scipio is depicted as hearing the "music of the spheres." In the classical Mediterranean world this idea goes back at least to Pythagoras: "Pythagoras, who in the sixth century B.C. discovered the orderly arrangements of the musical scale, had elevated that order to the heavens. Like the seven notes of the octave, the seven planets moved in a harmonic progression and so made a 'music' which, as tradition had it, Pythagoras claimed to have heard on several occasions."[53] By late antiquity the initiate was called upon "to enact with his body and with his voice the entire cosmic scheme" in "a song both human and divine."[54] Here the inner time of the performers is united with the inner time of the cosmos. Similar ideas can be discovered in sophisticated form in Hindu, Buddhist, and Sufi piety and in more general form probably very widely in the premodern world.

For some premoderns, and this idea has never entirely died out, music has not only personal and cosmic meanings but social meanings as well. This is the idea that music can bring social harmony, or, conversely, that the wrong kind of music can bring social breakdown. Allan Bloom, in his somewhat perverse book *The Closing of the American Mind,* argued the latter thesis with respect to the (rock) music listened to by contemporary college students.[55] Bloom, being a Platonist, probably got the idea from his master. In book 3 of the *Republic,* Plato wishes to regulate the musical modes in his ideal city. The psychological meaning of music is not missing here; indeed, it is central. Music brings order (or disorder) to the soul and thus attunes or fails to attune the individual to social and cosmic order.

This idea of music is shared by Confucius, who paired music with the rites as the most significant ways of uniting personal, social, and cosmic order. In earlier Chinese tradition the potentialities of music could be drastic indeed. Arthur Waley recounts:

Music, in the view not only of primitives, but in that of almost all non-European peoples, exercises a magic power not only over the heart of man (as we in Europe would to some extent admit), but also over the forces of nature. Everyone familiar with early Chinese books knows the story, existing in countless variants, of Duke P'ing of Chin and the baleful music—how drawn by the magic of an evil tune eight huge black birds swooped from the south and danced on his terrace, black clouds blotted out the sky, a tempest tore down the hangings of his palace, broke the ritual vessels, hurled down the tiles from the roof; and the king fell sick, and for three years no blade of grass grew in Chin, no tree bore fruit.[56]

Confucius's view of music was considerably more modest. Like Plato he saw music as having a central role in the education of the young. Like Plato he was conscious of the varying qualities of musical modes and melodies and the importance of regulating them for the sake of effective government. *Analects* 15:11 says:

Yen Yuan asked about the government of a state. The master said, "Follow the calendar of the Hsia, ride in the carriage of the Yin, and wear the ceremonial cap of the Chou, but, as for music, adopt the *shao* and the *wu*. Banish the tunes of Cheng, and keep plausible men at a distance. The tunes of Cheng are wanton and plausible men are dangerous."[57]

That Confucius himself was very susceptible to the right kind of music is indicated in another passage (7:14):

The master heard the *shao* in Ch'i and for three months did not notice the taste of the meat he ate. He said, "I never dreamt that the joys of music could reach such heights."[58]

Nomos, which means both ethical norm and musical measure, was at the heart of Plato's philosophy. Eric Voegelin describes his deathbed scene: "Plato died at the age of eighty-one. On the evening of his death he had a Thracian girl play the flute to him. The girl could not find the beat of the nomos. With a movement of his finger, Plato indicated to her the Measure."[59]

Whether we think of music as representing feelings, or as representing order (and disorder) in the soul, society, and the cosmos, music has a characteristic that is common to all forms of symbolization: it participates in that which it represents. If it signifies at all, it signifies intrinsically, not arbitrarily, by what it is, not only by what it points to.

Poetic Symbolization

Here I want to talk about symbolic language or linguistic symbolization. I am using the term "poetic" broadly to cover the nondiscursive uses of language, in the sense that Susanne Langer distinguishes between discursive and presentational forms.[60] Though we think of iconic symbols as intrinsically related in some way to what they symbolize, we usually think of the relation of words to what they symbolize as perfectly arbitrary: aren't "dog" and *chien* equally accurate and equally arbitrary ways of referring to the same thing? Yet we also know that an English poem about a dog doesn't go at all easily into French and that if the French translation succeeds, it is because the English poem has stimulated a new and genuinely French poem. It is not at all obvious to young children that the relation between words and things is arbitrary. Piaget recounts the following dialogue between an adult and a young child:

And how did we know that the sun is called "sun"?—*Because it's in the sky. It's not on earth. It gives us light in the sky.*—Yes, but how did we know?—*Because it's a great ball. It has rays. We knew it was called "sun."*—But how did we know its name was "sun"? We might have called it something else.—*Because it gives us light.*—How did the first men know it was called "sun" and not something else?—*Because the big ball is yellow and the rays are yellow, and then they just said it was the sun, and it was the sun . . .*—Then how did the first men know it was to be called sun?—*Because it's up in the air. It's high up . . .* How did the first men know the name of the sun?—*Because they had seen the sun.*

On the basis of many answers of this sort, Piaget offers an explanation:

These answers are very suggestive, for although they press nominal realism to its utmost limit they are not absurd. For indeed, although children may suppose they need only to look at a thing to know its name, it does not in the least follow that they regard the name as in some way written on the thing. It means rather that for these children the name is an essential part of the thing . . . the name sun implies a yellow ball that shines and has rays, etc. But it must be added that for these children the essence of the thing is not a concept but the thing itself.[61]

Wallace Stevens in a late poem rephrases the children's understanding when he says,

The poem is the cry of its occasion,
Part of the res itself and not about it.[62]

Schutz clarifies the distinction in poetry between the concept and "the thing itself," being part of the thing itself rather than about it:

A poem, for instance, may *also* have a conceptual content, and this, of course, may be grasped monothetically. I can tell in one or two sentences the story of the ancient mariner, and in fact this is done in the author's gloss. But in so far as the poetical meaning of Coleridge's poem surpasses the conceptual meaning—that is to say, in so far as it is poetry—I can only bring it before my mind by reciting or reading it from beginning to end.[63]

Archibald MacLeish makes the same point poetically when he says in "Ars Poetica" that a poem should be "mute," "dumb," and "motionless," that is, not talk *about* something. Rather,

A poem should not mean
But be

Susanne Langer explains:

Artistic symbols . . . are untranslatable . . . and cannot be explicated by any interpretation. This is true even of poetry, for though the *material* of poetry is verbal, its import is not the literal assertion made in the words, but *the way the assertion is made,* and this involves the sound, the tempo, the aura of associations of the words, the long or short sequences of ideas, the wealth or poverty of transient imagery that contains them, the sudden arrest of fantasy by pure fact, or of familiar fact by sudden fantasy, the suspense of literal meaning by a sustained ambiguity resolved in a long-awaited key-word, and the unifying, all-embracing artifice of rhythm.[64]

But it is not just that poetic symbolization, like all symbolization, participates in what it symbolizes. Poetry is a form of action, a way of "doing things with words."[65] As Mandelstam has said, "poetry is power," and as Rimbaud put it, "metaphor can change the world." More modestly, Helen Vendler has pointed out the "performative" character of much lyric poetry. Her discussion of Shakespeare's sonnets suggests that even in those sonnets that are not obviously "dramatic"—that is, addressed to another in praise, demand, or query—there is often an implicit rebuttal or defense against accusation or something of the sort, and if such "speech acts" go undetected, the poem may be seriously misunderstood.[66]

Just as images and sounds can "reach right into the body," so can heightened (or, as we shall see in a moment, "condensed") language. A doctoral dissertation gives a powerful instance. The author was the pastor of an urban California congregation:

A woman's mother was near death, but she didn't have a church home. She asked her neighbor, a member of the congregation I served, if she belonged to a church. The neighbor gave her my name and I visited her.

I met her at the door and the conversation went something like this. "I don't know why I called you, but my mother is near death and I thought maybe we should have someone from the church here" . . . She invited me into her home and we talked about her mother. I found out that the mother and daughter had been involved with a church many years ago. Then I suggested that we go into her mother's room and have a prayer. The woman suggested that we have the prayer in the living room because her mother had been in a coma for many days and couldn't participate. But I urged that we go in the room anyway. I offered a prayer and then asked if she knew the "Lord's Prayer." I invited her to join me. We had barely said, "Our Father who art in heaven," when her mother joined us through the rest of the prayer. She came out of her coma for a few days before she died and the mother and daughter had significant conversation.[67]

Here familiar, powerful words reach into the mother's body and pull her back into consciousness, at least for a few days.

In the young child the connection between language and action, what the body does, is a close one. As Bruner says,

The initial structure of language and, indeed, the universal structure of its syntax are extensions of the structure of action. Syntax is not arbitrary; its cases mirror the requirements of signaling about action and representing action: agent, action, object, location, attribution, and direction are among its cases. Whatever the language, the agent-action-object structure is the form soon realized by the young speaker . . . For what the child himself shows us is that initial development of language follows and does not lead his development of skill in action and thought.

Although later language becomes (in part) free from the context of action, as Bruner says, "to understand what a baby is saying, you must see what the baby is doing."[68]

The child learns to use language in contexts, which Bruner describes as "conventionalized into conventional forms and regularized as formats." What he means by a format is "a routinized and repeated interaction in which an adult and child *do* things to and with each other." The peekaboo game is a good example. But much adult language is also contextual and follows conventional formats. Bruner insists that such language is in a sense "constrained" so as to be "cognitively manageable."[69]

Bruner's talk of "contexts" that are "constrained" and that give rise to "formats" leads one to think of the work of Basil Bernstein, though Bruner does not make the connection. Bernstein, as is well known, distinguished two kinds of language codes, one a "restricted code," embedded in the concrete social relations of the people using it, and the other an "elaborated code," largely decontextualized and available for use between people with no intimate or particular relationship.[70] "Restricted code" is perhaps an unfortunate choice of terms, for such language can be very rich in overtones and implications and involve considerable virtuosity in use. I would prefer the term "condensed" to "restricted," and Mary Douglas, whose *Natural Symbols* is, in her words, "an essay in applying Bernstein's approach to the analysis of ritual," speaks of "condensed" versus "diffuse" symbols, as at least partially analogous to Bernstein's usage.[71] Condensed language, and here I would include the intimate language of parent and child, and of lovers, as well as of poetry, requires a world of shared experience that the words imply and that gives a surplus of meaning to any utterance. Poetry that has been learned by heart and been recalled in a variety of situations during a lifetime certainly has more meaning than a poem that is met on the page by the solitary reader for the first time. But even then, if the poem is to mean anything at all, it will almost certainly be because the reader knows something of the tradition of poetry out of which this particular poem comes and to which it will inevitably allude.

If condensed language is effective in forming identity in intimate contexts, in families, it also operates at the level of national identity, as Benedict Anderson points out:

> There is a special kind of contemporaneous community which language alone suggests—above all in the form of poetry and songs. Take national anthems, for example, sung on national holidays. No matter how banal the words and mediocre the tunes, there is in this singing an experience of simultaneity. At precisely such moments, people wholly unknown to each other utter the same verses to the same melody. The image: unisonance. Singing the Marseillaise, Waltzing Matilda, and Indonesia Raya provide occasions for unisonality, for the echoed physical realization of the imagined community.

Indicating how intense the experience of the "mother tongue" can be, Anderson, quoting from Thomas Browne, says that although up to a point the words can be translated, they "can bring goose-flesh to the napes only of English speakers."[72]

Religious language is often condensed, poetic, and, because of its involvement in ritual, performative. No more than any other kind of poetry can it be conceptually paraphrased without significant loss of meaning. Even a poet who has ostensibly left religion behind can catch the intensity of religious language, as when Stevens, noting that "There was a heaven once," goes on to say:

> There, too, he saw, since he must see, the domes
> Of Azure round an upper dome, brightest
> Because it rose above them all, stippled
> By waverings of stars, the joy of day
> And its immaculate fire, the middle dome,
> the temple of the altar where each man
> Beheld the truth and knew it to be true.[73]

Or late in life, after saying, in accordance with the teachings of Romanticism, "God and the imagination are one," he writes, "How high that highest candle lights the dark," returning to that symbolism of light and sun that haunts all his poetry.[74]

Narrative

Narrative is in one sense only a part of what I have been calling poetic symbolization. But there are aspects of narrative that make it transitional to my third category of representation, conceptual representation. Conceptual representation is always linguistic (or quasi-linguistic like mathematics), but not all language, as I have argued in the case of lyric poetry and related forms of condensed language, is conceptual. By conceptual I mean something like what Susanne Langer means by discursive. As she explains, "Language in the strict sense is essentially discursive; it has permanent units of meaning which are combinable into larger units; it has fixed equivalences that make definition and translation possible; its connotations are general, so that it requires non-verbal acts, like pointing, looking, or emphatic voice-inflections, to assign specific denotations to its terms."[75] One can imagine narratives that would be discursive in Langer's sense—that is, literal accounts of what actually happened. But many forms of narrative (including some that claim simply to recount what actually happened) are in fact governed by symbolic modes of organization. As Herbert Richardson says of myth, a significant form of narrative for our purposes, "mythical discourse rises at the level of the total story, the most complex level of linguistic utterance. The linguistic unit appropriate to myth is not the single word nor even the sentence, but the story."[76] Thus, the truth of a narrative in this sense does not arise from the "correspondence" of its words or sentences to "reality," but from the coherence of the story as a whole. Just as a poem cannot be paraphrased conceptually without irreparable loss, neither can such narratives be.

That the "total story" is the significant form of myth gives it a presentational quality, in Langer's sense, that overcomes the temporal sequentiality of its discursiveness. Lévi-Strauss nicely makes this point in relating myth to music:

> Myth and music [are both languages] which, in their different ways, transcend articulate expression, while at the same time—like articulate speech, but unlike painting—requiring a temporal dimension in which to unfold. But this relation to time is of a rather special nature: it is as if music and mythology needed time only in order to deny it. Both, indeed are instruments for the obliteration of time . . . Because of the internal organization of the musical work, the act of listening to it immobilizes passing time; it catches and enfolds it as one catches and enfolds a cloth flapping in the wind. It follows that by listening to music, and while we are listening to it, we enter into a kind of immortality.
>
> It can now be seen how music resembles myth, since the latter too overcomes the contradiction between historical, enacted time and a permanent constant.[77]

There are other features of narrative that anchor it in the symbolic or even in the enactive modes of representation. Stories can be acted out and often are in plays, movies, television, ritual. Even when the spectator is only an observer, something like the bodily response to music is also present. This is obvious with adventure movies, where we cringe, gasp, and so on with each turn of the plot even though we are sitting in the audience and the action is on the screen. But even a verbal narrative can do the same thing. Hold a young child on your lap as you tell the story of Little Red Riding Hood and you will feel the bodily response.

Another feature of narrative that links it to the symbolic is that the distinction between inner and outer, between self and world, is not as clear as in conceptual discourse. We *identify* with what is going on in the narrative. It is all very well to comfort a child by saying, "It's only a story," but at some level the child knows that the story has its own truth that such disclaimers don't reach. We are even drawn into narratives that purport to recount actual events. When we read in the newspaper or hear on television of someone who has lost an only child in a drive-by shooting, we cannot help, however briefly, feeling the pain, feeling "that could be me." This is not an aberration of "primitive" or "regressive" thinking. It is a normal human response.

Human beings are narrative creatures. Narrativity, as we shall see, is at the heart of our identity. One study of conversations at home between mothers and preschool children showed that narratives occurred every seven minutes, three-quarters of them told by the mothers.[78] The next time you are on public transportation or in a waiting room and can't help overhearing conversation, notice how much of it is narrative.

We not only tell stories to others, we tell them to ourselves, and this begins remarkably early. Bruner reports a study of soliloquies recorded from the crib of a child named Emily between the ages of 18 months and 3 years:

> Listening to the tapes and reading the transcripts repeatedly, we were struck by the *constitutive* function of her monologic narrative. She was not simply reporting; she was trying to make sense of her everyday life. She seemed to be in search of an integral structure that could encompass what she had *done* with what she *felt* with what she *believed*.[79]

From the ubiquity of narrative there emerged rather recently, as Bruner recounts it, the notion of "Self as a storyteller." Bruner quotes the psychoanalyst Roy Schafer:

> We are forever telling stories to ourselves. In telling these self-stories *to others* we may, for most purposes, be said to be performing straightforward narrative actions. In saying that we also tell them *to ourselves*, however, we are enclosing one story within another. This is the story that there is a Self to tell something to, a someone else serving as audience who is oneself or one's self . . . On this view, the self is a telling.

Psychoanalysts have discovered what writers of fiction have always known: that the stories we tell about ourselves, although based on our lives, contain "screen memories," even fictions, as well as fact. The truth they contain is not historical truth but *narrative* truth, and the task of the analyst is not archaeological recovery but assistance with the construction of a new narrative that will help the analysand deal more successfully with whatever trouble brought him to analysis, will help him redescribe his life.[80]

The self is a telling. And inevitably a telling about others as well as the self. Indeed, the self cannot be disentangled from significant others except ideologically, leading Bruner to speak, somewhat awkwardly, of a "distributed Self."[81] A distributed self is made up of the significant relations, "identifications," of a lifetime. A distributed self will behave differently in the different spheres and relationships in which it is engaged. If the distributed self doesn't fit too easily with the "deep self" of modern ideology, neither is it merely the shifting play of masks, the "presentations of self in everyday life," of Erving Goffman.[82] Narrative truth is no more secure than any form of truth, but it can be stable, reliable, even profound.

If personal identity resides in the telling, then so does social identity. Families, nations, religions (but also corporations, universities, departments of sociology) know who they are by the stories they tell. The modern discipline of history is closely related to the emergence of the nation-state. This is a peculiarly interesting example for our purposes. Families and religions have seldom been concerned with "scientific accuracy," with conceptual discursiveness, in the stories they tell. Modern nations have required national histories that will be, in a claimed objective sense, true. And unquestionably a great deal of accurate fact has been uncovered. But the narrative shape of national history is not more scientific (or less mythical) than the narrative shape of other identity tellings, something that it does not take debunkers to notice. Benedict Anderson in *Imagined Communities* recounts both the widespread establishment of chairs of history within a generation of the French Revolution and its unleashing of nationalist fervor and of the strange mixture of memory and forgetting that that history produced (not so strange to those familiar with other forms of self-telling).[83]

There is one other feature of narrativity that I want to discuss before coming back to the sense in which narrative is transitional to conceptual representation. In Bruner's account, Kenneth Burke in *A Grammar of Motives* describes a pentad of elements that can be found in any story: an Actor, an Action, a Goal, a Scene, and an Instrument—plus, according to Bruner, Trouble.[84] Trouble results when two or more elements fall out of harmony: the Buddha rejects the preordained Goal when he refuses marriage and the inheritance of his father's kingdom, or Jesus proclaims a radically new understanding of the Scene: the kingdom of God is at hand. These disharmonies

refused married life

are not fortuitous. There is something inherent in the order of human life, of the fact that it is a normative order, of the way things ought to be, that provokes or reveals disorder. The myths of the Australian Aborigines, as W. E. H. Stanner interprets them, express this "immemorial misdirection" of life.[85] Thus the Buddha discovers what his parents seek to keep from him: that human life inevitably involves old age, sickness, and death. And until after the resurrection, Jesus's disciples are too horrified to accept that Jesus must be crucified. So the denial of time in narrative is possible only by taking up time and its Trouble into the heart of narrative itself. The task of the Self's telling is to deal with the Trouble that is at the heart of every life, to find a form that makes it possible to go on in spite of suffering. And, as Benedict Anderson points out, national histories are centrally concerned with "our dead," who must be remembered in order that "they did not die in vain."[86]

If all were well and all manner of things were well, why would we need narrative? Unitive events with their profound sense of wholeness do not give rise to narratives, though they may form the culmination of a narrative, the discovery of a new order out of disorder. We have said, following Schutz, that the world of daily life is characterized by lack, by a fundamental anxiety. Narrative, like all the forms of representation we have discussed so far, does not operate under the terms of the world of daily life, but it does not avoid the fundamental anxiety. Rather it takes the fundamental anxiety into itself and, except in postmodern narrative, which leaves us more anxious than ever, transforms the anxiety into some kind of resolution: not necessarily a "happy ending," perhaps a tragic understanding. Because it is through religion, and religious narrative, that human beings have commonly dealt with the immemorial misdirection of life, we will return to these issues frequently.

Finally, as Bruner notes, "[Children] produce and comprehend stories, are comforted and alarmed by them, long before they are capable of handling the most fundamental Piagetian logical propositions that can be put in linguistic form. Indeed, we even know that logical propositions are most easily comprehended by the child when they are imbedded in an ongoing story. So one is tempted to ask whether narratives may not also serve as early interpretants for 'logical' propositions before the child has the mental equipment to handle them by such later-developing logical calculi as adult humans can muster."[87]

That even the narratives of early childhood are organized through relationships that are in some sense logical warns us against assuming that narrative, or symbolic representation generally, is "irrational." Art, music, poetry, and narrative are not just effusions of feeling. They are all forms of thought and are in principle as deeply rational as mathematics or physics. It is easier for adults as well as children (even for theoretical physicists) to think narratively than it is to think conceptually, so it is not surprising that logical relationships are often expressed in narrative form. Once again Kenneth Burke is helpful. In his commentary on the first three chapters of Genesis, he points out that narrative can be rephrased in terms of logical entailment: a God with authority to command and human beings with the capacity to choose lead to the logical possibility of disobedience and punishment. What is unfolded narratively in a succession of events can be restated logically as entailed in the initial formulation of the problem of order and freedom.[88] The logical restatement is by no means fully equivalent to the narrative, but it does help us see that the narrative, whatever else it is, is not illogical or irrational. Narrative, with its capacity to reach into our bodies and reformulate our identities, individually and socially, also contains, in its womb so to speak, conceptual possibilities. But the attainment of conceptual representation is an achievement in its own right.

Conceptual Representation

Jean Piaget has perhaps done more than anyone else to show how the child moves from symbol to concept in making sense of the world. The transition occurs (in mid-twentieth-century Switzerland) roughly between 7 or 8 and 11 or 12 years of age. The child moves from an egocentric (with the qualifications I have given to that term) world ("Oh, the sun has come with me") to a decentered world. The self and the sun are now seen as independent elements in a world of standard time and space. Even as late as 10 to 12, however, the child still attributes will and intention to a river or the sun (and, I would hold, in dreams and some moods so do adults of any age).[89]

Piaget notes, in a way reminiscent of George Herbert Mead, that the shift occurs in connection with social learning: "Only toward the end of the egocentric period does the child become capable of distinguishing between points of view, and thus of learning both to recognize his own (as distinct from other possible ones) and to resist suggestion."[90] It is also at this time that the child becomes adept at what Piaget calls "formal operations"— logical thought and mathematics.

The "decentered" world of late childhood approximates what we have called the world of daily life. It is not a world entirely controlled by what I will describe in a moment as conceptual representation, for narrative of a certain sort—realistic, literal narrative—and dialogue are indispensable resources for the world of daily life. But literal narrative is already halfway to conceptual representation, for it implies stable terms that correspond more or less accurately to a reality that is really there. Concepts are based on clear definition and accurate observation, so that they are concepts *of* something definite. When logic and observation are methodically combined, they render knowledge, *episteme* as the Greek philosophers put it, as opposed to *doxa,* opinion. Knowledge is based on demonstration; narrative does not demonstrate; rhetoric can persuade but not demonstrate. The world of daily life normally is constituted much more by opinion, by narrative and rhetoric, than by demonstration. Indeed, the world of strict demonstration, of science (the Greek *episteme* can also be translated as "science"), is as much an alternate reality relative to the world of daily life as is music or religion.

Nonetheless, a degree of practical demonstration is an indispensable part of the world of daily life. If the world of daily life is also the world of working, then accuracy in relating means to ends is certainly part of it. Often this feature of the world of daily life is referred to as rationality, as in rational choice or rational actor theory, but this is to use the term in its narrowed sense of instrumental rationality, important enough, but hardly exhaustive. It is equally unfortunate to refer to music, say, or religion, as irrational, or to attempt to explain them as "really" forms of instrumental rationality. Music and religion have their own rationality, which is not instrumental.

Some ability to use conceptual representation is characteristic of late childhood in every culture. Conceptual representation renders possible a world of objects independent of subjects, a world that is "decontextualized." This is part of the enormous power of conceptual representation, the ability to manipulate objects without being disturbed by subjective impulse, wish, or whim. But the independence of the world of objects is also the source of the limitation of conceptual consciousness. Everything is now an object, even one's own self, and certainly other selves. On the one hand, the emergence of conscious reflection (of the mature ego for the first time—which makes it problematic to use the term "egocentric" for small children), with the capacity to think clearly about objective reality, is a triumph. On the other hand, if conceptual representation is not reintegrated with the other forms of representation, then serious distortion may occur. This is not usually a problem in the world of daily life, where conceptual representation makes itself felt only momentarily and in fragments. However, in those cultures where conceptual representation has achieved significant spheres of dominance, difficulties can indeed emerge.

The discovery of the concept, in ancient Greece by Socrates or Plato, had powerful consequences. Plato used concepts to criticize myth but then reintegrated them into dialogue, narrative (the life and death of Socrates), and even myth (the myths near the end of several major dialogues). Greek philosophy, not without tension to be sure, could be fruitfully integrated with Christian religion for centuries. But in early modern Europe the liberation of the concept took a more radical turn. In connection with the rise of modern science the rejection of metaphor, symbol, and myth became explicit. Hobbes, for example, in a passage we could interpret as intended to refute Yeats's notion of embodied truth, which we considered above, said: "Now these words *true, truth,* and *true proposition,* are equivalent to one another; for truth consists in speech, and not in the things spoken of; and though *true* be sometimes opposed to *apparent* or *feigned,* yet it is always to be referred to the truth of a proposition."[91] In *Leviathan* Hobbes takes on the role of word policeman. In listing the abuses of speech, he writes: "Secondly, when [people] use words metaphorically; that is, in other sense than that they are ordained for; and thereby deceive others." He condemns talk of transubstantiation as a kind of "absurdity" that "may rightly be numbred amongst the many sorts of Madnesse." And he tells us that there is no such thing as "*Finis ultimis,* (utmost ayme,) nor *Summum Bonum,* (greatest Good,) as is spoken of in the Books of the old Morall Philosophers."[92] Reality is matter in motion and our language should conform to it. Thus, Hobbes would banish the language of poetry, theology, and traditional moral philosophy.

Descartes was as concerned as Hobbes to remove the vestiges of preconceptual thought. As Rosenstock-Huessy writes:

In his booklet on method, [Descartes] seriously, without any trace of humour, complained that man had impressions before his mind developed to the full power of logic. For twenty years, so his complaint runs, I was impressed confusedly by objects which I was unable to understand. Instead of having my brain a clean slate at twenty, I found innumerable false ideas engraved upon it. What a pity that man is unable to think clearly from the day of his birth, or that he should have memories which antedate his maturity.

Rosenstock-Huessy points out that Descartes's conceptual asceticism might have helped his mathematical and scientific studies, but "the truth is that the great Cartesius, when he obliterated the impressions of the child René, maimed himself for any social perception outside natural science."[93]

However problematic, something of the greatest importance was going on in the writings of the best minds of the seventeenth century in Europe. A radical shift from previous forms of thought was occurring. Ernest Gellner calls it the "Big Ditch" in the history of human cognition because it separates the modern West (and by now most of the world) from everyone else in history.[94] Just to suggest the magnitude of the change, we may turn to Lucien Febvre, as summarized by Stanley Tambiah, who pointed out that the following terms were not yet in use in the sixteenth century:

Adjectives such as "absolute" or "relative"; "abstract" or "concrete"; "intentional," "inherent," "transcendental"; nouns such as "causality" and "regularity"; "concept" and "criterion"; "analyses" and "syntheses"; "deduction" and "induction," "coordination" and "classification." Even the word "system" came into usage only in the middle of the seventeenth century. "Rationalism" itself was not christened till very late in the nineteenth century.[95]

But the process of scientific discovery has never been as pristine as Descartes and Hobbes would have liked. Michael Polanyi has written extensively of the "intellectual passions" that underlie any significant scientific discovery.[96] Jerome Bruner has developed the well-known distinction between scientific discovery, which is indeed passionate, sometimes chaotic, and often governed more by symbolic representation, by metaphor or even dream, than by conceptual reason, and the process of verification, or, as Karl Popper says, of falsification, where scientific method rules in all its stringency.[97]

Early modern science is full of examples where symbolic representation seems to be the midwife of conceptual discovery. Copernicus cannot be fully understood except in the context of Neoplatonic mysticism with its preoccupation with the heavenly bodies, especially the sun. In *De Revolutionibus* (1543) he wrote, "In the middle of all sits the sun enthroned. How could we place this luminary in any better position in this most beautiful temple from which to illuminate the whole at once? . . . so the Sun sits upon a royal throne ruling his children the planets which circle around him."[98] Kepler, expanding the Copernican theory by modeling the orbits of the planets, recounts his discovery in ecstatic terms:

> That for which I have devoted the best part of my life to astronomical contemplations, for which I joined Tycho Brahe . . . at last I have brought it to light, and recognized its truth beyond all my hopes . . . So now since eighteen months ago the dawn, three months ago the proper light of day, and indeed a very few days ago the pure Sun itself of the most marvelous contemplation has shown forth—nothing holds me; I will indulge my sacred fury; I will taunt mankind with the candid confession that I have stolen the golden vases of the Egyptians, in order to build of them a tabernacle to my God, far indeed from the bounds of Egypt.

Kepler's great work, from the fifth book of which this quotation is taken, was entitled, significantly, *Harmonice Mundi* (1619). Kepler speculates that "in the sun there dwells an intellect simple, intellectual fire or mind, whatever it may be, the fountain of all harmony." If the sun is itself *nous* (Reason, containing Plato's notion of measure, God), then it is the ultimate source of cosmic harmony in general and planetary harmony in particular. Kepler, as Polanyi tells us, "even went so far as to write down the tune of each planet in musical notation."[99] All this might be frivolous if Copernicus and Kepler had not laid the foundations of our modern understanding of the cosmos. There is something marvelous in the fact that the man who confirmed the Copernican heliocentric theory of the solar system actually "heard" the music of the spheres.

It is not surprising that metaphor should be so important in scientific discovery. Seeing something "as" something else, or "in terms of" something else, perhaps as something from an unexpectedly different realm, as Kenneth Burke explained the metaphorical process, provides the generative idea that can lead to a radically new hypothesis.[100] But new hypotheses must be tested (confirmed, falsified) in the much more mundane process of what Thomas Kuhn calls "ordinary science."[101] It is this process that operates under the constraints that Descartes and Hobbes proposed. It is here that the "positivist" process of testing theoretical propositions against real data takes the form of a commonsense correspondence theory of truth, whatever the philosophers may think.

Yet, as Gellner has reminded us, it is no good turning up our noses at such a process.[102] It has provided sure knowledge, knowledge that has allowed human beings to understand and transform the natural world—though, for reasons that should be obvious from the argument of this chapter, it has not yet similarly transformed, and is unlikely to transform, our knowledge of the human world, where scientific forms of knowledge, always appropriate, must be complemented by other ways of knowing, what we call the humanities. Yet it is not science as another reality that has transformed the world, but its application through technology, a form that unites scientific knowledge and the concerns of the world of daily life. Like the world of daily life, technology is preoccupied with lack and its overcoming, economically, politically, militarily. The instrumental reason of the world of daily life, armed with the new scientific knowledge, can become the victim of hubris and megalomania. Medicine is pushed to overcome death itself, but military technology is pushed to the brink of total annihilation. Given the enormous richness of human consciousness and culture, the multiple realities that the various forms of representation can call forth, the band of technology would seem to be narrow. Yet its discovery has consequences beyond calculation. Robinson Jeffers commented laconically on those consequences:

> A little knowledge, a pebble from the shingle
> A drop from the oceans: who would have dreamed this
>   infinitely little too much?[103]

For that little knowledge not to be too much, it must be reintegrated with the other forms of knowing that we have been considering in this chapter, and with ethical reflection, which itself unites conceptual thinking with forms more deeply embedded in human experience.

Yet science itself is without utilitarian concern, is an effort of pure understanding, however involved, as is every other sphere, in mundane preoccupations. The contemplative moment of sheer wonder is not limited to Copernicus and Kepler but occurs wherever the pursuit of knowledge bears fruit. At its highest level conceptual knowing returns to the symbolic, the musical, in the appreciation of pure form, or to the enactive, a sense of bodily delight. For the person who understands it, reading Aristotle's *Metaphysics* or Hegel's *Logic* can set off a subliminal dance. Bertrand Russell wrote, "The true spirit of delight, the exaltation, the sense of being more than Man, which is the touchstone of highest excellence, is to be found in mathematics as surely as in poetry."[104] A true understanding of science can be a barrier to our megalomania.

In this chapter we have considered the building blocks out of which will come ritual, myth, and theology (and the traditions of reflective thought of the non-Christian religions), the cultural forms around which religion develops. They will take on new meaning as we consider them in the life and history of actual societies.

2

Religion and Evolution

Chapter 1 was about religion and ontogeny. It was not an effort to understand the development of religion in the life course of the individual, though that would be a valuable undertaking; instead its purpose was to look at human development as the acquisition of a series of capacities, all of which have contributed to the formation of religions. This chapter is about religion and phylogeny, religion in deep history. When did religion begin? If only among humans, were there earlier developments that made its emergence possible, even in other species, and that might help us understand it? If we assume, as I do, that religion as defined in the Preface and Chapter 1 is confined to the genus *Homo* and perhaps even to the species *Homo sapiens,* where do that genus and species stand in relation to the whole story of evolution as far back as we can go? And what do I mean by evolution as a process that includes everything from single-cell organisms to contemporary human society and culture? That is what this chapter is about.

Stories

If we observe the history of human culture, we will find an abundance of myths of origin, some of which will be treated seriously in later chapters, but there is one story about origins that, at least among educated people, has a kind of priority today, and that is the story as told by science: in terms of the universe, scientific cosmology; in terms of life, evolution. These are extraordinary stories, and we will have to recapitulate some of them. But let us note, they are stories, narratives, and even, in a sense—because they have been given that sense— myths. Thus as we begin to consider these stories, we must also keep in mind what kind of stories they are and to what uses they have been and are being put.

44

There is a problem here, one that faces everyone who accepts the story of cosmic evolution as the metanarrative of educated people because it is the metanarrative of science with its overwhelming prestige in today's world; it is certainly my problem. As Geertz put it when trying to define science as a cultural mode, science requires, at least as an ideal, "disinterested observation." Even if it takes the form of narrative, as it does at times in most sciences, the narrative offered is backed up with evidence and argument. Each critical point in it must be demonstrated in the face of criticism and doubt and is revisable in the face of new evidence. The problem I alluded to above is that the very cultural form of narrative inevitably moves us beyond disinterested observation and established fact. Narrative is a pretheoretical form, one, as we saw in the last chapter, that is closely related to a sense of identity, both of self and of others. We are our story, and every group we belong to is its story.

David Christian is well aware of this aspect of narrative, though he is uneasy about it. He says that his big history is a story, indeed a creation myth, and the people it is "for" must be "modern human beings, educated in the scientific traditions of the modern world." But he notes parenthetically, "Curiously, this means that the *narrative* structure of the modern creation myth, like all creation myths, may appear pre-Copernican, despite its definitely *post*-Copernican content."[1] Exactly. As we will see in a moment, this modern creation myth inevitably gives rise, even in the modern scientifically oriented human beings most likely to believe it, among whom I include myself, to feelings and thoughts that are clearly pre-Copernican.

My whole book is awash in a sea of stories. I have, by calling my book *Religion in Human Evolution,* chosen to take as my primary metanarrative the modern creation myth that David Christian describes. As a social scientist I really have no other alternative if I am to be true to my calling, and, practically speaking, this is the only metanarrative that will allow me adequately to describe and compare all the other narratives and metanarratives that compose human history.

That does not mean it is the only story. In the course of writing this book, which is a history of histories, and a story of stories, I have become involved with many of the stories I recount to the point of at least partial conversion. In the extensive work that went into the four chapters dealing with the axial age—the chapters on ancient Israel, Greece, China, and India—each taking a year apiece, except two years for India where I knew the least to start with, I found myself morose as I completed each chapter, having come to live in a world I didn't want to leave but wanted to go on learning more about. Another way of putting it is that in each case I was learning more about myself and the world I live in; the stories were shaping my understanding. After all, that's what stories do.

But to tell the truth, I couldn't remain "disinterested," disengaged, even with the scientific metanarrative, where disengagement is an absolute methodological requirement. Here we have to face the fact that we can make category distinctions in principle that we can't completely adhere to in practice. The spheres of life that Geertz, following Schutz, described, in fact overlap. When it comes to telling big stories about the order of existence, then, even if they are scientific stories, they will have religious implications. It is better to face this fact head on than try to deny it. In fact I have discovered that some of my natural science colleagues find themselves crossing boundaries even when they don't intend to. Here is what Eric Chaisson, professor of physics and astronomy at Tufts University and author of *Cosmic Evolution,* has to say about the story he has told in his book:

Not least, we have also been guided by notions of beauty and symmetry in science, by the search for simplicity and elegance, by an attempt to explain the widest range of phenomena with the fewest possible principles . . . The resulting evolutionary epic, rises above the collection of its copious parts, potentially granting meaning and rationality to an otherwise unworldly endeavor. Intelligent life is an animated conduit through which the Universe comes to know itself . . .

Perhaps now is the time to widen the quest for understanding still further, to expand the intellectual effort beyond conventional science— to engage the larger, non-scientific communities of philosophers, theologians, and others who often resonate with the cosmic-evolutionary theme even if not in name, all in an ambitious attempt to construct a millennial worldview of who we are, whence we came, and how we fit into the cosmic scheme of things as wise, ethical, human beings.

Humankind is entering an age of synthesis such as occurs only once in several generations, perhaps only once every few centuries. The years ahead will surely be exciting, productive, perhaps even deeply significant, largely because the scenario of cosmic evolution provides an opportunity to inquire systematically and synergistically into the nature of our existence—to mount a concerted effort to a modern universe history *(Weltallgeschichte)* that people of all cultures can readily understand and adopt. As we begin the new millennium, such a coherent story of our very being—a powerful and true myth—can act as an effective intellectual vehicle to invite all cultures to become participants, not just spectators, in the building of a whole new legacy.[2]

Chaisson, in saying it is time to move beyond "conventional science," is himself recognizing that he is moving into another sphere, and we will note the clues to what sphere he is moving into. By using the word "epic" he suggests he is moving into the realm of poetry, which is surely part of the truth, but most of the signs point to the fact that he is moving into the realm of religion. When he speaks of a "millennial worldview," he is clearly pointing to one of Geertz's central elements in religion, an idea of a "general order of existence." When he speaks of the Universe with a capital U he suggests an element of the sacred upon which Durkheim's definition hinges; and at the end of the quoted passage, when he calls on "all cultures to become participants, not just spectators, in the building of a whole new legacy," he is drawing the further Durkheimian conclusion that "religion is a system of beliefs and practices relative to the sacred *which unites those who adhere to them in a moral community.*" He is, in fact, calling for a new church to go with his new religion.

I have no problem with Chaisson's endeavor—indeed, I have a lot of sympathy with it—but I would be happier if he had taken responsibility for what he is doing rather than implying that all this is still science, even if "beyond conventional science." And he falls into one of the pitfalls of all religions when he speaks of the story he tells as a "powerful and true myth," with the implication that other myths are not true, for truth is one of the marks that gives his religion its distinction. This leads perilously close to the implication that all the other religions are false. Then what happens to the vast majority of humanity that doesn't understand, much less believe in, his myth?

Chaisson would have avoided this error had he been clear about this: myth is not science. Myth can be true, but it is a different kind of truth from the truth of science and must be judged by different criteria, and the myth he tells, though it draws on science, is not science and so cannot claim scientific truth. I would argue that the myths told by the ancient Israelite prophets, by Socrates, Plato, and Aristotle, by Confucius and Mencius, and by the Buddha, just to stay within the purview of this book, are all true myths. They overlap with each other and with Chaisson's myth, but even in their conflicts, which are sometimes serious, they are all worthy of belief, and I find it possible to believe in all of them in rather deep but not exclusive ways.

Mary Midgley, in her analysis of the unavoidable overlap of science and religion when it comes to the theory of evolution, the best such analysis of its kind that I have come across, notes that there are two ways in which evolutionary theory becomes religious: cosmic optimism and cosmic pessimism.[3] She finds in a careful reading of Darwin himself that he could not avoid these resonances but, being more balanced than most of his supporters and most of his opponents, he held on to both responses, emphasizing one or the other, depending on the context.[4] Eric Chaisson has given us an example of cosmic optimism. Midgley turns to the Nobel Prize–winning French biochemist Jacques Monod for an example of cosmic pessimism:

> It is perfectly true that science attacks values. Not directly, since science is no judge of them, and *must* ignore them; but it subverts every one of the mythical or philosophical ontogenies upon which the animist tradition, from the Australian aborigines to the dialectical materialists, has based morality, values, duties, rights, prohibitions.
>
> If he accepts this message in its full significance, man must at last wake out of his millenary dream and discover his total solitude, his fundamental isolation. He must realize that, like a gypsy, he lives on the boundary of an alien world; a world that is deaf to his music, and as indifferent to his hopes as it is to his sufferings or his crimes.[5]

Although a distinguished scientist and one of the founders of molecular biology, Monod in the above passage has entered the world of metaphysical speculation and, perhaps not surprisingly, finds there the thought of a leading French existentialist. As Midgley says of him, he has created "a drama in which Sartrean man appears as the lonely hero challenging an alien and meaningless universe." To me it is especially poignant that Monod's first thought about the alien universe was that it was "deaf to his music," considering that he himself was a fine musician. With all due qualifications, I believe that we must also listen to Monod, a very intelligent man and a master of evolutionary biology. Even though, as is now widely believed, morality and religion are evolutionary emergents, evolution cannot tell us which one of them to follow. For those who can find meaning only in evolution, that must be a discouraging but indisputable truth.

Finally, though, to close these reflections on the inevitable area of overlap of evolution and religion, let me quote a charming passage from Oliver

Sacks, in which the prolific neurologist moderates his remarks within limits not respected by Chaisson or Monod, but also reveals what I would also consider an indisputable truth—namely, our kinship with all life.

> Life on our planet is several billion years old, and we literally embody this deep history in our structures, our behaviors, our instincts, our genes. We humans retain, for example, the remnants of gill arches, much modified, from our fishy ancestors—and even the neural systems which once controlled gill movement. As Darwin wrote in *The Descent of Man:* Man still bears in his bodily frame the indelible stamp of his lowly origin . . .
>
> In 1837, in the first of many notebooks he was to keep on "the species problem," Darwin sketched a tree of life. Its brachiating shape, so archetypal and potent, reflected the balance of evolution and extinction. Darwin always stressed the continuity of life, how all living things are descended from a common ancestor, and how we are in this sense all related to each other. So humans are related not only to apes and other animals, but to plants too. (Plants and animals, we know now, share 70 percent of their DNA.) And yet, because of that great engine of natural selection—variation—every species is unique and each individual is unique, too . . .
>
> I rejoice in the knowledge of my biological uniqueness and my biological antiquity and my biological kinship with all other forms of life. This knowledge roots me, allows me to feel at home in the natural world, to feel that I have my own sense of biological meaning, whatever my role in the cultural, human world.[6]

So for Sacks, biology doesn't answer every question; he still has to live in the cultural, human world. But feeling at home in the natural world is no small thing, and considerably happier than living like a gypsy on the boundary of an alien world. As I now move to trying to tell the modern scientific metanarrative in highly condensed form, let me just reaffirm my conviction that there is undoubted truth in all the reactions, including the rather different ones from these three scientists, but also those from many other scientists and nonscientists, to this extraordinary, and disturbing, metanarrative. I also believe that, in spite of our differences, we do not need to fall into culture wars in which we denounce and anathematize those with whom we disagree. This is a big universe; there is room for all of us.

What Followed the Big Bang

I want to recount briefly what modern cosmology has to say about the origin and history of the universe. Because of the nature of my story, I am more interested in biology than in physics, more in mammals than in other kinds of organisms, and more in humans than in other animals. Still, we, as modern humans trying to understand this human practice we call religion, need to situate ourselves in the broadest context we can, and it is with scientific cosmology that we must start. I am particularly concerned that we keep in mind the question of scale. We need not fall into Monod's pessimism, but it is an unimaginably huge universe in which we live and it began unimaginably long ago.[7] Where this universe is going we can't know for sure, but the best estimates today are not reassuring: dissolution of everything that exists into its constituent entities strewn at random in a dark and bitterly cold universe that will just go on expanding forever. Of course, that will be billions of years in the future, so we don't have to worry about it. And we can hope that science will discover other, happier, futures. Of one thing we can be sure: science offers us no final view of anything. We have Revised Versions of the Bible every generation or so, but the bible of cosmic evolution is revised every six months or even, probably, every day. Yet we still have to say that this grand metanarrative by which we are supposed to live is not, at least at the moment, terribly cheerful, looked at as a whole.[8]

Something like 13.5 billion years ago (the exact date is still in question but there is general agreement as to the approximate date), something infinitely dense and infinitely hot began to expand dramatically. That is why we speak of big-bang cosmology. Steven Weinberg describes the first one-hundredth second as "a state of infinite density and infinite temperature."[9] Under the conditions at the beginning, there were no atoms, only subatomic particles, and among them only elementary ones. Weinberg describes the situation at the end of the first one-hundredth second:

> We can estimate that this state of affairs was reached at a temperature of about 100 million million million million million degrees (10^{32} °K).[10]
>
> At this temperature all sorts of strange things would have been going on . . . The very idea of "particle' would not yet have had any meaning . . . Speaking loosely, each particle would be about as big as the observable universe![11]

I cannot say that I understand what Weinberg is describing, other than that it dwarfs any human scale of imagination. Still, from early in that first second, science can give us a rather specific and detailed description of what was happening as this infinitely small something expanded, at first more rapidly than the speed of light, so that by the end of the first instant it was larger than a galaxy.

We might well ask, what was happening before the big bang? Science really can't answer that question, but maybe it is not a meaningful question at all. Maybe there is no "before" to ask about. As this infinitely dense, infinitely hot something expanded, it created the time and space into which it expanded. Another possible explanation would be that a previous universe, after expanding for many billions of years, condensed again until it became this very small, very dense, very hot thing that exploded to form our universe. But really, earlier than the first hundredth second, there are only conjectures. If traditional myths of origin raise more questions than they answer, we should not be surprised that a scientific myth of origin should do the same. Science is nothing if not the continuous asking of new questions.[12]

Before giving a schematic account of the early development of the universe, we might try to get a sense of what 13.5 billion years might mean. (I can't even begin to imagine what 10^{32} °K of heat would mean.) In so doing I will draw on David Christian's ingenious idea of collapsing the history of the universe by a factor of 1 billion, so that each billion years is reduced to one year as a way of giving a human meaning to these vast expanses of time. Thus the big bang, beginning the universe, began 13.5 years ago; the sun and solar system, 4.5 years ago; the first living organisms on earth, single-cell organisms, between 4 and 3.5 years ago; multicellular organisms, 7 months ago; *Homo sapiens,* about 50 minutes ago; agricultural communities, 5 minutes ago; and the great explosion of science and technology, in the midst of which we live, within the last second.[13] Out of the 13.5 "years" of the life of the universe, historians have devoted themselves to the last 3 minutes and mostly to the last minute or less. This book is almost entirely dependent on historians, but if we are to set human history in the context of the modern scientific metanarrative, we need to look back at least a few "months," and, even if briefly, a few "years."

We have already noted that the universe began with something infinitely small, perhaps smaller than an atom, but an atom that was many trillions of degrees hot, that expanded with a speed faster than the speed of light, so that almost at once it had expanded to the size of a galaxy.[14] The extraordinary rapidity of this expansion ensures that most of the universe will never be observable from earth, as the light from it will be too distant ever to reach us. As the universe expanded, it began to cool. The entities and forces with which physics is familiar began to appear. After about 300,000 years, atoms of hydrogen and, in lesser quantity, helium, began to form. Once clouds of hydrogen and helium appeared, the force of gravity began to sculpt them into forms. A million years or so after the big bang, these forms attained new levels of complexity that gave rise to stars—and to galaxies composed of stars and cosmic dust, taking the form of flat rotating disks with arcs of matter streaming out from very hot centers. Gravity pulled the clouds of hydrogen and helium together, heated them up so that the stars burned with tremendous heat, using the atoms of which they are composed as fuels. It was in the intense heat within stars that all the other elements besides hydrogen and helium were formed: it was the stars that gave rise to chemistry. Very large stars quickly (in cosmic time) burned themselves up and exploded as supernovae, visible to our astronomers, spewing out a variety of chemical elements as they did so. About 4.5 billion years ago, perhaps as a result of a supernova explosion, our sun and solar system emerged, perhaps composed of the debris from the explosion.

David Christian notes that we have not taken seriously enough the meaning of this modern cosmology as it describes the sun and the solar system, including our planet. Copernicus was supposed to have unsettled human self-confidence by pointing out that the earth is not the center of the universe but revolves around the sun. Now it is quite clear that the sun isn't the center of anything much either. As Christian puts it: "Our sun, it seems, is situated in an undistinguished suburb in [the Milky Way] a second-rank galaxy (the Andromeda Galaxy is the largest in our local group), in a group of galaxies that lies toward the edge of the Virgo Supercluster, which contains many thousands of other galaxies."[15] How "decentered" can you get?

Our earth was just one of several planets that formed in the solar system revolving around this new star, our sun. The early history of the solar system, and of our planet, consisted of constant collisions of the variety of materials out of which the solar system was being formed. As Christian vividly describes it, "we must imagine the early earth as a mixture of rocky materials, metals, and trapped gases, subjected to constant bombardment by smaller planetesimals and without much of an atmosphere. The early earth would indeed have seemed a hellish place to humans."[16] As the earth increased in size due to the cosmic material that gravity was drawing to it, it heated up so that its interior became molten, with the heavy metallic elements such as iron and nickel forming a core and creating the earth's characteristic magnetic field, which shielded the earth from the high-energy particles that, had they been able to reach the earth's surface, might have interrupted the chemical processes that would eventually lead to life. As the metals sank to the core, the gases bubbled toward the earth's surface, making the earth a "massive volcanic field." As the earth cooled, the water vapor that had accumulated in the atmosphere "fell in torrential rains lasting millions of years," thus creating the oceans, where life would first appear.[17] There are probably millions of other solar systems just in our own galaxy, but whether any of them are likely to have planets like earth is a matter of dispute.

This is a very brief and inadequate description of the early history of the universe and ultimately of our own planet. Whether Eric Chaisson is justified in speaking of "cosmic evolution" is beyond my competence to decide. He believes that there is a continuity between the increasing levels of complexity involved in the emergence of galaxies, stars, and planetary systems, and the increasing levels of complexity in the evolution of life. Some biologists think that an increase in complexity is only one of the characteristics of biological evolution and not necessarily the most important. In any case it is worth remembering our old friend (or enemy), the second law of thermodynamics. There is a price to be paid for increasing complexity, cosmically or biologically: greater complexity requires greater energy input to sustain it. The stars will eventually all burn themselves up, even a middle-size star like our sun, which will last longer than the huge stars that burned fiercely and blew up as they (relatively) rapidly consumed their own fuel, but the same fate ultimately awaits all the stars, whatever their size.

The story I am about to tell, the story of life, is surely more intelligible to human beings than the story I have, in barest outline, just told. After all, we live on the earth and we see life all around us. That it has a long history is not so hard to imagine. That through much of the 4.5 billion years of its history the earth was wildly different from what we know begins to be hard to think about—it takes us close to the borderline of our imagination. But the history of the universe, in the midst of which we still live and out of which our earth came, is intimidating. It seems to intimidate even a Nobel Prize-winning physicist such as Steven Weinberg. Having described some of the competing cosmological models, he writes:

However all these problems may be resolved, and whichever cosmo-logical model proves correct, there is not much comfort in any of this. It is almost irresistible for humans to believe that we have some special relation to the universe, that human life is not just a more-or-less farcical outcome of a chain of accidents reaching back to the first three minutes, but that we were somehow built in from the begin-ning . . . It is hard to realize that this [earth] is just a tiny part of an overwhelmingly hostile universe. It is even harder to realize that the present universe has evolved from an unspeakably unfamiliar early condition, and faces a future extinction of endless cold or intolerable heat. The more the universe seems comprehensible, the more it seems pointless.[18]

Here we see the perils that narrative creates for the narrator. Weinberg's story creates in him, too, an "almost irresistible" desire for meaning. If, as Mary Midgley writes, "meaning is connection," then the desire for meaning is perfectly natural, for we are, however hard it is to understand, surely con-nected to the universe of which we are a part. Our need to find meaning in it is part of our "hunger for meaning," which is "central to our lives," as Midgley puts it. "It is the wider motive of which our theoretical curiosity is only a part. It is the impulse of our imaginations to order the world with a view to understanding and contemplating it—something which must be done before theory-building can even begin," she writes.[19] Weinberg, by pro-claiming that the universe is "overwhelmingly hostile" and in the end "point-less," wants to sweep any such hunger for meaning aside as something child-ish. But it could be that it is Weinberg who is being childish, that he is angry because he expected the universe to be nice and have a point, and is disap-pointed that it doesn't, almost like finding out that God, in whom he em-phatically doesn't believe, has let him down.[20] However, Weinberg can no more evade the search for meaning than the rest of us can. Like Jacques Monod, he has opted for cosmic pessimism as his meaning.

Not quite, though. He does find consolation: "But if there is no solace in the fruits of our research, there is at least some consolation in the research itself . . . The effort to understand the universe is one of the very few things that lifts human life a little above the level of farce, and gives it some of the grace of tragedy."[21] In these closing remarks of his book *The First Three Min-utes* (scientists frequently allow themselves rhetorical riffs in their final re-marks, which are often most revealing), what Weinberg has really done is to move from science as a cultural system to religion as a cultural system, and affirm the practice of science as his religion; fair enough, if it weren't quite so condescending to the rest of us who are left at the level of farce. But then religions are often exclusive.[22]

Although the history of the cosmos is much more intimidating than the history of life, would it not be possible, in the face of the cosmic pessimists, to take a position close to that of Oliver Sacks in relation to biological evolution? After all, our bodies are composed entirely of entities derived from those elementary particles that appeared in the first one-hundredth second after the big bang. We are, quite literally, part of the universe. It is not necessary to think that there was an intelligent designer who had us in mind to be grateful that the universe, after all, did lead to us, and that we can think about the whole of which we are a part. Of course, here I am talking about "worldview," not science, but I don't think there is such a thing as a "worldview of science," because science is not the cultural sphere of worldviews, though it gives rise to many.

Early Life on Earth

Once one begins to understand what the universe is like in which life on earth first appeared, a universe that was already nearly 10 billion years old at the time, it is not so remarkable that we don't yet fully understand life's origin. Even the possibility of thinking about this story that led to us is only a little over 150 years old, and it is a story that has been continually filled in almost daily ever since, though the problem of the origin of life is still far from solved. This and other unsolved problems serve to tempt those so inclined to invoke the intervention of a creator or intelligent designer, yet those hypotheses succeed only in increasing by several magnitudes the problems that need explaining.

Before we start thinking of miraculous interventions, however, what this relatively recent knowledge should do to us is to make us realize both what a gigantic cosmic history we are a part of and what very small and limited creatures we are in the face of it. Richard Dawkins, who is, when he is not bashing religion, a gifted science writer, has pointed out that we see the world through a narrow slit in the electromagnetic spectrum that is otherwise entirely dark to us and that reaches from radio waves at the long end to gamma rays at the short end. Other species have slightly different capacities: for example, some insects can see ultraviolet waves that we cannot see, and so live in an "ultraviolet garden" to which we are blind. But this is only one indication of our profound limitations:

> The metaphor of the narrow window of light, broadening out into a spectacularly wide spectrum, serves us in other areas of science. We live near the centre of a cavernous museum of magnitudes viewing the world with sense organs and nervous systems that are equipped to perceive and understand only a small middle range of sizes, moving at the middle range of speeds. We are at home with objects ranging in size from a few kilometres (the view from a mountaintop) to about a tenth of a millimetre (the point of a pin). Outside this range even our imagination is handicapped, and we need the help of instruments and mathematics—which, fortunately, we can learn to deploy. The range of sizes, distances or speeds with which our imaginations are comfortable is a tiny band, set in the midst of a gigantic range of the possible, from the scale of quantum strangeness at the smaller end to the scale of Einsteinian cosmology at the larger.[23]

Dawkins quotes J. B. S. Haldane, a great mid-twentieth-century evolutionary biologist, as saying, "Now my own suspicion is that the universe is not only queerer than we suppose, but queerer than we can suppose . . . I suspect that there are more things in heaven and earth than are dreamed of, or can be dreamed of, in any philosophy."[24] If Haldane is right that we live in a very strange universe, then we should not be surprised that very strange things happen, without needing to imagine external interference.

One of the stranger things about our universe is that we are present in it. One way of thinking about it, to stay at the planetary level, is called the anthropic principle, which starts from a simple, though in the larger scheme of things quite startling, fact that "we exist here on earth."[25] There are a great many things about our earth that make our existence possible, such as the presence of liquid water, essential to life, but if earth had had an orbit closer to the sun, that water would be boiling, or if farther, frozen. Further, the earth's orbit had to be close to circular rather than strongly elliptical or in some seasons our climate would have been too hot for life and in other seasons too cold. And, as Dawkins points out (contra Monod and Weinberg), if we live on a "friendly" planet, one that can support life, we also live in a "friendly" cosmos: "Physicists have calculated that, if the laws and constants of physics had been even slightly different, the universe would have developed in such a way that life would have been impossible."[26] But even with a cosmos and a planet that were in some deep sense "friendly" to life, the emergence of life itself is also extraordinarily strange. To quote Dawkins again, "The origin of life only had to happen once. We can therefore allow it to have been an extremely improbable event, many orders of magnitude more improbable than most people realize."[27]

It is true that the warm sea of 3.5 billion years ago was a kind of "chemical soup" with many of the molecules that could form parts of unicellular organisms already present. There are a number of theories about what had to happen before self-replicating organisms emerged, and many of them are plausible. So far laboratory experiments to recreate the conditions in which primal life originated have not succeeded in creating life, which is hardly surprising, given that we do not know exactly what that chemical soup was composed of or what exactly the conditions were on earth at the time. There are two main ways in which the problem of the origin of life is framed. One has to do with statistical probabilities, which I have already mentioned. Our sense of probabilities is based on a lifetime of less than a century, and it is in that framework that we necessarily and usefully think about probability. But if life appeared on earth spontaneously around a half billion years after our planet was formed, that gives an entirely different range of probabilities, so that something that would happen extremely rarely might still happen. That way of approaching the problem makes it a matter of a sheer chance encounter of just the right variables to produce life.

Another approach argues that sheer fortuitous accident as an explanation for the origin of life is difficult to imagine even at the most cosmic level of chance probabilities. This alternative approach turns to the phenomenon of emergence, in which apparently chaotic phenomena show the possibility of self-organization, again under just the right circumstances, yet more probable circumstances than sheer chance alone. There are a number of people who have pursued the idea of emergence in somewhat different ways. At the moment the jury is still out on how to explain the origin of life, but both theoretical and experimental work proceeds apace, so we will surely know more before long. In any case the emergence of radical novelty is a recurring theme in evolution, and we will return to it as we go along.[28]

The oldest surviving form of life on earth, though probably preceded by simpler forms, is the unicellular organisms called prokaryotes, whose DNA floats freely within the cell, with ribosomes that assemble proteins using instructions from the DNA. Prokaryotes multiply by cell division. For over a billion years these were the only organisms there were until, quite suddenly, 2.5 billion years ago, eukaryotes appeared, still unicellular though considerably larger than prokaryotes, and with a nucleus for the DNA and a number of other kinds of complexity, including new ways of multiplying. Both prokaryotes and eukaryotes often had tails that allowed movement. The division between prokaryotes and eukaryotes is the basic division of all life forms, for it is from the eukaryotes that multicellular organisms formed, and all multicellular organisms are composed of combinations of eukaryotes, and in an important sense are eukaryotes, having marginally and relatively recently branched off from the much more numerous unicellular prokaryotes.

But let us go back to the prokaryotes, often called bacteria, unicellular microorganisms that have been the most successful forms of life so far. They have made an incalculable contribution to other forms of life; not only have they created an atmosphere rich in oxygen through photosynthesis, but they are vital in recycling nutrients, with many steps in nutrient cycles depending on them, in the fixation of nitrogen from the atmosphere, and in putrefaction. Being mainly microscopic, they exist within animals and plants as well as independently, and, though some of them can cause disease, they also play significant positive roles, as in aiding human digestion. The fact that some of them cause disease has given bacteria a bad name, and has indeed led to the development, in multicellular organisms like ourselves, of immune systems to counteract them, though something like an arms race develops as both bacteria and immune systems evolve to fight each other. We know that antibiotic medicines that help our bodies fight some bacteria are also involved in such an arms race. Important as all this is, it should not distract us from trying to understand the remarkable phenomenon of bacteria.

We like to think of ourselves, of human beings, as the most successful of all biological species, of our age as "the age of man," or, at least, "the age of mammals," whereas in fact we live, as all life for 4 billion years has lived, in "the age of bacteria," as Stephen Jay Gould has put it. Bacteria are "the organisms that were in the beginning, are now, and probably ever shall be (until the sun runs out of fuel) the dominant creatures on earth by any standard evolutionary criterion of biochemical diversity, range of habitats, resistance to extinction, and perhaps, even in biomass." Gould then goes on to say, "The tree of life is, effectively, a bacterial bush. Two of the three domains [bacteria and archaea] belong to prokaryotes alone, while the three kingdoms of multicellular eukaryotes (plants, animals, and fungi) appear as three twigs of the terminus of the third domain."[29]

So we learn that not only is our sun a minor star in a not very interesting galaxy nowhere near the center of anything, but that our species, of which we are so justly proud, is far from the center of the biological universe, though a considerable danger to the survival of much of that universe—bacteria, however, being relatively safe from our depredations. Gould has long argued that the primary trend of biological evolution is toward diversity, variety, rather than toward greater complexity, which is only a marginal and minor development taking life as a whole.[30] Indeed, there has also been massive evolution toward decreased complexity, as among the vast number of parasite species that normally are less complex than their ancestors after they have offloaded functions onto their hosts. Gould often turns Darwin's image of the tree of life into the bush of life, as a bush shows less directionality in its widely branching stems. I am ready to agree with Gould in giving us another shock to our natural anthropocentrism, but I don't believe, and neither does Gould, that our sheer existence and our complexity are not worthy of the most careful study. However far out in right field (Gould was a great fan of baseball) we as a species might be, we are the only species that we are and we must surely try to understand ourselves. But, as I noted in the Preface, a vote of thanks to the bacteria is surely in order: "The Age of Bacteria transformed the earth from a cratered moonlike terrain of volcanic glassy rocks into the fertile planet in which we make our home."[31] And lest we underestimate these tiny organisms, invisible to the naked eye, we must remember what extraordinary capacities they have.

Although bacteria are still all around us as well as inside us (it is estimated that there are more bacteria in us than the number of our own cells, of which there are at least a trillion and maybe many more), let us return to the only slightly more complex organisms of which we are ultimately composed: the eukaryotes. It is true that bacteria can form colonies, referred to as biofilms, or, more colloquially, as slime, and that in their collective state they differ somewhat in their cellular structure from their state as independent organisms, but it is from eukaryotes that most multicellular bodies, including all the more complex ones, derive. Eukaryotes are on average 100 to 1,000 times larger than bacteria, so that the largest of them may be just visible to the naked eye. They represent a significant increase not only in size but in complexity compared to prokaryotes: they have an internal nucleus that contains the DNA and that is the result of some kind of cell symbiosis. Given the firm exterior surface of the prokaryotes, combining them in a new form was no mean feat. It took perhaps a half billion years for life to emerge from the seas of the early earth, but it took another 1.5 billion before the eukaryotes emerged.

Remembering Gould's strictures about the predominance of prokaryotes and eukaryotes, and the fact that multicellular organisms formed of differentiated eukaryotic cells are mere twigs on the bush of life, we may still consider the remarkable path that these twigs would take and the fact that one of them would eventually lead to us. John Maynard Smith and Eörs Szathmáry, in their book *The Major Transitions in Evolution*, describe the developments of unicellular organisms that we have noted above; the appearance of sexual reproduction among the eukaryotes; the appearance of multicellular eukaryotic organisms involving the differentiation of cells and leading to the three major divisions of fungi, plants, and animals; the development of colonies of multicellular organisms involving nonreproductive castes among some insect groups; the development of primate and then human societies; and finally the development of language among humans.[32] Smith and Szathmáry account for all of these transitions in terms of classical Darwinian natural selection.

Conserved Core Processes

Marc Kirschner and John Gerhart, in their book *The Plausibility of Life,* develop a conception of the organismic control of variation that does not deny but does extend the classical view of natural selection.[33] Because their focus is on animals, they will move us closer to human evolution as the background for understanding religion. Fungi and plants are enormously successful forms of multicellular life of great interest in themselves, but not essential for purposes of my story. In my attempt to translate Kirschner and Gerhart's very complex argument for the purposes of this book, I will inevitably oversimplify, so I warn the reader to consult this important book rather than rely on my summary.

The key to Kirschner and Gerhart's argument is the idea of facilitated variation, which involves much more selective activity by the organism than the usual notion of random mutation suggests. But facilitated variation makes sense only in terms of their other key concept: conserved core processes. What Kirschner and Gerhart stress is that mutations can occur only in organisms that are already structures—already have core processes that have persisted through long ages of evolutionary history—and that mutations, though inevitably random, will be accepted or rejected in terms of how they relate to the conserved core processes. The primary contribution of the book is to clarify how conserved core processes promote variation, that is, "facilitated variation," in ways that produce novel developments in phenotypes without undermining the continuity of the core processes. Stability and change, in this view, enhance each other rather than conflict with each other.

Although the book's main contribution is its spelling out of facilitated variation at the level of cell biology, its argument depends on the notion of conserved core processes, whose origin they do not claim to have fully explained. All of life is a development of the first core process, that of the prokaryote cell. "The most obscure origination of a core process is the creation of the first prokaryotic cell. The novelty and complexity of the cell is so far beyond anything inanimate in the world of today that we are left baffled by how it was achieved."[34] But as with all core processes, the emergence of the prokaryotes produced consequences that are still at work in all living organisms:

> The chemistry of the processes was evolved at least three billion years ago; the components and their activities have been retained unchanged to this day, transmitted to all offspring of this ancestor. It is an amazing level of conservation. After these millions of millennia of evolution, many metabolic enzymes in the bacterium *E. coli* are still more than 50 percent identical in their amino acid sequence to the corresponding human enzymes. For example, of 548 metabolic enzymes sampled from *E. coli,* half are present in all living life forms, whereas only 15 percent are specific to bacteria alone.[35]

Later core processes share certain characteristics: they occur relatively suddenly, they involve major innovations, and they do not consist of piecemeal accretions but involve whole suites of changes.[36] Speaking of the appearance of the second great conserved core process, that of the single-celled eukaryotes 1.5 to 2 billion years ago, Kirschner and Gerhart write, after describing some of the features of prokaryotes that are reorganized in eukaryotes:

> These cases suggest that the great innovations of core processes were not magical moments of creation but periods of extensive modification of both protein structure and function. The changes are not achieved by

facilitated variation of the regulatory kind we have described throughout this book. Instead, during great waves of innovation, preexisting components of prokaryotes changed their protein structure and function in fundamental ways to generate the components of new core processes of the eukaryotic cell.[37]

Kirschner and Gerhart describe "a period of rapid remodeling" that involved "enormous innovations" that are not "magical" but that don't simply follow the logic of facilitated variation that is central to their book. And again, as with the prokaryotes, the new core processes that emerge from this transition survive with remarkable stability in all subsequent eukaryotes, including the multicellular ones—fungi, plants, and animals, and, of course, us. In describing the suite of features that they speak of as the "invention" (their quotation marks) of eukaryotic cells, they write, "The most striking trait is their size and complexity. They are one hundred to one thousand times larger in volume than bacterial cells and have numerous internal membranes that wall off small compartments or organelles ('little organs'), which are specialized for different functions."[38]

The next "intimation of true novelty" comes from the period of perhaps a billion years ago "when multicellular eukaryotes, including animals, first arose." Here again we see the appearance of new conserved core processes: "A controlled fluid environment inside the multicellular epithelial organism was a novelty that promoted communication between animal cells via secreted and received signals." This worked out differently in fungi, plants, and animals, but to speak only of animals, they write, "The controlled internal milieu of animals must have provided the context for the elaboration of a greatly expanded set of signals and receptors, and indeed animals have evolved many kinds of cell-cell signaling." It is these signaling capacities that lead to the development of differentiated cell types, such as those for blood, muscle, and nerves. "The evolution of differentiated cells was a regulatory accomplishment involving new placements and increased amounts of old components. Once evolved, many of these cell types were conserved in metazoan [animal] evolution, from jelly fish to humans."[39]

The next and final set of conserved core processes in Kirschner and Gerhart's analysis has to do with the emergence of body plans among animals: "By 600 million years ago, fairly complex animals were probably present, branching sponges, radial animals such as jellyfish, and the first small bilateral animals (like us, with mirror-image left and right sides), perhaps rather worm-like in form, which left traces of their burrows in the muddy ocean floor, thereafter fossilized. This worm-like animal may have been the ancestor of all modern bilateral animals." But then:

> Rather suddenly, diverse macroscopic anatomy appeared on the Cambrian scene of 543 million years ago. By the Midcambrian, representative animals of all but one of the 30 major modern phyla were present according to fossil records.
>
> The abruptness of the emergence of so many complex anatomies may be an artifact of the special features of fossilization at that time or of some special environmental condition that favored large and more complex animals, or it may be the result of some breakthrough in regulatory control on the cellular level. Once again, a new suite of cellular and multicellular functions emerged rather quickly and was conserved to the present.[40]

We need not describe the details of animal body plans. Most of them share certain features, such as a mouth at the front and an anus at the rear, some kind of digestive system in between, some kind of heart and circulatory system, at least the beginnings of nerve connections, and so forth. It is worth noting that one phylum that shares features with our own vertebrate phylum, such as heads, often eyes, and so forth, even though some of these features evolved independently, has been notably successful, namely the arthropods. Stephen Gould reminds us, lest we seek to esteem our own class of mammals in the subphylum vertebrata too highly, that "mammals form a small group of some four thousand species, while nearly a million species of multicellular animals have been formally named. Since more than 80 percent of those million are arthropods, and since the great majority of arthropods are insects, [some] enlightened people tend to label modern times as the 'age of arthropods.'"[41] And the Wikipedia article "Crustaceans" points out that "Crustaceans are among the most successful animals, and are as abundant in the oceans as insects are on land." So, after the enormously successful unicellular organisms, among the multicellular organisms it is the arthropods who have most successfully radiated in an immense variety of species of significantly higher biomass than mammals.

Of body plans, which have extraordinary longevity and creativity in the production of variation, Kirschner and Gerhart write, "Although the body plan is an anatomical structure, it plays a central role in development, and it too should be called a conserved core process. It joins conserved processes such as metabolism and other biochemical mechanisms, eukaryotic cellular processes, and multicellular processes of development to make up the repertoire of conserved processes of bilateral animals."[42] Summing up, they write:

> If we follow the path from the bacterium-like ancestor toward humans, we find repeated episodes of great innovation. New genes and proteins arose in each episode. Afterward, the components and processes settled into prolonged conservation. The existence of "deep conservation" is a surprise. To some biologists it is a contradiction of their expectations about the organism's capacity to generate random phenotypic variation from random mutation. To some, it borders on paradox when held against the rampant diversification of anatomy and physiology in the evolutionary history of animals.[43]

But it is just Kirschner and Gerhart's point that random mutation, though essential for the production of variation, never acts through the isolated production of a genetic change. The genes, in fact, in spite of the popular belief reinforced by some science writers, are not little homunculi, "replicators" sitting in their chromosomes and "controlling" the organisms seen as "lumbering robot vehicles."[44] Rather, mutation takes place in phenotypes organized by conserved core processes that are able to produce efficient, and often quite remarkable, change without drastic disruption.

Instead of lumbering robots, organisms are actors in the process of evolution, even in the evolution of evolvability. Kirschner and Gerhart sum up:

> On the side of generating phenotypic variation, we believe the organism indeed participates in its own evolution, and does so with a bias related to its long history of variation and selection. Coupled with our already advanced understanding of natural selection and heredity, facilitated variation completes the broad outlines of the general processes of evolution, particularly for metazoan diversity.[45]

Toward the end of their book, Kirschner and Gerhart raise the question of the generalizability of their analysis beyond biology, recognizing the dangers of biological analogies in the past. Yet they do suggest a way in which their analysis could be useful for the present book on religious evolution:

At the very least, an analysis of evolvability by facilitated variation evokes different metaphors than does Social Darwinism, which stressed selective conditions, not variation. History is not just a product of selection, determined by the external environment or competition; it is also about the deep structure and history of societies. It includes their organizations, their capacity to adapt, their capacity to innovate, perhaps even their capacity to harbor cryptic variation and diversity.[46]

I mentioned in the Preface and will develop further below Merlin Donald's scheme of cultural evolution as involving successively the emergence of mimetic, mythic, and theoretic culture.[47] Perhaps each of these is a "conserved core process," never lost even though reorganized in the light of new core processes, each promoting variation, adaptive and innovative, but each essential to cultural integrity. That comes close to stating the central argument of this book.

Parenthetically, I might note that even Kirschner and Gerhart, in their novel and challenging analysis of conservation and variation, cannot avoid the question of religion. They actually begin their book by referring to William Paley's *Natural Theology* of 1809, where Paley develops the analogy of finding a watch on the heath and knowing that so complicated a mechanism had to have a maker, thus proving that the earthworm and the skylark must have had a maker too, what would later be called creationism. Our authors point out that the watch analogy is flawed: watches can be "made," can be taken apart and reassembled, but organisms grow and, if taken apart, die. Darwin had Paley in mind when he developed his idea of all life as descended from a single beginning and changing through natural selection.[48] But at the end of the book the authors "return to the heath" and imagine a descendant of Paley's, with an education in modern biology, who could explain to her ancestor if they could converse, how the watch analogy doesn't work and how we can understand the evolution of organisms in their own terms without the need of external intervention. But the authors do not want to exclude the question of faith; they simply want their young descendant to explain to her ancestor that we must now "draw the line between faith and science at a different place, one more defensible in the light of the modern understanding."[49] It seems, even when I don't expect it, that the relation of science and religion appears time and time again in the writings of the scientists I have been studying. Later in this chapter I will sum up what I have, quite unintentionally, discovered about the many ways in which scientists have of late thought about religion in relation to their own work.

The Evolution of New Capacities

Maynard Smith and Szathmáry in describing "transitions" and Kirschner and Gerhart in describing "conserved core processes" are both talking about the acquisition of new capacities. Stephen Jay Gould, in his opposition to the idea of progress in evolutionary history and his unhappiness with talk of higher and lower forms of life, quotes Darwin to similar effect and notes that Darwin for a long time avoided the word "evolution," preferring to speak of "natural selection" instead, because "evolution" had the built-in meaning of progress, as so clearly in the case of Herbert Spencer. In *Origin of Species* Darwin speaks of progressive change as a "vague and ill-defined sentiment" among paleontologists.[50] He accepts the idea only in the sense that descendants, due to the gradual accumulation of numerous small improvements, are more fitted for their environment than their ancestors and therefore more capable of surviving, though they too will in all likelihood become extinct. It seems that what worried Darwin was the idea of any inherent force for progress other than the slow workings of natural selection.[51] But perhaps it is possible to speak of the acquisition of new capacities simply as a fact in evolutionary history, however those capacities have been acquired, without implying any metaphysical direction, and recognizing that the preponderance of bacteria in the world today is not only evidence of their fitness, but, in their own way, of their progress, of their ability to adapt to the most amazing range of environments. They have made excellent use of the capacities they have, and they have had no need of the capacities that developed later.

If we may pick up from the point of Kirschner and Gerhart's final conserved core processes, the body plans of animals, twigs on the bush of life in which we happen to be very interested, we may note that in the early history of body plans, those of reptiles and mammals seem to be very similar. The earliest history of reptiles and mammals, some 320 million years ago (mya), more or less, is not entirely clear. Some classifications place the mammals as early descendants of reptiles, whereas others see both reptiles and mammals as diverging more or less at the same time from amniotes. In any case the early history of reptiles and mammals shows the clear predominance of reptiles. Large reptiles predominated in the Permian period (290–250 mya), though they were very nearly wiped out in the greatest extinction event known, the Permian-Triassic extinction event. However, the reptiles made a comeback, and the "age of the dinosaurs," as every schoolchild knows, followed. The dinosaurs were the dominant terrestrial animal from the late Triassic (about 230 mya) to the end of the Cretaceous (about 65 mya), when the Cretaceous-Tertiary extinction event finally wiped them out altogether, except for their descendants, the birds.

Stephen Jay Gould, in his intrepid war against anthropocentrism, has asked why, if mammals are so superior to reptiles as many have claimed, from the Permian to the end of the Cretaceous mammals remained small, rodentlike creatures but reptiles exfoliated into a tremendous variety of creatures, including the largest ones ever to have inhabited the earth. Even though mammals were warm-blooded and therefore presumably faster than reptiles, and had a considerably larger brain compared to body mass than reptiles, for a very long time they didn't seem to have much to show for it. If it were not for the Cretaceous-Tertiary extinction event some 65 mya, Gould notes, we (because we are mammals, speaking of our ancestors as "we") might be coexisting with, or rather scuttling around the feet of, much larger reptiles to this very day, or, if we confine "we" to human beings, we would not be here at all.[52] Only when really large reptiles (dinosaurs) were wiped out did the mammals finally come into their own and provide the megafauna of the more recent period.

A cautionary footnote here might be in order. Large size may open up possible new capacities, but large size is vulnerable. Mammals (and birds) were small, and like small reptiles such as snakes, lizards, and turtles, proved viable enough to survive the Cretaceous-Tertiary extinction event, as did, of course, the single-celled organisms. We don't usually think of humans as megafauna, but we are still on the large size if one looks at life as a whole, thus surely vulnerable to extinction in the case of a catastrophic event. Megafauna are variously defined, but the term is often used for any animals weighing more than a hundred pounds, and is widely used for any animals larger than humans. Ouch.

Though we will be primarily concerned with how mammals developed, especially since the Cretaceous-Tertiary extinction event 65 mya, we do need to say a word about birds, because birds developed, quite independently, some of the same capacities as mammals. Birds split off from dinosaurs in the Jurassic period, roughly 200 to 150 mya. By heredity they could still be called dinosaurs, the only dinosaurs to survive the Cretaceous-Tertiary extinction event. They are a highly successful class of animals, consisting of around 10,000 existing species, existing in every continent and region of the globe. Like mammals, they are warm-blooded, have a rapid metabolism, and need to have a large food intake to sustain their body heat and active life. Relative to body size, they have large brains, and some of them are quite intelligent—some crows even make tools. Most of them, like most mammals, are nurturant toward their offspring, building nests in advance of laying eggs, keeping the eggs warm by their body heat, and feeding their often helpless chicks until they are ready to take care of themselves. Most bird species are socially monogamous, and care of the eggs and the chicks is often shared between the parents, perhaps more often than among mammals. They have vocal capacities unmatched by all but a few other species, and use complex visual and aural signaling. Although the study of animal emotions is difficult and controversial, birds seem to share the capacity for emotion with mammals in a way that few other species do.

Mammals are warm-blooded, unlike reptiles but like birds, which means that they can inhabit regions so cold that reptiles could not survive in them. Most mammals also have hair or fur, which enables them to survive in cold climates. The very word "mammal" comes from the mammary glands, which seem to be unique to mammals. In the females of the species these glands produce milk for offspring, which are born alive. Even monotremes, the survivors of a very early mammalian line that reproduces by laying eggs, have mammary glands, whose purpose is not clear. Marsupials give birth to live offspring, but these are placed in the mother's pouch until they are able to function on their own. The great majority of mammals are called placental, as the embryos develop within a placenta in the mother's body. All placental newborns must suckle from their mother or some other female if they are to survive, but there is a difference between precocial species, in which the young are relatively mature and mobile from the moment of birth, and altricial species, in which the young are born helpless. The same difference is found in birds: there are a few bird species where the chicks are able to peck their way out of the egg and be on their own, but most require some degree of nurturance, in some cases quite extended.

I want to focus on parental care, a capacity that correlates with several other developments that have enormous potentiality, as Sarah Hrdy has pointed out. Just to name a few: increasing intelligence, sociability, and the ability to understand the feelings of others.[53] Related to this complex is what Frans de Waal calls "the co-emergence hypothesis," which describes the appearance at a certain point in human childhood of the capacity to recognize oneself in a mirror and thus have a sense of "positioning oneself in the world"

b.s. focus The
on vision as The
primary sense

at the same time that the child becomes capable of understanding that others, though separate from the self, have the same kind of feelings as oneself and so can be responded to in terms of their feelings, what de Waal calls "advanced empathy."[54] But de Waal does not mean that these interrelated capacities necessarily arose at the same time in evolutionary history or that they are confined only to humans:

> We are part of a small brainy elite that operates on a higher mental plane than the vast majority of animals. Members of this elite have a superior grasp of their place in the world and a more accurate appreciation of the lives of those around them. But however tidy the story may seem, I'm inherently skeptical of sharp dividing lines. For the same reason that I don't believe in a mental gap between humans and apes, I can't believe that, say monkeys or dogs have none, absolutely none, of the capacities that we've been discussing. It's just inconceivable that perspective-taking and self-awareness evolved in a single jump in a few species without any stepping stones in other animals.[55]

To relate de Waal's co-emergence hypothesis back to parental care, let us consider a comment of de Waal about the origin of empathy:

> Empathy goes back far in evolutionary time, much further than our species. It probably started with the birth of parental care. During 200 million years of mammalian evolution, females sensitive to their offspring outreproduced those who were cold and distant. When pups, cubs, calves, or babies are cold, hungry, or in danger, their mother needs to react instantaneously. There must have been incredible selection pressure on this sensitivity. Females who failed to respond never propagated their genes.[56]

Sarah Hrdy notes that some degree of parental care, usually from mothers but sometimes from fathers, can be found among fish, squid, crocodiles, and rattlesnakes, and notes: "Wherever parental care evolved, it marked a watershed in the way animals perceived other individuals, with profound implications for the way vertebrate brains were structured." But then she points to the special development of parental care among mammals:

> Nowhere have these cognitive and neurobiological transformations been more revolutionary than among mammals. Mammal mothers

fall in a class by themselves. Lactating mothers date back to the end of the Triassic, around 220 million years ago. This is when babies began to be born so helpless that mothers needed to be attuned to the smell, sounds, and slightest perturbations in the conditions of vulnerable young that had to be kept both warm and fed. Since any nearby newborns were likely to have issued from their own bodies, it was adaptive for mothers to perceive all neonates as attractive.[57]

The capacities that develop from the emergence of parental care are absolutely basic to the entire story I want to tell from here on, basic to the development of empathy and ethics, even among many species of animals, and ultimately religion among humans. However, it is important to remember that many other things were developing too. Aggression is to be found in almost every animal species (the bonobos may be the great exception, though even they can be quite unpleasant), and though much of this aggression can be interpreted as adaptive, much of it seems quite senseless, an end in itself gotten out of control. De Waal, in trying to defend himself from seeming to ignore the darker side of evolution, notes, "There's plenty of one-upmanship, competition, jealousy, and nastiness among animals. Power and hierarchy are such a central part of primate society that conflict is always around the corner." Yet just because others have emphasized this dark side, "nature red in tooth and claw," de Waal insists that we also recognize that that is never the whole story, and points out: "Ironically, the most striking expressions of cooperation occur during fights, when primates defend one another, or in their aftermath, when victims receive solace."[58]

I would like to turn to the work of an earlier ethologist, Irenäus Eibl-Eibesfeldt, to discuss some of the wider implications of parental care, implications that have recently been further spelled out by scholars like Hrdy and de Waal. As indicated by the very title of one of his best-known books, *Love and Hate,* Eibl-Eibesfeldt does not minimize the importance of aggression in the evolution of behavior. Following Konrad Lorenz and others, he notes that aggression is older than love and is, for example, found among reptiles, while love is not.[59] He also sees aggression as a site, curiously enough, for the development of ethics, even among reptiles, as we will note in a moment. But the origin of love he finds in parental care, which "unites the parents with their offspring and is clearly excellently united in reinforcing the bond between adults. We drew attention to the fact that only animals that care for their young have formed closed groups. They all do it by means of behavior patterns of cherishing which originate from parental care, and by making use of infantile signals which activate this behavior."[60]

Eibl-Eibesfeldt sees parental care as the basis not only of group bonding, but of individual friendship: "There is also, with few exceptions, no friendship without parental care."[61] He points out that friendships are initiated by behavior that draws on the repertory of parental care, as does, even more clearly, courtship behavior. Nuzzling, real or pretend feeding, kissing, are all borrowed from the repertory of parental care.[62] Eibl-Eibesfeldt seems to see sexuality and parental care as separate sources of bonding, with the latter more powerful than the former, but it would take only a cursory knowledge of Freud to see that these can be deeply related motives, though by no means always so.[63]

It would be possible to draw many more examples from Eibl-Eibesfeldt's rich natural history, of the way in which almost every form of love draws its substance from the repertory of parental care. He also notes that what he calls the flight drive, the natural response of a startled animal to seek refuge with a conspecific, particularly the most powerful conspecific available, is rooted in the child's rushing to its mother at the first sign of something unusual.[64]

Still, we must not forget the ubiquity of aggression. It would be well to take a glance at Eibl-Eibesfeldt's argument about aggression alluded to above, that relates it to norms that derive from self-preservation rather than love. What he calls ritualized aggression is found in many animals, including reptiles: "Fighting animals have often developed very complicated rules of combat that make it possible for them to fight without shedding blood." He gives the example of the marine iguanas of the Galapagos Islands: "The bloodless tournament begins with a threat display: the occupant of the territory raises the crest on his neck and back and shows himself to his opponent broadside on." He raises himself from the ground to make himself look larger, makes biting gestures and waves his head. If the intruder does not retreat, the defender rushes at him and they butt heads and try to push the other from the spot. The "fight" ends when one successfully pushes the other away, or when one acknowledges defeat by lying on his belly in a submissive gesture. Though they have large, sharp teeth and powerful jaws, no blood has been shed. Eibl-Eibesfeldt notes, "Rattlesnakes never bite one another, and rivals fight under strict rules." (And these rule obeyers are reptiles!) Similar ritualized fighting occurs in birds, fish, and mammals. We will need to consider such normative behavior further along. Eibl-Eibesfeldt points out the obvious adaptive explanation: fighting to the death could quickly eliminate fertile young males from the population, leading to early extinction.[65]

What Eibl-Eibesfeldt (or his translator) so charmingly calls "cherishing" behavior in the earliest and simplest examples of parental care must surely also have been adaptive, as de Waal and Hrdy noted above. But the fact that love in this rudimentary sense is "functional" does not mean that the extraordinary developments that ensued are mere functions of its origin. Hrdy writes, "Natural selection has no way to foresee eventual benefits. Further payoffs cannot be used to explain the initial impetus."[66] That parental care would lead to social bonding, the possibility of individual friendship, and even, eventually, to marriage and the family, are all unforeseen, and, though in turn adaptive, have given rise to meanings that go beyond adaptation. To find the origin of love in the adaptations of the earliest mammals and birds is not to reduce it to those origins but to marvel at the ways of nature in leading to something so central to our lives. Nonetheless, what humans have done with the practice and ideal of love should in no way make us overlook the whole evolutionary history or put down other species for not quite reaching some of the advances of our own. Frans de Waal makes the point that we cannot really understand ourselves if we limit our concern to our own line of development, even if we go back 2 million years to the increasing size of our frontal lobes: "Empathy is part of a heritage as ancient as the mammalian line. Empathy engages brain areas that are more than a hundred million years old. The capacity arose long ago with motor mimicry and emotional contagion, after which evolution added layer after layer, until our ancestors not only felt what others felt, but understood what others might want or need."[67]

As de Waal indicates when he speaks of "motor mimicry," empathy is in the body as much as in the head. It is in the body "where empathy and sympathy start—not in the higher regions of imagination, or the ability to consciously reconstruct how we would feel if we were in someone else's situation. It began much simpler, with the synchronization of bodies, running when others run, laughing when others laugh, crying when others cry, or yawning when others yawn."[68] And when empathy reaches the point of human love, though it is indeed in our heads, it is still very much in our bodies. As de Waal puts it: "Bodily connections come first—understanding follows."[69] To use the terms of Chapter 1, love is always, in part, enactive.

De Waal's approach helps him overcome a distinction that has become basic in much biological theorizing, though it arose from philosophical speculation—the distinction between selfishness and altruism. He gives the example of an animal mother, annoyed by the loud audible complaints of her pup, who suckles or warms it to shut it up. In such a case, "we can't exactly call empathy 'selfish,' because a perfectly selfish attitude would simply ignore someone else's emotions. Yet it doesn't seem appropriate either to call empathy 'unselfish' if it is one's own emotional state that prompts action. The selfish/unselfish divide may be a red herring. Why try to extract the self from the other or the other from the self, if the merging of the two is the secret behind our cooperative behavior?"[70]

He spells out further the "merging" aspect of empathy: "We can't feel anything that happens outside ourselves, but by unconsciously merging self and other, the other's experiences echo within us. We feel them as if they're our own. Such identification cannot be reduced to any other capacities, such as learning, association, or reasoning. Empathy offers direct access to 'the foreign self.'"[71] And the capacity for such identification can cross species lines: "The whole reason people fill their homes with furry carnivores and not with, say, iguanas or turtles—which are easier to keep—is that mammals offer us something no reptile ever will: emotional responsiveness. Dogs and cats have no trouble reading our moods and we have no trouble reading theirs."[72]

Given that many in our insanely individualistic American society would doubt that such empathy is possible, it should be more widely known that not only is it basic for human beings but that other animals have shared it for over a hundred million years. Just as "altruism" is a term that has invaded biology from philosophy with mixed results, so has the more recent philosophical idea of "theory of mind," the capacity to know what others know. De Waal calls it "cold perspective-taking" because it focuses on what another individual knows or sees, not with what the other wants, needs, or feels. For all his concern not to draw sharp lines between humans and other animals, or between different animal species, and in spite of the fact that the latest studies do show that apes in some situations are able to grasp the mental states of others, he is willing to admit that "the advanced forms of knowing what others know may be limited to our own species." Yet he feels that this is a "limited phenomenon" compared to the capacity to share the other's situation and emotions.[73] In other words, empathy remains a fundamental resource for a social animal such as ourselves, even though we also have more sophisticated ways of knowing.[74]

There are many other behavioral features besides the centrally important capacity for empathy that humans share with other animals and most especially with the great apes. Frans de Waal has probably done more than anyone else to describe these fascinating continuities in a series of important books.[75] But with limited space and the need to get to the genus *Homo* and the species *Homo sapiens,* I will limit myself to one other area that we share widely with other animals and that I believe is critically important for understanding the origin of religion—namely, play.

Play

If we are correct, following de Waal, in finding empathy, or following Eibl-Eibesfeldt, love, as the basis of all social bonding, then play will need to be understood as involving some kind of bond. But play, as we will see, is a kind of event, an activity that begins and ends, and it takes place in the context of daily life, from which it is to some degree differentiated. If mammals from a long time ago are often "social," as seems to be the case, though in varying degrees, what kind of society characterizes the daily life from which play is distinct?

The most obvious form of social bonding arises from the very practice that makes it possible: parental care. Although it varies by species, some relationship between mother and child and, less often, between father and child, continues after the offspring have become independent. Siblings, cared for by the same mother, can be rivalrous even in species with low social complexity: two pups may seek to nurse from the same breast. Yet siblings often appear to share a degree of trust that may be weaker in other relationships. In short, something like protokinship probably goes way back in the mammalian line, and can be found even among reptiles and fish.[76] Without language there can, of course, be no kinship terms, yet the recognition of kinship is often present. For example, though any other animal may be a play partner, siblings are especially likely to be; and the play between mother and child seems to be part of "cherishing" from very early on.

Yet kinship does not supply the only basis of social order of most mammalian societies, to the extent that they have societies, or bird societies either. In fact, the more social the species, the more likely it will be organized also in terms of a dominance hierarchy. Although the well-known pecking order in a group of chickens, where every single individual is ranked in terms of dominance to every other individual, is rare, some kind of ranking from the dominant male (and it is almost always a male) to middle-ranked members of the group, to the very lowest, who may be on the boundary of exclusion, is common. It was Abraham Maslow in early work with rhesus monkeys and chimpanzees in the 1930s who first coined the term "drive for dominance," and though he did not think there was a drive for submission, because all shared the drive for dominance, he did argue that submissive behavior in order to placate the dominant by admitting inferiority was certainly important.[77]

Dominance and the attempt to attain it when one doesn't have it would appear to mobilize aggression, not empathy. And because in almost all mammal societies that have dominance hierarchies it is males who are at the top or fight to be at the top, we might imagine that there are two moralities, differentiated by gender: females in terms of empathy, males in terms of dominance. This would be especially the case among primates, where male dominance hierarchies are highly developed and parental care is almost exclusively the domain of the mother. Yet things are seldom so simple. De Waal notes that dominant males enforce obedience to the rules of the group on younger members by inflicting punishment, occasionally severe, for transgressions, but then comments:

> There is no single individual from whom infants and juveniles receive more aggression, however, than their own mother. Usually, of course, it is of the nondamaging kind, but bites and even injuries do occur. Irwin Bernstein, a well-known American primatologist, interprets it as *socialization,* in which mothers teach their offspring to inhibit particular behaviors that may get them into trouble. Even though maternal aggression may not be to the youngster's immediate advantage, it promotes the caution and behavioral control required for survival in a hierarchically structured social environment.[78]

Also, counterintuitively or perhaps not, although males fight more often among themselves, they are better at resolving conflicts amicably than are females.[79] Dominant males are certainly looking out for themselves: they eat first and, if there is little, most; they attempt, almost always without total success, to monopolize mating with the females of the group. Yet by curtailing fights between their subordinates, sometimes taking the lead in hunting, and distributing resources, including social acceptance, they serve the group as well as themselves. (As usual it is both/and, not either/or.) Thus de Waal summarizes:

> Not surprisingly, given this integrative function, formalized hierarchies are best developed in the most cooperative species. The harmony demonstrated to the outside world by a howling pack of wolves or a hooting

and drumming community of chimpanzees is predicated on rank differentiation within. Wolves rely on each other during the hunt, and chimpanzees (at least the males, who are by far the most hierarchical sex) count on the other members for defense against hostile neighbors. The hierarchy regulates internal competition to the point of making a united front possible.[80]

De Waal finds that, especially among primates, dominance hierarchies are variable in their degree of despotism. Rhesus monkeys, for example, are despotic, and any challenge from below is severely punished. Chimpanzees, however, are quite different: "Even though we cannot go so far as to call chimpanzees egalitarian, the species has certainly moved away from despotism toward a social arrangement with room for sharing, tolerance, and alliances from below. Although high-ranking individuals have disproportionate privileges and influence, dominance also depends to some degree on acceptance from below."[81] It is even possible for a coalition of females to oppose an alpha male who is acting too harshly, and, because other males have their own reasons not to come to his rescue and females are large and strong enough that several of them can subdue a single male, the alpha has little choice but to back down.[82]

Having looked briefly at the social structure of ordinary life among highly social mammals, especially primates, we need now to look at play, an activity that by its very definition is *not* ordinary life. I want to focus on play because I think it is the first example in evolutionary history of one of Schutz's multiple realities other than the world of daily life. According to Johan Huizinga in his *Homo Ludens,* play is the ultimate source of virtually all human cultural systems: myth and ritual, law, poetry, wisdom, and science.[83] Cultural systems, as Geertz uses the term, are multiple realities at the human cultural level.

I will turn to Gordon Burghardt, whose splendid book *The Genesis of Animal Play* is the best recent treatment of the subject, for a fairly complex definition of play, complex because of the many dimensions that students of animal play have noted. Burghardt sums up by indicating five things that must in some way always be present before we can call something animal play:

1. Limited immediate function
2. Endogenous component
3. Structural or temporal difference

4. Repeated performance
5. Relaxed field[84]

The first criterion indicates that play is "not fully functional in the context in which it is expressed," that it "does not contribute to current survival."[85] If, according to Darwin, evolution can be characterized as "the struggle for existence," and according to Spencer as "the survival of the fittest," then play is something different from the "paramount reality" of the world of daily life in evolutionary history, and the something different is the first alternative reality.[86]

The second criterion is that play is something "done for its own sake," pleasurable in itself, spontaneous and voluntary; it is not a means to an end.[87] This is what Burghardt means by speaking of its "endogenous component." The third criterion, "structural or temporal difference," indicates that play may use behaviors from ordinary life, like fighting, chasing, wrestling, but without the aim that such behavior would ordinarily have. It uses features of ordinary life "playfully," for their own sake, and not to achieve the aim that they have in ordinary life. This is one of the bases for seeing play as not "serious," though that is an issue that will need further consideration. Burghardt points out that this criterion does not mean that play is "completely unstructured, free from rules," and, as a result purely "creative." Indeed, he says that "if these claims were true we would never recognize any behavior as play."[88] The fourth criterion is that play behavior is "performed repeatedly in a similar, but not rigidly stereotyped, form." It is, then, "something that is repeatedly performed, often in bouts, during a predictable period in the animal's life (which in some cases can be virtually lifelong)."[89]

The fifth and final criterion is related to the first one: play behavior "is initiated when an animal is adequately fed, healthy, and free from stress (e.g. predator threat, harsh microclimate, social instability), or intense competing systems (e.g. feeding, mating, predator avoidance). In other words, the animal is in a 'relaxed field.' "[90] This criterion is important for helping us understand the origin of play and the reason why it is limited, largely but not absolutely exclusively, to mammals and birds, and also why it is often limited to the young, though in some species it continues throughout life. One can think of a variety of conditions that would produce a relaxed field—we could almost say, analogously, relaxed selection—but an obvious one is parental care. Young animals whose primary needs are taken care of by others, who are fed and safe, are the ones most likely to play. Also a hierarchical social structure that provides some relief from aggression within the group and a more adequate defense against external dangers could provide conditions that encourage play, not only for the young, but for adults as well. This might be especially true for a hierarchical structure like that of the chimpanzees, one that has moved away from despotism toward something that begins to look like a "constitutional monarchy." The idea of a "relaxed field" doesn't explain why animals play, but it is a beginning.

Students of animal play have discerned three major forms of play: locomotor, object, and social play. Burghardt speaks of locomotor-rotational play as it can involve not only movement from place to place but movement in one spot, involving various kinds of turn. This is usually the earliest form of play in the life of the animal and is often solitary. Burghardt gives the example of "the gambols of foals released from barn stalls into a field."[91] Object play is also often solitary and involves an animal interacting with an object with no purpose other than to play. Anyone who has ever had a cat knows what object play is, but human infants interacting with toys is another obvious example. Social play involves at least two animals, but sometimes more. As Burghardt says, "social play can take many forms, but the most common are quasi-aggressive behavior patterns such as chasing, wrestling, pawing, and nipping." As to the salience of social play, he notes that it "is interesting to watch, involves many often complex and often balletlike movements, and appears to presage the use of these behavior patterns in more serious adult behavior."[92] Social play has the most possibilities for further development and will be discussed further below, but first we will need to consider one more of Burghardt's classifications of play, this one developmental.

Burghardt, organizing a great deal of previous work on animal play, speaks of primary, secondary, and tertiary play processes, all of which must meet the five criteria for the definition of play. Primary process play is not the result of direct natural selection and may have no selective consequences: it is the earliest form of play. Play of this type may have no role in subsequent behavior, or it "may serve as a 'preadaptation' or 'exaptation' providing variation that can be selected." If I may interpret Burghardt, it would seem that play is the result of something almost like "relaxed selection," such as parental care would provide, and it is just in situations of relaxed selection that genetic possibilities already existing, which is what "preadaptations" and "exaptations" indicate, previously suppressed because nonadaptive, are then released into behavior. Once play behavior has come into existence, it may be selected for various functions, which is what secondary and tertiary play processes describe, but some degree of primary play process survives in species that have also developed significant elaborations.

Secondary process play covers many of the functions that have been offered to explain the evolution of play. Secondary process play is "behavior that, once it occurred, evolved some role, although not necessarily an exclusive or even a major one, in the maintenance or refinement of normal development of physiological and behavioral capacities. Play may serve to maintain the precision of predatory, defensive, and social skills, neural processing, and physiological capacities."

Tertiary process play is "play behavior that has gained a major, if not critical, role in modifying and enhancing behavioral abilities and fitness, including the development of innovation and creativity." Although the transition between secondary and tertiary processes is not a sharp one but more of a continuity, tertiary process play points to the rich possibilities of the development of play among human beings where culture adds an array of possibilities for further elaboration.[93]

As we have seen, parental care seems to be an important precondition for the development of play. Burghardt makes some generalizations about the relation of kinds of parental care to the degree of play development. We have noted above the difference between precocial species, where the young are born virtually viable, and altricial species, where the young are born helpless. In some precocial species, such as cattle and horses, the mother usually gives birth to only one offspring and the offspring may stay with the parents longer than the offspring of some altricial species, where a large number of helpless infants mature quickly to independence. Thus "the parental care system as a whole needs to be considered. Nonetheless, altriciality may be a useful marker in identifying animals in which play is prominent because species with altricial young often play more, or more complexly, than even close relatives that are more precocial."[94]

Burghardt emphasizes the complexity of play and the very uneven development of research on key aspects of it, which make it difficult to account for the origin of animal play, yet he offers a tentative set of hypotheses that he calls "the surplus resource theory of play."[95] One aspect of this theory is that the longer the period of parental care, the more likely the offspring will have the energy and, often, the intelligence, to need some form of expression to avoid what we would call boredom.[96] It is in response to this more or less prolonged period of the relaxation of selection pressures that primary process play arises. Primary process play is a response to the absence of specific pressures, not to such pressures themselves. Nevertheless, the absence of selection pressures means that highly specific instinctual capacities to deal with the environment—predation, flight, mating—normally present from birth among animals lacking parental care, in their earliest appearance gradually atrophy through disuse among animals with extended parental care, that is, they tend to be genetically deselected. What takes the place of the deselected instincts, usually quite precise in their behavioral implications, are more generalized play behaviors, but ones that are now available to selection as secondary play processes—that is, play behaviors such as wrestling, running, chasing, and so forth—that could, in a general way, help to hone skills that will be useful in the "real world" once the young are on their own. Burghardt is clear that play did not originate to provide these functions, but that functions can develop out of play behavior as an activity whose good was originally not for any function at all. Once secondary play process has arisen, there is the possibility that play will give rise to novel activities not previously part of the species repertory. In other words, play is a new kind of capacity with a very large potentiality of developing more capacities, what Burghardt calls tertiary play processes, some of them quite extraordinary.

We need now to look at some of the features of social play among nonhuman animals to see just how some of these new capacities might have arisen. Our examples will come mainly from canids and primates, dogs and chimpanzees in particular, because those are the best studied. What is most striking in animals whose social structure is more or less strongly hierarchical is the equality that characterizes play. Marc Bekoff and Jessica Pierce put it strongly:

> We want to stress that social play is firmly based on a foundation of fairness. Play only occurs if, for the time they are playing, individuals have no other agenda but to play. They put aside or neutralize any inequalities in physical size and social rank. As we will see, large and small animals can play together, and high-ranking and low-ranking individuals can play together, but not if one of them takes advantage of its superior strength or status.
>
> After all is said and done, it may turn out that play is a unique category of behavior in that asymmetries are tolerated more so than in other social contexts. Animals really work at reducing inequalities in size, strength, social status, and how wired each is to play . . . Play is perhaps uniquely egalitarian. And if we define justice as a set of social

rules and expectations that neutralize differences among individuals in an effort to maintain group harmony, then that's exactly what we find in animals when they play.[97]

Burghardt notes some of the particular ways in which animal play is egalitarian. One common way is role reversal: "One animal chases the other; when the gap closes, the chased individual may suddenly swing around and begin chasing the chaser up trees, around bushes and rocks, and so on. One animal may be on top in a play wrestling match and then appear at the bottom."[98] In this example, role reversal occurs within a play bout, but the reversal may also occur across bouts: "That is, one animal may chase another one day and be chased the next."[99]

Burghardt calls the behavior of the older, stronger, or higher-status animal involved in play with a younger, weaker, or lower-status animal "self-handicapping," and notes that "self-handicapping implies some kind of mutual intentionality in aspects of animal social play."[100] De Waal comments on rhesus monkeys, who do not seem to notice temporary impairments in their play partners right away, but if the impairment lasts longer than a couple of weeks, they do take it into account and adjust to the impaired animal as they would to a younger one. "I always admire the complete control of adult males at play; with formidable canines, they gnaw and wrestle with juveniles without hurting them in the least."[101] De Waal argues that play inhibitions are probably produced by conditioning, are "learned adjustments": "From an early age, monkeys learn that the fun will not last if they are too rough with a younger playmate."[102] On this account play would be an expression of the plasticity and openness to learning that arises when parental care limits the need for early instinctive self-preserving behavior.

How do animals know how to behave during play bouts? This is far from perfectly clear, but there is evidence of a variety of forms of signaling behavior, beginning with the invitation to play, which in the case of dogs is known as the play bow: the dog crouches on its front legs and bows while its hind legs remain erect. This apparently means "I want to play," and will be reciprocated by a play bow from a possible partner.[103] Gregory Bateson referred to this behavior as "metacommunication" because it not only signals a willingness to play but indicates the kind of behavior that will follow, that is, not real fighting and such, but play fighting.[104] The canine play bow may be repeated during a play bout, which may mean "I still want to play." Primates have a variety of gestures that indicate a willingness to play and to abide by the rules of play. A common one among chimpanzees is a raised arm that is the equivalent of the play bow among dogs, though there are several other chimpanzee gestures the can indicate a willingness to play.[105] During the course of play a yelp or a nip may be telling the partner that he is getting too rough and to cut it out. If one partner persists in being too rough, the game comes to a sudden end, or turns into a real fight.

One reason animal play has been a problematic field, with some researchers even doubting the possibility of studying it, or denouncing other researchers as being anthropocentric in their interpretations, is that we know (or think we know) all too well what is going on. Indeed, a dog may give us a play bow and we may proceed to play with the dog. The social play of very young children is remarkably similar to social play in animals. It is in the act of play that we can see in animals just those things that many have said only humans have and have denied that animals have: a sense of self, an ability to understand what is going on in the mind of another, a capacity for very delicate and choreographed cooperation, for example, and, if these characterizations seem to be overreading, then certainly, at a minimum, shared intention and shared attention.

Science, as I will discuss further below drawing on Martin Buber, has some pretty clear rules that require an I–It relation between scientist and the object of study. The scientist must maintain an austere objectivity that inevitably makes the object into a thing. In the observation of play, and even more clearly in actually playing with an animal, it is almost impossible not to have an I–You relation, which arouses suspicions that one is not really doing science.[106] On the other hand, as de Waal has indicated at several places, something like an I–You attitude may be a valuable source of information, and treating animals as if they were pure mechanisms may blind us to what is really going on. One could see this as using an I–You relationship in a utilitarian way and thus undercutting its real meaning, but in reading de Waal and some of the other students of animal play as well, one senses both a genuine respect for the otherness, the You-ness, of the animals being studied, while also conducting careful objective research. After all, the multiple realities of which I–It and I–You are examples are never watertight but often overlap. It may be that such overlapping, as when a metaphor leads a scientist to a theoretical breakthrough as we saw in Chapter 1, can be the source of creativity.

A great deal of energy has been spent on showing how much humans differ from any other animal, and when it comes to language and, in any but a rudimentary sense, culture, humans really are different. However, I have made a considerable effort to show how deeply we are shaped by a very long biological history. Sex and aggression in some form or other go all the way back and are surely still powerful forces in humans today. Nurturance, in the form of parental care, the earliest behavior that we can call love, goes back to early mammals more than 200 mya. Dominance hierarchy is probably as old as mammal societies. Among behaviorally complex mammals, certainly among chimpanzees, patterns recognizably like ethics and politics have appeared, how long ago we don't know, but probably millions of years ago. And mammalian play, the seedbed of later capacities, goes back probably at least as far.

We did not come from nowhere. We are embedded in a very deep biological and cosmological history. That history does not determine us, because organisms from the very beginning, and increasingly with each new capacity, have influenced their own fate.[107] But our remarkable freedom, which I am happy to affirm, is embedded in a cosmological and biological matrix that influences everything we do. It is a science fiction fantasy that we, or mechanisms that we create, can simply jump out of this history into pure self-determination. We live in a world that includes our own minds and bodies, and we need to respect the world we live in. Remembering all these things, we can now consider how we are different, really different, from all other creatures.

Homo Sapiens

Some 5 million (or more) years ago the lineages leading to modern humans, *Homo sapiens,* divided from the ones leading to the chimpanzees. We have no reason to believe that members of the chimpanzee lineage 5 million years ago were identical with contemporary chimpanzees. They have evolved in that period just as we have. In spite of this period of considerable divergence, we do share a lot with the chimpanzees, more than with any other species, but there is a lot we don't share. We would like to have a clear picture of what happened to the lineages, now long extinct, that led to our genus after the separation from the lines leading to chimpanzees and gorillas; and what happened, some 2 million years ago or more, to the first members of the genus *Homo*—namely, *Homo habilis* and, a little later, *Homo erectus*—which are also extinct but much more recently so. But our evidence, consisting almost exclusively of skeletal fossils and stone tools, answers only a few of our many questions. The beginnings of richer arrays of archaeological evidence date back only to a period when, we believe, the speciation of *Homo sapiens* was already under way—some 250,000 years ago. Just how very late that is in geological time is indicated by James Costa: "Another approach compresses the geological timescale into a calendar year: reckoning from an earth origin [4.5 billion years ago in real time] at midnight on January 1, a simple calculation shows that all of human existence, from the earliest appearance of *Homo sapiens,* comes late on December 31, beginning about 11:49 PM."[108]

There has been much speculation about *Homo erectus,* because of the anatomical similarities to modern humans; *H. erectus* originally had a smaller brain, but it grew larger over time. There is a tendency to see them as something like modern hunter-gatherers, though with simpler technology and a language, if they had one at all, with a much simpler grammar than any known human language.[109] But hard evidence is scarce, so I will speak from here on mainly of our own species, whose early history is almost as obscure as the history of our earlier lineages, with only a glance over the shoulder, so to speak, at earlier members of our genus.

Although it is language and the cultural developments to which language contributed that most clearly differentiate us from our closest primate relatives, the origin of language is still an unsolved problem. As Peter Richerson and Robert Boyd have written, "A little scientific theorizing is necessary to convince us that the existence of human culture is a deep revolutionary mystery on a par with the origins of life itself."[110] I would like to defer consideration of culture and language until after I take a look at some of our physical differences from other primates, though it is always possible that some of those differences too may be partly due to culture.

Humans are an altricial species, that is, unlike precocial mammals, the young are born helpless, in a sense "premature," because developments that would have taken place in the womb are completed after birth in a state that needs constant parental care.[111] Humans, moreover, are born exceptionally prematurely. As a result of bipedalism—legs specialized for walking and running, another uniquely hominid feature among mammals—the pelvis of the mother is more constricted than in our four-legged ancestors, meaning that the baby must be born with its head small enough to come through the birth canal without serious injury to the mother. This is one of several design defects of human beings, causing the frequent deaths of mothers in childbirth throughout our history.

This very premature baby is born naked, as are other primate babies, but unlike our primate cousins who are soon covered with fur, humans remain naked throughout life, with the exception of hair on the head and around the genitals. This is one feature of what is called neoteny, the retention into adulthood of traits previously seen only in the very young. At birth the faces of chimpanzee and human babies are rather similar, but the flat face and high forehead of the juvenile is retained by humans, whereas chimpanzees develop jutting jaws, large teeth, and receding foreheads. Some speculate that another feature of neoteny is that the high learning capacity of the young is retained by humans throughout their lifetime. Others reject the "myth of juvenilization," another term for neoteny, and argue instead that human development shows "adultification," that is, a greater continuous development beyond that of comparable species.[112] Still others insist that human development is a "mosaic" of juvenilization and adultification, indicating that both processes have long been at work. For example, "Thus, against the ape background, we have hyper-adult brains and cranial vaults but juvenilized jaws."[113]

Extended parental care is characteristic of the great apes, particularly of the chimpanzees: compared even to other apes, chimpanzees mature slowly, remaining in contact with their mothers until 16 to 24 weeks as compared to about 4 weeks among baboons. They nurse until 4 or 5 years of age and are dependent on their mothers until the age of 8, though after weaning they forage for themselves.[114] In the great apes, births are spaced 6 to 8 years apart to allow the mother, who is resistant to allowing others to care for her offspring, to see it to maturity. Human infants may nurse that long, but usually less, as the space between births averages 3 years. For foragers who are constantly on the move, caring for even one baby is difficult for the mother, so others had to be involved in child care. Cooperative breeding—that is, shared parental care—is common among birds and known from a variety of vertebrates, including some primates, but, as noted, absent among the great apes.

Sarah Hrdy has argued that the emergence of cooperative breeding in our genus, probably several hundred thousand years ago, was a major transition with important consequences. She links cooperative breeding among hominids, well before the emergence of *Homo sapiens,* to the emergence of *emotional* modernity, that is, the capacity of human infants to relate to others with what de Waal calls, as we noted above, "a superior grasp of their place in the world and a more accurate appreciation of the lives of those around them." Great ape babies, whose mothers share their care with no others, have the capacity for a kind of direct emotional relation to their mothers, especially in their first few weeks of life, but never learn to generalize that capacity to others and even lose it in relation to their mothers at an early age. Human babies, from the beginning cared for not only by mothers, but by mothers' mothers, aunts, older female siblings, and possibly even by nonrelatives, do not lose this capacity for close emotional synchronization with others but go on developing and generalizing it. This development, Hrdy argues, began among hominids and significantly precedes development of the large brains that mark the emergence of our *anatomically* modern species, *Homo sapiens,* and *behaviorally* modern humans with the development of language and culture.[115]

Hrdy links the emergence of cooperative breeding and emotional modernity to the remarkable egalitarianism found among hunter-gatherers, as compared to either the other great apes or to human society after agriculture, which we will analyze more fully in Chapter 4.[116] But if Hrdy is right, the leading edge of the series of transitions that have led to humans becoming something radically new, what Terrence Deacon pointed to when he wrote that "biologically we are just another ape; mentally we are a whole new phylum of organism,"[117] turns out to be our turn toward greater involvement of the whole society in parental care and its attendant emotional developments.

The changes that take place in the structure of the chimpanzee head and face undoubtedly have to do with adaptations for feeding and fighting. The fact that the human head and face are structurally similar from childhood to adulthood is but one of many indications that humans lack the physical specializations of many other species. Other animals can outrun us and, with claws and teeth and sheer muscle strength, outfight us if we face them without weapons. It has sometimes been said that humans specialize in being generalists, and, of course, in being intelligent. However, we need to note some remarkable human bodily capacities that developed along with our growing cognitive capacities. Other apes lack two skills that are important for humans: the ability to throw accurately, undoubtedly helpful for hunting with weapons, and the ability to keep together in time, without which skillful dancing would be impossible. As Kathleen Gibson puts it:

> Humans are certainly surpassed by many other animals in strength and
> speed, and they fall short of most apes in arboreal locomotor skills and

in pedal manipulative capacity. It is doubtful, however, whether any animal exceeds humans in the ability to construct novel body postures and rapid, smoothly produced, sequences of novel postures, such as those that are used in dance, swimming, gymnastics, some complex tool-making-using endeavours, mime and gestural sign languages.[118]

As Gibson suggests, the capacity for rapid, flexible, and novel bodily movement goes together with the development of communicative skills, even when those skills may be prelinguistic. Although some might interpret the human lack of physical specialization as due to biological degeneration linked to neoteny, Gibson reminds us that such losses are compensated by the development of remarkable and unprecedented, though general and flexible, bodily skills.

Biologists have long noted some parallels between the effects of domestication of animals and features like neoteny among humans. Terrence Deacon has written, "We are in many ways a self-domesticated species. Would it be too humbling to see ourselves as a somewhat genetically degenerate, neurologically dedifferentiated ape? Reframing humanness in biologically degenerative terms is not to deny that we are in many ways more complex, both neurologically and behaviorally than other ape species."[119] Behind this statement is an argument too complex for me to go into here, but it arises from the recognition of developmental processes that, though under the general control of the genome, operate with considerable flexibility and, under certain circumstances, creativity, even as they act to buffer the impact of mutations on what Kirschner and Gerhart called "conserved core processes." From deep in the evolutionary past there is a balance, or a dialectic, between conserved structures and innovative variations. However, under conditions of "relaxed selection," when the genetic controls under the pressure of natural selection are relaxed, this dialectic may be enhanced. There is a release of "form-generating properties [that] derive from the self-organizing tendencies of molecular and cellular interactions rather than from relationships to environmental conditions. Paradoxically, this suggests that selection may actually hinder the evolutionary 'exploration' of alternative functional synergies, and that the relaxation of selection may play an important role in the evolution of increased functional complexity."[120]

I have argued that parental care among mammals has created a kind of relaxed selection from its very beginning, in sheltering newborns from direct selective pressures, and that animal play, with its innovative possibilities, is a response to that relaxed selection.[121] But if human beings are "self-domesticated," we can see the beginnings of something like self-domestication from the appearance of the first altricial mammals. If this is a correct interpretation, then it is probably an exaggeration to assume a radical separation of humans from all other animals in their freedom from instinctual control and their need to rely on learned behavior for controls supplied biologically in other animals.[122] Not only do other animals, at least some species of mammals, have a significant degree of freedom with respect to instinctual controls, but biological drives (to use a less loaded term than "instinct") are still powerful among humans: sex and aggression, nurturance and dominance, can be culturally influenced, but never eradicated. In evolution, it seems, continuity and innovation go together, even reinforce each other.

If the self-domestication of mammals leads to a childhood free enough to create intricate and innovative forms of play, the place of play in our own species, where in some important sense we never leave childhood, should be significant indeed. Let us take a look at the earliest evidence for what *Homo sapiens* was up to. Although simple stone tools have been found that date from more than 2 million years ago, the Acheulian stone industry, involving fairly sophisticated flaking of what are commonly considered axes, goes back perhaps to *Homo erectus,* almost 2 million years ago, and then the making of stone tools continues with increasing sophistication, but no significant change in form, right up to early *Homo sapiens,* who may have used such tools as recently as 100,000 years ago. Even though human brain size was growing markedly during this period, and a variety of cultural and social innovations that have not left physical traces may have occurred, the stability of the main tool industry leaves us without tangible evidence of significant cultural change.

Until relatively recently there has been a tendency to see this stability as having been interrupted some 40,000 to 50,000 years ago by what was called the "human revolution," when a whole array of evidence at European sites rather suddenly appeared. But beginning in the late 1990s a series of finds at African sites has either pushed the dates of the "revolution" back to 60,000 to 80,000 years ago or replaced the revolution idea altogether with the argument for the gradual development of sophisticated physical evidence from some 250,000 to 200,000 years ago, when the speciation of *Homo sapiens* was well under way.[123]

Sally McBrearty, who has been especially prominent in arguing for a longer and slower development of "modern" physical evidence, has held that the earlier revolution idea was Eurocentric and ignored African evidence.[124]

What is of particular interest from our point of view is that McBrearty cites evidence for red ochre and shell beads from well over 100,000 years ago. Of course we can't know for sure what these were used for, but ethnographic evidence suggests that they were almost certainly used for personal adornment as body painting and bead ornaments. Archaeologists have argued that both kinds of adornment probably acted as signals of group membership, important where group membership had become larger than face-to-face groups and where it may be important to know the difference between in-group members and strangers. Yet we can also use ethnographic evidence to indicate that such adornment could well have been used in collective celebrations or rituals, events for which participants usually "dress up." Could such celebrations or rituals have developed from the capacity for play that is deep in our biological heritage, but must have been enormously enhanced with the attainment of language and related cultural developments?

We don't know when modern grammatical language evolved, but we know that it occurred only among *Homo sapiens* at some point in its gradual speciation. In any case the study of contemporary human infants shows us the remarkable efflorescence of play behavior compared to any other animal, beginning before language use but then developing many new forms once language has been acquired.

Because play is central for my argument about religious evolution, I need to consider the prevalence of play among human children today, drawing particularly from Alison Gopnik's *The Philosophical Baby,* and then speculate about the evolution of play, especially after the emergence of language.[125] In my Preface, I wondered whether it might turn out to be functional to have spheres of life that are not functional. Gopnik, in summarizing and developing a great deal of recent work on the cognitive and emotional life of babies, suggests the same when she speaks of "useful uselessness":

> Adults and children spend their days differently—we work, babies play. Play is the signature of childhood. It's a living, visible manifestation of imagination and learning in action. It's also the most visible sign of the paradoxically useful uselessness of immaturity. These useless actions—and the adult equivalents we squeeze into our workday—are distinctively, characteristically, human and deeply valuable. Plays are play, and so are novels, paintings, and songs.[126]

She reminds us, and we should never forget it, that it takes a special kind of love to make this useful uselessness possible: "All the processes of change, imagination, and learning ultimately depend on love. We can learn from the discoveries of earlier generations because those same loving caregivers invest in teaching us. It isn't just that without mothering humans would lack nurturance, warmth, and emotional security. They would also lack culture, history, morality, science, and literature."[127]

A particularly important feature of "pretend play," in which children engage even before they can speak, is that it creates a whole range of "possible worlds," a term Gopnik uses as the title of her first chapter. She begins that chapter by saying, "Human beings don't live in the real world." It is clear that she doesn't mean that we do this all the time, but means instead that if we think of the importance of "dreams and plans, fictions and hypotheses," which are "the products of hope and imagination," then even adults spend a great deal of time in possible worlds that are not in the obvious sense "real."[128] Yet if adults spend a lot of time in possible worlds, children spend even more:

> From the adult perspective, the fictional worlds are a luxury. It's the future predictions that are the real deal, the stern and earnest stuff of adult life. For young children, however, the imaginary worlds seem just as important and appealing as the real ones. It's not, as scientists used to think, that children can't tell the difference between the real world and the imaginary world. It's just that they don't see any particular reason for preferring to live in the real one.[129]

Perhaps this is a moment as good as any to make a point stressed by Huizinga in his *Homo Ludens*—that the opposite of "play" is not "seriousness." Play can be very serious indeed. In spite of the fact that we say, "Oh, he's not serious, he's only playing," the noun "seriousness" lacks the substantive resonance of the noun "play."[130] The right contrast term—though, as we will see, it too has problems—is not "seriousness" but "work," as Gopnik indicates in my first quote from her above. Play is not, as Burghardt argued even with respect to animal play, the world of daily life, what Alfred Schutz called, "the world of working." As Gopnik points out, it has nothing to do with "the basic evolutionary goals of mating and predation, fleeing and fighting."[131] Although some forms of play are comical and diverting, others, including the derived forms Gopnik has mentioned but also the pretend play of children, are serious indeed.

Freud recognized this fact, while making another mistake, from my point of view, when he wrote, "Every playing child behaves like a poet, in that he creates a world of his own, or more accurately expressed, he transposes things into his own world according to a new arrangement which is to his liking. It would be unfair to believe that he does not take this world seriously; on the contrary, he takes his play very seriously; he spends large amounts of affect on it. The antithesis of play is reality, not seriousness."[132] But if the child is a poet, is poetry not real? Is King Lear not real? Far more real than an unfortunate domestic breakdown reported in the daily paper? So I will, along with James and Schutz, affirm the "reality" of "multiple realities." If, for methodological purposes, we must affirm the world of daily life as the "paramount reality," that does not mean that other possible worlds lack a reality of their own. Possible worlds, multiple realities, have consequences we could not live without.

Play and Ritual

Let us remember certain features of play as we turn to the question of the deep origins of serious play in human evolution. Play is delimited in time and space; Burghardt speaks of "play bouts," which begin and end, and notes that they occur often in socially central areas where the danger of predators is least. Whatever the arguments between Frans de Waal and Michael Tomasello as to how genuine and widespread real cooperation is in animals, even in our closest primate relatives, animal play is impossible without cooperation. Tomasello finds that "shared intentionality" is basic to human cooperation. But even in nonhuman animals, play is impossible without shared intentionality. In social play both parties must agree, through a play bow or a play arm gesture or in some other way, that they are about to engage in play, not fighting or something else. And in the social play of children, if someone doesn't want to play, or doesn't take the play "seriously," that is, doesn't share the intention to play, she may just leave or else become a "spoilsport" and ruin the play altogether.

If shared intention is a basic premise of social play, so is shared attention. In the wild games of running and hiding that some animals and almost all children play, it is essential that one attend to the rapidly changing and unpredictable behavior of the playmate or one will not be able to respond quickly and appropriately. Another feature of animal and human play is the presence of norms—in more complex human play, rules of the game—that apply only in the time and space of the game, but are mandatory there. Although there are more common features of play that we could mention, there is one final, but very important, feature: play is a practice, as that term is used by Alasdair MacIntyre when he says that the good of a practice is internal to the practice, not something with an external end.[133] We already saw that that was the case even with animal play.

Where all of this is heading in this book is pretty predictably that I think ritual is the primordial form of serious play in human evolutionary history—ritual because it is a defined practice that conforms to the terms described in the previous paragraph, rather than religion, which is something that grows out of the implications of ritual in a variety of ways that never leave ritual entirely behind.

Evidence for the early history of ritual is not easy to come by. I have mentioned red ochre as body paint and shell beads for body ornament as possibly having been devised for ritual occasions. Much more recently, perhaps 40,000 years ago, simple flutes turn up. Music is an ever-present accompaniment to ritual and almost always involves dance and song. Still we can't build much on these archaeological remains, which could have many meanings. From the time that we think language as we know it developed, we can think about ritual in terms of the many rituals observed among hunter-gatherers, problematic though that inference is. But there is reason to believe that in that long period when members of the genus *Homo* were developing forms of consciousness and behavior that were more complex than those of the great apes yet less than those of modern human language speakers, some kind of rituals probably evolved.

Michael Tomasello has a lot to say about nonlinguistic communication among children before they learn to speak, and even among adults perfectly capable of using language but who find themselves unable to use it—for example, when they are in a foreign country whose language they do not speak, or where there is a noise level so high that words could not be heard, or where discreet nonverbal communication between friends is preferred because of the danger of being overheard. He calls this kind of communication "gestural."[134] Merlin Donald, as we will see in detail in Chapter 3, has developed the notion of a mimetic culture in use before language, which involves gesture but also some kinds of vocalizations, song, and possibly some simple beginnings of language.

Ritualization in nonhuman animals is common and most frequently involves genetically fixed sequences of behavior that communicate intentions, usually in sexual or aggressive situations such as the fighting of the Galapagos Islands iguanas. But the kind of ritual that I am trying to understand as evolving from play is characterized precisely by a lack of genetic fixation, by the relatively free form and creativity that are features of mammalian play. So rather than turning to the iguanas for an example of nonhuman behavior that looks like incipient ritual, let us look again at our familiar cousins, the chimpanzees. Frans de Waal has observed chimpanzee events that he is willing to call "celebrations":

> When the chimpanzees see a caretaker arrive in the distance with two enormous bundles of blackberry, sweetgum, beech, and tulip tree branches, they burst out hooting. General pandemonium ensues, including a flurry of embracing and kissing. Friendly body contact increases one-hundred-fold, and status signals seventy-five fold. Subordinates approach dominants, particularly the alpha male, to greet them with bows and pant-grunts. Paradoxically, the apes are confirming the hierarchy just before canceling it, to all intents and purposes.
>
> I call this response a *celebration*. It marks the transition to a mode of interaction dominated by tolerance and reciprocity. Celebration serves to eliminate social tensions and thus pave the way for a relaxed feeding session. Nothing even remotely similar occurs in species that do not share.[135]

Although this kind of celebration is not designed by the animals but evoked by the arrival of bountiful amounts of food, it involves some elements of play behavior. Play events are often joyful and can look like pandemonium, though as de Waal points out in this case, they consist of meaningful interactions. Very significantly, there is a normative aspect to the event: it leads to a situation where hierarchy is (temporarily) overcome and replaced by "a mode of interaction dominated by tolerance and reciprocity," something characteristic of play in often otherwise dominance-concerned animals.

Could we see among prelinguistic but mimetically communicating hominids the emergence of something like this chimpanzee celebration as a deliberately devised form of serious play—serious in its meaning, though not without the expression of playful emotions? We know, and this will be described in more detail in Chapter 3, that group size was growing during hominid evolution. Among the great apes, kinship provided much of the group solidarity, and dominance hierarchies maintained order, though they also, in the competition for dominance, created disorder. But in hominid groups that were too large for kinship alone to provide solidarity, and that were also, perhaps, already moving away from dominance hierarchies toward more egalitarian solidarities among both sexes, ritual might have been just the innovation to provide the solidarity that was necessary but not otherwise provided.

The play features of such ritual would be evidenced in the fact that they would be discrete events, with beginnings and ends, that they would take place at particular times, perhaps when food was plentiful, and particular places, perhaps some place that had significant meaning to the group. The egalitarian norms of play, so essential in dyadic play, which must be "fair," would be in the case of ritual, as with the chimpanzee celebration, extended to the group as a whole. As in the case of dyadic play, the ritual would require shared intention and shared attention, developed well beyond the capacities of great apes, as both Tomasello and Donald point out.[136] The intention would be to celebrate the solidarity of the group, attending to the feelings of all its members, and probably marking the identity of the group as opposed to other groups. In-group solidarity and out-group hostility are recurrent human possibilities at every level, from foragers to schoolchildren to nation-states.

The intensity of the feelings aroused by such a ritual led Durkheim to speak of a sense of the sacred. Prelinguistically, however, this must have been rather vague, if we can speak of it at all. In any case such a ritual was not "worship," something that develops considerably later in much more complex societies, nor is there a worship of society, but at most a feeling of there being something special about the assembled group that, in the ritual, gave rise to what Durkheim called "collective effervescence."

Huizinga, in discussing the primordial significance of ritual, insists that we not forget that it was at first, and to some extent always, play:

> Archaic society, we would say, plays as the child or animal plays. Such playing contains at the outset all the elements proper to play: order, tension, movement, change, solemnity, rhythm, rapture. Only in a later phase of society is play associated with the idea of something to be expressed in and by it, namely what we call "life" or "nature." Then, what was wordless play assumes poetic form. In the form and function of play, itself an independent entity which is senseless and irrational, man's consciousness that he is embedded in a sacred order of things finds its first, highest, and holiest expression. Gradually the significance of a

sacred act permeates the playing. Ritual grafts itself upon it; but the primary thing is and remains play.[137]

Huizinga derives myth and ritual from play and then a great deal else from them: "now in myth and ritual the great instinctive forces of civilized life have their origin: law and order, commerce and profit, craft and art, poetry, wisdom and science. All are rooted in the primaeval soil of play."[138]

I think it is noteworthy that Huizinga never sees ritual in its early forms as devoted to a concern with "supernatural beings," so often used as the fundamental definition of religion. He speaks of a consciousness of "a sacred order of things," but in a nonverbal ritual it is hard to think that order was personalized. Nevertheless, especially after the appearance of fully syntactical language made narrative possible, characters in myths that were acted out in rituals could be other than human. Animals that can talk are found in myths and folktales all over the world. What are sometimes called "powerful beings" also often appear in myths, but it is problematic to call them "supernatural," especially in cultures that have no notion of nature for them to be supernatural in relation to.[139] It is especially dangerous to call powerful beings "gods," because of the loaded meaning of that term in a culture deeply influenced by biblical religion. Powerful beings are certainly not omnipotent or omniscient—they may even be injured or killed. They have powers that humans don't have, but are otherwise not significantly different. Often they are conceived of as ancestors who continue to appear after their death but are singularly concerned with the problems of their own familial descendants.[140]

Just how close powerful beings can be to humans is illustrated in the famous story in Genesis 32, of the occasion when Jacob wrestled all night with a man who turned out to be God, and Jacob was on the verge of winning when God touched him on the thigh and dislocated it. Still Jacob wouldn't let go until God gave him a blessing, which he did, telling Jacob that he had a new name, Israel, which perhaps means "God rules." Jacob then asked God his name, but God refused to tell him, blessed Jacob, and was released. We will find in Chapter 6 that "El" was the general Semitic word for a god, so that the tradition on which this story was based almost certainly did not refer to Yahweh, who did not give that name until his meeting with Moses much later in the biblical story. Yet El and Yahweh were merged, and later tradition saw them as names for the one and only true God. That the priestly redaction of Genesis left this story in is remarkable, because it surely shows

God as a powerful being only marginally stronger than a very strong man, whom Jacob was reputed to be. In short, the idea of divinity was one of the many things that evolved in the history of religion, and the idea of "supernatural beings" was lacking in its early stages. Even in later history the distinction was often not obvious.

Because Chapter 3 is concerned with the evolution of ritual and gives detailed descriptions of rituals among three tribal peoples, it is not necessary to discuss it any further at this point. But I would like to follow up on Huizinga's idea that play is a fundamental form of life, which I have related to the notion of multiple realities in James and Schutz, of cultural systems as Geertz used that term, and of practices as defined by MacIntyre.[141] As such it is a model from which many other forms of life develop, ritual and the related practices that we call religion being a kind of mediating case providing the pattern by which play can be transformed into other fields.

Geertz defined religion as providing a model of "a general order of existence," not far from Huizinga's "sacred order of things," and several other cultural systems have, over evolutionary time, developed out of that originally global and undifferentiated way of thinking, notably art, science, and philosophy, all of which are concerned in their different ways with the general order of existence and so possibly in competition with each other and with religion. In particular the question has arisen historically as to the relative status of the truths about the general order of existence that each of these fields has claimed to have discovered. It is hard to deal with this issue in the abstract, as the relation between these fields has changed so much over time. Art began almost always as a form of religious expression and, in the West, from the Pleistocene cave paintings until early modern times, continued to be so. In recent times as art has emancipated itself from religion, its claim to truth has been quixotic. On the one hand literature is quite happy to be viewed as "fiction," so that no truth claims seem to be involved, but then the question arises as to when fiction is truth or truth fiction, and we have not gotten very far with that issue.[142]

Philosophy in its early forms—in ancient Greece or China, for example—was in many ways a kind of religion. As Pierre Hadot has convincingly argued, philosophy was in its classical beginnings (and, I would argue, in China as well as the West) a "way of life," not just of thought, that dealt with all the problems of religion and that actually was a form of religion for its, usually educated elite, adherents.[143] Even some Enlightenment philosophies, if we may take Kant and Hegel as examples, were as concerned with ways of life as with ways of thinking. More recently philosophy has concerned itself almost exclusively with ways of thinking that almost, but never quite, ignore the fact that ethics and politics, say, are practices of life, not just forms of thought. Science, until quite recently, perhaps as late as the nineteenth century, was only a field of philosophy, seldom venturing to provide conceptions of "a general order of existence," until scientific cosmology and particularly Darwinian evolutionary biology came on the scene.[144] Though "natural philosophers" criticized forms of myth from ancient times, the war of science and religion is very much a modern phenomenon.

Religious Naturalism

As I noted early in this chapter, I was surprised to see how many distinguished contemporary scientists still concern themselves with religion and feel the need to take some stand in relation to it. Even more, I am impressed with those who seem to want to bring the war between science and religion to a peaceful conclusion or at least an amicable armistice. We noted in the Preface Stephen Jay Gould's distinction between religion and science as two non-overlapping magisteria,[145] and in this chapter that Kirschner and Gerhart "draw the line between faith and science at a different place, one more defensible in the light of the modern understanding,"[146] which seems very close to Gould's intention. The attempt to describe science and religion as two different "cultural systems" that work in different ways toward different ends seems to me right, but making clear the distinction and the ways in which they do and do not overlap (because all cultural systems overlap, and all of them have an impact on the world of daily life) is not easy.

I noted early on, following Mary Midgley, that the grand scientific metanarrative of cosmic and biological evolution could be viewed with cosmic optimism (Chaisson) or cosmic pessimism (Monod, Weinberg) or just with a kind of acceptance that this is the only world we have (Marcus Aurelius, Oliver Sacks). I need to report one other view I have found, which is in some ways similar to that of Chaisson but significantly moves beyond it: this is a view that accepts the scientific story as all there is, that explicitly disavows the supernatural, yet views nature from a religious perspective, thus giving religion a degree of autonomy that cosmic optimism in its unabashed version doesn't quite do. This version is sometimes called religious naturalism, recognizing that there is something religious about it but that it doesn't involve anything beyond nature.

Some of these views even use the word "God" though giving it a new meaning. The biologist Harold Morowitz offers a clear but rather startling view. He begins by accepting a kind of Spinozist pantheism, but he wants to move beyond the immanence of pantheism to some kind of transcendence. As a student of biological emergence, he is prepared to argue that the emergence of consciousness is a kind of transcendence: "We, *Homo sapiens,* are the transcendence of the immanent God . . . We are God."[147] He concludes his book with the following paragraph:

> To those who believe that we are the mind, the volition, and the transcendence of the immanent God, our task is huge. We must create and live an ethics that optimizes human life and moves to the spiritual. To do this we must use our science, our knowledge of the mind of the immanent God. I am reminded of the words of the Talmudist: "It is not up to you to finish the task: neither are you free to cease from trying."[148]

What I am trying to get at with this example is that, by calling the universe the immanent God and human beings the transcendent God, Morowitz has clearly gone beyond scientific language and has used explicitly religious language, even without positing any God beyond nature. In this sense his view can be called religious naturalism, which in his case means essentially using religious language to refer to aspects of the natural world.

Another version of religious naturalism is not quite so radical in its claims, even though it moves beyond cosmic optimism. Stuart Kauffman, a biologist who has done a great deal of work on complexity theory, in his book *At Home in the Universe,* which already, by its very title, indicates the optimistic turn, suggests something more in the book's final section, entitled "Reinventing the Sacred."[149] Here is a religious term, "the sacred," used in ways that most religious people would not recognize because they think the sacred is not something that can be invented or reinvented. In 2008 Kauffman took the title of the last section of his 1995 book, *At Home in the Universe,* as the title of a new book that spells out his views about science and religion in detail, *Reinventing the Sacred: A New View of Science, Reason, and Religion.*[150] Here Kauffman speaks not only of the sacred, but of God, though he gives that term a novel meaning: "God, a fully natural God, is the very creativity of the universe."[151]

Kauffman goes as far as he can to alleviate the fears of religious believers that science reduces everything to atoms. In a chapter entitled "Breaking the

Galilean Spell," which I in my ignorance thought was going to be a criticism of Jesus, Kauffman is actually criticizing Galileo and his numerous followers to this day who seek to reduce the complex invariably to the simple. As a proponent of emergence theory, Kauffman believes that emergent forms in evolution, cosmic and biological, cannot be reduced to or even fully explained by the entities of which they are composed: new forms of organization give rise to genuinely new and irreducible complexities. An essential aspect of the emergence of new forms of organization is their creativity, for they cannot be predicted in advance—in one sense they could even be said to be beyond reason, though they are fully natural. After considering the possibility that such a purely natural definition of God might offend some religious people, Kauffman affirms the genuinely religious meaning of his intention: "If we must live our lives forward, only partially knowing, with faith and courage as an injunction, this God may call to us as we step into mystery. The long history of life has given us tools to live in the face of mystery, tools that we only partially know we have, gifts of the creativity that we can now call God."[152] Kauffman, like most religious naturalists, is basically offering us a theory, a theory about what the term "God" could mean in a fully natural world. He makes clear that his God is fundamentally different from a Creator God who intervenes in nature from outside, so to speak, and so could not be a person.

Those who think religion is not primarily a theory, but a practice, would find it a little difficult to see how one could worship the creativity of the universe, how it could become the basis of a way of life, to use Hadot's term. Yet in the last passage from Kauffman quoted above he speaks of his God as "calling" to us and giving us "gifts." It almost seems impossible to avoid personalization once one has adopted religious language to the extent that Kauffman has, though he does not deal with the implications of what he has done. Like Chaisson, however, he does think there will be practical consequences if his proposal is widely accepted: it will "heal the split between reason and faith," and provide the basis of a "new global ethic."[153]

Most of those who propose some form of religious naturalism to meet the need for meaning in a world where science is viewed as incompatible with historical religions are not concerned to explain the evolution of religion, whereas most of those who have worked on the problem of the evolution of religion have not been concerned with the problem of religious naturalism. The reader may note that I have not cited the many works on religious evolution that have appeared in the last decade or two. This is largely because, as I said in the Preface, my concern is first of all to understand what religion is and then to consider the question of whether it is adaptive, maladaptive, or adaptively neutral in evolutionary terms. Most of the work in the field has been primarily oriented to these latter concerns, so they have not been very helpful in my project. Some have not been helpful at all, especially those coming from a particular strand of evolutionary psychology.[154] I have learned from some of those who have focused on the adaptive possibilities of religion, such as Robert Wright, in *The Evolution of God*, and Nicholas Wade, in *The Faith Instinct*, but I have found their focus too narrow ethnographically, too concerned with Judaism, Christianity, and Islam, with only passing reference to other kinds of religion, and even then lacking a subtle knowledge of their subject matter. The best of the books stressing religion as adaptive is Douglas Sloan Wilson's *Darwin's Cathedral*, whose focus on particular cases is often illuminating.[155]

However, there is one evolutionary biologist who has written both on the evolution of religion and on religious naturalism whom I have found particularly helpful. I have cited him in other contexts earlier in the chapter, but here I would like to discuss briefly what he has to say about religion. The scholar I have in mind is Terrence Deacon, evolutionary anthropologist and neuroscientist, who has written both as a religious naturalist and about the evolution of religion. The piece on religious naturalism that he wrote jointly with Ursula Goodenough, "The Sacred Emergence of Nature," expresses an emergentist view, as is clear from the title. It opens with a strong criticism of reductionism and an argument for the irreducibility of emergent forms. Like the emergentists discussed above, Morowitz and Kauffman, Deacon and Goodenough are cosmic optimists, whereas reductionists such as Monod and Weinberg are cosmic pessimists, suggesting, though my sample is small and not random, a correlation between emergentism and optimism, reductionism and pessimism. Deacon and Goodenough, however, make more moderate claims than Morowitz and Kauffman—they speak as "religious nontheists" and they avoid using the term "God."[156] Further, they are more aware than their fellow emergentists, or at least express themselves more clearly, that religion is not only often adaptive but can also often have very negative consequences, and that even short wrong turns can have long-term effects. As its title indicates, the main point of the article is to describe how emergence works and then to find meaning in celebrating it. They write, "Understanding the human as the emergent outcome of natural history allows us to understand who we are in exciting new ways." They then quote from an earlier article by Deacon:

Human consciousness is not only an emergent phenomenon, it epitomizes the logic of emergence in its very form. Human minds, deeply entangled in symbolic culture, have an effective causal locus that extends across continents and millennia, growing out of the experience of countless individuals. Consciousness emerges as an incessant creation of something from nothing, a process continually transcending itself. To be human is to know what it feels like to be evolution happening.[157]

They note a series of spiritual and moral responses to this understanding, but Deacon places them in an evolutionary context more explicitly in a second article, written with Tyrone Cashman, "The Role of Symbolic Capacity in the Origin of Religion."[158] After making the point that religion is found in no other species but our own, they link it to the evolution of symbolic capacities. They note three ways in which our symbolic abilities move us beyond the cognitive and emotional range of other primates. The first point they make is that only humans have the ability to create narratives, or, indeed, to have the memory, sometimes called autobiographical memory, of life as a series of related events. Other intelligent mammals have what is called episodic memory: that is, they can remember particular events when they are in a situation that calls them to mind, and they can act in the present on the basis of what they have learned in similar situations in the past. However, in animals, and in young children as Gopnik has shown, episodic memories cannot be recovered unless cued by some current circumstance that calls them to mind, and they are not linked to each other in any sequential way.[159] Our animal relatives have another kind of memory, procedural memory, that arises from repeated practice and the development of skill. For us, learning how to ride a bicycle or play tennis are examples of procedural memory, so embedded in our bodies that we cannot even explain them clearly except by acting them out, but they involve extended sequences rather than discrete situational memories such as episodic memory does. For early humans, learning how to make an Acheulian ax, a quite complex skill that takes a long time for moderns to master, would be an example of procedural memory.

What Deacon and Cashman argue is that learning a language involves procedural memory—that is, a great deal of memorization and practice until the ability to utter sentences, like riding a bicycle, is almost automatic. Sentences, however, are composed of words full of content that necessarily

constantly cue episodic memories. Language, therefore, involving a kind of
fusion of episodic and procedural memory, necessarily gives rise to narrative.
The emergence of narrative, based on language with its capacity for a syner-
gistic union of the two earlier forms of memory, is central for religion: narrative, as we saw in Chapter 1, is the basis of identity, personal and social, and
religion is more than anything else a way of making sense of the world, of
forming an identity in relation to the world. Deacon and Cashman are very
helpful as far as they go, though for the role of narrative in religion we need
to see it as deeply embedded in practice, above all ritual, a matter that will be
discussed in detail in Chapter 3.

In addition to the narrative contribution to the religious capacity to find
meaning in existence, Deacon and Cashman suggest that the very nature of
narrative could have led to ideas that life does not end with death: "The tendency to believe in an afterlife might be a natural by-product of the narrative
tendency."[160] This is an interesting suggestion, but one I would not be entirely ready to accept, particularly if we are thinking of early humans. The
afterlife can become obsessive in archaic societies—think of ancient Egypt,
which will be described in Chapter 5—and is important in one way or another in most of the historic religions. But hunter-gatherers are not necessarily interested in this issue, as, for example, the Navajo are not. Even those
who are, such as the Australian Aborigines, simply assume rebirth. The spirit
of Uncle X or Grandmother Y, now after their death resident in a local water
hole, may enter the womb of a woman and reappear in her newborn infant.
There is nothing supernatural to the Australians in this very natural belief in
the continuity of life. Gananath Obeyesekere, in his work on karma as a
significant element in Hinduism and Buddhism, has discussed at length how
widespread much simpler ideas of rebirth are among tribal peoples on every
continent.[161] I would even question the usual interpretation of graves of early
humans, sometimes with elaborate grave goods, as indicative of "a belief in
the afterlife." Such graves could be simply an expression of grief and the need
to remember. Strong feelings of grief are widespread among intelligent animals, who almost surely don't believe in the afterlife. Giving physical expression to such grief should not be overinterpreted without good evidence.

Deacon and Cashman make a second suggestion: that symbolism could
lead to a consciousness of a difference between "the visible world of real objects and living beings" and "a world of symbols that are linked together by
meaningful associations and constrained by the 'rules' of grammar."[162] The
dualism of thing and word, they suggest, might give rise to metaphysical

dualisms such as are found in many cultures both tribal and historic. But such dualisms do not need to be metaphysical—they occur often enough in the world of daily life, giving rise to many of our ordinary problems in understanding others. Further, this dualism is fundamental for science, where what appears is not the same as what science has discovered to be the truth: that the earth goes around the sun rather than that the sun goes around the earth, as appears to the naked eye. Even in a culture where "everyone" knows that the earth goes around the sun, there are very few people who could prove it—it is a belief based on faith in science even though it contradicts the senses. And scientific explanation depends heavily on invisible, at least to the naked eye, though natural, entities such as genes. Does that make common sense real and science imaginary?

Deacon and Cashman give the example of the Aboriginal Australian idea of the "Dreaming," which we will discuss in some detail in Chapter 3, as involving "a hidden reality for them, more real than the visible world." But it is more real, I would argue, because it is more condensed, and more powerfully expressed than the language of everyday, but it illuminates precisely the realities of the visible world, as science does in a different way. It is not an expression of illusory imaginations that draw people away from "the real world." It is the Dreaming that allows the Australian Aborigines, as one of their most astute students put it, "to assent to life, as it is, without morbidity." The metaphorical and analogical uses of language are very important for religion, as for several other cultural systems, including, in different ways, science and literature, but they can be strategic ways of understanding reality more deeply, not necessarily of avoiding it. Further, we may note, metaphor and analogy, along with other linguistic forms, are often used in the context of play. Huizinga devotes a whole chapter to "The Play-Concept as Expressed in Language."[163]

3   The third contribution of the symbolic capacity to the evolution of religion is to the development, out of the raw material of basic emotions shared with other primates and with other mammals as well, of more complex emotions such as "piety, awe, equanimity, self-transcendence, and spiritual renewal (to name a few)."[164] These complex spiritual emotions, together with moral intuitions such as compassion and even love of enemies, are not simply continuous with emotions that we continue to share with other animals but emergent in the context of cultural reformulation. Deacon's ideas about these emotions and their human importance is suggestive, and I think basically right, even though I cannot here go into them in detail. It is worth

noting, though, that it is just these complex spiritual and moral emotions that Goodenough and Deacon in the earlier article most strongly affirm. Religion, with its taint of supernaturalism, cannot be so easily affirmed as can spirituality, a tendency more widespread in contemporary thought than just among evolutionary biologists.

Why Is Religion So Often Concerned with the Personal?

I will now try briefly to relate what emergentist biologists can affirm (spirituality) to what they cannot affirm (theism) in my own conception of religion as a cultural system. I have insisted that the idea of gods and certainly of God is not primordial in the evolution of religion. But when members of a community enact stories, myths, in rituals, they are actors who represent humans, animals, or powerful beings (whether they should be called spirits, gods, or something else depends on the case). But it is surely the case that what rituals and the narratives they enact are about is personal. Many evolutionary biologists think human intelligence grew beyond that of any other species not because we were so clever technologically but because we developed very complex societies and the capacity for shared intention and shared attention that made an entirely new level of cooperation possible. Thus it is not surprising that what rituals and myths are about is socially interrelated "persons," their trials, foibles, and insights.[165]

I mentioned earlier, in connection with how we relate to animals, Martin Buber's distinction between the I–It relation and the I–You relation, noting that the You can even be extended under certain circumstances to animals. But in a species that has come to be what it is primarily because it is social, even, as some have said, supersocial, it is not surprising that the I–You relation would at the highest level of meaning trump the I–It relation. To put it bluntly, there is a deep human need—based on 200 million years of the necessity of parental care for survival and at least 250,000 years of very extended adult protection and care of children, so that, among other things, those children can spend a lot of time in play—to think of the universe, to see the largest world one is capable of imagining, as personal.

We see it appearing, spontaneously and unthinkingly, even among our scientists. When Steven Weinberg says that the earth "is just a tiny part of an overwhelmingly hostile universe," or Jacques Monod says that man lives in "a world that is deaf to his music, and as indifferent to his hopes as it is to his sufferings or his crimes," we must remember that only persons can be hostile

pah!

or deaf and indifferent. On the other hand, even someone like Richard Dawkins, who believes the universe is fundamentally meaningless, can still call it "friendly" when discussing the anthropic principle, and our emergentist friends believe in a universe whose highest form of emergence is the emergence of persons, and for whom our most highly evolved emotions have to do with respect for the dignity of others.

For Buber the I–You relation becomes the key to the understanding of reality. He does not deny the world of I–It; on the contrary, he affirms it. But he writes, "And in all the seriousness of truth, listen: without It a human being cannot live. But whoever lives only with that is not human."[166] The starting point of Buber's reflections on the I–You relation is the immediate presence of another: "When I confront a human being as my You and speak the basic word I–You to him, then he is no thing among things, nor does he consist of things. Neighborless and seamless, he is You and fills the firmament. Not as if there were nothing but he; but everything else lives in *his* light."[167]

Though the I–You relation exists between persons, Buber feels it can also exist in some other relations, such as between humans and animals and even between humans and trees.[168] In his answer to critics, written in 1957, 34 years after the original publication, he defends his position. With respect to animals he writes, "Some men have deep down in their being a potential partnership with animals—most often people who are by no means 'animalic' by nature but rather spiritual."[169] Even with a tree, it depends on the nature of the encounter whether there is an I–It relation or an I–You relation: "The living wholeness and unity of a tree that denies itself to the eye, no matter how keen, of anyone who merely investigates, while it is manifest to those who say You, is present when *they* are present: they grant the tree the opportunity to manifest it, and now the tree that has being manifests it."[170]

For Buber the You that can be encountered in humans and in nature is fundamentally a way of moving beyond the world of things into the world of ultimate reality, which is the eternal You:

In every sphere, in every relational act, through everything that becomes present to us, we gaze toward the train of the eternal You; in each we perceive a breath of it, in every you we address the eternal You, in every sphere according to its manner. All spheres are included in it, while it is included in none.

Through all of them shines the one presence.[171]

Buber speaks in a deliberately oracular and poetic voice. His translator, Walter Kauffmann, points out that his German, often uncolloquial, is distinctly odd. This is because Buber wants to avoid being too easily understood, too easily put in categories that people carry with them in advance. For Buber most talk of God is I–It talk: God becomes a thing whose nature people claim to understand, about which they can endlessly talk, but which is not the God of relation, which for him is the only God there is. He writes, "But whoever abhors the name [of God] and fancies that he is godless—when he addresses with his whole devoted being the You of his life that cannot be restricted by any other, he addresses God."[172] Buber spoke unabashedly out of the tradition of Judaism, but he was also speaking to the modern world, where nothing could be taken for granted in the sphere of religion or in language about God. What is important for my argument is his insistence on religion as a form of life, one based on relation, on presence, as opposed to the perfectly valid parts of our lives that are devoted to objects, to things. Confusing the two realms is to miss the point of both.

Although Buber did not discuss the relation between religion and science, I want to call another witness, one who was deeply involved in science and who couldn't think of religion except in relation to science. He was at once a major mathematician, a major scientist, especially in the realm of physics, and a major theologian. If there is another example of someone so distinguished in these three fields, I don't know who it would be. His name is Blaise Pascal and he lived from 1623 to 1662, in the seventeenth century when science as we know it was rapidly coming into existence. Pascal was a child prodigy in mathematics and published his first treatise on the subject, one that Descartes envied, when he was only 16. He helped to prove, against Descartes's argument, that a vacuum can occur in nature. He was an inventor and was most widely known in his early years for his mechanical calculator, which he invented for his father, who was an official involved in taxation. He was in correspondence with the leading thinkers of his day, and he was accepted as one of them.

On November 23, 1654, between the evening hours of 10:30 and 12:30 he experienced what we called in Chapter 1 a unitive event. He later sewed into his clothing a piece of parchment on which he had written an account of this event, if one can call a series of exclamations an account. The document begins, before the exclamations, with one word: "Fire." Fire is a central religious symbol in many cultures, but as a scientist Pascal was perfectly aware of its physical properties. The exclamations begin:

"God of Abraham, God of Isaac, God of Jacob," not of
    philosophers and scholars.
Certainty, certainty, heartfelt, joy, peace.
God of Jesus Christ.
God of Jesus Christ.[173]

and continue in the same vein for some 21 further lines, never becoming a connected narrative. Since 1646 Pascal and his family had come under the influence of Jansenism, a rigorist Catholic movement based on a religious community at Port Royal, and his previously conventional Catholic practice took a more serious turn. The international fame that his scientific work brought him and his growing friendship in aristocratic circles became matters of concern to him—he worried about the sin of pride.

After his conversion experience, however, he did not abandon science, for he continued to work on mathematical problems until he became too ill to go on. He did, however, give increasing time to religious matters, defending the Port Royal community against attacks mainly from members of the Jesuit Order, in the *Provincial Letters*. These letters, written in 1656 and 1657, purely as writing were said to have created modern French prose, but they were also substantively a searching critique of what Pascal believed were distorted views of the faith particularly among the Jesuits. In his later years he devoted himself to notes for a projected *Apology for the Christian Religion*, addressed to his elegant skeptical friends whom he wished to show what was missing in their lives. These notes were never drawn together as a continuous discourse, but when published after his death, where they were given the title of *Pensées*, "thoughts," they became the best-known and most influential of all his works, recognized as a literary, philosophical, and theological classic.

The question of how one of the leaders of early modern science could address matters of religion as his primary (though never exclusive) concern in his later years is one that has drawn a vast amount of comment. I want, simply and briefly, to note how Pascal himself viewed what he was doing, how he distinguished the various spheres of his life. The key sentence here is: *Le coeur a ses raisons que la raison ne connaît point.* Of the various translations, for me the simplest is: "The heart has reasons reason knows not of."[174] It would be easy to give this sentence an antirationalist interpretation, but only if we don't try carefully to understand what Pascal meant by heart and reason. Pascal had the idea that there are actually three orders of knowledge, which should not be confused because they operate on different levels: that of the body (the senses), that of the mind (reason), and that of the heart, which we will have to try to understand, as it is not as obvious as the first two. For one thing, Pascal was aware of the role of the heart in human anatomy, so the heart as a source of knowledge must be metaphorical, but then religious language is usually metaphorical and this metaphorical usage of "heart" was already ancient in Pascal's time, having a strong biblical base.

Pascal held that each kind of knowledge—from the senses, from reason, and from the heart—is each valid in its own way, but we should not confuse them. Of faith, which comes from the heart, and the senses, he wrote, "Faith certainly tells us what the senses do not, but not the contrary of what they see; it is above, not against them."[175] The heart is the source of innate knowledge, such as space, time, motion, and number, from which reason starts but which it cannot produce. It is also the source of love and, with the help of God, of faith. Faith based on reason alone is "only human and useless for salvation."[176] Consequently, Pascal believed that metaphysical proofs of the existence of God are useless.[177] Reason, however, can tell us a lot about the world:

> Let man then contemplate the whole of nature in her full and lofty majesty, let him turn his gaze away from the lowly objects around him, let him behold the dazzling light set like an eternal lamp to light up the universe, let him see the earth as a mere speck compared to the vast orbit described by this star, and let him marvel at finding this vast orbit itself to be no more than the tiniest point compared to that described by the stars revolving in the firmament.[178]

Not only can reason give us truth in it own sphere, as can the senses in theirs, but reason is a deep source of human dignity. In a famous passage Pascal wrote,

> Man is only a reed, the weakest in nature, but he is a thinking reed. There is no need for the whole universe to take up arms to crush him: a vapour, a drop of water is enough to kill him. But even if the universe were to crush him, man would still be nobler than his slayer, because he knows that he is dying and the advantage the universe has over him. The universe knows none of this.[179]

Pascal lived at a moment of a vast increase of our knowledge of the universe in which we live. The telescope and microscope were, with the help of reason, opening up realms unknown to earlier humans. Pascal could only marvel at the greatness and dignity that reason gives us. But in the end reason also gives us knowledge of our wretchedness, of our inability, unaided, to save ourselves. That is the business of the heart when it leads us to the presence of God. Only that presence can save us, as Pascal found out in November 1654. From the point of view of my argument Pascal gives an example of how a great mathematician and scientist can see knowledge as coming from several spheres. Without in any way denying the greatness and dignity of reason, he found that faith comes from the heart—it has reasons reason knows not of.

Religion as Play Again

To see Pascal's *Pensées* as play, even serious play, is not easy. It is a book full of anguish, and he even characterizes his conversion experience as Fire. Perhaps his mathematics, with which he was obsessed from an early age, was a kind of play for him. Many serious thinkers have had to admit that their most serious work was their play. We can close this chapter by turning to another great thinker, Plato, who gave us some of the most remarkable words about play that have ever been written. I have long been aware that book 2 of Plato's *Laws* is one of the brightest, most joyous passages in all his writings, and I could not help but wonder at it the more when I remembered that later in the *Laws* one finds some of the darkest passages he ever wrote. It was Huizinga's great book that reminded me that some of those bright passages I remembered are about play. In book 2 Plato explains the value of festivals and links them by origin to the play of children:

> This education [based on the proper ordering of passions in childhood] which consists in correctly trained pleasures and pains tends to slacken in human beings, and in the course of a lifetime becomes corrupted to a great extent. So, taking pity on this suffering that is natural to the human race, the gods have ordained the cycle of festivals as times of rest from labor. They have given as fellow celebrants the Muses, with their leader Apollo, and Dionysus—in order that these divinities might set humans right again. Thus men are sustained by their festivals in the company of gods.

It is necessary to see whether or not the things the argument is singing to us now are true according to nature. The argument asserts that
every young thing, so to speak, is incapable of remaining calm in body
or in voice, but always seeks to move and cry: young things leap and
jump as if they were dancing with pleasure and playing together, and
emit all sorts of cries. The other animals, the argument goes, lack perception of orders and disorders in motions (the orders which have received the names of "rhythm" and "harmony"); we, in contrast, have
been given the aforementioned gods as fellow-dancers, and they have
given us the pleasant perception of rhythm and harmony. Using this
they move us, and lead us in choruses, joining us together in songs and
dances; and that is why they bestowed the name "choruses"—from the
"joy" *(chará)* which is natural to these activities.[180]

Huizinga has brought another passage of equal or greater importance to
my attention, and I have found his translation the most satisfactory:

I say that man must be serious with the serious. God alone is worthy of
supreme seriousness, but man is made God's plaything, and that is the
best part of him. Therefore every man and woman should live life ac-
cordingly and play the noblest games and be of another mind from
what they are at present . . . For they deem war a serious thing, though
in war there is neither play nor culture worthy the name which are the
things we deem most serious. Hence all must live in peace as well as they
possibly can. What, then, is the right way of living? Life must be lived as
play. Playing certain games, making sacrifices, singing and dancing, and
then a man will be able to propitiate the gods, and defend himself
against his enemies and win in the contest.[181]

If, for Plato, Apollo and Dionysus lead humans in dancing and God seems
to want humans above all to play, what about Plato himself? Is he playing?
Plato often uses myths to express essential parts of his teachings. Huizinga
believes myths are part of the "play-habit of the mind" that we find in children: "Involuntarily we always judge archaic man's belief in the myths he
creates by our own standards of science, philosophy or religious conviction.
A half-joking element verging on make-believe is inseparable from true
myth."[182] He gives Plato as an example. Plato, even while often using myths
to make his most important points, will then say about the story that it is on

the whole true, or "something like the truth," or "likely," making clear that he is using the myth to get across an idea not a story to be set in stone. For example, in the *Statesman,* the stranger (who stands in for Socrates in this dialogue), after getting bogged down in a very abstruse argument, asks his youthful interlocutor whether they shouldn't turn to "ancient legends," which would involve "mixing in an element of play." The young man says to go ahead, and the stranger replies, "In that case, pay complete attention to my story, as children do; you certainly haven't left childish games behind for more than a few years."[183]

For Huizinga, myth is never far from the world of play. We can ask if Plato is ever far from play either. It is said that in his early life he wanted to be a writer of tragedies—of plays—even that, after beginning to understand Socrates, he burned his tragedies. Nonetheless, except for a few letters of doubtful authenticity, all his writings have a dramatic form: they are dialogues. From Huizinga we learn that according to Aristotle, the source of Plato's dialogue form was not tragedy, but farce; he claimed Plato followed "Sophron, a writer of farces—*mimos*—and Aristotle bluntly calls the dialogue a form of mimos, which itself is a form of comedy."[184]

One could argue that there is one "serious myth" at the very center of all of Plato's work: the life and death of Socrates, and that that myth is a tragedy. Certainly there is much of tragedy in the dialogues explicitly devoted to the trial and death of Socrates. Yet Socrates is never as serious as his friends when they are begging him to escape from the death sentence by leaving Athens as everyone expected him to do. At the age of 70, he declares that he has lived as a citizen of Athens and will die a citizen of Athens, and that he has no intention of fleeing. He also makes it clear that he has no fear of death. One is reminded of the discussion of tragedy and comedy at the end of the *Symposium,* when Socrates and Aristophanes are arguing about whether the same man could write tragedies and comedies. Aristophanes held that it would be impossible for one man to write both, but Socrates held that "the same man might be capable of writing both comedy and tragedy—that the tragic poet might be a comedian as well."[185] Is he describing not only himself, but Plato too?

So, with Plato, I have returned to the central theme of this chapter—the emergence of religion from mammalian play. I have gone deep into our evolutionary past to discover the origin of parental care and of play many millions of years ago, in the leaping and jumping of "young things," as Plato said. Play is so important to me because long before *Homo sapiens,* probably long before primates, play had already emerged in the evolution of mammals as a sphere sheltered to some degree from selectionist pressures, having its end internal to its practice, however much it may have proved adaptive in secondary and tertiary forms. Language and culture have given play the possibility of enormous creative elaboration, and, with the constant help of Johan Huizinga and with the passages in Plato that Huizinga pointed out, I have found ritual and religion emerging from play. Here, too, we find practices whose good, first of all, is internal to the practices, though they may have adaptive or maladaptive consequences as they reflect back on the world of daily life. But if ritual comes from play, many other spheres of life develop out of ritual and its cultural implications. I have tried above to indicate what a complex historical process this has been.

At several places relatively late in the day, science emerged as one of those spheres whose good is internal to it, and again leading to enormous adaptive consequences later on. In a culture that privileges theory, we have tended to think of these spheres, religion and science in particular, as cognitive, as ways of knowing above all. But I have been arguing that first of all they are practices, not theories, ways of living more than ways of knowing. In rereading this chapter the words of Steven Weinberg impressed me vividly with this point. Though the more he comprehends the universe, the more pointless it seems, the activity of inquiry, the "research itself," "the effort to understand the universe," even if what he understands is not comforting, is a good in itself, is a source of meaning in itself. In my reading for this chapter I have learned just how exciting the practice of natural science is, how much there is to learn, how many of the most important issues are still in dispute. The openness of the search, the sense that some new door will open soon, some new idea that no one had thought of before, of which Darwin's idea of natural selection is the archetype, creates an existential engagement with inquiry itself, regardless of where it will lead.

I wrote this chapter in a world where the culture wars between science and religion continue to rage, and it was only as I was completing it that Barbara Herrnstein Smith's excellent book *Natural Reflections* was published and I could take advantage of her calm, perceptive view of major aspects of these wars. I am interested to find myself on both sides of the far too polarized opposition, not only between science and religion, but between the methodologies of scientific explanation and humanistic understanding.[186] Smith places two figures that have influenced me enormously, Émile Durkheim and Max Weber, on the side of "naturalistic explanation," and she is surely right to do so, yet both of them, and Weber very explicitly, were also engaged in human-istic interpretation.[187] Weber called this method *Verstehen,* which can be loosely translated as "understanding" or "interpretation." The Wikipedia ar-ticle on *Verstehen* describes it as "nonempirical, empathic, or participatory examination of social phenomena," but there is nothing "nonempirical" about empathic or participatory examination of social phenomena. Such in-quiry involves the effort to put oneself in the place of the person or persons under scrutiny and try to see the world as they do. That seems eminently empirical to me, in that it is a valid effort to get at one rather central aspect of what is really going on among the people under study. One way of making the distinction between scientific and humanistic methodologies is to say that scientific explanations are concerned with the causes and functions of the ac-tivities under study; humanistic understanding is concerned with their mean-ing. It seems to me that both kinds of methodologies are required in both science and the humanities.

I have been very interested in the biological evolution of parental care and the "cherishing" behavior that developed between mother and child from the earliest mammalian times. Of course one can avoid such a word as "cherishing," though I got it from an ethologist, Eibl-Eibesfeldt, and it does seem to capture something important about what is going on. Frans de Waal somewhere says that when some biologists insist that one can speak of chimpanzees "raising the corners of their mouths," but not of them "smiling," they are actually limiting the possibility of full scientific understanding.

Another feature of the culture wars and methodological polarization, pointed out by B. H. Smith, is that it posits each side of a radical dichotomy to be monumentally homogeneous, whereas in fact each of them is such a miscellaneous array of activities, practices, beliefs, and claims to knowledge, that it is quite impossible to see them as unified wholes, but only as loosely related aggregations.[188] Some deny that the term "religion" is even useful, because it covers such a variety of things, and B. H. Smith herself believes that the distinction between science and technology is inapplicable through most of history, where they are aspects of a continuum with no simple differentiation.[189]

While I believe definitions, though always problematic, are unavoidable in order to delineate, however roughly, a field of inquiry, this whole book is a collection of very diverse cases, and anyone who reads it to the end will have a lively sense of how extremely variable this thing called "religion" is on the ground. But because religion deals with issues so central to human identity, to one's sense of self and world and the relation between them, a purely causal, functional analysis will leave out the most important part. I think this issue is very much related to the difference between reductionists and emergentists in the field of biology. The reductionist thinks an explanation is complete when it has uncovered the components and forces that have led to the phenomenon in question—when one has moved one level down to see where something came from. The emergentist thinks that many phenomena have properties that are genuinely new, not just an extrapolation of the properties of their components, and cannot be understood except at their own level. Kant made this point when he said that machines can be disassembled and put back together again but organisms, when disassembled, die. When Terrence Deacon speaks of complex emotions that develop among humans after the acquisition of culture and language, such as awe, equanimity, and self-transcendence, he notes that they are based on more rudimentary emotions that we still share with primates, such as fear and joy, but are not reducible to them, he makes a move that would be familiar to humanists.

Not only should various spheres of life, cultural systems, multiple realities, not be reified and imagined as more homogeneous than they are, but, contrary to Gould's argument about non-overlapping magisteria, we should note how much they not only overlap but participate in each other. B. H. Smith reminds us that religion and science were not always seen as being at odds, because for centuries what science there was took place in the West in universities founded by religious orders or other entities of the Catholic Church and was seen as part of a larger religious culture, not at war with it.[190]

As societies have grown in size and complexity, more differentiated spheres have developed, yet they have continued to intersect and influence each other. Nor should we forget that they all relate to and are influenced by Schutz's world of daily life. The remarkable (though relative) egalitarianism of hunter-gatherer cultures, noted above, is reflected in rituals in which the whole society participates, sometimes, as we will see, gender groups expressing their own identity in conflict and reconciliation with each other. As hierarchy returned to human societies, religions too became more hierarchical, often reinforcing a stronger male dominance than that found among hunter-gatherers. No student of Weber could fail to see both how the larger society, particularly in the fields of politics and economics, influences religious developments, but also the powerful influences in the other direction.

Just because religion is often so close to personal and group identity, the failure to understand or respect it either by those concerned only with what they believe is objective inquiry or by those who believe all religion is harmful and would best be eradicated, has given rise to great resentment from believers. Scientists have suffered similar blows to their own identity from those who would restrict science from certain kinds of inquiry (rather few in number), or offer their own kinds of science that should be taught together with "normal science," such as creation science (rather more numerous). I have accepted the validity of science as a provisionally accurate account of "nature," and see no point in trying to limit it or to imagine non-natural forces at work that would offer additional explanations. But again, B. H. Smith has pointed out not only that much of the world for a long time lacked an idea of "nature," but that even where it exists, definitions of it are problematic and involve the circular tendency to define nature as not supernature and vice versa, both depending on a far from clear definition of the other.[191]

I have insisted that the various spheres of life have their own practices whose good is internal to the practice, however often commandeered for other uses by outside forces. I have also argued that practice is prior to belief and that belief is best understood as an expression of practice. Thus scientific truth, about which I have no doubt, is an expression of scientific practice and has no metaphysical priority over other kinds of truth. When we find Buber speaking of the eternal You, who shines through the faces of other humans, sometimes the faces of animals, even at moments through trees, rocks, and stars, it would be easy to try to find a scientific explanation of why he would say that. But such an explanation, which might well be true, would in no way refute the truth of which Buber speaks. Similarly Pascal's encounter in November 1654, which he characterized as "Fire," has validity beyond any evolutionary psychological explanation of it. Science is an extremely valuable avenue to truth. It is not the only one. To claim it is the only one is what is legitimately called "scientism" and takes its place among the many fundamentalisms of this world.[192]

The story of cosmic and biological evolution, which I have tried to tell in very condensed form, is, to me and to many, powerful and convincing. For many scientists it leads to what they themselves express as a sense of awe. This is a perfectly natural and legitimate response, but, and here the religious naturalists I have described above would agree, it is a case where the religious sphere and the scientific sphere come together, indeed overlap. Given the level of tension in current discussions of these issues, I do not expect agreement, or even, necessarily, understanding. I am simply trying to be clear about where I stand.

In Chapter 3 I will describe the scheme of cultural and religious evolution that I have found most helpful, that is, the work of Merlin Donald. And then I will begin to consider the main subject matter of this book, the description of particular forms of religion and how they actually work.

3

Tribal Religion: The Production of Meaning

In Chapter 1 I offered a typology of religious representation—unitive, enactive, symbolic, and conceptual—to describe the ways in which religions have understood reality. The concepts of enactive, symbolic, and conceptual representation were adapted from the work of Jerome Bruner on child development. According to Bruner, who is in turn adapting his categories from Piaget, the child first learns about the world by acting on it. It is by holding, throwing, reaching for, that the children come to know the objects that surround them. In early language learning the symbol and the object are fused—the sun and the word for sun are not differentiated—and the commonest use of language is narrative. Although concept learning begins by 5 or 6 years of age, it doesn't become mature until adolescence. I argued that religion draws on all these forms of representation: just as the child continues to use enactive and symbolic representations, even after becoming conceptually sophisticated, so do religions. I prefaced Bruner's three stages of the development of representation with an initial stage, a kind of zero stage because it can't be represented, of unitive consciousness that turns up in religious experience in many times and places.

In Chapter 2 I located the evolution of religion in the deep history of the cosmos and of life on earth, concentrating on those features of mammalian evolution that provided the conditions for the emergence of ritual, possibly as a development out of animal play, but only alluding indirectly to the forms of religious representation described in Chapter 1. It is now time to consider how these ways of understanding may have arisen in evolutionary history and to look more closely at ritual and myth, and at the tribal and archaic religions where they are so prominent.

My task is greatly facilitated by the work of Merlin Donald, whose book *Origins of the Modern Mind: Three Stages in the Evolution of Culture and Cognition,*[1] offers a picture of the development of human culture that parallels phylogenetically what my typology of religious representation had described largely ontogenetically. His three stages of human culture—mimetic, mythic, and theoretic—parallel my enactive, symbolic, and conceptual types of religious representation, and his baseline prehuman but advanced mammalian stage, episodic culture, even has some possible resonance with my unitive type. In this chapter I want primarily to use his description of mimetic and mythic culture to help understand ritual and myth in tribal societies, followed in the next chapters by a discussion of ritual and myth in chiefdoms and archaic societies, but later in the book I will turn to Donald's idea of theoretic culture, which grows out of and significantly criticizes, but never abandons, the earlier stages.

Episodic Culture

I will begin with a brief look at Donald's baseline stage, episodic culture. It is an open question how far back one can push the idea of culture. Some have argued that all learned behavior, as opposed to what is genetically determined, even if learned by trial and error by the individual organism, can be seen as culture, though others would reserve culture for behavior that is transmitted, by imitation if not teaching, from one animal to another. Donald's description of episodic culture holds for many advanced mammalian species, but he draws his examples largely from nonhuman primates:

> Their [the great apes'] behavior, complex as it is, seems unreflective, concrete, and situation-bound. Even their uses of signing and their social behavior are immediate, short-term responses to the environment. In fact, the word that seems best to epitomize the cognitive culture of apes (and probably of many other mammals as well . . .) is the term *episodic.* Their lives are lived entirely in the present, as a series of concrete episodes, and the highest element in their system of memory seems to be at the level of event representation. Where humans have abstract symbolic memory representations, apes are bound to the concrete situation or episode; and their social behavior reflects this situational limitation. Their culture might be therefore classified as an episodic culture.[2]

What is cultural about episodic culture is that individuals learn from the experience of previous events what kind of event they are facing, how the elements in it are situated, so that an appropriate response is possible. For example, a chimpanzee menaced by a more dominant ape must decide whether to behave in a submissive way, or to flee, or to look for possible allies to resist the menace. Only a good memory of how such situations have worked out in the past will lead to a good decision in the present. A great deal of learning about how to respond to events goes on from early infancy, largely through the observation of the behavior of other chimps. What is learned in one band, because it is not genetically coded (though the capacity for subtle learning is), will be slightly different from what is learned by other chimps in other bands, and thus can be called culture.

I emphasized in Chapter 2 that two critically important features humans share with higher mammals are attention and intention, and their significance becomes clearer in the context of episodic culture. Apes must be fully attentive to what is going on in the here and now. Acute attention to the present situation, informed by memories of previous similar events, allows them to act effectively to fulfill their intentions—that is, to attain the goals around which their action is organized. Episodic or event perception remains significant for human beings—our understanding of the world also starts with episodic culture. Although on the whole the capacities for intention and attention are mutually enhancing, they are not necessarily simultaneous and may, of necessity, be both alternatives and alternating. The capacity for intentional behavior is certainly critical for any complex forager, but so is the capacity for attention. An excess of goal-oriented intentionality could lead to a failure of attention. A good forager, human or nonhuman, needs to cultivate the capacity for attention. John Crook points out that in a hunter-gatherer economy, "Attentiveness in the here and now would have high value when a hunter, weapon poised, and quietly moving through the landscape, heard a sound. At once, a totally focused here and now condition arises in which attention is wide open to the slightest situational change which might presage either the appearance of prey or of danger. This openness is quite unreflective for purposive intentionality has receded out of awareness."[3]

The much more complex cultural forms that we have developed over the last 2 million years or more, however, allow us to consider a significantly wider range of possibilities than are available to mammals more strictly confined to the here and now. Yet this more extensive cultural baggage (if I may speak from the point of view of episodic culture) may also get in the way of our immediate perception of the here and now. The incessant chatter of internal language may prevent us from seeing what is in front of our eyes. Thus some forms of religious practice, such as meditation, are designed to escape as much as possible from complex representations, particularly linguistic representations, in order to attain a "one-pointedness," to use Zen language, of immediate wordless perception of the here and now. Perhaps when such immediate perception becomes total we can speak of unitive consciousness, which, although it often involves seeing, is always beyond words, and can never be pointed to with words until after the fact.

I don't want to do more than suggest the possibility that the deepest kind of religious experience is rooted in our most elemental form of mammalian perception. I am aware that mammalian attention, finely honed and subtle though it is, is almost always at the service of utilitarian ends. It is designed to make animals fully present in the here and now so that they can relate more effectively to fellow members of their group, find food and mates, and improve their status in the band, as well as defend themselves from attack. Alert attentiveness is also a valuable asset for humans seeking to fulfill their intentions, including moral intentions that are far more than utilitarian.[4] But the concrete immediacy of a consciousness fully present in the here and now may also be a significant resource for the religious life.

Mimetic Culture

I want to describe at some length what Merlin Donald means by mimetic culture, a rather close parallel to enactive representation, because it makes intelligible what happened during a long period of human evolution, most likely the period between the appearance of *Homo erectus,* 1.8 million years ago, and the emergence of our own species, *Homo sapiens,* during the last 200,000 to 300,000 years.[5] As for the starting point, the period between the split in the hominid lineage from the lineage leading to modern chimpanzees, we know little about it except that hominids became bipedal and sometime before 2 million years ago began to make simple stone tools. They may have been more like modern chimpanzees than we are, but we cannot know how much that might be true. We begin to know a lot about the recent past from archaeology and history. But for what human culture was like in most of the last 2 million years, we have little direct evidence and will always have to rely on educated speculation. Even the early development of the culture of our own species—that is, between 200,000 and 50,000 years or so ago—

remains shrouded in uncertainty, although we have reason to believe that modern rapid language is at least 150,000 years old.[6]

One might challenge the starting point: after all, as close as we may be to the chimpanzees, they too have been evolving for the millions of years since our lineage branched off from theirs. How can we be sure that our ancestors were like the chimpanzees of today? Of course, we can't, but we do know that rates of evolutionary change vary enormously between species and that many species remain relatively stable over periods of time much longer than the 5 or 6 million years that separate us from the chimpanzees. It is also the case that the chimpanzees are remarkably similar in habitat and behavior to the other great apes that branched off from our common lineage much earlier than the time at which humans and chimpanzees separated.

Our closeness to the chimpanzees (how many times have we heard that "we share over 98 percent of our genes" with them?) has only become more evident as genetic research continues. Already in 1992 Jared Diamond argued that we are "the third chimpanzee" (along with chimpanzees and bonobos, or pygmy chimpanzees), although he thought the small genetic difference between us and the other two had enormous consequences.[7] Research reported in 2002 by Derek E. Wildman and colleagues suggests that we share over 99 percent of our genes with the chimpanzees and that "a movement is emerging in the scientific community to recognize the close evolutionary relationship between humans and chimpanzees by placing them in the same genus, which by the rules of zoological nomenclature must be *Homo*."[8] These authors do not, any more than does Diamond, wish to underestimate the enormous difference between ourselves and our chimpanzee relatives, but they attribute that difference to rapid evolutionary change of the regulatory sequences that control the timing and pattern of genic activity as well as to change in the structures of the proteins encoded in the genes, rather than exclusively to the less than 1 percent of our genes that we do not share with them.[9]

What are some of the changes that made mimetic culture, rudimentary at best among chimpanzees, into an elaborate and complex system in early humans? Significant anatomical changes are clearly involved. Bipedal locomotion goes a long way back, around 4 million years ago, beginning in the earliest hominid genus, *Australopithecus*. It was obviously an important step, but its adaptive function is in debate and need not detain us here. Ian Tattersall takes the cautious view that the Australopithecines were probably more "bipedal apes," in their cognitive as well as anatomical qualities, than anything very much like ourselves.[10] The descendants of the Australopithe-cines or other hominid species living at the same time—and we must remember that there were probably many species, most of which died out, rather than one simple genealogical line—began to change in several important respects. Brain size increased, and because large brains require a great deal of energy, a more efficient feeding system developed. That is, fruit, and increasingly meat, replaced leaves as primary foods, consequently allowing a smaller, more efficient gut, and releasing more energy for an ever-larger brain. As the brain increased in size, hominid babies had to be born at earlier stages of their fetal development; otherwise their heads would be too large to pass through the birth canal. Hominid babies began to be born, relative to other primates, "prematurely," that is, undergoing outside the womb development that in other mammals takes place before birth. The helplessness of these "premature" infants required much longer nurturing before they could look out for themselves.

These changes involving feeding habits and increasing brain size, which are most clearly exhibited in *Homo erectus,* contributed to a significant change in social organization compared to our primate relatives, probably somewhere between 1 and 2 million years ago, though possibly significantly earlier. A diet increasingly dependent on meat, and infants increasingly in need of prolonged care, led to the formation of relatively stable cooperative ties between a male and a female, or sometimes a male and several females, replacing the primate band dominated by an alpha male. An indication that pair-bonding was replacing single-male dominated bands was that sexual dimorphism—the difference in size and strength between males and females—declined. Robin Dunbar writes, "In mammals, striking sexual dimorphism [such as was still evident among australopithecines] is invariably associated with harem-like mating systems, where a handful of powerful males share all the females between them. The reduced sexual dimorphism in the later hominids, where males are only 10 to 20 percent heavier than females, suggests that females were shared more evenly among males."[11] Strong dimorphism, including much larger male than female canine teeth, is linked to conditions where intragroup fighting between males for access to females is intense, so that decreasing dimorphism suggests declining intragroup hostility between males.

But because there is no reason to think that *Homo erectus* was organized in isolated nuclear families and every reason to think that they required, besides male-female pair-bonding, a high degree of cooperation between males (in hunting and in defense against predators and other human bands) and a high degree of cooperation between females (in childbirth, child care, and gathering), an entirely new level of social organization beyond anything seen in nonhuman primates became necessary. Dunbar has found a strong correlation between increase in the neocortex (the primary area responsible for increasing hominid brain size) and group size, a correlation that holds not only for primates but for other mammals as well. His explanation is not that increasing brain size causes larger groups, but that members of larger groups need larger brains to cope with the increasing demands of group life.[12] We need to consider why growing social complexity requires increasing cultural complexity, and we can begin by considering the central argument of Dunbar's book, *Grooming, Gossip, and the Evolution of Language.*

Dunbar points out that the largest typical group size for our ape relatives, 50 to 55 members, is characteristic of chimpanzees and baboons. By projecting the correlation between size of neocortex and group size to *Homo sapiens,* he comes up with the number 150, which he finds not only comes pretty close to average group size among hunter-gatherers, but also turns out to be close to the basic unit size in many complex organizations: for example, the company, as the smallest military unit that can stand alone. Having discovered that grooming is perhaps the basic means for the creation of solidarity among primates, he raises the question of whether, given how time-intensive grooming is, it could possibly be effective in groups much larger than 50: "Grooming seems to be the main mechanism for bonding primate groups together. We cannot be sure exactly how it works, but we do know that its frequency increases roughly in proportion to the size of the group: bigger groups seem to require individuals to spend more time servicing their relationships."[13] Given human group size, however, and projecting from primate patterns, we would have to spend 40 percent of our time grooming one another, leaving precious little time for anything else, if grooming were our main source of intragroup solidarity. Is there another, more efficient way that humans could achieve the same end? "The obvious way, of course, is by using language. We do seem to use language in establishing and servicing our relationships. Could it be that language evolved as a kind of vocal grooming to allow us to bond larger groups than was possible using the conventional primate mechanism of physical grooming?"[14]

This is an interesting idea, and we will pursue it further below, but if Dunbar means by language, modern rapid language, which is only found in *Homo sapiens* (and we will see that he doesn't exclusively mean that), then there is still a huge gap of at least 2 million years between the first members of our genus and ourselves, a period in which, if Dunbar's projections are correct, group size was gradually increasing from 50 to 150, together with the neocortical increase that we know from fossil evidence was occurring during that period.

I think it can be argued that what was in fact providing the source of solidarity in these early groups was both more and less than what Dunbar suggests. It was less than language in that, although it may have involved much more complex and subtle vocalization than the great apes are capable of, it was still not modern rapid language. Some writers have spoken of "protolanguage," which is a kind of placeholder about which we can speak hesitantly at best. Nonetheless, a significant increase in the complexity of vocal communication is almost a necessary hypothesis if we do not believe in the sudden appearance of a "language module" of extraordinary complexity as a onetime mutation.[15]

But it appears that what provided solidarity before the appearance of modern language was also more than language. Donald uses the metaphor of "language piggybacking on culture" to suggest that the appearance of language required the prior development of a complex culture in terms of which the move to language would make sense.[16] It is the development of mimetic culture over a long period of time that in Donald's view provided greatly increased cognitive resources including the solidarity that grooming no longer, and language had not yet, provided.

In the midst of so much conjecture, it is perhaps wise to begin our description of mimetic culture with virtually the only hard evidence (excuse the pun) we have for it, namely stone tools. More than 2 million years ago *Homo habilis* was making simple stone tools, essentially "sharp flakes banged from smallish cobbles using a stone 'hammer.'"[17] Chimpanzees have been observed in the wild opportunistically using "tools," such as a stone to crack nuts, or a stick to get ants out of an anthill, but the deliberate production of even a relatively simple stone tool for future use indicates a cognitive advance beyond even the cleverest chimpanzee. Their relatively simple tools nonetheless allowed *Homo erectus* to butcher rather large animals, even elephants, quite quickly. Both the manual dexterity and the understanding of the material, such that just the right angle at which one banged one stone against another would produce a sharp chip, suggest considerable cognitive sophistication. What is most important, from the point of view of culture, is that this skill had to be learned, and part of the learning was practice, because it isn't easy to do it right on the first try. However simple, it was also a skill complex enough that it could not be learned on the fly—it could not be learned opportunistically as needed. The making of such tools had to be planned in advance of their use; the right material was not likely to be at hand at the moment of need. And the skill was difficult enough that it had to be taught. Yet it could be taught mimetically, without language.[18]

Donald describes mimesis as an increase in conscious control over action that involves four uniquely human abilities: mime, imitation, skill, and gesture.[19] Mime, he says, is the imaginative enactment of an event. Although apes have a rudimentary ability to mimic, mime involves acting out a sequence of events as in the pretend play of children, a form of action that breaks with the here-and-now concreteness of episodic action.[20] In mime, one can imaginatively act out something that has happened in the past or that one intends to do at a later date. However limited, it allows an escape from the present, a degree of freedom from immediacy. Imitation, in Donald's terms, involves something much more precise than mime. A child might "pretend to" make a stone tool, having seen an adult make one, but have no idea how to choose the right material or make the exact motions that would produce the necessary chip. Imitation of the actual process would usually involve teaching, and pedagogy emerges for the first time as part of mimetic culture. Skill, as Donald uses the term, involves mime and imitation but moves beyond them. It requires "rehearsal, systematic improvement, and the chaining of mimetic acts into hierarchies."[21] Donald uses the example of learning to play tennis, although *Homo habilis* was not likely to have played tennis! But learning to play tennis is largely a mimetic skill, though a very complex one if one learns to play well, putting together a number of simple action chains into complex sequences. A skilled tennis player appears to play effortlessly, "instinctively" knowing how to respond to each challenge, but skills that can later be called forth automatically were initially learned slowly and painfully by giving the most exact attention to the learning process. Finally, by gesture Donald wants to describe the way in which humans can call on all three earlier levels of mimesis in order to communicate with others. And it is gesture that originally provided the source of solidarity when group size grew beyond the capacity of grooming to do so, and still, Donald argues, plays an essential role in group bonding.

If we may stay with stone tools for a moment, it is worth mentioning that about 1.5 million years ago a marked improvement occurred with the appearance of the Acheulian hand ax and associated tools, "which were obviously made to a standardized pattern that existed in the toolmakers' mind before the toolmaking process began."[22] These new tools marked a considerable advance over the simple chips of earlier times. Donald says that they "required expert fashioning; archeologists require months of training and practice to become good at creating Acheulian tools."[23] Tattersall points out that though these new, more advanced stone tools appear in association with *Homo ergaster,* they do so only after *ergaster* had been on the scene for 200,000 years. He uses this as an example of the fact that in human evolution anatomical change proceeds, to a degree, independently of cultural change. Technological and other cultural changes survive even though species change, and in some cases follow by long periods the physical development that presumably was the necessary but not sufficient condition for them.[24] There is debate about dating both the emergence of modern *Homo sapiens* and language, but there are those who believe that the former, with all the brainpower and vocalization equipment needed for full modern language, nonetheless preceded modern language by perhaps tens of thousands of years.

It is easy to become fixated on growing technological sophistication as the key to understanding human evolution—it fits all too well with our penchant toward economic determinism in the understanding of history. But since the cognitive revolution in psychology of the last several decades, it appears that technology is more an indication of increasing cognitive capacity than a primary determinant in its own right, because cognitive capacity is the key to understanding human evolution. Although toolmaking is an important indicator of the emergence of mimetic culture, we need to understand much more about the whole of which toolmaking is a significant part.

Donald speaks of enculturation as a third factor in development, besides genes and environment, one that is unique to our species. He calls it "deep enculturation" in contrast to the shallower enculturation common to many other species, because deep enculturation reaches "deeply into the heart of human nature"—in a word, it structures our minds.[25] The entry point of enculturation turns out to be our old friend attention, which we saw was the key to episodic consciousness. For culture, the key move is the *sharing* of attention, and the very beginning of shared attention is when, in the earliest months of life, the human infant is able to return the parent's gaze, to share eye contact, followed not much later by the capacity to look where the parent is looking.[26] Donald describes the critical importance of shared attention in early infancy:

During early infancy, cultural influence rests chiefly with certain figures, such as the mother, father, and other close family members. These are powerful forces in the mental life of infants because they influence attention. They do more than dominate attention; they also train infants to share attention with them. Perhaps the most important lesson they teach their infants during the first year of life consists of the basic rules of attention sharing. Once this process is well established it serves very well as a fast-track social learning instrument, in a variety of situations. Joint attention develops into a primary cultural guidance device. It allows children to follow cultural signals that will become increasingly more abstract as they expand their horizons.[27]

It is important to remember that this early attention sharing is mimetic and not linguistic. This is as true for infants today as it was a million years ago. In describing the mimetic accomplishments of children, Donald suggests the nature of a period in human evolution when mimetic culture was all there was:

> Early in development, the child connects with a mimetic social network ruled by custom, convention, and role taking. The family is a small theater-in-the-round, featuring a series of miniplays, in which each member must assume various roles. Children understand these theatrical productions so well and so early that they can act out any role, within the limits of infantile acting. This is shown in their fantasy games, where they might chose to play the father, the mother, themselves, or even the dog or the family car. Children become excellent mime artists and actors, long before they can verbally describe or reflect on what they are doing.[28]

Gesture is the most complex form in which mimetic culture can create shared attention. It takes many forms: expressing emotion, asking for help, warning of danger, and so forth. It is so close to syntax that it is probably the primary road to language, especially if we include, as we must, vocal gestures. But at the moment I want to focus on one primary form of shared gesture, one that is basic to the creation of social solidarity: rhythm. Rhythm, which is already evident in the simple reciprocal mimetic games that parents play with very young children,[29] is the basis of group rituals that can mimetically define group identity and the roles of individuals within the group. Ours is the only genus with the capacity for "keeping together in time,"[30] and this biological capacity has been essential for the full development of mimetic culture. Whether premodern members of the genus *Homo* had the capacity to mimic animals, and thus represent not only their social context but also significant aspects of their natural environment, we will never know, but animal mimicry is common among historically known hunter-gatherers.

Mimetic action involves using one's body to represent oneself and others in some kind of event. It moves beyond mammalian episodic (event) consciousness by *representing* events through embodied action, an event about an event, so to speak. But there is no reason to think that, because premodern members of the genus *Homo* did not have modern language, their mimetic action was silent (as the word "mime" might imply). On the contrary, there is every reason to believe that vocalization had developed well beyond the simple cries in use by the great apes. Donald argues that some form of voluntary voice modulation—what he calls prosodic control of the voice—was a necessary step along the way to the evolution of language. He writes: "Prosodic control of the voice—that is, regulation of volume, pitch, tone of voice, and emphasis—is logically more fundamental than, and prior to, phonetic control; it is much closer to the capabilities of apes than phonology. It is close to what Darwin thought might have been the origin of the speech adaptation, a kind of rudimentary song."[31]

I will return to the question of song, but now want to turn to Leslie Aiello's interesting distinction between speech and language, and his suggestion that they evolved separately: "Many of the unique anatomical features involved in the ability to produce human speech, as well as some of the cognitive precursors of human language, significantly precede the appearance of fully developed modern human language involving syntax, symbolic reference and off-line thinking."[32] Even Dunbar, who argues that language replaced grooming as the basis of social bonding as human groups grew larger, indicates that "a steady flow of vocal chatter" whose "content would have been zero," in other words speech without language, might have been an intermediate phase between the conventional contact calls of the advanced Old World monkeys and apes and genuine language. And when he says "zero content," he means zero abstract symbolic content, and not zero social content, for even "primate vocalizations are already capable of conveying a great deal of social information and commentary."[33]

If there was speech before language,[34] as our several experts agree was likely, and if it was prosody—that is volume, pitch, tone, and emphasis—

that characterized this nonlinguistic speech, then if it was not "song"—and Dunbar gives a variety of reasons why song as we know it probably developed only late in evolutionary history—what was it?[35] Steven Brown offers another interesting alternative that might stand up to scrutiny. Brown starts from the point that, though language and music today are clearly different in that their primary locations in the brain are different, nonetheless, even in terms of brain physiology, there is a great deal of overlap between them. He then suggests that language and music form a continuum rather than an absolute dichotomy, with language in the sense of sound as referential meaning at one end, and music in the sense of sound as emotive meaning at the other.[36] From this continuum, from features of their overlapping location in brain physiology, and from parsimony in explanation, Brown argues that rather than music and language evolving separately, or emerging one from the other, the likeliest account is that both developed from something that was simultaneously protolanguage and protomusic, which he calls "musilanguage."[37] If we postulate that musilanguage was also enacted, that is, involved meaningful gesture as well as sound, then we could see ritual as a primary evolutionary example of musilanguage and note that even today ritual is apt to be a kind of musilanguage: however sophisticated its verbal, musical, and gestural components have become, they are still deeply implicated with each other. And, in terms of the argument of Chapter 2, we could suppose that play had developed many of these features as it formed the matrix out of which ritual developed.

[margin handwriting: musilanguage / gesture / ritual]

However committed to the idea that it was language that replaced grooming, and however doubtful he might be about the idea of musilanguage, Dunbar is ready to admit that words alone, even after the evolution of modern language, are inadequate to supply the solidarity necessary for human groups:

> Trying to hold together the large groups that the emerging humans needed for their survival must have been a trying business. We still find it difficult even now. Imagine trying to coordinate the lives of 150 people a quarter of a million years ago out in the woodlands of Africa. Words alone are not enough. No one pays attention to carefully reasoned arguments. It is rousing speeches that get us going, that work us up to the fever pitch where we will take on the world at the drop of a hat, oblivious of personal costs. Here, song and dance play an important part: they rouse the emotions and stimulate like nothing else the production of opiates to bring about states of elation and euphoria.[38]

A society engaged in mimetic ritual, without language, would seem to be an almost pure case of Durkheim's "elementary form," for the bodies of those engaged in the ritual cannot represent much beyond themselves and the society they compose. Possibly the elation and euphoria that Dunbar mentions might point beyond society, but if so, inarticulately, to say the least. Because for Durkheim collective effervescence is an expression of society, here we would seem to have the pure case: society enacting itself. Still, can we say that society creates the ritual, or do we have to say that the ritual creates society? Mimetic ritual would seem to be constitutive of the very society it makes possible.

In modeling the society itself as well as its constituent roles, mimetic culture provided the necessary resources for moving beyond the rather anarchic chimpanzee band to a larger group capable of controlling in-group aggression, such that pair-bonding and same-sex solidarity in various contexts could result. In-group solidarity did not mean these mimetic-culture-based societies were peaceful. There is every reason to believe that they were not, that there was endemic conflict between groups—even cannibalism shows up in the fossil record—and probably in-group aggression was only relatively successfully controlled.[39]

The limitations of mimetic culture are evident. Donald writes:

Mimesis is thus a much more limited form of representation than symbolic language; it is slow moving, ambiguous, and very restricted in its subject matter. Episodic event registration continues to serve as the raw material of higher cognition in mimetic culture, but rather than serving as the peak of the cognitive hierarchy, it performs a subsidiary role. The highest level of processing in the mimetically skilled brain is no longer the analysis and breakdown of perceptual events; it is the modeling of these events in self-initiated motor acts. The consequence, on a larger scale, was a culture that could model its episodic predecessors.[40]

It is well to remember that we humans are never very far from basic mammalian episodic consciousness. Mimetic culture, as I have said, is an event about an event. Narrative, which is at the heart of linguistic culture, as we will see, is basically an account of a string of events, organized hierarchically into larger event units. But the moment when our predecessors first stepped outside episodic consciousness, looked at it and what was before, around, and would be after it, was a historic moment of the highest possible importance. Other higher mammals, although they are social, are locked each in their own consciousness.[41] They are, as Donald says, solipsists. But humans, once mimetic culture had evolved, could participate in, could share, the contents of other minds. We could learn, be taught, and did not have to discover almost everything for ourselves. Mimetic culture was limited and conservative; it lacked the potential for explosive growth that language would make possible. But it was the indispensable step without which language would never have evolved.

Further, mimesis is, though in many respects less efficient than language, indispensable in its own sphere. As Donald writes, mimesis "serves different functions and is still far more efficient than language in diffusing certain kinds of knowledge; for instance, it is still supreme in the realm of modeling social roles, communicating emotions, and transmitting rudimentary skills."[42] Maybe not just rudimentary skills, for mimesis is basic for the teaching of quite complex skills in such fields as athletics, dance, and possibly other arts. Finally mimesis remains indispensable in "the collective modeling and, hence, the structuring" of human society itself.[43]

Mythic Culture

We are so fascinated with ourselves as language users that we think discovering the origin of language is the key to understanding human evolution. It is one of the great virtues of Merlin Donald's work that he takes culture, the ability to escape our solipsism and connect with a larger shared consciousness, as the key to what makes us unique. It is in this context that his idea that language "piggybacks" on culture makes sense.[44] Language acquisition in the individual is social: even if there were such a thing as a language module, it could become operative only in a socially provided linguistic context. Isolated children do not learn spontaneously to speak. Jerome Bruner, as Donald reminds us, has shown convincingly that language learning requires an external support system, a linguistic milieu, to be effective.[45] The question is, what was the "external support system" that made language possible in the first place?

Terrence Deacon, a biological anthropologist and neuroscientist, in his book *The Symbolic Species*,[46] subtitled "The Co-evolution of Language and the Brain," tries to understand the emergence of language by *Homo erectus*, whose brains were not organized for language use, although, as we know, our nearest primate relatives can, with the most enormous effort and external training, be taught at least a rudimentary use of words. But, as Deacon puts it, "The first hominids to use symbolic communication were entirely on their own, with very little in the way of external supports. How then, could they have succeeded with their chimpanzeelike brains in achieving this difficult result? In a word, the answer is ritual."

Deacon makes the case for the parallel between teaching symbolic communication to chimpanzees and the origin of language in ritual as follows:

> Indeed, ritual is still a central component of symbolic "education" in modern societies, though we are seldom aware of its modern role because of the subtle way it is woven into the fabric of society. The problem for symbolic discovery is to shift attention from the concrete to the abstract; from separate indexical links between signs and objects to an organized set of relations between signs. In order to bring the logic of [sign-sign] relations to the fore, a high degree of redundancy is important. This was demonstrated in the experiments with the chimpanzees . . . It was found that getting them to repeat by rote a large number of errorless trials in combining lexigrams enabled them to make the transition from explicit and concrete sign-object associations to implicit sign-sign associations. Repetition of the same set of actions with the same set of objects over and over again in a ritual performance is often used for a similar purpose in modern human societies. Repetition can render the individual details of some performance automatic and minimally conscious, while at the same time the emotional intensity induced by group participation can help focus attention on other aspects of the object and actions involved. In a ritual frenzy, one can be induced to see everyday activities and objects in a very different light.[47]

Although it would seem that Deacon is on the right track in arguing that ritual provided the "external support system" necessary for original language learning, one can see that it makes the most sense in the context of Merlin Donald's version of the origin of language. The problem with Deacon's story is that "ritual" seems to come out of nowhere, and if language is difficult for "chimpanzeelike brains," so would ritual be. Donald's idea of a very long period during which mimetic culture developed and the human brain reached something far larger and more complex than that of chimpanzees, provides what Deacon's argument implies: ritual as an external support system for language.

Deacon is surely right that the key to language is the ability to make sign-sign connections that abstract from the immediate connection of sign and object, but Donald is also right in his insistence on how deeply grounded language is, not only in mimetic, but even in episodic consciousness. Giving his own interpretation to the idea of universal grammar, Donald shows how closely language reflects event perception:

> How else can we represent space than by somehow specifying up, down, beside, and above? The parts of speech and the rules by which they are governed seem to emerge naturally from the progressive differentiation, or parsing, of event perceptions. In this case, we can say that language begins by simply putting labels on specific aspects of an episodic perception. In fact, it is the latter, episodic cognition, our vestigial mammalian inheritance, that has imposed this universal frame on language.[48]

Donald cites George Lakoff and Mark Johnson, who argue for the fundamentally metaphorical nature of language: "Lakoff and Johnson have suggested that metaphoric expression taps a cognitive vein that is much more fundamental than language itself. In effect, metaphor is a dead giveaway (to use a metaphor) of the episodic roots of language."[49] Donald writes:

> Linguistic universals spring from the context in which real-world languages are learned and, more important, in which they evolved. Like any other set of conventions, linguistic conventions are shaped by the situations in which they originated. They have mimetic origins. Thus, once we change our paradigm, the features of universal grammar emerge smoothly from a close analysis of gesture, mime, and imitative behavior. The "language instinct" exists, but it is a domain-general instinct for mimesis and collectivity, impelled by a deep drive for conceptual clarification.[50]

But why this drive toward conceptual clarification? Donald suggests that there was a need for a more coherent representation of the world than was possible through mimesis. "Therefore," he writes, "the possibility must be entertained that the primary human adaptation was not language *qua* language but rather integrative, initially mythical, thought. Modern humans developed language in response to pressure to improve their conceptual

apparatus, not vice versa."[51] Myth is a profoundly ambiguous word, so it
would be well to be clear what Donald means by it:

> Mythical thought, in our terms, might be regarded as a unified, col-
> lectively held system of explanatory and regulatory metaphors. The
> mind has expanded its reach beyond the episodic perception of events,
> beyond the mimetic reconstruction of episodes, to a comprehensive
> modeling of the entire human universe. Causal explanation, prediction,
> control—myth constitutes an attempt at all three, and every aspect of
> life is permeated by myth.[52]

It is because of, in a sense, the primacy of myth over language that Donald
calls the stage after mimetic culture, mythic culture.

Donald, in emphasizing the cognitive role of myth, approaches the view
of Claude Lévi-Strauss, the anthropologist who, more than any other, has
emphasized the intellectual function of myth. Lévi-Strauss, nonetheless,
thinks of myth, not as a form of science or as a primitive precursor of it, but
as having a different cognitive function:

> To say that a way of thinking [myth] is disinterested and that it is an
> intellectual way of thinking does not mean at all that it is equal to sci-
> entific thinking . . . It remains different because its aim is to reach by
> the shortest possible means a general understanding of the universe—
> and not only a general but a *total* understanding. That is, it is a way of
> thinking which must imply that if you don't understand everything,
> you can't explain anything.[53]

That is a view of myth that would indeed see it as "impelled by a deep drive
for conceptual clarification," one we will explore further below.

Although Donald mentions ritual among the resources of mimetic culture, he does not make it central, as Deacon does, to the emergence of language. But I think on Donald's own terms we could see that Deacon is right.
If myth moves just beyond the most complex form of mimesis, isn't ritual
the likeliest candidate for that most complex form? Mimetic ritual models
society, and conceivably even some of society's environment, such as animals. But even at the mimetic stage, cannot we imagine something more?
Ritual, after all, does not just mirror reality. It gives a picture of reality as it
ought to be.[54] In mimetic ritual the society overcomes all the incessant bick-

ering, the factional disputes, the injury, anger, and resentment, that are endemic in any society, and shows society united instead. Even if mimetic ritual could have been complex enough to show disorder as well as order, as all known (linguistically linked) rituals do, it would be disorder transcended that would be the message of the ritual.

Among the disruptions to which Paleolithic society was heir, illness must have been very important, especially if we mean by illness not only somatic, but also psychosomatic and sociosomatic disorders. Children in such small and fragile societies must have been especially vulnerable, and the loss of an adult through illness or death would have placed a great burden on other members of the group. Thus healing rituals would likely have been significant from early times, as they have remained so to this day. Without getting into the problem of shamanism, which to some is endemic in all ancient cultures and to others is a figment of the Western mind, the earliest ritual specialist was probably the curer, the one who knew curing ritual, a ritual that could vividly present the experience of health in the face of the existing trouble.[55]

If, however, it is right to imagine mimetic ritual as straining to present an idea of society not as it is but as it ought to be, then Donald's notion that language emerged in the effort to attain a larger understanding of the world through myth makes a great deal of sense. Jonathan Z. Smith characterizes (linguistically related) ritual in a way that perhaps helps us understand the "drive toward conceptual clarification" that led to myth:

> I would suggest that, among other things, *ritual represents the creation of a controlled environment* where the variables (i.e., the accidents) of ordinary life may be displaced *precisely* because they are felt to be so overwhelmingly present and powerful. *Ritual is a means of performing the way things ought to be in conscious tension to the way things are in such a way that this ritualized perfection is recollected in the ordinary, uncontrolled, course of things.*[56]

In ordinary life things keep coming apart. Of ritual, what the Mazatec Indian shaman said, "I am he who puts together,"[57] undoubtedly applies not only to physical healing, but to healing in general.

For over a hundred years the argument as to which came first, ritual or myth, went on without resolution. It was one of those arguments that many felt would be best abandoned because irresolvable. If scholars like Donald and Deacon are right, however, the argument is at last over. Ritual clearly precedes myth. But, although examples of ritual without myth have been discovered among various peoples, ritual as we know it is deeply embedded in myth, and usually unintelligible without it. On the other hand myth, though it has often come loose from ritual, is still recognizably liturgical in origin in many instances. It might be useful to look at some instances in which the connection is exceptionally close.

One of the things that is of interest when we look at ritual and myth in relatively small societies with oral cultures is the fact that ritual is often remarkably stable, whereas myth has many, not entirely compatible, versions. It is not that ritual doesn't change; there is nothing in any society that doesn't change. But ritual seems to be more resistant to change than is myth. Perhaps we can see it as the mimetic marker from which language in the form of myth took flight, as it were. I would like to turn to Roy Rappaport's *Ritual and Religion in the Making of Humanity*, the most serious effort to think about ritual to appear in recent years, to consider his highly condensed, definition of ritual: *"the performance of more or less invariant sequences of formal acts and utterances not entirely encoded by the performers."*[58]

Rappaport's stress on "invariant sequences of formal acts and utterances" brings us back to features of musilanguage that may have been essential in the transformation of meaningless sound sequences into highly condensed, in the sense of undifferentiated, but still referentially-emotively meaningful, sound events, only a step away from myth. A key aspect of these transitional events is redundancy, essential in helping humans move from indexical to symbolic meaning. According to Bruce Richman, musical redundancy is communicated in three forms: (1) repetition, (2) formulaicness ("the storehouse of preexisting formulas, riffs, themes, motifs and rhythms"), and (3) expectancy "of exactly what is going to come next and fill the upcoming temporal slot."[59] In the redundancy created by expectancy, the most important element is tempo, the rhythm that may be created by drumming, the stamping of feet, or other means. We have already noted the uniquely human ability to "keep together in time." In any case it is closely related to the "more or less invariant sequences of formal acts and utterances" that are central to Rappaport's definition of ritual. These aspects of ritual will be illustrated shortly with the example of the Kalapalo of South America, where ritual is entirely musical; myth provides the context but not the content.

I need to make a brief aside to defend my choice of cases. I don't want to argue that the groups I will describe resemble in any exact way groups of humans from 50,000 or more years ago. Just as chimpanzees have evolved during the same number of years that humans have, so these groups have evolved for as many years as any other surviving human group. Nevertheless, not to look at some groups of hunter-gatherers or horticulturalists with a wholly oral culture as telling us something about earlier stages of human evolution would seem to be perverse, and though this is exactly what anthropologists who oppose the idea of cultural evolution do, their arguments have not been persuasive to archaeologists or other scholars for whom human evolution is an undeniable fact. The harder problem is, which tribal societies should we choose? Some have been tempted to see the tightly organized, heavily ritualized, "Durkheimian" tribal societies as late, and loosely organized, "individualistic" groups, lacking much in the way of ritual or myth, as representative of early stages of human evolution.[60] Mary Douglas, rejecting evolutionary sequences altogether, argues that some tribal societies are quite "secular," having little to show in the way of religion. She does, however, give a reason why some tribes are strongly ritualized and others nearly secular. In her own Durkheimian way, she links degree of religiosity to intensity of social organization. Where, in her terms, grid and group (we need not here worry about her way of thinking about social organization) are high, we can expect ritual to be prominent; but where they are weak, ritual will be largely absent.[61]

The question is, if we ask, in spite of Douglas's objections to evolutionary schemes, which type is older, it is not obvious that we must choose the more loosely organized. It may turn out that small, loosely organized societies do not represent the main line of evolution. Dunbar's inferential argument for 150 as the group size for *Homo sapiens* would suggest as much. Let us take one of Douglas's examples of a secular tribe, the Basseri nomads of Iran as described by Fredrik Barth. Douglas writes: "Should not one suppose that a society which does not need to make explicit its representation of itself to itself is a special type of society? This would lead straight to what Barth says of the independence and self-sufficiency of the Basseri nomadic household which, enabling it to survive 'in economic relation with an external market but in complete isolation from its fellow nomads, is a very striking and fundamental feature of Basseri organization.'"[62] Basseri society cannot, however, be taken as exemplary of early human society. For one thing, true pastoral nomadism, of which the Basseri are indeed exemplary, is a late phenomenon, becoming possible only after the emergence of agricultural societies, and always symbiotic with them. The symbiosis is clear in this case in that it is the market that allows the Basseri household to live in "complete isolation from its fellow nomads."

I would argue that the Basseri, or any society in which households are completely isolated, would not have been able to attain mythic culture; I doubt that they would even have attained mimetic culture. Groups like Colin Turnbull's Mbuti pygmies, or other pygmy groups found in various parts of the world that are extremely loosely organized, are generally symbiotic with agricultural neighbors (Mbuti) or are refugees defeated by and fleeing from enemy tribes, eking out a bare subsistence, and cannot be good exemplars of early *Homo sapiens* evolution.[63] For different reasons neither can the Inuit or other small groups who live in the subarctic. The Inuit are the most recent arrivals in the New World and could only have occupied their territory after highly sophisticated technology involving hunting gear, clothing, and boating had evolved, only a few thousand years ago at most.

Both mimetic and mythic culture most probably evolved in the richest areas for hunting and gathering, areas that have long been taken over by agriculturalists. These are just the areas that would have supported the population density necessary for cultural innovation. In most of the world, hunter-gatherers have been driven to the peripheries, and no longer occupy the areas of original cultural florescence. But there is one notable exception: Australia. Except for very recent European incursion, the Australian Aborigines have gone their own way, not without some outside cultural influence to be sure, for 50,000 years or more. They are not "typical" of hunter-gatherer societies, as has often been pointed out, but they may be closer to our ancient heritage than any other such societies.[64] The other possible candidates are from the New World, where Mesoamerican civilizations influenced, but perhaps did not decisively transform, hunter-gatherer and horticultural societies on their outer perimeters.

As a thought experiment, I would like to look at several cases, one from Australia, one from South America, and one from North America, to see what mythic culture, relatively uninfluenced by archaic, much less historic, civilizations, might have looked like.

The Kalapalo

My first example is a Carib-speaking group in the Upper Xingu Basin of central Brazil (Mato Grosso state), the Kalapalo, as studied by Ellen Basso.[65] When Basso lived with them in 1966–1968, the population of the village was 110, but it had been severely depleted by a measles epidemic in 1954; when she returned to do the fieldwork for her second book in 1978–1980, the population was around 200, so during the whole period it hovered around Dunbar's hypothetical norm of 150. The Kalapalo are one of eight villages in the area that share a common culture and are linked by significant ties of kinship and ceremonial, although they speak several different and mutually unintelligible languages. They live in an area so remote that they have been little disturbed since precontact times. At present they are within the borders of Xingu National Park, within which "non-Indian settlement, missionary activity, commercial exploitation of natural resources, and even casual tourism were prohibited." The result of this policy, according to Basso, was "the continued cultural vitality of a basically healthy population, in many important respects unchanged from the time" they were first discovered by Europeans in 1884.[66] At the time the park was formed, however, the Kalapalo had to move to their present location within the park boundaries. They still return to their old village location, some three days' journey away, to collect fruit from the trees there and to see again sites with great sentimental interest because of their association with specific events in Kalapalo myth.[67]

The Kalapalo are horticulturalists, whose main crop is manioc, but they get a significant portion of their food from fishing and gathering wild plants. Their year is divided into two seasons, wet and dry. During the dry season, roughly between May and September, there are many ritual events that last for weeks and sometimes months. In nonritual contexts Kalapalo society is organized in terms of households and kinship networks, but in the time of ritual, social organization shifts to a more inclusive community level, transcending kinship and affinity. Economic activities are organized by ritual officers more intensively and productively than in nonritual contexts, and the products are shared by the community at large.

What is particularly interesting is that Kalapalo ritual is primarily musical, with myth operating more as comment than scenario, yet the idea of the dominance of music is itself embedded in myth. The Kalapalo classify various beings according to the sounds they make. The "powerful beings," who were there "at the beginning," express themselves though "music." Human beings use "speech." Other animate beings, including animals, have "calls." Inanimate things make "noises."[68] Among the powerful beings are Agouti, Taugi, Thunder, Jaguar, and others. "Agouti is a sneak and a spy, Taugi an effective trickster who can penetrate illusions, Thunder the most dangerous of powerful beings, Jaguar a violent bully who is easily deceived."[69] Some of the powerful beings have animal traits, as is evident from their names, and they utter "calls" as well as speech, though music is their preferred form of expression. Along with the powerful beings are the Dawn People, human beings who existed at the Dawn Time and who interacted easily with the powerful beings.

According to Kalapalo cosmogony, human beings were created by Taugi, the trickster, "who speaks deceptively about himself," which is why human speech is always potentially deceitful, and people are concerned to give evidence for their truthfulness, including frequently an expression that means something like "that's no lie."[70] The earliest human beings, the Dawn People, lived in close relation to the powerful beings and were in many ways like them. People today, descended from the Dawn People but lacking their ability, must be wary of powerful beings, with their enormous creative but also dangerous energy.[71] They can appear in dreams or in unusual circumstances, usually in human form, but sometimes in animal form, and such encounters often require protective ritual because of the danger involved. Nonetheless it is the powerful beings who are the focus of ritual life and their form of expression, namely music, which provides almost the entire content of the rituals.

According to Basso, the world of the powerful beings and the Dawn People involved language, but above all music:

> This world is reproduced during ritual performances, in which Kalapalo collectively adopt the powerful mode of communication through which they engender the experience of a unity of cosmic forces, developed through the unity of sound formed by creative motion. In rituals, too, they most vividly realize their powers of presence. For by collectively performing music, they not only model themselves upon their images of powerful beings, but they feel the worth of those models by experiencing the transformative powers inherent in human musicality.[72]

The great festivals, which take weeks—in some cases as much as a year—of preparation and rehearsal, involve elaborate body painting, flower decoration, and sometimes masks. Integral to the musical performance is its accompanying bodily movement, which Basso calls "shuffling" rather than dance, and the lines of performers change direction as the musical lines shift. While the performers enact the powerful beings, they also charm them, for music calms and soothes them and contains the dangers of their otherwise unrestrained power. It is clear that the powerful beings are not "gods" and that ritual is not "worship." Rather, as Basso puts it:

> Musical performance is associated with powerful beings and is a means of communicating with them although it is not directly addressed to them . . . Communication may be said to occur not by singing *to* a powerful being but by singing it *into being*. Highly focused mental images of the powerful being are created in the minds of the performers by means of the performance . . . There is a consequent merging of the self with what is sung about; just as in myth powerful beings participate in human speech, so in ritual humans participate in *itseke* [powerful being] musicality and thereby temporarily achieve some of their transformative power. In public ritual, this is power of community. Rather than implying danger and ambivalence, however, it is collective solidarity emerging out of a performative experience of social restructuring and communal labor, representing a transformative power with markedly creative effects, including the ability to create its own social organization and to help cure the most seriously ill.[73]

Basso discusses the intense "communitas"—she uses Victor Turner's term for the communal emotion of the ritual—that she finds among the Kalapalo not so much as a kind of "anti-structure," as Turner argued, but rather as an alternative structure. Rituals last too long and involve too much highly organized economic effort to be seen as brief periods when the differentiations of everyday life are overcome. Rather they move the people from their usual nonritual divisions of households and lineages, with all the jealousies and conflicts that that implies, into a period of intense collective effort in which they identify as Kalapalo, not as family members. The ritual dance groups deliberately separate siblings; husband and wife dance in different sets. "Common humanity," which may extend to no more than the Kalapalo and their neighboring allied tribes, takes over from the divisions of everyday life. Thus Kalapalo communitas, though temporary, is, according to Basso a "structured order . . . The appropriate attitudes underlying and creating effective collective work are communicated by collective, repeated, patterned musical performance, in which the joy of collective experience is realized. This collective musical performance allows the economic events to be successful, indeed, to occur."

What this new self-identity implies ("I am Kalapalo" as opposed to "I am Kambe's daughter-in-law," for example) is a moral sense of equality or "identity of participation."

> Economically, it means that everyone is obligated to participate, but everyone receives regardless of contribution. *Ifutisu,* the most basic value of Kalapalo life (subsuming the notions of generosity, modesty, flexibility, and equanimity in facing social difficulties, and respect for others)[74] is extended beyond the domain of family to all people in the community.[75]

The world of this purely oral culture is clearly organized by ritual and myth. The Kalapalo cosmos is coherent: in the beginning were the powerful beings; they created the Dawn People with whom they lived at first; they now dwell in a "sky village," near the sun rise, not far from the earthly habitations of present-day people who are descended from the Dawn People; after death, people go to the sky village and become powerful beings. This "cosmic history" has no great depth in time or space.[76] But ritual overcomes even this rather limited sense of temporal unfolding, for the powerful people become now and us. Basso cites the philosopher of music, Victor Zuckerkandl, to show how music helps to provide this sense of union between self and world. For Zuckerkandl, music creates "a sense of 'space without distinction of places' and 'time in which past and future coexist within the present,' that is, of the movement of tones which is music itself."[77]

The Kalapalo use the very recurrence of mythic time as a subtle way of understanding their reality. What happened "in the beginning" can always happen. Strange behavior on the part of an individual can be likened to some action of a powerful being in a myth, and so interpreted. An eclipse of the sun or moon recalls stories in which the sun or moon are "being killed," but also reassures in that in the stories they do not die, but return to their normal state. Basso argues that Kalapalo myth is not a kind of "charter," as Malinowski thought, that provides a model or rule to be followed. Instead myth is an account of the way things are, a reference frame for understanding the world. She points out that Westerners, even anthropologists, are used to explanations that take a didactic, logical, or evidentiary form, and so think of mythic "explanation" as irrational, failing to note the subtle and complex uses to which narrative thinking can be put.[78] We will see that this condescending attitude toward mythic explanation is typical of the theoretic mind, which is at best incipient among the Kalapalo.

Basso gives plenty of evidence that life among the Kalapalo, whatever ritual is supposed to do, by no means runs smoothly. If it did, ritual would hardly be necessary. Some rituals focus on adolescence—puberty rites for both boys and girls are important, and are preceded by periods of seclusion involving ascetic practices and athletic training. By successfully completing the arduous and lengthy period of seclusion that precedes the puberty rite, the young person can turn him- or herself into

> a pleasing object, neutralizing the evil forces within, thereby becoming a cherished and respected person and in rituals the active symbol of a community's moral worth . . . The Kalapalo adolescent can thus serve as a particularly apt image of moral as well as physical beauty . . . Yet in the myths these are the very people who most often provoke jealousy and anger in others and who in response withdraw from society or in various ways are especially responsive to the suggestions of powerful beings, thereby providing a test for themselves as well as for certain members of their families.[79]

Closeness to powerful beings is ambiguous. Some, through dreams or otherwise, are called to be shamans, who, after a rigorous period of training and a major public rite, can serve as curers and diviners for the people, having the ability to visit the sky village where the powerful beings dwell.[80] But the power of powerful beings is ambiguous. It can be used for evil as well as good, and the Kalapalo believe that there are witches who use this power to kill.[81] Death sets off prolonged rituals of grief, during which suspicions as to those possibly responsible for the death are roused.[82] Killing of suspected witches is not unknown.

One place where conflict comes into ritual itself is the major rites performed by each gender alone. As Basso says, "the symbols [these rituals] call to mind emphasize the differences and antagonisms between the sexes through their reference to the dangerous powers inherent in human sexuality. Yet at the same time the music effects communication between the performers (of one sex) and the listeners (who are of the opposite sex), a situation of communicative control over these dangerous powers." The worry about deceit, which is endemic in Kalapalo communication and a frequent feature of myth, enters into the ritual exchange. The performers try to move the listeners to a situation of shared feeling, but the listeners remain doubtful as to whether they can trust the performers.

Yet the listener, who is also a participant some other time, has a double experience of assertion and doubt . . . Since music is multiply interpretable, it is effective when there is a need for communication between beings who cannot, or will not, bring to a communicative event the same presuppositions about the truth of what is being said. This multiplicity of interpretation and distinction between performer and listener emphasizes boundaries created by classification and opposition, while at the same time paradoxically fusing the bounded and opposed into a unity of performative discourse, a domain of discourse which the Kalapalo represent by their ideas about powerful beings.[83]

Basso sums up her interpretation of Kalapalo ritual and myth by pointing out that ritual performance recapitulates the mythical relation of powerful beings and humans. Human life derives ultimately from the powerful beings, and both understand the primary mode of communication of the other: music and language.

When people perform music, they have the ability to move powerful beings because the latter can thereby most clearly recognize something of themselves in humanity . . . In ritual performance, the unity of persons is effected through musical expression, wherein the body is an important musical instrument that helps to create a feeling about the motion of sounds in space, and understanding of a particular sense of time and of the most intense expression of life itself, which is the experience—however transient—that one is indeed a powerful being.

Through sound symbols, ideas about relationships, activities, causalities, processes, goals, consequences, and states of mind are conceived, represented, and rendered apparent to the world. It is through sound that cosmic entities are rendered into being and represented by the Kalapalo—not as object-types but as beings causing and experiencing action in a veritable musical ecology of spirit.[84]

The Kalapalo example illustrates much of the argument about mimetic and mythic culture developed earlier in this chapter. Though myth, by providing a framework for interpreting the world, does give the Kalapalo the "conceptual clarity" of which Donald spoke, Kalapalo ritual remains overwhelmingly mimetic, using wordless music, gesturally rather than linguistically. I chose the Kalapalo as my first example because of the mimetic nature of their ritual, but they are, though perhaps extreme, not unique. Not only is ritual always, by definition, mimetic, myth seldom lacks a mimetic dimension. In describing the formal recitation of myths outside of ritual, Basso emphasizes that though they are not sung (occasionally songs may be interspersed in the recitation), they have a strongly rhetorical (gestural) element. They are performances, rhythmical and poetic, requiring an audience skilled enough to participate with appropriate responses, sometimes with the equivalent of the "amen" with which an Evangelical congregation responds to a sermon, sometimes with questions that spur the reciter to more intense expression.[85] If Kalapalo myth recitation, though clearly "speech" and not "music" even in their own classification of sounds, still carries mimetic overtones, so does almost all spoken language, even the driest of academic lectures.

Thus Kalapalo ritual illustrates Rappaport's condensed definition of ritual as involving "invariant sequences of formal acts and utterances," but it also illustrates many of the broader features in his analysis. For our purposes, the most important of these have to do with the creation of social conventions, a moral order, a sense of the sacred, and a relationship to the cosmos, including beliefs about what lies behind the empirical cosmos.[86] Rappaport, like most other writers on ritual, is aware of the wide variety of actions that can be classified under this term. One defining feature of ritual for him is performance.[87] In his usage of this potentially ambiguous term, performance carries the sense of what is called in the philosophy of language performative speech: something is not simply described or symbolized, but done, enacted. The sheer act of participating in serious rituals entails a commitment with respect to future action, at the very least solidarity with one's fellow communicants. Thus, as Rappaport uses the term, it would explicitly not be the same as participating in a dramatic "performance," where the actor sheds the "role" as soon as the performance is over, and the audience, however moved, goes away knowing it was "only a play."[88] On the contrary, serious ritual performance has the capacity to transform not only the role but the personality of the participant, as in rites of passage.[89] The fundamental relationship between saying and doing Rappaport sees as establishing "convention in ritual" and the "social contract and morality that inhere in it." This is the ground, he argues, for "taking ritual to be humanity's basic social act."[90]

If we can see wordless ritual as mimesis at its most complex, because, through gestures, it comes close to narrative form, we can imagine how potentially liberating a fully linguistic narrative might be. Variations, alternatives, speculations become possible when myth attains a degree of linguistic autonomy, that would be far less possible in the "invariant forms" of ritual, still marked by its mimetic birthplace. The Australians, with their luxuriant development of myth, give evidence of some of these possibilities.

The Australian Aborigines (The Walbiri)

As anthropologists have pointed out, there are many tribes, clans, and local groups in Aboriginal Australia, and because particularity is a significant feature of their cultures, to lump them all together is to distort their reality. Still there are common features of Aboriginal culture that contrast with other hunter-gatherer cultures. I will follow a middle path by talking of Aboriginal culture and religion in general to some degree, but will use as my chief example a central Australian desert society, the Walbiri.[91] My reasons for choosing the Walbiri are twofold. Although no Australian group has escaped the trauma of alien intrusion to the same degree as the Kalapalo, Walbiri culture was among the most intact of existing Australian groups when studied in the 1950s by M. J. Meggitt and Nancy D. Munn, the ethnographers on whom I am relying most.[92] The second reason is that the peoples of the central desert, of which the Walbiri are one, are closer to what Tony Swain calls the "trans-aboriginal 'architectonic idea'" than those of other regions vulnerable to a variety of outside contact earlier than the peoples of the central desert.[93] I am not at all claiming that the Walbiri represent the ancient, unchanging, "true" Aboriginal tradition—everything we know about Aboriginal culture suggests it was, like all other cultures, always open to continuous change—but rather that the Walbiri and other central desert tribes probably tell us most about what the continent-wide Aboriginal culture was like 200 years ago, on the verge of contact.

Unlike the Kalapalo, who lived in a village (although they alternated between summer and winter villages) and combined horticulture with hunting and gathering, the Australian Aborigines were seminomadic hunters and gatherers whose society was organized primarily in terms of locality and kinship. Because intense attachment to specific localities is central to Aboriginal culture, we must understand what it means to be "seminomadic." As Durkheim noted in *Elementary Forms,* Aboriginal society alternated in time between smaller foraging groups and larger ceremonial groups, but in neither case did they form permanent villages. They circulated in a fairly stable route among a number of camps that were usually associated with water holes. Very sacred locations that might be uninhabitable most of the year because of extreme drought could become the locus of large ceremonial encampments during the seasons when they were well watered and fertile. What gave people (the word "tribe" is particularly unhelpful in Australia) their identity was their relationship to "country"—to locations to which they had a particular ancestral affiliation—because they believed that they had themselves come from their country and would after death return to it. Thus it is impossible to understand Aboriginal society without getting into ideas that ↳ place we would call religious.

In Australia, myth and ritual normally entail each other. Although W. E. H. Stanner has described what he calls riteless myths and mythless rites, he believes that even in these cases the missing partner is implied.[94] The Aboriginal understanding of myth is usually expressed in the term "Dreaming," although we must use the word with caution. In some central desert groups, including the Walbiri, the word for myth and the word for dream are the same, but this is not the case in many other groups. Even where the word is the same, the Dreaming that takes one into the world of ancestral beings is clearly differentiated from ordinary dreaming. According to Nancy Munn, the Walbiri "use the term *djugurba,* which also means 'dream' and 'story,' to denote . . . ancestral inhabitants of the country and the times in which they traveled around creating the world in which present-day Walbiri now live."[95] The contrast term, *yidjaru,* denotes the ongoing present or events within living memory. It also refers to "waking experience in contrast to dreaming."[96] To use Schutz's terms described in Chapter 1, *yidjaru* might be described as "ordinary reality" and *djugurba* as "non-ordinary reality." The Schutzian terms help us overcome the idea that the difference between the two realms is primarily temporal, because although *yidjaru* refers to the ordinary present, *djugurba* also becomes present during ritual enactment or even when the myths are told. Tony Swain argues that Aborigines think of their world in terms of *"rhythmed events"* more than in terms of unfolding or even cyclical time, and that the Dreaming can be seen as a class of events, namely *"Abiding Events"*—formative events that underlie reality without respect to time but are always located in specific places.[97]

Swain further argues that the Aboriginal understanding of being is oriented not so much to space (undifferentiated extension within which particular things occur) as to particular places, understood as conscious and alive—as living traces of ancestral beings. An ontology of rhythmic and abiding events occurring in particular places obviates the necessity of thinking about time and history. It thus obviates any idea of cosmogony: the ancestral beings do not so much "create" the world, as Munn puts it, as form the world, for there is no idea of a beginning before creation, or even of creation. The forming activity of the ancestral beings is as much present as past. Swain retrieves an archaic word "ubiety," "thereness," to characterize Aboriginal ontology.[98] Ubiety so obliterates time that in the Dreaming, past, present, and future are not differentiated: there is only, in Stanner's apt term, "everywhen."[99] And even life in ordinary existence can be understood as a transition from birth out of the Dreaming to Death as a return into it.

The emphasis on places is not, however, monadic. The Walbiri idea of country is indicated iconographically by circles, indicating water holes and camps, and lines indicating the tracks between them. Although in one sense the circles are "centers," they are not seen, as in later archaic societies, as world centers. As Munn puts it:

> It should be noted that this centre symbolism, unlike that of cosmic models in some other cultures, does not refer to the centre of the world *as a whole,* but only to a single place. Walbiri country consists of many such life centres linked together by paths. There is no single locality that focalizes all the others. Walbiri do not really give conceptual shape to the world as a whole in the sense of a single, centralized structure, but conceive of it in terms of networks of places linked by paths.[100]

Fred Myers describes a similar attitude among the Pintupi, a people just south of the Walbiri:

> It is impossible to listen to any narrative, whether it be historical, mythological, or contemporary, without constant reference to where events happened. In this sense, place provides the framework around which events coalesce, and places serve as mnemonics for significant events. Travel through the country evokes memories about a fight that occurred at a nearby water hole or a death in the hills beyond. No temporal relation but geography is the great punctuator of Pintupi storytelling . . .
>
> Thus the world is socialized by the Pintupi, although they do not build a spatially centered cosmos of domesticated culture and wild nature as many more settled people have done. A social life with so much movement seems to preclude such a construction. Instead, they seem truly at home as they walk through the bush, full of confidence. A camp can be made almost anywhere within a few minutes—a wind-

break set up, fires built, and perhaps a billycan of tea prepared. Unmarked and wild country becomes a "camp" *(ngurra)* with the comfort of home. The way of thinking that enables a people to make a camp almost anywhere they happen to be, with little sense of dislocation, is a way of thinking that creates a universe of meaning around the mythologized country.[101]

Because *djugurba* (Dreaming) means "story" as well as "myth" (as in *mythos,* the Greek original of our term "myth"), it is not surprising that even when Ancestral Beings are involved, the stories remain very close to daily life. Of the stories that women frequently tell to each other and illustrate with sand drawings, Munn writes:

> Occasional tales include behavior of an extraordinary kind, such as the transformation of a man into a snake, which Walbiri do not believe happens today; but such occurrences are exceptional. A large part of story behavior consists simply of the action patterns of daily life; food acquisition, mourning rites, ceremonies of various kinds . . .
>
> While all these stories are regarded as traditional accounts of ancestral activities, it is obvious that we have here a narrative projection of the cyclical day-after-day experience of daily routine and a recounting of the sorts of incidents and behavior also possible for the most part in the ongoing present of Walbiri daily life. It is, in effect, this repetitive daily existence that is going under the label *djugurba,* ancestral way of life.[102]

The myths that serve as the scenarios of rituals and are told by the men who "own" those rituals are only somewhat more elaborate versions of the stories told by women. The same daily round—sleeping, hunting, eating—provides the substructure of the myths, but they focus on the actions and in particular on the travels of named Ancestral Beings from specific place to specific place. The complex designs on sacred stones and boards as well as painted on the bodies of ritual dancers use the same basic graphs as the women's sand drawings, but in more elaborate form. The lines that represent the tracks from camp to camp are more prominent than in women's drawings which focus on the circles which indicate the camps themselves. The ritual myths tell of how the Ancestral Beings formed the landscape—rivers, hills, or water holes—or how they became themselves some remarkable rock formation or other geographical feature. Nancy Munn sums up what she calls the Aboriginal "world theory" as the "coming-out" and "going-in" of the Dreamings: as Swain summarizes it, "something came out of, moved across, and went into, the earth," forming the world as it did so.[103] Though the Aborigines sometimes say that when an Ancestral Being went into the earth (or became some remarkable feature of the landscape), it "died," at the same time it remains fully present at all the sites of its wandering. Swain quotes T. G. H. Strehlow as saying that the Aranda, another central desert group, believe "in the simultaneous presence of the Ancestor at each of the many scenes which once witnessed the fullness of his supernatural powers."[104]

If in the myths the Ancestors are described as forming the natural world, they are also seen as forming the social world, establishing customs and rituals as they travel though the landscape. Although we speak of "Ancestral Beings," the Walbiri do not think of themselves as biologically descended from such beings. Rather they believe that such beings scattered *guruwari*, fertility powers or powers of generation, and left them in the soil as they traveled. Women then become impregnated by these powers, so that their children have the spirit of the Ancestral Being.[105] *Guruwari* also means the design, and its associated song, which represents the Ancestor. Boys during the initiation ceremonies touch objects with the design and are thus born again from the Ancestral *guruwari*. Thus human beings are linked to each other by their relationship to these beings; patrilineages derive from their connection to the Ancestral Beings, kinship being less fundamental than association with place.[106]

But not only is society formed through linkages between humans and the Ancestral Beings, so is the entire moral order. Another and even more common way the Aborigines refer to what I have been calling the Dreaming is the Law or the Ancestral Law.[107] Marcia Langton, herself an Aborigine, describes what Aboriginal Law entails:

> What our people mean when they talk about their Law, is a cosmology, a worldview which is a religious, philosophic, poetic and normative explanation of how the natural, human and supernatural domains work. Aboriginal Law ties each individual to kin, to "country"—particular estates of land—and to Dreamings. One is born with the responsibilities and obligations which these inheritances carry. There are many onerous duties, and they are not considered to be optional. One is seen to be lazy and neglectful if these duties are ignored and the respect,

authority and advantages, such as arrangements for good marriages, opportunities for one's children, are not awarded. As many of our people observe, Aboriginal Law is hard work.[108]

Among the Walbiri, Meggitt describes the Law as follows:

> There are explicit social rules, which, by and large, everybody obeys; and the people freely characterize each other's behaviour insofar as it conforms to the rules or deviates from them. The totality of the rules expresses the law, *djugaruru,* a term that may be translated also as "the line" or "the straight or true way."[109] Its basic connotation is of an established and morally-right order of behaviour (whether of planets or of people), from which there should be no divergence . . .
>
> As the law originated in the dreamtime, it is beyond critical questioning and conscious change. The totemic philosophy asserts that man, society and nature are interdependent components of one system, whose source is the dreamtime.[110]

If the Dreamings give accounts of how the cosmos is formed, they also give accounts of how one should act in society. For example, a central desert story tells of how an Ancestral Being was attracted to a woman of a kin category that made her a potential mother-in-law to him, and thus sexually taboo. He was so overcome with desire that he raped her, but she closed her legs in such a way that her vagina dismembered his penis. The Aborigines can show you the rock that represents her vagina with the stone-penis still embedded in it. The Ancestral Beings, it seems, were no better than we are, but what happened to them can be exemplary of how the Law functions.

Even though the Law may entail "hard work," and we should note that Aboriginal ceremonial life, in which the Law is reenacted, requires indeed a great deal of hard work, its end is renewed vitality. The Walbiri associate feelings of "happiness and well-being" with ceremonial, and believe that, after a social disturbance, a ritual performance will make people "happy" again.[111] One of the commonest forms of Walbiri ritual is the *banba,* or "increase" ceremonies, performed for the animal or plant species "owned" by a patrilineal group or at least by the patrilineal moiety to which the group belongs. These are indeed "totemic" rituals, but we need not get involved in worrying about the meaning of "totemism."[112] The totem of a patrilineal group is simply the Ancestral Being in its animal form and its geographic place with which the group is identified. As Meggitt has pointed out, the ceremonies are not intended so much to "increase" the relevant species as to ensure its normal maintenance, so "cosmic maintenance rituals" might be a better designation than "increase rituals."[113]

The particular totem does indeed "belong" to a particular group, but it does so in a context of many totems belonging to many groups, all of which are needed if cosmos and people are to survive.[114] In *banba* ceremonies, not only are "owners" necessary, but "workers" from the opposite moiety are also necessary, indeed do much of the work of preparing the ceremony. And the vitality of the species that the ceremony is intended to enhance serves the welfare of all the people, not just the "owners." That Aboriginal ideas of ownership do not fit Anglo-Saxon property law has given rise to many painful misunderstandings. "Owning" a site does not mean exclusive rights to its economic exploitation; on the contrary, it means the obligation to maintain its fertility for the use of all. What the actors in the ritual are doing is recreating the *guruwari,* the creative potency, of the Ancestral Beings. As Munn puts it: "Through their performance, the masters [what I have called the "owners"] realize the generative potential of the ancestral forms: it is as if they change ancestors into descendents, and so maintain the continuity of species and persons."[115]

In describing the Kalapalo, I concentrated on ritual and its central form, music. In treating the Australian Aborigines, I have moved to a greater concern for narrative, but the centrality of narrative is only relatively greater than among the Kalapalo, and ritual in general, and song in particular remain prominent. I have already mentioned that every *guruwari,* ancestral potency, has its associated song. The Ancestors leave songs behind in each place they visit and the songs, in turn, are reminders of the larger narrative of which they are a part. In Cape York there is an account of an Ancestral Being who, under Melanesian influence, is on the way to being a "hero" of an un-Aboriginal type, yet his proclivity to sing links him to the continental pattern:

He go, he go, he go.
Come out in the river mouth.
Him say, 'Well, I think I go now leave this place' . . .
He look back, 'Oh, country there I leave him long way', he say, 'right
    to south'.
He start make one sing there, make sing then.

He still go . . .
He never stop
Em keep sing.[116]

Dreamings are, as Paul Ricoeur would put it, redescriptions that add something, emplotment, to what they describe.[117] What is remarkable about Aboriginal narrative, at least of the central desert variety, is how little it adds, even though that little is critically important. Abiding Events and ordinary events overlap to a remarkable degree. It is in this sense that for the Aborigines life is what Stanner calls "a one-possibility thing."[118] As he says, "their Ideal and Real come very close together."[119]

It is not that the Aborigines lack "the metaphysical gift," the ability, as Stanner puts it, "to transcend oneself, to make acts of imagination so that one can stand 'outside' or 'away from' oneself, and turn the universe, oneself and one's fellows into objects of contemplation." Nor do they lack a drive "to 'make sense' out of human experience and find some 'principle' in the whole human situation."[120] Nonetheless, "the overruling mood is one of belief, not of inquiry or dissent."[121] "This is why, among them, the philosophy of assent, the glove, fits the hand of actual custom almost to perfection, and the forms of social life, the art, the ritual, and much else take on a wonderful symmetry."[122]

But Swain argues that this symmetry, this closeness of the Ideal and the Real, this emphasis on abidingness, persists and can persist only as long as ubiety reigns. Once place is lost, or even threatened, there is a "fall" into time and history, the glove no longer fits, and the yearning for another time, another place begins. He illustrates this "fall" with several Aboriginal cases, which I cannot here pursue at length, but two of which I must at least mention.

Aboriginal Australia has been cited, notably by Mircea Eliade, following Pater Schmidt, as an important case of *Urmonotheismus,* primeval monotheism, because of the "High Gods," or "Sky Gods" to be found there.[123] But among the central desert peoples that I have focused on there are no High Gods, indeed no gods at all. The Ancestral Beings, like the powerful beings of the Kalapalo, are not worshipped but identified with in ritual enactment. It was the absence of gods, worship, even prayer, that led early Western observers to declare that the Aborigines had no religion at all, thus missing entirely the rich web of belief and practice that in fact characterize Aboriginal life. So where are these High Gods, this primeval monotheism?

Eliade does argue for the existence of such among one central desert group, the Aranda, but Jonathan Z. Smith has pretty completely demolished the evidence Eliade cited for that argument.[124] The main evidence for High Gods, even "Supreme Beings," is to be found in Southeast Australia, which, as Tony Swain points out, suffered the earliest and most devastating incursions of European colonization.[125] Indeed, the context for the emergence of High Gods in Southeast Australia was "devastation, death and dispossession."[126] Once removed from the "country," which was itself alive with the traces of Ancestral Beings, the remnant population of Aborigines, having lost 80 percent or more of their people to infectious disease for which they had no immunity, if not to massacre, borrowed from their conquerors a different cosmology from their traditional one. A creator God, often called Baiami (the first report of this deity was from the Wellington Valley Mission in the 1830s) was said to have abandoned the earth and removed to the sky. Because the earth is devastated, the land of fertility and plenty is now located in Heaven, where the Aboriginal people can go after death. Baiami is the All-Father, not located anywhere in particular, ubiquitous, not ubietous, but definitely not of this earth. The split between earthly place and Heavenly ubiquity is mirrored in another most un-Aboriginal split: between good and evil. But far from simply mimicking their conquerors, this split is not between those who do good and those who do evil (the very idea of evil is un-Aboriginal) but between Aborigines and whites: only Aborigines go to Heaven. The loss of locative grounding led to a new un-Aboriginal concern with time. Not only was Baiami a creator, there was also the possibility, not envisaged in the central desert, of an end time, indeed a Millennium, in which all the whites would board their ships and sail away, leaving Australia once again to its native inhabitants. Swain does not argue that these new beliefs were "syncretistic," even though they borrowed the ontology of the conquerors, but rather that they were a revolutionary leap in Aboriginal thinking brought on by catastrophic conditions. Only in the late twentieth century were Baiami beliefs harmonized with Christianity.[127] Although Swain does not generalize his argument beyond a careful reassessment of the material on Southeast Australia, I think it not unlikely that the popular view of the religion of native North Americans—namely, that they believe in the Great Spirit and that after death they will go to the Happy Hunting Ground in the sky—is, to the extent it represents any Native American belief at all, a result of catastrophic contact conditions.[128]

The second case that differs from the central desert peoples is the Northwest where changes were, as in the Southeast, stimulated by the incursion of strangers, coming at about the same period as the whites to the Southeast, namely, late eighteenth to early nineteenth centuries, but in this case from the island of Sulawesi in present-day Indonesia.[129] The people that the Aborigines called "Macassans," but who probably included several ethnic groups from Sulawesi, were far less intrusive than the whites in the Southeast: they came in search of trepang, the sea cucumbers that were profitable in the China trade. They did not so much want to take Aboriginal land as to establish coastal enclaves for reprovisioning. Whereas the Aborigines failed utterly and to their consternation to bring the white invaders in the Southeast into any relation to the Law, the Macassans were uneasily but successfully included in it, even to the point of establishing some intermarriage.

Contact with the Macassans did not result in a sense of profound loss, but rather of vague uneasiness, an awareness that the world is larger than the "country" so essential to Aboriginal consciousness. And the ritual response, though significant enough, was less drastic than in the Southeast. That ritual response took the form of a cult of the All-Mother, as opposed to the All-Father of the Southeast. The All-Mother was not a Sky God, certainly not a Supreme Being, but simply a Being who arrived on the northern shore from across the water (Swain indicates she may have been a creative Aboriginal adaptation of a Sulawesi agricultural goddess, a "Rice Mother")[130] and now journeyed from place to place much like other Ancestral Beings. But her cult became, like Macassan contact, "international," namely spreading from group to group, even reaching the central desert by the late nineteenth century, though it is interesting that by the time it reached the Walbiri the central figure had become male: as Meggitt says the Walbiri *Gadjari* rite had become a Mother-cult without the Mother.[131]

The best description of a Mother-cult is W. E. H. Stanner's account of the *Punj* initiation ritual and the myth that goes with it among the Murinbata, a people who live not far from the Northwest coast. The myth is about Mutjinga, the Old Woman, who unaccountably swallows the children and must be killed in order that the children can be recovered from her womb (not her stomach). The myth has an overtone of sadness, of "sad inevitability," as Stanner puts it, for it is an account that illustrates the "immemorial misdirection" in human affairs.[132] The Aborigines have no explanation of why Mutjinga went wrong: they say, "she should have lasted a long time"; "the people did not want to kill her"; "she went wrong herself"; and ultimately, "it is a thing we do not understand."[133] The Murinbata, says Stanner, "have stopped short of, or gone beyond, a quarrel with the terms of life. Their myths are evidence that they reflected and felt a fatal impairment, but the rites are evidence that they met the issue in a positive way."[134] Summing up, Stanner says that Murinbata ritual is not just ceremonial but celebration and that "it allows them to assent to life, as it is, without morbidity."[135] Nevertheless, the overtone of sad finality that correlates with the transplaceness of the Mother-cult suggests a shift, far subtler than the drastic symbolic revolution in the southeast, from the soberly sanguine life of the desert. Life for the Murinbata may still be a one-possibility thing, but it had become more tenuously so.

One feature of Aboriginal life has struck many of its most careful observers: the almost complete lack of imperial ambition. There are almost no cases of war for territorial expansion throughout the whole continent. This does not at all mean that the Aborigines weren't violent. The chances of being murdered in an Aboriginal society were probably higher than in most contemporary societies, but the killings were for revenge, for alleged sorcery, for sexual infidelity, and so on, not for territory. Although there were many linguistic groups, "tribes" did not really have boundaries. Ancestral Beings wandered all over the continent and their tracks could be traced through the territory of many groups. But the "owners" of sacred places were merely their custodians, and the places would not yield their fertility to those ignorant of the local ritual, so there was just no point in territorial expansion.

For this and for other reasons, some of which should be evident even in my brief summary, several serious students of Aboriginal culture have concluded that, far from being "primitive," Aboriginal culture is in some ways superior to our own. (I am not speaking of "New Age" enthusiasts for Aboriginal "spirituality," who seldom understand it and instead read into it their own presuppositions about "Eastern" thought.) One of these serious students, David H. Turner, and he was a student even to the extent that he learned to play a difficult Aboriginal musical instrument, has published an article entitled "Australian Aboriginal Religion as 'World Religion,'" a title that speaks for itself.[136] Turner has published a trilogy of books that get at, among other things, the "complementary opposition" that allows the Australians to avoid our proclivity toward ever greater and ultimately self-destructive expansion.[137] Another is Deborah Bird Rose, who defends Aboriginal ultimate pluralism against our Western tendency toward imperial monism.[138] Tony Swain, in seeing the emergence of Sky Gods as a "fall" from ubiety, does not find that such a fall represents "progress." I wish to join these distinguished scholars in affirming that the world still has much to learn from the Aborigines.

Because I wanted to emphasize narrative, and to situate it in the particular Aboriginal ontology of place, I have not mentioned many parallels between the Kalapalo and the Aborigines. Concern for sickness and healing would be one example. There are curers in Australia, sometimes called "clever men" or "men of high degree," who specialize in curing rituals.[139] There are also witchcraft beliefs, means for discerning who is exercising witchcraft, and retaliation, either by violence or by countersorcery. Even wordless, or perhaps better, meaningless music is to be found among the Aborigines, though not as pervasively as among the Kalapalo. Stanner writes, "Many of the songs have no meaning . . . but they are not sung less lovingly,"[140] and Munn indicates that Walbiri song words often take "special forms" or are "foreign terms" that are very hard to translate.[141] It is quite possible that the Kalapalo, who live among peoples whose languages they do not understand, have also borrowed foreign songs that are to them "wordless." Another possibility is that ritual language, particularly in songs, has become so archaic as to be unintelligible to contemporaries. In the great traditions, there are specialists to interpret archaic liturgical language; among the nonliterate the meanings may simply be forgotten. The most significant omission in my description of Aboriginal religion is initiation ritual, which is at least as important as among the Kalapalo, although among the Walbiri, and in most but not all of Australia, it is boys and not girls who undergo initiation.

On the other hand, the discussion of the Aborigines suggests some reappraisal of the Kalapalo. Basso more than once suggests that powerful beings are located in particular places, and the Kalapalo attachment to place is strong. The political necessity of moving the village has not lessened the attachment of the Kalapalo to their former location and its significant sites. And among the Kalapalo, as among the Aborigines, temporal distance is shallow to nonexistent. Powerful beings and Dawn People become here and now in the rituals and may be thought of more as Abiding Events than as "creators" who lived "in the beginning."

Indeed, "ubiety" may turn out to be much more widespread as a religious premise than the Aboriginal example alone would suggest. Even where, in archaic societies, in contrast to the beings with whom the Kalapalo and the Aborigines identify, gods and goddesses who are worshiped and who receive prayers and sacrifices indubitably do exist, they are still profoundly local. In Mesopotamia, Egypt, and the ancient Mediterranean world, for example, generally the gods are first of all city gods, close to their people, and continuously active among them. The idea of "the Goddess," of which we have heard so much of late (as well of course as any idea of "the God"), was only incipient among archaic peoples. There were mainly particular goddesses and gods, though it was possible to see in a foreign god or goddess the equivalent of a familiar one. The New Age reappropriation of Aboriginal religion has, in the name of retrieving the past, come up with significant novelties. Although land in the sense of place was central in Aboriginal thinking, and Mother-cults, as we have seen, were not unknown, as Swain puts it, "Up until the early 1980s, we have no evidence of Aboriginal people referring to 'Mother Earth.'"[142] Once eco-feminists had embraced Aboriginal spirituality, and in a situation where many Aborigines had lost all contact with their hereditary place, it was not strange to find Aborigines themselves embracing a term that made emotional sense but had no genuine connection with their tradition. Ubiety suggests the absence of categories not only of time but of space (such as a generalized idea of Earth, much less Mother Earth) that we take for granted, so that the idea of ubiety is difficult for us to grasp, yet it may be central to the way of life of tribal and archaic peoples.

Another feature shared by the Kalapalo and the Aborigines that may have much wider significance is, as I said of the Kalapalo, the lack of Malinowski's idea of myth as a "charter," that is, a set of explicit rules to be followed. It might seem that the Law or Ancestral Law of the Aborigines is just such a charter, but that would be to understand it too quickly in terms with which we are familiar. Students of Aboriginal culture have assured us that there is no overall mythical "system" that integrates all the disparate stories. Nor is there a "moral code" accepted by all Aborigines. There are stories and there are examples of how to act and not to act, but they vary from group to group and their level of abstraction is minimal. This is what I was trying to suggest when I said that Abiding Events are close to the rhythmed events of daily life. Stanner makes the point and also suggests some of the reasons why:

> Many myths, one cannot say all, had a homiletic effect; perhaps the Aborigines drew a moral lesson from them; but to all appearances a strong, explicit religious ethic was absent, probably for the same reason that a religious creed was absent. Three vital preconditions were missing—a tradition of intellectual detachment; a class of interpreters who had the prerogative or duty to codify principle; and a challenge that would have forced morals and beliefs to find anatomies.[143]

I don't like arguments from absence, but because we will see all three preconditions Stanner mentions gradually emerge in archaic civilizations, and because we take these presuppositions so much for granted that we can hardly imagine their absence, in this case Stanner's point is valuable. The Kalapalo and the Aborigines know the difference between right and wrong as well as we do, but they lack any generalized idea of good and evil, and so both groups lack any notion of rewards and punishments in the afterlife, an idea that it-self is vague enough for them in any case.

Although I have made most of the points that I think are essential to the understanding of what I am calling, more than a little uneasily, tribal religion, I want to add one more example, in part to show another part of the world that shares the basic pattern, in part for more personal reasons: the Navajo of the American Southwest. If the Kalapalo are on the Southeastern periphery of archaic civilization in South America, the Navajo are on the Northwestern periphery of archaic civilization in North America. To be more personal, Clyde Kluckhohn, one of the great experts on the Navajo, was one of my undergraduate teachers, and my undergraduate tutor and the-sis advisor, David Aberle, was also a Navajo specialist. Under Aberle's direction I wrote my undergraduate thesis, *Apache Kinship Systems*.[144] The Navajo are simply the largest of the Southern Athabascan speaking tribes of the Southwest, all the rest of whom are called some kind of Apache, so it is natu-ral to include the Navajo in the Apache label. In the course of my thesis re-search, as well as in several anthropology classes, I studied the Navajo closely. Because my academic career began with the Navajo, it seems fitting that in this, my last major work, I should return to them, for their intrinsic interest and as piety toward my teachers.

The Navajo

The Navajo, like the Australian Aborigines, are a much-studied people and justly so. They are the largest Native American tribe in the contiguous United States (according to the 2000 Census, some 300,000 people) with by far the largest reservation, spanning parts of Arizona, New Mexico, and Utah. Although a good percentage of Navajo people still speak the language, many children are losing it, so the future of the language is not assured, even though it is being increasingly used in written publications, both periodicals and books. Although they have absorbed an enormous amount from other Indian tribes, especially the Pueblos, but also Plains Indians, and from the Spanish, the Mexicans, and Anglo-Americans, their indigenous traditions, including religious traditions, survive with considerable vigor. They justly call them-selves the Navajo Nation.[145]

Of particular interest from the point of view of the concerns of this book is the fact that the Navajo subsume many of the themes of Native North American religion. They compose, together with the several Apache tribes, the Southern Athabascan linguistic group, related at no distant time to the Northern Athabascans, who at the time of contact inhabited large areas in Alaska and northwest Canada, and also to several Athabascan-speaking groups on the northern Pacific Coast of California. It appears that the Southern Athabascans left the Subarctic area of the MacKenzie Basin in Canada sometime about 1000 CE and moved south either through the high plains or the Plateau and Great Basin areas or both, arriving in the Southwest around 1500, not long before the Spanish. At that time they began to diverge into the several Apache tribes and the Navajo. They were certainly hunters and gatherers, though they may have picked up some rudimentary horticulture on the high plains, and their religion was probably a version of the generic shamanism so common in hunter-gatherer North America, traces of which are still evident among the Apache and, only slightly less obviously, among the Navajo as well. But the Navajo (and to a lesser extent some of the Apache groups) underwent a long period of acculturation to the Pueblo cultures that had already occupied the land into which they were moving. In the course of this acculturation the Navajo picked up significant elements of Pueblo religion, which, in turn, was the Northwestern-most version of a religion centered on horticulture, and corn in particular, whose focus was in Mesoamerica. The Pueblos are in my terms still tribal peoples, yet, partly because of the influence of the archaic civilizations to their south, they show incipient archaic features. To the extent that the Navajo have become "Puebloized" they form a bridge to the treatment of archaic religion in the following chapters.

Compared to the Kalapalo or even the Australian Aborigines, we have a much fuller sense of Navajo history and are not confined to the single frame of the "ethnographic present" as is so often the case with tribal peoples. I want to argue that the Navajo, like the Kalapalo and the Aborigines, give us some sense of what human culture was like many thousands of years ago, in particular the focus on ritual and myth. But no tribal people provides us with a fossilized specimen of early human culture; all are the product of often drastic historical change. The very fact that the Kalapalo are Carib speakers and thus far distant from the main body of Carib speakers to the north, tells us that they must have undergone an eventful history, even though we cannot reconstruct it. For the Australian Aborigines we have somewhat more than two centuries of mainly catastrophic history that gives us only a little sense of the kinds of changes that were certainly taking place before the Europeans and the Indonesians arrived on their shores. For the Navajo, however, we have not only the linguistic linkage with Subarctic peoples in the fairly remote past, but five or six centuries of history in the Southwest, the earlier part of which can only be deciphered from spotty archaeological and historical records, to be sure. Even though some of this history was catastrophic, particularly the incarceration of over 9,000 Navajo by the United States Army in what can only be called a concentration camp at Fort Sumner, New Mexico, from 1864 to 1868, the Navajo have been able to shape their own fate to a degree rare among tribal peoples. This is due not only to their remarkable resourcefulness but also to the fact that their home territory was among the least appealing in North America to white settlers.[146]

The most fundamental impact of a "foreign" culture on the Navajo was not from any kind of European, but from the Pueblos, beginning with the earliest contact around 1500. This was evident in the increasing importance of horticulture under Pueblo influence among these hunter-gatherers, and of the many material (for example, pottery) and ideal (for example, mythology) cultural elements that came with it. What was occurring through the normal process of contact was intensified by particular historical events. The great coordinated Pueblo rebellion against the Spanish of 1680, which drove the Spanish—missionaries, soldiers, and settlers alike—out of New Mexico for twelve years, was followed by a Spanish reconquest of all the Pueblos except for the Hopi, as a result of which many Pueblo people took refuge with the Navajo, hoping for an eventual return to their native towns. When it became clear that further resistance was hopeless, some of these people did return to their home villages, while others intermarried with the Navajo. During the eighteenth century, drought drove some Hopi to take refuge with the Navajo, with a similar result. During this period matrilineal clans, widespread among the Western Pueblos and some of the Eastern Pueblos, became established among the Navajo, some with linkages to Jemez and perhaps Hopi clans. For a century after the Pueblo rebellion there grew up in northern New Mexico and Arizona a modestly prosperous and populous horticultural society that appeared to blend Navajo and Pueblo traits. Not the least of these was the building of pueblo-type stone buildings, "pueblitos," in proximity to hogans, the traditional Navajo house type. The ethnohistorian and archaeologist David Brugge suggests, however, that in the mid-eighteenth century the Navajo underwent a revitalization movement[147] in which they rejected some features of Pueblo culture, notably painted pottery, and reorganized their ritual system so that, while still incorporating Pueblo elements, it has a distinctively non-Pueblo cast, with a new central ritual, Blessingway, which we will discuss more later.[148]

During this period ecological changes continued apace. The Spanish had brought with them livestock not native to the New World, and through them the Navajo acquired sheep and horses. As sheep pastoralism became more important than horticulture in the Navajo economy (hunting and gathering had never ceased to be significant sources of food), the concentrated settlements that had supported the pueblitos became less important: pastoralism allowed the return to a more dispersed and seminomadic pattern, in some ways closer to the old hunter-gatherer pattern than to the Pueblo horticultural pattern. The acquisition of horses greatly increased the mobility of the Navajo compared to any previous period. We must remember that Northern New Mexico is on edge of the high plains and that from the seventeenth to the nineteenth centuries a great cultural efflorescence was occurring there brought on by the acquisition of horses, later of guns, and the presence of vast herds of buffalo, far easier to exploit than they had previously been. Both the Navajo and the Eastern pueblos were vulnerable to raiding from Plains Indian groups, notably the Comanche, and were at a considerable disadvantage as the French in the eighteenth century made guns available to plains tribes, whereas the Spanish managed to keep guns largely out of the hands of Indian groups under their jurisdiction. Nevertheless, the Navajo, along with other Apachean groups, although never rivaling the plains tribes in warfare, became efficient raiders, capturing livestock and occasionally slaves from Pueblo and Spanish settlements, and retaliating with large war parties when they suffered losses. After the successful invasion by the United States Army in 1846 during the Mexican-American War, Navajo raiding was systematically curtailed, to the point where the Navajo were more often the victims than the aggressors, ending only with their incarceration of 1864, already mentioned, and the return to Navajo country in 1868.[149] Navajo sheep herding, the heart of the Navajo economy, expanded greatly until the 1930s, when the United States government required the limiting of Navajo herds on the grounds that their size was causing erosion in a vulnerable environment. Subsequently the Navajo have become more and more dependent on wage labor, although sheep herding remains the focus of the traditional culture.

Given this eventful history during the last several centuries, what can we say about Navajo religion? Until the late nineteenth century, when the first records of Navajo myths and ceremonies were made, we are confined largely to conjecture. Even with increasing documentation during the twentieth century, the very size of the record and the variations arising from time and place of documentation, as well as who the Navajo informants were and who made the records, leaves room for many conflicting interpretations.[150] I will have to depend on those students of Navajo religion who seem most reliable and deal with alternative interpretations when appropriate.

Several writers have attempted to reconstruct the hunter-gatherer religion of the early Apacheans by looking for comparative material among the Northern Athabascans and the groups through whose territory the Southern Athabascans must have passed before reaching the Southwest.[151] Luckert posits the idea of a "prehuman flux" as a kind of baseline for hunter beliefs, not only in North America, but perhaps everywhere. By this term he points to a "time" when all things were interchangeable: not only powerful beings, humans, and animals, but insects, plants, and features of the natural environment such as mountains, were all "alive," and could take the form of one another. Eventually some of the powerful beings shaped the earth and separated the "peoples" (including animals, plants, mountains, and so on) into their present forms. However the primordial flux is not really in the past, but can be returned to through ritual and the trance states that accompany ritual.[152] Luckert argues that the sweat house, so widespread among North American hunters and still in use among the Navajo, had a particular function—its ritual use transformed human hunters into predatory animals, that is, particularly efficient hunters. In this view, the ritual sweat bath marks a transformation that allows humans to engage in the hunt, protecting them from the possibility of illness from contact with dangerous animals (that is, spiritually, not just physically dangerous). The ritual sweat bath is repeated after the hunt to transform the hunters, who have now become dangerous themselves, back into ordinary Navajo.[153] A whole mythology accompanies these hunter rituals, a mythology that tells of protective beings who aid hunters and help them reach the game that other beings are withholding from them, as well as trickster beings (Raven, Crow, Coyote) who sometimes aid and sometimes hinder human intentions.

Accompanying these hunter beliefs is the equally widespread idea and practice of shamanism. To put it in simplest terms, a shaman is an individual who either seeks or is sought by a powerful being for a direct experience through which some of the being's power becomes available to the shaman, usually for the purpose of curing. Ruth Benedict has shown that the idea of an individual relation to a "guardian spirit" is widespread in North America and more general than shamanism as usually understood, in that not only curing powers, but many other powers such as hunting success, may be conferred by the Being with which the individual is in contact.[154] The "vision quest," in which the person undergoes austerities in some remote spot, often a mountaintop, in an effort to find such a guardian spirit, is one aspect of this complex, though in other instances the spirit takes the initiative in "calling" the individual.

Although most of these features of the hunter tradition can still be found among the Apache groups, and are more widely shared with many North American hunter-gatherer cultures, the religion of the Pueblos is quite different. Hunter-gatherer groups, and the pastoral Navajo, were organized in extended families usually living in close proximity, and in larger groupings—local groups or bands—of up to several hundred people, coming together temporarily for particular reasons, which might range from ritual to warfare. The Pueblos, however, lived in settled villages, ranging in size from several hundred to several thousand, and were largely dependent on the produce of their surrounding fields. Their villages were often quite compact, sometimes built on the top of a mesa for defensive purposes. In these villages, rituals were organized not by individuals who had received their teaching from personal experience with powerful beings, but by priestly societies that handed down their teaching to each succeeding generation. Although curing rituals existed, they were carried out by societies of curing priests, not by individual shamans. The major rituals, each of which belonged to a particular priestly society, were calendrical, organized in relation to the solstices and the equinoxes, and linked to the annual growth seasons of the corn. Origin myths of the Pueblos were much more elaborate than among the hunter-gatherers and focused on the emergence of humans on the present earth after various vicissitudes in several underworlds. Pueblo religion was highly spatial in its orientation, with the home village seen as a kind of world center, and with sacred mountains marking the perimeter of sacred space in the four directions. Though some anthropologists speak of Pueblo "gods," I believe that such figures are closer to powerful beings than to the gods of archaic societies, in that they are more invoked than worshipped, more identified with than sacrificed to. The Pueblos did, however, have a more coherent and anthropomorphic pantheon than hunter-gatherers with their rather amorphous group of sometimes human, sometimes animal, sacred beings.

Where do the "Puebloized" Navajo fit in? Although in all the Apache groups there are individuals who receive ritual instruction from powerful beings, either through vision or dream, they are almost absent among the Navajo, being found only among diviners. The most important ritualists, called "singers" as they officiate at ceremonials that are called "sings," learn the rituals as apprentices to established singers and function more like priests than shamans, though there is no society of singers and each operates on his or (less frequently) her own. There is no ritual calendar, but rituals are performed when particular individuals or groups have need of them. Usually these are curing rituals, though the definition of illness is much broader than our own, except for the most central ritual of all, Blessingway, which is performed on a variety of occasions to be described below.

The Navajo myth of origin, recorded in many not entirely identical versions, is clearly derived from Pueblo sources, as it is a myth of emergence involving several, usually four, underworlds through which people traversed before emerging on "earth surface," as the Navajo refer to our world. Even so, hunter figures such as coyote pop up in places where they would not be expected in Pueblo myths. Though shamanism is absent among the Navajo, the myths for the major curing ceremonials have a strongly shamanistic character. They recount the adventures of a human boy or (less frequently) girl, who, through a variety of misadventures, incurs harm at the hands of powerful beings but who, through spiritual helpers, is able to undergo curing rituals from the very beings who had harmed them. These rituals they then bring back to their earth families and teach them, often to a sibling or close relative, before departing again to join the sacred beings. Though Navajo ceremonials are handed down from singer to singer, they were originally learned by humans who had direct experience with sacred beings in a highly shamanistic manner. Thus shamanism, though almost absent among the Navajo in practice, continues to exist, encapsulated, as it were, in the mythological scenarios of curing rituals.

Although the Navajo have no calendrical ceremonies (most rituals can be performed only in the summer or the winter, but at no particular time other than not during a solar or lunar eclipse), they have a strongly Pueblo-like orientation to space. The four directions with the four sacred mountains are central in Navajo ritual and are associated with colors, times of day, seasons, and particular sacred beings. Because the Navajo are widely dispersed, there is no center quite in the Pueblo sense, but the land within the sacred mountains (Navajoland, or Dinetah) is "central" in the Navajo understanding of space.[155] Also the dwelling or hogan where the ceremony is performed is a kind of microcosm of the universe (like the Pueblo kiva, though the kiva is not a dwelling), and in that sense a center.[156]

The most general term for sacred beings among the Navajo is *diyin dine'e,* usually translated as "Holy People," but students of Navajo religion are quick to remind us that in this case "holy" does not mean ethically good or even necessarily benevolent, but rather powerful. Because of their power they are dangerous, and if improperly approached can be harmful, even though with the proper ritual they may be helpful. The Holy People are quite a heterogeneous group, some coming from the old hunter tradition (exactly which ones is in dispute) and some obviously borrowed from the Pueblos. Of the latter the clearest instance is the *ye'i,* or masked gods, who are the Navajo version of the well-known Pueblo kachinas. These masked gods appear in certain sequences of a frequently performed ceremonial, Nightway, but are absent from the most important ritual, Blessingway.

Let us now consider Blessingway and why it is central and rather different from all other ceremonials. Although Blessingway is rooted in the Navajo origin myth—the narrative that gives the world its meaning—its most important feature, as in the case of all Navajo ritual, is song. Without song (remember that Navajo rituals are called "sings") no ritual can be effective. Thus we can understand why Blessingway is called "the spinal column of songs."[157] Gladys Reichard emphasizes the importance of song by a passage from Blessingway: "Changing Woman taught songs to her two divine children, admonishing them, 'Do not forget the songs I have taught you. The day you forget them will be the last; there will be no other days.'"[158] Gary Witherspoon has pointed out that all Navajos sing and many of them have composed songs—not ritual songs, which must be meticulously learned—but songs for various occasions.[159] Thus, as in the case of the Kalapalo and the Aborigines, we are in the midst of a singing culture. Indeed, wealth may be indicated by the number of songs one has, and poverty expressed by saying: "I have always been a poor man. I do not own a single song."[160]

Song, however indispensable, is embedded in narrative, and here too Blessingway is central. John Farella expresses its centrality with the metaphor of the "main stalk":

> Navajos commonly conceptualize and refer to their philosophical and ceremonial system as a corn plant. The junctures where the plant branches are the branching off of the major ceremonials. The "roots" extend into the underworld and, of course, refer to the pre-emergence stories. The main stalk is, on the one hand, a reference to hozhooji [Blessingway],

and, on the other hand (but really the same thing), a reference to the essence or the synthetic core of the philosophy.[161]

The narrative basis of Blessingway is the story of events just after the emergence onto the present earth-surface world, and before the adventures of the protagonists of the great curing ceremonials. It is the ambiguous relation of this narrative to anything we might call history, and its constitutive nature, that tempts Farella and others to speak of "philosophy," a term I would like to reserve for a theoretic culture almost completely absent among the Navajo.[162] The Navajo narrative of origin is not lineal history in the usual Western sense of the term. Rather, as Maureen Schwarz puts it, quoting from a paper by Rik Pinxton and Claire Farrerr: "The ancestral knowledge contained in the Navajo origin stories is 'just one more element of present reality, not an objectified, distanced, inert position of wisdom or truth.' For Navajo individuals, history is 'not an attribute or vehicle of an objectified representation of knowledge about reality' but 'the process of what is constantly in the making.'"[163] In this sense, the Navajo origin myth recounts Abiding Events, to borrow Swain's term for the Aboriginal Dreaming, so that the ideas of "before" and "after" have only a relative, not an absolute, meaning. In the ritual, everything in the narrative is potentially present.

Nonetheless, although there are references to pre-emergence events in many rituals, it is what happened after the emergence that organized the world as we know it.[164] When First Man and First Woman and other Holy People first emerged from the Fourth World, the earth surface was covered with water and was formless. Winds (themselves Holy People) dried the land, and the first thing that was done was to create a sweat house. Inside the sweat house First Man unwrapped the medicine bundle he had brought from the underworld. It contained precious stones in the form of grains of corn, soil from the sacred mountains in the underworld, and other objects. From the bundle First Man formed many of the features of the world as we know it, creating the first hogan as a kind of microcosm of the universe, its four main poles marking out the cardinal directions and the sacred mountains.

First man then covered certain sacred objects from his bundle with sheets of "dawn, evening twilight, sunlight," and "a spread of darkness," the four times of day.

When he had covered them four times as described, a young man and woman first arose from there. Absolutely without their equals in beauty, both had long hair reaching to their thighs . . . To fix your gaze on them was impossible, the glare from them was surprisingly bright. "This is the only time that any of you have seen them, from now on none of you will see them again. Although they are right around you, even though they are taking care of your means of living to the end of your days right around you, none of you will ever see them again," he told them.[165]

According to one version, it was these two young people who gave birth to a baby, placed on the top of one of the sacred mountains where First Man discovered it. He took it home to First Woman and, with advice from other Holy People, they nurtured the baby with pollen from clouds and plants and with flower dew. "Owing to this special care, the baby matured at an accelerated rate: in two days she walked, in four days she talked, and in twelve days she began to menstruate."[166]

The baby was Changing Woman, and her first menstruation was a cause of great rejoicing, and the occasion for the first Blessingway ceremonial. Girls' puberty rituals were common among North American hunter-gatherers and were undoubtedly brought with them when the Southern Athabascans entered the Southwest. But these older rites focused on the pollution caused by menstrual blood and the subsequent harm to hunting that contact with it might cause, so they involved the isolation of the girl during her menses. The Navajo rite, a form of Blessingway, was more of a celebration of the vitality and fecundity that Changing Woman was bringing to the people.

Changing woman was impregnated by the Sun as she lay resting on a rock. She subsequently gave birth to the Warrior Brothers, Monster Slayer and Child-of-Water. Although the appearance of Changing Woman was auspicious, the world was still a dangerous place as various monsters, produced by unseemly acts in the Fourth World, had also come to Earth Surface and were destroying its new inhabitants. The Warrior Brothers, who with great difficulty learned who their father was and how to find him, were after many trials endowed by Sun with the power to slay the monsters. This Monster Slayer, with backup from his younger brother, proceeded to do. All the monsters were slain except for Hunger, Poverty, Old Age, and Lice. Each of these, though unpleasant, has a function in human life: without hunger there would be no pleasure in eating; without poverty there would be no pleasure in getting new things; without Old Age (and death) the earth would become too crowded and birth itself would cease; without lice there would be no incentive to show friendship and love for other humans by picking lice from their heads.[167]

Changing Woman asks for and receives First Man's medicine bundle, but he has another one that he takes with him as he and First Woman return to the lower world. These figures, who had been so important in the story from the beginning, now take on a sinister aspect, for the bundle they take back with them is the witchcraft bundle.[168] From now on the nurturant figure of Changing Woman is at the center of Navajo ritual, but even she can be dangerous if her rules are not respected, and the Navajo world is always a mixture of benevolent and dangerous forces.

After the slaying of the monsters, Changing Woman wished for companionship:

> The White Bead Woman [who is most often considered to be one and the same as Changing Woman] wished now to have her own people. She wished to have a people that she could call her grandchildren. They would carry on the lore that she would teach them. They would respect and hold holy the prayers and chants that she would give them.[169]

Changing Woman rubbed skin from various parts of her body, and breathed life into what she had rubbed off. These were the Navajo, to whom she taught all the lore they needed. Then at the Sun's behest, she left the Earth Surface People and went to the West. Neither Changing Woman nor the other Holy People really leave, however, because in the rituals they are present and those undergoing the rituals can become one with them.

Important though Changing Woman is, the very heart of Blessingway, and according to interpreters such as Witherspoon and Farella, of Navajo life, is personified in the "beautiful ones" who were the parents of Changing Woman. Witherspoon, drawing from Wyman, recounts what First Man said to them at the beginning:

> "Of all these various kinds of holy ones that have been made you the first one will be (represent) their thought, you will be called Long Life [Sa'ah Naaghaii]," he was told. "And you who are the second one, of all the Holy People that are put to use first, you will be (represent) their speech, you will be called Happiness [Bik'eh Hozho]," he was told. That much so happened. "You will be (found) among everything (especially ceremonial affairs) without exception, exactly all will be long life by means of you two, and exactly all will be happiness by means of you two," was said to them.[170]

The centrality of *sa'ah naaghaii bik'eh hozho* is inadequately rendered either by the personification of them or by the translation "long life, happiness." The phrase is at the heart of Blessingway and is used in the Blessingway section with which almost every ceremonial ends. The term *hozho,* which is variously translated as "blessing," "beauty," "health," "wholeness," and so forth, and combines the ethical with the aesthetic, has been seen by many as the key term in Navajo culture. Farella reminds us that *hozho* always implies its complement, *hochxo,* variously translated as "evil" or "ugliness," but which is as necessary a part of Navajo life as *hozho.* The Navajo do not absolutize a contrast between good and evil but seek order in the midst of inevitable disorder. The ceremonial system, with Blessingway and *sa'ah naaghaii bik'eh hozho* at its center, brings meaning and order in this dangerous world.[171]

Farella suggests how the attitude toward the Holy People can change through an individual's life:

> A youth, particularly an adolescent boy, will violate taboos with impunity to show that he is not afraid and that he has courage. Then a misfortune occurs and he begins to believe. It is at this point when one begins to believe but has no knowledge, that the world is most fearful. One then begins to learn the stories and the ceremonies in an effort to transcend this fear. During the initial phases of this learning, the teacher protects his pupil, until he has acquired the control himself. Subsequently, a point is reached where fear is no longer the predominant emotional coloring of one's relation with diyinii [Holy People]. That fear is replaced with respect. This respect describes a relationship between equals or near equals, whereas fear characterizes a relationship of subordination.

Those individuals in later life who are most knowledgeable, as Farella notes, often are not ritual practitioners:

> They seem to be rather satisfied with things, not totally satisfied by any means, but accepting of the way things are. They do employ ritual, not to alter, but in the form of minor celebrations for what exists. At the same time the relationship of these men with diyinii is rather more intimate than is the relation of the ritual practitioner. They have a direct experience of the "powerful ones" as a part of them, and themselves as a part of the "powerful beings." . . .

With these more knowledgeable men, this boundary between self and diyinii, never very strong for the Navajos, has become nearly non-existent. The men I knew who attained this state were very old, and I suppose that death brought the final dissolution of this boundary. But, their state of mind on approaching death was one of peace, not of anxiety.[172]

As this account of an ideal Navajo life implies, the meaning of *saʼah naaghaii bikʼeh hozho* is completeness, but not, as Farella points out, the completeness of the isolated individual. *saʼah naaghaii bikʼeh hozho* can be equated with *nilchʼi*, the wind, air, or breath that animates all things. It is by means of Wind that we are connected to all beings. Another way of putting it is to say that *saʼah naaghaii bikʼeh hozho* links us to all beings, not only humans, as kin, *kʼé*.[173]

Perhaps this is the moment to counter the stereotype that the Navajos are "individualistic" whereas the Pueblos are "collectivistic." It is true that in a sheep-herding culture people are on their own more often than in a densely populated agricultural village, and that Navajo have a strong sense of respect for everyone, even children, to make important decisions for themselves. But the ideal Navajo is not like an Anglo individualist, seeking his own interest or "realizing himself" first of all. Rather the ideal is one who reciprocates blessings and takes responsibility for others. Even though Navajo rituals are all organized around "the one sung over," and thus have an apparently individualistic focus, even the curing ceremonies have a much wider concern:

Although Navajo healing ceremonies purport to focus on "the patient," the individual is not singled out for treatment. Instead, as Harry Walters notes, the "whole sphere" within which the patient is intimately connected on the personal, social, and cosmic realms is treated. "In the ceremony you don't just treat the physical being, you treat the mental, plus the spouse, the children, the household, the livestock, you know, the air that the patient is going to breathe, the earth that he is going to walk on, the water he is going to drink, the fire that he is going to use. Everything, you know, like you're, in this sphere you are one individual. So the treatment is to treat all of those, the whole sphere."[174]

Even Blessingway, whose uses include far more than curing, requires "one sung over" even if the purpose is preeminently for "the whole sphere." As

Wyman says, no matter what the occasion, the aim is "for good hope," "to avert potential misfortune, to obtain the blessings which man needs for a long and happy life."

> Blessingway practice therefore embraces birth and adolescence, the home or hogan, weddings, maintenance and acquisition of properties, protection against accident . . . No other ceremonial in the Navajo system offers the native assistance in every walk of life as Blessingway does . . . Its ritual is simple. It adapts itself to any emergency, dream, fancy, human frailty.[175]

When we consider the relation between Navajo sacred narratives and ethics, we will discover that they present an explicit moral code no more than do those of the Aborigines. The Holy People neither give moral injunctions nor act as moral exemplars: if they teach, it is as often by what they do wrong as by what they do right. Nonetheless, again as in the case of the Aborigines, the narratives do serve not only to make sense of the world but to provide a conception of moral order. Sam Gill, drawing on the pioneering work of Katherine Spencer, puts it well when he says that the sacred stories "serve as a guide to the moral life":

> Where in the era of creation the concern is with the establishment of proper places and relationships for things in the world, the era of the origin of the ceremonials is concerned with how one lives in that world. It deals with the boundaries of both places and relationships. It deals with the relationships which are necessary for life, such as the relationships between hunter and game, between a man and wife and women who are not his wife, between in-laws, between the living and the dead, between a Navajo and a non-Navajo, between a person and the plants and animals in his environment, between Earth Surface People and Holy People. The stories which tell of this era define the Navajo way of life. They deal with life in progress through time and across space. They test limits and thus reinforce those limits.[176]

In her valuable book *Navajo Lifeways* Maureen Schwarz shows how Navajo religion as embodied in the sacred narratives is still the source of meaning for Navajos today. She gives a number of instances in which the Navajo bring an active interpretation of the myths to the understanding of difficulties they are facing, difficulties dating mainly in the 1990s. The outbreak of the deadly hantavirus epidemic in the Four Corners region killed a number of Navajo. This outbreak was interpreted as a return of the "monsters" of mythical time, whose devastation could be countered only by a return to traditional Navajo forms of behavior and an increase in performances of Blessingway. Relocation of Navajos from land that had been judged as belonging to the Hopi, illnesses arising from uranium mining, and the continued plague of alcoholism were further instances where the application of understandings derived from the myths helped in dealing with current challenges. Perhaps the most interesting instance arose from an "appearance" of two Holy People to a woman in a remote part of the reservation. Though many, including some top officials of the Navajo Nation, used this apparition as a stimulus for ethnic renewal and ethnic pride, leading to an unprecedented development of the pilgrimage of thousands to the site of the appearance, others pointed out that Navajo sacred narratives explicitly say that the Holy People, though they are all around us, will remain unseen. They further criticized the notion of pilgrimage and offerings at the pilgrimage site, when the proper thing to do is to give offerings in the sacred places near where one lives. This lively hermeneutical controversy gave evidence of the continued vitality of the tradition, though it also gave occasion for some warnings that the true tradition is being lost, with possibly devastating consequences.[177]

What is remarkable is that with the increasing use of English by young people, who mainly work in nontraditional occupations, and with inroads by a variety of Christian denominations, including the Mormons, as well as the Native American Church (Peyote),[178] the old ceremonial pattern survives as well as it does, attracting many of those who have ostensibly adopted other religions. Perhaps its history has given Navajo religion the flexibility to survive even under great challenge. The strong Pueblo component has provided a coherence to the narrative and ritual that more fragmentary hunter-gatherer religions in North America seem to lack. But the very fact that the tradition, though Puebloized, has not been pinned down to the specificities of calendrical time and particular place—that a Puebloized religion has remained portable, as it were—gives it the capacity for a continuing flexible response to the many difficulties that Navajo people face. If Navajo intellectuals, working with extensive written texts, develop the "Navajo philosophy" that is already in part implicit in the oral tradition, there is no predicting what the future may hold.

Out of the enormous range of possibilities, I have chosen three to provide examples of how cultures, even today, can be organized primarily through narrative rather than theory, and how ritual, and its inescapably musical base, continues to provide primary meaning. The Navajo, indeed all three cases described in this chapter, suggest that cultures organized primarily in terms of ritual and myth can be effective in the present world, and that we must treat them as equals from whom we have much to learn.[179] Even when theory becomes centrally important, as we will see, ritual and myth survive in surprisingly vital new forms. But before considering that, and to better understand how humans have gotten from mythic culture to theoretic culture, we need to see how narrative and ritual have coped with problems presented by much larger and more stratified societies than those we have considered so far, and bent but did not break as they did so. For that we must turn to societies that have moved beyond hunter-gatherer egalitarianism toward differentiations of power.

4

From Tribal to Archaic Religion: Meaning and Power

The culture of ritual and myth described in Chapter 3 will eventually come in for dramatic attack—antiritualism and demythologization—from those seeking a more universal answer to the question of meaning (although the attackers themselves will never entirely escape from ritual and myth), but now we must consider how the resources for the production of meaning developed in tribal societies can be expanded to deal with much larger and more stratified societies through the development of new forms of ritual and myth, new understandings of the relation between cosmos, society, and self. These new understandings stretch the resources of ritual and myth to the breaking point but do not transcend them.

The Disposition to Dominate

In small-scale societies such as those we considered in Chapter 3, differentiations of power and status were minimal—but not lacking. If we now want to understand how ritual and myth help to organize large-scale societies, we can begin by looking more carefully than we have done so far at the differences of power and status that exist even in small-scale societies. But first we must consider what is most striking about small-scale societies—hunter-gatherers, but also many horticultural and pastoral societies—namely, how egalitarian they are. If we put *Homo sapiens* in evolutionary perspective, this is hardly what would be expected. All our nearest relatives, the several species of great apes, are more despotic than egalitarian, though we have seen that the chimpanzees have a qualified despotism. That is, they have status hierarchies that rank-order individuals from the strongest, the alpha male, or in the case of the bonobos, the alpha female, to the weakest. Chimpanzees and gorillas rank all males above all females; the bonobos rank females higher than males, but this doesn't make them less despotic or quasi-despotic, because they too have a clear status hierarchy. Among the chimpanzees, the alpha male not only on occasion physically abuses weaker males, he attempts to monopolize mating opportunities, mating promiscuously with the females in the band and preventing as far as possible the other males from mating at all. Under these conditions nothing like the family as we know it is possible. At most one can speak of long-term solidarities between mothers and children and some solidarity between siblings, but there is no continuing relation between parents and no significant relation between fathers and children.

For all that we have in common with the chimpanzees and the bonobos, our form of family is indeed different. Frans de Waal has summarized succinctly the main differences: "Of three main characteristics of human society—male bonding, female bonding, and the nuclear family—we share the first with chimpanzees, the second with bonobos, and the third with neither . . . Our species has been adapted for millions of years to a social order revolving around reproductive units—the proverbial cornerstone of society—for which no parallel exists in either *Pan* species."[1] What accounts for this difference? The absence of a disposition for dominance? Not likely. Rather, a different kind of society has made possible a different kind of family. Here I want to draw on the work of the anthropologist Christopher Boehm, particularly his book *Hierarchy in the Forest: The Evolution of Egalitarian Behavior.*[2] Boehm argues that we share with the chimpanzees and the bonobos a tendency toward despotism, that is, a disposition toward dominance. We also share with them two further dispositions, the disposition to submit when it looks like confrontation is likely to fail, and the disposition to resent domination once one has submitted.[3] But, Boehm asks, if we are a species with despotic tendencies, that is, a strong disposition to dominate whenever possible, how is it that the simplest known societies, namely the nomadic hunter-gatherers, are uniformly egalitarian, and probably have been so for thousands if not millions of years? Boehm's answer is not that hunter-gatherers lack dominance hierarchies, but that they have what he calls "reverse dominance hierarchies"—that is, the adult males in the society form a general coalition to prevent any one of their number, alone or with a few allies, from dominating the others.[4] Male egalitarianism is not necessarily extended to females—the degree to which females are subject to male despotism varies, even among hunter-gatherers. But what the reverse dominance hierarchy prevents is the monopolization of females by dominant males, and what it therefore makes possible is the family as we know it, based on (relatively) stable cross-gender pair-bonding and mutual nurturance of children by parents, precisely what is missing in our closest primate relatives.

Boehm insists that human egalitarianism does not come easily, that it is not the absence of the disposition to dominate; rather, it requires hard, sometimes aggressive, work to keep potential upstarts from dominating the rest. Egalitarianism is a form of dominance, the dominance of what Rousseau would have called the general will over the will of each. The hunter-gatherer band is not, then, the family enlarged; rather it is the precondition for the family as we know it. Boehm summarizes: "There appear to be two components of this kind of egalitarian social control. One is the moral community incorporating strong forces for social conformity . . . The other ingredient is the deliberate use of social sanctioning to enforce political equality among fully adult males."[5] I would add ritual as the common expression of the moral community without which the process of sanctioning would make no sense. Boehm is especially good on the way the sanctioning works. Potential upstarts are first ridiculed, then shunned, and, if they persist, killed. Boehm describes in detail how this system of increasingly severe sanctions works, with examples from every continent. He is perhaps less good at what I think is equally necessary, that is, the strong pull of social solidarity, especially as expressed in ritual, that rewards the renunciation of dominance with a sense of full social acceptance.

Everything in Chapter 3 helps us understand what happened. When Boehm describes the essential basis of hunter-gatherer egalitarianism as the emergence of a moral community, he is pointing to what mimetic and mythic culture made possible. In this moral community, powerful norms negatively sanctioned despotic behavior and protected the family. Although culture is the key resource making such a reversal possible, Boehm insists that the reversal is not quite what it seems. Despotic tendencies in human beings are so deeply ingrained that they cannot simply be renounced. We did not just suddenly go from nasty to nice. Reverse dominance hierarchy is a form of dominance: egalitarianism is not simply the absence of despotism, it is the active and continuous elimination of potential despotism.

But if egalitarianism is virtually universal among small-scale societies, how is it that with chiefdoms and particularly with the early state we seem to have a return of despotism more ferocious than anything to be seen among the great apes? There is a U-shaped curve of despotism—from the despotic apes to the egalitarian hunter-gatherers to the reemergence of despotism in complex societies—that needs to be explained.[6] Why the long history of egalitarianism based on the reverse dominance hierarchy came to an end in prehistoric times with the rise of despotic chiefdoms and early states, and why despotism, though challenged, has continued to some degree ever since, is a question we must address in this chapter.

Although hunter-gatherers have, on the whole, successfully checked upstarts, subsequent human history is peppered with successful upstarts. Many—one thinks of Julius Caesar, Napoleon, Shaka Zulu, Mussolini, among others—came to a bad end, though some died in bed. The tendency of upstarts to try to monopolize females and undermine the family is illustrated by the ancient Hebrew upstart David, who took Bathsheeba to wife and had her husband killed, although Machiavelli warned potential upstarts not to fool with other men's wives as that can spark instant rebellion. For an upstart to become a legitimate ruler there must be a reformulation of the understanding of moral community and new ritual forms to express it, so that despotism becomes legitimate authority and therefore bearable by the resentful many who must submit to it, a consideration that leads to the next step in my argument.

In order to understand why this U-shaped curve is not quite what it seems, we need to make a distinction between dominance (or despotism) and hierarchy, terms that get elided in most discussions—an elision that is hard to avoid, but that needs to be avoided if we are to understand what really happened. I want to use dominance (despotism) to describe the straightforward rule of the stronger and hierarchy to describe status differences that are actually sanctioned by the moral community—that is, I want to define hierarchy as legitimate authority.[7] It is part of the central paradox of human society that dominance and hierarchy have gone together from the beginning.[8] Even though they always go together it is important that we separate them analytically. Boehm's term "reverse dominance hierarchy" contains both elements: moral community justifies the hierarchical element (the group over the upstart), and the ultimate sanction of violence against the upstart has an inescapable element of dominance.

I want to turn to the Australian Aborigines to consider how hierarchy and dominance work out in an egalitarian hunter-gatherer society with which we are familiar from Chapter 3. Rather than discuss hierarchy among the Walbiri, however, I will consider a neighboring Western Desert group, the Pintupi, among whom Fred Myers has considered hierarchy more extensively than have any of the ethnographers who have worked with the Walbiri. Myers places his discussion of hierarchy in the context of the three major patterns of Pintupi social life. One is what he calls "relatedness," which he defines as "extending one's ties with others outward, being open to claims by others, showing sympathy and a willingness to negotiate." Relatedness is essential for hunter-gatherers, among whom the isolated nuclear family would be far too fragile to survive for long. The second major pattern is autonomy, an unwillingness to be imposed on by others, and in particular an assertion of the ability of adult men and women to conduct their family affairs as they wish. The third major pattern, which serves to mediate the inevitable tensions between the first two, is the Dreaming itself, a pattern of myth and ritual that has an authority that transcends the wills of individuals and provides stability in the midst of the constant renegotiation of which Pintupi society is composed. Myers emphasizes that Pintupi society is not by nature corporate, with discrete boundaries of membership. Relatedness extends far beyond local camps but consists of one-to-one ties more than common membership. It is only ritual and the norms that ritual affirms that create anything like region-wide solidarity.[9]

Though adults will defend their autonomy to the point of violence if necessary, there is one kind of authority that is always acceptable. Those who "look after" others, who "hold" them as a nursing mother holds her infant, have, at least within certain spheres, legitimate authority. Myers specifies the spheres of such legitimate authority: "Far from being absolute, such authority is situated primarily in the domains of ritual, sacred sites, and marriage where older persons can look after younger ones by passing something to them. In these particular domains, elders have considerable power over their juniors, but outside these areas, social relations are more egalitarian, access to natural resources remains relatively free, and there is no monopoly of force."[10] Pintupi will always agree that one will have to "listen to" fathers and mother's brothers, who have "taken care" of one since infancy. But more generally, it is not only senior members of one's close family who have authority; it is elders in general, insofar as they "take care" of the younger generation by handing on to them the legacy of the Dreaming. Myers sums up how such handing on reconciles autonomy and authority:

> Pintupi experience the life cycle as a continuous progression toward autonomy and potency, a progression toward greater identification with the most encompassing dimensions of the moral order. Younger males

consent to the authority of the older in expectation that there is value to be gained—both for them and for the entire society. To carry the Law is something they do for themselves, but something they do also for the continuation of life itself. Women, too, recognize the social value of male initiation and accede to its necessities. The power and authority of older men in this context are considered necessary to make everyone conform to the cosmic plan.

What men display is the ability to "look after" people. Of course, at the same time, they define what it means for men to "look after" others: One does so by carrying and passing on the Law. Ultimately what older men give to younger is the ability to participate with other men as equals. Although this autonomy is not usually viewed as personal aggrandizement, the Law that they pass on as value still serves as the instrument of their power. Through it, men exert authority without accusation of being egotistical. They only mediate the Dreaming.[11]

Because the younger generation, which is being cared for and to whom the Law is being passed, will become the older generation and in turn care for and pass on to a still younger generation, authority, except for that of the Dreaming itself, is temporary, is indeed the means by which dependent youngsters attain adult autonomy and responsibility. A similar pattern exists among many Aboriginal groups and is sometimes referred to as gerontocracy, the rule of the elders. Such authority can be abused, can turn into domination, when it is used to withhold potential marriage partners from young men, or takes the form of sadistic initiation practices, but according to Myers this is not the case among the Pintupi.[12]

Yet the disposition toward dominance is not missing among the Pintupi. Men who put themselves forward beyond the circumscribed limits of legitimate authority are a major cause of "trouble." Rather than confront a potential upstart, the Pintupi prefer to leave the area where he is trying to assert himself, a common method for handling upstarts among hunter-gatherers, what Boehm refers to as shunning. Myers says, "asserting oneself too much is fraught with danger," and cites the case of a man who was widely criticized for his presumption; when the man died suddenly during an initiation, it was believed that he had been sorcerized.[13]

If legitimate hierarchy and the disposition toward dominance that it seeks to control are in evidence among the most egalitarian societies, where authority is temporary and minimal, but by no means absent, then it is not surprising that they will be found in more complex societies as well. Let me turn to another of the groups we considered in the last chapter, the Kalapalo, for an example of authority that is not circulating and temporary, but permanent insofar as it can be inherited, though in this case it hardly ruffles the waters of a still-pervasive egalitarianism.

Ellen Basso speaks of "hereditary ritual officers known collectively as *anetaū* (singular *anetu*) who manage, organize, and plan the ritual process."[14] During the sometimes lengthy preparation for rituals, the *anetaū* extensively organize and coordinate the labor required to prepare the resources that will be used in the ritual. But, as in the case of the Pintupi, the authority of the *anetaū* "represents community consensus and is motivated by community rather than personal goals." Indeed, the *anetu* is supposed to personify the central Kalapalo ideal of *ifutisu,* as specified in the virtues of generosity and conciliation, virtues that operate to deny a desire to dominate.[15]

In the village Basso studied, two *anetaū* men, aspiring to leadership, divided the community into competing factions. Nonetheless, outside the ritual context the *anetaū* play no role; economic and social life "being organized around households and networks of relatives."[16] Although a third to a half of villagers are of *anetu* descent, only certain individuals among them, such as the men mentioned above, ever play the role of ritual officer. Even so, all *anetaū* have a degree of honor or respect, what is referred to as rank, in that their funerals are more elaborate than those of other Kalapalo, and become the occasion for some of the central rituals of the people. How such ranking ever got started in the first place—and there are ranked societies without states or even chiefdoms in many parts of the world—is not easy to explain. The *anetaū* are not said to "own" rituals the way patrilineages in Australia own rituals, but they are indispensable to the organization of ritual life, which, in turn, tells the Kalapalo who they are. It is hard to believe that it is not the connection to ritual that sets apart the *anetaū* from the rest of society.

Although the increase in economic surplus does not determine the form that hierarchy and domination will take, it is true that increasing economic surplus from horticulture and agriculture (and even from hunting and gathering in cases like the Northwest Coast of North America where the resources, in this case fishing, were especially plentiful) does correlate with the growth of hierarchy and domination (we will consider some possible reasons for this correlation later). The Kalapalo, it will be remembered, have a modest amount of horticulture, along with hunting and gathering, and so more surplus than the Pintupi. But even though outsiders have sometimes referred to the *anetaū* as "chiefs," Basso says "they are not necessarily village *leaders* and are frequently without any political influence whatever,"[17] and so cannot serve as an example of even simple chieftainship. We might turn to the Pueblo Indians, neighbors of the Navajo, the third group described in detail in Chapter 3, to find clearer instances of at least incipient chiefdoms, but the Pueblos are so diverse and their ethnography so enormous that it has seemed wiser to turn in an entirely different direction.[18]

Polynesia is a kind of laboratory for the comparative study of chiefdoms. Ancestral Polynesian culture emerged some 2,500 years ago in the area of Samoa and Tonga, what is called Western Polynesia. Over the next 1,500 years Polynesians spread to Central Eastern Polynesia—the Society Islands (including Tahiti), the Marquesas, and other nearby archipelagos—as well as north to Hawai'i, southeast to Rapa Nui (Easter Island), south to New Zealand, and west to what are called the Polynesian Outliers. Except for the Outliers, all the islands were uninhabited when the Polynesians arrived. In the Western Outliers, Polynesians replaced or merged with populations who had arrived in the earlier Lapita colonization, from which the Polynesians themselves had evolved.

What makes Polynesia so helpful for present purposes is that Ancestral Polynesian Society has now been rather thoroughly reconstructed by Patrick Kirch and Roger Green.[19] Its social form was a simple chiefdom. All the complex chiefdoms in Polynesia developed endogenously from this beginning, having been subject to no outside influence before the arrival of Europeans. Hawai'i, which we will consider as an early state, was particularly isolated and had had no communication even with other Polynesian groups for about 500 years before European discovery at the end of the eighteenth century. The emergence of complex chiefdoms is difficult to understand, but we can at least be sure that in Polynesia the process was entirely endogenous.

Tikopia

We can begin with the simple chiefdoms of the small island of Tikopia (three square miles), studied by the great twentieth-century ethnographer Raymond Firth.[20] Though Tikopia is no fossil—it is a Western Outlier with a history of occupation going back some 3,000 years—it is an example of what is referred to as a conservative Polynesian society, exhibiting some of the features of Ancestral Polynesian Society, even though it is not by any means an unchanged continuation of it.[21]

Even though extended kinship is important in egalitarian band societies, the residential group is usually the decisive unit, as we have seen among the Pintupi. In rank societies, however, kinship becomes central, for it is lineages and clans that are ranked. Tikopia is a small, somewhat isolated island, southeast of the main Solomon Island group, and it had a population of 1,281 when Firth undertook a census in 1929.[22] It was divided into four clans, each with several lineages, and although lineages tended to be localized, landholdings, which belonged to lineages, could be anywhere on the island. Each clan had a chief and, although there was no paramount chief, there was a ranking of clans and their associated chiefs so that the Ariki Kafika, the chief of the highest-ranking clan, the Kafika, was said to represent "the whole land" of Tikopia, although he had no political authority in clans other than his own. The highest-ranking lineage within the clan bore the name of the clan, and the chief was chosen from this lineage. But there was another dimension of ranking in Tikopia, particularly striking in such a small-scale society, namely the distinction between chiefs, who were true aristocrats, and everyone else, who were commoners.

Even though the chief had to come from the highest-ranked lineage in the clan, there was no automatic succession by lineal descent. The eldest son of the chief was the presumptive heir, but he, like everyone else in the clan except the chief, was a commoner. Nor was it certain he would ever become anything else, for another member of his lineage might be chosen instead. At least nominally, the chief was elected by the people. As the Ariki Tafua (chief of the Tafua clan) told Firth: "When a chief is elected, he is made *tapu* by the body of the people. While he is still living as a common man, he is only an executive [*maru*], but when he is taken as chief he has become *tapu* indeed. When a chief is going to be elected all the people gather together. Then the expression is uttered 'He is made *tapu* by the body of the people.'"[23] *Tapu*, the Polynesian word from which our word "taboo" comes, can in this case not too inaccurately be translated as "sacred." The respect with which the chief, and the chief alone in Tikopia society, was treated suggests that he was indeed a sacred object: he was not to be touched by others; one bowed or kneeled in his presence; one never turned one's back on him, and when leaving his dwelling one backed out the door. The chief remained aloof, visited by others but not visiting them, and certainly not eating with them. As Firth indicates, there was something kingly about the Tikopia chief—something redolent of supreme authority, even divinity—though we will see in what ways those implications must be qualified.[24] How are we to account for this extraordinary status of a chief of only a few hundred individuals, so without parallel in egalitarian band societies? What were the practical implications of this status? In particular, what was the balance between legitimate authority and the power to dominate?

Perhaps the first thing to be said is that the chiefs were also the high priests of Tikopia: there was no differentiation of sacred and secular power. As high priests they were the intermediaries between the major divinities and the people, and they also appointed subordinate priests, elders, in the other lineages of the clan who were responsible for mediation between their people and the lesser divinities tied to their own lineages. The authority of Tikopia chiefs derived primarily from their role as priests. As Firth puts it:

> The chief of Kafika was acknowledged to be the first among the chiefs of Tikopia in the traditional religious system, and in secular as well as in sacred contexts he was given pride of place. *Primus inter pares,* he regarded himself, and was regarded by his people, as having the prime responsibility for the prosperity and welfare of the land as a whole. Though in secular contexts the Ariki Kafika was conceded priority, it was through his special relation with powerful gods that he was be-lieved to exercise his superior role in the social and economic as well as in the religious spheres.[25]

The Tikopia chiefs, even the Ariki Kafika, could be said to lead but not to dominate. They were well off by Tikopia standards, but others might have more land. They worked their land or fished like everyone else, and Morton Fried wrote, quoting Firth, " 'Most of their food comes from their own exer-tions.' By initiative and example a chief inspires and directs community production. He gives elaborate feasts, and this generosity 'sets the seal upon his status.' "[26] The chief appointed a few close relatives as executive officers (*maru*) with authority to break up fights, settle minor disputes, and so on, but if force was needed, he had to call on the men of his clan—he had no military force of his own—and the chief himself was supposed to refrain from violence. The chief, then, appears neither to have exploited his followers nor to have tyrannized over them, but to have "ruled" by example and gen-erosity. His followers retained the ability to decide for themselves whether to do what he wanted.

In all these regards the chief seems little different from the self-limiting upstarts called Big Men in small horticultural societies, particularly in Highland New Guinea. Big Men gain prestige through generosity, one of the few acceptable avenues for leadership in egalitarian societies. Through marriage alliances and loans to others that can be called in later, they accumulate vast quantities of yams and pigs, which are then distributed in great feasts, bringing honor to their giver. The Big Man exhausts himself in the accumulation of resources and has little chance of passing on his prestige to his offspring. What is significant in comparison to Tikopia chiefs is that the prestige of the Big Man is unrelated to his lineage, and not dependent on any religious function, though he may be abetted by men with spirit powers.[27]

Not only was the Tikopia chief a priest, but his religious role indicates a significant shift in the understanding of the relation between humans and powerful beings from anything we saw in Chapter 3. For the first time, and not entirely clearly, one can detect along with the numerous powerful beings still present in the land, beings that can tentatively be called gods. Although the Tikopia had nothing like history in our sense, they did have a conception of several major time periods. First was the age of the gods, when most of the major deities appeared, deities many of whom were still central for worship as long as the traditional religion survived. These gods had homes in the sky, though they were interested in the land of Tikopia, even fought each other for domination of it. Eventually the gods gave birth to men who founded the major lineages. The next period was one in which gods and men both walked the earth and interacted with each other face to face. Finally the gods retreated to their spirit abodes, from which they could still intervene in human life (sending a good harvest or a hurricane), and from which they also could be summoned by the performance of the proper ritual and the utterance of the proper name in order to receive human requests.[28] This sequence is somewhat similar to that of the Kalapalo, for whom "in the beginning" there were the powerful beings, then the Dawn People who could interact directly with powerful beings, and then ordinary people whose interaction with powerful beings was mainly through ritual. But whereas the Kalapalo imagined the Dawn Time as only a few generations ago, the Tikopia have a much more extensive sense of quasi-historical time. Because lineage is so important to them, and priority of ancestry is related to the status of the lineage, they have accounts of as many as ten generations of ordinary human succession, which Firth estimates as the equivalent of at least 250 years. The mythical time before that is not intelligible in terms of successive generations. The

Tikopia, like the groups described in Chapter 3, is an entirely oral culture—there is no written record of the stories of gods or men that has any definitive authority. Therefore it is not surprising that there are many names for the same god and many versions of the same myth, depending on who is speaking, in particular from the point of view of which lineage or clan. None of this represents anything different from what we have seen before.

What is different in the Tikopia case, and what marks, however incipiently, a transition to archaic religion, is that the central rituals are no longer enacted collectively; the people no longer become one with the powerful beings through music and dance. Although the whole community is involved in the ritual process, the chief alone performs the ritual, acting as an intercessor between the people and the gods. And the praise, thanksgiving, and requests for blessings offered by the chief acting as priest are what allow us to speak of these rituals as worship and the objects of these rituals as gods. The central ritual occurs in an open-air temple with the priest presiding. Food offerings, which women and children have helped prepare, have been baked in a large oven. Kava, a mildly narcotic drink, is the most important offering—indeed, it gives its name to the rituals, each chief having his own "Kava"—and it requires an elaborate preparation for which even children are enlisted. The food offerings are distributed to the people after the ritual, but the kava, which was a ritual drink among a number of Polynesian societies, is not drunk but entirely poured out as a libation to the god or gods to whom the ritual is oriented. Particularly in connection with the major ritual cycles called the Work of the Gods, performed twice yearly, there is general feasting, singing, and dancing, which does not take place in the temple. Dance was still very important in Tikopia, as everywhere in Polynesia—the gods were depicted as particularly enjoying the dance—but dance was not the center of the ritual.

Although, as I have said, there is general participation before and after the central ritual, the ritual itself is performed by the chief alone with a few senior men in attendance. It consists of the priest offering the food and the kava to the god or gods while reciting the sacred litany requesting blessings. We have spoken of the Tikopia *ariki* as *tapu*—sacred—but the source of his sacredness is his *manu* (Proto Polynesian *mana*).[29] Firth explains the connection between *manu* and chiefly ritual as follows: "The quality of *manu* [*mana*] was one which could be manifest in some circumstances by ordinary men, but above all it was the property of chiefs. 'No common man is *manu* in his lips.' The prosperity of fruiting breadfruit and coconut, health for the people, etc., was conceived to arise from the 'lips' of the chief, from his recital of the ritual formula . . . The origin of *manu* lay with the spirits, the gods and ancestors."[30] Much of what the chief says is inaudible even to the few in attendance, for the words, and especially the names of the gods, are secret.

The purpose of ritual is highly practical. As Firth writes: "The Tikopia religious system was openly and strongly oriented towards economic ends, drew largely upon economic resources and served as a channel for their redistribution. It was also intricately interlocked with the system of rank. Chiefs and other lineage heads, in a broadly graded hierarchy, were not only the most prominent operatives in the religious system, they were also the legitimate representatives of the people and directors of group activities."[31] As we have also noted, due to their ritual connection with the gods, the chiefs were sacred; indeed, during the high rituals the god being worshipped might temporarily enter the body of the chief, so that, for that moment at least, he became divine.

The highest god in Tikopia, the Atua i Kafika, is unusual among Polynesian divinities: he was, in the age when both gods and men walked the earth, a man, the son of the Ariki Kafika, but also a culture hero who brought new kinds of food and new techniques to Tikopia. He was killed in a land dispute and was told that if he did not retaliate against his killer, he would be elevated to the highest divinity. It is on his model that later Kafika chiefs, his descendants, refrained from violence. Irving Goldman describes the centrality of the Atua i Kafika by saying that his forms "symbolize the social cosmos": "As *Atua* he is a god, the 'high' god of Tikopia; as ariki Kafika he is the high sacred chief; and as *Kafika* he is the name of one of the four major descent groups and of its leading lineage, and of its temples. *Kafika* is god, chief, organic assemblage of people, and sacred place. He is the center of religion, of rule, of social and economic life. All else is dependent and peripheral—but not subsumed under Kafika."[32]

Although ritual activity involved the general participation of the people, and "the mobilization of individual effort toward the common ends did imply a moral responsibility of every person for the welfare of others,"[33] the major responsibility rested with the chief himself. It was believed that the worship of the gods secured benefits for members of the group as a whole:

Prosperity for the leader meant prosperity for his family and lineage. If the prosperity of any group seemed to lag behind that of other groups, this was regarded as due to the leader's lack of power with the spirits [*mana*] . . . The prestige of a leader was involved in the prosperity of his group, and if this prosperity failed his reputation and his secular power to get his commands obeyed suffered. The structure of the lineage and clan system was such that people could not easily transfer their allegiance to other leaders; they simply failed to attend and support their leader's rites. In rites where the reference was to the whole Tikopia society and not simply to one sector of it this kind of judgement also applied.[34]

If we compare Tikopia beliefs as expressed in ritual and myth with those of the groups we described in Chapter 3, we will see some significant differences. Powerful beings among the Kalapalo, Australian Aborigines, and Navajo were often, though not always, alpha male figures, who could be terribly destructive when crossed, even inadvertently, but with whom people could identify if they followed the proper ritual, and, through identification, their power could become, at least temporarily, benign. Some powerful beings were viewed largely as nurturant mothers, as in the case of Changing Woman, but this was hardly the norm in tribal mythology. If the myths do describe a moral order, a Law, as the Aborigines put it, it is not because powerful beings are always reliable or even moral. The myths are an effort to understand the nature of reality. Their narrators must use the analogies that lie at hand, analogies from their own social experience, with all its inner tensions and inconsistencies.

Among the Tikopia, a different kind of society found itself reflected in a different conception of powerful beings. As Firth puts it: "One thus has an image, strongly visualized by the Tikopia, of the major spirits, the gods, behaving like the Tikopia conception of chiefs, but in an invisible, spiritual world. They had control of followers, and of major spheres or enterprises; they came and went at their own will; they could be terrible in anger; they dispensed benefits and punishments; their decisions, though conceived as arbitrary, could be swayed by appeals to their sympathy; there were distinctions and ranking among them, as among men."[35]

Every god was the god of some lineage, and showed preference for his or her own, so that the morality for which they stood was one of clan and lineage loyalty, not generalized norms. The Tikopia gods look a little more like the gods of Homer than what we have seen before. The accounts of their doings are full of the discrepancies and disagreements depending on who is speaking that we have already mentioned, but there is perhaps a new degree of articulation. As Firth puts it:

Ideas of Tikopia spirits were then conceptualizations of power and control. They objectified and personified principles of randomness in human affairs, but they also encapsulated ideas about the structure of Tikopia society—of filial respect and paternal authority, of the status of chiefs, of differentiation of roles between men and women. They also expressed in a symbolic way a recognition of less clearly formulated interests and imaginings—notions about sex and human frailty; underlying anxieties about failure of achievement, about loss of bodily vigour, illness and death. This whole set of concepts was related to a set of specific social groups and social situations, and constituted an elaborate systematic framework with considerable logical articulation.[36]

If we speak of these beings as gods, however, it is not because they are so radically different from the powerful beings we have already encountered, but because their relation to humans, as exemplified in their role in ritual has shifted: they are now worshipped. "Worship," as Firth puts it, "ordinarily implies respect, even admiration to a high degree, demonstrated by symbolic actions which indicate the asymmetrical relationship—as by reduction of bodily posture by obeisance, kneeling or prostration; or by presentation of objects in offering. These symbolic acts are prompted not only by recognition of status discrepancy but also by desire to be associated in some way with the position, actions or personality of the exalted one."[37] As we have noted, the Tikopia chief had few prerogatives of wealth and power; he was obeyed only when the people wished to obey him; but it is he alone, as representative of his people, who worshipped the gods. In Tikopia, a new degree of hierarchy—between gods and men, between chiefs and people—had come into existence, but little evidence of domination. The modest role of the Tikopia chief, however, was open, under other circumstances, to elaborations that would have enormous implications.

The Tikopia seem remarkably peaceful. And why wouldn't they be, in their small society on their small island? Polynesians were warriors, and it appears that Tikopia did not escape their endemic warfare, even though, for generations even before the arrival of Europeans, disorder seems to have been rare. The island's early history, however, was not so quiet. There are tales of repeated Tongan invasions that were finally repelled, but also, as Firth puts it: "Internally, Tikopia men of rank seem to have been almost obsessed by a thirst for prestige and power, and a hunger for land, and ready to resort to violence to secure their ends. This was a time, so Tikopia say, when there were many *toa* (strong men, warriors), and they were trying, by main force or by stratagem, to kill one another off so that each might rule singly, and the land own obedience to him alone."[38]

Even more disturbing are stories about the extermination and expulsion of major groups of Tikopia themselves. In accounts that Firth believes are substantially true, two major groups, the Nga Ravenga and the Nga Faea, who may have been late-arrived foreigners, were eliminated in about 1700 and 1725, respectively. Land hunger on an island of small size and perhaps growing population is an obvious reason, though the Tikopia indicate that the immediate reason for the attack on the Ravenga was their insolent suspension of tribute. The details are quite horrifying: the Ravenga were exterminated, man, woman, and child, with only one survivor, though he did become the ancestor of a significant lineage; and the Faea were so threatened that, with their chief and most of their people, they went to sea on what was inevitably a suicide mission, leaving only a remnant behind.[39] The stories were still recounted anxiously in Firth's time lest something similar ever happen again. At least retrospectively, the Ariki Kafika was exempted from having ordered these dreadful measures. The chiefs as Firth knew them were more priests than warriors and were indeed not tyrants. But an island paradise Tikopia was not.

Although, as a chiefdom, Tikopia is a hierarchical, not an egalitarian society, egalitarianism is not left entirely behind. The choice of a new chief even has a "democratic" aspect—the people must acclaim him. Neither the preference of the old chief nor any religious ritual substitutes for the popular will. The role of privileged rank in Tikopia can be seen in important respects as similar to that of the Dreaming among the Pintupi, in that it provided a superordinate reference point capable of moderating and mediating the tensions of daily life. As Goldman puts it: "A primitive community under aristocratic leadership is essentially a religious community, acknowledging in the religious sense the inherent superiority of a ruling line. Under these conditions, subordination in such a community is no more demeaning than is subordination before an ancestral figure, a god, or a spirit. Such subordination is accepted as part of the natural order."[40] The very fact that lineage is continuous, given, and not negotiated, provides it with the possibility of embodying overarching norms. But lineage alone does not make a chief: he must be effective. Egalitarian sentiments, as well as the ever-present possibility of challenges from upstarts, ensure that "neither the arrogant nor the weak among the chiefs survives for long."[41] But the equilibrium characteristic of

Tikopia, uneasy though it undoubtedly was, characterizes neither Polynesia as a whole, nor, as we will see, Hawai'i in particular.

The Disposition to Nurture

Before looking more closely at Hawai'i, let me amplify a bit the discussion of the disposition to dominate that links us to our closest primate relatives and is probably a part of our biological heritage. Its prototype may be the chimpanzee alpha male, but we should remember the bonobo alpha female, who shows us that the disposition to dominate is probably gender neutral, although despotism would be far too strong a word to characterize bonobo dominance.[42] We have also seen how the disposition to dominate was modified, though not eliminated, among egalitarian hunter-gatherer bands, through a culturally mediated moral community as well as sanctions against upstarts.

In our description of leadership in egalitarian societies as well as of the incipiently hierarchical Tikopia, we have come across another disposition that seems as basic as the disposition to dominate: the disposition to take care of, to "hold," as the Pintupi say, using the analogy of a nursing mother holding her child, that is, the disposition to nurture. Among both *Pan* species as well as the earliest members of the genus *Homo,* the long period of infant dependency required that the mother not only nurse the child for several years, but look after it and help it find food for several years after that. Among chimpanzees and bonobos, fathers do not seem to participate in this activity, although whether or not they have a latent disposition to nurture is not clear. Males do engage in grooming behavior and in some other forms of concern for others that might suggest something of the sort is present.[43]

If we look closely at the cases we have considered so far, we will see that the disposition to nurture is linked to the disposition to dominate in ways we might not at first have expected. A moment's reflection makes it obvious that a mother nurturing a child is also, inevitably, dominant over it. What dominance there is among the Pintupi elders is expressed as the elders caring for the younger men. And the Tikopia chiefs were seen as caring for their people, not only by channeling the benevolence of the gods, but also by organizing the great rituals that were inevitably redistributive. The chiefs organized the accumulation of foodstuffs in preparation for the rituals (as the *anetaū* did among the Kalapalo) that were then redistributed in the collective feasting. Redistribution is, however, not necessarily as egalitarian as it sounds.

People are obligated to prepare food for the great rituals; the chiefs are generous in redistributing it in the name of the gods. The generosity of the Melanesian Big Man brings him prestige, but the contributions of his relatives
and dependents that made his generosity possible are not equally acknowledged. We may not like to think of it when we say "it is more blessed to give
than to receive," but it is the giving that creates dominance. As Marcel Mauss
reminds us: "To give is to show one's superiority, to show that one is something more and higher, that one is *magister*. To accept without returning or
repaying more is to face subordination, to become a client and subservient,
to become *minister*."[44] The archetypal *minister* is the child, who cannot repay
what he or she receives, at least not until much later if ever. Thus if nurturance is linked to dominance, receiving is linked to submission. These elementary facts of human life must surely be kept in mind as we consider the
relation between gods and men, rulers and people, in hierarchical societies.

If the disposition to dominate and the disposition to nurture are part of
our biological heritage, they have been partially transformed by culture. In
egalitarian bands, the disposition to dominate has in part become a disposition toward autonomy. Even in such intensely cooperative societies, each
adult must make his or her own decisions; no one can tell one arbitrarily
what to do. If men do submit to authority, as they do in Pintupi and many
other such groups in the process of initiation, the ultimate intent is to make
them into responsible, caring adults, able to act on their own and, in turn, to
exercise authority over younger men when appropriate. Although all Pintupi
males can become elders, not all Tikopia males can become chiefs—far from
it. Even so, all are included in Tikopia society—Firth's famous title *We the
Tikopia* carries a profound truth. In stratified Polynesian societies, only the
aristocrats have lineages; lack of lineage is the very definition of commoners.
In this sense all Tikopia are aristocrats; incipient hierarchy has not overcome
a basic egalitarianism. It was not inevitable that it would ever have changed;
it seems the Tikopia had tried other alternatives and in the end preferred to
remain "traditional" in Goldman's terms. But elsewhere in Polynesia the
story was very different and we must attempt to understand why.

Through Polynesia

With late precontact Hawai'i we come to a truly terrifying example of the
return of despotism that we spoke of early in this chapter: a stark distinction
between social classes, even the existence of an outcaste class; heavy taxation

of commoners; land expropriation at the will of chiefs; and—perhaps symbolic of the kind of society Hawai'i had become—frequent human sacrifice. Compared to Tikopia, hierarchy was greatly intensified—chiefs, as we will see, had become sacred indeed; but domination, only barely apparent in Tikopia, was extreme. Chiefs ruled by divine right but also by force; and they could be conquered and killed by force. And yet most of what was evident in late precontact Hawai'i was potential in Tikopia; it is possible, even probable, that early Hawai'i looked more like Tikopia than what Captain James Cook observed when he was the first Westerner to visit the islands in 1778.[45]

Whether Hawai'i in 1778 was a state or not is a question we can postpone until later. That it was a deeply inegalitarian, stratified society, however, goes without question. Starting out from hundreds of thousands of years of egalitarian hunter-gatherers, and much more recently from only very incipiently hierarchical horticultural societies like the Kalapalo and the Tikopia, how did societies like Hawai'i become possible? Returning briefly to the Pintupi, as close an ethnographic example to early hunter-gatherers as we are likely to get, I have pointed out their need to balance relatedness and autonomy (autonomy in this case meaning the autonomy of adult males and their families). Marshall Sahlins has made the thought experiment of imagining households in such societies as genuinely autonomous. Following Christopher Boehm I have argued that society, even in the loose sense of Pintupi local groups and extended relationships, would be necessary to prevent upstarts from destroying families by abusing or killing weaker men and mating randomly with women. But society in such cases is not just a defense against upstarts. It is also, as I suggested in discussing the Pintupi, a necessary safety net for families that would be too fragile to survive alone. Sahlins underlines this point in discussing why his idea of a "domestic mode of production"—production by and for the household alone—though a useful ideal type, is a performative impossibility:

> It never really happens that the household by itself manages the economy, for by itself the domestic stranglehold on production could only arrange for the expiration of society. Almost every family living solely by its own means sooner or later discovers it has not the means to live. And while the household is thus periodically failing to provision itself, it makes no provision (surplus) either for a public economy: for the support of social institutions beyond the family or of collective

activities such as warfare, ceremony, or the construction of large technical apparatus—perhaps just as urgent as the daily food supply.[46]

We will want to look at "warfare" and "large technical apparatus" more carefully in a moment—neither of them appears central for hunter-gatherers—but some public provision, cycled through extended kinship and religious ritual, is indeed essential for the survival of the simplest known societies (remembering that no human society is in any absolute sense simple). That should be obvious in each of the three examples described in Chapter 3. Agriculture, however, requires greater planning, effort, and discipline than hunting and gathering—that is why hunter-gatherers have often not been eager to adopt it.[47] Even hunting and gathering expeditions require some leadership, however unpretentious. If we can take the Kalapalo and Tikopia examples as suggestive, horticulture requires more clearly institutionalized leadership. The Kalapalo *anetu* and the Tikopia chief organize economic activity for the sake of ritual, activity that produces a surplus that is then redistributed to the people at large. In both cases leadership operates to intensify economic activity beyond what households alone would produce, but leaders gain in prestige rather than in enhanced material rewards: their gain is more from what they give than from what they keep. As Sahlins puts it: "And in a larger vantage, by thus supporting communal welfare and organizing communal activities, the chief creates a collective good beyond the conception and capacity of the society's domestic groups taken separately. He institutes a public economy greater than the sum of its household parts." Yet, as Sahlins also notes, "what begins with the would-be headman putting his production to others' benefit, ends, to some degree, with others putting their production to the chief's benefit."[48]

It would be easy to argue that other Polynesian societies are more hierarchical than Tikopia because of the presence of a "large technical apparatus," in this case elaborate systems of irrigation, found in many of the larger islands and in Hawai'i in particular. But Timothy Earle and others have shown that even the most elaborate Polynesian irrigation systems required only local leadership, no more oppressive than that of Tikopia chiefs; they reject the "hydraulic theory" of Karl Wittfogel, the argument that irrigation systems lie at the origin of the state (or of complex chiefdoms).[49]

What about "warfare," that other "collective activity" that Sahlins linked to the need to transcend the domestic mode of production? Warfare and chiefdoms are linked for reasons that are becoming increasingly clear. Although there is no peaceable past to hark back to—hunter-gatherers often have homicide rates higher than our inner cities—war does seem to be correlated with economic intensification and to emerge in relatively recent prehistoric times. Much depends on what we mean by war: homicide, revenge, even occasional raiding are not rare among hunter-gatherers. But organized warfare oriented to territorial conquest does seem to appear only where rich economic resources are locally concentrated and other options are less appealing. And organized warfare is usually associated with the appearance of chiefdoms.[50]

Earle's comparison of the archaeology of three cases where chiefdoms emerged shows that the earliest levels of settlement in the Thy region of Denmark, the Mantaro Valley of Peru, and Hawai'i lacked both warfare and chiefdoms: early settlers could just move on if they found the good land taken. But all three groups were agriculturalists—the Danish group was also pastoralist—and when there was no more good land to be had, then fighting over what there was began. Undoubtedly organized warfare requires leadership, so it is not surprising that chiefdoms emerged in all three cases. But in only one case, Hawai'i, did there emerge a paramount chiefdom approaching the level of an early state. In the Peruvian highlands the Mantaro small chiefdoms fought each other for centuries, some rising, some falling, but none ever amounting to much until the Inka conquest.

To take a Polynesian example, the Maori of the North Island of New Zealand were divided into dozens of small chiefdoms constantly at war with each other, but no larger entity emerged. The Maori chiefs were richer and more powerful than Tikopia chiefs, but remained united by bonds of kinship with their followers. Goldman quotes Firth as saying of the Maori chief, "His wealth was utilized for his own aggrandizement and influence, but in so doing it contributed greatly to the material benefit of his people."[51] Goldman places the Maori together with Tikopia as "traditional" Polynesian societies. Although the North Island of New Zealand was larger than any other Polynesian Island, and reasonably productive economically (most of the South Island was too cold for the Polynesian subtropical agricultural array, and the Maori there became thinly settled hunter-gatherers), the fusion of religious and secular aspects of chieftainship and the unity of chiefs and people kept them closer to Ancestral Polynesian Society than in many other cases. Warfare, though endemic, did not create political entities larger than simple chiefdoms and did not fundamentally alter the traditional Polynesian pattern.[52]

Even where warfare had more dramatic social consequences, it did not inevitably lead to large-scale social formations. For Kirch, "The case of Mangaia [one of the Southern Cook Islands] is instructive, for though a relatively small high island, it is a sort of microcosm for a Polynesian society in which politics, as well as economics and religion, had come to be thoroughly bound up with warfare."[53] In the case of Tikopia we have heard stories of a time when *toa,* warriors, threatened to overturn the political order. In Mangaia this is exactly what happened. With a population never more than about 3,000, early Mangaia was probably divided into several small chiefdoms, in which chiefs combined religious and secular authority, as in Tikopia or New Zealand. But at some point the chiefs were challenged by warriors, reduced to purely priestly functions, and replaced by a new kind of chief who was in effect a "military dictator."[54] The prize was the small area, 2 percent of the island, that could be irrigated. This land was redistributed as spoils of victory, its previous occupants being deprived of any hereditary claim to it.[55] We have noted that *mana,* traditionally inherited in chiefly lineages, could also be manifested in others. Success in war was such a manifestation of *mana,* and could produce, as it did in Mangaia, a "secular" chief, a successful upstart who nonetheless had a thin veil of religious legitimacy. Lacking, however, what Weber called "hereditary charisma,"[56] there was no form of routine succession—every new chief came to office only through military victory.

This political revolution was mirrored by a religious revolution. The god Rongo, who elsewhere in Eastern Polynesia was a peaceable god of agriculture, became a god of war and the high god of the island. Rongo required human sacrifice at the accession of each new military ruler. According to Kirch, the archaeological record suggests that cannibalism was common in late prehistory. He sums up the situation by saying, "Late precontact Mangaian society became, to a pervasive degree, a society based on terror."[57] The small size and population of Mangaia prevented the emergence of a complex stratified society, but it is an example of some of the possible though not inevitable consequences of militarization.

Scholars such as Kirch and Earle who have intensively studied chiefdoms, simple and complex, agree that their emergence was neither inevitable nor due to a single causal mechanism. There are, however, necessary but not sufficient conditions: an economy whose productive intensification beyond the household level required a significant degree of leadership; occupation of available land so that there was no open frontier to which the dissatisfied could move; highly productive land the use of which it was worth fighting over; and a degree of religious legitimation for economic-political-military leadership so that warfare did not threaten the continued existence of society. In New Zealand low-level endemic warfare seems to have been manageable, but in Mangaia, certainly in recent centuries in Rapa Nui (Easter Island),[58] and perhaps in the Marquesas as well, the intensity of conflict threatened the very viability of society. Society is a fragile achievement: societies, like individuals, are vulnerable. No historically known society has lasted forever; we would be wise to remember than no society existing today is likely to be an exception.

Hawai'i

Though one of the remotest parts of Polynesia, Hawai'i was the richest, and, next to New Zealand, the largest of the island groups. Size and density of population are among the conditions for the development of complexity, necessary but not sufficient. Kirch estimates that at contact the population of Hawai'i was at least 250,000 and perhaps considerably higher.[59] The next-largest Polynesian population was New Zealand, estimated at 115,000. However, the population of the "maximal political unit" in New Zealand was only 3,500, whereas the Hawaiian paramount chief, Kalaniopu'u, when he met Captain Cook at Keakakekua Bay in February of 1779, headed a chiefdom of at least 60,000 and possibly as many at 150,000 persons.[60] Thus the large population of New Zealand did not lead automatically to large political units with complex chiefdoms, though all the complex chiefdoms in Polynesia were in areas of large and dense populations: besides Hawai'i, Tonga, Samoa, and Tahiti.

Of course, the population of Hawai'i did not start out large. At settlement, sometime in the early centuries CE, its population was probably a few hundred at most and maybe as small as 50. For centuries, as the land was being gradually occupied and developed, simple chiefdoms similar to the Ancestral Polynesian model prevailed. From 1100 to 1500, however, population and agricultural intensification both rapidly increased, and fiercely competitive regional chiefdoms appeared.[61] Small, local temples, devoted to agricultural deities, and similar to what we have seen in Tikopia, are found almost from the beginning, but it is only after about 1100 that archaeologists date the building of large regional temples, devoted, if we can use ethnographic analogies, to the god of war, and indicative of the existence of complex chiefdoms.[62]

The emergence of the particular Hawaiian system of class stratification most likely correlated with the development of warlike complex chiefdoms. The Hawaiian term *ali'i* is cognate with Proto Polynesian *ariki,* priest-chief, but, in Hawai'i, even though it was still the term for chief, even paramount chief, it also applied to chiefly lineages in general, so it came to mean something like nobility as well. Unlike "conservative" societies like Tikopia and New Zealand, this chiefly nobility denied any genealogical linkage to the common people. One probable source of this split can be extrapolated from historical times: local chiefs had no genealogical relation to their locality; they were appointed by victorious paramount chiefs in return for their service in war. Thus the tie between the local community and its leader was broken. This break was reinforced by the prohibition (*kapu,* Hawaiian cognate for *tapu*]) of commoners keeping lineages going back before their grandfather's generation.[63] The loss of lineage and of lineal connection with the local chief had quite practical consequences: it entailed the loss of any right to the land. The new conquering chief might keep the existing farmers on as long as he could extract sufficient surplus from them, but the farmer served at the will of the chief or his local agent, the *konohiki.* He could lose his land or his life at the whim of either.[64] Below the commoners was an outcast class, the *kauwā,* composed mainly of war captives and transgressors of *kapu,* from whom human sacrifices were taken. To commoners the *kauwā* were polluted and to be avoided at all cost, but not to the *ali'i.* The *kauwā* were beyond *kapu* because of transgression; the *ali'i* because of divinity; and thus they could enjoy a familiarity that neither could have with commoners.[65]

The sanctity of the *ali'i* was not based on lineage as such, but on divine descent. As Goldman puts it: "[Sanctity] was specifically a quality of the gods and, in graded proportion, of their human descendents. Deference was thus to the gods and to the divine-descended. The offspring of high rank sibling marriages acquired the highest *kapu* because they were in fact gods. Like the gods they were said to be fire, heat, raging blazes. In the hierarchy of sanctity, gods and their human descendants were included in a single order." Although the distance between *ali'i* and commoners was (almost) absolute, there were a number of grades within the large *ali'i* class. Some women of the highest level "had so much of rank that they dared not rear children for fear their power would either cripple the new-born infant or kill it. Such women gave their children away to relatives for rearing."[66]

The *kapu* surrounding the paramount chiefs and others of the highest rank was extreme compared to the *tapu* of the Tikopia *ariki.* The paramount chief was, for all practical purposes, supposed to be invisible: he did not leave his dwelling except at night when he would not be seen. He was even supposed to remain immobile, exercising his *mana* by his mere existence, not by any action. We will see that the chief could on occasion appear and even act with explosive energy, but the underlying sense of his extreme sanctity is expressed by these beliefs in his immaterial *mana*.

The paramount chief was concerned with agriculture and played an important role, as we will see, in agricultural ritual, but he was far removed from the world of daily work. He was surrounded by what can only be called a court, consisting of relatives (consanguineal and affinal), officials, retainers, and a fairly extensive bodyguard. Just to supply the needs of his court the chief had to levy exactions on the commoners in his territory, but he also levied corvée labor for the construction of irrigation systems for taro and of fishponds in sheltered areas along the shore, as well as for the building of major temples. Although military leadership came from the *ali'i* class, commoners could be enlisted in wars. It was in the great rituals, which themselves required the mobilization of extensive resources, that the paramount chief's sanctity and power were most publicly expressed.

Before briefly describing the major rituals I must say a word about the gods to whom they were addressed. Traditional Hawaiian "theology" was much more developed than the beliefs we have seen in Tikopia. As Valerio Valeri says, "the highly systematic nature of the Hawaiian pantheon should not be surprising given the existence of a powerful class of priests, that is, of professional intellectuals."[67] (In Tikopia the chief passed on his ritual knowledge to his son, and it was vulnerable to loss due to such things as untimely death of the father, poor memory of the son, and so on.) The priests, who were themselves of *ali'i* rank, though not of the highest, were among the retinue of the court. Their existence did not mean that the chiefs were "secular" as in Mangaia. The chiefs continued to officiate at the most important ceremonies, indeed were essential for their efficacy, but they were assisted and even instructed by the professional priests. The role of the priests in developing a systematic view of the pantheon also did not replace the role of ritual leaders among the commoners who continued to have their own local temples, beliefs, and rituals, not necessarily correlated with the official ones.

The four major Hawaiian gods were Kū, Lono, Kāne, and Kanaloa, ranked in that order, at least on the island of Hawai'i (Kāne appears to have been the highest god in Kaua'i). I will discuss only Kū and Lono, the foci of the two most important ritual cycles. Each of the major gods presided over broad sectors of nature and of human activity. Kū was the god of war, fishing (a dangerous activity), and sorcery, whereas Lono was the god of agriculture, fertility, birth, and medicine.[68] The opposition between Kū and Lono comes out clearly in the contrast between their ritual cycles.

The Makahiki or New Year's festival is devoted to the god Lono.[69] According to Valeri, "Lono is preeminently the god of growth, of horticulture, of rain (he is associated with the clouds) and presides over the life of the people in general. As such he is the nourishing god. He is offered the first fruits of the land, particularly taro, which he helps to produce." The gourd is one of Lono's bodies and, according to Valeri, is "the one that perhaps better than all others condenses the different manifestations of this god. In fact, the fruit of the gourd evokes the roundness of that which is developed, full, or pregnant, as well as the form of rain-bearing clouds." A gourd containing kava is placed around the neck of Lono's image, and "the two mainstays of life, poi (taro puree) and water, are ordinarily kept in gourds."[70] Although Lono is male, the references to roundness, pregnancy and fertility strongly suggest a feminine aspect. The major male gods have female consorts, but the consorts are not the objects of significant rituals.

The Makahiki festival begins the Hawaiian year and lasts for four months. At the end of the old year the temples of Kū are closed and war and all forms of killing (including human sacrifice) are forbidden for the four months of the festival. There are moments in the Makahiki cycle that have a strong quality of Carnival-like status reversal, or, if not reversal, status leveling. As Valeri says, "the enthronement of Lonomakua [the image of Lono at the center of the festival], who is engendered by feasting, includes the dethronement of the [paramount chief][71] and his gods, who are engendered by violent sacrifice." The paramount chief and those closest to him remain secluded in their houses while Lonomakua reigns.[72] A high point of the festival is the ritual bathing *(hi'uwai)*. After an evening of feasting and kava drinking, nobles and commoners alike go to bathe in the ocean. This is the only time when the commoners see the most sacred *ali'i,* who, during the rest of the year, remain invisible. All the *kapu* that separate nobles and commoners are suspended, as the bathing becomes an orgy in which sexual relations between persons of different status are permitted.[73]

During the four days and nights that follow the *hi'uwai* rite, it is forbidden to work; the time is given over to feasting, mockery, obscene and satirical singing, and, above all, to dancing, in which hundreds, perhaps thousands, participated. Laughter overcomes *kapu,* and sexual advances during the dancing cannot be refused. Valeri writes that "these marvelously coordinated dances" realize "a perfect fellowship" that reconstitutes society itself. All of this takes place in an atmosphere of "hierarchical undifferentiation."[74] It is as though, for a while at least, the old egalitarianism reappeared.

Not all was egalitarian during the Makahiki season, nor was the paramount chief absent from some of the most important events. The chief escorted the Lonomakua, or impersonated the god himself, in a circumambulation of the island, collecting first-fruits offerings from each district as he entered it. Most of the offerings went into the chiefly treasury or were distributed to his retainers, but at some moments the commoners were fed, a remnant of the old "redistribution."

The *kāli'i* rite occurred toward the end of the Makahiki cycle. After bathing in the ocean for the first time in four days, the paramount chief and his men go by canoe to meet the god. When the chief lands he is met by Lono priests who menace him with spears. Several spears, which he evades, are thrown at him and a mock battle ensues. The party of the chief "wins" and he subsequently escorts Lonomakua back into his temple. A little later, a tribute canoe filled with offerings, also called Lono's canoe, is set adrift and Lono is said to return to Kahiki, the land of the gods, from which he came.[75] The Makahiki festival is over and work and hierarchy are once more in control.

The remaining eight months of the year belonged to Kū, whose most important ritual was the ritual of the *luakini* temple. As opposed to the public bathing, dancing and joking of the Makahiki festival, the solemn, even terrifying, *luakini* temple ritual took place within the precincts of the temple itself, dedicated to the war god Kū. Unlike most Polynesian temples, the major Hawaiian temple compounds were walled, so that no one besides the officiants could see what was going on, though we may be sure everyone knew what was going on.[76]

The archetypical *luakini* temple ritual occurred at the inauguration of a new paramount chief, when the temple was built, or more likely, rebuilt, but the ritual was repeated periodically to reaffirm the position of the ruler. The rite is too complex to be summarized here.[77] Human sacrifice, forbidden during the Makahiki festival, occurs at every stage of the *luakini* ritual. Valeri's central interpretation of this long and elaborate ritual is that it involves the "taming" of the war god Kū, even his transformation into something more like Lono. Human sacrifice is quite bloody in the early stages but is bloodless nearer to the end (death by strangulation rather than decapitation).

The archetypical *luakini* ritual occurred after the new paramount chief had achieved victory over his opponents, often rival claimants to the throne, sometimes brothers or half-brothers, whose bodies became part of the sacrifice, so that it was not just Kū who was being tamed, but the new ruler (who was, after all, both Kū and Lono) as well. The ritual helped to transform him from a "wild" warrior into a "tame" leader of civil society. Because, however, the new paramount chief often sought to affirm his leadership with new wars of conquest, the oscillation between wild and tame, as well as the *luakini* temple rituals, were a continuous feature of chiefly rule.

Although most serious students of ancient Hawai'i affirm the traditional Hawaiian belief that the paramount chiefs (and to some extent all the higher ranks of *ali'i*) were considered gods, many observers, including some anthropologists, prefer to believe that the notion of a divine ruler was purely metaphorical, that no one really believed it literally, a sentiment shared by Christian Polynesians in Hawai'i and elsewhere, ashamed of their pagan ancestors.[78] The problem arises, I believe, from a far too absolute meaning given to the word "god" in cultures deeply influenced by monotheism. In archaic societies, complex chiefdoms, and the tribal societies described in Chapter 3, gods, powerful beings, ancestors, and humans exist on a continuum—there are no absolute breaks between these categories. As in Tikopia, gods and chiefs were thought of in terms of one another, so in Hawai'i, as Valeri says, "Not only the *ali'i* are represented as gods, the gods are represented as *ali'i*."[79] Nonetheless, when the paramount chief was taken to be Kū in person, it was a matter of no small consequence.

We must try to understand more clearly the role of the Hawaiian paramount chief. He was simultaneously divine and human and the mediator between the divine and human realms. As Valeri writes, "the [paramount chief] is the supreme mediator between men and gods. Direct contact with the most important gods of the society is possible only for the king and his chaplains."[80] This direct contact was manifested above all in sacrificial ritual, especially human sacrifice, which unites gods and humans like no other action. Only the paramount chief could authorize human sacrifice, and he was, in a sense, sacrifier (the one on whose behalf the sacrifice is performed), sacrificer (the priestly officiant at the sacrifice), and, symbolically, the sacrifice, for the victim, through his sacrificial death, "becomes" the chief, particularly in instances I will note below.

That the paramount chief remained high priest is illustrated by a story that Valeri takes from a nineteenth century Hawaiian authority:

At the time of a volcanic eruption, King Kamehameha sent for a priest of Pele to seek his advice on what he should do. "You must offer the proper sacrifices," said the seer. "Take and offer them," replied the chief. "Not so! Troubles and afflictions which befall the nation require that the ruling chief himself offer the propitiatory sacrifice, not a seer or a kahuna [priest]." "But I am afraid lest Pele kill me." "You will not be killed," the seer promised.[81]

As this instance indicates, the paramount chief as divine-human mediator acts for the common good at a time of affliction. In one aspect he was seen as "father" of his people,[82] even implicitly as "mother," insofar as he was seen as the source of fertility. Offerings to the chief as Lono, even when not physically redistributed, were seen as repaid by his mana of fertility.

But the chief also had a terrifying, destructive side, as indeed did the gods. A favorite image of the chief as devourer was the shark. According to Valeri, "a shark was sometimes called chief, and a chief called a shark." He cites the following chant as a typical example of this usage:

A shark going inland is my chief,
A very strong shark able to devour all on land;
A shark of very red gill is the chief,
He has a throat to swallow the island without choking.[83]

A term used traditionally to designate the paramount chief was *ali'i 'ai moku,* "chief who eats the island."[84]

The "terrifying" side of Hawaiian chieftainship was in part a reflection of practical political reality. Succession to the paramountcy was never clear. Though seniority counted, in a polygamous family the son of a mother of higher rank than the mother of the oldest son might be considered to outrank his older half-brother. And with marriage to sisters or half-sisters favored by chiefs trying to maintain the highest possible rank of their offspring, the genealogical complications were considerable. In any case the death of a paramount often set off a civil war, and challenges from a pretender could come at any time. By killing and sacrificing his brothers and/or half-brothers, the paramount could absorb their mana, become them, so to speak, so as to concentrate the genealogical rank of his generation in himself. But more broadly, according to Valeri, the chief's "human sacrifice is always a fratricide: either a literal one—because his most likely rivals are his

brothers—or a metaphorical one—since every transgressor implicitly identifies with him and therefore becomes his 'double.'" Through incestuous marriages to sisters or half-sisters, he could also absorb the mana of the women
of equal rank. Thus the chief reproduces his legitimacy through fratricide and
sororal incest.[85]

By the same token, a defeated chief has obviously lost his mana, is no longer divine, is polluted. Rule depends on linage, but lineage, as we will see,
can be fabricated. Rule must be proven, must be actively affirmed, which is
why so few chiefs met a natural death. Even though claimants to the throne
of a ruling paramount were his brothers, they could still be considered upstarts, for their legitimacy remained to be proved. And upstarts were not always relatives of the ruler, not even always *ali'i*. The legendary 'Umi, archetypal usurper and conqueror, who, perhaps around 1500, conquered the whole
island of Hawai'i, was of commoner birth. He did not, however, attempt to
reign as a "military dictator," but claimed that an earlier paramount chief
had secretly slept with his mother, so that he was truly an offspring of the
chiefly line on his father's side.[86] Chiefs kept genealogical specialists who
could confirm *ali'i* rank and status or on occasion fabricate a needed genealogy. So, though ideologically the genealogical principle remained dominant,
according to Valeri, "*actual* relationships of subordination and political alliance tend to be more important, in the long run at least, than the genealogical relationships."[87] In other words, though upstarts who came to power
through sheer military force abounded in Hawaiian history (though there
were probably more unsuccessful upstarts who met an untimely end), they
sought genealogical and ritual legitimacy once in office.[88]

The critical reader might well ask how much of what I have written about
Hawaiian rulers was ruling class ideology and how much was shared by
commoners. Indeed, what did commoners think of all these goings-on? One
of the advantages of Hawai'i as a case is that we have some information
about such things from those who lived under the old regime. Of great value
in this regard is the book of David Malo, *Hawaiian Antiquities,* written in
the 1830s in Hawaiian and translated into English in 1898. According to
Valeri, "Malo's work is the most important source on ancient Hawaiian culture."[89] Malo was of *ali'i* lineage, born probably in 1793, and in his young
manhood was attached to the household to the high chief Kuakini, brother
of the powerful Queen Ka'ahumanu. He had personal knowledge of what he
spoke, and, though his possible bias as a Christian convert must be taken
into account, he also had some critical distance from the society he described. So let us consider Malo's testimony:

The condition of the common people was that of subjection to the chiefs, compelled to do their heavy tasks, burdened and oppressed, some even to death. The life of the people was one of patient endurance, of yielding to the chiefs to purchase their favor. The plain man *(kanaka)* must not complain.

If the people were slack in doing the chief's work they were expelled from their lands, or even put to death. For such reasons as this and because of their oppressive exactions made upon them, the people held the chiefs in great dread and looked upon them as gods.[90]

Yet commoners not only judged between chiefs, they could on occasion rebel against them.

There was a great difference between chiefs. Some were given to robbery, spoliation, murder, extortion, ravishing. There were a few kings[91] who conducted themselves properly as Kamehameha I did. He looked well after the peace of the land.

On account of the rascality *(kolohe)* of some of the chiefs to the common people, warlike contests frequently broke out between certain chiefs and the people, and the commoners killed many of the former in battle.[92]

It was the king's duty to seek the welfare of the common people, because they constituted the body politic. Many kings have been put to death by the people because of their oppression of the *makaainana* [people of the land].[93]

From other information and from the examples that Malo himself gives, *ali'i* claimants, who undoubtedly used popular dissatisfaction with the reigning chief to gather an opposition force, led such popular rebellions. In any case, as in all such situations in traditional societies, such a revolt was not a revolution, not an effort to change the nature of the regime, but an effort to replace a bad ruler with a good one. As Malo writes: "If the people saw that a king was religiously inclined *(haipule)*, strict in his religious duties, that king attained great popularity. From the most ancient times, religious kings have always been greatly esteemed."[94]

Malo's testimony is invaluable. It is apparent from what he wrote that commoners had their own ideas about the high and mighty, and were prepared to act on them. Yet the most they could hope for was a good, "religious" ruler. Whether through fear or admiration, the *ali'i* were godlike to them. In nonliterate societies known only archaeologically or even in literate societies where the surviving documents derive solely from the ruling class, we would have almost no idea what the common people thought.

Another indication of the importance of the paramount chief to the entire population was the breakdown of social order following the ruler's death. Valeri speaks of such a death as involving "radical subversion and violent anarchy" that "removes the foundation of the system of social rules." In short, the system of *kapu* that ordered sexuality and respect for person and property collapsed. Nothing and no one were safe. Nor was this the benign Carnival-like status leveling of the Makahiki festival, but rather a period of extreme fear for life and limb.[95] Is it not possible that many, even commoners, identified with the apparent omnipotence of the paramount chief, who combined the divine and the human in his own person, but who was also the enforcer of the system of *kapu?* If so, it is not surprising that the chief's death brought on the collapse of the normative order, both internal and external. One can imagine that even the most skeptical commoner would wish for the rapid installation of a new paramount chief to bring the disorder to an end.[96]

Another extraordinarily valuable testimony of something we could have no knowledge about where we are entirely dependent on archaeology is Malo's description of "prophets," *kāula.* This is the Hawaiian cognate of the Proto Polynesian *taaula,* whose various meanings include "priest, spirit medium, shaman, sorcerer, or prophet."[97] Firth translates the cognate Tikopia term, *taura,* as spirit medium, which seems to be the most general term for a phenomenon that takes different, though related, forms in various Polynesian societies. Unlike *tahunga* (Hawaiian *kahuna*), priests of the official cult, spirit mediums can be of any status and either gender. This is a "democratic" role, as the spirit may choose whomever he or she wishes (male spirits usually choose male mediums and female spirits female mediums). Firth devotes a chapter to spirit mediums in *Rank and Religion in Tikopia,* but, as the almost sole function of such mediums had to do with healing within the lineage of the medium, they were rather peripheral. The Hawaiian *kāula* is another matter altogether. Let us hear Malo: "The *kāula* were a very eccentric class of people. They lived apart in desert places, and did not associate with people or fraternize with any one. Their thoughts were much taken up with deity." *Kāula,* prophets or foretellers as Malo calls them, forewarned of such events as "the death of a king, or of the overthrow of a government."[98] One noted *kāula* of the eighteenth century is reported to have prophesied:

That which is above shall be brought down;
That which is below shall be lifted up;
The islands shall be united;
The walls shall stand upright.[99]

Valeri quotes another early authority, S. M. Kamakau, as saying "The prophets were independent people, and were inspired by the spirit of a god. They spoke the words of the god without fear before chiefs and men. Even though they might die, they spoke out fearlessly."[100]

The potential opposition between chief and prophet arises from their fundamentally different relation to deity. As Valeri puts it, "the *kāula* represents a totality directly accessible to the individual and thus in opposition to the social hierarchy; the king represents a totality consubstantial with the social hierarchy."[101] Both chief and prophet are in a sense upstarts: the chief because he came to power by force; the prophet because he affirms his message in the face of king and people. But the chief does not rule by force alone and the prophet's weapon is not force but speech. The figure of the prophet, who claims a direct relation to a god in a society like Hawai'i where social hierarchy overwhelmingly mediates the relation between the divine and the human, is shadowy indeed. He will return.

What links Hawai'i to comparable cases of early states or early civilizations is the absolutely central role of the priest-king. The fusion of powerful beings, nature, and the society as a whole, characteristic of ritual in what I have called tribal religion, though it reappears at moments in a society like Hawai'i, for instance in the Makahiki festival, has become to a remarkable degree concentrated in one person in early civilizations.[102] Human sacrifice, which turns out to be the sole prerogative of the priest-king in such societies, and which is almost absent from societies at any other stage of development, epitomizes the enormous fusion of power in one person. As David Malo put it:

The edicts of the king had power over life and death. If the king had a mind to put someone to death, it might be a chief or a commoner, he uttered the word and death it was.

But if the king chose to utter the word of life, the man's life was spared.[103]

The word of life and death is a divine word, and it is not surprising that the one who exercised it was considered a god.[104] He was a god who was also a man, for he represented humans to the gods as well as the gods to humans. His arbitrary power and the oppression of the common people over whom he ruled represent a remarkable breakdown of tribal egalitarianism and a return of a particularly harsh form of despotism, made possible by the increasing size of the social unit with its attendant loss of face-to-face community, by the increased surplus due to agricultural intensification, and by the rise of militarism now that there was so much to fight over. The disposition to dominate was triumphant in the king as Kū in his wild state.

But Hawai'i was not Mangaia or Rapa Nui, where terror reigned almost without restraint. Terror existed, but it was ritualized, institutionalized, limited. The king as Kū was tamed and became, at least part of the time, the king as Lono, who, as Valeri said, "is the nourishing god." So in Hawaii, the *ali'i nui,* the high chief, combined the disposition to dominate with the disposition to nurture, domination with hierarchy, as has every government since. Yet when despotism first reappears, the representation of cosmos, society, and self in one person, a person who combines both terror and benevolence, places that one person under almost unbearable tension. All archaic societies are monarchical, center around one person, but later archaic societies find ways to diffuse the intensity, to give it broader sociocultural institutionalization, so that the focus becomes more on rule than on ruler. We will consider such changes below.

But was the Hawaiian high chief an archaic king? Was Hawai'i before Kamehameha I a state (or rather four states, as high chiefs reigned on each of the four major islands)? These are obviously matters of definition. One critical element in deciding whether a paramount chiefdom has made the transition to statehood is whether or not it has broken decisively with the kinship system. In 1972, Marshall Sahlins argued that Hawai'i had not made such a break: "They had not broken decisively with the people at large, so that they might dishonor the kinship morality only on pain of a mass defection."[105] And in 1984 Patrick Kirch agreed with him: "the ruling elite . . . never managed to sever completely the *kinship* bond between chiefs and people that Hawai'i inherited from Ancestral Polynesian Society."[106] By 2000, Kirch acknowledged that his opinion on this issue had "subtly changed over the years," and that he had come to think that "even prior to Captain Cook, Hawaiian society constituted an 'archaic state.' The development of class stratification as well as the alienation of land rights from producers, not to mention the forms of absolutizing religious ideology (including the war cult of human sacrifice) and the regular exercise of military force are all typical of state-level social formations."[107]

Lawrence Krader's definition of the state as a "secondary formation" is helpful in solving this definitional problem. He holds that "social integration, internal regulation, and external defense" are functions of all societies, but that "the state combines these functions with the promotion and preservation of its own existence as an end in itself. Thus the state is to be viewed as a *secondary formation* for the achievement of the aforementioned social ends."[108] I think that it can be argued that by late precontact times the court around what we can now call the Hawaiian *king* was such a secondary formation: it had the power to administer, tax, levy corvée, and conscript for military service, for its own ends, not necessarily the ends of the people. If we use functional analysis, as in sociology we always must, we must be careful to ask, functional for whom? What was functional for the state was not necessarily functional for the people, or indeed for society as a whole. There are all too many such examples in human history, so we must leave the degree to which the state is functional for society as an empirical question that will vary from case to case.

One last typological remark: Hawai'i seems to be a good example of what Max Weber called the patrimonial state, and which he defined as a state growing out of the household (court) of the king. Here again there is a matter of degree. It is only when the king's "household" reaches the size and effectiveness that enable it to function as a genuine secondary formation that it can be called a patrimonial state. I would argue that in ancient Hawai'i it had reached that stage.

5

Archaic Religion: God and King

In my discussion of tribal religion I chose three examples for close examination: the Kalapalo, the Australian Aborigines (the Walbiri), and the Navajo. From the thousands of tribal peoples, this choice could not be defended as "representative," even though each was chosen from a different continent. In considering chiefdoms as the form of organization intermediate between the tribal and the archaic, I chose to look mainly at Polynesia because of the clarity of the record there in which archaeology and ethnography combine to give a sense of development over many centuries, starting with Neolithic villages and ending with an early state in Hawai'i. Still, given that we have data for hundreds of chiefdoms in many parts of the world, the choice of Polynesia can be defended as strategic but not as representative. With early states or early civilizations, what I have chosen to call archaic societies, we are in a very different situation. Though exactly how many there are can be argued, the number is surely quite small compared to tribes or chiefdoms, and those for which data is adequate are fewer still. Looking ahead to what follows the archaic, namely the axial age, there are only four cases: ancient Israel, ancient Greece, India in the second half of the first millennium BCE, and China in the same period. I have therefore decided to look closely only at those archaic societies that significantly contributed to axial ones: ancient Mesopotamia and Egypt, which influenced both Israel and Greece; and Shang and Western Zhou China, from which there is a smooth transition to the Chinese axial age. Had the data been adequate I would have included the Indus Valley civilization in India as well.

I have, of course, in Chapter 4, already considered at length one other archaic society, Hawai'i. This I have used as an example of the transition to an early state, with the advantage that we know more about it at an early stage than any other case. For none of the archaic societies we will consider in this chapter was there anyone like David Malo around to report on their early stages, nor can we reconstruct the probable developmental sequence for over 2,000 years before their emergence as early states with the clarity we now have about Polynesia. For studying the beginning of an archaic religion, the Hawaiian case is invaluable because of the wealth of information we have about it, not available for any other case.

Before turning to the cases with which this chapter will be concerned, it will be useful to consider Bruce Trigger's instructive survey, *Understanding Early Civilizations,* a compendious comparative analysis of seven cases: Old and Middle Kingdom Egypt, Mesopotamia from Early Dynastic III to Old Babylonian times, China in late Shang and early Western Zhou times, the Aztecs from the late fifteenth to early sixteenth centuries, the Classic Maya, the Inka kingdom during the early sixteenth century, and the Yoruba peoples of West Africa from the mid-eighteenth century to the late nineteenth century.[1] Trigger has chosen his cases largely because they are the ones for which there is adequate data; the inability to understand the Indus Valley civilization on the basis of archaeological evidence alone (what little writing there is has not been deciphered) has forced him to exclude this important case, rightly in my view.[2] Trigger's sample is of mature states; because he does not include Hawai'i, he has no example of a really early state. Of course we should remember that the "early state" is more a process than an event—it is almost always impossible to "pinpoint the precise moment of the birth of the state."[3] Even in Hawai'i the state was clearly forming well before Western contact, though the process is more evident than in any of Trigger's cases, and for this reason the Hawaiian case remains invaluable.

One of the defects of my sample of archaic societies is that it excludes all the New World cases, so a summary of Trigger's findings—three of his seven are from the New World—can go a little way to make up for that deficiency. It will be useful to begin by considering what Trigger means by "early civilizations," because his definition is very close to what I mean by archaic societies:

Anthropologists apply the term 'early civilization' to the earliest and simplest forms of societies in which the basic principle governing social relations was not kinship but a hierarchy of social divisions that cut horizontally across societies and were unequal in power, wealth, and social prestige. In these societies a tiny ruling group that used coercive powers to augment its authority was sustained by agricultural surpluses and labour systematically appropriated from a much larger number of agricultural producers. Fulltime specialists (artisans, bureaucrats, soldiers, retainers) also supported and served the ruling group and the government apparatus it controlled. Rulers cultivated a luxurious style of life that distinguished them from the ruled.[4]

If we think of Hawai'i, the distinction between the *ali'i* and the commoners is just such a clear class distinction. Another way of making the same point without focusing quite so centrally on class is to say that the key distinction is between the state as a secondary formation and the rest of society. That this is close to what Trigger means is clear when he writes, "wealth tended to be derived from political power far more frequently than political power was derived from wealth."[5] So it is not class as defined in terms of relation to the means of production that is critical in these societies, but class as defined in relation to political power.

Also important for Trigger is the point that kinship, although remaining significant in different ways for both the rulers and the ruled, no longer, as in tribal and chiefdom societies, is the "basic principle governing social relations." He adds one further point of great importance: "Just as class has replaced real and metaphorical kinship as a basis for organizing society, so religious concepts replaced kinship as a medium for social and political discourse."[6] Of course, symbolic action and expression that can be called religious appear at every level of social organization, but something new in the religious realm appears in archaic societies: gods and the worship of gods. My reading of Trigger's study reinforces my sense that what makes archaic society different from its predecessors is a complex religio-political transformation that gives rise to two ideas that are essentially new in the world: kingship and divinity, in many ways two parts of a single whole.

Hawaiian society as we described it focused on the king and his relation to, even identity with, the gods, particularly Kū and Lono. Kingship is central in every one of Trigger's cases, and everywhere the king had a unique relation to the gods, was frequently considered a god himself. Some form of divine kingship can be found in Old Kingdom Egypt, the Aztecs, Mayas, Inkas and Yorubas, and in Zhou China the king was the "Son of Heaven," though he was not himself considered divine. In Mesopotamia, the earliest period of what was probably priest-kingship is obscure, but there were sporadic claims to divine status by kings in the Akkadian and Ur III dynasties in the third millennium BCE, and perhaps even in the Old Babylonian dynasty in the first half of the second millennium.[7]

Human sacrifice associated with royal ritual was present in some form in every case, and was, as in Hawai'i, always an indication of the extraordinarily exalted status of kingship, although the extent of it was variable. The commonest form was what is called retainer sacrifice, in which wives and retainers, sometimes in large numbers, were buried with the dead king. In Egypt this practice was found in the First and probably the Second Dynasties; in Mesopotamia only in the Early Dynastic royal burials at Ur—in each case no later examples are known. Although the numbers decreased markedly in China after the Shang, some retainer burial was practiced for centuries. But in most cases human sacrifice in rituals other than funerals was not uncommon: Shang China, the Mayas, Inkas, and Yorubas, and most extensively of all, the Aztecs, where thousands of war captives were sacrificed at the great temple at Tenochtitlan right up until the Spanish conquest.[8]

The extraordinary exaltation of the ruler puts Hawai'i firmly in the category of (early) archaic society, where such exaltation everywhere went to extremes unknown in earlier or later periods, but there are other features that we normally consider indicative of archaic society that were not present in Hawai'i: urbanism and writing, for example. Trigger argues, however, that cities are not an indispensable marker of early civilizations; rather, such civilizations divide into two types, city-states and territorial states. Whereas Mesopotamia, the Yorubas, the Aztecs, and the Mayas were city-states, Egypt, China, and the Inkas were territorial states.[9] City-states were large, multipurpose, urban conglomerates, usually located near highly productive agricultural areas, and from which larger states were sometimes formed, usually by subjecting other such cities to tribute status. In territorial states it was the court, not the city, that provided the center, and the court was often peripatetic. There were important ceremonial centers, but the court could visit them only intermittently or move from one to another. Hawai'i was clearly in the category of the territorial state, building its empire across the archipelago rather than reaching out from a single city. Of course, established territorial empires eventually gave rise to cities, though cities were not the basis of state structure. Conversely, city-states sometimes became territorial states, though extending city institutions to a large territory usually proved a daunting and often in the long run an impossible task, Rome being the great exception.

When we use the word "civilization," as we inevitably must in speaking of archaic societies, we usually think of writing as an essential criterion. But in

Trigger's seven cases, writing was entirely absent among the Inkas and the Yorubas, and rudimentary among the Aztecs, Mayas, and perhaps the Shang Chinese (though there may have been more extensive writings than the oracle bones, on which our knowledge of Shang writing depends, they have not survived). Even in Mesopotamia, where writing was "invented" around 3200 BCE, it was first used mainly for accounting and for lists, and continuous texts cannot be deciphered until about 2500 BCE.

Another feature of most archaic societies is the presence of monumental architecture, mainly for ritual and/or royal use. The Hawaiian *heiau* (temple) was a modestly monumental structure, one of the largest of which, on the island of Maui, was over 4,000 square meters in area and required an estimated 26,000 labor-days for construction during ten separate occasions.[10] Such temples do not compare with the Mesopotamian *ziggurats,* the Aztec, Maya, or Inka temples, or, of course, with the Egyptian pyramids. But neither the Shang Chinese nor the Yorubas appear to have produced monumental architecture much more impressive than the Hawaiian *heiau.*

Trigger indicates that when he began his study he expected to find economic practices to be the most constant in his sample and religious beliefs and practices the most variable. In fact he found the opposite: subsistence patterns varied quite widely due to differences in ecological context, whereas religious beliefs and practices were remarkably comparable across his seven cases.[11] Comparable, but, as we shall see, still significantly different. In Chapter 4 we saw how the relation of religion and power, only incipient in tribal societies, came to a kind of climax in Hawai'i. Having used Trigger's book as an introduction to the field of mature archaic societies, we can now try to understand better the relation of religion and power, of god and king, in such societies by taking a closer look at three of them.

Ancient Mesopotamia

On the face of it, Hawai'i and Mesopotamia could hardly have had more opposite starting points. Hawai'i was located in just about the remotest spot on the planet, out of contact with any other society for centuries before the arrival of Europeans. Mesopotamia (literally, "the land between the rivers"—the Tigris and Euphrates—present-day Iraq contains all of ancient Mesopotamia) was at the center of the vast Eurasian (and North African) land mass and was never out of touch with its many neighbors, near and far. This geographical difference alone helps account for the fact that the Mesopotamian

state began about 5,000 years before the Hawaiian state. Not only geographically, but in terms of other variables as well, Hawai'i and Mesopotamia are
far apart among archaic societies, so that beginning the consideration of
mature archaic societies with Mesopotamia allows maximal contrasts to
appear.

Archaeology reveals that, in spite of their many differences, in both cases
settlement began on largely virgin territory. After about 4000 BCE, in the alluvial plain of Southern Mesopotamia, only very sparsely settled before, a
large number of fairly large settlements appeared rather suddenly, and by
about 3200 BCE the first true cities in the world had emerged.[12] These cities
focused on monumental temple compounds but also had palaces, markets,
and extensive residential quarters. The new level of population density that
these cities evidenced was made possible by extensive cultivation of the alluvial soil. But the economic basis of these cities was not just local irrigation
agriculture, but area-wide economic innovations that Andrew Sherratt has
called the secondary products revolution, a transformation that he believes
was as significant as the beginnings of plant and animal domestication
themselves, at least 4,000 years earlier.[13]

Early animal domestication was at first simply for the purpose of having a
stable meat supply. With the secondary products revolution, for the first time
animal power began to replace human power in agriculture. (It is worth remembering that, due to the absence of cattle and sheep, there was no secondary products revolution in the New World, or, of course, in Hawai'i). Yokes
and harnesses were invented so that cattle could pull plows and carts. Sherratt
estimates that the plow, because it can go deeper into the soil, is four times
more efficient than the hoe in preparing the soil for sowing.[14] And carts make
it much easier to bring grain in from outlying fields. These inventions appeared first in northern Mesopotamia by about 4000 BCE, in the old zone of
agricultural settlement, but they helped to make possible the rapid urbanization in the south, which followed soon after. The changes involved in the
secondary products revolution were not only agricultural; they involved a new
kind of pastoralism as well. For the use of milk and milk products (yogurt,
cheese) originated at about this time, as did the use of sheep to supply wool
for textiles, earlier textiles being of vegetable fiber. Again, Sherratt estimates
that the use of herds as a source of milk products is four to five times more
efficient, in the amount of protein and energy produced relative to the same
amount of feed, as using them only for meat.[15] Although southern Mesopotamia had rich alluvial soil that could be very productive when irrigated, and

lands beyond the possibility of irrigation that would support pastoralism, it had little else: no wood, no stone, no metal. In spite of great ingenuity in the use of resources indigenous to the area, it is clear that trade, including long-distance trade, was essential from the very beginning. Thus a region-wide economy, involving plow agriculture and intensive pastoralism, together with a considerable amount of trade, had appeared by the end of the fourth millennium BCE.

Susan Pollack catalogs some of the developments in southern Mesopotamia evident by the end of the Uruk period (4000–3100 BCE):

> The Uruk period witnessed a massive increase in the number of settlements. Although many of them were small villages, others grew rapidly into towns and cities. By the end of the Uruk period, some larger settlements were walled. Temples and other public buildings became larger and more elaborate, and their construction must have employed large workforces for lengthy periods . . . Mass production was introduced for manufacturing some kinds of pottery using technological innovations such as mold manufacture and wheel-throwing. Systems of accounting . . . were elaborated and diversified, and writing—the premier accounting and recording technology—was invented toward the end of the period. Representations of men with weapons and bound individuals, presumably prisoners, attest to the use of armed force. The repeated depiction of a bearded individual with long hair, distinctive style of headdress, and skirt engaging in a variety of activities suggestive of authority is among the indications [of] the public exercise of power.[16]

By 2900 BCE the city of Uruk, perhaps the most important city of Sumer, had become enormous by the standards of ancient cities. Hans Nissen shows that it was larger than Athens in 500 BCE or Jerusalem in 50 CE, and almost as large as Rome in 100 CE.[17] It has been estimated that by 2500 BCE the population of Uruk was about 50,000. The main temple of the city was immense, with a stepped tower that had been rebuilt several times, each time with increased height.

With only archaeological evidence (the script was used almost solely for accounting and contains no decipherable narratives) to go on, we simply cannot say what the structure of authority in Uruk and other comparable cities emerging at the same time was like. Hans Nissen details some of the previous theories: that the early rulers, entitled *en,* or *ensi,* were in effect priest-kings; that later, temporary military leaders called *lugal* (meaning "the great man") were appointed, and these over time became permanent "kings," rivaling the chief priests for dominance in the city. Nissen feels the whole terminology of *en, ensi,* and *lugal* is too inconsistent in the surviving records to support such a theory and that we simply do not know how power was wielded in the earliest period. By the early dynastic period (2900–2350 BCE) it is clear that there were royal dynasties in the major Sumerian cities, but that great temples were the focus of both wealth and power, and indeed their upkeep was a major royal responsibility. Both temple and palace have been referred to as "great households" or "great organizations" because they were major landowners, had large staffs, and in some cases engaged in textile manufacturing, the major Mesopotamian export.[18]

It is also generally agreed that besides the temple and the palace there was a vigorous "private sector," perhaps led by lineage elders who also had a say in city government, though the idea of what Thorkild Jacobsen called "Primitive Democracy"[19] has not been widely accepted. In any case, relative to most other early states, early Mesopotamia does seem to be a case of "heterarchy," that is, a nonegalitarian society with several competing centers of power, rather than one with a single dominance hierarchy.[20] The fact that Mesopotamia was the least isolated of any of the early civilizations, and the most dependent on long-distance trade due to its lack of local resources, is perhaps related to the existence of multiple power centers within its many cities. Although leadership in the Sumerian period is not as clear as it would later become, in quite early Sumerian mythology it is said that "kingship came down from heaven," even though the king himself did not claim to be a god.[21]

The absence of divine kingship in the earliest history does not mean that this ubiquitous archaic idea was entirely absent. It appears, not surprisingly, in dynasties attempting to unite the city-states and create territorial empires. As Oppenheim puts it:

In Babylonia from the time of Sargon of Akkad [ca. 2350 BCE] until the time of Hammurapi[22] [1792–1750 BCE], the name of the king was often written with the determinative DINGIR ("god"), used normally for gods and objects intended for worship. We also know, from Ur III texts and, sporadically, from later documents, that statues of deceased kings received shares of the offerings in the temples. The sanctity of the royal person is often, especially in Assyrian texts, said to be revealed by a supernatural and awe-inspiring radiance or aura which, according to the literature, is characteristic of deities and of all things divine.[23]

And the claim by a number of Assyrian kings to be "king of the universe" would seem to imply a power more than human.[24]

But even when, as was more often the case, the king was characterized as the "servant" or "slave" of the god (a usage that, in an entirely different context, will reappear in Christianity and even more extensively, in Islam) rather than as divine himself, it was his closeness to divinity, not his "secularity," that was emphasized. In his inscriptions the king endlessly recounted all he had done for the gods—building or rebuilding temples, presenting lavish offerings, holding festivals, and so on—and attributed the prosperity of the land and even his military victories to the benevolence of the gods, particularly the patron deity of his city. Here, as in all early civilizations, the religious and the political are not different spheres, but aspects of a total understanding of cosmos and society, which does not mean that we cannot observe variations in how these aspects were phrased.

As in Hawai'i, the Mesopotamian pantheon was enormous, but a few gods were particularly important: Anu, the father of the gods; Enlil, his son and actual ruler of the gods; Ninhursaga, the goddess of birth; Enki, the god of fresh water, but above all the god of intellect and cunning, and of all the productive arts.[25] Each city had its own patron god: Uruk was devoted to Anu; Eridu to Enki; Ur to Nanna; and so on. The patron god of Lagash was Ninurta, son of Enlil, warrior god, but also god of the plow. Although each god was related to particular aspects of nature (Anu to the sky, Enki to fresh water, and so on) and to aspects of human life, all of them had a great concern with economic prosperity, so that what Firth said of Tikopia, "the religious system was openly and strongly oriented towards economic ends," is also true of Mesopotamia, as the following hymn to Ninurta from the end of third millennium Sumer, indicates:

> Ninurta whom Enlil has named!
> I wish to celebrate your name, O my king!
> Ninurta, I, your man, your man,
> I wish to celebrate your name!
> O my king, the sheep has given birth to the lamb— . . . ,
> And I, I wish to celebrate your name!

O my king, the goat has given birth to the kid— . . .
And I, I wish to celebrate your name! . . .
You fill the canal with perpetual water, . . .
You make the speckled barley grow in the fields,
You fill the pool with carp and perch[?], . . .
You garnish gardens and vineyards, with honey and wine!
And you will grant the palace a longer life![26]

I don't want to imply that the gods were always benevolent—far from it. They were not infrequently the cause of what Jacobsen calls "paralyzing fear."[27] As in Hawai'i, they were not so far from the powerful beings of tribal peoples. They were the source of great abundance, but also the cause of storm, flood, and pestilence. They could bring victory or defeat in war. Above all, the gods were kings and queens, and the temples were their courts. The "service to the gods"—demanding, difficult, but joyous and rewarding—was at the center of life in Mesopotamia.[28] A large sector of the economy was organized to serve the gods and goddesses presiding in major temples, their relatives and retainers, all of whose images had to be lavishly "fed," clothed, adorned with jewelry, and, occasionally, during festivals, paraded through the streets or taken on boat trips to neighboring temples.[29] Because the economic and political prosperity of the city depended on the benevolence of the gods, their generous service was the first obligation of both kings and people.

The nature of the relationship between gods and men is epitomized in the mythical "Story of Atrahasīs."[30] Although the text dates from Old Babylonian times (first half of the second millennium BCE), Jacobsen believes it represents ideas that go back at least to the third millennium. In the initial division of the world, Anu was allotted the heavens, Enlil the earth, and Enki the waters under the earth. As the gods had to be fed, Enlil put his many children, the lesser gods, to work carrying out the hard tasks of irrigation agriculture. The poem begins:

When Ilu (i.e., Enlil) was the boss
they were burdened with toil,
    lugged the workbasket;
the gods' workbasket . . . was big,
    so the toil was heavy,
    great the straits.[31]

The gods had to dig out the Tigris and Euphrates rivers as well as the irrigation canals, and they found it all too much. They decided to revolt against Enlil, and having burned their work tools they surrounded his house. Enlil, frightened and barricaded at home, called on Anu and Enki for advice as to what to do. He felt like abandoning earth altogether and joining his father in the sky. But Enki, always the clever one, had a suggestion: why not create men to do the work the lesser gods found so tiresome? He killed one of the lesser gods, We-e, perhaps the ringleader of the rebellion (could we call it a strike?), and, mixing his blood with clay, fashioned the first human beings.[32]

Enki's plan worked almost too well: men took over the work of the gods, but greatly prospered in doing so. Their growing population became so noisy ("the land bellowed like a bull"), that Enlil could get no sleep. He sent a plague to wipe the people out, but the wise man Atrahasīs consulted Enki who told him to keep the people quieter and give more offerings to the gods, and the plague ceased. Again the people increased and the noise level rose. This time Enlil sent a drought, but again Atrahasīs persuaded Enki to intervene. The third time was really too much and Enlil sent a great flood to kill every human being. Enki, however, was one step ahead of him and had Atrahasīs construct an unsinkable boat, load it with every kind of animal, and last out the flood. When Enlil discovered what Enki had done he was furious, but meantime the decimation of the people had left the gods with no offerings, and they were beginning to starve. Enlil finally realized that humans were indispensable to the gods, and, having arranged several methods of birth control, allowed Atrahasīs and his people to resettle the earth.

One might think, says Jacobsen, that Enlil cut a rather poor figure with his fear, impulsiveness, and insensitivity, but to the ancients the story illustrates Enlil's ultimate power, his stunning capacity to create a flood that could potentially destroy every living thing. Jacobsen concludes: "All the same it is clear that the myth views absolute power as selfish, ruthless, and unsubtle. But what is is. Man's existence is precarious, his usefulness to the gods will not protect him unless he takes care not to be a nuisance to them, however innocently. There are, he should know, limits set for his self-expression."[33]

In ancient Mesopotamia the idea of the state organized the life of both gods and humans and the relation between them. After the creation of human beings, it was they, not the lesser gods, who "lugged the workbaskets." Or rather, it was the lot of most men to do so; some humans led a godlike existence—they were "served" as the gods were served. Even so, kings were portrayed as working on the great building projects, though we may doubt how much time they actually spent doing so, and they, like everyone else, were servants of the gods, except for those relatively rare moments when they identified themselves as gods. Dominance was a major theme; mostly it was dominance cloaked in the mantle of legitimate hierarchy; but both gods and kings were capable of irrational anger against "undeserving" targets. Jacobsen identifies Anu with "authority" but Enlil with "force," and it was Enlil who in fact ruled the world.[34] It is true that Enlil's force was supposed to be "legitimate force,"

> Yet, because Enlil is force, there lie hidden in the dark depths of his soul both violence and wildness. The normal Enlil upholds the cosmos, guarantees order against chaos; but suddenly and unpredictably the hidden wildness in him may break forth. This side of Enlil is truly and terribly the abnormal, a scattering of all life and life's meaning. Therefore, man can never be fully at ease with Enlil but feels a lurking fear which finds expression frequently in the hymns which have come down to us.[35]

Yet nurturance, expressed as a concern for a certain kind of justice, was increasingly evident in the third millennium and the first half of the second, reaching a kind of climax in the so-called "code" of Hammurabi. Already in the middle of the third millennium we have a king of Lagash who proclaims himself "as the righter of social wrongs and defender of the weak": "Uruinimgina [the king] solemnly promised Ningirsu [the god] that he would never subject the waif and the widow to the powerful."[36] A poem written after the fall of the Akkadian dynasty of Sargon criticizes its kings for allowing "injustice and violence to set foot in the land."[37] In the Ur III dynasty there was periodic remission of debt: "The tablets that enshrined the debtors' obligations to their creditors were then collected and broken, thereby dissolving the debt."[38]

The "code," which Jean Bottéro argues is not a set of laws but a summary of Hammurabi's verdicts, and thus not really a code, is justly famous. Bottéro points out that it is the prologue and epilogue that give us the clearest insight into the meaning of justice in ancient Mesopotamia. In the prologue Hammurabi writes:

> When (my god) Marduk [who had for the Babylonians replaced Enlil as ruler of the gods] had given me the mission to keep my people in

order and to make my country take the right road, I installed in this country justice and fairness in order to bring well-being to my people.

And in the epilogue:

> The great gods have called me, and I am indeed the good shepherd who brings peace, with the just scepter. My benevolent shade covered my city. I have carried in my bosom the people of Sumer and Akkad. Thanks to my good fortune (literally: the divine protection of which I am the object) they have prospered. I have not ceased to administer them in peace. By my wisdom I have harbored them. In order to prevent the powerful from oppressing the weak, in order to give justice to the orphans and the widows.[39]

The rhetoric of nurturance here is powerful: the image of the good shepherd will occur again in the history of religion. Needless to say, kings were seldom as benevolent as they claimed to be—the exorcism texts give examples of grave injustices coming from the palace. But neither was this "just rhetoric." A standard was set that would have consequences.

We can speak of the idea of justice in ancient Mesopotamia, but we must be careful to understand that our word is not entirely cognate with their thought. For one thing, justice was personified, was a god. Justice was the sun god, Utu in Sumerian, Shamash in Akkadian, who, by lighting up, making visible, all actions, could discover which were just and which unjust. As Bottéro points out, there was no real idea of law in ancient Mesopotamia, but rather of decision, the decision of gods or kings: justice was not abstract, it was visible only in the particular case. The Akkadian term for justice, *mêšaru*, was closely associated with kingship: "The gods have commissioned him [the king] *to make appear (to make shine) in the land mêšaru,* i.e. order at the same time as justice."[40] *Mêšaru* derives from the word *êšêru*, which means "to go straight, in the right way; to be in order."[41] Because justice was embedded in a whole way of life, an elaborate set of obligations and prohibitions including spheres we would consider having little to do with morality, we cannot equate it simply with our understanding of the term.

We know from the vast number of exorcism texts and penitential hymns that justice was often discerned retroactively: that is, if one suffered from some physical complaint or moral injustice, it must be because one had done something wrong. Divination was resorted to in an attempt to discover the "sin" one had committed, the mistake one had made, the tabu one had violated, and specialists could prescribe the right rituals and petitions that might reverse the suffered wrong. But the way of thinking about life was indelibly hierarchical. As Bottéro put it:

> Not only by virtue of the affirmed ontological superiority of their gods, whose inscrutability no one could overcome, but also by virtue of the gods' role as masters and governors of the world, they recognized the gods' sovereign privilege of complete freedom of decision and action. All the expressions and all the demonstrations of the gods' will were thus accepted within the same "civic" spirit, as it were, like the orders of the kings by their subjects: without discussion, without protest, without criticism, in a perfect and fatalistic submission, with the clear consciousness that one does not resist that which is stronger. The gods were considered too clever, too equitable, and too irreproachable for them ever to be called arbitrary or for their decision ever to be questioned. In that land, even in words, no one ever really rebelled against the most pitiless of all decisions: our universal condemnation to death.[42]

Well, not quite "no one," as we will see in a moment. There were a few prophets who foretold the fall of kings.[43] And there were intellectuals, such as the writer of the so-called "Babylonian Theodicy," who did raise questions about the justice of the gods:

> Those who do not seek the god go the way of prosperity,
> While those who pray to the goddess become destitute and
>   impoverished.[44]

Although the Mesopotamian equivalents of Job's friends do seem to get the upper hand in this dialogue, there are texts in which the mystery of reward and punishment is declared beyond human understanding:

> What seems good to oneself,
>   is a crime before the god.
> What to one's heart seems bad,
>   is good before one's god.
> Who may comprehend the minds of gods
>   In heaven's depth?

The thoughts of (those) divine deep waters,
  Who could fathom them?
How could mankind, beclouded,
  Comprehend the ways of gods?[45]

In one important respect, ancient Mesopotamia is like all the societies we have observed so far, in the last two chapters and in this one: there are notions about some kind of survival after death, but there is no idea of rewards and punishments in the afterlife, and, on the whole, such existence as there is, is uninviting. For the ancient Mesopotamians, the "netherworld," where all spirits go, varies between bad—gloomy somnolence—and worse—a realm of fierce demons. Though Bottéro is indeed right that most people took death as unquestionable, the greatest of Mesopotamian poems, the Epic of Gilgamesh, is about a legendary king who literally goes to the ends of the earth to escape death, a reality brought home to him by the premature death of his dear friend Enkidu (both Gilgamesh and Enkidu are classic upstarts). Gilgamesh, the only ancient Mesopotamian writing to have made it into the canon of world literature, and that uncertainly, is far too complex a narrative to summarize here.[46] For all the vigor of his protest and the enormous risks he takes to overcome death, Gilgamesh is at last faced with the reality that his quest is impossible, and that he has no alternative but to submit: "mere man—his days are numbered; whatever he may do, he is but wind."[47]

The term "civilization" is difficult to define, as it has been used in many ways. I am not using it as a contrast term to "uncivilized," any more than I am using the term "culture" as a contrast to "uncultured." As used descriptively, civilization is usually confined to societies that have states. The comparable term for nonstate societies is "culture area." Polynesia is a culture area, though Hawai'i might in time have given rise to Hawaiian civilization. Just as there are diverse societies speaking unrelated languages in a culture area, the American Southwest for example, so there may be many states speaking different languages within a single civilization, and, of course, none of these entities is static—all change over time.

Mesopotamian civilization was from the beginning a multi-city-state civilization. There was a common language, Sumerian, a common pantheon, and a common writing system. Early on, perhaps even from the beginning, there was a different language spoken in some of the northern cities, Akkadian, an early Semitic language (Sumerian is related to no known language group). Not only did the Akkadians share the same culture, they used the same writing system, the cuneiform system that by 2500 BCE had developed out of the original pictographs. Sumerian and Akkadian, written in cuneiform, were the classic languages of Mesopotamian culture, and tablets written in both languages were copied and studied until the end.

Efforts to create a unified state in Mesopotamia emerged in Sumer first, and then among the Akkadians: Sargon founded a new city, Agade (or Akkad), to the north of Sumer, as his capital. Later, Babylon, not far from Akkad, unified Mesopotamia, and identified its patron deity Marduk with Sumerian Enlil. The Babylonian language was a dialect of Akkadian, and Babylon claimed to be the primary exponent of classic Mesopotamian culture. Assyria, beginning in the city of Assur, well to the north of the old Mesopotamian heartland, had a more ambivalent relation to the tradition, but by identifying its patron god, Assur, with Marduk, and by amassing a great royal library of classic cuneiform literature, it, too, claimed the cultural heritage of Sumerian/Akkadian culture.

Even when, by 2000 BCE at least, Sumerian had been replaced by Akkadian everywhere in Mesopotamia as the spoken language, Sumerian texts continued to be handed down, copied, and recopied, even in Assyrian times. In the first millennium, Aramaic gradually replaced Akkadian as the spoken language, but it was written in the new alphabetic script and the guardians of the traditional culture did not use it. After the Mesopotamians lost their political independence, first to the Persians (538) then to the Greeks (330) and then to the Parthians (247 BCE), scribes continued the cuneiform tradition. The last known text written in cuneiform script dates from 75 CE, and is taken to mark the end of Mesopotamian civilization.

In an important sense, all culture is one: human beings today owe something to every culture that has gone before us. Mesopotamian culture certainly had an influence on its neighbors, notably Persia, Israel, and Greece. Some, including some notable Assyriologists such as Jean Bottéro, have wanted to see it as the first act of "Western Civilization." Others, notably Leo Oppenheim, who gave his book *Ancient Mesopotamia* the significant subtitle *Portrait of a Dead Civilization,* have wanted to emphasize the strangeness, the difference, of Mesopotamian civilization from ours.[48] An argument could be made for either position, but it would seem that Mesopotamian civilization as a comprehensive way of life did come to an end, and the last cuneiform text may be a convenient point to mark its demise, just as the last hieroglyphic text can be seen to mark the death of ancient Egyptian civilization.

Though writing is a convenient marker for a given civilization and has often been seen as an essential element in the definition of a civilization, we must be cautious in using it as such. We must be especially cautions in imagining that the invention of writing instantaneously created a "literacy revolution." If that term has any validity—if it implies a change in *mentalité*—and we will consider that possibility in a later chapter, it hardly applies to ancient Mesopotamia, Egypt, or Shang China. For one thing, early writing had quite limited usage. The archaeologist Hans Nissen goes so far as to say, "the invention of writing [in Sumer] did not mark any particularly historical turning-point."[49] In Mesopotamia, writing, together with a developing number system, was originally used primarily in registering the contributions to temples and palaces and the rations paid out by them. Still, the use of writing and numbers in accounting practices was no mean achievement, whether or not it was a "historical turning-point," and may be related to the fact that of all early civilizations, Mesopotamia had the most far-flung trade and the most developed market economy.[50] Early writing was also useful in the development of bureaucracy: orders could be transmitted to distant regions with some security that the exact instructions would reach the intended destination.[51] However, given that cuneiform (and hieroglyphic) writing was a very difficult practice, requiring years of special training, there had to be scribes in the palace or temple who could write the instructions, and scribes at the other end who could decode them. Even priests and kings might not be able to read.

Once more literary texts began to be written, often myths or hymns, segments of important rituals, they remained very close to spoken language. Their constant repetitions with minor variations show that they were frequently verbatim transcriptions of oral texts. In short, ancient civilizations, even when difficult writing systems had appeared, remained largely oral cultures throughout their history.[52] Writing did not mean the end of oral tradition; not even printing did more than make a dent in it. Although today oral tradition in most developed societies is pushed to the margins by the ubiquity of print and electronic media, it survives in many nooks and crannies in all existing societies. Because the gods—mostly benevolent, sometimes in their "wild" moods terrifying, always in the end inscrutable—were the center of concern for Mesopotamians throughout their history, perhaps the end of Mesopotamian Civilization was marked, not by the last cuneiform document to be produced, but by the last prayer to be uttered to Marduk or Assur, but of that we have no record.

Ancient Egypt

Jean Bottéro claimed ancient Mesopotamia as the "first act" of Western Civilization, but how much more often has Egypt been cast in that role? Jan Assmann in *Moses the Egyptian*[53] has traced the image of Egypt held by the ancient Hebrews and Greeks, through many centuries when knowledge of Egyptian writing was lost but fascination with Egypt continued, up until recent times when such distinguished non-Egyptologists as Thomas Mann and Sigmund Freud found Egypt foundational for the understanding of Western culture. It has been my intention in this book to try to understand each religion in its own cultural context, so far as possible as its adherents understood it. This admittedly utopian enterprise itself, however, is culturally situated, made possible only by cultural developments, including massive scholarly advances, in recent times.

Nonetheless, when it comes to Egypt the baggage of preconceptions, even of prejudice, is heavy. A strongly negative picture pervades the opening books of the Hebrew Bible, particularly Exodus (the Joseph story in Genesis is a bit more nuanced), with Egypt as the very archetype of idolatry, the primary sin that the children of Israel must avoid at all cost, but also the archetype of oppression and slavery. Even a recent book that I admire, Michael Walzer's *Exodus and Revolution*,[54] makes ancient Egypt the very symbol of everything we want to get away from, even to this day. On the opposite side—from Plato to the present—Egypt has been seen as the source of ancient wisdom, the origin of human culture. I will try to avoid the tendency either to demonize ancient Egypt or to idealize it, and to approach it as much as possible not from what followed but from what came before, from the point of view, say, of Tikopia, Hawai'i, or ancient Mesopotamia.

Barry Kemp, the distinguished archaeologist of ancient Egypt, states well the situation in which anyone who undertakes what I have undertaken finds himself, however well intentioned: "I am aware as I write this book that I am creating in my own mind images that I hope correspond to the way things were in ancient Egypt. I also know that the more I try to make sense of the facts, the more what I write is speculative and begins to merge with the world of historical fiction, a modern form of myth. My ancient Egypt is very much an imagined world, though I hope that it cannot too readily be shown to be untrue to the original ancient sources."[55] I would only add that history *is* our myth—as Jan Assmann puts it: "History turns into myth as soon as it is remembered, narrated, and used, that is, woven into the fabric of the present. The mythical qualities of history have nothing to do with its truth values."[56] To put it in one word, as William McNeill does, what we are doing is "mythistory."[57] Looking at our project in these terms should bring us into closer sympathy with cultures such as ancient Egypt in which myth is a primary cultural form. To the extent that we are also creatures of myth in that "we are what we remember,"[58] we are in the same boat as the ancient Egyptians.

Another German Egyptologist reminds us that we are even one step closer to the ancient Egyptians. Not only do we still have our own myths, we cannot escape theirs:

> Any sort of contact with the world of the Egyptians silences one question, that of the reality and existence of these gods. Egyptian religion lived on the fact that gods exist. If we remove the gods from the Egyptians' world, all that remains is a dark, uninhabited shell that would not repay study . . . In order to understand the forces that circumscribe the very closed and homogeneous world of the Egyptians, we must inquire after their gods and employ all our conceptual armory in order to seek out the reality of these gods—a reality that was not invented by human beings but *experienced* by them.[59]

Given that "we" are the product of all previous human culture, we have, at some level "already" experienced those gods, as we have "already" experienced the powerful beings of tribal peoples. If we are truly to understand ancient Egyptian religion (or any religion), it will be part of our task to "remember" what we have forgotten, but which in some sense we already know.

If Mesopotamia in many ways looked like the antithesis of Hawai'i, predynastic Egypt provides more than a few parallels, improbable though that may seem. Egypt was certainly not as isolated as an island in the mid-Pacific, but compared to Mesopotamia it looks isolated. Egypt is effectively the Nile Valley from the First Cataract to the Mediterranean. Due to the yearly inundations of the Nile bringing new alluvial soil and avoiding both the need for irrigation and the problem of salinization, the valley was one of the most fertile strips of land in the world. It was bounded, however, on both sides by virtually impassable desert, and was thus much less vulnerable to incursions from without than was Mesopotamia. It was, however, vulnerable in several spots: from the upper Nile region known as Nubia, from Libya to the northwest, and from the northeast region, that is Palestine and beyond, inhabited by what the Egyptians called "Asiatics." It was also vulnerable to the sea along the coast of the Nile Delta. For the first 2,000 years of its dynastic history the vulnerable frontiers were breached only once, by Asiatics known as the Hyksos, who managed to rule the delta for a hundred years in the mid-second millennium BCE. Egypt's partial isolation was only definitively breached in the first millennium BCE when the surrounding world had become more "developed." Not only were there Nubian and Libyan rulers, but disorienting conquests by Asiatics—the Assyrians, and for a longer period the Persians—by the Greeks, that is, Alexander the Great and the Ptolemaic Empire that followed, and finally by the Romans. The first millennium BCE in Egypt was a period of considerable creativity and innovation even though the country was under unprecedented outside pressure and influence, but before that Egyptian civilization had developed for 2,000 years with little outside influence and with continuity of language and population. This among other reasons makes ancient Egypt remarkable. It was the longest lasting, most continuous, and best documented of the archaic civilizations and as such has to be Exhibit A when considering them. It also illustrates the considerable capacity for transformation within such civilizations as well as the limits beyond which those transformations apparently could not go.

Although dynastic Egyptian civilization seems to burst on the scene with stunning brilliance at the end of the fourth millennium BCE, it was not without centuries of preparation. An agricultural population of rather homogeneous culture grew gradually from about 5500 BCE to the end of the fourth millennium. During the last centuries of that millennium, and more clearly in Upper Egypt[60] than in the delta, there were growing signs of hierarchy and stratification, mainly indicated by the appearance of elite graves with luxury grave goods. Graves and tombs, as we will see, were matters of great importance to the Egyptians from the earliest times.

In the immediate predynastic period, that is, circa 3100 BCE, several paramount chiefdoms or early states appear to have emerged in Upper Egypt, the most important of which were Hierakonpolis and Naqada.[61] There is every indication that warfare between these polities was intense and that the unified state was the result of the military victory of one of the competing polities. Ideology was significant from the beginning: Naqada was associated with the god Seth and Hierakonpolis with the god Horus. When Hierakonpolis conquered Naqada to form what Kemp calls the Proto-Kingdom of Upper Egypt, the union was symbolized by the association of Horus and Seth as the expression of the unity of the "two lands" (later extended to mean

Upper and Lower Egypt), followed by the conquest of the whole country and the founding of the First Dynasty, with its new capital at Memphis, not far from present-day Cairo, where the delta begins to diverge from the main stream of the river.

The whole process of transition is obscure. There was some writing, in particular names of kings and deities, but continuous texts do not appear for several centuries, so no textual account of the founding exists until long after the historical fact. The first several dynasties saw a remarkable flowering of culture and the creation of cultural forms in several realms that would continue, not without some change, until the end of Egyptian civilization in the early centuries CE. The details, however, are far from clear: there is argument about the names and order of the early kings. Toby Wilkinson, among others, postulates a Dynasty 0, from about 3100 to 3000 BCE.[62] The first three dynasties, generally called protodynastic or early dynastic, lasted until 2600 BCE, when, with the Fourth Dynasty, the Old Kingdom begins.

Michael Hoffman offers a number of reasons for the cultural florescence that accompanied the rise of a unified Egyptian state at the beginning of dynastic history. He cites the long period of population growth leading up to significant demographic concentrations in several parts of Upper Egypt; the extraordinary productivity of the land and the possibility of aggregating resources through taxation and storage; the rapid development of sophisticated craft production and architecture; and perhaps above all the centrality of the mortuary cult already in the first two dynasties, that will remain, through many vicissitudes, such an identifying characteristic of Egyptian culture:

> As Egypt consolidated from local chieftainships into regional kingdoms, into the world's first national state, it developed the royal tomb as its flag: a symbol of political integration under god . . . From our brief exposure to the study of known mortuary practices and monuments, we can conclude that the development and function of the royal mortuary cult in late prehistoric and early historic Egypt (between about 3300 and 2700 BCE) was one of the most socially, economically, and politically sensitive indicators of the rise of the state and was one of the most important reasons why Egyptian civilization emerged when it did and in the fashion that it did.[63]

In the absence of continuous texts until well into the Old Kingdom, that is, toward the end of the Fifth Dynasty, around 2400 BCE, it is difficult to reconstruct religious belief and practice. Many local gods are known, and the centrality of some of the gods, such as Horus and Seth, as mentioned above, is clear, but we know little of the context of myth in which these gods may have been embedded. For instance, the name of Osiris, known as the father of Horus in later times, is missing in the early dynastic period and even his existence then can only be inferred indirectly. On the other hand the relation between Horus and the king is clearly central. The naming of Egyptian kings is complex and became more so over time, but from the very beginning Horus figured prominently in the name of every king. Horus's emblem is the falcon, but it would be a mistake to call him a "falcon god." The name Horus means "the one on high." The falcon then, rather than an exclusive identity, associates him with the sky, perhaps even with the sun. In any case, as Kemp puts it, "Horus is the one deity whose figure appears unambiguously in association with Early Dynastic kings. The figure of the falcon . . . stands alone above a heraldic device containing the principal name of the king."[64]

A critical question for us in trying to understand archaic religion is the question whether the king is Horus in a strong sense—that is, is he divine, an instantiation of the god himself? This question has been answered variously. Henri Frankfort has argued for divine kingship,[65] whereas Georges Posener has held that the king is only metaphorically a god.[66] Jan Assmann in a number of works has argued for a changing understanding of the king's divinity, from god to son of god, to chosen by god, to servant of god. Perhaps the key is a changing understanding of divinity itself. In the Old Kingdom (third millennium BCE), ritual was not an interaction between gods and human beings, but an interaction between "gods" themselves. As Assmann puts it, ritual *"was not conceived of as a communication between the human and the divine, but rather as an interaction between deities."*[67] What this means in practice is that ritual language is "uttered as divine speeches by priests who play the roles of the deities in question as they carry out the respective cultic acts. The words uttered while performing the cultic acts are thus the words of the deities, sacred words whose radiant power makes it possible to illuminate the otherworldly meaning of what is happening in this-worldly events."[68]

This begins to make sense if we see that the "gods" of early dynastic Egypt are only incipiently differentiated from the "powerful beings" of tribal people, and that they are more identified with than worshipped, so that Assmann's "otherworldly" and "this-worldly" are only aspects of a largely undifferentiated cosmos. In this context it makes sense to say that the king *is* Horus, in that he enacts Horus rather than worships him. Thus we could perhaps say that the early Egyptian king is Horus in the sense that the Hawaiian king is Kū. With the sun god Re of the Middle Kingdom things were undoubtedly different, as they perhaps were even in the later Old Kingdom when Re had become central and the king was said to be "the son of Re" rather than Re himself. But even though the relation between king and god evolved over time, Assmann also reminds us that the idea of the divinity of the king persisted. In the first four dynasties, "The ruler is not an image of god, he *is* god," but in later times things are not entirely different: "Even in its classical, representative form, pharaonic kingship never entirely relinquished the idea that the pharaoh, son of god, was the incarnation of god. The god embodied by the pharaoh, however, was typically demoted to a filial rank: the pharaoh did not embody Amun, Re, or Ptah, but Horus, the son of Osiris, and as such the Son."[69] But of course Horus was the god of kings before Amun, Re, or Ptah came on the scene and probably before Osiris was clearly established as his father.

The fusion of the divine and the human in the person of the king is perhaps the central expression of the "compact symbolism" which Erich Voegelin sees as characterizing tribal religion and only gradually differentiating in the history of archaic societies, not to be radically broken through until the axial age.[70] The king, whether as incarnation, son, or servant of the gods, is the key link between humans and the cosmos such that the weakness or absence of the king is a sign of profound cosmic and social disorder; the proper functioning of the king is the primary guarantee of life and peace.

Just as the powerful beings of tribal peoples were violent as well as benevolent, and in ancient Mesopotamia one never knew what Enlil might do, so chaos and disorder were never far from the consciousness of the ancient Egyptians. Erik Hornung describes an Egyptian understanding of reality going back as far as the Fifth Dynasty of the Old Kingdom in which chaos, defined as limitless waters and total darkness, preceded the coming into being of the first god, surrounds the finite universe, and will ultimately prevail when the cosmos grows old and is reabsorbed into it. Further, chaos not only surrounds the cosmos but penetrates it continuously, requiring equally continual human action to deal with it.[71]

This human action, focusing on the king, takes two main forms. One is the "hostile confrontation" with "the powers that belong to the nonexistent outside creation but invade creation and must be driven out of it. It is the duty of the king and the gods to do this."[72] Such negative powers can be represented by foreign enemies—Libyans or Asiatics—as well as by domestic rebels, or, indeed by anyone who transgresses the proper order of the world. From the earliest beginnings of Egyptian kingship there appears the image of "the smiting of the enemies," often a painting or relief of the pharaoh holding a number of enemies or rebels by the hair while wielding a weapon with which he will destroy them. Military power was always associated with the Egyptian state and had a powerful symbolic justification in holding the line against chaos.

But there was another aspect of the confrontation with chaos or the non-existent, namely its essential role in "fertility, renewal, and rejuvenation."[73] Unless the sun, which grows old at dusk, descends into the utter darkness of the underworld, it will not be reborn at dawn; unless the land is submerged by the inundation of the Nile, it will not bear new crops; unless all things, including humans, die, life will not continue. All these transactions with chaos are dangerous and must be acted out with meticulous ritual propriety, but it is only through them that life as we know it can go on. As the sun, from the Fifth Dynasty on, became ever more central in Egyptian religion, solar ritual became the primary focus of the cult. Unless the ritual was properly enacted, that is, carried out every hour of the day and night, in principle by the king but usually delegated to his priestly deputies, the very source of life would be endangered.

It is this second kind of confrontation with chaos, dangerous but not hostile, indeed essential, that helps us understand the importance of mortuary ritual and royal tombs in Egyptian history. The apparent Egyptian preoccupation with death was in reality a preoccupation with life. Because the death of the king was the greatest threat to human order, special precautions needed to be undertaken to be sure that it rendered life and not death. Tombs were not built, pyramids were not constructed *after* the death of the king, but such construction began early in his reign. The king's son was obligated to complete the work and undertake the funeral ritual, but we know that the tombs of kings who died early were seldom impressive. Royal tombs, above all the great pyramids of the Fourth Dynasty, which remain among the wonders of the world, were monuments to the life of the king, before and after death. We could even refer to them as the reified rituals of divine kingship, the "flags" in Kemp's analogy, of the ancient Egyptian state.

When we first find decorated tombs in the Fifth Dynasty and later, the scenes depicted are full of life, not only the daily life of humans, but the life of animals and plants as well. In later centuries the preoccupation with the netherworld grew and representations of daily life were no longer so evident. But the "afterlife" to the ancient Egyptians was not viewed as a radically other world, but as a continuation of this one. From this point of view, as Hornung emphasizes, the relation between order and chaos was "anything but negative," because the right relation between them was the very source of everything the Egyptians most valued.[74]

John Baines, among others, has taken pains to remind us that the lives of most of the ancient Egyptians were hard and, all too often, brief. In a population of 1 to 1.5 million, the real elite was a "close-knit group of a few hundred . . . The core elite together with their families numbered two or three thousand people." Even when including secondary elites and local administrators who had some degree of literacy, together with their families, the "ruling class" only composed 3 to 5 percent of the population.[75] Although Baines argues that the daily life of the great majority was little different from that of Neolithic villagers, and local identification, particularly with the local deities or local versions of widely known deities, remained important throughout Egyptian history, the centralized Egyptian state reached into the village economically in the form of taxes, politically through military conscription or corvée labor, and almost certainly culturally. Especially during the early dynasties the royal court was peripatetic, regularly voyaging up and down the Nile, so that most villagers would have had some experience of the royal presence in their neighborhood. The contrast in style of life between that of the court and that of the villagers would indeed have given most people the impression that the king was a living god.

In Egypt as in other early archaic states, centralization of power under the leadership of the king was associated with remarkable cultural creativity in the development of writing, art, and architecture, but also with experiments in pushing the limits of human power. Evidence for human sacrifice in late predynastic and early dynastic Egypt is not plentiful, but is sufficient to make it clear that it was practiced. Retainer sacrifice of wives, officials, and servants occurred in the First and Second Dynasties, but then ceases.[76] Retainer burial is a marker of the extraordinary status of the king, who can take his closest associates with him into the afterlife, unlike ordinary mortals.

But the most extreme example of pushing the limits of power must be the building of the great pyramids of the Fourth Dynasty, after retainer sacrifice had been abandoned. Impressive tombs are a hallmark of Egyptian culture before and after the Old Kingdom, but nothing in Egyptian history or that of any other archaic society comes near to equaling the colossal undertaking involved in the construction of the great pyramids of Cheops and Khephren at Giza in the middle of the third millennium BCE, engineering feats not equaled again in human history until the twentieth century CE. The wealth and manpower of the whole country must have been mobilized for decades to complete these enormous projects. The workmen who actually produced these monuments were not slaves, but ordinary villagers from all over the country who were required to spend given periods of time at the construction site. If there was no "national economy" earlier, this vast building project surely created one. But it also undoubtedly strained the early state to its limits. Just as retainer sacrifice had been abandoned earlier, so such gigantic construction projects were never repeated. Jan Assmann views the building of the great pyramids as a kind of culmination of the building of the early state:

> In a sense the great pyramids of Giza represent the culmination of a process that began in Naqada [late predynastic period]. The tombs become increasingly monumental and the power of the chief (later the pharaoh) becomes greater and greater, taking on divine dimensions until the pharaoh becomes akin to the Supreme God. This increasing divinization of the ruler finds visual expression in the development of the royal tombs—a process that reaches its logical conclusion at Giza . . . The state provides the immense forces and organizational resources without which the architecture would be impossible. Thus the pyramids also symbolize and visualize the organizational prowess of the state, as embodied in the king, whose will is strong enough to move mountains.[77]

These great pyramids, visible to anyone traveling up or down the Nile for the last 4500 years, made, as Herodotus put it, even time afraid. They too will pass away, but unlike most Egyptian monuments, not any time soon.

It is ironic that, because we have no inscriptions associated with them, we know little about the exact meaning of the great pyramids. In Egypt as in Mesopotamia many centuries pass from the "invention of writing" until the appearance of continuous texts. Even when such texts do appear in the Fifth and Sixth Dynasties, their subject matter is very limited: administration and temple, above all mortuary, ritual. For one thing the literate class was still extremely small. For another, oral culture does not disappear with the invention of writing—far from it—and much cultural knowledge was still entrusted to living memory rather than writing. Early writing gives us insight only into fragments of a whole way of life, a way of life primarily transmitted not only orally but mimetically, that is, by example.[78]

But the Old Kingdom, destined to remain forever enclosed in more than a little mystery, in spite of its claim through the great pyramids to overcome time, did in fact come to an end, and was followed by what is known as the First Intermediate Period at the end of the third millennium, that is, roughly 2150 to 2040 BCE. Because in archaic societies there is no such thing as "religion" or "politics" (we use those terms only analytically to describe dimensions of what was concretely a single whole), societal collapse and religious crisis are two ways of describing the same phenomenon. When the centralized state disintegrated and whoever claimed to be king exercised no effective power, then local upstarts appeared. Assmann speaks of an alternation in Egyptian history between the "monocentric surface" of the centralized state and the "polycentric deep structure" that reappeared whenever the surface structure crumbled. Not only did the geographic entities of the predynastic period reemerge, but something of the ethos of the earlier period appeared as well: namely the culture of the "violent hearted," for upstarts rule by force and survive only by military victory.[79]

Nonetheless, centuries of dynastic history could not be obliterated and what at first glance looks to be a period of regression was in fact a period of marked cultural advance. Local power claimants could no longer act as appointees of the king: they had to seek other sources of justification. Naked power may have been the initial basis of local rule, but was not alone sufficient. Rather than claiming appointment by the king, local rulers claimed to have been appointed by the local god, and local cults flourished at the expense of the high gods. Rulers gave evidence of their divine chosenness by their capacity to bring order and even justice to the local scene.

Endemic civil war interrupted the smooth transmission of oral and mimetic culture; a new flowering of written texts arose to fill the gap. Austere and relatively brief autobiographical texts from late Old Kingdom tombs have been found, often perfunctorily listing the magnanimous deeds of the deceased. But such autobiographical texts flourish in the first Intermediate Period. They give a dark picture of surrounding conditions in order to highlight the achievements of the local ruler. The autobiographical inscription of one such ruler, the Nomarch[80] Ankhtifi of Hierakonpolis and Edfu, states:

I am the vanguard of men and the rearguard of men. One who finds the solution where it is lacking. A leader of the land through active conduct. Strong in speech, collected in thought, on the day of joining the three nomes. For I am a champion without peer, who spoke out when the people were silent, on the day of fear when Upper Egypt was silent.[81]

Already in the Old Kingdom norms of moral obligation to the common people were reiterated in mortuary inscriptions. Ankhtifi resumes and expands this tradition when he claims:

I gave the hungry bread
And clothing to the naked,
I anointed the unanointed,
I shod the barefoot,
I gave him a wife who had no wife.[82]

But with Ankhtifi these acts were not merely the reiteration of established moral norms. In a time when people were dying of hunger and even eating their children, every norm of ordinary morality was being violated. Thus when Ankhtifi asserted:

I rescued the weak from the strong,
I gave ear to the matter of the widow.

he was engaged in what Assmann calls "saving justice."[83] He was not a bureaucrat operating under established moral norms, but a patron protecting, indeed saving, his clients from disaster and expecting loyalty in return. Assmann sees in this the emergence of a new rhetoric: "The rhetoric of crisis and salvation foregrounds the patron as a savior whose achievements have preserved the nome from the certain disaster seen everywhere else."[84] If crisis conditions place a new emphasis on loyalty to the patron, they consign the disloyal to destruction. Assmann believes that the culture of loyalism created in the disastrous circumstances of the First Intermediate Period, became central to the culture of the Middle Kingdom, when fear of chaos was used to justify rule long after the country had been successfully reunited.

Assmann sees a shifting pattern of Egyptian values accompanying the oscillations between monocentric and polycentric polities. "Integration" was the norm in periods of unity; "competition" in periods of disunity. It was the task of the Middle Kingdom (2040–1650 BCE) to move the new cultural rhetoric of the First Intermediate Period from the context of competition to the context of integration. But times had changed. The centralized state was not the isolated pinnacle that it had been in the Old Kingdom, when all faces were turned to the center. The center had to attract the loyalty of the newly independent and vigorous peripheries by cultural, not just military means. Assmann describes the problem:

> On the one hand, it was necessary to reestablish the norms of integrative ethics and self-effacement so radically challenged by the collapse of the Old Kingdom. On the other, these norms had to be universalized: the ethic of a tiny privileged minority had to be transformed into the ethic of a broad cultural elite representing Egyptian ideals and sustaining the existence of the state. Something akin to "education" was needed. Indeed, the Middle Kingdom was the first to find that it required a systematic education policy as part of its project of political restoration.[85]

Education required schools and standard texts, as well as new genres of writing. It is from the Middle Kingdom that we begin to find "wisdom" texts, hymns and tales. "Literature" is a dangerous word as its origins are so recent in the West, but if we use the word cautiously, then we can begin to speak of Egyptian literature from early in the second millennium BCE. Of particular importance are the so-called "instruction texts" in which often a father imparts worldly wisdom to his son, but which also contain significant new religious ideas. To students of ancient China this focus on moral education for a bureaucratic ruling class, with a high regard for certain "classic" texts, will sound more than a little familiar, even though Confucianism in China developed many centuries later. As we will see, the differences are as important as the parallels.

The ancient Egyptian system of moral norms was summed up in a single term: *ma'at*. The term has been variously translated as order, justice or truth. None of these translations is wrong, but none is adequate, for, as Eric Voegelin puts it, "The symbol is too compact to be translated by a single word in a modern language. As the Maat of the cosmos it would have to be rendered as order; as the Maat of society, as good government and justice; as the Maat of true understanding of ordered reality, as truth."[86] Assmann proposes the translation "connective justice," emphasizing the element of reciprocity that forms communities and establishes obligations. He cites a royal inscription from around 1700 BCE:

> The reward of one who does something lies in something being
>   done for him.
> This is considered by god as *maʿat*.[87]

If *maʿat* points to the generalized reciprocity that is central for tribal societies and found in most moral systems subsequently, for the Egyptians it became substantial in the form of a goddess. Its "religious" status is indicated by the frequent depiction of the king offering *maʿat* as a small statue of the goddess to the god being addressed, who is said to "feed on" *maʿat*. Such a small statue of the goddess appears frequently in depictions of the judgment of the dead where the "heart" of the deceased is put on the scales opposite to the statue of the goddess. A heart lacking in *maʿat* will sink, thus condemning the deceased to nonexistence.

The appearance of the heart as a central symbol in ancient Egyptian religion is itself a symptom of the changed relation between god, king and humans after the First Intermediate Period. The "loyalism" that linked the local ruler to his god and his followers to him was generalized in the Middle Kingdom to the realm as a whole. The idea of kingship growing out of this way of thinking was closer to the Mesopotamian model of rule than to that of the Old Kingdom.[88] None of the old symbols were abandoned: the king was still Horus, and the son of Re. But the emphasis now was on the king as steward of the god, as chosen by the god; it was the god who was the real ruler.

But the king was also, on a grand scale, the patron and protector of the people. If Assmann uses the term "savior," he does not mean a savior from this world, but a savior in this world. In summing up he says, "Egyptian civilization needs no Redeemer, only a 'good shepherd' protecting his sheep from the wolves."[89] Concomitantly, the king requires a more consciously willed loyalty than would have seemed necessary in the Old Kingdom. Assmann describes a kind of history of the heart, remembering that in Egyptian heart means more than it does in English: it includes mind and will as well as feeling. In the Old Kingdom the elite ideal was the "king-guided individual." There is no mention of the individual heart for "the heart of the king thinks and plans for all." In the Middle Kingdom the ideal is the "heart-guided individual," the person whose loyalty has been internalized, whose veneration of the king has become part of his innermost self. The New Kingdom will see another development, the "god-guided individual," but that must await consideration until a bit later.

Assmann argues that the Egyptian emphasis on the role of the ruler as protector of the weak against the strong, of the poor against the wealthy, as the upholder of any semblance of order against the chaos of civil discord, was a kind of Hobbesian justification of what was in some ways a police state in the Middle Kingdom.[90] Yet he is also aware that we are not talking about a Neolithic village where village elders could maintain order, much less a hunter-gatherer band ruled by a general will. When large-scale agricultural societies break down, violence and horrors of all sorts not infrequently erupt. One may doubt how many of the weak and poor the pharaoh really protected against the privileged of the land, but that his rule kept mayhem at bay may not have been just ruling class propaganda. It may have been appreciated, and not only by elite classes.

It is in the New Kingdom (1550–1070 BCE) that something that at least incipiently can be called theology flowers, but conscious reflection on religious meaning begins in the Middle Kingdom if not before. In order to understand the nature of Egyptian religious reflection, there are certain things we must consider. In *The Search for God in Ancient Egypt,* Assmann describes three dimensions of what he calls implicit theology, that is, aspects that appear primarily in practice: the local or cultic, the cosmic, and the mythic. He then describes what he calls the "fourth dimension," explicit theology. He warns us early on that there was no "theoretical discourse" in ancient Egypt,[91] which makes his use of the term "theology" problematic. Eric Voegelin suggests a term for reflection that pushes mythical thinking to its limit—to the verge of theoretical reflection without ever quite crossing the boundary—mythospeculation.[92] This might be a better term for Assmann's fourth dimension than explicit theology.

The three dimensions of implicit theology, which, Assmann says, were "confined entirely to the sphere of practice,"[93] comprise the basic continuity that makes it possible "to speak of 'the' religion of ancient Egypt, in the singular."[94] Although Egyptian religion had its unique features, it is not entirely wrong to see it also as a species in the genus "polytheistic religions of the ancient Near East," as long as we realize that such religions "represent highly developed cultural achievements that are inseparably linked to the political organization of the early state and are not to be found in tribal societies."[95] As in other archaic societies, the king had a central role in each of the dimensions of religious practice.[96] The king was responsible for the performance of cult and the construction and upkeep of the temples where cult was performed, not only in the capital, but throughout the country. Although tombs were important in every period of Egyptian history, after the Old Kingdom, temples replaced tombs as the site of major construction under royal patronage, a practice that continued well into Ptolemaic times. Temples were so important and so numerous that in a late text Egypt was called "the temple of the whole world."[97] The king through ritual was also responsible for the maintenance of cosmic order, the daily passage of the sun and the annual inundation of the Nile. Finally, the king was at the center of the "central myth" that sustained the Egyptian state, namely, the myth of Horus as the son and successor of Osiris, but also as the beloved of all the gods.[98] The centrality of the king in every dimension of religious practice, however differently phrased in each society, was something common to all archaic societies.

Myth as a symbolic form was basic to Egyptian religion, but myth in the sense of extended narrative does not appear to have been as highly developed as in Mesopotamia, where it largely supplied what secondary reflection on religious meaning there was. Although allusions to aspects of the myth of Isis, Osiris, and Horus can be found in many Egyptian texts, it is indicative that the only "complete version" of the myth is Plutarch's hellenized version, written in Greek in the second century CE.[99]

Mythospeculation (Assmann's explicit theology), however, not unknown in other archaic societies, was particularly highly developed in Egypt, and underwent significantly more historical change than did religious practice (Assmann's implicit theology). Its social location was the educated, literate elite, largely a product of the Middle Kingdom and later. In the New Kingdom the existence for the first time of a professional priesthood as a subgroup of the literate elite gave further impetus to mythospeculation. I will consider two texts of the Middle Kingdom to give some sense of what early Egyptian mythospeculation was like. It is important to notice that both texts either describe or are the words of "the god." Much ink has been spilled as to whether they give evidence of a latent "monotheism," a discussion that Erik Hornung has pretty well disposed of.[100] The existence of the gods is taken for granted in both texts, so in that sense they are polytheistic. But they are also clearly addressed to a god who cannot be subsumed among the other gods and whose status is the focus of the mythospeculation. The "Instruction to Merikare" is attributed to the First Intermediate Period, but is almost certainly a product of the Middle Kingdom. After a good deal of worldly advice this Instruction has a "theological" coda of considerable interest:

> Well tended is mankind—god's cattle,
> He made sky and earth for their sake,
> He subdued the water monster,
> He made breath for their noses to live,
> They are his images, who came from his body,
> He shines in the sky for their sake;
> For them he made plants and cattle,
> Fowl and fish to feed them.
> He slew his foes, reduced his children,
> When they thought of making rebellion.
> He makes daylight for their sake;
> He sails by to see them.
> He has built his shrine around them,
> When they weep he hears.
> He made for them rulers in the egg.
> Leaders to raise the back of the weak.
> He made for them magic as weapons
> To ward off the blows of events.
> Guarding them by day and by night.
> He has slain the traitors among them,
> As a man beats his son for his brother's sake,
> For god knows every name.[101]

One cannot but observe in this passage themes that appear to be parallel to themes in the Hebrew Scriptures: mankind in God's image, for example, and the combination of loving care and punishment of rebellion. But this is not Yahweh. What "god" means in such passages is problematic.

Apparently a notion of the divine as having a concern for the welfare of humans was widespread enough to arouse reproaches during the First Intermediate Period, or in the memory of it in the Middle Kingdom. The "Admonitions of Ipuwer" complains that not only the king, but also "the god" have been derelict in their duty of taking care of the people. Ipuwer reproaches the god who brought human beings into existence: "Where is he today? Is he asleep? His power is not seen."[102]

But a remarkable defense of the "all-lord" is mounted in Coffin Text 1130 from the Middle Kingdom, a text that Assmann believes belongs in the developing tradition of wisdom literature. The text is an apology for the god against such accusations as Ipuwer's. In order to "still the anger" the god recounts his "four good deeds":

> (1) I performed four good deeds in the threshold of Light-land:
> I made the four winds,
> So that everyone could breathe in his time.
> That is one of my deeds.
> (2) I made the great flood,
> so that the poor man would have use of it like the rich man.
> That is one of the deeds.
> (3) I made each one like his fellow
> and forbade that they do evil.
> But their hearts resisted what I had said.
> That is one of the deeds.
> (4) I caused that their hearts cease forgetting the West,
> so that offerings would be made to the deities of the nomes.
> That is one of the deeds.[103]

What is striking about this text is the emphasis on equality. One can see in this text a remarkable forerunner of the assertion that "all men are created equal." The god has given the wind (the prevailing north wind brings blessed coolness to Egypt's otherwise desert heat), and the inundation of the Nile to all, rich and poor alike. And he made all humans alike, forbidding them to do evil. It is humans, not the god, who have created oppression and caused the difference between rich and poor, strong and weak.

Significant in these early texts is their intertextuality: they represent a continuing dialogue about the nature of god and the relation between god, morality, and existing social conditions. The king is not missing—the Instruction to Merikare indicates that the god has created rulers to protect the weak—but the focus is not on glorifying the king but on justifying the god. If the form is not theoretic, it is surely forensic, and forensic is probably one of the sources from which theoretical discourse developed. It is worth noting the importance of the forensic mode in the Hebrew scriptures.[104] All of this is to suggest that the axial age (mid-first millennium BCE), to be discussed in Chapter 6, did not come into the world unprepared. Much Egyptian mythospeculation is at least proto-axial, and we will have to return to it when we reach the axial age.

The New Kingdom (1550–1070 BCE) was founded by Ahmose, who succeeded in driving the Hyksos out of Egypt and reuniting the country. But the early rulers of the Eighteenth Dynasty not only drove the "Asiatics" out, they pursued them into their hinterland, establishing what is often called the New Empire, including Palestine, parts of Syria, and even, more briefly, northern Iraq. It was thus one of the first multiethnic empires (the Hittite Empire being another) already in the middle of the second millennium BCE, a phenomenon that would be increasingly important in the first millennium BCE. Even while recognizing that there were other realms, particularly in the northeast, the Egyptians laid claim to universal rule, a development that has often been linked to the increasing sense of universality in the Egyptian understanding of divinity. With the New Kingdom the promising beginnings of Middle Kingdom mythospeculation became far more explicit.[105] Without becoming God in the sense of the monotheistic religions, the god (who is often unnamed, but who could be identified as Re, Amun-Re, Ptah,[106] or others) has a kind of reality that transcends not only humans but "the gods." Without ever losing connection to the social order and its earthly upholder, the king, the god becomes more clearly than ever, the god of individuals, and, although the evidence is uncertain, almost surely the god of ordinary people, not only the cultured elite.

A priest of Amun composed the following hymn to Amun (whose name means literally, the hidden one) in the 1330s:

> Turn back to us, O lord of the plenitude of time!
> You were here when nothing had come into being,
> and you will be here when "they" are at an end.
> You let me see darkness that you give—
> shine for me that I might see you!
> Oh, how good it is to follow you,
> Amun, O lord,
> great to find for the one who seeks him!
> Drive off fear, place joy
> in the heart of humankind!
> How happy is the face that beholds you, Amun:
> it is in festival day after day.[107]

Amun fulfils the old understanding of divine assistance to the poor and the weak, but the idea is now personalized, available to the individual. It is a passage like this that allows us to understand why Assmann says that in the New Kingdom the ideal has changed from the king-guided individual and the heart-guided individual to the god-guided individual, so that in another text, something like the idea of "salvation" appears:

> You are Amun, lord of the silent,
> who comes at the call of the poor.
> I called to you when I was in sorrow,
> and you came to save me.
> You gave breath to the one who was imprisoned,
> and saved me when I was in bonds.
> You are Amun-Re, lord of Thebes,
> you save the one in the netherworld.
> You are the one who is gracious to him who calls on him,
> you are the one who comes from afar![108]

Here the god, Amun or whoever, seems almost to be outside time and beyond the cosmos (you were here before the beginning and will be here after the end), but another side of late Egyptian mythospeculation, never seen as contradicting the side tending toward transcendence, symbolizes the god not as beyond the cosmos, but *as* the cosmos:

> Your two eyes are the sun and the moon,
> your head is the sky,
> your feet are the netherworld.
> You are the sky,
> you are the earth,
> you are the netherworld,
> you are the water,
> you are the air between them.[109]

Seeing the god as the cosmos, particularly as the sun, allows for a sense of human participation in the divine life, for the light of the sun, which surrounds us, is the presence of the god. As one hymn to the sun puts it: "All eyes see through you. They can do nothing when Your Majesty goes down."[110] Assmann cites a passage from Goethe that picks up the theme of human participation in the light of the sun:

> If the eye did not partake of the sun
> How could it gaze on the light?

If we did not share in the power of God
In the godly we could not delight.[111]

It is the very capacity to think of the creator god now as Amun, now as
Ptah, as beyond the cosmos and identical with the cosmos, as distant from
humans yet participating in them, without worrying about apparent contradictions, that keeps this remarkable tradition of reflection within the realm
of mythospeculation rather than theoretical discourse.

Except for one brief moment: Akhenaten (1352–1338) and his so-called
(from the name of his capital city) Amarna religion.[112] The pharaoh Ameno-
phis IV changed his name to Akhenaten, obliterating Amun from his name,
and, in intention, from the whole of Egypt, proclaiming Aten, the sun disk,
as the sole god. The experiment lasted twenty years at most and by fifty years
after Akenaten's death had been obliterated from conscious memory, only to
be rediscovered by archaeologists in the nineteenth century. Though clearly
indebted to the mythospeculation that had arisen in the Middle Kingdom
and flourished in the New Kingdom, Akhenaten's religion prefigures and is
perhaps even subterraneously related to axial religions, in particular the religion of Israel, and had best be considered in Chapter 6. But however radical
the Amarna religion was in some respects, it was regressive in one respect
that links it indelibly to the archaic, not the axial, religious moment: there
was no way the people could relate directly to Aten; knowledge of him came
only through pharaoh; and even if there was one god, pharaoh, as his son,
and even pharaoh's wife, were also divine.

However variously the relation between the divine and the human was
figured in archaic religions, the role of the king was always central. Even
when, as in Egypt, piety had become democratized and private devotion was
widespread, the formation of religious community depended on kingship.
The conquerors of Egypt knew this well: the Persians, Alexander, and the
Ptolemies, even the Romans, took the role of pharaoh as essential for the
maintenance of religio-social order in Egypt. Only when Christianity had
decisively replaced the ancient religion could the vestigial role of pharaoh be
abandoned altogether.

Shang and Western Zhou China

The first thing to note with respect to ancient China in comparison with ancient Mesopotamia and Egypt is that the absolute chronology of the archaic

begins significantly later. The earliest writing we have from China dates to about 1200 BCE, nearly 2,000 years later than in the Middle East. Nonetheless there is every reason to believe that archaic civilization in China was largely indigenous and owed little to any other civilization. The Chinese Neolithic is exceptionally well known so that we have a picture of a long gradual development toward a stratified society and an early state by the middle of the second millennium BCE, with little indication of significant influence from the outside.[113] Chariots certainly and metallurgy possibly were introduced from the outside, but well into the second millennium BCE. And, although early Egypt shows a number of Mesopotamian influences, early China's writing, art, and architecture show no influences from abroad. It is of course possible that some influences from the Middle East or the Indus Valley could have reached China via Central Asia in the third and early second millennia, but we have no evidence that they were extensive, and the great distances and geographical barriers involved suggest that such influences were unlikely, even though in later times significant trade routes through Central Asia would be developed. But perhaps the most powerful argument for indigenous Chinese development is the unique style of Chinese society, culture, and religion, which sets it markedly apart from the cases discussed so far.

Linked to the fact that Chinese culture is indigenous and unique is its unparalleled continuity. Although in the archaic cases we have considered so far it is not difficult to trace continuities from the Neolithic to the early state, in every such case, and this is true of the New World archaic cultures as well, the axial "breakthrough," though not without precursors in the archaic cultures, occurs outside them and leads eventually to their demise, marked most clearly by the loss of their writing systems and thus their literature, not to be recovered until modern times. China is the one case, however, where there is a continuity not only from the Neolithic to the archaic, but from the archaic to the axial, a continuity marked by the persistence, not without development to be sure, of the same writing system from the archaic to the present.[114]

In our current postmodern mood, questions have been raised about such perhaps reified denominators as "Mesopotamia" and "Egypt," not to speak of "Israel" and "Greece," and there have been some who have questioned what "China" is as well. Yet major scholars in the field seem more than ready not only to preserve the term, but to push it ever farther back in history. The *Cambridge History of Ancient China,* published in 1999—though not definitive, it is as close to definitive as for a while we are likely to get—

contains a remarkable series of assertions from its various authors about when "China" begins. Kwang-Chih Chang, a distinguished archaeologist, writes that "By 3000 BCE, the Chinese interaction sphere can properly and appropriately be called China."[115] David Keightley, a leading specialist on the Shang, writes a bit more hesitantly, "It is only with the late Shang and its written records, however, that one can, for the first time begin to speak with confidence of a civilization that was incipiently Chinese in its values and institutions."[116] Edward Shaughnessy, a specialist on Western Zhou, however, writes that although many features of later Chinese culture may have had roots in the Neolithic and the Shang, "nevertheless, if those earlier periods can be said to be the foundation of Chinese history, necessary, to be sure, but underground and all but invisible throughout most of that history, then surely the Western Zhou would have to be called its cornerstone."[117] And of course there are many who would date "Imperial China" only from the Qin (221–206 BCE) and Han (206 BCE–220 CE) dynasties. No one, however, has claimed a sharp break from the Neolithic to the present. Such continuity surely puts China in a class by itself.

Though the Chinese development is clearly unique, there is a problem in defining its uniqueness. Chinese civilization in the axial age is extraordinarily rich, providing a wealth of material and a diversity of views that make comparison with other axial civilizations most rewarding. Unfortunately, such is not the case with the Chinese archaic, particularly with its earliest phase in the Shang dynasty (ca. 1570–1045 BCE), but even for the Western Zhou (1045–771 BCE) the evidence is spotty and its interpretation contested. For Shang culture we are dependent, as far as written records are concerned, almost exclusively on the so-called oracle bones (there are a few inscribed bronze vessels), that is, the 100,000 or so inscribed cattle scapulas and turtle shell fragments that survive from the Anyang period (ca. 1200–1045 BCE). The texts, numerous but mostly quite brief, are evidence of an elaborate practice of ritual divination. Fortunately the subjects of divination are diverse so that a considerable amount of interesting information can be derived from careful analysis of the texts. Nonetheless many of the things we would most like to know are simply absent from this data. With regard to religion, the primary subject of this book, David Keightley has written, "the inscriptions provide a flat and abbreviated view telling us more of the notes of Shang cult than of the music of Shang belief."[118] Given the great importance of the later Chinese development, we must use the limited information we have to try to understand its background.

One source of frustration is the lack of myths from surviving archaic texts. Large books have been written on Chinese mythology, but they derive their data largely from texts composed late in the pre-Han period, in the Han dynasty (206 BCE–220 CE) itself, or even later.[119] Some of this material may date from Shang and Western Zhou times, but we cannot know exactly what. There is a little data from the Western Zhou, though even that is hard to date, but the oracle texts are entirely devoid of mythic narrative.

These texts, however, are not devoid of data significant for the understanding of Shang history, most importantly data about royal genealogy. From them we can construct a list of six predynastic kings and twenty-nine dynastic kings.[120] It is only from the time of the twenty-first dynastic king, Wu Ding, that we have archaeological and textual data because it was only under Wu Ding that the Shang ceremonial center at Anyang was established, a site extensively excavated in modern times. For kings earlier than Wu Ding we have only the order of succession, and the relationship between predecessor and successor, that is, whether the successor was a brother or a son of his predecessor. For Wu Ding and later kings, scholars have established approximate dates: Wu Ding's death date is given as 1189, and the last Shang king, Di Xin, is said to have ruled from 1086 to 1045. Several sites have been suggested as earlier Shang capitals, but without writing associated with them it is impossible to be sure when or if they were indeed capitals. Thus most of what we know of Shang society derives from its final approximately 150 years when the capital was at Anyang.[121]

Shang Society was, in Weber's terms, a patrimonial state, that is a state organized as an extension of the ruler's court, augmented by associated lineages and various kinds of servants. Incipiently, at least, it was a patrimonial bureaucracy in that a variety of appointed civil and military officers served under the king, though such officers were only incipient bureaucrats insofar as they were merely an extension of the personal rule of the king, lacking a strong sense of responsibility to the office itself. Paul Wheatley argues against those who see the Shang polity as feudal insofar as the king appointed local officials in outer regions of the realm and even recognized as subordinates some chieftains beyond the borders. Wheatley holds that these appointments should be seen as "benefices," dependent (in theory at least) on the pleasure of the king, and entailing no legal rights of the local ruler, as true feudalism would.[122]

One of the specific features of Shang society was the emphasis on lineage in general and the royal lineage in particular. Kinship is never unimportant in early states, but the absolutism of royal rule often took precedence over lineage loyalty so that the importance of kinship relations was markedly reduced. It is quite possible that the preoccupation with lineage in Shang China was confined largely to the ruling class, and the royal lineage in particular, as in Hawai'i. But the Shang emphasis on lineage left a permanent legacy for all later Chinese culture, of which the Confucian emphasis on kin relationships was an expression. Ancestor worship, so central in Shang cult, has continued at the domestic level to this day.

The focus on the Chinese ruler was as strong as in any of the archaic cases, but the formulation of it differed significantly from Ancient Mesopotamia or Egypt. It has not been uncommon to refer to the Shang regime as a theocracy, but that does not mean that the king himself was considered divine, at least not in the sense that such was the case in Egypt or some other archaic societies. Ancestor worship was central in Shang religion, unlike the cases we have considered so far. The worship of ancestors and the understanding of them as indispensable intermediaries with high gods was, however, present in several other early states: the Yoruba of West Africa, and, in slightly varying ways, among the Aztecs, Mayas, and Inkas of the New World.[123] Nowhere, however, was worship of the royal ancestors so central as in Shang China.

References to gods are not missing in the oracle-bone texts, but they are not numerous and their significance is not entirely clear. Most important was Di ("the god" as we may call him, following our usage for ancient Egypt), also rarely Shang Di ("the god above"), whose power over weather, harvest, and war gave him the most extensive dominion of Shang deities. Significantly, however, Di was not worshipped directly, but rather through the royal ancestors as intermediaries. The actual nature of Di, and particularly the question of whether Di was a kind of primordial ancestor, is in dispute, but need not detain us. It is reasonably clear that the Shang did not view Di as a lineal ancestor—with their powerful concern for the royal lineage, if they had believed they were descendants of Di they would almost surely have said so. But with his lack of particular characteristics (at least as far as we know, not having myths from the Shang period), and the fact that his worship was indirect, he was perhaps similar to some of the otiose high gods known from other cultures. Because Di could intervene in battle for or against the Shang, he was surely not entirely otiose, and his Western Zhou successor, Tian (Heaven), was considerably more active. In addition to Di there were a number of nature deities, river and mountain gods, for example, a sun god who may have been conceived as multiple (ten suns being a calendrical unit), and various local deities as well. Though such deities did receive occasional sacrifice, their worship was not the main focus of the Shang cult as we know it from the oracle-bone inscriptions.

At the center of the Shang cult was the worship of the Shang royal ancestors, who were considered to be powerful deities in their own right and also to have the capacity to intercede with Di in matters of great importance. Ancestors of other lineages were probably also conceived as continuing to intervene in earthly life, but their jurisdictions would have been limited to their descendants. Only the royal ancestors were seen as intervening in matters of concern to the realm as a whole and to the king in particular (for example, in matters of his health or whether his wife or consort would give birth to a son or daughter). But if the gods, including Di, were viewed largely impersonally, having little in the way of individual personality, such was also the case with the ancestors. They were classified by distance from the present (the more distant, the more powerful), and by whether they were direct ancestors (more important) or collaterals, that is, kings succeeded by nephews rather than by sons (less important), and, of course by whether they were male (more important) or female (less important—and lineal mothers of kings were the only females mentioned). On the whole the cult was directed not to the parental generation, but began with the grandparental generation.

Wu Ding is the rare case of a ruler whose conquests made him stand out from the ranks of the largely anonymous ancestors, and receive worship immediately after his death. Wu Ding's own divination texts show a wide variety of recipients being asked many kinds of questions, but under his son, Zu Jia (ca. 1177–1158 BCE), a process of increasing routinization set in, in which the cult was organized in terms of a calendrical cycle, with each ancestor assigned to a particular day, and asked a limited number of questions.[124] Questions concerned the weather, the success of the harvest, the outcome of military expeditions, or simply will there be any calamity during the next period of time. The answers were determined by reading the cracks that appeared after the scapulas or turtle shells had been subjected to heat, and then the charges and replies were inscribed.

If the existing king was not divine, he was proleptically so, for he would, after his death, become an ancestor whose power would only increase with each successive generation. As Wheatley puts it, "the ruling monarch was a member of a lineage which coexisted ontologically on earth and in the heavens above, and he was a pivotal figure in all ritual procedures."[125] Divination and sacrifice, even if carried out by others, were always performed in the name of the king, who alone was the intermediary between the earthly and the divine realms. It is in this connection that the Shang king referred to himself as "I, the one man" *(yu yi ren)*. But if the ancestors were impersonal, so, in a sense, was the king. Keightley quotes David Schaberg as saying of Shang and Zhou kings, "There was no provision in Chinese ritual language for naming a living king; until he received a posthumous title, the word for him [*wang*] was the word for all kings, and he was indistinguishable, at least on the level of language and ideals, from that generalized role."[126] It was, then, the ritual role of the king that was decisive, not his personality. And however mysterious the high god Di may be to us, there was a unique relation between the god and the king. As Keightley tells us, "What distinguished both Di and the king was that, at least in the limited world of the divination inscriptions, Di focused his attention on no other living individual and his activities. Welcome or unwelcome though this attention may have been, it cannot have failed to enhance the king's status in the religious and political hierarchy."[127]

But if the king's authority was enhanced by his special role with respect to Di and the ancestors, Keightley also points out that the king's power was limited by "a network of spiritual obligations and attentions," such that "the king was no despot, free to act as he pleased." Indeed, the pressures on the king and the king alone that led to his use of the phrase "I, the one man," might well, Keightley suggests, have meant, "I, the lone man."[128] Keightley characterizes the consequences of the king's embeddedness in a ritual-social order as follows: "The wishes of these various Powers—particularly those of the ancestors, whose jurisdictions appear to have been arranged more systematically and comprehensibly than those of Di or the Nature Powers—may have served as a kind of unwritten constitutionalism, just as later Confucian traditions may have limited the options available to an Emperor."[129]

If the Shang king was no despot, neither was he in any sense a democrat. As with other archaic societies, the distinction between ruler and ruled was stark. Keightley points out that although in the Chinese Neolithic there is little evidence of human sacrifice, in the Shang dynasty, "the burial of mutilated and beheaded human victims, and the ritual slaughter of dozens of captives, became a regular part of man's spiritual, and political, repertoire."[130] Some Shang elite tombs were of enormous size and had complex structures as well as splendid furnishings,[131] all of which had to be created by dependent labor of some sort. On the basis of our scanty evidence we do not know if there was a sense of obligation on the part of the king for the welfare of the common people, such as we will encounter in the Zhou dynasty, but the divination concerns as expressed in the oracle bones have more to do with the welfare of the ruling elite than that of society as a whole.

The Shang dynasty presided over a realm of significant if shifting size in the Yellow River Valley of North Central China in the last centuries of the Second Millennium BCE. New regions for agriculture were opened up and population grew; cities were built and the arts cultivated, particularly the art of bronze casting, a most sophisticated technology. Our chief visual knowledge of Shang culture comes from bronze vessels of exquisite beauty that have survived in significant number. Whether this rich but imperfectly known civilization saw the beginning of the moral concerns that would be central to all subsequent Chinese culture, we cannot presently say.

At least in later memory, the Zhou conquest of the Shang began with what we can only call a moral explosion whose echoes can still be heard. According to records of uncertain date, the early Zhou kings, Wen (r. 1099–1050 BCE) and Wu (r. 1049/45–1043 BCE), justified their effort to replace the Shang with a new doctrine, expounded with particular clarity by King Wu's brother, the Duke of Zhou (Zhou Gong), the doctrine of the Mandate of Heaven *(Tian ming)*. As we have seen, the high god Di did, on occasion, predict success for the enemies of the Shang king, but there is no indication that such action was considered punishment for the king's faults. The Zhou continued on occasion to use the term Di or Shang Di (Shang here means "above," and is not the same graph as the one for the Shang dynasty) for the high god, but much more frequently referred to him as *Tian* (Heaven), a term not used in that sense in the Shang inscriptions.[132] The Zhou viewed Heaven as intensely concerned with the moral quality of human beings, kings in particular.

King Wen, who was the first Zhou ruler to take the title king *(wang)* even though he was from the Shang point of view a rebel, was viewed in the Zhou tradition as a model of ethical behavior *(wen* means, roughly, "culture'), whereas the last Shang king was viewed as morally depraved. King Wu *(wu* means, roughly, "military") completed the conquest of the Shang, a conquest consolidated by his son, King Cheng, for whom, due to his youth, King Wu's brother, the Duke of Zhou, acted as regent in the first seven years of his reign. King Wu and the Duke of Zhou were also viewed by later generations as paragons of morality. A Heaven deeply concerned with human morality could and did transfer the Mandate *(ming)* from one dynasty to another if the ruler of the previous dynasty became too degenerate. The Zhou doctrine of the Mandate of Heaven was extended back before the Shang dynasty, which, the Zhou ideologists claimed, had itself been given the Mandate of Heaven due to the moral faults of the last rulers of the Xia dynasty, about which we know nothing from Shang inscriptions themselves. Although effective in legitimating the newly installed Zhou dynasty, the doctrine of the Mandate of Heaven proved a two-edged sword, as it could be turned against the Zhou themselves, and against every succeeding ruling house throughout Chinese history. One of the Major Odes of the *Shi* or *Book of Songs* begins with the following stanza:

> Mighty is God on High,
> Ruler of His people below;
> Swift and terrible is God on high,
> His charge has many statutes.
> Heaven gives birth to the multitudes of the people,
> But its charge cannot be counted upon.
> To begin well is common;
> To end well is rare indeed.[133]

The ode continues with a series of invectives attributed to King Wen describing the crimes of the Shang, and ending by invoking the deserved end of the preceding Xia dynasty as well, yet the Ode affirms the conditional nature of royal rule, which could not help but apply to the Zhou themselves.

In most respects, the transition from Shang to Zhou shows a great deal of continuity. The early Zhou kings conquered a larger area than that over which the Shang had ruled, but lacked the capacity to rule most of it directly. Members of the royal lineage, brothers and nephews of kings, for example, were given subject domains. In some instances existing local rulers were recognized as subject to the Zhou court; in particular the descendants of the Shang ruling house were established in what became the state of Song. This arrangement has frequently been referred to as feudalism, though Wheatley has the same reservations about this term as in the case of the Shang, and prefers to consider the Zhou regime as patrimonial, with benefices established for royal relatives. Feudalism, argues Wheatley, drawing from European history, requires some kind of contract between lord and vassal, missing in Zhou as in Shang.[134]

Herrlee Creel, however, argues for the usefulness of the term "feudalism," properly understood, for the Zhou period. He offers his own, somewhat minimalist, definition: "Feudalism is a system of government in which a ruler personally delegates limited sovereignty over portions of his territory to vassals."[135] But, in fact, his analysis is very close to that of Wheatley. According to Creel, the Zhou claimed they were creating a centralized administration, that their "vassals" were not autonomous, but subject to the royal will, and that the Zhou court taxed, administered justice, and in theory, though not often in practice, removed vassals from their domains, especially in the early years when there were strong monarchs.[136] This is not far from what Wheatley means by a patrimonial regime that gives benefices to subordinates. What Creel wants to stress is that the later idealization of the early Zhou kings was not entirely misplaced. As he says, "it was no part of the intention of the early kings to establish a realm of which they were not in full control. They had not conquered 'all under heaven' merely for the sake of giving it away."[137] Their failure to establish, except relatively briefly, a centralized regime was due to the lack of techniques of control to do so, not, at least in the eyes of later thinkers, to lack of intention. It was their putative intention that lived on, though it would not be again realized until 221 BCE.

Though the beginnings of patrimonial bureaucracy were present in the Zhou royal court, as they had been in the Shang court, as well as in the newly established subject states, neither Shang nor Zhou were effectively centralized: the process of decentralization of the Zhou kingdom that became complete in the Warring States period (481–221 BCE) had set in early on. For convenience, the Western Zhou period is said to end with the fall of the Western Zhou capital in 771 BCE and the reduction of the Zhou court to political impotence thereafter. The transition from archaic to axial, which is the primary concern of this book, was taking place between the end of Western Zhou and the establishment of the centralized empire by the Qin in 221 BCE. We need not draw any sharp line in this period of 550 years, but, as we shall see in a later chapter, it may be convenient to take the life of Confucius (551–479 BCE) as a turning point.[138]

Unfortunately, it is very difficult to date the texts that purport to come from the period between the Zhou conquest and the lifetime of Confucius, so we can only conjecturally trace the development of thought in that period. Two of the most important bodies of texts that Confucius himself referred to with respect, and so at least parts of which must precede him, are the *Book of Documents* (sometimes referred to as the *Shujing*—I will refer to this as the *Shu*) and the *Book of Songs* (sometimes referred to as the *Shijing*—I will refer to this as the *Shi*). The *Shu* purports to contain speeches and dialogues from the early years of the Zhou conquest, some of which, if they may not be the actual words of the alleged speakers, are nonetheless almost certainly of Western Zhou date and even early in that period.[139] It is in the "Da gao" ("Great proclamation") chapter, attributed to King Cheng, that we find the first mention of the Mandate of Heaven, and in the "Shao gao" ("Proclamation of Shao Gong") that we first find reference to the emperor as Son of Heaven *(Tianzi)*. The latter passage is worth quoting:

> August Heaven, the Lord on High, has changed his eldest son and this great state Yin's [Yin was the term the Zhou sometimes used to refer to the Shang] mandate. It is the king who has received the mandate.[140]

In this passage we can see how the Zhou absorbed the Shang high god Di into their primary reference to Heaven, and how the emperor is not only the son, but the "eldest son," of Heaven.

Shaughnessy holds that two of these early chapters of the *Shu* contain an argument on the nature of government between Zhou Gong (The Duke of Zhou) and his half-brother Shao Gong, also referred to as the Grand Protector Shi. Zhou Gong, perhaps protecting himself from the accusation of usurping power during his regency for young King Cheng, argues in the "Jun Shi" ("Lord Shi," that is, Shao Gong, in this case the addressee of Zhou Gong's speech) that the Mandate of Heaven is given to the Zhou people in general and that virtuous kings (he cites Shang kings as well as Kings Wen and Wu as precedents) have always relied on meritorious ministers for successful rule. Shao Gong, replying in the "Shao gao," argues, as noted above, that the mandate was given to the king and that he alone can rule. As Shaughnessy notes, this argument would continue throughout Chinese history, with Confucius and his followers taking the part of Zhou Gong, and royal absolutists the part of Shao Gong.[141]

What is of interest here is how far these early chapters of the *Shu* anticipate later, perhaps axial, developments. There is no doubt, though the argument must await a later chapter, that for Confucius the idea of Heaven and its Mandate did have axial implications. I think it can be argued, however, that in the early days of the Western Zhou the axial implications were incipient at best. What was at stake was an intra-elite argument about the legitimacy of one royal lineage, that of the Zhou, replacing another royal lineage, that of the Shang, at the highest level of authority, in the face of centuries of predominance of the Shang house. All the actors in this drama were members of royal families and the archaic idea that it is only the ruler who can mediate between the high god and the people was not in question. Even the dispute between Zhou Gong and Shao Gong in its original form was only about the relative power of members of the ruling family. It would be hundreds of years later, with Confucius and his successors, that early Zhou terminology would be used to formulate a much more generalized conception of the relation between the divine and the human. Cho-yun Hsu and Katheryn M. Linduff have put it well when they write, "The Zhou contribution provided the cornerstone for their own political legitimacy, but it opened the course for the long Chinese tradition of humanism and rationalism and may be thought of as the first step toward a Jaspersian breakthrough."[142]

Even if the early Zhou proclamation of the idea of the Mandate of Heaven was only a first step, it had implications for the understanding of the relation of ruler and people as well as ruler and Heaven significantly different from anything we know about the Shang. In the "Jun Shi" Zhou Gong is supposed to have said: "If our sons and grandsons cannot be respectful above and below [toward Heaven and the people], and destroy the glory that our ancestors have brought to our house—if they do not remember that Heaven's Mandate is not easy to keep, and that Heaven is not to be relied upon, they will overturn the Mandate."[143] What respecting the people entails can be discerned from a number of chapters in the *Shu*. For example, in the "Zi Cai" King Wu admonishes one of his sons to "attend even to the helpless and solitary, attend even to pregnant women . . . from of old the kings have done so."[144] If I may paraphrase Bernhard Karlgren's rather awkward translation of this chapter, the son is told to set an example for the people, to care about and encourage them, to avoid capital punishment, and, indeed, as far as possible to avoid punishments altogether.[145] We may doubt how far such injunctions were carried out, or how the kings actually attended to pregnant women, but it is the ideal that is of interest here.

The poems in the *Shi* are no easier to date than the so-called authentic chapters of the *Shu,* but many of them give a vivid picture of how rulers ought to act as well as how they in fact do act. For example:

Happiness to our lord
That is the father and mother of his people.
Happiness to our lord!
May his fair fame be forever.[146]

But not all rulers were judged so worthy. Another song warns:

> Oh, our people are exhausted,
> Would they have but a little respite!
> Treat the middle kingdom with kindness,
> Then peace will reign in all the lands.[147]

Or the judgment may go beyond warning:

> Big rat, big rat,
> Do not gobble our millet!
> Three years we have slaved for you,
> Yet you take no notice of us.
> At last we are going to leave you
> And go to that happy land;
> Happy land, happy land,
> Here we shall have our place.[148]

In early China, people were more valuable than land, so that oppressed peasants could, as it were, "vote with their feet." Though they may have sought a "happy land," the most they were likely to find was a somewhat more benevolent lord.

If the *Shi* gives us a remarkably frank picture of Zhou political life (at moments, as in the "Big Rat" poem, rivaling David Malo's picture of early Hawai'i), it also is our best source for pre-Confucian piety. One of the "Zhou Hymns," generally believed to be the oldest texts in the collection, gives an idea of the centrality of Heaven in Zhou belief:

> Reverence, reverence!
> By Heaven all is seen;
> Its charge is not easy to hold.
> Do not say it is high, high above,
> Going up and down about its own business.
> Day in, day out it watches us here.
> I, a little child,
> Am not wise or reverent.
> But as days pass, months go by,
> I learn from those that have bright splendor.
> O Radiance, O Light,

Help these my strivings;
Show me how to manifest the ways of power.[149]

The phrase "I, a little child" indicates that it is the king speaking; the king sometimes even refers to himself as an orphan. Such usages are probably related to the phrase "I, the one man," which the Zhou as well as the Shang continued to use.

What is significant in this hymn is the idea that the king is the humble servant of Heaven. No Shang inscription implies any such relation of the Shang king to Di. Indeed Di almost completely drops out of late Shang inscriptions, which are addressed almost exclusively to ancestors (though under Wu Ding ancestors were sometimes viewed as intercessors with Di). References to ancestors are not missing in the *Shi,* but they are rare, particularly in comparison to the many references to Heaven. That ancestors were still viewed as potentially influencing their descendants is indicated by the opening verse of a Minor Ode:

The fourth month was summer weather;
The sixth month, blistering heat.
Have our ancestors no compassion
That they can bear to see us suffer?[150]

Another Ode describes an ancestral sacrifice in great detail, and observes:

Every custom and rite is observed,
Every smile, every word is in place.
The spirits and Protectors will surely come
And requite us with great blessings
Countless years of life as our reward.[151]

Oracle bones are very different sorts of texts from the hymns, odes and airs of the *Shi,* so we are, in a sense, comparing apples and oranges. For all we know there were Shang hymns to Di that have not survived. But from the existing evidence, it does appear that Zhou piety from fairly early on, though it continued to observe ancestor worship, developed significantly new preoccupations with Heaven and the human-divine interaction. We have, for example, in an Ode in the *Book of Songs,* an accusation of Heaven that reminds us of the Egyptian accusation of the god:

Broad and vast is mighty Heaven,
Yet it keeps its grace from us,
But rather brings death and famine,
War and destruction to all the states.
Foreboding Heaven is a cruel affliction,
It does not ponder, does not plan.
It pays no attention to the guilty,
Who have committed their crimes.
But the ones who are innocent,
These, without exception, suffer.[152]

But here, too, Heaven has its defenders:

The hardships of the folk here below
Are not brought on by Heaven;
No, nice to meet, then a stab in the back.
Violence comes from the acts of man.[153]

What we have here is at least incipient theological argument. When Confucius said he was "a transmitter, not a creator" (*Analects* 7/1), he surely had a point, because he was indeed trying to conserve and interpret the traditions of the "three dynasties" (Xia, Shang and Zhou), but particularly that of Zhou:

The Master said, Zhou could survey the two preceding dynasties. How great a wealth of culture! And we follow upon Zhou.[154]

As I have noted, in no other case does the axial follow the archaic with such continuity.[155]

I have referred to the despotic founders of early states, who came to power through blood and terror as they almost always did, as upstarts of the kind that tribal society usually managed to repress. As opposed to Girard's theory, it would seem that the first killing among culturally organized humans was not the killing of a scapegoat, but the killing of an upstart who genuinely threatened to revive the despotism of the old primate alpha male. We have argued that hunter-gatherer egalitarianism is not the abandonment of dominance, but a new form of it, the dominance of all against each. Effective dominance, however, brings on not only submission but resentment, and a desire to resist dominance. That is why upstarts wishing to re-create despotism can be found in every society. We do not need to go to sociobiology for an understanding of the ubiquity of upstarts: modern philosophy has had more than a little to say about this human proclivity. Hobbes spoke of the "desire to be foremost," Hegel of the fundamental human dialectic of "master and slave," Nietzsche of the "will to power."

But though upstarts are found in all societies, successful upstarts appear only in complex societies. Two aspects of complex society help to make this possible. An increasing agricultural surplus allows larger groups to form—groups beyond the face-to-face bands of hunter-gatherers—and the age-old techniques of dealing with upstarts are harder to apply in such large societies. But the opening wedge for the successful upstart is most often militarization. Large, prosperous societies are almost always in danger from the have-nots at their fringe, or from other prosperous groups who would like to become even more prosperous. In a situation of endemic warfare, the successful warrior emanates a sense of mana or charisma, and can use it to establish a following. Thus in Polynesia, the *toa* (warrior) could challenge the *ariki* (priest/chief). "Heroic ages" in many parts of the world have seen the rise of such warrior chiefs. The brave warrior alone could not challenge the old egalitarian consensus. As Hobbes pointed out, the strongest man can be overcome by a coalition of others, even by someone weak when the strong man is asleep. It is when the outstanding warrior can mobilize a band of followers that he can challenge the old egalitarianism and, as a successful upstart, free the disposition to dominate from the controls previously placed on it. The warrior band, however, can turn out to be a self-defeating project if all it does is stimulate the creation of other warrior bands leading to an ever escalating increase in violence (a real possibility—the "nightmare of history" of which James Joyce spoke).[156]

Chiefdoms are notoriously ephemeral, but early states are also quite fragile. It is only when a successful warrior can fashion a new form of authority, of legitimate hierarchy, that he can break the cycle of violence and hope for lasting rule, perhaps one to be inherited by his offspring. But this involves a new relation between gods and humans, a new way of organizing society, one that finds a significant place for the disposition to nurture as well as the disposition to dominate. This is the task that archaic religions and societies have to complete if they are to be even briefly successful. In doing so they elaborate a vast hierarchical conception of the cosmos in which the divine, the natural, and the human are integrated.

Even societies in which the old hunter-gatherer egalitarianism was maintained by an informal system of increasingly severe sanctions against incipient upstarts, required a pattern of myth and ritual that would provide meaning and solidarity "above the fray," so to speak, of everyday life. That was the role of the Dreaming in Australia and the other tribal groups we considered had similar practices and conceptions. We then found that in societies where agriculture was increasingly important and population was growing, ranked lineages could provide, as we said, "a superordinate reference point capable of moderating and mediating the tensions of daily life." The Kalapalo and the Tikopia had such ranked lineages, even though they were basically egalitarian.

There are clear continuities between tribal and archaic religions: in the moments of collective effervescence in the great festivals of archaic society, the solidarity of the social whole was reaffirmed. But most of the time in archaic societies hierarchy, not collective solidarity, provided the organizing principle. As Lewis Mumford writes:

> At this point, human effort moves from the limited horizontal plane of the village and the family to the vertical plane of a whole society. The new community formed a hierarchic structure, a social pyramid, which from base to pinnacle included many families, many villages, many occupations, often many regional habitats, and not least, many gods. This political structure was the basic invention of the new age: without it, neither its monuments nor its cities could have been built, nor, one must add, would their premature destruction have so persistently taken place.[157]

Archaic societies were much larger than preceding societies had ever been. If they were to maintain any stability at all they had to find forms of solidarity that were based on more than tribal festivity on the one hand or warrior force on the other. The solution that every archaic society of which we have adequate knowledge found was a new conception of kingship and divinity that moved beyond old ideas of ranked lineages and powerful beings. In Hawai'i as in the societies we have examined in this chapter, kings acted like gods and gods acted like kings. The cosmos, as Jacobsen said, was seen as a state, and the state as an essential element in the cosmos.[158]

But perhaps we need to move back a step. Once upon a time there was no state and no cosmos seen as a state. How did we get from a society, even a ranked society, in which chiefs and people were still linked by strong kinship ties, to a society in which a genuine secondary formation, a state, no longer linked to the common people by kinship, could appear? It would seem that that shift from tribal to archaic society only became possible when one man focused so much attention on himself that he could claim that he and he alone was not only capable of rule, but capable of maintaining society's relationship to the gods—or, before long—to "the god." When the Shang king spoke of himself as "I, the one man," he expressed a profound truth about archaic kingship. The new secondary formation, the state, was to express his will alone, and it was he alone who stood before the god(s), maintaining the right ritual relationship to the divine. It is as though the king, himself divine or semidivine, was the necessary fulcrum to move society to a new level of social organization. Or, to change the metaphor, it is as though the archaic king unleashed an explosion of atomic energy, capable of moving what had for millennia not been willing to move. But, once achieved, the archaic state had quickly to weave a web of institutions and structures of power, but also of rituals and conceptions of the cosmos, which would make it seem both natural and inevitable.

In archaic society traditional social structures and social practices were grounded in the divinely instituted cosmic order, and there was little tension between religious demand and social conformity. Indeed, social conformity was at every point reinforced with religious sanction (taboo). Nevertheless the very notion of powerful kings and well-characterized gods acting toward men with a certain freedom introduced an element of openness that was less apparent at the tribal level.[159] Once kings claim to be protectors of the common people questions can be raised when the common people suffer, and the basis of political legitimacy is open to argument. Once gods have replaced powerful beings as the focus of ritual and myth, dramatic symbolic reformulations are at least conceivable. "In all polytheism there is a latent monotheism, which can be activated at any time," Eric Voegelin goes so far as to say, "if the pressure of a historical situation meets with a sensitive and active mind."[160]

In the section on ancient Mesopotamia, we argued that archaic societies, even when they had writing, probably did not undergo a "literacy revolution." Rather, orality remained the dominant mode of communication during archaic times and long after. Still, we need to consider whether the existence of writing did not allow at least the beginnings of more reflective and systematic thought than could have been carried on by oral tradition alone. Although riddles, aphorisms, and maxims are standard features of oral tradition, the more developed arguments that we find in the so-called wisdom literature of the ancient Near East, or in some of the writings that survive from Western Zhou, did perhaps depend, at least in part, on writing. Narrative is central to oral tradition, but written narratives could be ordered and revised to give them a weight they might not have had in oral recitation. Hymns could become the vehicles of mythospeculation. Whatever aids to reflective thought that the technology of writing supplied were limited to the scribal class. Early literacy has been called craft literacy, because it was a specialized craft that only a few could master. Those few, however, may have been essential for the self-understanding of archaic society and for what was to come.

Voegelin was reminding us that even in massively conformist archaic society, where, as Jacobsen puts it for Mesopotamia, the "prime virtue" was obedience,[161] there were "sensitive and active" minds—prophets, priests, scribes—who, even within the confines of the cosmos as a state, could think new thoughts. The reality of archaic civilization was centralization of political power, class stratification, the magnification of military power, the economic exploitation of the weak, and the universal introduction of some form of forced labor for both productive and military purposes.[162] As against these undeniable realities we must also cite the major achievements of archaic society: the maintenance of peace within the realm, more productive agriculture, the opening up of markets for long-range trade, and significant achievements in architecture, art, and literature. But equally important was, with the help of a literate elite, a new effort to give political power a moral meaning. The archaic king was almost always depicted as a warrior, as a defender of the realm against barbarians on the frontiers and rebels within; as such he embodied a powerful element of dominance. But he was also seen, and probably increasingly as archaic societies matured, as the defender of justice, in Mesopotamia and Egypt as the good shepherd, in Western Zhou as father and mother of his people. Gods as well as kings were increasingly thought of not only as dominant but also as nurturant. The very appeal to ethical standards of legitimacy for both gods and kings, however, opened new possibilities for political and theological reflection. In the axial age a new kind of upstart, the moral upstart who relies on speech, not force, would appear, foreshadowed as we have seen, by voices already raised in archaic societies.

6

The Axial Age I: Introduction
and Ancient Israel

INTRODUCTION

Ritual in tribal societies involves the participation of all or most of the members of the group—in classic Durkheimian fashion, if the ritual goes well, it leaves the group filled with energy and solidarity.[1] Some are more active than others, but many are involved, and even when, as in the case of the Navajo, the ritual centers around someone who is being cured, the whole network of people with whom that person is involved participates in and benefits from the ritual. In stark contrast, ritual in archaic societies focuses above all on one person, the divine or quasi-divine king, and only a few people, priests or members of the royal lineage, participate. The rest of society acts sometimes as audience, but sometimes knows of the great rituals only by hearsay, because their presence would profane the high mysteries. Whereas tribal societies consist of small face-to-face groups, or of a few adjacent ones, archaic societies were territorially extensive and could include millions of people. It would seem that maintaining the coherence of such large and extensive societies required that the attention and energy that tribal ritual focused on the whole society now be concentrated on the ruler, elevated beyond normal human status, in relation to beings who were now not only powerful, but required worship. The elevation of rulers into a status unknown in tribal societies went hand in hand with the elevation of gods into a status higher in authority than the powerful beings they were gradually replacing. Of course, most people in archaic societies continued to live in small face-to-face groups and to have a ritual life of their own, only loosely articulated with the great royal rituals at the imperial center, and resembling in many ways the ritual life of tribal societies.

Both tribal and archaic religions are "cosmological," in that supernature, nature, and society were all fused in a single cosmos. The early state greatly extended the understanding of the cosmos in time and space, but, as Thorkild Jacobsen argued, the cosmos was still viewed as a state—the homology between sociopolitical reality and religious reality was unbroken.[2] As we have seen, the establishment of the early state and the beginning of archaic society destroyed the uneasy egalitarianism of hundreds of thousands, if not millions, of years of hominin evolution, but in so doing made possible much larger and more complex societies. A dramatic symbolism that combined dominance and nurturance produced a new sense of divine power combined with social power, enacted in entirely new forms of ritual, involving, centrally, sacrifice—even human sacrifice—as a concrete expression of radical status difference.

If the balance of tribal egalitarianism had never been easy to maintain and began to give rise to modest status differences long before the emergence of the state, the state itself and its religio-political symbolization gave rise to new forms of instability. Intermediate periods, as we have seen, raised serious questions about the cosmological order: Where is the king? Where is the god? Why are we hungry? Why are we being killed by attackers and no one is defending us? Once political unity had been reasserted, these questions could be smoothed over, but the cracks remained, and new insights appeared, such as the idea that rule is conditional on divine favor and may be withdrawn from wicked rulers, or that individuals might appeal directly to the gods without the mediation of the ruling cult. Such insights would be clearly expressed in the axial age, but in archaic society they remained only cracks in a continuing cosmological unity.[3]

In dealing with the axial age, roughly the middle centuries of the first millennium BCE, we will need to consider a number of definitional issues and the degree to which apparently parallel developments were really similar. But I would like to begin the consideration of the axial phenomena rather concretely. As we have seen, king and god emerged together in archaic society and continued their close association throughout its history. It is not surprising, then, that the axial age sees some dramatic new twists in the relation between god and king. It is not that these symbols or the close relation between them were abandoned, but they were transformed in remarkable new ways. One of the questions that recurs is, Who is the (true) king, the one who really reflects divine justice?

In Greece, Plato tells the Athenians not to look at Achilles, the hero of aristocratic Greek culture (we should remember that Achilles was a kinglet and his mother a goddess), but at Socrates, not an aristocrat at all, but a stonemason and a busybody, asking questions people would rather not think about. For it is Socrates, the lover of wisdom, the philosopher, who should be king, who would be the only truly legitimate king.

In China, it is Mencius, living 200 years after Confucius (conventional dates, 551–479 BCE), who tells us that Confucius, the failed official who gathered a few followers as he traveled from state to state in ancient China, never achieving real influence anywhere, who was the uncrowned king, the one around whom the empire could have been rightly ordered, and by implication, he, Mencius, was another who ought to have been crowned, though his worldly success was no greater than Confucius's.

In India, who was the Buddha? He was the son of a king and ought to have succeeded his father, but instead he abandoned his kingdom and his family to become an ascetic in the forest seeking enlightenment.

In Israel, the tension between God and king was endemic in the period of the monarchy: at times God seems to have made an eternal covenant with the House of David, giving the monarchy quasi-divine status, but often kings, including David, are portrayed as sinners or even enemies of Yahweh who were punished for their bad deeds. Yet in the Babylonian exile, when the Davidic monarchy, the Jerusalem temple, and the land itself were all lost, Yahweh was proclaimed as the only God there is, and a God who can chose whomever he wants to serve his purposes—even the Persian king could be God's messiah. Christianity played its own changes on this theme, using the old royal epithet of the king as Son of God (and Jesus's Davidic lineage was affirmed) in a new way, proclaiming the reign of Christ the King even on the cross. And Muhammad, God's chosen prophet, was, like Moses, a king and not a king, but surely a ruler of a people. Those who led the community after Muhammad's death would affirm their claim to rule as successors *(khalifa)* to the prophet.[4] The old unity of God and king was broken through dramatically in every case, and yet reaffirmed paradoxically in the new axial formulations.

At this point it might be well to remember one of the central principles of this inquiry: Nothing is ever lost. Just as the face-to-face rituals of tribal society continue in disguised form among us, so the unity of political and religious power, the archaic "mortgage," as Voegelin called it,[5] reappears continually in societies that have experienced the axial "breakthrough." Kings who ruled "by divine right," are obvious examples, but so are presidents who claim to act in accordance with a "higher power." At every point as our story unfolds, we will have to consider the relation between political and religious power. But one thing is certain: the issue never goes away.

As a first approximation to an understanding of the axial age, let us turn to the elegant prose of Arnaldo Momigliano, who has this to say of "the classical situation of the ancient world between 600 and 300 BC":

> It has become a commonplace, after Karl Jaspers's *Vom Ursprung und Ziel der Geschichte*—the first original book on history to appear in postwar Germany in 1949—to speak of the *Achsenzeit,* of the axial age, which included the China of Confucius and Lao-Tse, the India of Buddha, the Iran of Zoroaster, the Palestine of the Prophets and the Greece of the philosophers, the tragedians and the historians. There is a very real element of truth in this formulation. All these civilizations display literacy, a complex political organization combining central government and local authorities, elaborate town-planning, advanced metal technology and the practice of international diplomacy. In all these civilizations there is a profound tension between political powers and intellectual movements. Everywhere one notices attempts to introduce greater purity, greater justice, greater perfection and a more universal explanation of things. New models of reality, either mystically or prophetically or rationally apprehended, are propounded as a criticism of, and alternative to, the prevailing models. We are in the age of criticism.[6]

Momigliano points to two aspects of the axial age that we will have to consider in more detail. One is the background features of societies that are in several ways "more developed" than the societies that preceded them. The other is new developments in the realm of thought—political, ethical, religious, philosophical—that he sums up with the significant term "criticism."

If we turn to Jaspers himself, we will find that he, like Momigliano, is interested in a historically empirical description of the axial age, but his concern is primarily existential—where are we in history?—as the title of his book in English, *The Origin and Goal of History,* implies. His dates are slightly different: He finds that the "axis of history is to be found in the period around 500 BC, in the spiritual process that occurred between 800 and 200 BC." It is there, he writes, that "Man, as we know him today, came into being."[7] Both Jaspers and Momigliano say that the figures of the axial age—Confucius, Buddha, the Hebrew prophets, the Greek philosophers—are alive to us, are contemporary with us, in a way that no earlier figures are.

Our cultural world and the great traditions that still in so many ways define us, all originate in the axial age. Jaspers asks the question whether modernity is the beginning of a new axial age, but he leaves the answer open. In any case, though we have enormously elaborated the axial insights, we have not outgrown them, not yet, at least.

Before attempting to define more carefully the nature of the cultural innovations of the axial age, we must consider in a bit more detail the social context in which they arose. Several features mentioned by Momigliano—central government, town planning, international diplomacy—were already present in archaic societies, as were literacy and metallurgy. But there were significant changes in these last two features. Iron was replacing bronze in both agriculture and warfare, but the transition was uneven and gradual: the "Iron Age" was not itself the cause of the other changes. In particular it would seem that iron was more important in increasing the efficiency of warfare than in transforming the means of production. Still, the use of iron tools must have contributed to the gradual increase of population that characterized the first millennium BCE and the use of iron weapons to the ferocity of first-millennium warfare. And although literacy goes back as far as 3000 BCE, it is true that it remained largely a craft literacy, confined to small groups of scribes, until well into the first millennium. Alphabetic scripts were replacing Mesopotamian cuneiform and Egyptian hieroglyphics, and were in use in Greece, Israel, and India, considerably widening the circle of literacy. China maintained the use of characters that might seem to rival cuneiform and hieroglyphics in difficulty, but although they required a great deal of memory, they were easier to use than the archaic scripts of the West, and literacy was clearly growing in late first-millennium China.

An important feature that Jaspers emphasizes is that none of what he calls the axial "breakthroughs," a term we will need to consider further below, occurred in the centers of great empires. Rather, in all cases, "there were a multitude of small States and cities, a struggle of all against all, which to begin with nevertheless permitted an astonishing prosperity, an unfolding of vigour and wealth."[8] We will have to examine more carefully how this situation worked out in each case, but in general the competition between small states created the possibility for the emergence of itinerant intellectuals not functioning within centralized priesthoods or bureaucracies, and therefore more structurally capable of the criticism that Momigliano found central to the axial age, and that Jaspers defined as the capacity for "questioning all human activity and conferring upon it a new meaning."[9]

Jaspers's mention of the combination of prosperity involving an increase in wealth and vigor with incessant warfare brings up two additional points about the axial age that require mention. Although standard weights of precious metals had been used in economic transactions in archaic societies, it is only in the axial age that coinage became widespread, originating perhaps in Asia Minor, but rapidly coming into use in the Greek and Phoenician cities, the Near East, India, and China. The Phoenicians invented the earliest form of the abacus. What these developments tell us is that trade was increasing all across the old world. The market economy was surely only incipient in the middle of the first millennium, and many rural areas were largely unaffected by it, but we know that market relations tend to destabilize long-established kinship and status relationships, so this too has to be added as a background factor contributing to the social volatility of the axial age.[10]

Jaspers's reference to warfare amounting almost to a war of all against all seems to refer to the incessant warfare between small states as we see it in early Greece, the Israelite monarchies, northern India, and northern China in the axial age. But there was another factor adding to military instability: the rise of large territorial states militarily more efficient than their Bronze Age predecessors, especially in the Near East. These impinged on and acted to destabilize the incipient axial societies. The first obvious example is the Neo-Assyrian Empire (934–610 BCE).[11] As anyone familiar with the Hebrew Bible knows, Assyria destroyed the northern Israelite kingdom, the Kingdom of Israel, in 722 BCE, and made the southern kingdom, the Kingdom of Judah, a vassal state through most of the seventh century. Assyrian pressure on the Phoenician cities on the Mediterranean coast stimulated Phoenician colonization on the North African coast, where the most important colony, Carthage, was founded early in the millennium, in Sicily, and throughout the western Mediterranean. Though the Assyrians did not impinge directly on the Greeks, the Phoenician expansion helped stimulate Greek colonization from the Black Sea coast to the western Mediterranean. The brief neo-Babylonian expansion finished off the Kingdom of Judah in 587 BCE, immediately followed by the Achaemenid Persian Empire (ca. 550–330 BCE), which became the territorially most extended empire in history up to its time, powerfully influencing Judah in the postexilic period, thoroughly challenging the Greeks in their homeland, with major cultural consequences, and ruling the Indus Valley in India at just the moment of axial efflorescence in the Ganges Valley. Thus all the axial cases except China experienced Persian pressure at critical moments in their development. Persia itself is often included as an axial case, but everything about Zoroaster (including his dates, which vary, according to different authorities, from the middle of the second millennium to the middle of the first), Zoroastrianism (including the contents and dating of Zoroastrian scriptures), and the degree to which and the way in which Zoroastrianism was institutionalized in Achaemenid Persia, is in dispute due to enormous problems with very limited sources. For this reason I will regretfully omit Zoroastrianism from my discussion of axial cases in this chapter. We are left in the uncomfortable position of recognizing a significant Persian impact on three of the four well-documented axial cases, while Persia itself remains largely a historical cipher.[12]

Although Jaspers credits Alfred Weber as one of the sources of the idea of the axial age, almost certainly Max Weber, an important early associate of Jaspers's, was also an influence. Though Max Weber's comparative treatment of the world religions implies something like the axial-age hypothesis, the only place in his writings where I have found a definite assertion of something like the axial age is his reference to a "prophetic age," involving prophetic movements in the eighth and seventh centuries BCE, reaching even into the sixth and fifth centuries, in Israel, Persia, and India, with analogues in China. Such movements appear to be the background for the later emergence of the world religions.[13]

After mentioning Max Weber as a precursor, I need to mention two other scholars who developed Jaspers's idea further after he had put "the axial age" on the map. One of these is Eric Voegelin in his massive five-volume *Order and History*,[14] where he speaks of "multiple and parallel leaps in being" in the first millennium BCE. Specifically, a leap in being describes a movement from compact cosmological symbolization, characteristic of what we have called archaic societies, to a differentiated symbolism of individual soul, society, and transcendent reality in the axial cases. Voegelin does not mention Jaspers until volume 2, and then critically, but he appears to owe him a larger dept than he acknowledges.[15]

The other scholar influenced by Jaspers who deserves mention is S. N. Eisenstadt, who has done more than anyone to make the axial age central for comparative historical sociology. Eisenstadt focuses on one central aspect of Jaspers's analysis, the "basic tension between the transcendental and mundane orders," and on "the new type of intellectual elite" concerned with the possible restructuring of the world in accordance with the transcendental vision.[16] He emphasizes the appearance of what he calls "reflexivity," the capacity to examine one's own assumptions, in the axial age, which is similar,

I believe, to what Momigliano meant by "criticism." Eisenstadt has stimulated scholars in many fields to write about the axial age, and in what follows I will often be drawing on their work as well as on that of Eisenstadt himself.

I will return, after examining the individual cases, to the question of how much we can generalize about the social conditions that were the context of axial developments. But it is necessary, before considering the cases, to characterize a bit more specifically the cultural content of the axial age: in a word, what made the axial age axial? This question has stimulated more than a little disagreement and some questions about whether we can even speak of an axial age at all, given the differences among the several cases. For example, Eisenstadt's emphasis on the distinction between transcendental and mundane has been questioned in the case of China because of its inveterate "this-worldliness."[17] Johann Arnason has pointed out that Jaspers's "most condensed statement" of the axial age, describing it as the moment when "man becomes conscious of Being as a whole, of himself and his limitations," and "experiences absoluteness in the depths of selfhood and in the lucidity of transcendence," is remarkably similar to Jaspers's own version of existential philosophy.[18] In discussing the axial age it is all too easy to read in our own presuppositions or to take one of the four cases (usually Israel or Greece) as paradigmatic for all the others. Is there a theoretical framework in which to place the axial age that will help us avoid these pitfalls as much as possible? I believe there is: the framework of the evolution of human culture and cognition that I outlined in Chapter 3.

We saw there that Merlin Donald describes the evolution of human culture as unfolding in four stages. Earliest is episodic culture, in which humans, along with all higher mammals, learn to understand and respond to the immediate situation they are in. Then, perhaps beginning as early as 2 million years ago, came mimetic culture, the prelinguistic, but not necessarily prevocal, use of the body both to imaginatively enact events and to communicate with others through expressive gesture. Then, some 100,000 or more years ago, with the development of language as we know it, came mythic culture, which Donald describes as "a unified, collectively held system of explanatory and regulatory metaphors. The mind has expanded its reach beyond the episodic perception of events, beyond the mimetic reconstruction of episodes, to a comprehensive modeling of the entire human universe." Every aspect of life, he says, "is permeated by myth."[19] Although myth gives a comprehensive understanding of life, it does so exclusively by the use of metaphor and narrative. Also, mythic culture until very late in its history was, except for drawings of various kinds, an exclusively oral culture. In Chapter 3 I referred to, but did not describe, theoretic culture, the most recent of Donald's stages. It will be my argument that the axial break-through involved the emergence of theoretic culture in dialogue with mythic culture as a means for the "comprehensive modeling of the entire human universe," so I must now turn to a description of theoretic culture.

Donald begins his description of theoretic culture negatively, telling us that it involved "a break with the dominance of spoken language and narra-tive styles of thought,"[20] but a break with dominance does not mean the abandonment of earlier forms of cognitive adaptation. Humans are still epi-sodic, mimetic, and mythic creatures, although, as in earlier transitions, the emergence of a new form of cultural cognition eventually involves reorgani-zation of the earlier forms.

The key elements of theoretic culture developed gradually; they consisted in graphic invention, external memory, and theory construction.[21] Graphic invention began relatively early, with body painting, sand painting, the great Paleolithic cave painting, and such, but its key contribution to the emergence of theoretic culture was its ability to provide external memory storage—that is, memory outside the human brain. Early writing is clearly a significant step beyond painting in the amount of cognitive information that could be stored, but the unwieldy early writing systems and the limited number of people who could use them meant that they were precursors to, rather than full realizations of, the possibilities of theoretic culture. Not sur-prisingly, Donald sees Greek culture in the first millennium BCE as the place where theoretic culture first clearly emerged, and the efficient external mem-ory system provided by a fully alphabetic writing system as an aspect (not a cause) of that emergence. He describes the importance of external memory as follows:

External memory is a critical feature of modern human cognition, if we are trying to build an evolutionary bridge from Neolithic to modern cognitive capabilities or a structural bridge from mythic to theoretic culture. The brain may not have changed recently in it genetic makeup, but its link to an accumulating external memory network affords it cognitive powers that would not have been possible in isolation. This is more than a metaphor; each time the brain carries out an operation in concert with the external symbolic storage system, it becomes part of a network. Its memory structure is temporarily altered; and the locus of cognitive control changes.[22]

But graphic invention and the external memory it makes possible are only the essential prerequisites for the development of theoretic culture, which is the ability to think analytically rather than narratively, to construct theories that can be criticized logically and empirically. Donald cites Bruner as describing the two modes of thinking evident in modern humans as narrative and analytic.[23] And Bruner himself recognizes a distinguished precursor when he uses as the epigraph for his book the following passage from William James: "To say that all human thinking is essentially of two kinds—reasoning on the one hand, and narrative, descriptive, contemplative thinking on the other—is to say only what every reader's experience will corroborate."[24] So analytic or theoretic thinking does not displace, but is added to, narrative thinking, a point essential to our understanding of the axial age.

In one sense something like theoretic thought, the capacity to draw conclusions from instances outside a narrative context, goes all the way back: mimetic stone flaking surely required a degree of inferential thinking. At a practical level, "primitives" were as logical as we are, a major reason why Lucien Lévy-Bruhl's idea that they were "prelogical" has attracted such scorn.[25] Even if we narrow our definition to something like conscious rational reflection, we can find instances earlier than the axial age. The practical need for calendrical accuracy in agriculture led even some preliterate societies to a kind of "primitive astronomy," in which, Donald argues, many elements of modern science were incipient: "systematic and selective observation, and the collection, coding, and eventually the visual storage of data; the analysis of stored data for regularities and cohesive structures; and the formulation of predictions on the basis of these regularities . . . Theory had not yet become as reflective and detached as it later would; but the symbolic modeling of a larger universe had begun."[26] Begun, but, as perhaps in such fields as metallurgy as well, theory remained at the level of craft specialization, not challenging myth at the most general level of cultural self-understanding; there myth in the sense of ethically and religiously charged narrative remained largely unaffected by the new developments.

What made first -millennium Greece unique in Donald's eyes was "reflection for its own sake," going "beyond pragmatic or opportunistic science" and eventuating in "what might be called the theoretic attitude."[27] Donald does not relate his argument to the problem of the axial age, because he singles out Greece alone as the place where the theoretic attitude first arose, but Yehuda Elkana, while also focusing on Greece, relates his argument to the general axial problem in his contribution to the 1985 book edited by Eisenstadt, *The Origins and Diversity of the Axial Age.* His paper is entitled "The Emergence of Second-order Thinking in Classical Greece," and what he means by "second-order thinking" is close to Donald's "theoretic attitude."[28] Following Donald, I am using the term "theory" in distinction to the term "narrative." Elkana is concerned less with the distinction between narrative and theory than with, in Donald's terms, the distinction between theory and "the theoretical attitude." For Elkana, first-order theory can be quite complex, as can, for example, mathematics and the beginning of algebra in Babylonia, or the calendrical astronomy noted above, but it involves only straightforward rational exposition, not reflection about the basis of the exposition. Second-order thinking is "thinking about thinking"; that is, it attempts to understand how the rational exposition is possible and can be defended. One of the earliest examples is geometric proof, associated with Pythagoras in early Greece. Geometric proof asserts not only geometric truths, but the grounds for thinking them true, that is, proofs that in principle could be disproved, or replaced by better proofs. For Elkana the arguments of several of the pre-Socratic philosophers that the universe is formed from water or fire or mind, although clearly theories and not myths (we will have to ask later about the relation between such theories and myths), do not imply second-order thinking, as they do not seek to disprove the alternatives. One would think they did so implicitly, as each pre-Socratic offered in turn his alternative theory. The value of Elkana's position, however, is not in the details, but in the help he gives us in seeing that "theory" precedes the axial age, at least in selected areas such as astronomy and mathematics, but that it is precisely the emergence of second-order thinking, the idea that there are alternatives that have to be argued for, that marks the axial age.

Elkana quotes a passage from Momigliano that I cited earlier to make the decisive point: "New models of reality, either mystically or prophetically or rationally apprehended, are propounded as a criticism of, and alternative to, the prevailing models."[29] Here we have, not theories about limited realms of reality, not even second-order thinking about a limited area of reality such as geometric proof, but second-order thinking about cosmology, which for societies just emerging from the archaic age meant thinking about the religio-political premises of society itself. It is second-order thinking in this central area of culture, previously filled by myth, that gave rise to the idea of transcendence, so often associated with the axial age: "Transcendental breakthrough occurred when in the wake of second-order weighing of clashing alternatives there followed an almost unbearable tension threatening to break up the fabric of society, and the resolution of the tension was found by creating a transcendental realm and then finding a soteriological bridge between the mundane world and the transcendental."[30] But here Elkana, a historian of science, is, I think, skipping a beat. In the history of science the effort to make sense of what has come to be recognized as empirical anomalies that don't fit existing ideas, leads to the creation of a new abstract theory, a new "order of reality" if you will, that succeeds in making sense of those anomalies. But "creating a transcendental realm" involves something more substantial than a scientific theory. Because transcendental realms are not subject to disproof the way scientific theories are, they inevitably require a new form of narrative—that is, a new form of myth. In Chapter 5 I noted that "mythospeculation"—myth with an element of reflective theory in it—already appeared in several archaic societies. The transcendental breakthrough involved a radicalization of mythospeculation, but not an abandonment of it.

Akhenaten's religious revolution in the middle of the fourteenth century BCE vividly illustrates the difference between myth and mythospeculation. It is not at all true that in a mythic culture there is no change—even the gods change. Some are forgotten, some demoted, some elevated to primacy. In Egypt the position of highest of the gods was indeed unstable: first Horus, then Re, then Amun or Amun-Re, then Ptah, then, in Ptolemaic times Isis, and so forth. None of these changes was traumatic; none of the gods who lost their primacy was denied existence. The way to change a mythic culture is to tell a different story, usually only a somewhat different story, which does not involve denying any previous story. The commonly remarked "tolerance" of polytheism, as noted by David Hume, for example,[31] is not the moral virtue of tolerance as we understand it today, but is part of the very structure of mythic culture. Some myths and the gods whose actions they recount may be more central than others, but the issue of truth and falsity doesn't arise. The very idea of myth as "a story that is not true" is a product of the axial age: in tribal and archaic societies, believers in one myth have no need to find the myths of others false.

But that is just what Akhenaten did: he declared that all the gods but Aten were false; he raised the criterion of truth and falsehood in a way that drove a dagger into the heart of traditional Egyptian religion. As Jan Assmann puts it:

The monotheistic revolution of Akhenaten was not only the first but also the most radical and violent eruption of a counter-religion in the history of humankind. The temples were closed, the images of the gods were destroyed, their names were erased, and their cults were discontinued. What a terrible shock such an experience must have dealt to a mentality that sees a very close interdependence between culture and nature, and social and individual prosperity! The nonobservance of ritual interrupts the maintenance of cosmic and social order.[32]

But though Akhenaten cut to the root of traditional myth, he did not leave the mythic mode and, in some ways, was even quite conservative. The prime source of our knowledge of Akhenaten's thought is "The Great Hymn to Aten," which is still fundamentally narrative.[33] Yet the "cognitive breakthrough" is clear enough. The Aten, the sun disk, is the source of light, and light is the source of life and of time itself. Ritual and myth are not abandoned, but they focus exclusively on Aten. James Allen has argued that, in finding light to be the fundamental reality of the cosmos, Akhenaten was more a "natural philosopher," a precursor of the pre-Socratics, than a theologian.[34] But Akhenaten was both. And what made him conservative was that he believed that Aten revealed himself only to him, the pharaoh, and only through the pharaoh to the people. In popular devotion, Aten was depicted together with Akhenaten and his wife, Nefertiti, all three as gods. In this respect Akhenaten's religion reaffirmed the archaic unity of god and king, and however much a precursor, it failed to raise the critical question of the relation between god and king, the very hallmark of the axial age. Moreover, Akhenaten's claim to be the exclusive channel for the relation of god and people took place in an age when personal piety, the direct relation of individuals to the gods, was on the rise.

For many reasons, Akhenaten's revolution failed: knowledge of his very existence was wiped out not long after his death, only to be rediscovered in modern times by archaeologists. The primary reason for the collapse, besides the fact that the revolution was far too radical for its time (other radical movements have survived on the margins of societies that rejected them) was that it was exclusively the intellectual product of its founder. When Akhenaten died, there were neither priests, nor prophets, nor a people to continue in the faith. Nonetheless, the fact that mythospeculation had made a cognitive breakthrough that would not be repeated for nearly a thousand years is indeed remarkable. It is an indication of the fact that, however slowly and painfully, the axial breakthroughs were the children of the archaic cultures from which they arose.

But what I want to get at now, and what we will see more clearly when we examine the individual cases, is that "breakthrough," that problematic word, does not mean the abandonment of what went before. Theoretic culture is added to mythic and mimetic culture—which are reorganized in the process—but they remain in their respective spheres indispensable. Theoretic culture is a remarkable achievement, but always a specialized one, usually involving written language in fields inaccessible to ordinary people. Everyday life continues to be lived in the face-to-face interaction of individuals and groups and in the patient activities of making a living in the physical world. It is first of all mimetic (enactive, to use Bruner's term) and not in need of verbal explanation, but if linguistic explanation is necessary, it will most often be narrative, not theoretic.

I have mentioned the fact that the face-to-face rituals of tribal society continue in disguised form among us. As an example, let me take the ritual handshake that is so much a part of our daily life. Arnaldo Momigliano tells us that the ancient Roman handshake, *dexterarum iunctio,* was an old symbol of faith, *fides,* that is, faith as trust or confidence, and that from very early times Fides was a Roman goddess. He says that there are good reasons for thinking that handshaking in Greece was an expression of *pistis,* the Greek equivalent of *fides.* Though normally the handshake simply confirmed the trustworthiness of an agreement, with perhaps an aura of divine protection, Attic grave reliefs suggest a further extension of the idea for they "show handshaking as a symbol of Faith at the parting between the dead and the living. Thus handshaking was not only a sign of agreement among the living, but the gesture of trust and faith in the supreme departure."[35] With us the handshake is hardly a conscious gesture, but nonetheless one does not expect to be attacked by someone with whom one has just shaken hands. A refusal of a proffered handshake, however, would make the ritual gesture conscious indeed: breaking the ritual raises ominous questions that would require an explanation.

No one has argued more persistently than Randall Collins, following Durkheim and Erving Goffman, that daily life consists in endless "interaction ritual chains." "Ritual," he says, "is essentially a bodily process." He argues that ritual requires bodily presence, and asks, rhetorically, whether a wedding or a funeral could be conducted by telephone or videoconferencing. His answer is, clearly, no. One could videotape a wedding or a funeral, but without the physical presence and interaction of the participants, no ritual could occur.[36] But mimetic (enactive, embodied) culture does not just continue to exist alongside theoretic culture: it reclaims, so to speak, some of the achievements of theoretic culture. Hubert Dreyfus has shown in detail how skills learned with painstaking attention to explicit rules, through becoming embodied and largely unavailable to consciousness, are in the end far more efficient than they were at the beginner's stage.[37] His examples include driving a car and expert chess playing. In such cases the experienced practitioner knows "instinctively" what to do in challenging situations. "Critical thinking" (theoretic culture) at such moments would only disrupt the flow and produce serious mistakes. One can imagine such a process of embodiment going all the way back to Paleolithic stone chipping. What was initially learned by painful trial and error became, with practice, "second nature," so to speak, even before there was any language to describe it. If we imagine that "moderns" live in a "scientific world" and have left behind such primitive things as ritual, it is only because we have not observed, as people such as Goffman, Collins, and Dreyfus have, how much of our lives is lived in embodied rituals and practices. This is not to say that ritual has gone uncontested: antiritual tendencies and even movements occurred in most of the axial breakthroughs, and periodically ever since. This is something we will have to consider closely as we go along. But in every case, ritual, when thrown out at the front door, returns at the back door: there are even antiritual rituals. Our embodiment and its rhythms are inescapable.

If mimetic culture has interacted vigorously with theoretic culture once the latter has appeared, such is also the case with narrative culture. There are things that narrative does that theory cannot do. In Chapter 1 I noted that narrative actually constitutes the self, "the self is a telling."[38] Not only do we get to know persons by sharing our stories, we understand our membership in groups to the extent that we understand the story that defines the group. Once theoretic culture has come into existence, stories can be subjected to criticism—that is at the heart of the axial breakthroughs—but in important spheres of life, stories cannot be replaced by theories. Because stories really have been replaced by theories in natural science, some have come to believe that such can occur in all spheres. Though efforts to create a science of ethics or politics or religion have rendered critical insights in those spheres, they have not succeeded in replacing the stories that provide their substance. When Aristotle, surely one of the greatest theorists of all times, begins his *Ethics,* he asks the question, what do people consider the highest good, and finds that the common answer is happiness. In short, he starts from opinion, from the stories people tell about what leads to happiness, and though he criticizes those stories, he doesn't reject their substance. Aristotle agrees with the common opinion that happiness is the highest good—he brings his critical insight to bear in seeking to discern what will lead to true happiness. In short, he seeks to improve the common story with a better story, not with a theory. Some modern moral philosophers have sought to create an ethics based on "reason alone." But when utilitarians say that ethics should be based on the consideration of the greatest good for the greatest number, they require a substantive account of the good to get started: they still need a story about the good. When deontologists try to get around this objection by distinguishing between the good, which is culturally variable, and the right, which is universal, they still require a story about the right that reason alone cannot produce. Efforts to create a "religion within the bounds of reason alone" run up against the same problem: they end up replacing old stories with new ones.

Narrative, in short, is more than literature, it is the way we understand our lives. If literature merely supplied entertainment, then it wouldn't be as important as it is. Great literature speaks to the deepest level of our humanity; it helps us better understand who we are. Narrative is not only the way we understand our personal and collective identities, it is the source of our ethics, our politics, and our religion. It is, as William James and Jerome Bruner assert, one of our two basic ways of thinking. Narrative isn't irrational—it can be criticized by rational argument—but it can't be derived from reason alone. Mythic (narrative) culture is not a subset of theoretic culture, nor will it ever be. It is older than theoretic culture and remains to this day an indispensable way of relating to the world.

Donald noted that through most of its history, narrative culture has been oral, and that the development of writing as an external symbolic storage system is an essential precondition for the emergence of theoretic culture. Though the earliest writing seems to have been largely utilitarian, keeping accounts of income and outgo in temple and palace economies, when writing was used for extended texts, those texts were more apt to be narrative than theoretic or even quasi-theoretic. They recorded, but did not replace, spoken language. Writing was meant to be read aloud (silent reading is a quite recent development) often because most people, even royalty, remained illiterate and needed scribes to tell them what was written. In short, though writing was a precondition for theoretic culture, and widespread literacy in a society does produce significant cultural change, oral culture has survived as an indispensable supplement to literacy.

We have noted that face-to-face culture always involves the body, even if only slight wariness about strangers in public places. Human interaction is often physical: we have noted the common ritual of the handshake, but a pat on the back, a hug, or a kiss imply increasing degrees of intimacy. Spoken language is embedded in mimetic, enactive culture. Walter Ong has noted that the spoken word "has a high somatic content." He writes: "The oral word, as we have noted, never exists in a simply verbal context, as a written word does. Spoken words are always modifications of a total, existential, situation, which always engages the body. Bodily activity beyond mere vocalization is not adventitious or contrived in oral communication, but is natural and even inevitable. In oral verbalization, particularly public verbalization, absolute motionlessness is itself a powerful gesture."[39] Not only the right gesture, but the spoken word, is essential in many rituals. In a wedding it is the exchange of "I do" that makes the ritual effective. The words of consecration are equally indispensable for a valid Eucharist.

The special significance of the spoken word in religious life long after the advent of writing is indicated by the widespread emphasis on memorization and recitation, sometimes involving the body, as in the forward-and-backward rocking of the torso in Hassidic Jewish prayer. The value attached to the spoken word could lead to a suspicion of writing, as though the highest truths could only be communicated orally—Plato's Seventh Letter is perhaps the most famous expression of this qualm. Certain traditions—Zoroastrian, Hindu, and Buddhist—have insisted on oral transmission of texts over extended periods even after writing was well known. None of this should make us doubt the importance of the written word; it should only make us aware that orality and literacy have always overlapped, and that the full cultural impact of literacy is quite recent. Nor do I want to equate narrativity with orality, even though narrative was long embedded in oral language. Once written down, narratives could more easily be perused and compared, thus increasing the possibility of critical reflection.

The axial age occurred in still largely oral cultures, with only incipient literacy and only the beginnings of theoretic reflection, yet radical conclusions, more radical than those of Akhenaten, emerged in each case. One last time, before turning to the cases, we may ask, how did this happen?

Eric Weil, in an interesting contribution to the 1975 *Daedalus* issue on the axial age, asked whether breakthroughs are related to breakdowns, whether breakdowns might not be the necessary condition for breakthroughs.[40] Breakthroughs involve not only a critical reassessment of what has been handed down, but also a new understanding of the nature of reality, a conception of truth against which the falsity of the world can be judged, and a claim that that truth is universal, not merely local. Why would anyone in a secure and settled society be tempted to make such radical reassessments? Weil's argument is that periods of severe social stress which raise doubts about the adequacy of the existing understanding of reality, in other words, serious breakdowns, may be the necessary predecessors of cultural breakthroughs. Necessary but not sufficient: "Unfortunately for those who crave general explanations, breakdowns in history are extremely common; breakthroughs extremely rare."[41] He suggests it was the threat of the Persians to the kind of city that the Greeks thought necessary for human life that may have stimulated the Greek breakthrough; the pressure of Assyria, Babylonia, and Persia on the ancient Israelites that made them seek a transcendent cause; and possibly similar disruptions in ancient China and India that lay behind the axial innovations there. The negative cases, however, are many. One of the most puzzling is the Phoenicians, who suffered from pressures from the great empires at the same time Israel, their linguistic cousin, did, and later, in Carthage, faced a life-and-death struggle with Rome. Yet this remarkably versatile, economically innovative, highly literate culture experienced no breakthrough, unless, and this is highly unlikely, all evidence of such a breakthrough has been lost.

Weil reminds us of another point: those responsible for the most radical innovations were seldom successful. In the short run they usually failed: think of Jeremiah, Socrates, Confucius, Jesus. Buddhism finally disappeared in India, the Buddha's home ground. Jaspers sums it up starkly: "The Axial Period too ended in failure. History went on."[42] So breakthroughs were not only preceded by breakdowns, they were followed by breakdowns. History indeed. The insights, however, at least the ones we know of, survived. The very failures that followed them stimulated repeated efforts to recover the initial insights, to realize the so far unrealized possibilities. It is this that has given such dynamism to the axial traditions. But important though these traditions are to us, and Weil reminds us that any talk of an axial age is culturally autobiographical—the axial age is axial because of what it has meant to us[43]—these traditions give us no grounds for triumphalism. The failures have been many and it is hard to gauge the successes. It is hard to say that we today, particularly today, are living up to the insights of the great axial prophets and sages. But it is time to take a closer look.

ANCIENT ISRAEL

Although everyone who has seriously discussed the axial age has included ancient Israel as an axial case, it is clear that theory, if we define it narrowly as "thinking about thinking," was not an Israelite concern. The wisdom tradition, already present in archaic Mesopotamia and Egypt, was well developed in Israel, but only incipiently engaged in logical argument as compared, say, to Greek philosophy. Nonetheless, ancient Israel clearly meets the standard for which we argued in the introductory section if we remember the importance of external memory, the preoccupation with and criticism of texts, and the conscious evaluation of alternative grounds for religious and ethical practice. To use Momigliano's language, as cited above, the texts that were being put together in ancient Israel did indeed contain "new models of reality" that operated as "a criticism of, and alternative to, the prevailing models." Though these new models were still usually expressed in narrative form, they involved such fundamental rethinking of religious and political assumptions that they had a powerful theoretic dimension. It will be our task here to see how exactly these new models came into existence.

From the point of view of a modern historical approach, the data concerning ancient Israel, and the scholarly interpretations of the data, are very nearly baffling. What we have to work with is essentially the Hebrew Bible, what Christians call the Old Testament, with some archaeological evidence and some appearance of Israel in the archives of neighboring societies, but, in the end, it is the Bible that is the primary source. The problem is that after 200 years of intensive scholarship there is still only weak and contested consensus on such elementary facts as the dating of various biblical texts. Much of the Bible presents itself as history—not, of course, in the modern sense of critical historiography but as a more or less continuous narrative extending from the creation to the fifth century BCE. But every page of that narrative serves some religious purpose and can only be of use for the reconstruction of "what really happened" by the most painstaking scholarly analysis, if at all. And the "if at all" is not a minor addendum: one tendency in contemporary biblical scholarship is to say that we will never know what really happened and that we must deal with the Bible as it is, namely a collection of stories, some of which may have some connection with actual individuals who lived in ancient Israel, but we don't know what. This is not an escape open to me. My comparative historical undertaking requires that I give some historical reality to the data or not use it at all. My strategy is to follow as far as possible some reputable scholars, while putting aside after careful consideration the views of others, and to use my common sociological sense of what is probable and what is not probable when the scholarly guidance is conflicting.

What I have found has been in many ways surprising to me, and, though not surprising to experts in the field, may be surprising to readers of this book. Some scholars believe that the entire history of Israel was created out of whole cloth in the Persian period (538 BCE to 333 BCE) or even in the Hellenistic period (333 BCE to 165 BCE).[44] It seems apparent to me that we know very little indeed about the premonarchical history of Israel, with only a little evidence for late-premonarchical society. This means that the five books of Moses—the Pentateuch or the Torah—is folktale, legend, and epic, created or, at best, elaborated from the sketchiest of fragments, in the monarchical period or later. The transition from tribal to monarchical society as described in Judges through 1 Kings, seems to me in outline plausible, though in detail often dubious. To one raised on the idea that what made Israel different from its predecessors was that it was based on history, not myth, it has come as a shock that the single most central figure in the Hebrew Bible, Moses, has no more historicity than Agamemnon or Aeneas.[45] But that the epic—the story of Moses, the Exodus, and the revelation at Sinai—was given its present form in the monarchy, perhaps in the seventh century, many centuries after the supposed events to be sure, seems much more likely to me than the so-called minimalist scenario that it was the product of an even much later date.

The reason I can't believe the so-called minimalist scenario is that I see no reason why the inhabitants of a small colonial province under Persian or Greek rule would have any need to create the history of the united, then divided, then obliterated monarchy, or the Moses/Exodus epic either. The issue that almost the entire Hebrew Bible deals with is the issue of God and king, the central issue of archaic society, in a couple of marginal kingdoms under tremendous strain in the tumultuous mid-first millennium BCE. To be sure the Babylonian exile gave rise to an enormous sense of loss, but I fail to understand the depth of that feeling if nothing at all had really been lost, if the kingdoms of Israel and Judah were largely fictions of the Persian or Hellenistic periods. I am thus inclined to go with a quite modified traditional chronology rather than with the radical revisionists. I am aware that what I am calling a "modified traditional chronology" will still seem quite radical to many readers.

A condensed chronology may help the reader follow the discussion:

Mid-13th c. BCE	Moses (traditional dating)
1208	First mention of Israel in Egyptian records
ca. 1200–1000	Premonarchical tribes of Israel and Judah
ca. 1030–1010	Saul as king of Israel
ca. 1010–970	David as king of Judah and Israel
ca. 970–930	Solomon as king of Judah and Israel
ca. 930–722	Divided monarchy of Judah and Israel
722	Assyrian conquest of (northern) kingdom of Israel
640–609	Josiah as king of Judah
587	Babylonian conquest of (southern) kingdom of Judah
587–538	Babylonian exile
539	Conquest of Babylonia by Cyrus the Persian
538	First exiles return to Judah
333	Alexander conquers Persian Empire, including Judah
140–63	Hasmonean monarchy
65	Roman conquest of Palestine

Even though some traditions, particularly in the book of Judges, may go back to the premonarchical period, only one particular text, written in the oldest Hebrew in the Bible, namely the song of Deborah (Judges 5), may possibly be dated to the premonarchical era.[46] Nonetheless, even if memories of a premonarchical past were recorded only in monarchical or later times, the fact that such memories play such a prominent role in the Hebrew Bible is itself of great significance. In ancient Mesopotamia and Egypt the divine creation of order out of preexisting chaos involved integrally the institution of kingship. Although we know from archaeological evidence that there was in both cases a long period of premonarchical development, that fact has been elided from the cultural memory. Of course the Israelite monarchy was a latecomer—monarchy in Mesopotamia and Egypt was thousands of years old by the time of Saul, David, and Solomon. Still, that the premonarchical period—remembered, elaborated, or invented—should have had such a prominent role in Israel (the first seven books of the Bible are concerned with it) requires an explanation. Several plausible explanations have been given: (1) premonarchical stories were used to legitimate the monarchy; (2) premonarchical stories were used to criticize the monarchy; (3) after the fall of the monarchy, premonarchical stories were used to assure the Israelites that they could continue to exist after the monarchy as they had before it.[47] There is probably some truth in all these explanations.

Given that every motive for "remembering" the premonarchical period was tendentious, it is hard, even with the help of archaeology, to say very much about premonarchical society. If there were a people called Israel in the hill country of northern Palestine in the late thirteenth century, as the victory stele of Pharaoh Merneptah indicates, it was of marginal importance, as it never appeared again in Egyptian (or any other) records in the premonarchical period.[48] In all likelihood it was only one of several groups of inhabitants, of various origins, among whom a collective identity formed only gradually—Judah, for example, not being a part of Israel until the time of David. Although the power of New Kingdom Egypt in Palestine was in steep decline after 1200 BCE, sporadic efforts to defend trade routes from highland raiders led to Egyptian incursions involving occasional deportation of Palestinians to Egypt.[49] Memories of such deportees who managed to return may have provided the nucleus of the Exodus/Moses narrative, though beyond the fact that Moses is an Egyptian name, there is little evidence to go on. But that we have any of Moses's own words, much less that the enormous corpus of laws contained in Exodus, Leviticus, Numbers, and Deuteronomy were literally delivered by Moses, is believed by almost no scholars today. Yet the Torah, the first five books of the Bible, has been at the heart of Jewish worship for over 2,000 years. Where did it come from and how did it attain its centrality? These are not easy questions to answer, if we can answer them at all, but even trying to answer them may lead us closer to what we most need to know.

Let us start by shifting from the opening books of the Bible—however central they are, they are not historical in the modern sense of the term—to what we can say with at least a little historical confidence about early Israelite society. If we can use the books of Judges and 1 Samuel to give us some sense of what late premonarchical society was like, we can say that the term "Israel" perhaps applied to a collection of hill peoples in central and northern Palestine, organized mainly by kinship into lineages, clans, and tribes. Although the idea that there were twelve tribes is a fiction—even in the Bible the lists of the twelve vary considerably—and we don't know exactly of what a tribe consisted, there were no stable structures above the tribal level. Several tribes might unite under a charismatic war leader, such as Gideon or Jephthah, when threatened by neighboring peoples, but these alliances did not survive the crisis, nor was the relation between "Israelite" tribes entirely free of conflict. I put the term *Israelite* in quotes because there is little ground for asserting a strong ethnic identity in the premonarchical period. In language and culture the Israelites were virtually indistinguishable from their "Canaanite" neighbors. The isolated appearance of the term "Israel" in the Merneptah Stele of 1208 BCE tells us little or nothing about continuity or identity. Indeed, we might almost say that the Israelites were Canaanites who lived in the hills, and Canaanites were Canaanites who lived in the lowlands and along the coast (the Phoenicians are often identified as "Canaanites"), or maybe it would be best to call them all simply Western Semites.

Alexander Joffe, arguing entirely from archaeological data, suggests that the period from roughly 1200 to 1000 BCE, in what he calls the Levant, saw the collapse not only of the Egyptian and Hittite empires that had previously contested the area, but of many local city states organized around a palace economy, the Phoenician cities being virtually the only ones able to maintain continuity through this period. In a pattern seen earlier of cyclical urbanization and ruralization, the decline of cities was concomitant with a significant increase in settlements in the hill country, where agriculture and herding were combined. Joffe believes that these growing hill settlements were not the product of significant in-migration, though populations in the ancient Near East were seldom without a variety of forms of movement, but were composed mainly of indigenous "Canaanites."[50] By the beginning of the tenth century BCE, he notes, the revival of urban settlements, either the recovery of old towns or the establishment of new ones, was well under way, but rural settlements were numerous enough and strong enough to play a part in subsequent political development: "The emergence of a rural component, with strong networks of connections, also created for the first time in the Southern Levant a meaningful social counterbalance to the power of cities. The Iron Age is the uneasy fusion of both urban and rural, where loci of politics, economics and culture are in constant tension."[51]

But surely Israel was characterized by a distinct religion, long before the monarchy—think of Abraham, Isaac, and Jacob, much less Moses. For decades the idea of religious distinctiveness in early Israel has steadily eroded. Yahweh, it seems, is not the original God of Israel, but a latecomer, arriving from, of all places, Edom, and generally identified with the south: not only Edom but Midian, Paran, Seir, and Sinai (Judges 5:4; Habakkuk 3:3; Psalm 68:8, 17).[52] The original God of Israel was El, not Yahweh, as is evident in the patriarchal narratives: the name Isra-el means "El rules," not "Yahweh rules"—that would be Isra-yahu.[53] Or maybe not El, the personal name of the old urban Canaanite high god, but el, the generic West Semitic term for god, spirit, or ancestor. Perhaps in Genesis 32, Jacob at the ford of the Jabbok was wrestling with a tribal "powerful being," not the transcendent God, nor the convenient later resolution of the problem, an angel.

If in premonarchical times even tribes were not clearly defined, the real focus of piety was on the family and the lineage. Recent scholarship has emphasized the importance of family religion, not only in ancient Israel but throughout the ancient Near East. Families worshipped ancestors (also called *elim,* plural of *el*) and local gods, the "gods of the fathers," or "household gods," who might be represented by images, as in the case of the teraphim of Laban, stolen by Rachel (Genesis 31:30–35). Karel van der Toorn has usefully characterized this early religion:

> In the earliest phase of Israelite religion it would seem that religion was predominantly a matter of the family or the clan. The settlers of the central hill country lived in self-contained and largely self-sufficient communities . . . Family religion was focused on the god of the settlement. This god was the patron of the leading family and, by extension, of the local clan and the settlement. Allegiance to the clan god was concomitant with membership of the clan. The clan god was commonly a god of the Canaanite pantheon, El and Baal being the most commonly worshipped. The occurrence of Yahweh as clan god seems to have been exceptional.[54]

Our knowledge of the "Canaanite pantheon" comes mainly from the rich trove of texts from the city of Ugarit in northern Syria in the second millennium BCE.[55] There are clear continuities with Israelite religion, but also clear discontinuities—Ugarit was destroyed well before our earliest evidence for Israel and was a city well to the north of the Israelite hill country, so, though continuities can be found, they must be used with caution. In addition, the term "El" could be used as a proper name for the Ugaritic high god, or simply as the generic word for "god." Similarly Baal, the proper name of an important Ugaritic god, is also simply the word for "lord" or "master." Thus Rainer Albertz cautions against reading too much into terminological similarities:

> However, regardless of the names of the gods whom the families chose to be their gods, at the level of family piety they lost any specific characterization. Whether the early Israelite families worshipped El-Shaddai or El-'Olam or another El, as a family god this god had little more in common with the great god of heaven in the Ugaritic pantheon than the name. The cultic, local, historical and functional differentiations

within the world of the gods, which are a reflection of political and social differentiations [in urban Ugarit], hardly play any role at the level of
the family with its relatively simple social structure.[56]

Just as the Madonna of one village in rural Italy was not viewed as the same
as the Madonna in the next village, the El of one locality was not necessarily identical with the El of another: for example, the El of Bethel relative to
El Elyon of Jerusalem. The same was true for Baals and even local Yahwehs
in early times.

It is tempting to see the religion of early Israel, with its local, decentralized, clan "gods," as similar to the tribal religions described in Chapter 3,
and there is probably some truth in that idea. Early Israel was not, however, an isolated society or one surrounded only by tribal peoples. It was,
rather, one of several "frontier societies," as they have been called, close to
and inevitably influenced by archaic societies with highly differentiated
religious systems. Probably in premonarchical and certainly in early monarchical Israel something of archaic polytheism was present.[57] Most unsettling has been the discovery that El's consort Asherah was inherited by
Yahweh when El and Yahweh were merged (more on that shortly). The existence of a Mrs. God, so unseemly to Jewish and Christian orthodoxy, has
become widely, though not universally, accepted.

There is reason to believe that Yahweh became important only with the
early state, a matter we must carefully consider. (Tribal societies under great
external pressure have come up with "prophetic movements" oriented to
high gods, as we saw in Australia in Chapter 3, so that remains a theoretical
possibility in premonarchical Israel. But the near marginality of Yahweh in
earliest Israel argues against that possibility in my view.) Certainly Yahweh
as the national god did not displace the lineage and local gods, at least not
for a long time. Albertz points out that family religion persisted well into the
monarchical period, perhaps all through it. Personal names often referred to
gods, but, he writes, "It is still in no way customary in the early monarchical
period to give one's children names containing Yahweh; this only changes in
the late period of the monarchy."[58]

The Early State

If we can speak of premonarchical Israel at all, it was a congeries of decentralized local kin groups of various sizes, primarily hill dwellers, some of whom
came together fitfully under charismatic war leaders to defend themselves

against incursions from neighboring groups such as the Ammonites and from the coastal cities of the Philistines. Like similar groups everywhere, such people treasure their autonomy, resist even permanent chieftainships, and devote themselves to evading state control. It would seem that increasing military pressure, particularly from the Philistines, finally stimulated the emergence of an early state as a means of more effective self-defense. Alexander Joffe refers to Israel and Judah, as well as the trans-Jordanian states of Ammon and Moab that also emerged in the early first millennium, as secondary states, developing out of interaction with older and more developed states in the area.[59] Joffe characterizes these emerging states as "ethnicizing states," suggesting that they are less the creation of state structures for pre-state ethnic groups, than part of the very process of the creation of ethnicity, which had not only political but economic and cultural, especially religious, sources.

Evidence for Israel and Judah as independent states dates only from the ninth century. According to the Bible, they splintered from the "united monarchy" of Saul, David, and Solomon in the late tenth century. Working only from archaeological data, Joffe argues that there was indeed a fairly large tenth-century state that included what would later become Israel and Judah and probably trans-Jordanian areas as well, but that it was weak and ephemeral, a creation of a local elite influenced by Phoenician models, but lacking a clear ethnic basis. Like some other ancient Near Eastern monarchies, it was a heterogeneous creation of a ruling elite, and included within it quite diverse groups of which Israel and Judah, or their component elements, as it is debatable whether these had yet become entities, were only part. This tenth-century state probably tried to establish some kind of royal ideology, but according to Joffe, it was "a fragile and perishable Potemkin Village, with a royal establishment that was not especially powerful."[60] Joffe cautions against a premature effort to relate archaeological and literary evidence, but if his archaeological argument is sound, Saul, David, and Solomon sink into the sands of legend, if not entirely, then almost so. But Joffe himself points out that, however inadequate this tenth-century state was at the time, the memory that there had been such a state may have had powerful ideological consequences, not only leading to the later provision of its alleged founders with fascinating biographies, but supplying a source for an ideological unity that was almost surely lacking at the time.

In any case some significant actors in the ninth-century states of Israel and Judah, which began to take on a degree of historical substantiality lacking in their tenth-century predecessor, argued for a common religious culture between the two, even though a contested one. Archaeological evidence suggests that widespread literacy was lacking in Israel and Judah until the eighth century, so that earlier accounts were orally transmitted, always a problematic process, though written documents from the eighth or even the seventh century went though such a long process of editing and rewriting that they are scarcely more reliable than oral accounts.

I have tried to show just how fragile our knowledge of the early monarchy is, and even more of the premonarchical period. And yet because of the importance of premonarchical Israel for all later Israelite and Jewish/Christian/Muslim history, we must try to characterize some of its significant features. One such feature is that premonarchical Israel was, or was remembered as being, antimonarchical. The "judges," who combined a number of roles, including law giving, were primarily war leaders, often with a charismatic aura. None of them, however, attempted to establish a chiefly, much less a royal, lineage. When the Israelites said to Gideon after he had led the successful war against the Midianites, "Rule over us, you and your son and your grandson also," Gideon refused, saying, "The Lord will rule over you" (Judges 8:22–23). But when Gideon's son, Abimelech attempted to make himself king, there were rebellions that finally ended in his death.

After Abimelech had proclaimed himself king, Jotham, his younger brother, before fleeing for his life, told the fable of the trees, satirizing kingship:

> The Trees once went out
> to anoint a king over themselves.
> So they said to the olive tree, "Reign over us."
> The olive tree answered them,
> Shall I stop producing my rich oil
> by which gods and mortals are honored
> and go to sway over the trees?"

The fig tree prefers to produce its delicious fruit and the vine to produce the wine that "cheers gods and mortals" rather than rule. Then the bramble accepts the offer, suggesting absurdly that the other trees "take refuge in my shade," though he is likely to burst into flame and devour the other trees (Judges 9:7–15).[61]

The most famous warning of the dangers of kingship came from Samuel just before he anointed Saul, the first king of Israel. Samuel is himself a complex figure, the last of the "judges," but also priest and "seer," that is, a prophet who can, among other things, foresee the future. Indeed, 1 Samuel tells us "the one who is now called a prophet was formerly called a seer" (1 Samuel 9:9). It would seem that Samuel, the last of the seers, was the first of the prophets, and that, as Frank Cross has argued, prophecy and kingship in Israel were born together and died together.[62] In any case, Samuel's response to the popular demand for a king is prophetic in the classic sense.[63] When the people demanded that Samuel give them a king, Samuel was displeased and prayed to the Lord. The Lord told Samuel, "Listen to the voice of the people in all that they say to you; for they have not rejected you, but they have rejected me from being king over them." Then Samuel reports the words of God's solemn warning to the people:

> These will be the ways of the king who will reign over you; he will take your sons and appoint them to his chariots and to be his horsemen, and to run before his chariots; and he will appoint for himself commanders of thousands and commanders of fifties, and some to plow his ground and to reap his harvest, and to make his implements of war and the equipment of his chariots. He will take your daughters to be his perfumers and cooks and bakers. He will take the best of your fields and vineyards and orchards and give them to his courtiers. He will take one-tenth of your grain and of your vineyards and give it to his courtiers. He will take your male and female slaves and the best of your cattle and donkeys, and put them to his work. He will take one-tenth of your flocks, and you shall be his slaves. And in that day you will cry out because of your king, whom you have chosen for yourselves; but the Lord will not answer you in that day. (1 Samuel 8:6–18)

If there are premonarchical memories here, we cannot be certain what they are. That Yahweh was considered king in tribal Israel and that the choice of a human king was a kind of apostasy is almost surely a later idea. Samuel's graphic picture of royal oppression could represent the experience of the Israelites under the monarchy, but tribal Israel knew what monarchies were like—they had spent a good deal of energy avoiding them—so this negative image could be premonarchical. In the back and forth over the choice of a king the attitude of the Lord is not wholly negative. In telling Samuel to choose Saul, he seems to recognize the perils of the situation: "He shall save my people from the hand of the Philistines, for I have seen the suffering of my people, because their outcry has come to me." (1 Samuel 9:16)

Even if the biblical account of Saul, David, and Solomon cannot be taken at face value, the depiction of these three figures may give us some idea of the process of creating the early state in Israel. First of all, Saul was not exactly king of "all Israel"; he was king over "Gilead, the Ashurites, Jezreel, Ephraim, and Benjamin" (2 Samuel 2:9). Neither the northernmost tribes nor Judah were included. He seems only modestly more powerful than the "judges" who preceded him: he ruled not from a capital city but from his own estate; he relied on levies from the tribes under his control but had no army of his own; he apparently had no system of taxes and corvée. In terms of what we saw in Chapter 4, Saul looks more like a paramount chief than a king.

With David we begin to see the outline of an archaic monarchy: he had a personal army including non-Israelite troops (though we can't read too much about ethnicity into this early period); he captured Jerusalem, a Jebusite city, that then belonged to him personally (the city of David) rather than to any tribe; in a rather strange addendum to the David story (2 Samuel 24), David ordered a census as the first step toward more intense political control, but he subsequently repented of it and God punished him for it.[64]

With Solomon the outline was substantially filled in. With the help of Phoenician artisans he built a temple to Yahweh in Jerusalem, with an adjoining palace for himself. He established extensive relations with neighboring powers and undertook matrimonial alliances with several of them. Whereas David financed most of his activities with war booty, Solomon had to rely on taxation and forced labor. Whether the Solomon we know in the Bible was a real king or an archetype of kingship in Israel, his actions approximated Samuel's dark warning to the Israelites about what life under a king would be like.

According to 1 Kings 11–12, when Solomon died, the northern tribes requested of Rehoboam, Solomon's son and successor, that he "lighten the yoke that your father put on us." Rehoboam, however, ignoring the advice of the elders of Judah and following the rash advice of his age-mates, threatened the northern tribes with increasing, not lightening, their burden (heavy taxation and forced labor). The ten tribes of Israel thereupon revolted and chose Jeroboam to be their king. According to Rainer Albertz, one can see the revolt of Jeroboam and the northern tribes as an effort to return to the lighter rule of Saul, closer to the old tribal ideal of independence. A royal residence as a permanent power base in the north was not constructed for fifty years after the separation from Judah. It also seems that there was a reference to an early version of the story of Moses and the Exodus as part of the effort to legitimate the northern kingdom—the life of Jeroboam was even seen as paralleling the life of Moses as a liberator of his people from autocratic oppression.[65] Again, whether these accounts contain some contemporary evidence or were constructed only considerably later, they testify to the continued ambivalence in the tradition about the institution of kingship.

But in Judah, whether from David and Solomon or only later, the full outline of archaic Near Eastern kingship gradually took shape. Much of the symbolism of sacred kingship comes down to us as focusing on the figure of David, founder of the royal lineage of Judah, and of Solomon, his son and first successor, even if in fact the development was only gradual. Although elements of the old high pantheon of West Semitic gods had been known to tribal Israel, they became adapted to monarchical institutions in the developing royal theology of the early monarchy. Mark S. Smith has carefully described the process. El, the original god of Israel, was, in ancient Ugarit married to Athirat and surrounded by their children, including morning and evening star gods, as well as sun and moon gods, but also the somewhat ambiguous figure of Baal, sometimes seen as a son of El, sometimes as an outsider. In the Israelite version El had a consort, Asherah, and various children, including Astarte and Baal, but also Yahweh. This gave rise to a kind of cosmopolitan theology in which El or Elohim was the father of the gods of various peoples. Smith sees a remnant of this older idea surviving in the old poem included as chapter 32 of Deuteronomy:

When the most high (Elyon) allotted peoples for inheritance,
When He divided up humanity,
He fixed the boundaries for peoples,
According to the number of divine sons:[66]
For Yahweh's portion is his people,
Jacob his own inheritance. (Deuteronomy 32:8–9)

Other sons of El were gods of other peoples. In the context of this "world theology" the reputed presence of chapels to the gods of Solomon's various foreign wives would not be blasphemous, but would represent on the level of divinity the pattern of international relations established by the new monarchy. In this schema, Baal, the god of Tyre, but long known in premonarchical Israel, would be no particular threat.[67]

This rather tolerant cosmopolitan theology, appealing to moderns on that account,[68] was, however, to be replaced gradually by something else sufficiently different that reconstructing the earlier pattern has been difficult. Mark Smith characterizes the change as involving two parallel processes: convergence and differentiation.[69] The primary example of convergence was the growing idea that El and Yahweh were two names for the same God; but it also involved the absorption into the figure of Yahweh of characteristics that had earlier belonged to Baal (storm god, war god). Differentiation involved the idea that two gods, Yahweh and Baal, for example, were incompatible, that it was wrong to worship both of them, even though the existence of the rejected god was not denied. It was convergence, not differentiation, that dominated the royal theology. In this it was similar to ancient Mesopotamia and Egypt, where it was common to elevate one god above the others, or to combine in one the attributes of others.

Karel van der Toorn speculates that it was Saul who first raised Yahweh to the status of the national God, even suggesting an Edomite strain in Saul's genealogy that would account for the elevation of this hitherto rather marginal god. Van der Toorn also notes that the place from which David brought the ark of God to Jerusalem was Kiriath-jearim, in the heart of Saul's home territory.[70] By bringing the ark into Jerusalem and placing it on the site where the temple would later be built, David unmistakably claimed Yahweh as the God of his own kingship.

That Yahweh was the patron deity of the Judahite monarchy, and was exalted above all other gods, would seem to be the case, but does not imply that Yahweh was the only god. Psalm 89, one of the royal psalms, has the following to say in verses 3 to 7:

You said, "I have made a covenant with my chosen one,
　　I have sworn to my servant David:
'I will establish your descendants forever,
　　And build your throne for all generations.'"
Let the heavens praise your wonders, O Lord,
　　your faithfulness in the assembly of the holy ones.
For who in the skies can be compared to the Lord?
　　Who among the heavenly beings is like the Lord,
a God feared in the council of the holy ones,
　　great and awesome above all that are around him?

The idea of a high god, above all other gods, but still a god among gods, is part of the old Near Eastern royal pattern. What this pattern looked like in

Mesopotamia is suggestive of what was coming to be in Jerusalem: "It is no exaggeration to state that ancient Mesopotamian civilization idealized static urban cultures, where kingship, temple cult, and the status of privileged citizens maintained their formal *Gestalten* in the face of shifting political fortunes, and monumental architecture strove to replicate itself across the centuries as an anchor of collective civic vitality."[71] One additional feature was central in Jerusalem: the temple of Yahweh was located on a holy mountain: Mount Zion, a mountain whose name summed up the Judahite royal complex.

If we can speak of a royal theology it is because the king is at the center of it: God's chosen king, in the temple, on the holy mount, in the sacred city, in the land that, by extension, can as a whole be called Zion. We can see—less in the narrative accounts of Samuel, Kings, and Chronicles, more in many of the psalms—the image of a king who is so close to the Lord that he is (almost) divine, that is, we can see in Judah what was common in the archaic Near East.[72] At one place only in all the Hebrew scriptures, Psalm 45, verse 6, the king is addressed as God:

> Your throne, O God, endures forever and ever.[73]
>   Your royal scepter is a scepter of equity;
>   you love righteousness and hate wickedness
> Therefore God, your God, has anointed you
>   with the oil of gladness beyond your companions

If the king is only once called God, his closeness to divinity is affirmed repeatedly: he is begotten by God (Psalm 2:7); he is the firstborn of God (Psalm 89:27); he is seated at the right hand of God (Psalm 110:1).[74] The notion of divine kingship in Israel is contrary to our preconceptions and is almost always denied. Steven Holloway, writing about a similar tendency among scholars of ancient Mesopotamia where divine kingship has also often been denied, writes, "The problem is not the elastic conception of the divine in ancient Mesopotamia but our modern rigid notion of the meaning of godship, and the misleading translations and interpretive shortfalls it occasions."[75] For us, and in good part because of later developments in the religion of Israel to which we are heir, there is an ontological chasm between the divine and the human that simply wasn't there in the archaic mind. There was a whole hierarchy of gods: high gods, their wives, children, and grandchildren, their messengers—even the spirits of the dead were called "gods." If mountains could be divinized, so could extraordinary humans, and who more likely than the king? That "David," meaning David's lineage, should be chosen for kingship "forever" is already so extraordinary that it points to a significant difference that puts the king "beyond your companions," as Psalm 89 has it. I don't mean to deny that the king was often depicted as the servant of God, or that the king could be chastised by God. In that same Psalm 89 which so exalts the king, God says that if David's children "violate my statutes," he will "punish their transgression with the rod," but still God says, "I will not remove from him my steadfast love . . . I will not violate my covenant" (Psalm 89:30–33).[76] The promise of "forever" transcended the sins of those to whom it was made, raising the question of conditional versus unconditional covenants that will have to be considered later. The destruction of the dynasty by the Babylonians caused a crisis for ancient Israelite theology, but one they were able to surmount, as we will see.

There is clearly a tension between the narrative account of the origin of kingship in ancient Israel and the symbolism of kingship as reflected in psalms that were perhaps written for enthronement ceremonies in the temple. In the narrative, kingship had a quite specific historical beginning. In the coronation hymns, not only will the kingship last forever, its origins are in the creation itself. Jon Levenson finds that "the cosmic-mythological symbols of creation," so closely linked to ancient Near Eastern kingship, but supposedly absent in Israel, were in fact present there as well. He quotes Psalm 89:25 in this regard:

I will set his hand upon the sea,
His right hand upon the rivers.

In the ancient Ugaritic myths, the high god El overcame the chaos of the waters, seas and rivers, in the act of creating the world (fragments of this version of creation are found in various places in the Hebrew scriptures, and even alluded to in Genesis 1:1 which suggests that chaos was present at the beginning of time and that God brought order into it). In Psalm 89:26 the king is described as participating in this divine act of creation, leading Levenson to note, "Creation, kingship, and temple thus form an indissoluble triad, the containment of the sea is the continuing proof of their eternal validity (e.g., Psalm 93)."[77]

Some scholars interpret these mythological overtones to the Zion complex as a result of the absorption of Jebusite beliefs by the Israelites after their conquest of Jerusalem, which was an old Canaanite city. The point is not that the Israelites absorbed ethnically alien ideas, but that tribal Israel was becoming an urban kingdom, and absorbing an urban kingly ideology. There may already have been a temple in Jerusalem before the conquest, and Zadok, David's choice as one of the two high priests, may already have been the Jebusite priest of that temple (though he was later given an Aaronic lineage). The other high priest was Abiathar, who had served as David's high priest before the conquest. In any case, Psalm 48:2 identifies Zion with the Peak of Zaphon, the mountain of the gods in northern Syria known from the Ugaritic texts, and not with Jerusalem.[78]

There are two further implications of the cosmic-mythological nature of the Zion-temple-city-king complex that require noting. One is the idea of inviolability—concretely, the inviolability of Jerusalem. Levenson suggests that the cryptic statement of the Jebusites just before David's attack on Jerusalem that "you will not come in here, even the blind and the lame will turn you back" (2 Samuel 5:6) implies that the Jebusites already had the idea that Jerusalem was impregnable, an idea that the Israelites would take over from them. Levenson writes, "The note of absolute security in the face of the grimmest military facts becomes a central theme in the hymns of Zion that were sung in the days of the Judahite monarchy."[79] The eventual destruction of Jerusalem and the temple in 587 BCE was traumatic and had enormous consequences, but the inviolability of Zion could be maintained if Zion and the city of Jerusalem were seen as transhistorical realities.

The other implication of the Zion complex worth noting is empire. In retrospect David and Solomon were said to have ruled from the river (the Euphrates) to the borders of Egypt. But if the king of Judah was the Lord's anointed, and Yahweh ruled over all the gods, then, in principle, all the nations must bow down to Zion. The Lord of hosts rules "to the ends of the earth"; he is "exalted among the nations, exalted in the earth" (Psalm 46:10). In the Near Eastern royal tradition, the great king, the king of kings, is, in principle, the ruler of the cosmos. That Judah was a small state, often subservient to powerful empires, did not keep the Davidic royal theology from making universal claims, claims that would eventually be seen as to be realized only in the end times.[80]

Yahweh Alone

What we have seen so far is the emergence in Israel, or at least in Judah, of a classic Near Eastern monarchy, with all its attendant ideology. Israel has moved from being a tribal society to being an archaic society with an early state. As secondary states, Israel and Judah did not need to invent archaic culture from scratch—they could take much of it over from the surrounding high cultures, giving what they borrowed a new twist, the dominance of the god Yahweh for example, though his uniqueness is not evident from the early monarchical period. But if the early Israelite states were typically archaic, of what interest would they be in trying to understand the axial age? Something did happen to shake the archaic pattern to its foundations, something that would restructure it, though not destroy it. It is to that change that we must now turn.

If one read only the five books of Moses, the Torah, the heart and soul of Israelite and Jewish religion since the fifth century BCE, one could discern the archaic pattern only with difficulty, only as a shadow. The shadow cast over the archaic pattern, and over Mount Zion, is the shadow of Sinai, and the shadow cast over the figure of David is that of Moses.[81] I am quite aware that the Bible says that Sinai and Moses long preceded Zion and David, and I would not deny that some fragmentary knowledge may be quite old, though more likely of Moses than of Sinai. But the great edifice of the Torah is late monarchical at the earliest and probably much of it is exilic or postexilic. Because the Bible has no interest in showing us how the Torah evolved, we must look to other, more perilous, means to discern the process.

The most obvious place to look is the emergence of the idea of Yahweh as the only God that it was legitimate for Israelites to worship, in place of the cosmopolitan theology that, although placing Yahweh first among the gods, did not deny that other gods could still legitimately receive their due. What we see here is what Mark Smith calls differentiation, in contrast to the convergence that seems to have been characteristic of the royal theology. El, as we have noted, was never conceived as "foreign," and was accepted by all parties as a synonym for Yahweh; other gods, certainly Baal and Asherah, came to be denounced as alien, and their worship as a rejection of Yahweh, who was to be differentiated from them. Although this process has often been characterized as "the growth of monotheism," it is probably better to refer to it with the term introduced by Morton Smith, the Yahweh-alone movement, for devotion to Yahweh did not mean the denial of other gods, only the obligation not to worship them.[82]

The data as usual are highly problematic, but it would seem that the Yahweh-alone movement appeared first in the north, in the kingdom of Israel. What historical reality lies behind the legends of Elijah and Elisha in ninth-century Israel is hard to say—they exist in a world of remarkable miracles—but their devotion to Yahweh and their fierce hostility to all other gods is the most notable thing about them. The stories about them seem to float free from the Deuteronomistic framework in which 1 and 2 Kings place them. They denounce above all the Baal worship of King Ahab's wife Jezebel, and warn of the punishments that will follow such disloyalty, thus following the pattern of Deuteronomistic history that characterizes all the books from Joshua to 2 Kings, but the ecstatic intensity of their hostility seems to transcend the interpretive framework and to suggest the early emergence of an extreme devotion to Yahweh alone. An adequate explanation for this development is beyond us, but there are a few background factors that might give us some context for such a development.

If the traditions concerning Jeroboam have any validity, Israel (as opposed to Judah) was religiously conservative, rejecting the incipient royal theology centered on Jerusalem, its temple and its king. The Bible denounces Jeroboam for setting up "golden calves" at Bethel and Dan. It is very possible that these old Israelite sanctuaries already had such images. The "molten sea" in Solomon's temple was said to stand on "twelve oxen" (1 Kings 7:25), but no one claimed they were worshipped, which was the charge against the images at Bethel and Dan, hard to adjudicate at this remove. In any case Yahweh was the national God of Israel, and, calves or not, was the God worshipped at Bethel and Dan. But monarchy was less firmly established in Israel than in Judah: assassination followed assassination; dynasty followed dynasty, many too brief even to be called dynasties. Internal troubles were matched with external troubles. Israel was exposed to attack from the Arameans of Damascus, and the growing threat of Assyrian imperial power from the ninth century. On top of all this, enmity with Judah was constant, broken only by occasional truces.

The legends of Elijah and Elisha indicate fervent devotion to Yahweh and bitter opposition, not only to the worship of other gods, particularly Baal, but to any worship of Yahweh that involved images or other practices similar to the worship of other gods. Although Elijah refers to Abraham, Isaac, and Jacob, often thought to be ancestors of various northern lineages, combined in one line of descent only later, there is no mention of Moses or Sinai. Elijah was famously called to go south to Mount Horeb (Deuteronomy's term for Sinai) to receive a revelation, one that comes not through storm or earthquake but through the "still, small voice" of Yahweh, yet there is no explicit reference to Moses at Horeb, and some have even suggested that the Moses story was based on the Elijah story rather than the other way around.[83] The traditions indicate severe tension between the prophets and the royal house, particularly Ahab and even more, his queen, Jezebel. It is possible that the practices sanctioned by the royal house were quite ancient and it was the prophets who were the radical innovators, but the social location of the struggle between prophet and king/queen is difficult to reconstruct from the evidence we have.

From the middle of the eighth century BCE, when prophets appeared who for the first time left written records, the social situation in both Israel and Judah was showing signs of severe stress. All across the Near East and Eastern Mediterranean the eighth century seems to have been a time of considerable economic growth, the social consequences of which were destabilizing. The commercialization of agriculture meant that large land holdings were profitable, whereas smallholdings devoted solely to subsistence, were becoming anachronistic. In times of drought or other difficulty, small farmers had to resort to moneylenders, often large landholders. The laws of credit were such that small farmers became in effect debt slaves, or were even sold into slavery to meet their creditors' demands. All of this greatly undermined the effectiveness of the extended kinship system. Because Israel was larger and richer than Judah, these conditions may have been worse in the north. In addition, Assyrian intervention in the Levant, sporadic since the ninth century, was growing more intense in the closing decades of the eighth. The literary prophets were reacting strongly both to the growth of social injustice and to the problems of foreign policy.[84]

Two of the early literary prophets, Amos and Hosea, appeared first in the north, though Amos came originally from Judah. They are just as concerned with the proper worship of Yahweh and just as hostile to his rivals as were the Elijah/Elisha legends, but there is a new note of personal intensity because we have their own words (of course it is always difficult to know what are their own words and what was added later). I have already noted the importance of family or personal religion in the ancient Near East and in early Israel,[85] but that is not what Amos and Hosea are expressing. Rather they are describing a personal relation between Yahweh and the children of Israel that seems strikingly different from anything before. Hosea's metaphors are particularly intense: Israel is the unfaithful wife of Yahweh, rejecting Yahweh's love, although Yahweh is willing to take her back in spite of her unfaithfulness. God tells Hosea to enact the relation of Yahweh and Israel by taking a prostitute as his wife as a parable to the people: "And the Lord said to me, 'Go again, love a woman who is beloved of a paramour and is an adulteress;

even as the Lord loves the people of Israel, though they turn to other gods'"
(Hosea 3:1).

Even more poignant is Hosea's picture of God as a rejected parent:

When Israel was a child, I loved him,
    and out of Egypt I called my son.
The more I called them,
    the more they went from me;
they kept sacrificing to the Baals,
    and burning incense to idols.
Yet it was I who taught Ephraim to walk,
    I took them up in my arms;
    but they did not know that I healed them.
I led them with cords of compassion,
    with the bands of love,
and I became to them as one
    who eases the yoke on their jaws,
    and I bent down to them and fed them. (Hosea 11:1–4)

Although I think such passages are essential to understanding Hosea, they
are quantitatively outweighed by far by invective against the sins of the
people and the description of the judgments that will come down upon
them, as is true of all the prophets. The prophets were angry men speaking
for an angry God, yet, critically, a loving God, willing to forgive the truly
repentant.

Although the sins that provoked Elijah and Elisha were almost entirely cultic, there is a significant new note in the literary prophets, most clearly discerned early in Amos, though characteristic of all of them: the sins they denounce are not just cultic, but ethical, especially the oppression of the weak
and the poor by the strong and the rich. Amos, like Hosea, stresses the special
relation between Yahweh and Israel, making Israel's unfaithfulness all the
more terrible: "You only have I known/ of all the families of the earth;/ therefore I will punish you/ for all your iniquities" (Amos 3:2). Among those iniquities are the following:

Thus says the Lord:
"For three transgressions of Israel,
    and for four I will not revoke the punishment;

because they sell the righteous for silver
    and the needy for a pair of shoes—
they that trample the head of the poor into the dust of the earth,
    and turn aside the way of the afflicted." (Amos 2:6–7)

Not only did Amos and the other prophets criticize cultic sins, they were critical of ritual altogether if people imagined it could outweigh ethical failures. In a famous passage Amos transmits the word of God:

"I hate, I despise your feasts,
    and I take no delight in your solemn assemblies . . .
Take away from me the noise of your songs;
    To the melody of your harps I will not listen.
But let justice roll down like the waters,
    and righteousness like an ever-flowing stream. (Amos 5:21, 23–24)

And Amos sees God as the God of all peoples, even if the relation with Israel is special:

Are you not like the Ethiopians to me,
    O people of Israel? Says the Lord.
Did I not bring Israel up from the land of Egypt
    and the Philistines from Caphtor
    and the Arameans from Kir?
The eyes of the Lord God are upon the sinful kingdom,
    and I will destroy it from the face of the earth
    —except that I will not utterly destroy the house of Jacob.
(Amos 9:7–8)

As noted above, prophecy coexists with monarchy in the history of ancient Israel (we will have to consider the special case of Moses below) as part of the same syndrome. Can we see a struggle for the very definition of the relation between Yahweh and people going on between prophets and kings? The royal theology, in classic archaic form, sees the relation of God and people as necessarily mediated by the king. Individuals and families may have their own cults, but the kingdom as a whole relates to God only through the king. It is this understanding that the prophets challenge: for them God relates directly to the people. From the beginning, prophets kept their distance from the king; had their own channel to Yahweh, so to speak. Samuel criticized Saul; even David was criticized by Nathan. It would be wrong to see the prophets as simply opposed to the kings: they existed together in an uneasy symbiosis. What the prophets insisted on was that the king had no monopoly in relation to Yahweh. At times the conflict was intense, as between Elijah and Jezebel, but only Hosea in the last catastrophic moments of the northern kingdom rejected kingship altogether:

> I will destroy you, O Israel;
>   who can help you?
> Where now is your king to save you?
>   where are all your princes to defend you—
> Those of whom you said,
>   "Give me a king and princes"?
> I have given you kings in my anger,
>   and I have taken them away in my wrath. (Hosea 13:9–11)

The prophets, the earliest exponents of the Yahweh-alone position, claimed that they were more truly "called" by Yahweh than were the kings. Prophecy in the sense of a personal call, or even possession by the divinity, is widespread, not only in the Near East, but among tribal and archaic peoples generally, as we have seen.[86] But in most cases prophets were marginal, answering the needs of the common people, or offering advice and support to rulers, as many prophets did in Israel. The capacity of the great prophets of Israel to challenge kings directly is an indication of the weakness of monarchy, especially in the north, both internally and in face of external threat, and the consequent inability of kings to control various groups of their literate subjects. The great prophets claimed to be called, but the message with which they were entrusted was one of judgment and hope directed to both kings and people, and it was above all the demand to worship Yahweh alone.

So far we have concentrated on the prophets oriented to the northern kingdom, Amos and Hosea, and Hosea is important not only in himself but also for the strong continuity between his language and that of Deuteronomy. Still, we cannot forget Isaiah, also a late eighth-century prophet. Isaiah, in many senses the quintessential prophet, was of Jerusalemite priestly background and, rather than rejecting the Davidic royal theology, managed to transcend it from within. His call, as recounted in Isaiah 6, occurred in a magnified vision of the temple, but it was Isaiah as prophet, not the king, who was called. Nonetheless Isaiah, whose denunciations of kings and people for both ethical and cultic sins were no less emphatic than his northern confreres, remained loyal to the ideal of Zion, the inviolability of Jerusalem, and the continuation of the Davidic kingship, even if only as an ideal projected into a future "Day of the Lord," when all things would be put right. How much of this goes back to Isaiah himself and how much was developed later by the tradition stemming from him is hard to say, but it is in good part due to Isaianic tradition that the idea of King/Jerusalem/Zion was never wholly replaced by the idea of Moses/Sinai/Covenant.[87]

In their demand for the worship of Yahweh alone, the prophets were a distinct minority as is evident from the Bible itself where generation after generation of both kings and people are condemned for worshipping other gods. Ziony Zevit suggests that the evidence for the worship of several gods, and of Yahweh with his consort in particular, is widespread in the archaeological record, not only in the "high places" of popular worship, but in the Jerusalem temple: "The Jerusalem temple itself reflected this polydoxy. Along with the YHWH cult, for most of the history of the institution, other deities were also worshiped."[88] But if, at least until the exile and perhaps even then, only a minority heeded the prophetic admonition, it was, nonetheless, a significant minority, one with the capacity to elaborate the tradition well beyond what the early literary prophets themselves had said. Although 1 and 2 Kings suggest that several kings, in Judah though not in Israel, notably Hezekiah and Josiah, were sympathetic to the Yahweh-alone movement and instituted reforms in accordance with its program, the first clear indication that such a movement had been gathering strength comes during the reign of Josiah, when, during renovations to the temple, a book was discovered that is widely believed to be an early draft of what we know as the fifth book of Moses, Deuteronomy.

The Deuteronomic Revolution

The book of Deuteronomy as we have it has certainly gone through several recensions, but the text is distinct enough in both form and content that it is a critical reference point for looking back at the first four books of Moses and forward to the historical books. What have come to be called "the Deuteronomists" have been seen as contributing a central, perhaps the central, strand of Israel's faith, but who were the Deuteronomists? Who exactly created the tradition that took its first definitive form with the discovery of "Deuteronomy" in the temple in 621 BCE we cannot know, but Geller, following 2 Kings 22, gives us an important indication: "It is worth noting that the committee that brought the Book of the Law to Josiah's attention consisted of Hilkiah the high priest and Shaphan the scribe. It was then confirmed as true by Huldah the prophetess. The list may be viewed as an indication of the major wings of the Deuteronomic coalition."[89] The prophetic background is clear, for the zeal that characterized the prophetic Yahweh-alone movement was at the center of Deuteronomic faith. But the presence of the high priest and a royal scribe is also significant. Each was located within a tradition that overlapped with the prophetic tradition but was not wholly absorbed into it. The priestly tradition with its focus on the temple, the sacrifice and the actual encounter of the high priest with the presence of God in the Holy of Holies in the temple, gave rise to its own literary tradition, one that perhaps completed the editing of the Torah. And royal scribes were educated in the Israelite form of the ancient Near Eastern tradition of wisdom, handed down in such biblical books as Proverbs, Ecclesiastes, and Job. The wisdom tradition was above all one of instruction, of teaching, and of the relation of teacher and student, all of which were taken up into the Deuteronomic understanding of Israelite religion.

The very core of the Deuteronomic tradition, one that gave the religion of ancient Israel its fundamental definition, was the Covenant. Where did this idea come from and what did it mean? We have already seen how central the idea of covenant was in the Judahite royal theology, where the covenant was above all between Yahweh and the house of David. Covenant was a widespread feature of ancient Near Eastern ideology. At one time it was thought that the Hittite suzerainty treaty of the second millennium BCE provided the model on which the Mosaic covenant was based.[90] More recent work, including the exhaustive study of Moshe Weinfeld, suggests that it was the Assyrian treaty model that had the decisive influence on Deuteronomy.[91] The possibility of a powerful Assyrian model for central elements in Israelite religion requires that we back up for a moment to consider the international situation that gave rise to both the literary prophets and the Deuteronomists.

The Assyrian Empire (more properly the Neo-Assyrian Empire, 934–610 BCE) represented a new level of intensity, both militarily and ideologically, compared to previous Near Eastern empires.[92] By the eighth century the ferocity of the Assyrian conquest, involving wholesale destruction and deportation, roused both fear and a desperate desire to resist in all the Levantine states, including Israel and Judah. The military menace of Assyria was paralleled by intense ideological pressure. Although the Assyrians worshipped more than one god, Aššur was the god of king and empire, par excellence, and all subject peoples were required to recognize his predominance. The enormous creativity of Israelite religion from Hosea to Jeremiah and including the early versions of the Pentateuch (that is, late eighth through the seventh centuries) must be seen, then, as in part responses to the Assyrian challenge.

Religious resistance to Assyria took the form of an exclusive reliance on Yahweh, as against the pressure to recognize Aššur; if the Yahweh-alone movement originated before the period of intense Assyrian pressure, it was greatly strengthened in response to it. Isaiah's advice to Judah's kings Ahaz and Hezekiah to avoid both anti-Assyrian alliances and submission to Assyria, but instead to rely on Yahweh alone, is an expression of an intense, if not entirely realistic, religious resistance.

Once Hezekiah submitted to Assyria, followed in the same course by his son, the long-lived Manasseh, they were linked by a suzerainty treaty to accept not only the Assyrian king as ruler, but the primacy of his god, Aššur.[93] Such a treaty involved stipulations that the vassal must follow, and also blessings and curses, often most terrible curses, for any breach of the treaty, any disloyalty. Further, it was the obligation of the vassal to "love" his suzerain, a love not reciprocated by the Assyrian king, for love in this case meant loyalty, required of the vassal but not of the suzerain.[94] It is this kind of treaty, particularly the vassal treaties of Esarhaddon, that Deuteronomy took over and transformed, as we will consider shortly.[95]

Weinfeld contrasts the vassal treaty, which sets up obligations on the part of the vassal and is thus conditional, with the grant treaty, which is an unconditional grant from the suzerain to a follower given as a reward for faithfulness. He finds the covenant with Abraham, involving the promise of land and progeny, as well as the covenant with David, involving the permanent succession of David's house, to be examples of grant covenants, but in both cases he finds that biblical language follows Assyrian models. Thus when God commends Abraham for having "kept my charge" (Genesis 26:5), the language echoes that of Aššurbanipal's grant to a servant, as does the language of "serving perfectly," having "walked before me," and so forth. The language of covenant is, as noted above, ancient in the Near East—it goes back to Sumer and is found among the Hittites and others besides the Assyrians—but the biblical language is especially close to the Assyrian prototypes. This suggests something about the dating of even the apparently "early" covenants with figures such as Abraham and David. We must not, however, overlook the sea change in the Israelite usage: Assyrian covenants were between ruler and subject; Israelite covenants were between God and human beings.[96]

Though the unconditional grant covenants were fundamental to Israel's identity, it was the vassal covenants that provided the basic structure of Deuteronomy and its central formulation of Israelite religion. In both Assyrian and Israelite versions of the vassal covenant the subordinate must keep the stipulations of the treaty or face the most disastrous consequences: in Israel God, in Assyria the gods, will inflict leprosy, blindness, violent death, rape, and invasion by "a nation you have not known" if the subordinate is disloyal.[97] In short, Deuteronomy (and perhaps most of the Pentateuch) comes out of a situation of unparalleled violence in which the northern kingdom had already been destroyed and many of its inhabitants deported, and Judah hung by an uneasy thread in a vassal relation to Assyria. In one reading, Judah, too, had felt the terrible wrath of Assyria in Sennacherib's campaign against Hezekiah in 701 BCE. Baruch Halpern argues for the historicity of the Assyrian claim that they destroyed the whole Judean countryside and all forty-six fortified towns except for Jerusalem, depopulating the rural areas in so doing.[98] Thus, when Hezekiah finally submitted to Assyrian suzerainty, Judah was only a shadow of its former self. Although the countryside was denuded, the population of Jerusalem was swollen with refugees from the northern kingdom after its fall in 722 and from rural Judah from the campaign of 701. Inevitably such drastic population shifts shattered the already weakened kinship ties still further.[99] The memory of the Assyrian horror would linger, and dread of a new catastrophe that would finally engulf Jerusalem itself, would grow. If the prophets often threatened "terror," one of Jeremiah's favorite terms, the Assyrian example, in Jeremiah's time replaced by the equally merciless Babylonians, was all too ready at hand.

Though the book of Deuteronomy was "discovered" in 621 at the time of King Josiah, its beginnings might well date from the time of King Manasseh (687–643) when Esarhaddon (681–669) was ruling and his vassal treaty would have been known in Judah. It is worth noting that the great early prophets for whom texts survive—Amos, Hosea, Isaiah, Micah—are all mid- to late eighth century, the time of the first great Assyrian onslaught. During the seventh century, however, no major literary prophet appeared until Jeremiah began his preaching in 627, when Assyrian power was in decline and new upheavals were on the horizon. It might not be too wildly hypothetical, therefore, to imagine that while public prophecy was in abeyance under the long, repressive rule of Manasseh, circles of those who would come to be called Deuteronomists were already privately at work creating a counter-text to the dominant Assyrian ideological order.

The critical turn, and we can find the beginnings of it in the eighth-century prophets, was the claim that though the kings of Israel and Judah were subordinate to the great kings of Assyria, Yahweh was by no means subordinate to Aššur. On the contrary, Assyria was in Yahweh's control, not Aššur's. Levantine kings often broke their covenant with Assyria, usually with disastrous results. But for the incipient Deuteronomists, the covenant that counted was the covenant between Yahweh and the Children of Israel, and it was the betrayal of that covenant by the Israelites that gave them into the power of the Assyrians, who could only act in accord with the will of Yahweh.

What the eighth-century prophets held about the primacy of Yahweh was spelled out in detail not only in Deuteronomy but in Exodus. The figure of Moses, shadowy and marginal before, took on heroic proportions, narratively in Exodus and "theologically" in Deuteronomy. Eckart Otto points out how much of the Moses story derives from Assyrian sources, the episode of Moses in the bulrushes based on the birth legend of Sargon,[100] for example—yet was given a dramatically different meaning:

> Transferring the structure of events derived from the neo-Assyrian account to the people of Israel under Moses' guidance, the authors of the Hebrew account denied prestige and authority to the Assyrian king. In the Moses-Exodus account, Moses figured as his anti-type due to the fact that it was Moses who, as a figure of Israel's primeval history, mediated between his people and the divine realm. That means that the royal function of mediation was transferred to an ideal figure of Israel's past. With the denial of the concept of sacral kingship, its corresponding ideas of society and its constituents were rejected. For the authors of the Moses-Exodus account, "Israel" was constituted not by a state hierarchy with the king as its central personality but by a covenant between YHWH and his people. This was not an idea of Judaean groups during the exile but a Judaean counter-programme of the seventh century BCE, which rejected Assyrian claims to loyalty.[101]

What the Deuteronomists created was surely motivated by a desire to resist Assyrian ideological domination, but it went far beyond that. The Moses who emerged at the center of the new movement was not only the antitype of the Assyrian (and Egyptian) kings, but of Israelite kings as well.

No one has spelled out the pivotal role of Moses better than Michael Walzer. The great institutional achievement of Israel was to found a society not on the rule of one man who claimed to unite heaven and earth, but on a covenant between God and a people. That is the significance of the events at Sinai after the Exodus from Egypt. But such a new community, like the old one, had to be simultaneously political and religious—there was as yet no clear distinction between these realms—and therefore had to have a leader. But in starkest contrast with Pharaoh, Moses was no divine king. He was God's prophet, nothing else. Yet his sheer responsibility as leader in so desperate an enterprise made him at times look like a king and even act like a king. Walzer points out that there were two sides to Moses as leader: a Leninist side and a social-democratic side.[102]

The Leninist side is most clearly evident in the incident following Moses's discovery that while he was on the mountain receiving the commandments of the Lord, the people had made for themselves a golden calf which they proceeded to worship, an indication of disloyalty, of failure to "love" God, at the very beginning of the formation of Israel as a people. Moses called to those "on the Lord's side" and the sons of Levi gathered around him. Then Moses said to them:

> Thus says the Lord, the God of Israel, 'Put your sword on your side, each of you! Go back and forth from gate to gate throughout the camp, and each of you kill your brother, your friend, and your neighbor.'" The sons of Levi did as Moses commanded, and about three thousand of the people fell on that day. Moses said, "Today you have ordained yourselves for the service of the Lord, each one at the cost of a son or a brother, and so have brought a blessing on yourselves this day. (Exodus 32:27–29)

The Exodus narrative insists that Moses was not a king, a critically important point, but in Exodus 32 he acts like a king. As David Malo, a member of the old Hawaiian aristocracy, put it with respect to the Hawaiian king:

> The edicts of the king had power over life and death. If the king had a mind to put someone to death, it might be a chief or a commoner, he uttered the word and death it was.

But if the king chose to utter the word of life, the man's life was spared.[103]

Moses claimed that the word was the Lord's, but its human voice was Moses's, and on this earth it is the state that authorizes the word of life and death; the spokesperson of the state is always, somehow or other, a king.

Exodus 32 is not the only place in the Exodus narrative where terrible things happen to those who oppose Moses, but Walzer insists the Leninist side is not the whole story. There is another Moses, a social-democratic Moses, who leads by teaching, exhortation, and example, not by violence; who defends the people from the wrath of God, asking the Lord not to make a catastrophic end to the project that He had initiated.[104] Most important, however, what emerged was a new political form, a people in covenant with God, with no king as ruler. Moses is a teacher and a prophet, not a king, and the Torah underscores this point, not only by God's prohibition of Moses's reaching the promised land, but by the account of his death. Moses died in the land of Moab, and "no one knows his burial place to this day" (Deuteronomy 34:6). Walzer points out that there could be no greater contrast to the Egyptian Pharaoh, whose tomb was so central to his identity. Moreover, Moses was not the father of kings—the Bible tells us almost nothing about his descendants.[105] Machiavelli famously asked whether former slaves could have been transformed into a covenant people without the rule of a prophet armed.[106] If, however, we see the Moses narrative not as a historical account but as a charter for a new kind of people, a people under God, not under a king, an idea parallel to Athenian democracy though longer lasting, then we might see Moses as a kind of "transitional object," as a way for people who knew only monarchical regimes to give up the king and begin to understand what an alternative regime might be like.

In the end it was Moses as the one who mediated the covenant who eclipsed Moses as ruler, for covenant was the key to the new society that these proto-Deuteronomists envisioned as coming into being. If Exodus recounts the story of the Exodus and the revelation at Sinai, the covenant and the core terms to which the people must adhere, it is Deuteronomy that spells out the implications of the covenant, its meaning for king, prophet, and people.

It is because Deuteronomy is explicit about these matters that it can be called "theology," but the term must remain in quotation marks because Deuteronomy is rhetoric rather than philosophy—it is the farewell speech of

Moses before the children of Israel enter the promised land and he must be left behind to die. Its purpose is persuasion rather than logical argument. Deuteronomy sums up the sense in which the Torah represents something new relative to the old Near Eastern royal theology, Israelite or other. Although the point of the new dispensation is to recognize God and only God as king, there is reserve even in the use of this basic Hebrew metaphor for God: out of the forty-seven times the metaphor of God as king is used in the Bible, only twice in the Torah is God referred to as king—once in Numbers, once in Deuteronomy—though he is frequently depicted in terms of a majesty that must suggest royalty.[107]

Deuteronomy recognizes the necessity of human kingship, but of so remarkably circumscribed a character, indeed, as something like a "constitutional monarchy," that it is hardly recognizable in ancient Near Eastern terms. In Deuteronomy 17:14–15 Moses says to the people, "When you have come into the land that the Lord your God is giving you, . . . [you] may indeed set over you a king whom the Lord your God will choose." Not "you *will*" but "you *may*." The king must be an Israelite, not a foreigner, must not acquire many horses, many wives, or much silver and gold. Thus not exactly a David or a Solomon. But most importantly:

> When he has taken the throne of his kingdom, he shall have a copy of the law written for him in the presence of the levitical priests. It shall remain with him and he shall read in it all the days of his life, so that he may learn to fear the Lord his God, diligently observing all the words of this law and these statutes, neither exalting himself above other members of the community nor turning aside from the commandment, either to the right or to the left, so that he and his descendants may reign long over the kingdom in Israel. (Deuteronomy 17:18–20)

Reign long, not forever. That's it. That's all Deuteronomy or anything else in the Torah has to say about a king. Not exalt himself above others? One wonders why a king whose sole function is to observe the commandments is needed at all.

If Deuteronomy is reserved about kingship, then it is also reserved about prophecy. On the one hand Moses is exalted above all the prophets to such an extent that Stephen Geller's term "superprophet" does not seem inappropriate;[108] on the other hand, though Deuteronomy says that each generation will have a prophet "like Moses," the restraints on such later prophets are severe. "Never since has there arisen a prophet in Israel like Moses, whom the Lord knew face to face," says Deuteronomy 34:10, echoing Numbers 12:6–8, where God says that he has appeared to other prophets in visions but spoke with Moses face to face. Further, God asserts the finality of the revelation to Moses: "You must neither add anything to what I command you nor take away anything from it, but keep the commandments of the Lord your God with which I am charging you" (Deuteronomy 4:2). So beware the prophet who speaks something other than what Moses has spoken. As to future prophets God has this to say to Moses:

> I will raise up for them a prophet like you from among their own people; I will put my words in the mouth of the prophet, who shall speak to them everything that I command. Anyone who does not heed the words that the prophet shall speak in my name, I myself will hold accountable. But any prophet who speaks in the name of other gods, or who presumes to speak in my name a word that I have not commanded the prophet to speak—that prophet shall die. (Deuteronomy 18:18–20)

How can we tell if the word is really from the Lord? "If a prophet speaks in the name of the Lord but the thing does not take place or prove true, it is a word that the Lord has not spoken" (Deuteronomy 18:22). One wonders if Deuteronomy would not just as soon leave Moses as the only necessary prophet.

Although the Assyrian references convince me that at least some basic ideas of Deuteronomy date from the seventh century, surely more was added in the exile and even later. What we can know about its context and dating is hypothetical, and it is doubtful that we will ever have anything but more or less plausible hypotheses. What is critical, however, is that we try to understand what Deuteronomy, and by extension the Pentateuch, the Torah, is doing, for that is the heart of all subsequent Jewish piety. If there was an "axial breakthrough" in Israel it is here if anywhere that we will find it. The disastrous international situation was surely the breakdown. What was the breakthrough?

More than any of my sources, Stephen Geller has struggled with this question and it is to him that I will turn for help. Taking off from the inevitable comparison with Greek thought, Geller asserts that though the Hebrew Bible is not "theory," does not proceed by syllogistic reasoning, still "in some passages, at least, there is an attempt at real intellectual argumentation, however unsystematic its presentation." He goes on to say:

> The problem of interpretation lies in finding a method for uncovering those ideas and arguments that avoids imposing Hellenic concepts of logic anachronistically on the more diffuse structures of biblical thinking, while also translating them into an idiom that we moderns find comfortable . . . It follows that the tool proper to the understanding is not logical argumentation but literary interpretation, not abstract analysis but concrete exegesis. The result will be less a logos, a theory about God, and more a lexis, a reading of Him and His ways as the biblical thinkers conceived of them, sensitive to the lineaments of the text and proceeding step by step with it.[109]

This Geller does by a close reading of Deuteronomy 4, which he dates, by the way, to the exile, in the decisive chapter of his book, a reading I cannot replicate here. What is fundamental is that the Torah is a covenant between God and his people, constitutive of a new understanding of self and world. But also key is that the covenant is contained in a text, a text that in critical respects supersedes kings, prophets and sages, though not the necessity of interpretation. Deuteronomy 4 makes an extraordinary claim for the text of which it is a part:

> See, just as the Lord my God has charged me, I now teach you statutes and ordinances for you to observe in the land that you are about to enter and occupy. You must observe them diligently, for this will show your wisdom and discernment to the peoples, who, when they hear all these statutes, will say, "Surely this great nation is a wise and discerning people!" For what other great nation has a god so near to it as the Lord our God is whenever we call to him? And what other great nation has statutes and ordinances as just as this entire law that I am setting before you today? (Deuteronomy 4:5–8)

Such statements lead Geller to say, "The first part of Deuteronomy 4 establishes a new form of religion in which the text is raised to the level of God Himself, in a sense *is* God."[110] God is in the Word, and if the people hear the Word and keep it they are in right relation to God, regardless of anything else that is going on in the world.

A religion of the text is a portable religion. For all its preoccupation with the promised land, it is notable that neither in Deuteronomy nor anywhere in the Torah is Jerusalem mentioned. Even when the centralization of sacrifice is commanded, the temple is referred to only as "the place where the Lord your God will choose to put his name."[111] Though "statutes and ordinances" concerning priests and sacrifices are copious in Deuteronomy, one must say that as with kings and prophets, they are treated with restraint. Although the priestly texts of Leviticus and Numbers indicate the presence of God in the tabernacle, Deuteronomy speaks only of his name being there. God, for the Deuteronomists, is always in Heaven; only his Word is at hand. Scholars have long held that the Pentateuch is made up of several strands: the J and E documents that are primarily narrative, and two documentary strands that include large cultic and legal codes together with interpretations of their meaning, P (Priestly) and D (Deuteronomic). It is wrong to consider the Priestly teachings of Leviticus and Numbers as "primitive," or even as exclusively "cultic," for in the very midst of Leviticus, the central chapter 19, are the two great ethical commandments: "You shall love your neighbor as yourself" (Leviticus 19:18), and "You shall love the alien as yourself, for you were aliens in the land of Egypt" (Leviticus 19:34). Mary Douglas, drawing on a long line of scholars, has argued that the text of Leviticus, far from being a jumble of unrelated rules, is a great cosmological vision of the right ordering of existence, organized around the living presence of God in the tabernacle.[112]

Sacrifice in the tabernacle (in the Pentateuch standing in for the temple) was essential to the Priestly vision as it was the central way in which the people could communicate with its God and remember how near at hand he is. The Priestly strand was far too prominent in the Torah ever to be abandoned, and according to many scholars it was P that gave the Torah its final recension. One of the great prophets, contemporary with Jeremiah but living in Babylon in the early exile, Ezekiel, clearly reflects the Priestly tradition, which would live on as long as the temple survived, and in different forms, was influential in Christianity and in both Jewish and Christian mysticism.[113] But D got the last word and found its ultimate triumph in rabbinic Judaism. The great rolling rhetoric of Deuteronomy, the Word of God through Moses himself, became the decisive touchstone for the meaning of the Torah, a book that Jews could take anywhere. The land was never forgotten, but many other Near Eastern peoples would disappear once their land was lost, whereas the Jews could survive and prosper wherever they were as long as they had the Book and a community to interpret it.

The Axial Turn: Covenant, People, and Person

We have argued that the axial breakthrough in Israel occurred when the relation of God and the Children of Israel was seen as a covenant, as analogous to the old Near Eastern vassal treaty between king and vassal, though having dramatic new meaning because it dispensed with the role of king as mediator. Geller has argued for the paradoxical quality of this affirmation—a text that views God as transcendent and beyond any image has at the same time created a gigantic anthropomorphism, a God deeply concerned with a people. God is shown as king in the very text that hesitates to call God a king. "I argue that it was the creation of a new level of anthropomorphism, derived, for the most part, from royal imagery, but attaining, ultimately, a new picture of a divine personality, that synthesized the conflicting aspects of divinity."[114]

Geller offers a close analysis of the Shema, the Credo of Judaism, Deuteronomy 6:4–5, to substantiate his claim. The Shema, "Hear O Israel, The Lord our God, the Lord is one" (one possible translation) has often been taken as the very foundation of Israelite "monotheism," the positive version of the negative injunction of the first commandment, "Thou shalt have no other gods before me" (Exodus 20:3, KJV).[115] Although monotheism is at this point in history probably an unavoidable term, it is the burden of Geller's analysis that God is not an "ism," not a logical deduction, but is defined in relationship. After going over all the possible grammatical interpretations of the Hebrew, Geller ends up arguing that the first clause (6:4), "Hear, Israel, since Yahweh is our God, Yahweh is one (i.e. supreme)," is to be understood in relation to the second clause (6:5), continuing, "thou shalt love Yahweh, *thy* God [with all your heart *(lēb),* and with all your soul *(nepeš),* and with all your might *(mě'ōd)*]."[116] For the second clause Geller turns to the archaic language of the King James Version to emphasize that even though the assertion in the first clause is collective ("our God'), the command in the second clause is second-person singular, a nuance that "thy" correctly translates but "your," being both singular and plural in modern English, does not.

Geller's argument is that, though the relation to God defines Israel as a people, that relationship is also, and critically so, with each Israelite as an individual:

> My thesis is that under the guise of declaring God's oneness, what is also, or really, being demanded is that one achieve unity of the self, both of one's mind ("heart," *lēb*) and one's appetites/emotions/life *(nepeš),* through singular attachment to God. The covenant members must be one, whole

with and wholly with God. In other words, monotheism involves not just God but also the personality of the believer. The two unities proceed hand in hand. In fact, the numerical nuance of "one" in the Shema is also true, not only in regard to God, but also to the believer.[117]

Given our contemporary, and particularly American, proclivity to think that individual and community are in a zero sum relation, we must work hard to see that for the ancient Israelites the relationship between God and people and God and the individual were mutually reinforcing. Nowhere more than in the great resurgence of prophecy at the end of the monarchy, particularly in Jeremiah and Ezekiel, where conflict between individual prophet and reprobate people seems most intense, is it clearer that the prophet is never a "private individual." The pathos of his situation is that he is a representative of God to the people and of the people to God. His inability to escape from either responsibility led Jeremiah to the terrible outcry, "Cursed be the day / on which I was born!" (Jeremiah 20:14).

Timothy Polk in *The Prophetic Persona* gives an instructive analysis of Jeremiah as in his very self an exemplar and a metaphor for the people he is called to try to reach.[118] Perhaps the key term for Jeremiah is "heart" *(lēb),* which we have noted already in the Shema. A rightly ordered heart would be one ruled by love of God. But this is just what the people lack, so God tells Jeremiah to proclaim to the people:

> Hear now this,
> > O people foolish and without heart
> Who have eyes but do not see,
> > ears but do not hear . . . (Jeremiah 5:21)
> But this people has a stubborn and rebellious heart;
> > they have turned aside and gone away. (Jeremiah 5:23)[119]

The book of Jeremiah is so full of predictions of disaster that it is sometimes hard to remember that these are warnings that could be heeded, unlikely though that seems. It is therefore worth considering one of the rare passages that balances the curse with the hope of blessing:

> Thus says Yhwh:
> Cursed is the man who trusts in man,
> > and makes flesh his arm,
> > whose heart turns from Yhwh.

For he is like a shrub in the desert
    and cannot see when good comes.
And he will dwell in the parched places of the wilderness
    in a land of salt, uninhabited.
Blessed is the man who trusts in Yhwh,
    whose confidence is in Yhwh.
For he is like a tree planted by the waters,
    stretching out its roots by a stream.
He will not fear when the heat comes,
    but his leaves will remain green;
nor in the year of drought will he be anxious,
    or cease to bear fruit. (Jeremiah 17:5–8)[120]

For Jeremiah, again and again meeting only misunderstanding and turning away, the truth seems to be, "The heart is deceitful above all things/ and desperately corrupt. Who can understand it?" (Jeremiah 17:9).[121] When hope for a return to Yahweh fades in the present, Jeremiah dreams of a future when God himself will change the inconstant hearts of men: "But this is the covenant which I will make with the house of Israel after those days, says the Lord: I will put my law within them and I will write it upon their hearts; and I will be their God and they shall be my people" (Jeremiah 31:33, RSV). A passage that calls to mind the even more vivid image of Ezekiel: "A new heart I will give you, and a new spirit I will put within you; and I will take out of your flesh the heart of stone and give you a heart of flesh" (Ezekiel 36:26, RSV).

In Polk's analysis, Jeremiah is not a great personality who happens to be a prophet; it is just in the demanding role of prophet, demanding because he must speak for both God and people, that Jeremiah comes to know and to be a true person. When the pressure becomes too unbearable, in the great Confessions of Jeremiah, we hear, indeed, the private voice that tells God it is all too hard. Yet it is from God that the strength to continue comes:

Therefore says the Lord:
"If you return, I will restore you,
    and you shall stand before me.
If you utter what is precious, and
    not what is worthless
you shall be as my mouth.

They shall turn to you,
    but you shall not turn to them.
And I will make you to this people
    a fortified wall of bronze;
they will fight against you;
    but they shall not prevail over you,
for I am with you
    to save and deliver you,
        says the Lord. (Jeremiah 15:19–20, RSV)

It is in the extraordinary role of intercessor that the prophet models the relation to God for all the people.[122] After Jeremiah and Ezekiel the prophetic voice is not stilled, but becomes largely anonymous, adding new material to old collections. Perhaps most important is the exilic collection that scholars call "Second Isaiah," Isaiah 40–55. According to Mark Smith,

> This work modifies the old royal theology in many respects. First, the Judean king vanishes from the picture, and in turn Yahweh freely uses the royal means available to exercise the divine will on behalf of Israel. Cyrus the Persian becomes Yahweh's "anointed" [messiah] in the new divine plan of salvation for Israel and the nations (Isaiah 45:1). Second, Israel itself, instead of the Judean king, becomes the new servant who is to mediate blessing. Israel is the bearer of the old "eternal covenant" (2 Samuel 23:5) now to the nations (Isaiah 55:5).[123]

Smith's third point is "monotheism"—that is, as Yahweh is exalted, the existence of other gods is denied, their cults are denounced as the stupid worship of inanimate, man-made objects. "Yahweh is not just the god of Israel (both as land and people), but of all lands and nations."[124]

"Second Isaiah" continued the transformation of the royal theology that the eighth-century Isaiah had begun. What seems to have happened in exilic and postexilic times is that the Deuteronomic and transformed royal theologies were largely merged. The Torah—instruction or law—remains as important as ever, but the note of redemption, the hope of return and recovery, mitigate the unrelieved ferocity of much of the great prophetic writing. It is as though Israel has finally accepted its life as a people whose only king is God—the promise to the house of David will be realized only through divine action in the messianic future. The commandments did not enslave, as

Paul at moments thought, but gave Israel a higher law that freed it from ultimate bondage to any earthly law. Judaism, a religion of the book that can survive anywhere on earth, was beginning to emerge.

If in an important sense Deuteronomy, with its transcendent God known above all in his Word, and its conditional covenant calling forever for the people to be faithful to the commandments of the Lord, carried the day, the unconditional covenants were not forgotten. They remained forever as the horizon within which this people lived. God's promise to Abraham and to Jacob/Israel meant that, in however frightful the situation, God's love for Israel would not be abandoned. God's promise to David meant that sometime in the future a truly good way of life would exist on this earth.

Axel Honneth has given us an extremely fruitful analysis of the struggle for recognition as a powerful dynamic in human history,[125] one that may help us deal with what must always be a problem for non-Jews: Why is Israel and Israel alone the chosen people? Honneth posits the need for recognition as proceeding in three phases. First there is the need for recognition as love, without which there can be no self-confidence. Then there is the need for recognition as justice, without which there can be no self-respect. Then there is the need for recognition as creator of value, without which there can be no self-esteem. Recognition does indeed seem to be at the heart of the Israelite religious dynamic. God's recognition of this particular people calls in turn for the recognition of God by the people. Only by this mutual recognition, which is first of all the recognition of love, can people and self be constituted. Only God's initiative made the whole process possible. But the recognition of love must be personal, it cannot be general. God must recognize someone, to begin with, and if from that someone something new comes into being, a people constituted not by loyalty to an earthly ruler but by loyalty to God, that too must be a particular people. Certainly the religion of ancient Israel moved powerfully toward the recognition of justice, and here the beginnings of a larger context, how one treats the aliens, for example, developed. But without the continuing insistence on particularity it is hard to see how the Israelite axial breakthrough could have been preserved.[126] It is also well to remember that the particularity of Israel is only relative: the two "universal" religions that emerged from Israelite origins had their own quite particular beginnings that have defined them ever since. Both Christianity and Islam are religions of the book for whom the distinction between believers and unbelievers is hardly unimportant.

Stephen Geller puts another dimension of particularity in context by reminding us that the "Arnoldian distinction between Hellenism and Hebraism as polar opposites" is far from the whole truth:

> Both world views share an exclusive claim to validity, the chief outward expression of the tremendous energy released by the new insights. Both developed a new view of community, a new ethic of education and new institutions to support it. Gymnasium and synagogue are both unprecedented forms of communal organization. To be sure, an immense gap separates biblical faith from Greek logos, the kind of tension-filled dialectic we have studied from the calm assertions of absolute, eternal verity that philosophy and science came to postulate.[127]

But, just as we have seen several far from easily reconcilable strands of Israelite religion contributing to its dynamism, the very gap to which Geller points, the gap that would make the Western tradition forever at least dual, would prove enormously fruitful for the many generations that sought to cross it.

Before concluding, let us sum up what we have found about the ways in which an axial breakthrough occurred in ancient Israel. To the extent that we have made theory, second-order thinking, the criterion of axiality, Israel remains a problematic case. But the Hebrew scriptures have marshaled a number of resources to do something quite similar to the achievements of the other axial cases, most notably Greece. Rhetoric, which, for all its tension with philosophy was part of the axial transition in Greece, was highly developed in Israel, notably in Deuteronomy. Further, Israelite rhetoric was developed in a forensic context. Walter Brueggemann has organized his magisterial *Theology of the Old Testament* along the lines of testimony, countertestimony and cross examination.[128] If the ancient Israelites finally made the case for Yahweh as the only God there is, they did so argumentatively. They were not even averse to arguing with God himself. The clearest example of argument is the book of Job, essentially a complex dialogue, involving, finally, the voice of God himself. Out of all this argument and counterargument emerged an idea of God unique in the world and with enormous historical implications. An utterly transcendent God, of whom there is to be no image, is both loving and righteous and demands love and righteousness from his people, and, insofar as his people is to be a light to the nations, from all the world as well. The powerful beings of tribal peoples and the gods of archaic civilizations were all in critical respects embedded in the social world in which they existed. In archaic societies the critical embeddedness was the relation, approaching identification, of god and king. In the early monarchy the relation of god and king was more than a little analogous to that relation in the great Near Eastern archaic civilizations. In the end, however, the children of Israel did not need "kings of flesh and blood" as the rabbis called them, to relate them to God who is the only real king. A God who is finally outside society and the world provides the point of reference from which all existing presuppositions can be questioned, a basic criterion for the axial transition. It is as if Israel took the most fundamental symbolism of the great archaic civilizations—God, king and people—and pushed it to the breaking point where something dramatically new came into the world.

Yet this profound historical shift, this gift of ethical freedom to a people who could see that God's justice is itself the highest expression of ethical freedom,[129] was attained through a cultural medium that never gave up narrative as the fundamental framework for cultural understanding. This leads us to ask if the ancient Israelites were not using narrative in a new way, to do what would today be called "narrative theology," that was effectively a functional equivalent for theory—not, to be sure for the analysis of nature, but for the understanding of human existence. Much in the Hebrew Bible is similar to, sometimes identical with, the myths, legends, folktales, sayings and poetry of other Near Eastern peoples. Yet the great enveloping narrative moves from the Creation to the Babylonian captivity, and, with the apocalyptic passages in the late prophets, projects into the future when on "that day" the Lord will set all things right. With its reiterative theme of promise, unfaithfulness, punishment, and redemption, this great narrative was something new: a way of placing believers in relation to a story that gave them meaning and hope. The very opening of the first book of Moses, Genesis 1–2:4a, even if it was the late product of the priestly school and even if it did not contain the doctrine of *creatio ex nihilo,* is a powerful and austere account of creation, unique in ancient Near Eastern creation stories.[130] Indeed, the whole book of Genesis is a narrative masterpiece, incorporating old fragments but making them into a prologue for everything that will follow—as is sometimes said, it is the Old Testament of the Old Testament.

Taken as a whole, the historical framework of the Hebrew Bible is metanarrative big time, to be sure, but a metanarrative that no culture that has received it has ever been able to escape. And a metanarrative powerful and flexible enough so that movements and countermovements, establishments and heresies, could all turn to it to justify ethical/social/political programs,

programs that would contribute, not always to the good, to all subsequent historical dynamics. Here, too, we find a new cultural form so powerful in its consequences that we must understand it as part of the axial transformation.

Finally, as a result of both the rhetorical and narrative innovations accomplished by ancient Israel, we must understand the social achievement of peoplehood without monarchy, of a people ruled by divine law, not the arbitrary rule of the state, and of a people composed of responsible individuals. Here, as Geller noted, the postexilic emergence of the synagogue was crucial: a religious community that could come into being wherever a quorum of Jews was gathered, a community that would be subordinate in outer things to whatever state was in power, but which provided an alternative rule of life to the believers. This was the chrysalis of both the Christian Church and the Islamic Umma. It was not "the differentiation of church and state," but it was the entering wedge that would make that idea thinkable.

What this summary suggests is that in our quest to understand what makes the axial age axial, we will need to look, surely, at the emergence of theory wherever it arises, but we must also look at the possible transformation of older cultural forms into new configurations, and at the social consequences of such transformations.

In this chapter I have tried to understand the religion of ancient Israel as an axial breakthrough. It may be worth closing this section with what amounts to a confession of faith by a contemporary Jew, Jon Levenson, that contains even today all the dynamic terms of God, king, and people that we have seen as decisive from the beginning:

> There is, therefore, no voice more central to Judaism than the voice heard on Mount Sinai. Sinai confronts anyone who would live as a Jew with an awesome choice, which, once encountered cannot be evaded— the choice of whether to obey God or to stray from him, of whether to observe the commandments or to let them lapse. Ultimately, the issue is whether God is or is not king, for there is no king without subjects, no suzerain without vassals. In short, Sinai demands that the Torah be taken with radical seriousness. But alongside the burden of choice lies a balm that sooths the pain of decision. The balm is the history of redemption, which grounds the commandments and insures that this would-be king is a gracious and loving lord and that to choose to obey him is not a leap into the absurd.[131]

7

The Axial Age II: Ancient Greece

Ancient Greece would seem to be the easy case when it comes to the axial age. Greece gave rise to a form of democracy based on decisions made after rational argument in the assembly; to philosophy, including formal logic (second-order reasoning); to at least the beginnings of science based on evidence and argument; not to mention that it also gave rise to extraordinary artistic and literary achievements. Some have been so overwhelmed by the culture of ancient Greece as to imagine a "Greek miracle" emerging, without forerunners or rivals, full-blown from the head of Zeus so to speak. The Greeks were just inherently "rational."

In recent years such extreme enthusiasm has been countered with vigorous debunking, the enthusiasts charged with being Eurocentric or Western-centric, with failing to recognize how much the Greeks got from Asia or Africa (mathematics, astronomy, and so on). And the critics insist that Greek "democracy" wasn't very democratic after all—it applied only to the minority of the population who were citizens and excluded women, slaves, and resident aliens. Greek philosophy, they say, led to the blind alley of "metaphysics" that kept philosophers for centuries preoccupied with wholly illusory issues. And Greek science, by rejecting experiment, never amounted to much. I heard Carl Sagan in one of his television broadcasts on the history of science declare that "Plato set back European science by 1500 years." Quite a trick, but by far not the only baneful influence that has been attributed to Plato.

So where are we? I think it best to treat ancient Greece as just one of our four axial cases, try to understand how it developed, how it was similar to and different from the other cases, and end with a brief reference to what it contributed to the future. It might be well to begin with a paragraph from Louis Gernet,[1] student of Durkheim, friend of Mauss, and teacher of Jean-Pierre

Vernant, around whom in recent years, a remarkably creative group of French classicists has formed:

> Is this not the secret of Greece: that it allowed the least number of its legacies to die, and fused the largest numbers of its ancient values? In any case, one of its most authentic successes was to conceive as one an ideal of heroism and an ideal of wisdom. The two easily cohere in figures in whom a benevolent and organizing activity dominates, or in those vaguer ghosts of the founders of the sanctuaries and cities who were the welcoming hosts of men and gods. In the obscure regions where ideals are fashioned, the experiences of a thousand years count for something. A vivid feeling flourishing in the past, a sense of joyous participation in a commerce with humanity and nature according to accepted rhythms of life. In contrast to the brutalities of daily life, the myth of the Hyperboreans [a people in the far north still living in conditions of the Golden Age] could, at a very early date, evoke from the distant past the image of a tranquil, just people engaged in the delightful hospitality of the *agapai*.[2]

The point here is that the continuities in Greece from pre-state to, in the Greek case, quasi-state conditions, although evident in all the axial cases, are particularly easy to recognize in the survival of pre-state institutions and beliefs.

In particular the myths, many of which are similar to the ancient Near Eastern myths that also underlie the Hebrew scriptures, but are visible only in fragments there, have been preserved in great detail. Although they contain occasional references to an early period when gods and men participated in the same feasts, an idea that Gernet believed was still being lived out in rural festivals, the primary picture of the divine–human relation as depicted in Homer and other early texts is quite different, and startlingly different from the relation between Yahweh and the children of Israel that we saw in Chapter 6. According to Hugh Lloyd-Jones:

> In the *Iliad*, as in all early Greek poetry, the gods look on men with disdain mingled with slight pity. "I should not be sensible," says Apollo to Poseidon when he meets him in the battle of the gods, "if I fought with you on account of wretched mortals, who like leaves now flourish, as they eat the fruit of the field, and now fade away lifeless." Nothing says

Zeus himself, "is more wretched than a man, of all things that breathe and move upon the earth."[3]

Lloyd-Jones goes on to say that the gods "treat men as the nobles of an early stage of a rural society treat the peasants."[4] In the heroic age and later, there is no indication that the gods, though they have their favorites, to be sure, "love" human beings in general or any particular group of them. The Greeks as a whole are not "chosen," though, again, particular individuals may be, and the Greeks are not shown as better than their enemies.[5] On the contrary, Troy is treated with more sympathy than the Greeks in the *Iliad;* certainly Hector is shown as more admirable than Achilles or Agamemnon.[6] So the most fundamental feature of the divine-human relation in Israel—God's love for Israel and the obligation to return that love, "Thou shalt love the Lord thy God . . ."—is completely missing in Greece. Aristotle said: "For it would be strange for one to say that he loved Zeus," and held that *philia* (love, friendship) was impossible between man and God.[7] Justice is another matter. The gods in general and Zeus in particular are indeed concerned with justice, something we will have to consider at length below.

   Although there were many tensions evident within the Hebrew scriptures, and sharp differences developed over the centuries in their interpretation, the Torah achieved a normative authority that had no equal in ancient Greece. Homer and Hesiod were central texts in Greek education throughout antiquity, but they never had the authority of the Hebrew scriptures. Old myths were reformulated by poets and tragic dramatists; criticized and reformed by philosophers; and new myths, gods, and goddesses from a variety of sources were introduced from time to time without causing undue disturbance. Ancient Greek religion was in every sense more fluid than that of ancient Israel, and we will have to consider the social causes and consequences of such fluidity.

Early Greek Society

We have noted the central significance of the god–king–people complex in all the archaic societies and the fact that each axial case had to come to terms with this complex, so it is significant that ancient Greece in the period of the axial transition was the only case where actual kings were absent, though not absent in the cultural imagination. In short, the polis, problematically translated as "city-state," the dominant institution in the period from the eighth to the fourth centuries BCE that saw the flourishing of ancient Greek culture and the axial transition, was not ruled by kings. Tyrants there occasionally were, but as we will see, they were quite specifically not kings. It is not as though the idea of kingship was lacking. Even though, by the eighth century, the Greeks no longer had a very clear idea of the Mycenaean civilization that had preceded them in the second millennium BCE, they did know the Mycenaeans were ruled by kings. On the basis of our modern archaeological knowledge of that Mycenaean civilization, we know that those kings were divine, semidivine, or priestly on the model of archaic Near Eastern culture, of which Mycenaean civilization was only a western extension. Not only did the polis-dwelling Greeks know that there had been kings in their past, but they were aware that there were kings in Scythia in the north, in Assyria and Persia in the east, and in Egypt to the south. But their ideas of kingship were formed not only by external models but by central figures in their own myths and legends: the *Iliad* is a story of a Greek army under the ostensible rule of a king, namely Agamemnon, referred to on occasion by the word *anax,* which is descended from the Mycenaean word for king, *wanax.*[8] The later Greek word for king, *basileus,* is used loosely in Homer for king, noble, or, simply leader.[9] Agamemnon does not seem to be much of a king—half the time he looks more like a paramount chief. Zeus is also referred to as *anax,* though in the *Iliad* not as *basileus,* and he is a king, though a bit like Agamemnon, not one who can ignore the feelings of his divine subjects. Interestingly enough, Zeus is referred to in Homer more often as *pater,* father, than as king.[10] After Homer the powers attributed to Zeus grew even stronger, so that we are confronted with a situation where a king of the gods is not mirrored by a human king, a situation unique to the Greeks.[11]

But if the Greeks were not organized in kingdoms, what kind of society did they have? The earliest Greek society is, if anything, even more obscure than that of the Israelites. Somewhere around 1200 BCE the Mycenaean cities were either overrun or abandoned, due to internal collapse, climate change, or external conquest. If the last, it was not by "the Greeks," as the Mycenaeans, as we know from the Linear B syllabic script, had been Greek speakers for some centuries. Greek speakers of the Dorian dialect, and thus called "the Dorians," have sometimes been blamed for the fall of Mycenaean civilization, but there is not enough evidence to make that more than speculation.[12] In any case, Linear B and the other achievements of Mycenaean civilization disappeared after 1200, and the next 400 years are generally referred to as the Dark Age. It is at least dark to us, as archaeology has yielded only sparse findings in this period and evidence of a considerable decline in population. There are hints in some places that trade with the Near East had not ceased altogether. The Athenians maintained a tradition that their city, not an especially eminent one, alone among the Mycenaean cities escaped conquest, and they also believed that it was from Athens that a considerable number of refugees, perhaps around 1000 BCE, emigrated to the Anatolian coast, where they established towns that would be significant centers of the reemerging Greek culture in the eighth century. But if Athens was never destroyed, still it shrank to a very small town in the centuries after 1200.

The low point of the post-Mycenaean period seems to be 1100. Ian Morris tells us that after 1100:

> Much of the countryside was probably abandoned, or left very thinly settled. Most people lived in small hamlets, occupied for anything from 50 to 300 years . . . [T]he disasters around 1100 may have impoverished central Greece, with what little wealth was left falling into the hands of village headmen, the heirs of the last Mycenaean local officials . . . Central Greece had become something of a ghost world. Practically every hilltop and harbor had had earlier occupants, and by 1050 the landscape was dotted with the ruins of a more glorious age. Just listing examples cannot evoke the atmosphere of those days . . . If any part of the Iron Age deserves to be called a Dark Age, then this is it. From some perspectives, such as that of the lower classes who built the Mycenaean palaces and labored to meet their quotas, or that of the local aristocrats held in check by the *wanakes* [plural of *wanax*] and their officers, the destruction around 1200 may have been a blessing. But by 1050 the costs of change—not just the loss of high civilization, but also disruption and massive mortality—outweighed the benefits to any group. Egyptian documents record crop failures at just this time.[13]

Although it is very hard to reconstruct social structure from archaeological data alone, and using Homer as a source of data is fraught with problems, it is reasonably clear that the Dark Age saw the collapse of the strongly hierarchical Mycenaean order and its replacement with a much more egalitarian society.[14] A number of authors have argued that the political structure of the Dark Age was one of low-level chiefs, heavily dependent on followers who did not fail to voice their own views, with perhaps an occasional and evanescent paramount chief. Such societies are balanced between low-level hierarchy and considerable egalitarianism. Walter Donlan uses evidence from the *Odyssey* to describe what these societies were like:

I doubt there exists a clearer description in all ethnography of a low-level chiefdom, and of its internal stresses, than in these books of the *Odyssey*. The chief possesses considerable authority, but he must bend to the collective will of the fighting men, who are naturally disposed to be critical of his leadership. It is important that we understand that the epic tradition constantly underscores the fact that the leader-people tension is the cause of social dysfunction. Odysseus is consistently represented as being as good a leader as a people could realistically hope for; yet the message is unmistakable, that personal leadership is fragile and unstable and that the intrinsic opposition between the two social vectors of autocracy on the one hand and egalitarianism on the other, is a frequent prescription for social breakdown.[15]

In spite of the emphasis in Homer on outstanding individuals, we can still see a society with only the beginning of the idea of hereditary rank. Terminology with respect to leadership was in flux. As noted above, *basileus* was a term of such varied usage that it more often meant "leader" than "king." Although Hesiod will refer to the Homeric leaders as "heroes," in the Homeric texts themselves even the rank and file could be called heroes or *aristoi* ("best," the origin of our term "aristocracy").[16] Still, many of the leaders had a special relation to the gods: Achilles or Menelaus or Odysseus or Patroclus can all be called *diotrephes*, "Zeus-nurtured," or *diogenes*, "Zeus-born." Some leaders (for whom the term "heroes" would later be reserved) were literally Zeus-born—Sarpedon, for example. But lineage, even divine lineage, did not itself provide status, nor did divine favor. Paris was Aphrodite's favorite, but because of his inadequacy as a warrior, Greeks and Trojans alike despised him. When it came time for Sarpedon, beloved son of Zeus, to die, Zeus pondered intervening to save his life, but Hera prevailed on him not to do so as it would cause strife among the gods, many of whom would then want to save their children from fate-appointed death. This incident indicates that Zeus's monarchy was far from absolute. Homer shows us a society in which status was based on valor, but also one in which leaders, *basileis*, could be seen as "godlike," and therefore superior to common men.

There was a clear understanding, however, that the warrior elite owed its position to the services it provided to the larger community: the leaders were part of society, of a whole greater than its parts, even its leading parts, an idea the Greeks would never abandon before the Macedonian conquest. Like many others the Greek aristocracy began as a warrior aristocracy. Sarpedon's words to Glaukos in the *Iliad,* however, express the social basis of their claim to high status:

> Glaukos, why is it you and I are honoured before others
> with pride of place, the choice meats and the filled wine cups
> in Lykia, and all men look on us as if we were immortals,
> and we are appointed a great piece of land by the banks of Xanthos,
> good land, orchard and vineyard, and ploughland for the planting of
>   wheat?
> Therefore it is our duty in the forefront of the Lykians
> To take our stand, and bear our part of the blazing of battle,
> so that a man of the close-armoured Lykians may say of us:
> "Indeed, these are no ignoble men who are lords of Lykia,
> and drink the exquisite sweet wine, since indeed there is strength
> of valour in them, since they fight in the forefront of the Lykians."[17]

Despite our need to moderate the notion of a monarchical past in early Greece, there were still some reminders of a kind of rule that was closer to the old Near Eastern magico-religious pattern than had actually been the case for a long time. In the *Odyssey* we find Odysseus disguised as a beggar praising Penelope with the words:

> your fame goes up into the wide heaven,
> as of some king [*basileus*] who, as a blameless man and god-fearing,
> and ruling as lord over many powerful people,
> upholds the way of good government, and the black earth yields him
> barley and wheat, his trees grow heavy with fruit, his sheepflocks
> continue to bear young, the sea gives him fish, because of
> his good leadership, and his people prosper under him.[18]

And in Hesiod's *Works and Days* we have a similar picture of a good *basileus,* paired with an opposite one of the bad *basileus,* whom he often characterizes as "bribe-devouring":

> But those who give straight verdicts and follow justice,
> both when fellow citizens and strangers are on trial,
> live in a city that blossoms, a city that prospers.
> Then youth-nurturing peace comes over the land, and Zeus

who sees afar does not decree for them the pains of war.
Men whose justice is straight know neither hunger nor ruin,
But amid feasts enjoy the yield of their labors.
For them the earth brings forth a rich harvest; and for them
the top of an oak teems with acorns and the middle with bees.
Fleecy sheep are weighed down with wool,
and women bear children who resemble their fathers.
There is an abundance of blessings and the grainland
grants such harvests that no one has to sail on the sea.
But far-seeing Zeus, son of Kronos, is the judge
of wanton wrongdoers who plot deeds of harshness.
Many times one man's wickedness ruins a whole city,
If such a man breaks the law and turns his mind to recklessness.
Then the son of Kronos sends a great bane from the sky,
Hunger and plague, and the people waste away.
Women bear no children, and families dwindle
through the counsels of Zeus the Olympian,
the son of Kronos, who punishes wrong by wiping out
large armies, walls, and ships at sea.[19]

In a fascinating passage near the beginning of his *Theogony*, Hesiod writes of the gifts that the Muses, the daughters of Zeus, can give to kings:

And if the daughters of great Zeus honor a king [*basileus*]
cherished by Zeus and look upon him when he is born,
they pour on his tongue sweet dew
and make the words that flow from his mouth honey-sweet,
and all the people look up to him as with straight justice
he gives his verdict and with unerring firmness
and wisdom brings some great strife to a swift end.
This is why kings are prudent, and when in the assembly
injustice is done, wrongs are righted
by the kings with ease and gentle persuasion.
When such a king comes to the assembly he stands out;
Yes, he is revered like a god and treated with cheerful respect.[20]

Hesiod then goes on to say that the muses give similar wisdom and persuasive speech to the "singers and lyre players of this earth" (*Theogony*, 1.94), thus implying a link between the singing poet and political power in a way we will need to examine further below.[21] In Homer and Hesiod, then, echoes of a kind of kingship that had long been vestigial in Greece can still be heard.

If Walter Donlan, as we have seen, saw Odysseus and his band of followers as archetypal of early Greek society, W. G. Runciman does something similar with Odysseus's Ithaca. Runciman describes Ithaca as a "semi-state" rather than a "proto-state"—that is, a kind of society with some rudiments of statehood but no sign of an inevitable development in that direction. Ithaca had "passed the stage at which political and kinship roles are coterminous but also [had] evolved roles to which authority attaches which is superior in both kind and degree to that of the lineage head, the village elder or the leader of a hunting band." It was a society in which "the combination of heroic prowess and eloquence in debate (*'auctoritas suadendi'* was just what Odysseus possessed to the full) is the basis of leadership."[22] Runciman's point is that no independent set of political roles had emerged in such a society, no "secondary formation" as we have called it, so that the "semi-state" depended very much on the personality of its leader, and in Odysseus's absence tended to fall apart altogether. We will have to consider the degree to which the polis ever transcended the limits of what Runciman calls a semi-state, and the fact that the polis never developed a full-fledged secondary formation, as keys both to its cultural dynamism and its ultimate political demise.

In trying to understand early Greek society, we need to keep a number of things in mind. We could, almost by default, call it a tribal society, though that doesn't get us very far. Unlike many tribal societies, or even axial China, extended kinship does not seem to have been a major focus of social organization. The lineage, *genos* (pl. *gene*), was of some significance among the nobility, but not among the common people. The household, *oikos,* whose core was a nuclear family, but which could include three generations, unmarried females, and non-kin dependents, was the basic kinship unit among both nobles and peasants. A village was a collection of households, but when did a village become a polis?

The Eighth Century

In the eighth century we begin to see unmistakable signs of cultural revival, so much so that scholars have begun to speak of "The Greek Renaissance of the Eighth Century BCE."[23] "Renaissance" is a problematic word if we take the analogy too seriously. The Italian Renaissance involved the revival of classical culture on the basis of a great many classical texts as well as the survival of ancient architecture and sculpture. The eighth-century Greeks had no texts (Linear B script would not have been legible to them if they had seen it) and only fragments of Mycenaean architecture and sculpture. Nonetheless, the text of Homer as we have it (long preceded by oral recitation), dating from around 700 and even perhaps committed to writing by that date, does project an image of some sort of Greek society purportedly from that earlier age but more likely reflecting mainly social conditions in the more recent past.

Homer is one element in an aspect of the eighth-century revival that is referred to as Panhellenism—that is, a consciousness of the Greeks as Greeks, even though there was no political unity among them. The *Iliad,* in which the Greeks are not yet called Hellenes, being referred to by several names, most commonly as Achaeans,[24] depicts a Greek army, composed to be sure of highly diverse elements, but under the command of a single king, Agamemnon, and pitted against a city on the Anatolian coast, Troy, that differs little from the Greeks in culture, yet that unites the Greeks in their common effort to destroy it. The *Iliad* is the story of men more than gods, but the gods are everywhere evident within it, and it is the great Panhellenic Olympian gods—Zeus, Hera, Apollo, Aphrodite, Hermes, and so forth—who are in evidence, not the diverse local deities of every village and hamlet that we know actually existed at the time. And there was unity not only at the level of legend and myth, but of cult as well.

The first firm date we have in Greek history is that of the first Olympiad, 776 BCE (not uncontested), and we should remember that the Olympic games were first of all ritual occasions, inaugurated by sacrifices to Zeus and celebrated as religious festivals. Although local authorities managed the games, their participants came from all the Greek communities. The four-year cycle of games was later augmented by the cyclic Nemean, Isthmian, and Pythian games, also open to all Greek contestants. Perhaps even more important in the long run was the emergence of the Delphic Oracle, located at the remote site of Delphi and not controlled by any major city. The Oracle was consulted by people from all over greater Greece and had a significant influence on policy, in particular supporting the deliberate colonization of much of the Mediterranean and Black Sea coastline from about 750 to 600 BCE.

Yet the very same period that saw the rise of Panhellenic ideology, ritual, and institutions also saw the emergence of a new social form, the polis, which emphasized local loyalty and solidarity as strongly as the Panhellenic institutions emphasized a common Greek identity. The eighth century saw for the first time the building of temples all over Greece, temples that, with the festivals associated with them, were the very symbols of the unity of the polis. It also saw the emergence of significant civic officials and institutions, not the least important of which was a strong military organization as the expression of the autonomy of the polis.

Because the polis is a unique Greek institution, a society without a king, though variously governed, related clearly to the Greek cultural achievements that were to come, we would like to know where it came from and how it developed. We would especially like to know how a strong Panhellenic identity and a strong local polis identity emerged at the same time, and whether they reinforced each other or were a source of conflict, or perhaps some of both.[25] We have little written evidence from the eighth century, for alphabetic writing was in its earliest stages even late in that century and not much more written information from the seventh century. However, for these centuries as well as for the dark ages before the eighth century, archaeology continuously provides us with new data.[26]

It would seem that the polis was the primary residence of the nobles, though they may also have had country seats.[27] Thus the distinction between nobles (*agathoi,* "the good") and the common people (*demos,* but also, pejoratively, *kakoi,* "the base," or "bad"), was in part between town-dwelling landowners and country-dwelling peasants, yet the polis was fundamentally a people, one that included the peasants, so the distinction between town and country was never as great as in medieval Europe. We must also remember that, in spite of claims of immemorial attachment to their locale, both nobles and people had been in more or less continuous movement for centuries. It is difficult to look at a map of Greek dialects without seeing that people had been moving around a lot, and moving meant fighting—even after they settled down there was still a lot of fighting going on between neighboring poleis. So perhaps the first claim to noble status was based on taking the lead in warfare.

Perhaps the Greek nobles were originally warrior bands who emerged after the fall of Mycenaean royal legitimacy, not too different from the warrior bands that replaced the fall of chiefly legitimacy in some of the Polynesian islands described in Chapter 4. Still they laid claim to a shadow of the ancient past in several ways. As noted above, the term *anax,* derived from the Mycenaean *wanax,* meaning "great king," survived in Homer, where it was applied, however problematically, to Agamemnon and Priam, as well as occasionally to other Greek leaders, and the term *basileus,* applying to officials of some sort in Mycenaean times, was used as a general term for leaders in Homer and Hesiod, but retaining some degree of legitimacy beyond the sheer attribute of force. Hesiod, whose text is usually dated to around 700 BCE, distinguishes between good *basileis,* whose actions are in accordance with *themis,* customary law, as bringers of prosperity through natural fertility as well as social harmony, and bad *basileis,* who give rise to drought and famine as well as social unrest. They thus represent, in however attenuated a form, the relation between this world and the world of the gods that was the case with high chiefs and archaic kings. Not surprisingly they also often functioned as priests. A hereditary priest in Athens was called *basileus,* though his religious importance was not great and he had no political power at all.

Even though groups of nobles ruled most Greek poleis before the rise of democracy in the fifth century, and even after that often supplied the leaders in democratic or quasi-democratic poleis, we should not exaggerate their power, their cohesion, or their closure to other groups. They were landholders, but not great landholders in comparison, say, with the senatorial class in Rome. The poleis themselves were on the whole quite small in both territory and population, with only a few that could be called cities. Athens, the largest, had a population of no more than 250,000 at its height. The degree to which slave labor was used in agriculture is debated, but it seems unlikely that Greek nobles ever had vast slave estates. Noble families had clients and tenants, but seldom amounting to any great number.

Very significant is the fact that nobles were a far from cohesive group: they viewed themselves as equals and resisted domination by any particular family. They competed for excellence and virtually created the culture of athletics as we know it even today, in which winning was of enormous importance. But the effort of one family to dominate the polis would be resisted by other noble families, even more, initially, than by non-nobles.

Although the nobility were the prime movers in creating the polis as we know it from the eighth century, it was they who took the lead in creating Panhellenic culture and institutions as well.[28] Members of noble families, though always jockeying for power in their own poleis, were also often abroad, cultivating guest-friendships with noble families in other parts of Greece, and contracting marriages with such families as well. The tyrants who controlled a number of poleis, usually briefly, mainly in the sixth century, were nobles who mobilized support from the people against their fellow nobles, but who also called on their friends and relatives abroad to help them take power by force. Their lack of cultural legitimacy and the resentment they aroused among the nobles as well as the common people combined to make their rule relatively short: none created a stable monarchy.

The Greek conception of status hierarchy was complex, but because it was the context of Greek cultural innovations, we must try to understand it. At the highest level there were the immortal gods. In the heroic age they had coupled with mortals, and the children of these unions were often the founders of noble lineages, but the days of divine–human intercourse were long over and perhaps the most important distinction of all was between mortals and immortals. Even so, Sarpedon said to Glaukos, "All men look on us as if we were immortals." Great men—leaders in war and peace, major poets, wise men—could be called "godlike," though it was not until Alexander that the idea of divine parentage as against divine descent reappeared in Greece under foreign influence. But even the children of a divine–human coupling were mortal, and it was human mortality that created the great divide between gods and humans.

The distinction between the immortals and mortals provided a template for how the nobles (*agathoi,* the good) viewed the demos (*kakoi,* the base), yet the nobility was never closed to new members, and wealth could lead to noble status in no great period of time. But the citizens, including the people as well as the nobles, could view themselves as radically distinguished from another group, the slaves. The extent and degree of slavery in ancient Greece is debatable, but the definition of slaves was that they were, in contrast to citizens, unfree. Orlando Patterson has argued persuasively that the very idea of freedom so central in Greece and in later Western civilization, was intelligible only in contrast to the unfree status of slaves; that is, a society without slaves would not have developed that particular notion of freedom.[29] Perhaps the drastic inequality of immortals and mortals made it easier for the Greeks to accept the distinction between slaves and free without question. Indeed, the gods might be characterized as having hyperfreedom, being free of many human limitations, notably mortality. Relative to the gods, even free humans could be considered slaves.

There were other status distinctions as well. Unlike Rome, no Greek city readily extended its citizenship to foreigners, so that resident aliens, particularly in a great commercial city like Athens, were an important group, often rich, but without political rights. And, of course, women, though they played a significant role in mythology, drama, and occasionally even in philosophy, were excluded from political participation. They were, however, full participants in many of the rituals that to an extraordinary degree defined the polis. We can say that they were cultic citizens, even though not political citizens.[30] The wise and warlike divinity who protected Athens was, of course, the goddess Athena. Nor was Athens alone in this regard: Hera was the goddess of Argos and Samos, for example.

Having given a sense of what Greek society was like in the first centuries after the eighth-century renaissance, we must ask: Why did so many new developments occur in the eighth century? In answering this question it is important to remember that early Greece, whose geographical extent was constantly changing at least from 1200 to 600 BCE, was part of the "Orient," as Mycenaean civilization had been. There was as yet no "Europe." When the archaeologists discovered that the town of Lefkandi in Euboea was a significant center of commerce from 900 if not earlier, it was commerce with the Near East.[31] The Greeks who had established themselves along the west coast of Anatolia before or after 1000 BCE were in constant contact with peoples to their east, and it was no accident, as they say, that these towns, such as Miletus, would be in the forefront of cultural innovation in the earliest phase. There is, for example, a tradition that Homer came from the island of Chios off the Anatolian coast. But rather than seeing the Greeks, as nineteenth-century scholars tended to do, as Indo-Europeans who were "influenced" by the Orient or even "Orientalized" to some degree, we should see them from Mycenaean times on as the western periphery of "the Orient," indelibly part of it, and only gradually creating a distinct civilization of their own. In this they are more closely parallel to ancient Israel than we usually imagine.

So when we speak of the Dark Age in Greece, we should be aware that the centuries from 1200 to 800 were dark in much of the Near East outside of the Mesopotamian and Egyptian heartlands. Palestine from 1200 to 900 is as obscure as Greece. If we can speak of "retribalization" among the early Israelites, so can we among the Dark Age Greeks: both were responses to the breakdown of the great Bronze Age palace cultures of the second millennium BCE. What happened not long before 800 that would shake up the entire region was the rise of a new kind of efficient military empire, the Neo-Assyrian Empire (934–610 BCE), which in the late ninth and eighth centuries reached the Mediterranean and, as we have seen, played a significant role in the history of ancient Israel. Unlike the case of Israel, the impact of Assyria on Greece was indirect; it was nonetheless powerful.

The mediator of Assyrian influence to the Greeks was primarily the Phoenicians, though some of the inland Anatolian kingdoms may also have been involved. It was the increasing demand of the Assyrians for tribute, especially metals, but for a variety of other goods as well, together with the desire to escape their immediate control, that sent the Phoenicians into the far reaches of the Mediterranean, leading to the foundation of Carthage in 814 BCE, but of many other cities in North Africa, Sicily, Italy, and Spain. In Cyprus, Crete, and perhaps other places as well the Phoenicians came in contact with the Greeks, stimulating them in a variety of ways (the Greeks adapted their alphabet from the Phoenicians in the eighth century), but particularly offering them a market for a variety of goods ultimately demanded by the Assyrians. Mogens Larsen has spoken of the "grand Assyrian vacuum-cleaner."[32] It was this "vacuum cleaner" that set both the Phoenicians and the Greeks in motion, but the motion became self-propelling once begun. From about 750 to 600 the Greeks emulated the Phoenicians in establishing outposts all over the Mediterranean and Black Sea coasts.[33]

What is remarkable in this burst of activity beginning in eighth-century Greece is that a growing cultural unity[34] (overlying but never replacing local heterogeneity) was not linked to political unity: the increasing numbers of poleis retained their autonomy with great tenacity, so much so that Greek expansion cannot except metaphorically be called colonization. The newly established poleis had only a sentimental attachment to their cities of origin and were not politically subordinate to them. Societies that were, in a sense we will be examining shortly, politically primitive, were becoming increasingly culturally advanced. It is this early archaic period to which the term "Orientalizing" is most frequently applied, though I have tried to indicate that Greece was part of the Near Eastern *oikumene* from the second millennium on, and that contact, as the Lefkandi site indicates, was never lost.[35] It is clear that we are not faced here with an either/or: that the Greeks were isolated innovators or that they got it all from Asia and Africa. To the contrary, they were innovators indeed—that is the subject of this chapter—but they would never have achieved what they did if they had been isolated, small, retribalized societies. Much of what is remarkable about them derives from the fact that they were cosmopolitan, small, retribalized societies, in one sense closed in on themselves, in another open to the whole wide world.

I have described early Greek society as "ranked," with a distinction between nobles and common people (slaves were probably few until the seventh or even sixth centuries BCE, but the distinction between slaves and free was sharper than that between nobles and commoners). Still, from the earliest times, the pride of a self-styled nobility was always matched by a strong

sense of egalitarianism, and the notion that all free citizens were full participants in society. Our earliest texts, Homer and Hesiod, give evidence of the
existence but also the fragility of the ranking system in early Greek society.
The *Iliad* has been described as "conservative" or even "reactionary," but it is
hardly a simple celebration of the Greek nobility. From the beginning something is very wrong among the aristocrats. Richard Martin has seen Achilles
as the figure with whom the poet identifies, and through whom he relentlessly
criticizes Agamemnon and by implication the hierarchy of the Greek leadership, such as it was.[36] Achilles attacks Agamemnon as selfish, as taking more
than he deserves while leaving the hard fighting to others. Peter Rose sees the
conflict between the two as reflecting the resistance of an older culture based
on reward of merit (Achilles) and a newer one based on material wealth
(Agamemnon).[37] Though Martin and Rose tend to see "Homer" siding with
Achilles, Achilles is hardly portrayed as an unblemished hero. When overcome by irrational anger, he is far from reflecting the virtues of Greek aristocrats. And when he tells Patroclus that he wishes all the Trojan and Greek
warriors would die and only the two of them survive, he is revealed as more
selfish than Agamemnon.[38]

Greek political organization is far from clear in the *Iliad,* but on important occasions an assembly of all the troops had to be called. Normally only
the leaders spoke, and the one occasion where a commoner (Thersites, a real
kakos, not only abusive in speech but ugly and deformed as well) speaks, only
to be beaten and humiliated by Odysseus, is often given as an example of
Homer's aristocratic prejudice. It is worth remembering, however, that Thersites was allowed to conclude his speech—the text indicates that this was not
the first time he had spoken—and that the content of his remarks, a strong
criticism of Agamemnon's selfishness and near-cowardice, was very similar
to that of Achilles. The Thersites incident, thus, cuts two ways and is not as
"reactionary" as it might at first seem.

Our other earliest author, Hesiod, clearly does not speak for the aristocracy. We have quoted his nostalgia for the good *basileus,* but, particularly in
the *Works and Days,* the *basileis* of his own day, again leaders more than
kings, are subjected to merciless criticism and Hesiod's denunciation of their
oppression of the poor rivals that of his near contemporary, Amos. Those
whom the self-styled good *(agathoi)* styled as the bad *(kakoi)* would more
likely think of themselves as the middling *(mesoi)*—small farmers, able to
fight in the ranks, and unwilling to take abuse from anyone. From the point
of view of the *mesoi,* the privileges of the *agathoi* had to be earned, and abuse

from them was unacceptable.[39] Those without property, the *thetes,* had less standing, but the boundary between them and the poorest farmers was permeable and their claim to dignity—less easily heard than that of the *mesoi*—would not ultimately be ignored.[40] Thus, it was possible for the members of the emerging polis of the eighth century to see themselves as a community *(koinonia),* composed, in spite of status differences, of political equals *(homoioi).* It is this situation that allows Ian Morris to make the following remarkable statement:

> I will argue that in the eighth century the Greeks developed a radically new concept of the state, which has no parallels in any other complex society. The Greeks invented politics, and made political relationships the core of the form of state which they called the polis. The essence of the polis ideal was the identity of the citizens with the state itself. This had two important results. First the source of all authority was located in the community, part or all of which made binding decisions through open discussion. The second consequence was that the polis made the definition of the state as the centralized monopoly of force tautologous; force was located in the citizen body as a whole, and standing armies or police forces were almost unknown. The polis' powers were total: there were no natural rights of the individual, sanctioned by a higher authority; the idiom of power was political, and there was no authority beyond that of the polis . . . Of course in practice there were contradictions between the plurality of the citizen society and the unity of the state, but the contrast between the ideal of the polis as a political community of citizens and the ideals of the states of ancient Mesoamerica, Mesopotamia and even China could hardly be greater. The ethic of the polis was almost a stateless state, autonomous from all dominant-class interests by being isomorphic with the citizen body. The citizens *were* the state.[41]

Of course, if the citizens were the state, that puts the very meaning of "state" in question. It is this situation that has led Runciman to say that the polis wasn't a "city-state" but a "citizen-state," in that the citizens indeed were the state, and necessarily, from Runciman's point of view, a fragile and ultimately nonviable one.[42] It is this situation that led Paul Cartledge to write that "with the partial exception of Sparta ancient Greek poleis were technically 'State-less political communities.'"[43] Finally, Christian Meier, quoting

Thucydides saying that to the Greeks "the men were the *polis*," asserts both that the polis was a citizen-state and that that very idea called in question the notion of a state at all: "There was no way in which anything resembling a state could establish centralized power or state institutions that were divorced from society."[44]

But if we take the statement "the citizens *were* the state" literally, then the assembly of (in principle) all of the citizens must have been the ruling body.[45] I take it that Morris's point is that such an assembly already effectively existed in the eighth century and could not be ignored, but not that it actually governed because that would have meant the emergence of democracy much earlier than Morris or other specialists have argued. Early poleis were governed by groups of nobles (oligarchies) but always contingent on the explicit or tacit approval of the assembly. That is what makes the citizens the state even in this early period (eighth to fifth centuries BCE). Morris sees a drift toward ever greater participation of the whole citizen body in most of the poleis during these centuries.[46] Athens made a significant start in the eighth century, but then reverted to older oligarchic patterns during much of the seventh century, only to undergo the first of several major reforms under the leadership of Solon in the early sixth century. Of that we will have more to say below.

Although most of the poleis had popular participation through the assembly, genuine democracy was a late and relatively rare achievement. Oligarchy, the effective rule of noble families, was the dominant form of government, but these oligarchies were, except for Sparta, usually weak, permeable, and unstable. We have already noted that tyrannies were transient, and often served to include the previously excluded rather than to establish strong central control. In short, it is only from the polis, visible first in the eight century, that Greek democracy, that rare and remarkable phenomenon, could, in fifth-century Athens, find its first full development. So far we have looked at early Greek society primarily in structural terms; to understand it adequately we need to consider its cultural, indeed religions, dimension.

Poetry and Its Ritual Context

I have used texts such as those of Homer and Hesiod as sources of information, which, of course, they are; we must also consider what kind of texts they are: first of all they are poems. Poetry is common in oral cultures for works of any length because poetry is easier to memorize than prose. Few would dispute that the texts of Homer as we have them are the written results of a long history of oral recitation. One need not argue that writing had no effect on them—they were probably to a degree consciously transformed as they were written down—but oral traces are not hard to detect in them. Hesiod's poems, although most believe that Hesiod himself wrote them down, were also clearly intended for recitation, and could at first have been composed orally. "Bards" are already described in Homer—Demodocus in the *Odyssey*—as performers in ritual or semiritual situations. In sixth-century Athens the *Iliad* and the *Odyssey* were "performed" in their entirety as part of a major festival. Performance in this case points to the mimetic nature of the event: the bard was an actor, making the tales he recounted become real for his audience. The poet might be called a "singer," and though the Homeric poems were probably not sung, they may have been chanted, emphasizing the rhythmic nature of the texts.[47]

But what was the content of the tales? In our analysis of cultural evolution, following Merlin Donald, we have largely identified the mythic with the narrative: myths are stories, as the Greek word *mythos,* from which our word comes, implies. But, as we know from Vladimir Propp, Claude Lévi-Strauss, and others, stories are eminently migratory—the same stories can appear in many different cultures, some of them with close to worldwide distribution. There is no reason to search for one ultimate meaning in such stories: it is how they are used in particular societies at particular times that makes them effective myths of those societies. Thus Walter Burkert's definition is useful: *"Myth is a traditional tale with secondary, partial reference to something of collective importance."*[48] It is the tale as applied that does the work of myth. We can go on to make a problematic but significant distinction between tales about powerful beings or gods and their interaction with human beings as opposed to tales about what human beings did in the past, that is, in the narrow sense, between "myth" and "history." I put the terms in quotation marks because they can be distinguished only analytically—in practice they always overlap.[49]

If Homer and Hesiod deal in myths in both the wide and the narrow sense, they also share a source of authority, common to many early poets—one that ultimately became conventional, but that has to be taken seriously in early times—namely, that it was the muses, daughters of Zeus and goddesses themselves, from whom the poetry came. Thus, such texts, if not "revealed," were certainly "inspired." In contrast to the Hebrew scriptures, however, what the muses reveal is not necessarily reliable. Early in his *Theogony* the muses tell Hesiod:

Listen you country bumpkins, you pot-bellied blockheads,
we know how to tell many lies that pass for truth,
and when we wish we know to tell the truth itself.[50]

The poet himself may know what is true and what isn't, but he is reticent to say so. Hesiod (and perhaps Homer?) addresses himself to "the wise." How to understand him may not always be obvious, may require interpretation. In this respect poetry shares something with the character of oracles, such as those received at Delphi, notoriously ambiguous and in need of interpretation— even dangerous because a wrong interpretation could be disastrous. Marcel Detienne in *The Masters of Truth in Ancient Greece* has reminded us that *Alētheia* (truth) and *apatē* (deceit) are not to be taken in a positivist sense, that is, simply as contradictory, in these texts. Truth may be veiled; deceit may have a truthful purpose. We are in the realm of efficacious, not testable, speech.[51]

Poetic speech, long after writing had come into use, was performative, even creative; we could say it created its own "truth." It certainly created a world. Eric Havelock in his *Preface to Plato* has spoken of the "Homeric encyclopedia," the sense in which Homer conveys all that is worth knowing in the oral tradition.[52] Jenny Strauss Clay speaks of the two Homeric epics as having a kind of "totality," and quotes Gregory Nagy as saying, "Between the two of them, the *Iliad* and the *Odyssey* manage to incorporate and orchestrate something of practically everything that was once thought worth preserving from the Heroic Age."[53] Although in the Homeric encyclopedia, as Havelock calls it, almost every kind of knowledge can be found, what was most important, what made Homer the "teacher of Greece," was the form of life that it described, the *paideia* (education, culture, *Bildung*) that it modeled. It was this that aroused Plato's hostility, continuing a line of criticism of Homer that began at least with Xenophanes (late sixth, early fifth centuries), for Plato wanted to replace Homer, to make Socrates the teacher of Greece.

Havelock turns to Hesiod to describe the core of the poetic teachings. He finds the content of what the muses, through the poets, taught in lines 66–67 of the *Theogony,* which he translates:

They sing the laws and ways of all
even of the immortals do they celebrate (those).

The first line contains the words *nomoi* and *ethea,* which Havelock says can also be translated as "custom-laws" and "folk-ways."[54]

If in Hesiod the emphasis is relatively explicitly on *nomoi* and *ethea,* Homer, where the word *nomoi* (or the singular form *nomos*) is not to be found,[55] is more indirect, closer to the mythical systems of tribal and archaic societies, in depicting a moral world in which both gods and men act sometimes badly, sometimes well. If Homer and Hesiod are still primarily mythic in form, they are not merely expressions of "dominant ideology." Hesiod is quite explicitly critical of the nobility from the point of view of the "middling"; but Homer is quite critical as well: in the *Iliad* neither Agamemnon nor Achilles, nor even the gods, are wholly admirable; in the *Odyssey* the suitors, representatives of the nobility of Ithaca and neighboring islands, are depicted as almost wholly despicable. To the extent that Hesiod explicitly and Homer implicitly are critical of existing society and suggest that it could be different than it is, there is a hint of the axial already in these earliest Greek texts.[56]

So far we have been considering the form and content of the earliest Greek texts to emerge from a previously entirely oral tradition. To the extent that we have emphasized that these texts were performed, we have already set them in a mimetic/ritual context. We must now consider the religious changes that were occurring as these texts were first written down and that provide their larger context. One such context is the centrally important ritual of sacrifice that we have noted usually appears only in archaic societies. Sacrifice is old in the Greek world, and is probably one of the features it shares with the larger Near East of which it was a part. Modest sacrificial altars are to be found in Greece well back in the Dark Age, possibly continuous with Mycenaean usage. It is likely that these altars were used by the leader-priest of the noble household *(oikos)* for sacrifices that were shared with members of the *oikos,* their dependents and their guests (there are Homeric examples of such sacrificial feasts), on such occasions as weddings, funerals, or days appointed for worship of a particular deity.[57]

The eighth century sees changes in religious practice that correlate with (are in some sense identical with?) political changes we have already noted. Richard Seaford writes: "Excavation has shown that in the eighth century BCE there occurred a sharp increase in phenomena associated with the early development of the polis in various parts of the Greek world, notably the genesis of monumental temples and a massive increase in the quantity and quality of dedications made in public sanctuaries. It has become clear that another important function of these early temples, in addition to the storage of dedicated wealth, was the sacrificial feast."[58] Outside the *oikos*-sacrifice there is Homeric evidence for sacrificial feasts among warrior groups, with emphasis on the equal participation of all. But from the eighth century it appears that animal sacrifice becomes a central and defining ritual of the polis itself. Seaford writes: "The solidarity and articulation of the polis is expressed in its animal sacrifices, in which the principle of equal distribution (found in Homer) remains powerful. *Full citizenship and entitlement to participation in the sacrificial meal seem to be one and the same thing.*"[59] This is again a reminder that in archaic Greece we are dealing with a world in which our normal distinction of the spheres, in this case the religious and the political, simply doesn't work. We cannot speak of the "merging" of what has not been separated.

A further example of this principle is suggested by Seaford's argument that the word *nomos*, which we saw Havelock translate as "custom-law," derives from the verb *nemein*, "to distribute," and that therefore *nomos* meant "distribution, then the principle of distribution." *Nomos*, as we noted, is not found in Homer, but *nemein* is and is almost always used to mean distributing food or drink. Further, Seaford writes, "Even the distribution of urban space may use the terminology of dividing up an animal." He goes on to say that of the eight occurrences of the word *nomos* in Hesiod, two refer to sacrifice. And he concludes by saying that the word *nomos*, so central in the ethical thought of classical Greece, "originated in the widespread . . . practice of distributing *meat*."[60]

For present purposes, what is most interesting is that sacrifice, so closely linked to hierarchical authority in most archaic societies, in early Greece mirrors the polity in that it is oriented to the god, yes, but then to the community as a whole, not to ruler or priest. In fact, in most cases, anyone can carry out a sacrifice—there is no priestly, much less royal, monopoly. Thus Greek sacrificial feasts, the very core of ancient Greek religion, express the same egalitarian spirit as the political structure of the "citizen-state," and is as unusual religiously as the citizen-state is politically.

If egalitarian sacrifice (virtually an oxymoron) makes Greece markedly atypical, so is the fact that Greek religion was, in a sense, priestless. Walter Burkert writes: "Greek religion might almost be called a religion without priests: there is no priestly caste as a closed group with fixed tradition, education, initiation, and hierarchy . . . The god in principle admits anyone, as long as he respects the *nomos*, that is as long as he is willing to fit into the local community."[61] Of course there had to be people in charge of sacrifice and other rituals. What made Greece unique is that any citizen could serve.

Zaidman and Pantel describe how "priests" (and significantly "priestesses") were chosen:

> In most cases a priest or priestess functioned like a civic magistrate, exercising a liturgical authority in parallel to the legislative, judicial, financial or military authority of the city's officials. The methods of selecting priests and priestesses make clear their affinity to the status of magistrates. Most were appointed annually, and often by lot, and at the end of their term of office they were obliged to render account . . . Again, like magistracies, these priestly offices were typically barred to foreigners, including permanent residents, and open to all citizens.[62]

If religious officials were integrated into the structure of civic authority, this by no means is an indication that religious life was peripheral. On the contrary, the festivals that proliferated around the sacrificial feasts were central expressions of the self-understanding and solidarity of the polis. Greek festivals were many and various, and there is no space to describe them in detail here, but a few salient features need to be discussed. Important in most festivals was the procession, *pompe,* leading to the sanctuary where sacrifices would take place, but significant in its own right.[63] The procession could begin at the city gates or even at the border of the polis and approach a sanctuary in the middle of the city, or, conversely, it could begin in the middle of the city and end at an outlying sanctuary. The procession itself consisted of those most concerned with the ritual, but it was a very public event and attracted crowds of onlookers. Because at some level the whole city was involved, the procession could overcome, at least momentarily, the deepest divisions of Greek society: women, if they weren't already, as was the case in some important rituals, central actors, slaves, resident aliens, and children could all participate as onlookers in the festival atmosphere.

One particularly important type of festival was the agonistic festival consisting of a procession, a sacrifice, a contest *(agon),* and a banquet.[64] Contests in the context of ritual are present from the earliest times of which we have knowledge. The funeral games for Patroclus that Achilles sponsored featured a number of contests and races with Achilles awarding prizes to the winners (*Iliad* 23). We have already noted that the Olympic games were part of a great festival for Zeus. But the contests were not necessarily athletic alone: contests among singers, individual or in chorus, instrumentalists, rhapsodes (reciters of Homer), eventually dramatists, were common. Often the contestants represented different groups within the city (or, of course, different cities in the Panhellenic festivals), and thus could express rivalry and group hostility in the course of reaffirming group solidarity. Kin groups, local groups, and various kinds of associations all had their own festivals, involving primarily their own members.

Political/Religious Reform in Sixth-Century Athens

Athens was geographically the largest of the Greek poleis after Sparta, but Sparta's size was due to the fact that it included regions inhabited by helots, noncitizens kept in a condition of subjection and always potential rebels, whereas the Athenians consisted of all qualified citizens, not only in the city, but in the towns, villages, and countryside of Attica. Thus in terms of the citizen population, Athens was the largest polis from early on. Nonetheless, as we have seen, Athens lagged behind in the seventh century when striking cultural advances were taking place elsewhere—in Ionia and Sicily, for example. "Lagging behind" culturally and politically did not mean lagging behind economically, and it was economic advance that led to tensions between rich and poor, landlords and tenants, that were beginning to threaten the solidarity of the polis itself. In this context we can understand the important role of Solon, chief magistrate in 594–593 and instigator of major social and religious changes. Although we have a good bit of what many believe is authentically Solon's poetry, later on he became such a central figure in the self-understanding of the Athenians that we cannot always be sure what he actually did as against what was attributed to him as a semimythical refounder of the city. It is from the time of Solon that Athens begins its rise to the status of cultural metropolis of all Greece. This does not mean that important things were not happening elsewhere; but increasingly, those who were outstanding in any field were tempted to visit Athens, or even to take up residence there.

Solon, we are told, was given virtually dictatorial powers for a limited time to reform the polis, and it is those religio-political reforms that will concern us here. But Solon was also later considered to be one of the "Seven Sages" or "Seven Wise Men" of early sixth-century Greece, and wisdom was essential to his role as a reformer. After following the political and religious changes of the sixth and fifth centuries, we will return to the question of wisdom and its transformations from Solon's time until the fourth century.

Solon, of noble lineage but only moderately wealthy, placed himself "between" the aristocrats and the middling and lower classes and held that his reforms were concerned not to overturn existing social arrangements but to give to each group its due—in short, he was above all concerned with justice, *dike,* and with Zeus as guarantor of justice. Meier calls Solon's views a "third position," attempting to encompass the positions of the nobles and the commoners with the end of creating a just and fair polis for all.[65] In practice this meant attempting to moderate the dominant group and give the subordinates a greater role in political life. Important legislation is attributed to Solon, such as the canceling of all debts and the prohibition of servitude for debt. It is said that Solon ordered the return of Athenians who had been enslaved for debt, even if they had been sent abroad. Such acts were clearly intended to curb the oppression of the poor by the rich, but Solon knew that only a transformation of consciousness would make such reforms lasting. In his poetry he was as much preacher as politician, advising the well off to moderate their greed for the sake of civil comity, but also threatening them and/or their descendants with ruin *(ate)* if they violated the justice *(dike)* of Zeus.[66]

Just as there was ongoing tension over economic relations between the nobility and the middling, which Solon tried to address, so was there more than a little tension between rituals sponsored by the noble households *(oikoi)* and rituals sponsored by the whole city. Not only was the noble *oikos* a potential patrimonial state in waiting, and thus always a latent threat to the citizen-city, but the presence of several such *oikoi* in the same polis created the possibility, not infrequently realized, of civil violence. Funerals mobilized intense feelings among the group to whom the deceased belonged and could give rise to violence against rival factions. It is in this context that legislation, attributed to Solon but also to early lawgivers in other cities, sharply limited the number of participants and the kinds of activities that such noble funerals could include. Seaford suggests that though there were many motives for these laws, at least an important one was the need to curtail the power and proclivity to violence of the noble families. When such legislation was followed by the creation of citywide funerals or memorial rituals for the war dead, we can see the polis asserting its primacy over the noble households. There was also legislation against overly lavish weddings among the nobility, and the creation of festivals for young women that to some extent gave collective expression to what would otherwise be purely household celebrations.[67] If Solon was supposed to have curtailed the private rituals of the nobles, so a late tradition attributes to him the first comprehensive ritual calendar for the city as a whole.[68]

Although the example of Solon was etched deeply into the consciousness of the Athenians—Christian Meier calls him Athens's "first citizen," and Eric Voegelin calls him "the most important single person in Hellenic politics"—he clearly did not succeed in solving the problems that plagued the city.[69] The rivalry of the great families and the exclusion of the middling continued, so that by the middle of the sixth century the Athenians accepted the tyrant Pisistratus, over Solon's strenuous objections. After two unsuccessful attempts to gain power, Pisistratus's tyranny lasted from 547 until his death in 528; the tyranny of his sons was finally overthrown in 510. As in other cases, Pisistratus came to power as a solution to otherwise intractable problems, and though his reputation in later times was very negative, he extended privileges to the lower strata and worked hard to build the civic image of the city through the encouragement of festivals and a building program on the Acropolis. He was succeeded by two sons, the second of whom seems to have turned despotic, encouraging the opposition that led to the fall of the tyranny. In a sense, however, the extent to which Pisistratus promoted the interests of the common people and encouraged them to identify with the city undercut the very rationale for the despotism, and it was not long before reforms much more extensive than those of Solon moved the city ever more in the direction of radical democracy.

Though the very name of Athens points to its particular divinity, Athena was a generally recognized goddess and had cults in many places. Nonetheless, Athena's importance for Athens was very great and grew markedly in the sixth century when her temple on the Acropolis was increased in size and splendor. The Panathenaea, whose origins are obscure but which was already one of the great festivals of Athens in early times, was augmented in the first half of the sixth century (just before or just after the tyranny of Pisistratus— the dating is unclear) with the Great Panathenaea—that is, every fourth year the Panathenaea was expanded to include athletic games similar to those at Olympia, together with other competitions, including by the time of Pisistratus's son, Hipparchus, three-day recitations of the entire *Iliad* and *Odyssey*. These festivals were intended not only to celebrate the greatness of Athena for all Athenians but to appeal to a Panhellenic audience as well.

One remarkable event has been interpreted as an indication of just how important Athena was to the Athenians. Herodotus (1.60) reports that Pisistratus, in his second attempt to establish his tyranny in Athens (ca. 556 BCE, the dating is disputed), had a tall, beautiful woman dress as Athena in full armor and drive into the city in a chariot with heralds proclaiming that she was Athena and that she called upon all Athenians to accept Pisistratus as their leader. The stratagem worked, and Herodotus remarks on the gullibility of the Athenians, who were supposed to be the most intelligent of the Greeks. But Rebecca Sinos has pointed out that there was a long tradition of Athena serving as leader of a hero's procession, that the Athenians did not believe the woman portraying Athena was literally the goddess, but that they were participating in a drama that pleased them. In particular they wanted to believe that Athena had chosen not only Pisistratus but the Athenian people for a heroic role. She finds this a recurrent theme in later Athenian history.[70] This is a remarkable example, for if Sinos's interpretation is correct the Athenians felt themselves "chosen" by Athena over an extended period of time and this sense of chosenness gave them a feeling of pride and self-confidence greater than that of the citizens of many other Greek cities. But if Athena "chose" the Athenians, she was not a jealous goddess. She didn't seem to mind if her chosen people worshipped other gods, which they did in great numbers. Among the many who could be mentioned we should especially consider Dionysus.

It is part of the myth of Dionysus that he was an outsider, that he came from abroad, from Thrace or Phrygia, in historic times. Modern scholars as well as ancient Greeks tended to accept this part of the story as historically true, until the name of Dionysus appeared several times among the gods of the Mycenaeans in Linear B texts. So Dionysus is a very ancient Greek god, but he is "always" coming from abroad. He was very important in Athens, where a number of festivals, some of them very early, were dedicated to him. Robert Connor has seen the growth of Dionysiac worship in sixth-century Athens as a kind of religious preparation for the emergence of Greek democracy in the reforms of Cleisthenes beginning in 508–507.[71] Connor discusses the Dionysiac *thiasōtai* (confraternities) as among the many forms of voluntary association that made up something like "civil society" in sixth-century Athens—associations that were to some degree self-governing and that fostered the practice of group discussion and group decision making. It was the combination of the social practice nurtured in such associations with the spirit of Dionysiac religion that Connor sees as an important foundation for the democratic reforms, reforms that Cleisthenes nurtured but could not have created.

The structural reforms undertaken by Cleisthenes, or by the people of Athens under his leadership, are too complex for us to describe in detail. Suffice it to say that these reforms overcame some of the divisiveness that characterized Athens in earlier times and extended the participation of the common people in the government of the polis. What is significant for us is the fact that these political changes were accompanied by, were one aspect of, a general change that was religious as much as political. It is this religious side of the change that Connor characterizes as the increasing importance of Dionysiac religion.

The myth of Dionysus is complex and ambiguous, indeed ambivalent, with a dark side as well as a joyous one, but one of its foci is that of the outsider god who comes into a city and turns it upside down, leading to the destruction of those who oppose him but to a new solidarity among those who accept him. He is transgressive, to use a term common in current discourse, a boundary-crosser to be sure, but also integrative, the symbol of new community.[72] Connor believes that Dionysiac worship in the sixth century "is best understood as the first imaginings of a new type of community." More specifically, he writes:

> Dionysiac worship tumbles into carnival and carnival inverts, temporarily, the norms and practices of aristocratic society. While these inversions may provide a temporary venting mechanism and thereby help stabilize repressive regimes, in the longer run they can have quite a different effect. They make it possible to think about an alternative community, one open to all, where status differentiations can be limited or eliminated, and where speech can be truly free. It is a society that can imagine Dionysiac equality and freedom.[73]

Connor gives the example of features institutionalized in the political realm "that probably originated in religious practice, for example, 'outspokenness,' *parrhēsia,* and *isēgoria,* 'equality of speech.'"[74] Given the importance of Dionysiac cult groups and the spirit of Dionysiac religion, Connor finds it "not surprising" that the newly established Athenian democracy would express itself in a new festival, the City Dionysia, or festival of Dionysus Eleuthereus (that is, the Dionysus who came from the border city of Eleutheria, but also with the etymological implication of freedom). He argues that the City Dionysia was founded not under the Pisistratids but under Cleisthenes or shortly thereafter and so was a kind of "freedom festival" celebrating the fall of the tyranny.[75] Other specialists on Greek religion believe that the City Dionysia was founded under the Pisistratids, but that it underwent significant reform and enhancement at the time of Cleisthenes.[76] In that case, Connor's argument would still be applicable.

What from our point of view is most interesting is that religious practice not only made possible the idea of a different social reality than the one existing, but helped to actualize it as well. Although the capacity to imagine alternative social realities is part of what we have described as the axial transition, it is interesting that in this case it does not involve anything explicitly theoretical. Indeed, Connor writes: "The festival helps us understand why our texts contain no elaborate statement of Athenian democratic theory . . . The ancient Greeks did not write theory; they enacted it. They enacted it in particular through the City Dionysia."[77] We will have more to say about the role of the City Dionysia, to be sure, but what is interesting in this example is how far mimesis and narrative can prepare the way for the axial transition. Of course the Greeks *did,* as we will see, write theory, though not much in the way of democratic theory. But theory too, as well as democratic reform, arose from indispensable mimetic and narrative foundations.

Greek Tragedy

Because it was during the City Dionysia that tragedies were first performed, the uncertainty about the early history of the festival implies uncertainty about the origins of tragedy as well. The earliest tragedies, or something like them, must have been performed in the sixth century, and probably the contest in which three playwrights presented three plays on successive days was already in place. All surviving tragedies, however, date from the fifth century.

Aeschylus (ca. 525–456) produced his first tragedy in 499, won his first victory in 484, and his *Persians,* the earliest surviving Greek tragedy, was produced in 472. Sophocles (ca. 495–404) wrote the last of the surviving tragedies, *Oedipus at Colonos,* produced posthumously by his grandson in 401, having barely outlived his younger colleague, Euripides (ca. 485–407). Thus we have records of plays by the three great tragedians from virtually all of the fifth century and surviving plays from its last seventy years. The age of tragedy, therefore, almost completely overlaps with what has often been called the golden age of Athens: its move toward radical democracy; its remarkable victories in two wars with the greatest empire of the day, the Persians; the rise of the Athenian empire; extraordinary cultural achievements in many spheres of which tragedy was perhaps the pinnacle; the Peloponnesian War with Sparta, ending in complete and disastrous defeat in 404. Tragedy thus accompanied and commented on the political and cultural rise of Athens, its inner corruption, and its disastrous fall, including at the end two brief periods of tyranny. To say that tragedy was an intrinsic part of fifth-century Athens is in no way an overstatement, but we need to consider more closely how it was part of the very substance of the city.[78]

By the end of the sixth century the great festivals of the Panathenaea and the City Dionysia were in place and the reforms of Cleisthenes had greatly extended the participation of the people in running the city, when Athens had to meet an extraordinary challenge. The Persian Empire, which played such an important role in the return of the Israelites to Jerusalem beginning in 538, was in the 490s extending its control to western Anatolia and gradually conquering the Greek cities there. Athens, already the greatest naval power in Greece, annoyed the Persians by assisting the cities in Ionia to resist wherever possible. Therefore the great king Darius decided to conquer the whole Greek peninsula in order to consolidate the western provinces of the now huge Persian Empire by eliminating Greek interference. In 490 Darius invaded Greece and was defeated, mainly by the Athenians, at Marathon. In 480 his son Xerxes tried again, and was decisively defeated by the Athenians in the great sea battle of Salamis. In 479 a combined force including Athenians and Spartans defeated the Persians in a land battle at Plataea, putting an end to any further Persian incursion. Consequently the Athenians organized the Delian League, including most of the cities on the coasts and islands of the Aegean, as a defensive alliance against the Persians. As the Persian threat subsided, Athens turned the League into what was in effect an Athenian empire and became the strongest military power in Greece, thus rousing the envy of Sparta, which had long laid claim to that role.

It was in this context of increasingly radical democracy and growing imperial power that the flowering of Athenian culture occurred. Nor were these two aspects unrelated. As the Athenian navy, the backbone of Athens's military power, grew, so did the need for rowers; the lowest stratum of Athenian citizens, the unpropertied *thetes,* supplied these rowers. Previously when most battles were fought on land it was the hoplites who formed the infantry phalanx that composed the most significant non-noble group among the warriors, and the hoplites, coming mainly from prosperous farmers who had sufficient income to arm themselves, never lost their symbolic importance. But as the navy became ever more important, the *thetes* were increasingly drawn into the governance of the city. Because military pay was no small part of the income of the *thetes,* their democratic inclusion was complemented by their support of Athenian imperial power. Josiah Ober has argued against

Moses Finley that Athenian democracy did not depend on the growth of the Athenian empire, but some linkage was certainly there.[79] Thus the great tragedians were faced with the double development of democracy and empire and their complex interrelation and had to help the Athenians make sense of their rapid historic rise.[80]

Greek tragedies from the fifth century are performed not infrequently in our theaters today, and occasionally in films as well, so it is difficult for us to imagine how differently they appeared at the time of their origin. For us going to the theater is a purely private decision to enjoy a certain kind of "entertainment." For the ancient Greeks, drama was part of one of the greatest annual festivals, the City Dionysia, and was performed in the Theater of Dionysus on the southern slope of the Acropolis: it was simultaneously a form of worship and a civic obligation. Simon Goldhill has described it as follows: "The festival ran for four days at the end of February, beginning of March. Each day began at dawn. The audience was the biggest collection of citizens in the calendar . . . [B]etween 14,000 and 16,000 people regularly attended . . . Whereas the Assembly, the most important political body of democracy, regularly had around only 6,000 in attendance, and courts fewer still, the Great Dionysia was closer to the Olympic Games in scale."[81] On each of the first three days, three tragedies by one of the three playwrights was presented, plays of often nearly unbearable intensity, but the day was capped by a fourth, satyr play, about which we don't know very much except that it was cruder and perhaps reflected the kind of Dionysiac play out of which tragedy had developed, and though not necessarily comic, may have relieved the tension of the three previous plays. For a day beginning at dawn, this would have been quite an experience, especially because one would have to return at dawn for the next three days as well—not exactly like an evening at the theater. On the fourth day five comic plays were presented, often involving sharp political and cultural criticism, which both continued the self-reflection of the tragedies and relieved their seriousness with laughter.

Goldhill recounts how, before the plays were performed, a series of rituals defined the religious and political meaning of the event. Shortly before the beginning of the festival a procession brought the statue of Dionysus to the theater. The first day began, as we might expect, with a sacrifice: piglets were killed and their blood was scattered around the playing area and libations of wine were poured to the gods. The ten generals, the most important military and political leaders of the city, performed these sacrifices. There followed a reading out of the names of civic benefactors of the city in the preceding year, and their presentation with an honorific crown. The third ritual of the morning was the "parade of tribute," in which, in the days of the empire, bars of silver from the subordinate cities were paraded around the playing area. Goldhill quotes Isocrates saying in retrospect that this ceremony seemed to be "a precise way of being hated by everybody." Finally there was a parade of war orphans, young men who were being educated at state expense and who were expected to follow their fathers in battle for the sake of the city, reminding us that Athens, even in the time of its greatest glory, was a warrior city in which every male citizen was expected to play his part in military life.[82] When the plays began, the religio-political nature of the event was clear in everyone's mind.

What is truly remarkable is what the plays that followed were about: they were neither patriotic propaganda, nor bland moralistic tales; rather they called into question everything in heaven and on earth.[83] As Vernant puts it, "tragedy could be said to be a manifestation of the city turning itself into theater, presenting itself on stage before its assembled citizens," and doing so without fear or favor, showing its self-destructiveness as well as its grandeur.[84]

It has been asked, what has Greek tragedy to do with Dionysus, when almost none of the surviving plays (Euripides's *Bacchae* being the great exception) has explicit Dionysiac content. Vernant provides a suggestive answer:

> I have written elsewhere: "A consciousness of the fiction is essential to the dramatic spectacle; it seems to be both its condition and its product." A fiction, an illusion, the imaginary: Yet, according to Aristotle, this shadow play that the illusionist art of the poet brings to life on the stage is more important and true for the philosopher than are the accounts of authentic history engaged in recalling how events really occurred in the past. If we are right in believing that one of Dionysus' major characteristics is constantly to confuse the boundaries between illusion and reality, to conjure up the beyond in the here and now, to make us lose our sense of self-assurance and identity, then the enigmatic and ambiguous face of the god certainly does smile out at us in the interplay of the theatrical illusion that tragedy introduced for the first time onto the Greek stage.[85]

Among the remarkable things about Greek tragedy, so attuned to its immediate context, yet so relevant to us today, is how demanding on the audience their enigmatic and ambiguous quality was. Again, Vernant is helpful:

But the tragic message, when understood, is precisely that there are zones of opacity and incommunicability in the words that men exchange. Even as he sees the protagonists clinging exclusively to one meaning and, thus blinded, tearing themselves apart or destroying themselves, the spectator must understand that there are really two or more possible meanings. The language becomes transparent and the tragic message gets across to him only provided he makes the discovery that words, values, men themselves, are ambiguous, that the universe is one of conflict, only if he relinquishes his earlier conviction, accepts a problematic vision of the world and, through the dramatic spectacle, himself acquires a tragic consciousness.[86]

And it is perhaps the tragic consciousness of the depth and confusion of the self and the need for self-understanding, however difficult, that is the axial moment provided by Greek tragedy, one almost completely missing in Homer, where things are, by and large, what they seem. It is here that Eric Voegelin finds the tragic "leap in being," his terminology for what I am calling the axial moment.[87] If so, it is an axial moment that is still almost entirely mimetic and narrative, only latently theoretic.

Christiane Sourvinou-Inwood gives us a somewhat more specific anchoring of Greek tragedy in Dionysiac ritual in what she calls the "ritual matrix" of tragedy.[88] Based on inference from fragmentary evidence, she argues that the City Dionysia began in the sixth century as a celebration of the return and residence of Dionysus Eleuthereus to Athens, an event that occurred in mythic time but which became present again in the ritual. On the first appearance of Dionysus Eleuthereus (Dionysus from Eleutheria), bringing wine and revelry, he was rejected as causing disorder in the city. There followed afflictions, particularly to male sexual organs, and the realization that such afflictions could be overcome only by accepting Dionysus into the city as a resident deity. Due to the nature of the affliction, the presence of erect phalloi as a prominent feature in Dionysiac processions indicates that the malady had been cured.

At a deeper level the meaning of the ritual is that, in Sourvinou-Inwood's words, "It turned out that only by surrendering control and embracing disorder in the service of Dionysos can men ultimately maintain order and avoid catastrophic loss of control."[89] This paradox involves the very nature of Greek religion, which pushes the limits of human rationality. It also provides a paradigm or matrix for the exploration of religious paradoxes in general,

not only Dionysiac ones. The "tensions, problems, and human limits articulated in these myths of resistance to Dionysus" were "especially conducive to
religious exploration," explorations that could be extended to other myths
and to the problematic nature of human life in general.[90]

Thus the ambiguity and ambivalence that characterize Greek tragedy and
raise it to a level of transcultural human relevance, is rooted in a willingness,
indeed a necessity, to face the problematic nature of human life not obvious
in earlier Greek culture. In Homer, for example, Orestes was unambivalently
celebrated as a great hero for avenging his father's murder by killing his
mother's lover, Aegisthus. The fact that Orestes killed his mother, Clytem-
nestra, as well, is never explicitly mentioned, but only once hinted at. In Aeschylus's Oresteia, however, it is Orestes's moral obligation not to kill his
mother that clashes with his moral obligation to avenge his father that is at
the center of the action, and it is his guilt as a matricide that finally needs
absolving, without ever obliterating the horror of the deed. It is this that leads
Sourvinou-Inwood to argue that Greek tragedy is continuously involved in
"religious problematization." She demonstrates the "ritual matrix" of the plays
of Euripides as much as of those of Aeschylus, and argues that Euripides, far
from being an Enlightenment freethinker, was pushed to the limits to make
sense of what the gods, in whom he continued to believe, were up to in a dark
time.[91]

But if the tragic poets were involved in religious exploration, they were
simultaneously involved in political exploration, those being two sides of the
same coin, and the fact that tragedy and radical democracy in Athens coin-
cide is no accident, as they say. If Sourvinou-Inwood is right, from the very
beginning the chorus in the early Dionysiac rite represented both the Athenians in the myth of origin who rejected and then accepted Dionysus, and
also the Athenians of the day, who were once again welcoming Dionysus
among them; the chorus never lost this double role throughout the history of
tragedy. So if, as Vernant said, in tragedy the polis turned itself into a theater,
but a theater in which the people were both actors and spectators, then the
people were looking at themselves, however far away in mythic time or geographic space the action of the play took place. It is surely the sustained capacity of the city to endure such searching self-examination for a century
that is so remarkable.

Christian Meier complements Sourvinou-Inwood in giving us a political
reading of the plays to go along with her religious one. They turn out to be
two sides of a single whole. It is not possible in this chapter to give a reading

of individual plays in their specific historical context, but we might consider briefly the first surviving play, Aeschylus's *Persians*.[92] It was produced in 472, less than a decade after the great Athenian victory of Salamis in 480 and the Greek victory at Plataea in 479. It is the only surviving tragedy to be placed in real rather than mythic time, but the locus of the play is the far away capital of the Persian Empire, Susa. The play is set in 480 when the chorus of Persian elders is anxiously waiting news of events on the western front. The queen, widow of Darius who had led the invasion of Greece in 490 and mother of Xerxes who is still at the front, appears in order to express her profound anxiety and, after the first news of disaster has arrived, her wish is to consult the shade of her dead husband. Sourvinou-Inwood shows how much of the play is taken up with the ritual of the raising of Darius's ghost, and his subsequent appearance and utterances, an example of the importance of ritual in almost all surviving tragedy. Only near the end of the play does Xerxes himself appear, ragged and bloody, to describe the full measure of the defeat.

Aeschylus does not fail to have the Persians marvel at how the much smaller Athenian forces defeated their great armada, or to show their recognition of the undying love of the Greeks for freedom. But the play does not display hatred of the Persians. On the contrary, the audience is drawn into the dignity and suffering of the Persians, the experience of a great city in defeat. Darius's ghost explains the defeat in terms of hubris, of a lack of moderation, of crossing boundaries (the Hellespont) that ought not to have been crossed. But the effect is to turn the mirror on the Athenians, in 472 busily engaged in extending their power throughout the Aegean.

Meier finds Aeschylus speaking to his fellow citizens, saying that "the Athenians too would have to stay within their limitations . . . Darius' warning 'that man is mortal and must learn to curb his pride' (420) was meant for their ears too . . . The powerful experience of defeat . . . must have brought home to them the dangers of combat, as must Aeschylus' great lament on the pity of war."[93] Even Sourvinou-Inwood, who usually confines herself to the religious meaning of the tragedies, writes of *Persians* that "the overweening pride and overstepping of human limits was not only relevant to the Persian kings . . . [T]he exploration of this overconfidence and transgression, here distanced to, and located in, the enemy other, was of direct relevance to Athens."[94]

If there were space it would be interesting to look at other of the great tragedies for their religious/political meaning both in their own time and for us. Instead we must sum up this extraordinary conjuncture of city and poet. Probably only a democratic city could subject itself to such searching self-examination, and we must remember that the city never faltered in its pride and respect for its tragic poets, but the city did not heed what they were attempting to teach. Athens did gradually turn a self-defensive alliance into an oppressive, at moments brutal, empire. Though insisting on justice at home, it willingly behaved tyrannically to its subject cities. Pericles, or Thucydides speaking through him, justified brutality in the name of survival. As far as other cities were concerned, justice was the rule of the stronger. The voice of Plato's Thrasymachus was the voice of imperial Athens.

And just at the wrong moment, 451, when the empire most needed some sense of common purpose, Pericles proposed a new law that would make it a requirement of Athenian citizenship that both parents be Athenians. This at a time when inter-polis marriages had been common and only Athenian citizenship of the father had previously been necessary to guarantee the citizenship of the child. It was now clear to the subject cities that they would never be Athenians.[95] The contrast with Rome, which, in its hour of need, extended Roman citizenship to its allied cities, could not be clearer.

If Sophocles was more somber than Aeschylus, the younger Euripides at moments verges on the morbid or hysterical. Euripides is particularly vivid in showing the horrors of the enslavement of Trojan women after their men have been killed, as in his *Hecuba,* for example, where Hecuba has to bear the sacrifice of her daughter, whom Odysseus has refused to save. Given that the Athenians had sporadically killed the men and enslaved the women of recalcitrant cities in their empire, again we can see the mirror turned on the people, but the people not learning what their teachers were saying. When Pericles precipitated the war with Sparta, the Peloponnesian War (430–404), a war that may well have been inevitable, but did not live long enough to ensure that his cautious strategy would continue, the seeds of catastrophe were sown. The end was punctuated by two brief periods of tyranny, the oligarchy of the Four Hundred in 411 and the rule of the Thirty Tyrants in 404.

It is more than poignantly apt that the last surviving Greek tragedy was Sophocles's *Oedipus at Colonos,* written not long before his death in 404 but first produced by his grandson in 401, a fitting marker of the end of an era. The blind and aged Oedipus, accompanied by his daughter Antigone, comes to the Athenian town of Colonos to die. At first the townspeople, careless of his great suffering, want to drive this polluted man away, but Theseus, the

Athenian king, welcomes Oedipus, believing that his tomb in Attic territory
would be a blessing to the city. Through his life of wisdom and folly, power
and suffering, he had truly become a hero, that is, one who would live on
after his death. The astounding achievements of fifth-century Athens have
indeed lived on after the fall of the Athenian empire; it was truly a golden
age, but also an age of great suffering, suffering inflicted and suffering
undergone. Greek tragedy has been one of our greatest resources for dealing with suffering ever since, though its lessons are no easier to learn now
than ever.

Wisdom and the City

We have followed the history of the Greek poleis, and, from the sixth century, Athens in particular, politically, religiously, and through poetry, beginning with Homer and Hesiod and continuing through the poetic drama of
fifth-century Athens.[96] We have observed axial intimations at several points
so far, but they have remained at the level of the mimetic and the narrative,
though sporadically, as with Hesiod, Solon and certainly with the tragedians, we have seen something like mythospeculation. But if Greece is above
all the birthplace of theory, of philosophy and science, we need to backtrack
a bit to look at the beginnings of anything that could adequately be called
theory or seen as pointing to it. Surely the place to begin is with wisdom,
sophia, that we have already alluded to in the discussion of Hesiod and
Solon. From the earliest times poets, diviners (or interpreters of oracles), and,
as we saw in Hesiod, "kings," were counted among the wise.[97] A tradition
that originated probably no later than the fifth century, and was noted by
both Plato and Aristotle, referred to a group of Seven Sages or Wise Men
around the beginning of the sixth century, of whom, although the list varies
in later tradition, Solon was almost always one. As an indication of what
wisdom meant in a period later than Hesiod, it would be well to look a bit
more closely at these Seven Sages.[98]

If we think we will find among them the beginning of Greek "philosophy," we will be largely disappointed, for among them only Thales has later
been considered in that category. The list as we have it is, on the face of it,
curious. It most commonly included Solon, Thales, Pittakos, Bias, Chilon,
Kleoboulos, and Periander, and the only thing they have most obviously in
common is an involvement in political life. Pittakos was said to have been
aisymnētēs, a term Aristotle defined as an "elected tyrant," of Mytelene. He

was supposed to have been elected for a period of ten years to put the city in order, and was, similar to Solon, a moderate reformer. Chilon was a high official in Sparta, and Periander was tyrant of Corinth, variously described as brutally oppressive and as wisely moderate. Bias was known for his work in arguing legal cases, and Thales, whom we primarily consider as a thinker, played an active role in the politics of his home city, Miletus. Of the seven, only Kleoboulos of Lindus on the island of Rhodes seems to have had no involvement in politics. It appears, therefore, that wisdom was in early Greece primarily practical and political rather than theoretical.

As to the content of their teaching, almost all that we have from the sages are short gnomic statements with ethical intent. From Solon we have, of course, quite a bit of poetry, but his teaching was often summed up with such a phrase as "Nothing in excess," complemented by a phrase attributed to Kleoboulos, "Moderation is best." It would seem that politically the sages represented on the whole (Periander is a problem here) the "third position" of Solon, between the nobility and the middling, and by emphasizing moderation *(sophrosyne),* originally a middling value hardly shared by aristocrats, were helping to make this virtue central for all Greeks, so that it became a noble virtue as well as a popular one. Still Richard Martin finds that the political was only one of the roles of the sages and not necessarily the most important. He finds three features defining them as a type: "First, the sages are poets; second, they are involved in politics; and third, they are performers."[99]

Poetry was the normal form of expression in early Greece, so it is not surprising that the sages were poets, although it is only Solon's poetry that has survived. Martin gives the evidence that Thales wrote in poetry, even though none of it survives, and the accounts of the poetic achievements of the others, even Periander.[100] The significance of poetic expression for us is that it is more apt to be used for mythospeculation than for theory. Martin's emphasis on the sages as performers is of especial interest to us, as it indicates the continued importance of mimetic culture in the way they influenced their fellow citizens. He defines performance as follows: "By performance, I mean a public enactment, about important matters, in word or gesture, employing conventions and open to scrutiny and criticism, especially criticism of style."[101] Martin gives many examples of exemplary actions of the sages, often, though not always, combined with some brief verbal statement. One example, from Solon, will suffice: "Thus when the tyrant Peisistratos at Athens was already established in power, Solon, unable to move the people against him, piled his arms in front of the generals' quarters and exclaimed, 'My country, I have served thee with my word and sword!' "[102] Having said this, he promptly left Athens for Egypt.

Because the sages were known for their gnomic wisdom, often set in a performative context, Martin reminds us that Roman Jakobson once remarked that proverbs and sayings are "the largest coded unit occurring in our speech and at the same time the shortest poetic compositions."[103] Gnomic sayings, then, could be called one-line poems, often set in the context of Zen-like actions that underline the point being made. These sages could surely speak and argue, but they taught not so much with their words (Solon is here a considerable exception) but with their lives (here Solon is no exception). The performative dimension is, thus, not so much another dimension, as one that sums up the practical-political and the poetic and gets to the heart of what the sage was doing. These considerations drive Martin to add still a fourth feature: because the actions that the sages performed so often had explicit or implicit religious undertones, we must add to the other three features "religious importance."[104] Because the religious dimension consisted mainly in ritual activity, sacrifice or the interpretation of sacrifice, the dedication of gifts to Apollo, and so on, we can say that the overriding element of performance includes religion together with politics and poetry. This should hardly come as a surprise; throughout this chapter we have seen that religion and politics are so deeply intertwined that they resist separation in terms of our categories, and that Greek religio-political life was expressed above all in poetry and performance.

Martin argues that Greek thinkers after the time of the Seven Sages, up to and including Socrates (though he makes a significant qualification for Socrates) showed the same dominantly performative quality and therefore cannot be treated as disembodied "thinkers" as we are wont to do. I would make two significant additions to Martin's argument. One is the tragic poets, usually not treated as thinkers, though they were remarkable thinkers, who, if Sourvinou-Inwood is right, stood themselves initially in the role of protagonist in the earliest drama, directly addressing the people in their own words,[105] but who, even when they slipped behind the screen of skilled actors (who were also, we must remember, skilled singers), were still very much involved in creating a performance that would move an audience on many levels, of which the verbal, crucial though it was, was only one.

The other addition I would make is to add one more character to Martin's list, that is, not to stop with Socrates, but to add Plato as well. Was Plato not also a dramatist, and does he not seek to convince not only by argument but by example, above all the life and death of Socrates, but through the subtle human interplay of the dialogue as well?[106] The fact that Plato's dialogues were never, to my knowledge, performed, is not enough to remove them, in my view, from the category of the performative—in principle they *could* be performed.[107] One further point about Plato as performative: his suspicion of writing relative to the spoken word. Plato's point in the famous discussion of this issue in the *Phaedrus* is that real learning can occur only in face-to-face interaction, and that writing can only serve as a "reminder" of what one already knows, and may even serve to weaken memory. Here Plato is recognizing writing as a form of "external memory," to use Donald's term, but balanced on the cusp between oral and literate cultures as he was, he didn't seem to recognize the powerful resource such external memory could be. But here I want to emphasize the point that through the distinction between the written and the oral, Plato makes the performative, the enactive, primary:

> *Socrates:* Now tell me, can we discern another kind of discourse [besides writing], a legitimate brother of this one? Can we say how it comes about, and how much better and more capable it naturally is?
> *Phaedrus:* Which one is that? How do you say it comes about?
> *Socrates:* It is a discourse that is written down, with knowledge, in the soul of the listener; it can defend itself, and it knows to whom it should speak, and with whom it should remain silent.
> *Phaedrus:* You mean the living, breathing discourse of the man who knows, of which the written one can fairly be called an image. (*Phaedrus* 276a)[108]

Although Aristotle also wrote dialogues, we don't have any of them, and the treatises we do have could never be performed except as professorial lectures, though even that remnant of performance suggests that the performative category, like so much in human culture, is never lost.

The Beginnings of Rational Speculation

The discussion so far can be seen as preparatory for the consideration of what are usually referred to as the "Presocratic Philosophers," where, if anywhere, we should be able to discover the beginning of theory in ancient Greece, and therefore locate the axial moment. We might remind ourselves what we are looking for when we speak of theory. Following Merlin Donald, we have argued that human consciousness has developed sequentially, as the episodic culture that we share with higher mammals has been augmented, first by mimetic culture, and then by narrative culture—augmented, not replaced. Theoretic culture, which was not caused by literacy (it may have been the cause of literacy), but probably required literacy as a condition of its continuing development, is the most recent form of consciousness, and, like its predecessors, augments rather than replaces previous cultural forms, so that human consciousness is, as Donald puts it, a "hybrid system."[109] Donald characterizes the "fundamental change" that the emergence of theoretic culture involves as follows: "The human mind began to reflect on the contents of its own representations, to modify and refine them. The shift was away from immediate, pragmatic problem solving and reasoning, toward the application of these skills to the permanent symbolic representations contained in the external memory sources."[110] Surely the emergence of "philosophy" should fit the bill. We should, however, remember Donald's admonition that human consciousness is a hybrid system, and the axial transition may therefore involve more than simply the appearance of theory.

Right off the bat we have a problem with terminology. "Philosophy" is not a term we can take for granted: it emerges only in the fourth century BCE and was applied only retrospectively to earlier thinkers. It is not even clear if the term means the same thing in the modern world—that is, since the seventeenth century—as it did in antiquity. The Seven Sages were not (except for Thales of Miletus, and he only much later) referred to as philosophers, either in ancient Greece or in modern usage; rather the term "sage" translates *sophos* (pl. *sophoi*), literally "wise man," or the virtual synonym, *sophistes,* the term that will later be translated as "sophist" and that Plato so harshly criticized. Indeed, the term *sophos* could be used of one skilled in any craft or art.

The notion of wisdom *(sophia)* and of wise men in pursuit of it was for a long time quite vague and general, including poets and lawgivers along with those who speculated about the beginnings of things, as Thales was supposed to have done.[111] We have evidence that his possible disciple, at any rate his fellow Milesian of the next generation, Anaximander, certainly did engage in such speculation, as we have a fragment of his writing, among the very first Greek texts to be written in prose. But although, according to Aristotle, Thales, Anaximander, and Anaximenes (a third generation Milesian thinker) compose the Milesian school of natural philosophy, the very term "philosopher," as noted above, did not come into common usage until the time of Plato or just before, so not for 200 years after Thales. The meaning of the term "nature" *(physis)* from which "natural" philosophy is derived, cannot be taken for granted either.

Part of our problem is that much that we know of the Presocratics is contained in the writings of Aristotle, who, if anyone, was indeed a theorist. Was it not Aristotle who essentially created logic as we know it? Was it not Aristotle who reflected on the meaning of our representations in just about every field of knowledge? But it is just Aristotle's own achievements that bring into question his account of a series of Presocratic philosophers, emphasizing as he does the theoretical implications of their thought, and viewing them primarily as predecessors to himself. While using cautiously what Aristotle says about them, remembering that this is often all we have, we must remember also that they were religio-political performers, often writing in poetry, as close to the seven sages as to what will later be thought of as philosophers. And although we can see some kinds of development in their thought over two centuries, they don't line up in any neat succession.

Martin emphasized the competition between the seven sages—that's one reason there had to be seven of them. Competition *(agon)* was a feature of Greek culture from the earliest times—Hesiod mentions having taken part in a poetic competition—so it should not surprise us to see the "Presocratics" competing and criticizing each other. Though often active in their own cities, they tended to move around a lot, often ending up in places far from where they were born. Their freedom to think and criticize was due in part to the competitive culture and regard for "free speech" within the Greek polis, but also in part to their ability to move elsewhere when conditions for them became uncomfortable where they were. They were the ancient version of something like "free-floating intellectuals." These conditions both within the polis and from the fact that Greece was a multi-polis society undoubtedly have something to do with the remarkable diversity and creativity that we find in their thought.[112]

The conventional view has been that Thales, in the early sixth century, was the first philosopher, the one who threw off the cloak of myth and began the tradition of rational inquiry. But this view not only of Thales but of his Milesian followers, Anaximander and Anaximenis, requires more than a little qualification. The three Milesians, in the accounts we have of them, were in search of beginnings, of the *arche* of the universe, but that search was based neither on observation nor on deduction, but on speculation, indeed, seeing how close their thought was to Hesiod on the one hand and to Persian and Mesopotamian ideas on the other, their thought was at best midway between mythospeculation and theory.[113] After all, as Francis Cornford pointed out, Hesiod too began his *Theogony* with a cosmogony based on natural entities, not the gods. In the beginning there was Chaos, a "yawning gap" as Cornford translates it, and from Chaos came Earth and Eros, a god to be sure, but in this early context more like the principle of generation than an Olympian deity.[114] When Thales said the world began with Water[115] or Anaximenes, with Air, or Anaximander with the Unbounded (or the Indefinite, *Apeiron*), had they really moved so far from Hesiod? Geoffrey Lloyd has argued that Anaximander's astronomy was based on observation and began a tradition of gradually improving observation and analysis, but that the Milesian cosmogonies had no such basis or cumulative possibility.[116] In short, Anaximander contributed to early Greek science, but the Milesians as cosmogonists were doing something else, moving beyond, but not very far beyond, myth and toward, though not very near to, theory.

The evidence for the thought of the Milesians, given how little we know of their own words, is slight, and we are heavily dependent on much later texts for what we know of them. Nonetheless Charles Kahn has managed to reconstruct an account of the thought of Anaximander that is worth considering. At first glance he would seem to be very far from Cornford, or even Lloyd: "What the system of Anaximander represents for us is nothing less than the advent, in the West at any rate, of a rational outlook on the natural world. This new point of view asserted itself with the total force of a volcanic eruption, and the ensuing flood of speculation soon spread from Miletus across the length and breadth of the lands in which Greek was spoken."[117] On closer inspection, however, we find Kahn insisting that the "cosmological ideas of the old poets," primarily Homer and Hesiod, provide the indispensable background for the emergence of Milesian thought. Given the difficulty in interpreting the evidence for this early period of Greek thought, Kahn says: "It is only by placing the Milesians in between the two regions of light provided by archaic poetry on the one hand and classical philosophy on the other—by thus illuminating them, as it were, from above as well as from below—that we may have any hope of seeing a bit deeper into this dark period of transition and creation."[118]

Kahn makes still another point worth noting. It is probably no accident that Greek cosmological speculation emerged in Miletus, an important commercial port on the west coast of Anatolia, which the Greek inhabitants called Ionia. Ionia was the closest part of the Greek world to the world of the East: to Anatolian kingdoms long in contact with Mesopotamia, and eventually to the Persian Empire that extended over almost the entire Middle East. It was a natural point of entry for the advanced astronomy and mathematics that had long been developing in Mesopotamia. This external stimulus was so significant that Kahn gives it a vivid characterization: "The maternal soil of Hellas was fertilized by Mesopotamian seed."[119] This Mesopotamian stimulus is particularly important if Lloyd is right that it was the Milesian contribution to astronomy that laid the foundation for a genuine science in this field.

Two important features link the new natural philosophy with the past: a fundamentally narrative framework and a belief that the cosmos is alive. Anaximander, like Hesiod, was intensely interested in the beginnings of things. Indeed: "The arrangement of Anaximander's treatise followed an order which was essentially chronological. The life history of the world was described as a process of gradual evolution and differentiation out of the primordial *apeiron* [boundless] . . . This presentation of natural science as a kind of epic poem, with beginning, middle, and end, is characteristic of early Greek thought."[120] It is true that Anaximander's account appears to be both naturalistic and rational: everything is explained by impersonal forces, not only the origination of the universe, but the workings of the heavenly bodies, the weather, and other natural phenomena. The Olympian gods are nowhere mentioned. But we are still in the realm of narrative; the links back to Hesiod's *Theogony* can still be detected.

If we look more closely at the *apeiron,* the "scientific" nature of the thought of Anaximander becomes even more problematic. The *apeiron,* which, when translated as "the Boundless," might appear to be an abstraction, turns out to be a huge, inexhaustible mass totally surrounding the world. It is imperishable and ungenerated, itself the beginning *(arche),* both in space and time, of everything else, through the emission of a "seed," from which the heavens, the earth and all things gradually differentiated out. Summing up, Kahn makes it clear that although the *apeiron* may be a principle of nature, it is at the same time, a new kind of divinity:

> We see that, in addition to being the vital source out of which the substance of the world has come and the outer limit which encloses and defines the body of the cosmos, the *apeiron* is also the everlasting, god-like power which governs the rhythmic life cycle of this world. Thus it is not only the idea of the well-regulated cosmos which Greece owes to Anaximander, but also that of its regulator, the Cosmic God. And the

two ideas belong together. For the conception of the natural world as a unified whole, characterized throughout by order and equilibrium, gave rise to the only form of monotheism known to classical antiquity.[121]

Surely Anaximander did not yet differentiate science and theology, but we will probably want to bracket the word "monotheism" in this quotation, as it raises more problems than it solves. It might be better to think of the *Apeiron* as a kind of god above the gods, or the divine ground of a universe that is in some way or other divine altogether (Thales is reported to have said, "All things are full of gods").[122] Though Anaximander distributes most of the cosmic functions of the Olympian gods to "natural" forces, he nowhere denies the existence of the gods. His successor, Anaximenes, whose first principle was "air" in a sense too complicated for us to go into, said that "infinite air was the principle, from which the things that are becoming, and that are, and that shall be, and gods and things divine, all come into being."[123] In this way of thinking, because air is the source and origin of the gods, it could be considered "more divine" than the gods, but the existence of the gods is not in question, nor was it through most of the history of Greek thought, including in Plato and Aristotle. This is not to say that the Homeric gods did not receive criticism—we will need to consider that issue below—nor even that no one in ancient history denied the gods altogether, only that that was not the inevitable or even the very common result of the emergence of Greek "naturalism." Thus if we can speak of a Greek "monotheism" at all, it was very different from the Israelite one: the Cosmic God was no jealous God denying the existence of other gods. Even more important, the Cosmic God did not require the rejection of the cult of the Olympian deities, which continued to be performed, with hymns, prayers, and sacrifices, by the wise and the foolish alike, throughout antiquity.

I have put "naturalism" in quotes because what nature, *physis,* meant is not to be assumed as identical with the meaning of "nature" in contemporary English usage. *Physis,* a central term in the subsequent history of Greek thought, came to mean "the *essential character* of a thing," but it never lost its other meaning of development, of the idea that we "understand the 'nature' of a thing by discovering *from what source* and *in what way* it has come to be what it is."[124] Paul Ricoeur reminds us that it is dangerous to translate *physis* by "nature," because *physis* is "not some inert 'given,'" but rather *physis* is alive. We will not understand Aristotle's idea that art is the imitation *(mimesis)* of nature *(physis)*, Ricoeur says, if we think that through art we are imitating "that-thing-over-there," when rather we are actualizing something that is alive.[125] Perhaps another way of putting it would be to say that Greek thought lacked our strong dichotomy between subjectivity and objectivity, so that nature is something one lives with, something one is part of, not something "over there."[126]

All the qualifications I have been trying to make to the idea that the Milesian cosmology marks "the advent of a rational outlook on the natural world," by arguing that it is also a reformed mythology, do not mean that I want to downgrade its importance, or, indeed, its significance for almost all later thought. It did not mark a complete break with poetry, myth, and the Olympian gods, but it did usher in a whole new world of speculation that would open up many lines of development. The world of the wise was subject to many influences—political, economic, religious—but never again would a concern for "the essential character of things" cease to preoccupy the Greek mind.

The Axial Transition

It has been widely accepted that by the time of Plato and Aristotle "rationality" in something like the modern sense of the term, had clearly appeared in ancient Greece, although even this assumption is one that we will need to examine closely. Agreement as to how much earlier such rationality can be discerned, and who among the Presocratics most clearly expressed it, is much less general. If we can get clear about the emergence of rationality, or theory as Donald defines it, we may consider the role this emergence played in the Greek axial transformation. But we must always keep in mind the larger historical landscape of the efflorescence of ancient Greek culture during the 500 years from about 800 to about 300 BCE. Before looking at particular thinkers and movements it might be useful to survey briefly the background features of the period that might help account for the axial transition.

The emergence of the polis itself, usually dated to the eighth century, with its emphasis on the participation of all citizens in the assembly, even when political office was monopolized by a few, and the development of an inclusive polis religion, centering on sacrificial rites performed at ever more imposing temples devoted to the patron deities of the poleis, have been seen as the essential preconditions for the development of Greek rationality. With the development of ever more widely participatory political and judicial institutions, especially in the sixth and fifth centuries, there was a growing emphasis on argument in the assembly and in the law courts, which made argument and evidence matters of explicit concern. The very intensity of political participation in these developing poleis has been seen by a number of scholars as the indispensable precondition for the innovations in thought.[127]

It is worth remembering that literacy, once given significant causal status in this process, though now seen more as a necessary than a sufficient cause, closely accompanied the rise of the polis: the first writing, the poems of Homer, Hesiod, and the Homeric Hymns, dating from the late eighth or the early seventh centuries, and the beginning of prose texts, of which we have only fragments, from the early to middle sixth century.[128]

A third factor besides political developments and literacy, the invention of money, occurred in the late seventh or early sixth century in Asia Minor and so accompanied the beginning of Milesian speculation. Richard Seaford has argued forcefully for the importance of the world's first money economy as a stimulus to abstract thought in his 2004 book *Money and the Early Greek Mind*. Seaford moves the whole discussion of money beyond the usual haphazard treatment that applies the term to anything used as a measure of value, to a precise definition of what money, in fact, really is, a discussion too technical to repeat here, but which comes down to money as a circulating currency accepted on trust in the issuing authority.[129] Seaford argues for the Ionian Greeks as the inventors of money and as to its date of origin he says, "coinage spread in Greek Asia Minor from the late seventh or early sixth century and in the mainland from about the middle of the sixth century."[130] Seaford illustrates the influence of money on the Greek capacity for abstraction by citing the work of the Milesians and gives a number of specific examples such as the well-known saying of Heraclitus, "All things are an exchange for fire and fire for all things just as goods are for gold and gold for goods."[131] Whether money can play as dominant a role as a stimulus to early Greek thought as Seaford believes, is open to argument. That it was an important background factor is very likely true. It is also important to remember that money was issued by the polis, so was as much a political as an economic development.

A fourth factor in the increasing rationalization of Greek thought has been suggested by Robert Hahn: technology, particularly architectural technology.[132] Hahn points our that in the first half of the sixth century in Ionia, just when the Milesian teaching was taking shape and Anaximander was trying to formulate the structure of the cosmos, the first monumental stone temples in Greek history were being built there: the temple of Apollo at

Didyma near Miletus, the temple of Artemis at Ephesus, and the temple of Hera at Samos.[133] Hahn argues that, though much of the basic technology for building massive stone structures was learned in Egypt, whose ties with Ionia were close at the time, the Greek architects had to work out a number of problems to meet their own needs. Although they were building sacred edifices to the gods, they were also solving complex problems of geometry and engineering using human reason alone. Hahn believes that Anaximander's model of the universe used temple construction, particularly the structure of massive columns composed of large circular drums stacked on top of one another, as a kind of paradigm. We know that Anaximander thought the earth was cylindrical in shape, with a ratio of 3:1 for diameter and height, like the drum of a column, possibly implying an infinite column connecting all parts of the cosmos, of which the earth is only one segment, what Plato will later describe as a kind of *axis mundi*.[134] Hahn interprets the thought of Anaximander as involving the "rejection of supernatural explanations" and the "promotion of rational discourse," which may be true, but should not be taken to label Anaximander as a premature "secularist." His use of the religio-cosmological meaning of the temple column as the paradigm for his world picture would suggest that he was still living, in good part, in a myth-ological world, however much he learned from the rational reflections of the architectural engineers. Finally, if literacy and money seem to be closely cor-related with the rise of the polis, so is monumental temple architecture, the very symbol of the solidarity of the polis.[135]

These four suggested background features of the rise of something like rational reflection in ancient Greece are all more or less closely tied to the rise and efflorescence of the polis itself and of a larger society composed of a number of independent poleis. Because the polis society was unique, it is perhaps not surprising that it gave rise to unique cultural developments. In our introductory reflections to the problem of the axial age we suggested that breakdown was a usual precipitating factor to the axial transformation. So far we have viewed polis society as largely successful. It is true that in the first half of the sixth century, according to the scant historical information that we have, Miletus suffered several foreign invasions and severe internal con-flict. We simply don't know enough to say whether these difficulties were related to the Milesian innovations in thought. The issue of breakdown will return when we consider later developments. It remains to discuss some de-velopments in the sphere of religion, not all of which can be encompassed in what we normally think of as polis religion.

We have mentioned above the importance of the cult of Olympian deities as the focus of the solidarity of the developing polis. But we also noted another strand of the Greek religious tradition, the Dionysiac, as having increasing importance in sixth-century Athens. There was no unified, certainly no centralized, Greek religion; Delphi served as a transpolis religious center but its focus on Apollo and his oracles meant that it represented only one of many religious cults, practices and devotions. A variety of religious movements and/or charismatic figures appear fitfully in the very partial records we have from the sixth century throughout the Greek world. The best documented movement, and that not very well documented, is that of Pythagoras and his followers in Sicily and southern Italy.[136] Pythagoras, a shadowy figure from whom no writings survive, was of Ionian birth, and probably cognizant of Milesian thought, but he migrated to Sicily and began a movement there that was simultaneously religious and political.[137] Although his followers sought political control in several cities, his teaching, at least for the initiated, was secret and concerned with individual religious needs.

Mystery religions, of which the best known is the cult of Demeter at Eleusis near Athens, were also concerned with individual religious well-being ("salvation" would probably be too strong a word). These religious currents, which we can only discern with difficulty, were another significant influence on the developing wisdom tradition, one that, perhaps surprisingly to us, overlaps with the development of rationality. Aspects of the thought of Heraclitus and Parmenides have been traced to the influence of "mystery" religions. Shaman-like figures, often described as having magical powers, go back at least to Epimenides at the time of Solon (early sixth century), Pythagoras a generation or two later, Empedocles, who lived in the middle fifth century and who made significant contributions to Greek speculation, but who is also alleged to have dressed himself in extravagant garments, holding himself to be divine, and Socrates. If we look at the Socrates described by Alcibiades in the *Symposium,* we will find a man who could lose himself in standing meditation for 24 hours, who could walk barefoot comfortably on ice whereas his fellow soldiers had difficulty walking in boots, who was immune to alcohol, and who did not need sleep.

One primary difference between these religious currents and what Michael Morgan calls "Delphic theology," is that the Delphic theology emphasized the dramatic distance between gods and men, immortals and mortals (the Delphic motto, "Know thyself," was an admonition to remember that you are human and that it would be hubris to try to compete with the gods), whereas the mystery religions, with their emphasis on ecstatic rites, possession cults, and initiation rituals, saw the divine–human boundary as permeable, and divinization as a human possibility.[138] If one looks at the *Phaedo,* the *Symposium,* and the *Phaedrus,* one might well consider Plato to be in the latter camp.

We noted above that the Milesians ignored or accepted the existence of the Olympian deities, but did not criticize them. But the fact that they could build their cosmogonies with little but implicit reference to their predecessors, together with the fact that they felt free to modify drastically the views even of their own teachers, tells us something important about the Greek intellectual world. G. E. R. Lloyd, in a book comparing ancient Greek and Chinese science, points out the striking "*lack* of great authority figures for the writers of the [Greek] classical period," and contrasts "the famously agonistic Greeks" with "the less famously irenic Chinese," who normally sought ancient authority for their assertions.[139] Lloyd shows that even in the Hellenistic period, when schools attached to founders and their texts formed in Greece, the intensity of debate within schools, the tendency of later heads of schools to criticize their founders and for new divergent schools to form, as well as for individuals to shift from one school to another, was not mirrored in China, even though various forms of debate and argument can be found there as well.

Homer never lost his hold on the Greek mind, being the text that every literate Greek learned first, and efforts to allegorize his poems to bring them into conformity with later thought began surprisingly early, but Homer's influence was more as a kind of subtext even in writers who overtly criticize him (Plato in the *Republic,* for example) than as an external authority. If one thinks of Israel, the Greeks also stand in marked contrast. As a thought experiment in what might have been we can think of the close connection of Zeus and justice *(dike)* beginning, tentatively, in Homer, becoming quite explicit and central in Hesiod, powerfully applied to his immediate situation by Solon, and reiterated once again in the tragedies of Aeschylus. But although the concern for justice remains central for those we call the Presocratics, the connection with Zeus loosens drastically. We saw in the case of Israel that Yahweh emerged gradually from being one among other gods, even the greatest god, to the status of the one and only true God. Zeus never underwent that fate, even though the possibility was never entirely lost: witness the *Hymn to Zeus* of the early third century BCE Stoic Cleanthes.[140]

Xenophanes, who left his native Colophon (in Ionia) at the age of 25 probably after the Persian conquest of the city in 545 BCE, and lived for many
decades in various cities in Sicily and southern Italy, is the first figure we
know of to openly criticize the Olympian gods. He wrote poems that he recited himself in public in the various cities to which he traveled and was a
"true *sophistes* or sage, prepared to turn his intelligence upon almost any
problem."[141] His importance rests primarily in the fact that he drew a conclusion from Milesian speculation that the Milesians themselves had not drawn,
namely, that traditional views of the Olympian deities were false: "Homer
and Hesiod have attributed to the gods everything that is a shame and reproach among men, stealing and committing adultery and deceiving each
other."[142] It was not only the actions attributed to the gods that were "unseemly," but even their appearance, as if the gods were born, and had clothes
and speech and bodies just like mortals. Xenophanes pressed his attack on
anthropomorphism with a cultural relativist argument that "the Ethiopians
say that their gods are snub-nosed and black, the Thracians that theirs have
light blue eyes and red hair." He even argued that if horses and cattle could
draw, their gods would look like horses and cattle.[143]

Xenophanes developed a positive theology that may have been his extrapolation from the teachings of the Milesians:

One god, greatest among gods and men, in no way similar to mortals in
body or in thought.
    Always he remains in the same place, moving not at all; nor is it fit-
ting for him to go to different places at different times, but without toil
he shakes all things by the thought of his mind.
    All of him sees, all thinks, and all hears.[144]

Here we have an elaboration of the Greek Cosmic God that Kahn found to
be implicit in Anaximander, but "One who is greatest among gods and
men," not the only god. Xenophanes was fully conscious that Homer was the
man "from whom all men have learned from the beginning," so that his
criticism of Homer was tendentious indeed.[145] At least among the educated,
the Homeric gods, though not rejected, would never be entirely secure again.

Heraclitus and Parmenides

In the next generation after Xenophanes, the two most important and original thinkers were Heraclitus and Parmenides, living at roughly the same

time, the late sixth and early fifth centuries, one in Ionian Ephesus, the other in Italian Elea, who very probably did not know of each other's work. Unlike Xenophanes, whom we can see as simply developing the implications of his Milesian predecessors, both Heraclitus and Parmenides were struggling to turn an inherited poetic language into a language that could move beyond narrative to penetrate the timeless truth about self, society, and the cosmos. Although on the surface the two thinkers would seem to be utterly different, with Heraclitus believing the ultimate truth of the cosmos to be continuous change, and Parmenides believing it to be unmoving and unchanging being, the fact that both of them sought to describe a reality that differed from appearance made them, in the eyes of some, the cofounders of reason or theory and thus pivotal figures in the axial transformation.[146]

Of Heraclitus we have fragments of his "book," which was known for many centuries in antiquity, but which must have been a short collection of aphorisms of which we have perhaps a third to a half surviving. He was Nietzsche's favorite Greek thinker, and with Heraclitus's emphasis on paradox and conflict, it is not hard to see why.[147] He wrote in prose, but his aphorisms have the power of Jakobson's one-line poems. They probe the depths of person, society, and cosmos and the profound and conflictual relations between them, but they do not consist of sustained logical argument.[148]

Havelock emphasizes that Heraclitus, indeed, the Presocratics generally, were still living in a largely oral culture: Heraclitus speaks of hearing and speaking, not of reading and writing. Although, Havelock says, the aphorism is as old as poetry, the complexity of Heraclitus's condensed sayings would not have been as easy to remember as if they had been written in dactylic hexameters, even though they were often cadenced to the point of verse and used the devices of repetition, assonance, antithesis, and symmetry.[149] Heraclitus uses certain key terms repeatedly, but gives them unfamiliar meanings, words such as *logos* (whose many meanings range from "language" to the "cosmic order of the universe"), the wise *(to sophon),* and even such apparently obvious words as war and fire. Havelock says, "Out of a total of some one hundred and thirty sayings, no less than forty-four, or some thirty-four percent, are preoccupied with the necessity to find a new and better language, or a new and more correct mode of experience, or are obsessed with the rejection of current methods of communication and current experience."[150] Nevertheless Havelock also believes that Heraclitus provided "the prototype and ancestry for the achievement of the first philosophical prose."[151]

Kahn deepens Havelock's argument when he holds that Heraclitus expresses his profound philosophy with a literary artistry that is essential to understanding his meaning. It is not that there are no "arguments" in Heraclitus—Kahn reminds us that from Plato to the present he has been taken seriously as a thinker—but that his thought requires literary as well as logical interpretation if we are to make as much sense of it as we can.[152]

There is no space here for anything like an adequate exposition of the teaching of Heraclitus. I will only mention those aspects, though they are central ones for him, that have to do with what we would call the religious dimension. The idea of "the wise" *(to sophon)* is a central one, as in his saying that "the wise is one, knowing the plan by which it steers all things through all."[153] Kahn quotes Reinhardt as being right when he says, "Heraclitus' principle, what corresponds in his case to the *apeiron* of Anaximander and the *on* [Being] of Parmenides, is not fire but *to sophon.*"[154] And in one place Heraclitus plays with the possibility of thinking of Zeus as central: "The wise is one alone, unwilling and willing to be spoken of by the name of Zeus."[155] But, and here one must be cautious because there is little consensus among the experts, there are a number of terms that Heraclitus uses that seem to point to ultimate reality: *logos,* fire, war ("the father of all"), god *(theos),* but all of which can perhaps be subsumed in the idea of "unity in opposites." Opposites, according to Heraclitus, need each other, but also need to fight each other, so strife and unity belong together, in instances that may seem strange to us: day and night, the way up and the way down on a mountain road, the sea as nurturing to some (fish) but deadly for others (humans), and so forth. Heraclitus wants to insist both on the eternal change that involves all things, but also in their ultimate unity ("all things are one"; D. 50).

Edward Hussey in his valuable summary of the teachings of Heraclitus helps us keep the various levels straight: "We must then take the wise [*to sophon,* with which we began our discussion of the thought of Heraclitus] as something that stands above and apart from both cosmic opposites and cosmic unity, yet manifests itself both in the cosmic god and in individual souls."[156] Heraclitus believes that the truth *(logos)* is common and available to all, something shared between gods and humans, but that you have to be awake to know it and most people "are oblivious of what they do awake, just as they are forgetful of what they do asleep."[157] As it was put elsewhere, people have eyes but do not see, ears but do not hear. As Heraclitus put it, "Not comprehending, they hear like the deaf: absent while present."[158] Yet the possibility of our waking up, of our genuinely listening, is still there, otherwise why would Heraclitus write a book? Is it only that we must see the light of reason, or do we, as in the mystery religions, have to awaken from the dead?

When, as with Heraclitus, we are on the cusp of mythospeculation becoming philosophy, probably both.

With Parmenides we find something different. At first glance he seems to belong to the realm of mythospeculation along with the earlier Presocratics; he wrote in poetry, Homeric dactylic hexameters to be exact, and his one surviving poem (one of the most extended writings we have of these early thinkers) begins with a prologue recounting an ascent to heaven and an approach to an unnamed goddess who reveals to the youth *(kouros)*, who probably stands in for Parmenides, the Way of Truth and the Way of Opinion. The Way of Opinion turns out to be a cosmogony not dramatically different from those of his predecessors. The Way of Truth, however, introduces something radically new in the history of Greek thought. The goddess tells Parmenides that there are only two ways of inquiry and that one is thinkable, the other not. Eric Voegelin translates, "The one way, that *Is* and that *Not* it cannot be, is the path of Persuasion [*Peitho*] which is attendant upon Truth [*Aletheia*]."[159] For Voegelin the revelation of "Is!" could only have come through some kind of experience of transcendence. He argues that to translate this passage as "It is," or "Being is," is to miss the ecstatic apprehension of the "Is!" which Parmenides at first hesitates even to call "Being." He writes:

> That which comes into grasp through the Nous [mind] does not come into grasp in the manner of an object for discourse. The progress on the way toward the Light culminates in the experience of the supreme reality that can only be expressed in the exclamatory "Is!" When the philosopher is confronted with this overpowering reality the "Not is" becomes devoid of meaning for him. With the exclamation "Is!", we come closest to the core of the Parmenidean experience. The propositional expressions "Being is," and "Nothing cannot be," are already "clumsy" circumscriptions.[160]

For Nietzsche, too, Parmenides's discovery is of a sudden sort, but quite different from Voegelin's idea, that is, not an ecstatic experience but a logical revelation:

> Can something that is not, be? For the only form of knowledge which we trust immediately and absolutely and to deny which amounts to insanity is the tautology A = A . . . [Parmenides] has found a principle, the key to the cosmic secret, remote from all human illusion. Now,

grasping the firm and awful hand of tautological truth about being, he can climb down, into the abyss of all things.[161]

Both Voegelin and Nietzsche recognize that Parmenides does not (Nietzsche would say cannot) link the Being revealed as the Way of Truth to any worldly experience. Voegelin sees the logical argument that Parmenides develops to prove that Being is and Not Being is not as simply a defense of the transcendental experience that cannot be translated into empirical language. For Nietzsche it is an effort to create an absolutely logically consistent but completely dead sphere of pure Being out of which indeed nothing can come. In a sense they are merely recapitulating the different ways in which Parmenides was understood from his earliest successors to the present. But what they both would agree on, I think, is that Parmenides has delivered the first example in ancient Greece of an extended, tight, logical argument, and that all his successors will have to come to terms with that, either accepting it as the absolute road to truth, even while arguing for flaws in Parmenides's own argument, or placing logical argument as only one way of approaching the truth as the late Plato will do.[162]

Without in the least minimizing the logical achievements of Parmenides, it is still worth seeing him with at least one foot in the older mythic world. Alexander Mourelatos, intensely aware of the philosophical relevance of Parmenides's arguments, nonetheless reminds us of the poetic richness of the poem, its constant Homeric resonances, and its use of language and imagery especially from the *Odyssey* to make its philosophical point. Like Kahn's work on Heraclitus, Mourelatos's work on Parmenides shows that literary analysis can richly supplement philosophical analysis in helping us understand what the text is saying. The very title of his book, *The Route of Parmenides,* suggests the nature of his approach. What he calls "route" others have translated as "path" or "way," but Mourelatos is calling our attention to the fact that the young man making the ascent to heaven in the Prologue of the poem, is, like Odysseus, following a route, guided by the goddess, that will lead him "home," that is to a determinate end, the truth, but there is the danger of following a false route that will not be a route at all, only an endless wandering (the way of opinion or seeming). Mourelatos argues that Parmenides's use of epic material throughout his poem "involves rhetorical effects which give poetical force to his argument," through the use of metaphor, for example. And he makes a general point that will be applicable not only to the Presocratics but to philosophy generally: "But Parmenides's success in poetry need not be unrelated to his success as a philosopher. As modern literary criticism has taught us, a great deal of poetry—from all ages—shares common ground with philosophical analysis to this extent: in both approaches we find close attention, almost at the microscopic scale, paid to the implicit pictures, the aura, the suggestiveness, and the multiple meanings of words."[163]

Here we have space for only a little of Mourelatos's suggestive analysis. He points out that Parmenides speaks of a divinity who controls the identity and coherence of the what-is as having four faces: *Anangke* (Constraint), *Moira* (Fate), *Dike* (Justice), and *Peitho* (Persuasion), but the goddess who addresses the young man is "no other than Peitho, Persuasion, herself." What Peitho relies on is "the bond of fidelity," *pistis,* trust. What the metaphor of Peitho is saying is that the rightness of the what-is is "internalized: a necessity of autonomy," but the trust, though mutual, is not equal, for it is from "reality" (the what-is) that the trust comes and it pulls us toward it, almost with the force of *eros,* love, as Plato will later put it.[164] At an even deeper level, Mourelatos argues, we are beings attuned by nature to what-is, that our thinking is really "about, because of, for the sake of, what-is," but that most of the time we get lost in the what-is-not, we lose the true route or path, we don't see what it is our inmost nature to see.[165] Parmenides in his own way is as lonely as Heraclitus, trying to hold up a light, but not finding many who see. Mourelatos reminds us that the images and metaphors are not the ontology, which stands on its own logical rigor, but they point to real aspects of it. Nietzsche's notion that the what-is is a dead abstraction, a pure tautology, would seem to be very far from the truth, perhaps a symptom of his own wandering on the path of what-is-not.

In any case, if we are looking for the place where theory begins in ancient Greece, this would seem to be it, even more clearly than in the case of Heraclitus. Parmenides is not only giving a theory of truth, he is defining the form of argument that could lead to truth—he is thinking about thinking, he is giving a method (etymologically related to *hodos,* Greek for path or way) for finding the truth. Is this the axial breakthrough? The enigmatic nature of Parmenides's poem, its combination of mythic imagery, divine revelation, and rational argument, its lack of any connection between the "Is!" and the world we live in, would seem to limit its axial implications. But of this we can be sure: Parmenides has supplied tools that will be indispensable for the axial breakthrough, even if we have to reserve the completion of that breakthrough for the work of Plato and Aristotle.

But even though the word "philosophy" is relatively late, and, with our emphasis on theory, we may be inclined to consider Parmenides to be the first real philosopher in ancient Greece, we must remember that the transition from a practical/performative understanding of wisdom to what has been called, at least since Plato, philosophy, was a gradual one, and that Greek philosophy itself never lost a practical/performative side, not even in the work of its most self-conscious theorist, Aristotle. As Michael Frede puts it:

> If, because of our focus on the pursuit of theoretical understanding of the world, we do not see that those engaged in this pursuit felt committed to a much more broadly understood wisdom with at least a strong practical component, we will find it difficult to understand how Socrates could see himself, and be seen by others, as part of a tradition going back to the Milesians . . . From Socrates onward all philosophers in antiquity thought of philosophy as being practical in the sense of being motivated by a concern for the good life and as involving a practical concern for how one actually lives and how one actually feels about things.[166]

Crisis and Breakdown

If Xenophanes, Heraclitus, and Parmenides could be seen as responses to the Milesian cosmogonists, they in turn stimulated an ever-widening series of responses in the second half of the fifth century. Parmenides, in particular, led some to develop further his own position and others to try to reconcile being and change with as rigorous a logic as he had used to deny that possibility. There is no space here to describe what happened, except to say that the emergence of argument itself allowed the very form of argument to be used in many ways, not all of them rooted in an ethical ontology like that of the predecessors. Parmenides even lent himself to parody, as when Gorgias, the famous sophist, in his "On Not Being," held that "for anything you might like to mention: (1) that it is nothing, (2) that, even if it were something, it would be unknowable, and (3) that, even if it were knowable, it could not be made evident to others."[167]

In retrospect and under the influence of Plato we tend to distinguish the philosophers from the sophists, but at the time no such distinction was made. The wise and the skilled were denoted by the same term and, as usual in Greece, the aim was most often to refute the others and show oneself as truly wise. But in Athens in the last decades of the fifth century there was a growing sense of breakdown, something never far from the often-pessimistic Greek mind even in normal circumstances, but that had become all too real under the conditions of the protracted Peloponnesian War. Ancient Greece was a world of more than a little orthopraxy, that is, a sense of the right way to act, but very little orthodoxy, as we have seen. One could hardly appeal to the *Iliad* for help in a situation of bitter and seemingly interminable warfare. So a sense that everything could be called in question affected not only those who professed wisdom, but a tragedian like Euripides and a historian like Thucydides. The latter commented on the *anomia*, lawlessness, that made normal life nearly impossible in a period during the war when the plague was ravaging Athens: "No fear of god or law of man had a restraining influence. As for the gods, it seemed to be the same thing whether one worshipped them or not, when one saw the good and the bad dying indiscriminately. As for offenses against human law, no one expected to live long enough to be brought to justice."[168]

Fernanda Caizzi describes one kind of sophistic response to such situations, that of Antiphon. Those we have come to call sophists, who applied the work of such thinkers as Parmenides not to questions of ultimate reality but to ordinary human life, sometimes concluded that *nomos,* the ethical and legal code governing ordinary life, varied so much from one place to another that it could not be identified with *physis,* nature. Indeed, existing moral codes might be contrary to nature. As Caizzi puts it:

> Numerous of Antiphon's points seem to reflect experience of Athenian social life, perceived from the position emphasizing the inadequacy of its rules to answer the individual's needs, and confirmed by evidence that stared everyone in the face. The recourse to nature, in terms of life and death, as the only criterion of advantage and disadvantage; the linkage between useful and pleasurable, on the one hand, and between harmful and painful, on the other; the observation that law cannot protect individuals even when they adhere to it, and even less so when they are the innocent party; the reference to court proceedings and to persuasion's being much stronger than truth or falsehood—all imply a morality that is primarily egoistical and self-protective, skilful in justifying itself by pointing out the shortcomings of justice and law to give human beings security.[169]

Although Plato never mentions Antiphon, we can perhaps see him behind such figures as Thrasymachus and Callicles, men who believed that justice is the rule of the stronger and that conventional norms should not restrain them.

If, under the conditions of breakdown in Athens in the late decades of the fifth century, things actually came to this, we should not ignore—Plato does not ignore—earlier and influential sophists who never endorsed such amoralist views, even if their cultural relativism left the door open to such views. Indeed, at least since Hegel there has been a concerted effort to rehabilitate the sophists, even to show them as the creators of a form of education that continues to this day, and the inventors of the idea of culture, both in the sense of common culture and of high culture. The speculative thought of the late sixth and early fifth centuries, although never replacing the poetic tradition or the popular religion among the people, did create new needs among the elites, particularly in democratic poleis where the old aristocratic education no longer made sense. Neither Athens nor any other democratic city consciously created a civic education appropriate to its needs, but, according to the great authority on these matters, Werner Jaeger, it was the sophists who supplied what was missing, replacing the poetic education of the past with a rational, logical, and, above all, rhetorical education. Jaeger uses the Greek word *Paideia,* variously translated as "education," "culture," even "civilization," as the title of his three-volume magnum opus, and he gives pride of place to the sophists as the first to use *paideia* in the sense of "culture," the very idea that we still find indispensable.[170] Jaeger sees the sophists as the inventors of the trivium, the first three of what will later be the seven liberal arts, that focuses on language—namely grammar, dialectic (logic), and rhetoric—usually also adding mathematics.[171]

In a self-governing city, speech was essential to any who aspired to leadership. The services of sophists as teachers were needed especially by those who wanted to speak persuasively in public, so it was rhetoric above all that the sophists taught, though they did not neglect other subjects. Not only in Plato's mind but also in public opinion, it was rhetoric that made the sophists suspect. Could not one use rhetoric to make the worse cause appear to be the better? Aristotle would rescue rhetoric from its Platonic exile (though Plato was a great rhetorician), and it would be central not only to all education in antiquity, but right up into the nineteenth century in the West.

The views of the sophists with respect either to the traditional beliefs or the cosmic theology of the Presocratics is complex. There is the possibility that some of them were atheists, but on the whole they preferred to refrain from judgment on religious issues. They thus contributed to an incipient "secularization" of culture, for the first time in Greece, but also raised another issue for popular suspicion. They can be seen as the forerunners of the kinds of psychological, sociological, and anthropological views of culture in general and religion in particular that would explain them primarily in terms of their usefulness. Further development of such views in these fields had to wait until the nineteenth century, when secularization was once again on the agenda.[172]

There are those who want to make the sophists heroes, defenders of democracy and liberalism as against the supposedly reactionary views of Plato, and Plato does put "progressive" views into the mouth of Protagoras in the latter's Great Speech in the dialogue of the same name, though it can be argued that Plato actually agreed with much he attributed to Protagoras, improving his views in the retelling.[173] In any case, not all the sophists were democrats—Antiphon was executed for being the planner of the oligarchical revolution in Athens in 411 BCE.[174] Hegel perhaps gives us the best way to place the sophists in the development of Greek thought. He sees the earlier Presocratics, especially Parmenides and Heraclitus, as discoverers of objective being, reality in itself as against appearance.[175] The sophists borrowed their methods of thought for subjective ends, as providing "good judgment," in Protagoras's words, in both private and public life, but without any clear commitment to objective validity.[176] But it is the very faintness of their hold on truth that has called into question their status as philosophers. Yet, for Hegel, the sophists are the necessary precondition for the next turn in the history of Greek thought. It was not for nothing that popular opinion considered Socrates a sophist. For Hegel it is in and through subjectivity that Socrates (or Plato following him) was able to return to objective reason, but this time, because of incorporating the subjective moment, in a much richer form.

Socrates

Socrates and Plato, so difficult to separate one from another, signify the completion of the axial transition in ancient Greece. Dealing with them at all is enormously challenging because the scholarship is immense and the disagreements major. The following necessarily brief treatment must be restricted to those aspects relevant to the argument of this book.

The breakdown that preceded their breakthrough actually engulfed Socrates, who was executed in 399 BCE at the age of 70 after being tried and convicted for impiety (not recognizing the gods of the city and introducing new gods, *daimones*) and leading the youth of Athens astray. He is one of the most extraordinary figures in history, leaving an impression, not only on Plato but on many others, that changed the course of Greek and subsequently Western culture. In his lifetime (469–399) Socrates experienced the rise and fall of the Athenian empire and lived amid the currents that we now separate as philosophical and sophistic. Aristophanes in his play *Clouds* depicts Socrates as a typical sophist and teacher of rhetoric, but his portrait gives every evidence of comic distortion. That Socrates was a teacher no one doubts, but a new kind of teacher. The typical sophist claimed to be wise in all things, to be able to answer any question asked of him. Socrates claimed to know nothing, to be a seeker of wisdom, not a purveyor of it.

In his speech to the jury at the trial that would cost him his life, Socrates recounts the visit his friend Chaerephon made to Delphi to ask if any man was wiser than Socrates, and the answer he received, that none was. Socrates was perplexed by this reply (from Apollo, no less), because he knew that he was not wise at all. But on seeking wisdom from those who claimed to be wise, he discovered that none of them really was either, so that his superiority lay not in his own wisdom, but in his knowledge of his lack of it (*Apology* 21a–e). Socrates claimed not to know the answers but to know the questions: How can we care for our souls? What is the goodness or virtue that will lead our souls in the right direction? Socrates's questions were in a sense subjective, they were concerned with the self or soul, but not in the sense of the sophists, who made everything relative to the individual or the culture, for Socrates was searching for the truth not only of his own soul but of everyone's. In his defense he refers to his Daimonion, that "divine voice that made itself heard every time it wished to hold him back from an action."[177] But his quest for wisdom was in the end demanded by something greater than a spirit, it was demanded by god.[178] In his often-quoted answer to the possibility that the jury might acquit him if he would promise no longer to practice philosophy, Socrates tells the jury that he would say:

> Gentlemen of the jury, I am grateful and I am your friend, but I will obey the god rather than you, and as long as I draw breath and am able, I shall not cease to practice philosophy, to exhort you and in my usual way to point out to any of you whom I happen to meet: Good Sir, you

are an Athenian, a citizen of the greatest city with the greatest reputation for both wisdom and power; are you not ashamed of your eager-
ness to possess as much wealth, reputation and honors as possible while
you do not care for nor give thought to wisdom or truth, or the best
possible state of your soul? [And then he goes on to say:] I shall treat in
this way anyone I happen to meet, young and old, citizen and stranger,
and more so the citizens for you are more kindred to me. Be sure that
this is what the god orders me to do, and I think there is no greater
blessing for the city than my service to the god.[179]

Heraclitus had said that most people are asleep while awake (absent while
present; D. 34), and Parmenides that most people are wandering in the wilderness of what-is-not because they haven't found the path of what-is, and
Socrates seems to have been doing much the same in confronting the people
of Athens fairly directly with the fact that they had no idea about the truth.
Apparently doing this day after day in the agora was more annoying than
doing it in the privacy of one's own study.

It is also the case that Socrates really was calling into question the accepted answers to his questions and so calling into doubt the beliefs and
practices of his fellow citizens. Execution was an extreme penalty for such
behavior, but the period after the fall of the thirty tyrants was unsettled,
and, though Socrates had refused to collaborate with them, some of their
leaders had been his students. The paranoia that Eli Sagan has found democracies prone to was part of the atmosphere that led to the strange trial and
conviction of Socrates.[180] But even more than the trial and the conviction,
what made this event become paradigmatic for the whole history of philosophy was Socrates's willing acquiescence to his sentence, his belief that it was
his duty to obey the laws of his city, as recounted in the *Crito.* A willing
death in accordance with the laws of the city, but even more "in the service
of the god," of a man who, while living, had already had life-changing effects
on many of his students, completed the picture that would be indelible ever
after, leading Erasmus to place him among the saints when he wrote, "Sancte
Socrates, ora pro nobis!"[181]

That Socrates marks a great transition in Greek history is evident from
the fact that we call his predecessors "Presocratics," but it isn't evident in the
quality of his thinking what was so new—surely it was not his "rationalism," for rational argument had flourished in Greece at least since Parmenides. Of the efforts to account for his pivotal significance, several might

be considered. Hegel believed that Socrates really was guilty as charged, for his idea of divinity was new, and he was trying to lead his students to a way of life different from that of traditional Athens. And for Hegel it was Socrates's radical subjectivity, but one given an objective turn in the search for the good and the true themselves, that put him at odds with his city. Yet, Hegel says, the city was already guilty of the very things it accused Socrates of—wasn't it already rife with subjectivity and subversive ways of life?—and so repented of Socrates's death sentence almost as soon as it was carried out. Yet Socrates's death was in a critical sense the conclusive sign of the death of Athens—the bloom had wilted—for Athens could not find the objective political form to fulfill Socrates's new understanding of the soul. The old form of the polis could neither absorb it nor reject it, and so it was reduced to a shadow.[182]

Werner Jaeger, without mentioning Hegel in this regard, offers a somewhat similar interpretation. He sees Socrates as prefigured by such great Athenians as Solon and Aeschylus, each of whom in his own time led his fellow Athenians to a deeper understanding of their ethical calling. But Socrates was speaking in a new register, and the Athens of his day was not the Athens of old: "Was he the last embodiment of a harmony which, even in his lifetime was in process of dissolution? Whatever the truth may be, he seems to stand on the frontier between the early Greek way of life and a new, unknown realm, which he had approached more nearly than any other, but was not fated to enter."[183] Later Jaeger puts it only a little differently: "Socrates was one of the last citizens of the type which flourished in the earlier Greek polis. At the same time, he was the embodiment and the finest example of the new form of moral and intellectual individualism. Both these characters were united in him, without impairment of either. The former pointed back to a mighty past; the latter looked forward to the future. Thus, he was a unique event in the history of the Greek spirit."[184] This summary is to the point, but we must be careful of the word "individualism." Socrates was searching for the truth of the soul, his soul and that of those with whom he conversed, but that truth was not, to quote Heraclitus, private: it was common (D.2). If this be individualism, it was a very different species from that of Antiphon. Perhaps Hegel's cumbersome idea of subjective spirit reaching for objectivity puts it better than the single term "individualism."

We will give Eric Voegelin the last word. He writes, "In the *Apology* we have seen the multiple levels of action. On the political level Socrates is condemned by Athens; on the mythical level, Athens has been condemned by the gods. The dialogue is itself a mythical judgment."[185] For Voegelin, what this judgment meant was that the order *(kosmos)* of the polis was transferred to the soul of Socrates, who became the new order-bearer, and from Socrates this order of the soul once again, through Plato, became, potentially at least, the order of (a new kind of) society.

The Greek word *kosmos,* order, an important one for Plato, works equally well at the level of self, society, and universe. Gabriela Carone has argued that in the late dialogues of Plato, such as the *Timaeus* and the *Laws,* the idea was expressed that humans can take the order of the universe as the model for their own souls, so that every human, at least potentially, is a citizen of the universe, an idea usually attributed only later to the Stoics.[186] Kahn has shown that we know Socrates best only in the *Apology,* written soon after the trial and giving a picture that would have been unconvincing if far from the historical reality, but that even in the *Crito* we find elements that Plato may have added to the historical picture, and that in the early aporetic dialogues it is no longer safe to take the words attributed to Socrates as simple expressions of his actual views.[187] On the other hand one might ask, however far from the historical Socrates Plato wandered, did he ever abandon his spirit? Terry Penner has shown recently that, whatever discontinuities one can find between "Socrates" (the quotes signaling that anything we know of him is in the end conjectural) and Plato, there are also significant continuities right up to the late dialogues.[188] This is not the place to get into "the Socratic question," but to me it seems clear, however unknowable the details, that without Socrates there would have been no Plato. Plato, however, with his enormous range of interests, the living quality of his thought, and the vast corpus of his writings, which rival the Bible in length, completed an axial transition that had been long in the making and moved toward the institutionalization of an axial culture that would have enormous long-term consequences.

Plato

Plato's work is a shoreless sea, touching on almost every subject (even on natural philosophy in the late dialogues), and the touchstone for Aristotle and all later ancient (and modern) philosophy. I shall confine myself to only a couple of issues having to do with the theoretical concerns of this book.

If one of the defining aspects of axial culture is the capacity to imagine things different from what exists, Plato would seem to be the banner bearer of all axial thinkers.[189] The idea of Plato as a conservative, so widespread that it includes such diverse thinkers as Karl Popper and Leo Strauss, seems wildly off the mark if conservatism involves any kind of devotion to a traditional social order. Malcolm Schofield points out that "there is little *Republic* would preserve either of existing political structures or of conventional moral beliefs and practices."[190] Could insisting on radical gender equality, so that women as well as men participate in the guardian class and even in warfare, expropriating the property of the ruling class, so that they live an austere life, forbidden even to touch money, without families and without private dwellings, be called conservative? For Plato over and over again it is clear that the worst regime is tyranny, and that the tyrant is the worst human being. The utopia of the *Republic* is full of draconian rules, but it is not designed to allow one or a few tyrants to make the life of the populace miserable. The firmest discipline is directed to the guardians, to combine fierceness in defense of the city with gentleness toward the population as a whole. They are a kind of monastic order, taking the vow of poverty (significantly, the guardians have no slaves, nor does anyone else in the good city), obedience (to the philosopher king), and, if not the vow of chastity—breeding arrangements are indeed strange in the *Republic*—at least being saddled with the most profound consequences of the vow of chastity, namely the lack of a spouse or children of one's own. None of these restrictions apply to the rest of the population. Of the cardinal virtues, the philosopher king is above all capable of wisdom and the guardians of courage, but the whole city is to exemplify moderation and justice. Furthermore, though at first glance the *Republic* appears to be a caste system, Plato insists it is a meritocracy: if children of farmers or artisans appear to be exceptionally bright and spirited, they will be elevated to the guardians, and if the children of guardians prove to be slow, they will be sent to more menial jobs.

Plato does not make it easy for us to understand him. In the description of the good city above, the words are not Plato's, but Socrates's. As Simon Goldhill reminds us, Plato is full of "ironic hedging and careful withdrawal behind a mask (or two)."[191] Plato never appears in "Plato," as Goldhill says: "Plato names himself as *absent* from the scene of Socrates's last conversation, and in his dialogues he offers a play of different masks, from the intimate impersonation of Socrates in the first-person to the studied anonymity of the 'Athenian stranger.' (How *is* philosophy (to be) internalized?) Plato is veiled—absent and all-seeing—in 'Plato.' "[192] Nonetheless few would disagree that when Socrates speaks, something, at least, of what Plato believes comes through. There is much that is ironic and humorous in the *Republic*'s description of the good city. At times Socrates admits that he is not at all sure what comes next, and at the critical moment in book 6, when he is discussing the idea of the good, which is the source of the wisdom that makes the good city possible, he eludes the definition of what exactly the idea of the good is, disconcerting his hearers by using the simile of the sun, but not explaining exactly how it works. With all its hesitations, false starts, and dead ends, it is hard to think that Plato is describing a totalitarian state, which in all historical instances has been presided over by a tyrant, Plato's anathema, even though some of the Plato's rules are indeed coercive.[193] They coerce, however, the rulers far more than the ruled, and seem designed to avert rather than create tyranny. In any case, however playful the whole adventure of designing a good city is, allowing some to think his boldest proposals, such as the equality of women, are jokes, surely in the end Socrates wants his hearers to take his experiment seriously, and, if implementing it is not possible, "perhaps there is a pattern [paradigm] of it laid up in heaven for him who wishes to contemplate it and so beholding to constitute himself its citizen."[194]

We should remember that the whole experiment of creating "a city in words" was designed in the first place to make clearer to his two interlocutors, Plato's brothers, Glaucon and Adeimantus, the nature of justice in the soul by showing it in larger scale in a city. The *Republic* operates at many levels and is attempting to do many things, but at one fairly obvious level it is Plato's attempt at the conversion of Glaucon and Adeimantus to virtue in their own souls. Conversion is not too strong a word. The very heart of the dialogue, the parable of the cave in book 7, is about someone living in a cave and seeing only shadows cast on a wall until he is taken to the upper world, reality itself, and seeing the sun, even though he must be induced to descend to the cave again to help those condemned to live there. In the *Republic* the religious intention runs parallel to the political at every point, and we must always read it with an eye to several levels of meaning at once.

But if Plato is no conservative when it comes to political structures or moral conventions, what is even more revolutionary about him is his rejection of the central Greek cultural heritage, exactly what conservatives are supposed most lovingly to hold to their breasts. Homer, the teacher of the Greeks, is ignominiously expelled from the good city, and with him Hesiod and the great tragic poets as well. Why is the defining literary tradition of Greece expelled from the good city? Because its form is poetry and its content is myth. Luc Brisson argues that Plato was the first to distinguish between *muthos* and *logos,* between myth and rational argument, that before him *muthos* and *logos* were virtual synonyms, both meaning a story or an account.[195] Brisson describes the critical distinction that Plato made: "By contrasting *mythos* to *logos* as nonfalsifiable discourse to falsifiable discourse and as story to argumentative discourse, Plato reorganizes, in an original and decisive way, the vocabulary of 'speech' in ancient Greek, in accordance with his principal objective: that of making the philosopher's discourse the measure by which all other discourses, including and especially that of the poet, can be determined."[196]

Myths are inherently unreliable because they recount stories, not arguments, and because the stories they recount, handed down orally, occurred so far in the past than no one can possibly know if they are true or not. Plato was of (at least) two minds about the distinction between orality and literacy, sometimes arguing as in the *Phaedrus,* for example, that the truth can only be transmitted orally, but insisting in the *Laws* that all children be taught to read and write and that the laws themselves must be written.[197] With respect to the very important myth of Atlantis in the *Timaeus,* Plato holds that, though it was for a long time handed down orally (it recounts events that occurred 9,000 years previously), its reliability rests on the fact that it was written down in Egypt long ago. In any case the myths that Plato would dismiss were handed down orally by Homer, from whom Hesiod and the tragic poets drew (there are those today who think the tragedies were first composed orally and only later written down), and this is part of their unreliability. Even more important, however, is the content of the myths, particularly their characterization of the gods as having all the moral defects of humans, often in an exaggerated degree. This cannot be true, according to Plato, and thus the good city must get rid of them.

Because we have argued that the emergence of theory is critical to the axial transition, we can hardly be surprised that a great axial figure like Plato would rely above all on argumentative discourse and not on mythic narrative, and he often says that this is exactly what he is doing. Yet his blanket rejection of a poetic tradition that much of the world treasures to this day staggers the imagination. Plato himself says, in book 10 of the *Republic,* that since childhood he has loved Homer and still stands in awe of him. But this only emphasizes the radical and violent nature of his rejection. Hans-Georg Gadamer summarizes the charges: "[Homer] is said to be a sophist and magician who produces only deceptive appearances of things. And what is worse, he ruins the soul by stirring up in it the whole range of its passions." After pointing out that Aeschylus had engaged in an effort to purify the myths by presenting the gods as exemplars of morality, not immorality, Gadamer says that Plato was going much further:

Plato's criticism is no longer poetic criticism of myth, for unlike the poets he does not preserve ancient poetry in a form purified by criticism. He destroys it. To that extent his criticism becomes an attack on the foundations of Greek culture and on the inheritance bequeathed to us by Greek history. We might perhaps expect something of this sort from an unmusical rationalist but not from a man whose work itself is nourished from poetic sources and who cast a poetic spell which has enthralled mankind for thousands of years.[198]

Charles Kahn confirms Gadamer's point: "Plato is the only major philosopher who is also a supreme literary artist . . . Plato is the only Socratic writer to turn this popular genre [the dialogue] into a major art form, in rivalry with the great works of fifth-century Attic drama."[199] Kahn gives us the clue to how Plato, the great poet, can reject the entire poetic tradition. Plato, as I would expect in terms of my argument about the axial transition, by no means rejects the mimetic and the mythic—indeed, he sees that without them he can never make his theoretic insights effective. What he rejects is not the mimetic and the mythic as such, only the entire tradition of them! Plato would abandon Homer and Hesiod, Aeschylus and Sophocles—and replace them with what? The *Symposium* ends with most of the participants in the previous night's discussion awaking with hangovers, only to find Socrates and Aristophanes engaged in argument, as though they had never slept at all. And what was the argument about? Whether the same man could write tragedy and comedy, with Aristophanes saying it would be impossible and Socrates arguing that it should be possible. And who was the man who wrote comic tragedies or tragic comedies?

So Plato, the man who rejected tradition (and so can in no way be called conservative), knew that humans cannot live without tradition. What he created was a new tradition (oxymoron though that is), one in which Socrates replaced Achilles, and his own dialogues replaced the epic and tragic poets (we might add, in size as well as contents). Did he pull it off? Not completely, to be sure, and thank God for that, but he did indeed establish his new tradition, one that continues to our day. For any lesser man (and who could we name as greater than Plato), the very project would be that of a madman. Yet Plato was not mad. In the scope and depth of his thought he can be compared, perhaps, to only one man, his pupil, Aristotle.

But we need to say more, though not much more, about how Plato kept the mimetic and mythic aspects of tradition along with the theoretic. (And we should not forget that Plato did not reject all of his Greek inheritance:

Heraclitus and Parmenides escape, not his occasional criticism, but his censure, and he owed a great deal to Parmenides, who, after all, wrote in dactylic hexameters, but neither did he reject the great lawgivers, Solon in particular, but Lycurgus and others. With Solon he even recognized a form of poetry that need not be banned.) Plato knew that education *(paideia)* was key to his reform effort: a new kind of person had to be educated to make possible a new kind of city. He took the traditional elements of Greek education, *gymnastike* (not too far from our "athletics") and *musike* (including our music, singing, and dancing, but the arts generally) and gave them a new form. With *gymnastike* his reform was primarily negative: one was not to overemphasize athletic competitions (so dear to the Greeks), because that could lead to the exclusion of what is really important, and even to a kind of sloth. Care of the body remained important so long as it contributed to health, vitality, and good looks, but beyond that it was only a distraction.

With *musike,* too, he began with tradition, but then replaced the substance. In both the *Republic* and the *Laws* Plato emphasizes that the right kind of music, singing, and dancing (and for children, games) begin the ordering of the soul that makes rational reflection possible at a later age. Book 2 of the *Laws* is the place where Plato most fully spells out his views on musical education. For example:

> *Athenian:* So, by an 'uneducated' man we shall mean a man who has not been trained to take part in a chorus and we must say that if a man has been sufficiently trained, he is 'educated.'
> *Clinias:* Naturally.
> *Athenian:* And of course a performance by a chorus is a combination of dancing and singing?
> *Clinias:* Of course.
> *Athenian:* And this means that the well-educated man will be able both to sing and dance *well?*
> *Clinias:* So it seems.[200]

Of course the Athenian stranger, who speaks (we think) for Plato, goes on to describe in more detail what moral elements are involved in singing and dancing *well.* But the experience of participating in a chorus is not just for educating the young; it essential for everyone:

> Education, then, is a matter of correctly disciplined feelings of pleasure and pain. But in the course of a man's life the effect wears off, and in

many respects it is lost altogether. The gods, however, took pity on the human race, born to suffer as it was, and gave it relief in the form of religious festivals to serve as periods of rest from its labors. They gave us the Muses, with Apollo their leader, and Dionysus, by having these gods to share their holidays, men were to be made whole again, and thanks to them, we find refreshment in the celebration of these festivals.[201]

Plato knows that only a few can devote their lives to rational argument, however important that is to the good life for everyone, and that narrative—myth—remains the primary mode of expressing truth.[202] Here things get tricky indeed, and I cannot solve arguments that have perplexed many, but Plato, though holding that his "new" myths are on the whole true, or "something like the truth," or "likely," and thus provide an important supplement to rational discourse even for the most advanced students, can also admit that he is on occasion lying—for a beneficial purpose to be sure, but still lying. The most famous and most vilified instance is the "noble lie" in the *Republic,* intended to convince the various classes in the city that their position is "natural." It is beyond my purpose to get into this argument, except to say that this untrue myth (as opposed to the "true myths," such as the one about Atlantis in the *Timeaus*) is, it seems to me, more intended to convince the guardians that their "golden" nature is sufficiently wonderful that they don't need the metal, gold, or the properties and households that go with wealth, rather than to convince the lower classes, who can have all these things, that they are "naturally" subservient.

Yet, for all Plato's distinction between the poetic myths (Homer, and so on) that must be abolished and the poetic myths (his own) that are basic to the good city, there is an element of myth, maybe several elements, that never come to the surface of discussion. It would be unwise to imagine that Plato, in every way so sensitive and intelligent, was unaware of them, but had his own reasons for not pointing them out. For one thing, in the sense of myth as a story or account, never lost in Plato, there is a basic myth in the whole corpus of his dialogues: the myth of the life and death of Socrates. It is this above all that Plato is holding up; it is surely in his eyes a true myth, even when he attributes thoughts to Socrates that he might logically have had though he didn't actually have them. And Socrates is not an argument; he is a person with a story, a narrative. What does that do to the idea that theory triumphs in Plato? And regardless of whether one thinks it a good or a bad thing if it did?

There is then the fact that though Homer and Hesiod are thrown out at the front door, they keep sneaking in at the back door. In an interesting essay on poetry in the *Republic,* David O'Connor points out the poetic allusions that underlie so much of the action. He points in particular to Plato's use of Odysseus's "Visit to the Dead" (*Odyssey,* book 11) as an implicit model for much of the *Republic,* but for the parable of the cave in particular. After having excoriated Homer's account of the visit to the dead in book 3 (386a–d), he actually uses it positively in relating the parable of the cave where he cites the *Odyssey* (516d–e) in support of the idea that one who had once reached the surface of the earth would never want to return to the cave, where all one sees are "shadows," Homer's word for the dead in Hades. Homer as banished; Homer as authority (Plato in many dialogues, in passing, cites a line of Homer, often to clinch a point); Homer as subtext for the whole structure of a dialogue. O'Connor also develops Plato's elaborate use of Hesiod's "Races of Metal" from the *Works and Days* as providing the substructure of his account of the various regimes, the kind of human being appropriate to each, and their successive decline in books 8 and 9 of the *Republic,* an argument well worth pursuing if we had space, but only reinforcing the idea that what Plato threw out so unceremoniously in book 2 remains fundamental to the whole structure of the dialogue, at least subterraneously, or, for Greeks who often knew much of Homer and Hesiod by heart, not so hard to see at all.[203] What is that telling us about the relationship of theory and narrative?

Finally, as Gadamer, Kahn, and others have pointed out, it is the dialogues as the rivals of Homer and Sophocles, the *Apology,* the *Symposium,* the *Phaedrus,* the *Republic,* even the *Laws* if read rightly, that pull us into the philosophical life; whereas the arguments are often disconcerting, ending in mid-air, as when Socrates in the *Republic* just won't tell us what the idea of the good really is, or the arguments need recasting, often in the same dialogue, sometimes in a later one.[204] In his outline of the highest level of education in the *Republic,* I know that Plato puts mathematics, and particularly geometry, very high, because there the truth is evident to the mind alone and needs no confirmation from the senses, and then he puts dialectic, logical argument, even higher, and here one thinks of Plato's revisions of Parmenides's arguments for Being. None of that do I deny. But if that were all, would Plato be Plato?[205] Would he not be just another interesting early logician? My point is that the power of Plato is his reform of the whole of what Donald called the cultural "hybrid system," the system that includes mimetic, mythic, and theoretic in a new synthesis, but not the replacement of mimetic and mythic by the theoretic alone.[206] Such a replacement is an experiment that no one central to the axial transition in any of the four cases undertook; that awaited the emergence of Western modernity in the seventeenth century.

I have referred to Aristotle as perhaps the second greatest mind of all time, so it would seem churlish not to give him equal or almost equal space with Plato, but we don't have such space. Aristotle is an effective writer—at times, such as in the *Nicomachean Ethics,* an almost great one—but he is not the artist that Plato was. What he did, however, with enormous enthusiasm and energy, was to sketch out most of the fields of inquiry that would preoccupy later thinkers, and do it so well that the Middle Ages came close to treating him as a final authority, something neither Aristotle himself nor the ancient Greeks and Romans ever did. Along the way, he rehabilitated poetry (especially admiring tragedy in his *Poetics*), and he rehabilitated rhetoric, when he saw, if used properly, that it could indeed serve ethical ends.[207] He had no need to throw out received myths—in his *Metaphysics* he saw the early poets' interest in the origins of things as foreshadowing philosophy—or to replace them with true or untrue myths of his own. Nor did he have Plato's need to start everything from scratch, relying only on deductive argument—not that Plato really carried out such a project. Aristotle often allowed himself to start from opinion, from common experience, and refine it with critical reflection and argument, but never move too far from the world as given. It would be condescending to say of so great a thinker that he was a man of eminent common sense. Yet the Plato who sometimes seems to be a man of smoke and mirrors, more concerned to startle us than to help us, was not imitated in these respects by Aristotle. There is a long tradition of choosing one or the other of them, as if that involved the choice of two different kinds of life, but I think we need make no such choice: we still need both of them.

One way of thinking about Aristotle is to say he was a post-axial thinker. Plato had gone through the great struggle to break with what he had inherited from the past in the light of Socrates's search for wisdom. He used every resource that a great mind and a great artist could muster to open up the possibility of a new kind of person and a new kind of society, not only a new kind of thought. And he did so with a brilliance that must still have been vivid in Aristotle's day. But what Plato did, Aristotle did not have to do.[208] Most remarkably, instead of being overwhelmed by his predecessor, as most gifted persons would have been, Aristotle was able calmly to look around the new world that Plato had opened up and explore its many possibilities, without rancor, though certainly not evading a good argument when he needed one. There was very little he did not see. Though less "religiously musical" than Plato, as Max Weber would have put it, we must not think of Aristotle as secular. He had a theology as well as a logic and a metaphysics, a variation on the idea of a Cosmic God as first dimly discerned by Anaximander, and developed richly in Plato's late dialogues, a theology that would be very influential in later times. And certainly, like Plato, he thought of philosophy as a way of life.[209]

The philosophic schools were indeed the organizational form for the education of the Hellenistic and Roman elites. None of the schools ever became orthodox even to the extent that Confucianism did in China, and they always had to compete with poetry and rhetoric for the allegiance of members of the elite. The extent to which philosophy as a way of life penetrated non-elite strata is an open question. There the old Olympian myth and ritual pattern never entirely lost its hold, even though increasingly interpreted allegorically.[210] But that classical culture after Plato and Aristotle was axial seems beyond dispute.

"Doomed to Extinction"

We saw earlier Eric Voegelin viewing the trial of Socrates as the death sentence not only of Socrates by the city, but of the city by the gods. Obviously Athens did not collapse in 399 BCE, though the final conquest by Macedonia in 322 did end its independence, and Paul Veyne has argued that even earlier than that the Athenian democracy was turning into the rule of the notables that would characterize most Greek cities in the Hellenistic age, even if their outer forms, as Athens's did, remained democratic.[211] The "spirit" of the golden age, however, did not disappear, it simply moved out of the polis as such. If the order of the polis was transferred to the soul of Socrates and then to that of Plato, we can see that happening sociologically in the emergence of the Platonic Academy, to be followed by other philosophical schools later in the fourth century, notably Aristotle's Lyceum, but also Stoics, Epicureans, and others in time.

W. G. Runciman helps us understand what happened to the Greek polis in the fourth century, and it had to do with the end of an extraordinary geopolitical anomaly rather than the death of Socrates, with which it correlates only "in spirit." Runciman's basic point is that the Greek polis was "an evolutionary dead-end," able to survive as long as it did only because of its special geopolitical situation—close enough to learn from neighboring civilizations, but too remote to be conquered by them: witness the basically logistic failure of the Persians, which we can recognize without minimizing Greek heroism. The dead end of the polis was the very fact that made it so culturally creative: it never became a state, and for sure, it never became a state of states. This citizen state, which was its citizens, wasn't even a city-state. For all Plato's attacks on Athenian democracy (we should remember that Plato also bitterly attacks oligarchy, the only realistic alternative to democracy other than tyranny in the Greek polis), he affirms in the *Republic* that other than in the good city, philosophy could arise only in a democracy; and for all his sympathy for Sparta, when he tries to found the second-best city in the *Laws,* the primary speaker is not a Spartan stranger, but an Athenian one. One could not imagine a Spartan speaking so long. It is the very uniqueness of the Greek sociopolitical form, particularly its democracy, that made it the germ of so much that we still value culturally, its combination of the very primitive and the ultrasophisticated, unique in world history, but this was also its fatal weakness when finally faced with the much more resilient form of a large scale monarchy, this time, much closer than Persia, namely Macedonia. Runciman argues that only a monarchy, or a very strong oligarchy such as Rome or Venice, of the kind the Greeks never had, could mobilize the power to compete effectively in the political world of antiquity. The Greek poleis were just too small and too divided to withstand a major challenge. If there is a Greek miracle, it is its geographical situation that allowed the Greeks for almost five centuries, from the eighth through most of the fourth, the freedom to carry out their extraordinary experiment without having to pay the price for their political/military vulnerability.[212] For that we can only say, Halleluiah!

Runciman has pointed out that evolution occurs at more than one level. Biological, social, and cultural evolution are interdependent, even interpenetrative, processes, but are not identical.[213] The failure of the polis as a social experiment did not mean the failure of Greek culture. And, of course, culture never survives without some kind of social carriers. We have already indicated the social vehicle for the survival of Greek culture: the schools, in the first place the gymnasia, in the second the various schools of philosophy, but also of medicine and other arts. Long after Athens lost its political independence, it remained a center of culture, of the schools to which Greeks and later Romans from all over came to study. Of course, another factor of critical importance was that both the Macedonians and the Romans deeply admired

Greek culture, imitating it rather than attempting to destroy it. And it was also the good fortune for the survival of the tradition that Christianity, not inherently friendly to the Greek ethos or to philosophy in particular, was, even in the letters of Paul if not earlier, gradually Hellenized, so that much of Greek culture and Greek thought survived inside the church, even though the intolerant church once in power closed not only the temples but the philosophical schools as well.

What survived would be reborn again and again. And what survived depended very much on organization. Chance, to be sure, played a part, but it can hardly be entirely by accident that Plato and Aristotle survive almost entire, but of Heraclitus's little book, so small, but so precious, we have perhaps less than half, not to mention the great majority of Greek tragedies that are lost. But enough, surely enough, of what was created, especially in those first decades after Socrates, survived to make the world forever a different place. And when the traditions of axial Israel came together in a strange love-hate relation with the traditions of axial Greece, the result was, to more than a small degree, and for evil as well as good, the world we have.

8

The Axial Age III: China in the Late First Millennium BCE

One of the more remarkable things about classical Greece is that it seemed to go from a tribal society (actually a retribalized society) to something on the verge of modernity within a matter of generations. The sheer rapidity of the change has been seen as having something to do with the vigor of the ultimate flowering. There had, of course, been a Bronze Age palace society, the Mycenaean, in second-millennium BCE Greece, with powerful rulers, monumental buildings, and a written script. All that had been largely forgotten during the Greek Dark Age from roughly 1200 to 800 BCE, with only the foggiest memories surviving, and, significantly, the complete loss of writing. The monuments of that earlier culture were strange outcrops on the landscape, in need of invented legends to make sense of them.

Ancient China could hardly have been more different. In Chapter 5 we considered pre-axial China—the Shang dynasty in the late second millennium BCE and the Western Zhou in the early first millennium BCE.[1] We noted that the continuity between pre-axial and axial culture in China was without parallel in Greece or Israel (we will consider the question of such continuity in India below). This continuity is signaled by the continuity of the writing system—the graphs that we have from the Shang dynasty are recognizably ancestral to all subsequent Chinese writing. Confucius is said to have taught his students selections from what we know as the *Documents* and the *Odes,* which in their present form were edited long after Confucius's death, but parts of which probably date to the early Zhou, and were in existence in the lifetime of Confucius.[2] The continuity in writing signals an even more significant continuity in cultural content. We have a much clearer understanding of Shang and Western Zhou society than we have of Mycenaean and Dark Age Greece, because we have not only rich archaeological material but significant textual continuities.

And yet, China from the time of Confucius (conventional dating, 551–479 BCE) to the Qin unification (221 BCE) was as stunningly innovative as was ancient Greece. It was the time of the flowering of the "hundred schools," in their variety as well as in their content presaging modernity, differently but to the same degree as the classical Greeks. The Confucian *Analects,* and those who subsequently venerated Confucius as their teacher, idealized the culture of early Zhou and made it a standard to which later China should return, but in the guise of returning to the old they opened up remarkably new possibilities. China in the late first millennium was undergoing a dramatic transition from the "feudal" (in the sense described in Chapter 5) regime of the Zhou to the centralized bureaucratic regime of the Chinese Empire. Because the society that the Confucians idealized differed significantly from the society we take for granted as Chinese, we must first try to understand what it was like, returning briefly to some of the themes of Chapter 5. China's axial transition occurred when a society ruled by warriors was being transformed into a society ruled by imperial bureaucrats. What was that society ruled by warriors like?

Before Confucius

As we noted in Chapter 5, Western Zhou (1045–771 BCE) society, though in its decentralization similar to what we think of as feudal, was actually a lineage society in that "fiefs" were not based on a contractual relation between lord and vassal, but were "gifts" from the king, usually to kinsmen, sometimes to other loyal vassals, that were in principle conditional, such that they could be revoked at any time.[3] In Weberian terms it was a decentralized patrimonial society, and using the term "feudal" points only to its decentralization. We must remember that early first-millennium BCE China was more thinly populated, and less economically developed and urbanized, than would be the case by the end of the millennium. Non-Chinese "tribes" were interspersed with Huaxia (Chinese) peoples, and much of the land had yet to be cultivated.

Under these circumstances the early Zhou monarchy probably maintained a degree of centralized control only for a century or two. Centralized rule would, with the passage of time and the increasing distance of lineal ties, gradually disintegrate. The decline of central authority was signaled by, though in fact it had almost surely preceded, the fall of the Western Zhou capital in 771 BCE and the move of the capital from the Wei River valley in western China, which had long been the home of the Zhou people, to Louyang in the east, where the power of the Zhou became largely ceremonial and depended on the goodwill of the more powerful, now in fact independent, eastern states.

The ensuing Chunqiu (Spring and Autumn) period, named after a chronicle that spans the years 722 to 481 BCE, saw a gradual descent into incessant warfare, leading into the Warring States period (450–221 BCE) when a series of new developments changed the nature of Chinese culture and society and led to the elimination of the warrior aristocracy that still dominated in the Spring and Autumn period.

Confucius himself lived at the end of the Spring and Autumn period and viewed the society in which he lived with critical apprehension. He idealized the early Zhou, and he was the first to "use the old to criticize the present," a practice that never ceased among his followers and that many rulers, including the first Qin emperor, strongly condemned. By looking more closely at the reality of Spring and Autumn society, we can see what tied Confucius to it and what he condemned in it.

Mark Edward Lewis describes the "great services" that were the primary concern of the Spring and Autumn aristocracy: sacrifice, war, and hunting.[4] These three services were heavily ritualized and interrelated; ceremonial was at the heart of this, as of many other aristocratic societies. Though *li,* ritual, would come to have very different meanings in later Confucianism, it was, in the form of the "great services," at the very heart of the early Zhou culture that Confucius claimed to venerate. The central service, of which war and hunting were extensions, was sacrifice itself. The great sacrifices to the spirits and the ancestors were the forms in which Zhou society enacted itself to itself. Because our Western view of China is so much influenced by the central figure of the civilian scholar-bureaucrat in imperial China, it is important to recognize that in Western Zhou and Spring and Autumn China we are dealing with a warrior society, one different from, but perhaps of the same genus as, premonarchical Israel (think Samson and the David of the David and Goliath story), Homeric Greece, and the India of the Mahabharata. It was the warrior who carried out the sacrifices so central to the society's self-understanding, in this respect similar to early Greece, but not to early Israel or India, where the priestly class carried out the sacrifices. As Lewis puts it:

In the Spring and Autumn period political authority was derived from the worship of potent ancestral sprits and the gods of locality through regular offering made at the altars of the ancestral temple and the state. The actions that set the rulers apart from the masses were the "great services" of those altars, and these services were ritually directed violence in the form of sacrifices, warfare, and hunting. These activities, symbolically linked through the ceremonial exchange and consumption of meat, reached their common culmination in the offering up of living beings at the altars. Thus the noble was above all a warrior and sacrificer, a man who took life in order to feed the spirits who gave him power.[5]

Lewis then quotes from the *Zuo zhuan,* a text probably assembled in the fourth century BCE but drawing on older materials and still our best source for the Spring and Autumn period:

The great services of the state are sacrifice and warfare. In the sacrifices one takes the meat from the sacrifices in the ancestral temple, and in warfare [before setting out on a campaign] one receives the meat from the sacrifices at the *she* altar. These are the great ceremonies of the spirits.[6]

Sacrifice and warfare (hunting was ancillary to both, providing some of the meat for the sacrifice and training for warfare) defined the warriors against the common people, who participated in neither. Further, sacrifice reflected the organization of the warrior class, divided into lineages as it was, and organized hierarchically in lineage terms.

In this patrilineal society, primogeniture was a significant factor: the eldest son succeeded, in principle though often not in fact, to his father's position, but younger brothers would be granted domains of their own. In the domains of younger brothers, their younger sons would receive still smaller domains. A formal system of ranks, depending on where one stood in the lineage system, was expressed ritually by rules governing the kind and number of ritual implements appropriate for each level of the hierarchy and the degree of elaboration of the ceremonies.

Archaeology has discovered that the so-called Zhou ritual system, the one that Confucius idealized, probably was not established at the founding of the dynasty but was the result of a major ritual reform dating to around 850 BCE, which standardized the form of ritual implements and the number of them appropriate for each rank, a reform that very rapidly established itself all across the Chinese cultural world, but that is not described in any text. Lothar von Falkenhausen, in his important synthesis of decades of archaeological discovery, has argued that what he calls the Late Western Zhou Ritual Reform was probably an effort to restore coherence to a system of lineage relationships that had become confused after 200 years of Zhou rule, in that the demographic increase in aristocratic lineages created a situation that was hard to represent ritually. The Reform drastically restricted the number of lines of descent that carried significant status, reducing many nobles to a kind of low-level elite status represented by the term *shi,* often translated as "knight," to which Confucius may have belonged. Falkenhausen further speculates that this drastic Reform was justified on archaistic grounds as going back to the founding period of the Zhou, and that it was only during that Reform that Kings Wen and Wu and the Duke of Zhou took on their archetypal significance, and even that the earliest parts of the *Shangshu (Documents)* and the *Shi (Odes)* were initially codified only in this Reform period.[7]

Whatever the actual date of the Zhou ritual system that Confucius saw himself as renewing, what is significant is the extreme importance of ritual from the earliest historical times, that is, in the Shang dynasty as well as in Western Zhou. Because ritual *(li)* is at the center of the thought of Confucius and the Confucian tradition, this should not be a surprise, yet it is important to realize that *li* in the Western Zhou did not mean exactly what it would later mean to the Confucians. Falkenhausen helps us understand this early importance of ritual:

> One instance in which archaeology has independently verified preexisting textual knowledge is the revelation of an extremely close connection between the social order and the ritual practices required by the ancestral cult of the Zhou elite—a connection abundantly attested by the material evidence . . . Such a nexus is, of course, a common phenomenon in early societies. Yet a direct linkage of social status to ritual privilege may very well have been taken more for granted in early China than in other early civilizations.[8]

The ritual reform of about 850 BCE was an elaborate effort to stabilize the political ranking of the aristocratic lineages by dictating the forms and implements appropriate to each lineage level in its sacrificial rituals devoted to the ancestors. Certain forms were reserved only for the Zhou king; others for the great branch lineages of the royal family and its highest ranking allies that had been established in various parts of north China; and still others for subsidiary lineages in the service of the king or the rulers of the various domains.

It is probable that the standardization that the ritual reform created with remarkable thoroughness was an effort to bring order into a disorderly situation. After two centuries of Zhou rule, dozens of small domains and a few larger ones were increasingly independent. Culturally there was remarkable unity among the elite—the widespread success of the Reform shows that—but politically it was more and more difficult for the Zhou king to organize any kind of concerted action among polities that were increasingly independent. Further, as in many aristocratic societies, one's honor and, through one's actions, the honor of one's ancestors, was a major concern. War was one of the great ritual services and was often brought on by some real or imagined slight to the honor of one's lineage.

Lewis notes "the highly ceremonial character of military campaigns. Every stage of the campaign was marked by special rituals that linked the actions in the field to the state cults and guaranteed the sacred character of battle."[9] Critically important was the formal declaration of the reasons for the campaign:

> Before every battle the warriors would assemble and be told why the will of Heaven, the imperatives of duty, the honor of the state, and the spirits of the ancestors demanded that this battle be fought. Together with the divination before the tablets of the ancestors, the battle prayer, and the ceremonial command *(ming)*, this oath fixed the day's carnage within the political and religious framework. It stipulated the rules of discipline, but did so in a form which bound both the commanders and the warriors to the common service of their ancestors and the gods.[10]

As one might expect in such ritualized combat, there were rules that gave warfare a formal quality: an invading army was to be greeted with gifts; a time and place for combat was set; if an army had to cross a stream and was in disarray, the opposing force would wait until order had been restored before attacking; if the lord of a state had died, an invading army was supposed to withdraw in order not to "increase mourning."[11] It goes without saying that this kind of warfare was fought by an aristocratic elite. Commoners might be involved in supportive roles, but they did not participate in the fighting. Similarly, though commoners might fish and hunt for small animals, only the ceremonial hunts of the aristocrats had as their quarry large or dangerous animals. Because our texts concern the warrior elite virtually exclusively, we know little about the farmer and artisan classes. Some of these latter may have been of non-Huaxia cultural background, and in any case they were attached to the territory they inhabited and "belonged" to those who controlled the territory. Early Zhou society was, then, in many ways very different from what later Chinese society would be like. And though ritual would be central both early and late, its meaning would change dramatically over time.

The early Zhou establishment of branch and allied lineages in various parts of the country was a way to spread their dominion over a greater territory than the Shang had ever controlled. But in the sparsely settled and largely uncultivated countryside, the lineage heads would be established in towns and controlled only the closely surrounding territory. The original meaning of the term *guo*, which later came to mean "state," was the "capital," if that is not too grandiose a term, of such a lineage, namely, the location of the ruler's "palace" and, above all, of the ancestral temple, the locus of the all-important sacrifices. As population grew and more and more land was brought into cultivation, something more like a territorially defined state gradually developed.[12] Warfare that originally had been largely ceremonial became more in earnest, and small states began to be annexed by larger ones. In this process, and especially in the Spring and Autumn (Chunqiu) period, the capacity of the Zhou kings to bring about any semblance of order collapsed. Not only was there fighting between incipient states, there was serious dissension within lineages (there had always been succession struggles), but also between lineages in a single state, and even between the sublineages within the lineages. The ritual system that was supposed to bring order to the society was increasingly violated, and although honor would never cease to be a source of conflict, wars were now fought for power, even hegemony, and not just for the ancestors. As Yuri Pines puts it: "Indeed, the Chunqiu was the age of disintegration. The continuous usurpation of superiors' prerogatives by their underlings resulted in incessant strife among the states, among the major lineages within each state, and often within the lineages. The history of Chunqiu political thought may be summarized as the statesmen's painstaking efforts to put an end to the disintegration, prevent anarchy, and restore hierarchical order."[13] But as Pines goes on to say, the restoration of ritual *(li),* which still meant the hierarchical forms of the Zhou system we have described above and not yet the conceptual reformulation of the Confucians, was the "universal panacea" offered to achieve these ends, a panacea, however, that never seemed to work. Confucius, living at the very end of the Chunqiu period, symbolizes the moment when the need for a dramatic reformulation emerged, even though it would be couched in terms of a return to the time of the early kings.

Before we summarize the legacy of Spring and Autumn thought for the emergence of philosophical reflection in the following period, it would be well to look at some deep underlying socioreligious changes that had occurred before the Warring States period, which can help us understand the new developments then. Falkenhausen argues that these changes are more obvious in the archaeological record than in the texts. There were two major shifts, each succinctly summarized in the titles of chapters 8 and 9 of Falkenhausen's book: "The Separation of the Higher and Lower Élites (ca. 750–221 BCE)" and "The Merging of the Lower Élite with the Commoner Classes (ca. 600–221 BCE)."[14] The Late Western Zhou Ritual Reform of around 850 BCE "had the effect of demoting the vast majority of the ranked elite from the upper stratum of a two-tiered society, dominated by the contrast between the ranked and commoner members of its constituent lineages, to a newly created middle layer sandwiched between the increasingly powerful rulers above and the unranked commoners below."[15] Part of the problem of the Chunqiu period was that the increasingly powerful elite was deeply divided between ever more powerful states and within these states between ruling lineages and ministerial lineages—it was these divisions that made the society so unstable.

The Middle Spring and Autumn Ritual Restructuring of around 600 BCE had the further consequence of augmenting even more the privileges of the upper ranks while reducing the privileges of the lower elite, to the point where their very difference from commoners was nearly obliterated and would be obliterated in the Warring States period.[16] As Falkenhausen puts it, "The formation of a specially privileged subgroup within the elite preceded, and no doubt paved the way for, the full emergence of despotic rulers during the Warring States."[17] What this double shift downward of the lower elite meant was that the very nature of the warrior society that we described as existing in early Western Zhou gradually ceased to exist, and the meaning of the three services that defined that society was gradually lost.

One feature of the earlier warrior society noted especially by Lewis was particularly vulnerable to these shifts, namely the basic egalitarianism of the warrior elite. Lewis remarks that the carefully graded ranks of the warrior nobility should not obscure to us the fact that "these gradations were based on incremental additions to a fundamental nobility common to all members of the elite on the basis of their kinship and joint participation in the 'great services.'"[18] Further, the *shi,* the lowest level of the noble hierarchy, was nonetheless a generic term for nobleman, so that higher ranks were "added on" so to speak, to one's basic definition as a *shi.* "The king was at the top of the nobility and the *shi* at the bottom, but the language and ritual procedures of the period insisted that the two shared a common noble nature, that they were divided in degree but not in kind."[19] Confucius was probably a *shi* in a time when the term was, as we shall see, taking on new meanings. If the newly powerful rulers of the Warring States ruled a society of equals, it was because all would be equally subject to the ruler. Confucius would make new distinctions, but on the basis of moral qualities, not lineage.

It is now time to sum up what the immediately preceding period gave Confucius to work with as he rethought the cultural basis of Chinese society. Here we face a dilemma concerning our principal textual source for the Chunqiu period, the *Zuo zhuan.* This text is one of the three canonical commentaries on the *Chunqiu,* the so-called *Spring and Autumn Annals,* actually the Annals of the state of Lu, which attained primary canonical status because, almost assuredly mistakenly, its compilation was attributed to Confucius. The *Zuo zhuan,* unlike the other commentaries, is a large continuous history of the period, only uncomfortably and partially unsuccessfully accommodated to the form of a commentary on the *Chunqiu.* Although it is generally agreed that it was compiled only in the fourth century BCE, there is disagreement as to the authenticity of the sources from which it was compiled.[20] If it was written or rewritten extensively by Confucians in the fourth century, it can hardly be used as describing the historical "background" from which Confucian thought derived. If, however, the speeches contained in it really do predate Confucius, they give us a sense of the cultural resources available to Confucius. I am in no position to make an independent judgment of this technical issue, although the arguments for the authenticity of at least some of the *Zuo zhuan* seem convincing to me. But for my purposes whether the *Zuo zhuan* recounts what preceded Confucius or only the views of the early Confucians is less important than the developments themselves.

Two changes in the terminology of social status that are compatible with the long-term changes described by Falkenhausen largely on the basis of archaeology are the shift in meaning of the term *shi,* described above as the lowest level of the ranked aristocracy but now taking on the meaning of "official," even low-ranking official, on the basis of status rather than birth. At a time when in the larger Warring States, officials were chosen on the basis of merit rather than birth, and we know of instances where merchants were given high office, this is an indication of the declining significance of hereditary lineages at all but the highest levels of status. The term *shi* gets further generalized to apply simply to an educated person, or even to scholars as a class.

Another term that we have not mentioned so far shows a similar development from late Spring and Autumn times to early Warring States times, the term *junzi.* Etymologically the term means "son of a lord," and thus a noble. But in the *Zuo zhuan* we find even high ministers using the term with moral overtones, using the term to distinguish ethically outstanding nobles from those who, though noble by birth, were not *junzi* in their actions. The standard translation of *junzi* in the *Analects* is "gentleman," though other translations, such as "superior man," are sometimes found. In any case the term in the *Analects* is invariably used to refer to ethical, not lineal, distinction. What these two terminological shifts indicate is a society in which noble lineage, except at the highest level, has largely lost its significance, but one in which to a considerable extent the lineally unranked population can now share the cultural forms previously the exclusive prerogative of the elite, though altering their meaning in so doing.[21]

One interesting phenomenon of the late Chunqiu period, one that provides just a flicker of resemblance to the Greek polis, was the brief emergence of the capital population in the various states as a political actor. The capital populace *(guo ren)* consisted of the *shi* as well as of merchants and artisans. According to Lewis, "The capital's inhabitants came to play a decisive role in the internecine struggles between the various lineages of the nobility and often decided the succession to the throne . . . In times of crisis the entire populace could be assembled in order to decide the policy of the state."[22] Once the centralizing tendencies of the Warring States period took hold, with stronger rulers and weaker ministerial lineages, the capital populace is no longer heard from.

If terminological and other changes associated with them, which will be described below, were already "in the air" a century or more before Confucius, this lends further credibility to his claim to be a transmitter rather than a creator.[23] Nonetheless, the *Zuo zhuan* provides us only with anecdotal accounts. There was no formal discussion of these changes before the *Analects,* indeed no "private thinkers" or "peripatetic philosophers" before Confucius.[24] Whatever changes were under way, he was the first to think of them systematically or, as it were, "objectively." Even though the *Analects* is more aphoristic than systematic, it is surely right to see Confucius as inaugurating the Chinese axial age.

Still, the extent to which Confucius thought of himself as embodying the traditional culture of Zhou, and the record seems to indicate that some of what we think of as his innovations may have been developing well before him, suggests that Benjamin Schwartz was right in asserting that Confucius and his followers "more truly represented some of the *dominant* cultural orientations of the past than did some of their later rivals."[25]

Confucius

We began this chapter with a contrast between Greece and China with respect to continuity with the archaic past. We begin our discussion of Confucius with another contrast with Greece: if there is any figure in Chinese history who has exerted influence comparable to that of Plato in the West, it is surely Confucius. Whitehead famously said that all Western philosophy is nothing but a series of footnotes to Plato; we could say the same of Confucius: all Chinese philosophy is nothing but a series of footnotes to Confucius. Although all Chinese thought is surely not Confucian any more than all Western thought is Platonic, it is still true that every major Chinese thinker of whatever "school" has had to come to terms with Confucius. The contrast is where the two are located in the unfolding of their respective axial transformations: Plato at the end of a long development beginning with Thales, the first Greek thinker whose name we know; Confucius at the beginning of a long development, but occupying the position of Thales, that is, the first Chinese thinker whose name we know, though with the influence of Plato.

How to understand this, at first glance, striking contrast will become easier if we look more closely at the *Lun yu,* the *Analects,* the only book we have of Confucius and virtually our only source of knowledge about him. The *Analects* surely resembles in size and style one of the early pre-Socratics, say Heraclitus, particularly if we had the whole text of Heraclitus. The *Analects* isn't very long, much of it is aphoristic, and it is surpassed as sustained argument by several later Warring States texts: *Mozi, Mencius (Mengzi), Zhuangzi, Xunzi,* as well as by collective books such as the *Guanzi* and the *Lüshi chunqiu*. So, formally, the *Analects* does indeed look "early," even if its influence has been enormous. But we are not even sure how early the text is. The conventional dates for Confucius are 551–479 BCE, but we have no reason to think that Confucius wrote anything. What we have was written down by his disciples, perhaps in his lifetime, perhaps after his death, and it is almost universally agreed that the book as we have it is not all from the same period. Books 3–10 or 4–9, or generally the early books, are widely believed to be closest to the time of Confucius himself; the later books, 11–20, but often including books 1–2 or 1–3, are felt to be later additions by disciples or disciples of disciples, but how much later is in dispute, some believing that the whole text is from a generation or two after Confucius, or, the extreme case, E. Bruce and Taeko A. Brooks, in their *The Original Analects,* argue that the text extends over most of the Warring States period with later additions only ceasing with the Qin conquest of Lu in 249 BCE.[26]

Brooks and Brooks see in the later books of the *Analects* responses to much of the later development of Warring States thought. The chief objection to this idea is that the later books never attain the quality of sustained argument characteristic of late Warring States thought. While noting these differences of opinion and occasionally referring to them, I do not need to take a position on them. That the *Analects* is a central text, perhaps *the* central text, is not in dispute, and all later Chinese thinkers treated the text as a whole, constructing a "Confucius" who may never have existed except in the minds of all literate Chinese for over 2,000 years.

Looking at the *Analects,* our only secure source, we are still not sure who exactly Confucius was. If he was a noble, he was surely a *shi,* the lowest level of nobility, at a time when the distinction between *shi* and commoner was fading. He was a teacher, for he had students, disciples. What he taught was probably some version of what came to be known as the Six Arts—rites, music, archery, charioteering, writing, and arithmetic—"the polite arts of the aristocracy,"[27] and that educated commoners were at that time also interested in learning. The Six Arts would much later be eclipsed by the Five (or Six) Classics, but it is clear that they were not texts, but skills. For example, one did not learn *about* ritual and music, but how to perform ritual and music, actually two closely related activities. Archery and charioteering were military arts, and Brooks and Brooks argue that the earliest level of the *Analects,* book 4, has a military ethos, though that is not obvious to me.

There were undoubtedly many teachers of the aristocratic arts and had been for a long time before Confucius. What made him unique, the beginning of a new phase of Chinese culture, is that he was not interested only in teaching specific arts, even rites and music that would be so central in the Confucian tradition, but was above all consciously concerned with what we might call the "formation" of his students, their ethical development as persons and their ethical stance in the world. He was also concerned with the sad state of society in his time, and with the loss of traditions that, in his view, had once provided greater stability and greater dignity for all people. What is clear is that Confucius was a man of extraordinary integrity who made an impression on his students that later generations never forgot.

In trying to reconstruct his teaching, we must begin with the argument as to which of the two most central terms, *ren* (which Waley translates as "goodness") and *li* (which Waley translates as "ritual"),[28] is the most important and even ask if we really have to choose between them. According to Brooks and Brooks, *ren* is a key term in book 4, which they believe is the earliest book, and the only one that we can be relatively sure recounts the actual views of the historical Confucius. In that book, *ren* appears in a number of passages, whereas *li* is mentioned only once and in passing. Everyone agrees that *ren* is extremely rare in any text earlier than the *Analects,* but very common there. Its pre-Confucian meaning is not easy to establish from its rare occurrences. It is always noted that the graph for *ren* consists of the graph for person, human being, also pronounced *ren,* and the number two. Its early usages may have meant "handsome," "valiant," or possibly, as a play on the related term for human being, "manly," and was probably an aristocratic quality, not an ethical virtue. In the *Analects, ren* is clearly ethical and yet its meaning, as the many different translations of it indicate, is not entirely clear.

If book 4 is the earliest and the one closest to Confucius, we find in it right from the beginning something mysterious, something elusive about *ren:*

> The master said, For my part I have never seen anyone who loved *ren* and hated the not-*ren*. One who loved *ren* would put nothing else above it. One who hated the not-*ren* would himself be *ren;* he would not let the not-*ren* come near his person. Is there anyone who for a single day has put forth all his strength on *ren?* For my part I have never seen anyone whose *strength* was not sufficient for it. There may be some, but, for my part, I have never seen one. (4:6)[29]

Nor did Confucius himself claim to be *ren:*

> The master said, "How would I dare consider myself a Sage *(sheng)* or
> *ren?* What can be said about me is that I continue my studies without
> respite and instruct others without growing weary. (7:34)[30]

And when the disciples ask for a definition of *ren,* the answer is usually eva-
sive, or whether such and such a person is *ren,* the answer is usually in the
negative. Yet Confucius tells us that *ren* is not remote:

> The Master said, Is *ren,* indeed so far away? If we really wanted *ren,* we
> should find that it was at our very side. (7:30)[31]

What we can make out from these passages is that, although *ren* is near,
and one who loved it would put nothing else above it, yet no one, not even
Confucius himself, has been able to put it into practice, though no one lacks
the strength to do so. Particularly in the later books of the *Analects* the substance of *ren* gets filled in considerably, leading us to believe that *ren* is the
highest virtue because it includes all the others and then some, but it never
entirely loses its mysterious quality. There is something about it that puts it
above ordinary life. It is one of a number of indications that the *Analects* is
not entirely the secular text that both Chinese and Westerners have often
taken it to be.

If we think about some of the common translations, Waley's "goodness"
gets the generality of the term, as does the common translation "benevolence," which, as Graham points out, is appropriate as the primary translation only from the time of Mencius,[32] but both goodness and benevolence
are too easily identified with our own moral vocabulary and, as Ames points
out, lack the richness of the term: "*ren* is one's entire person: one's cultivated
cognitive, aesthetic, moral and religious sensibilities . . . *Ren* is not only mental, but physical as well, one's posture and comportment, gestures and bodily
communication." *Ren,* he writes, "does not come easy . . . It is something we
do, and become."[33] *Ren* is surely ethical, the highest ethical term in Confucianism as Heiner Roetz, points out,[34] yet it is not theoretical, at least not in
the first instance: it is performative, enactive, mimetic, though it gives rise to
thought.

Taking account of its closeness to *ren,* human being, we can now translate
ren, the virtue, as, following Roetz, "humaneness," but not, as is sometimes

done, as "humanity," thus agreeing with Ames's objection to the translation "humanity" as implying it to be a general human characteristic. "Humaneness" attempts to capture the element of aspiration to an ideal that, though close at hand, is not easily realized in practice. It is nonetheless a norm or standard, indeed *the* norm or standard with which to judge human behavior. Though rooted in embodied, social, life, it is nonetheless universal.[35] Herbert Fingarette, who is generally believed to subordinate *ren* to *li*, nevertheless gives a definition of *ren* that epitomizes its claim to universality: "society is men treating each other as men."[36] Almost Kantian, treating other human beings as ends in themselves. Perhaps we will understand better how humaneness works in Confucian practice after we consider its complementary term, *li*.

What is striking about *ren* in its earliest appearance, that is, if Brooks and Brooks are right, in book 4, is that it appears nearly contextless. Whatever "arts" Confucius was teaching to his students, he was deeply concerned with their personal formation and he set for them a high, almost unattainable ethical goal. We will see eventually that *ren* does have a context, however stark its first appearances. But the substance of what Confucius taught was surely *li*, and we can hardly introduce a discussion of *li* without some concern for its context. Fingarette argues cogently that the key context is *Dao*, the Way. *Dao* is an important term in the *Analects* as it is for most Warring States thinkers, but its meaning varies with the thinker and we should not identify it everywhere as having the meaning given to it by those we have come to call Daoists. In the *Analects* the *Dao* is not so much the Way of the Cosmos as it is the Way of the ancients, the Way of the former kings, the Way of the gentleman *(junzi)*. In the *Analects* the *Dao* is paired with the term *de* (power, potency, virtue), as it will be quite differently in the *Daodejing*. In the *Analects,* following fairly closely the early Zhou use of the term, *de* is the "charisma" of the ruler, a power that draws people to him and brings them to the practice of the Way. Confucius does indeed attribute *de* to the early kings, creators, he believes, of an ideal form of government, but he generalizes it as a quality of the gentleman, of any sincere follower of the Way.[37]

The Way has a dignity of its own, nowhere expressed so clearly as, again, in book 4, "The Master said, In the morning hear the Way; in the evening die content" (4:8, trans. Waley).[38] Fingarette nonetheless argues that the acts that are necessary in following the Way are specified in the *li*, and in its primary meaning, "ritual."[39] By late Chunqiu times, if we can place any confidence in the *Zuo*, the idea of ritual, epitomized in the "Great Services" of the early Zhou, had become generalized and extended to a wide variety of situations, still including high religious ceremonies, but now also including many areas that we would think of more in terms of manners or politeness, and yet all seen as, if properly performed, the basis of social stability. The *Analects,* especially but not exclusively in book 10, does include many heterogeneous examples of *li,* some of them, to us, rather trivial—for example, "He must not sit on a mat that is not straight" (10:9, trans. Waley).[40]

If Confucius began as an instructor in ritual, it would have probably been in the details of sacrifice, but also of appropriate action in various social situations, that he would have specialized. But in his concern for the formation of his students, he moved, tentatively at least, to generalize *li* as a way of relating to the world and one's fellow humans, expressive in its own way of the same ethical depth as *ren.* At the opposite extreme to the straight mat, Confucius describes the correct action, in its minimalism, nonaction *(wuwei),* of the sage ruler Shun, earlier even than the Xia, Shang, and Zhou dynasties: "The Master said: 'Shun was certainly one of those who knew how to govern by inactivity [*wuwei*]. How did he do it? He sat reverently on the throne, facing south—and that was all'" (15:5, trans. Leys). Simon Leys, whose translation I am using here, makes the point in his notes that "inactivity" could also be translated as "noninterference," and that the ethical aspect of what Shun did lies in his "setting a moral example, and his virtue *(de)* radiates down to the people."[41] Putting the sayings about the straight mat and facing south together, we can see that how you sit can be far from trivial.

Ritual, then, is a way of relating and a way of governing. In the *Analects* it is often contrasted with rule by punishments. In the ideal society there would be no punishments, no executions or mutilations, as people would act in accord with ritual: "The Master said: 'Lead them by political maneuvers, restrain them with punishments: the people will become cunning and shameless. Lead them by virtue *(de),* restrain them with ritual *(li):* they will develop a sense of shame and a sense of participation'" (2:3, trans. Leys). But it is not only the ruler who can find ritual effective. The gentleman *(junzi)* who acts in accord with ritual will also influence those around him: "The Master wished to live among the barbarian Nine Tribes. Someone said, 'They're uncouth. What about that?' He said, 'If a gentleman lived among them, what uncouthness would there be?'" (9:14, trans. Graham).[42]

If *li* is not just a heterogeneous collection of customary behavior that can be summed up, as Roetz sometimes does, as "conventional ethics," it is because Confucius locates it in a new vision. Fingarette here seems to me right in not accepting the usual (in modern culture) derogatory meaning of such terms as "convention" and "tradition," but instead seeing the extent to which the man who claimed to be a transmitter and not a creator was actually saying something new, never said before in Chinese history. According to Fingarette, Confucius was offering a

> new ideal of a universalistic community based upon shared conventions. The *content* of his proposal was to found the new community as a tradition. But he also found ready to hand a powerful *formal* mode of discourse in which to propagate the ideal; indeed he used the most deeply rooted mode of discourse in human culture—the narrative and especially the narrative myth or anecdote of an ancient past . . .
>
> Confucius perceived humanity through the imagery of ceremony and thus of tradition. It was peculiarly appropriate for him to turn to the narrative mode of formulation in its most common form—the narrative of an ancient past. Thus the content of his teaching was perfectly congenial to the oldest and probably the most evocative of all forms of thinking about life's meaning. Although the narrative mode used in this way is an "archaic" form of thought, it is not any more an archaism in Confucius than it is in a contemporary novel or drama. Confucius used narrative of a mythic past in the service of a new ideal grounded in radically new insights into man's essential nature and powers.[43]

Fingarette rejects the common view of tradition as the dead hand of the past, intrinsically given, unquestionable, for a more accurate view of tradition as it actually operated in most "traditional" societies, that is, as in a state of constant revision and reinterpretation in the face of new circumstances. He cites a key passage from the *Analects* to show that this was Confucius's view: "The master said, He who by reanimating the Old can gain knowledge of the New is fit to be a teacher" (2:11, trans. Waley). Fingarette's point is that it is only through tradition or convention (what the anthropologists call culture) that human beings can act in ways not determined by instinct or conditioning alone, but that new conditions always require that tradition be rethought, "reanimated." Without reanimation, tradition is indeed dead, but the *li* transmitted by Confucius was alive, at work, as Fingarette puts it, in "reuniting" human beings.[44]

We might return briefly to what Fingarette called the "formal mode" of discourse in which the *Analects* roots the vision of the new community, the narrative of an ancient past. Much of the content of that narrative, though reworked for the needs of the time, is contained in the section on Shang and Western Zhou China in Chapter 5 and in the first section of this chapter. Fingarette calls it a "narrative myth," and it is that, but it is told as history and it clearly has a relationship to history as we know it. When Confucius talks of the culture of the Shang, and of the early Zhou, especially King Wen and the Duke of Zhou, he is talking about things that we believe actually existed. He also talks of a Xia dynasty, which so far has no historical substantiation, and of kings earlier than the Xia such as Yao and Shun, where we are surely in the realm of myth. But the distinction between myth and history is never an easy one, and the fact that Chinese myth is presented as history, is itself significant. Later thinkers will come up with even earlier kings to appeal to as legitimating their positions. Although the content is quite different, China resembles Israel and differs from Greece and India in its attachment to history, or should we say mythistory, as a defining cultural form.[45]

It is now time to return to our question as to which is more important, *ren* or *li*. There are two passages in the *Analects* that are taken to give diametrically opposite answers to that question. We must remember that the *Analects* is an aphoristic book, at best anecdotal, that it is not a systematic work, that it does not itself ever develop systematic connections between its key terms. Under these conditions, apparent contradictions are numerous and varying interpretations inevitable. But let us turn to the passages:

> Yan Yuan asked about *ren*. The Master said, "To overcome one's self and to return to *li* is *ren*. If for one day one will overcome the self and return to *li*, then the whole world will turn towards *ren*. *Ren* can only come from the self—how could it come from others?"
>
> Yan Yuan said, "I beg to ask for the concrete steps." The master said, "Do not look at what is contrary to *li!* Do not listen to what is contrary to *li!* Do not speak what is contrary to *li!* Do not put into action what is contrary to *li!*
>
> Yan Yuan said, "although I am not smart, I wish to serve these words." (12:1, trans. Roetz)[46]

Here *li* seems to take precedence over *ren*, because "returning to *li*" seems to be the very definition of *ren*. But here is the other passage: "The Master said, A man who is not *ren*, what can he have to do with *li*? A man who is not *ren*, what can he have to do with music (*yue*)?" (3:3, trans. Waley).[47] Here *ren* seems to be the essential precondition of *li*, without which it would be mean-ingless, and so takes precedence over *li*.[48]

Perhaps Fingarette can show us that what seems to be a contradiction is really a complementarity, and he uses music, so often coupled with *li* in the *Analects,* to do so:

> Acts that are *li* are not just rote, formula-conforming performances; they are subtle and intelligent acts exhibiting more or less sensitivity of context, more or less integrity in performance. We would do well to take music, of which Confucius was a devotee, as our model here. We dis-tinguish sensitive and intelligent musical performances from dull and unperceptive ones; and we detect in the performance confidence and integrity, or perhaps hesitation, conflict, "faking," "sentimentalizing." We detect all this *in* the performance; we do not have to look into the psyche or personality of the performer . . .
>
> Analogously, an act may be seen as *ren* if we look to see how *this* per-son does it, and more specifically whether it reveals that he treats all persons involved as of ultimately equal dignity with himself by virtue of their participation along with him in *li*.[49]

We can see that for Fingarette *ren* and *li* are part of a single package, each implying the other.

Roetz also sees the complementarity, yet he wants to give *ren* a "higher" moral status than *li*. For him *li* points to conventional morality (*Sittlichkeit* in Hegelian terms) whereas *ren* represents postconventional morality, morality based on universal ethical principles (*Moralität* in Hegelian/Kantian terms), and he uses Lawrence Kohlberg's stages of the development of moral rea-soning in the child to rank *li* as applying to stages 3 and 4, the conventional level, and *ren* as applying to stage 6, the highest stage of postconventional moral reasoning.[50] Roetz also pairs another "postconventional" term with *ren*, namely *yi*, often translated as "right," "rightness," or, as Roetz prefers, "justice." In any case, *yi*, like *ren*, is found in what Brooks considers the old-est part of the *Analects,* book 4: "The Master said, The gentleman's relation to the world is thus: he has no predilections or prohibitions. When he regards something as right, he sides with it" (4:10, trans. Brooks). "The Master said, The gentleman concentrates on right; the little man concentrates on advan-tage" (4:16, trans. Brooks). We will have more to say about *yi* when we dis-cuss the *Mencius*.[51]

I am sympathetic with Roetz in his effort to rescue Confucius and Confucianism from those who deny them ethical universalism and categorize Confucian ethics as "group ethics," lacking any standard by which individuals can judge group conventions. But I would argue, contra Roetz, that Fingarette, despite his insistence on the Confucian self as a social, not a psychological, self (an argument that I don't want to get into), does not think of Confucian ethics as "group ethics" in this derogatory sense. On the contrary, I think Fingarette, with his emphasis on the revisability of tradition in the light of new circumstances, is actually raising up *li* to the same stage of ethical universalism as *ren*.

Still, I would like to go a bit further along with Roetz in emphasizing the universal ethical element in the *Analects*. Starting from *ren* again, something new is added in *Analects* 12:2:

> Zhonggong inquired about *ren*. The Master replied, "In your public life, behave as though you are receiving important visitors; employ the common people as though you are overseeing a great sacrifice. Do not impose on others what you yourself do not want, and you will not incur personal or political ill will."[52]

Here we have one of several versions of the golden rule to be found in the *Analects*. It follows and amplifies the admonition to treat others in one's private and public life with the greatest dignity, and it is given as an explanation of *ren*.

However, there is another key term that also turns up in golden rule sayings, one we haven't mentioned before but adds to the richness of the Confucian vocabulary:

> Zigong asked, "Is there something which consists of a single word and which, because of its nature, can be practiced for all one's life?" The Master said, "I should say this is *shu*: What you do not want for yourself, do not do unto others." (15:24, trans. Roetz)[53]

Roetz leaves *shu* untranslated as he wants to question the usual translation of "reciprocity" as potentially implying utilitarian calculation, a lower level of moral reasoning than he thinks is involved here. He points out that the term *shu* is more usually translated "forgiveness" or "indulgence," and he suggests the best translation would be "fairness," emphasizing its universality as a norm. *Shu* turns up in another key passage, 4:15, which Roetz translates:

The Master said, "Shen! My way *(dao)* is pervaded by one." "Yes!" said Zengzi. When the Master had gone, the disciples asked, "What does he mean?" Zengzi said, "The way of our teacher is benevolence and fairness *(zhongshu),* and that's all."[54]

Here is *shu* again, paired with *zhong,* usually translated as loyalty, but having a range of meanings such that here "benevolence" seems more apt. Roetz's point is that the golden rule is a formal procedure, not a virtue, and as such is universalizable and not context-dependent.[55] Yet it still needs the background assumption of a universal ethical concept governing what it is that one does or does not want done to one. It is just this that *ren, shu,* and *zhong* (humaneness, fairness, benevolence) are providing.

Fingarette has emphasized the place of *li* in the *Analects,* and argued that Confucius interpreted *li* as a sense of life as ceremonial, within which and only within which human beings can become human. It is in this vision that he sees "the secular as sacred," the subtitle to his book. Yet we don't want to let this idea simply reinforce the notion of Confucianism as a secular philosophy and not a religion. It is probably right to see something that only modern Westerners have called an "ism" as not to be called, as again only modern Westerners have called it, "a religion."[56] But we cannot deny the adjective "religious" to Confucianism. Many of its key terms—*Tian, Dao, de, ren, li* (after all, *li* never loses its basic meaning as religious ritual)—point beyond the mundane world, have an aura of the sacred about them that they never lose, and that will be reaffirmed much later by neo-Confucianism.

There is one unmistakably religious term that does not appear often in the *Analects,* but that is nonetheless present at certain key moments, and that is *Tian,* Heaven. Even here there is an effort to argue for the secularity of Confucianism by holding that *Tian* no longer has any religious meaning, but is simply a term for "nature." "Nature," however, in all premodern cultures is normally a religious term—even *physis,* Greek for "nature," meant something alive, growing, and worthy of respect. But the specific appearances of Heaven in the *Analects* imply something clearly other than any meaning we can normally give to "nature." For example:

When the Master was trapped in Kuang, he said, When King Wen perished, did that mean that culture *(wen)* ceased to exist? If Heaven had really intended that such culture as his should disappear, a latter-day mortal would never have been able to link himself to it as I have done. And if Heaven does not intend to destroy such culture, what have I to fear from the people of Kuang? (9:5, trans. Waley)

What made Confucius not simply one more teacher of the Six Arts, was his mission—his "mandate" we could say, thinking of later ideas that Confucius was the uncrowned king, the real holder of the Mandate of Heaven—to transmit and, we must add, to reanimate, the tradition of the ancients, with all that that implied. Elsewhere we find Confucius claiming what we can only call a "personal" relation with Heaven:

The Master said, "There is no one, is there, who recognizes me." Zigong said, "Why is it that no one recognizes you?" The Master said, "I neither resent Heaven nor blame man; in learning about the lower, I have fathomed the higher. The one who recognizes me, wouldn't it be Heaven?" (14:35, trans. Graham)[57]

And when his favorite disciple died he grieved with such abandon that he startled the other disciples (11:10) and turned to Heaven:

When Yan Hui died, the Master said, "Alas, Heaven has abandoned me, Heaven has abandoned me." (11:9, trans. Graham)[58]

Because Heaven is concerned with the human moral order, and in this sense Confucius's thought is continuous with that of Western Zhou, there is a relationship between Heaven and the Way, *Tian* and *Dao*. Yet Confucius never uses the term "Way of Heaven" *(Tiandao)*.[59] Graham argues that this is perhaps because diviners and others who used it to refer to the course of the heavenly bodies had at that time preempted the term.[60] Confucius had little interest in cosmology; for him both *Tian* and *Dao* were concerned above all with the human moral order.

In spite of the agreement of many scholars that Chinese thought is basically "optimistic," Confucius, though relying on Heaven and the *Dao,* is, if not pessimistic, at least in doubt. He can feel, as we just saw, abandoned by Heaven. And his concern with the *Dao* is very much with its absence: "The Way does not prevail" (5:7, trans. Leys). "The world had lost the Way" (16:2, trans. Leys). As with other axial thinkers, Confucius believes the world is out of joint, that it is his task to do what he can to set it right, but that, win or lose, above all he must hold on to his principles, he must behave in accordance with *ren* and *li.*

So what are we to make of this extraordinary man, and of the book at-tributed to him? Was he a political activist, attempting to revive a just politi-cal order that had fallen into decay? Was he the founder of a new sect, seek-ing the moral purity of its members, but basically withdrawing from society? Or was he, like Socrates, a critic of the social and political practices of his time, a seeker of truth rather than office, who through his example drew to himself disciples who would in various ways carry on the tradition that he established? Robert Eno considers that Confucius's achievement was to es-tablish a new understanding of education, one that through the knowledge and practice of *li* would lead to the transformation of his students into "ethi-cal and wise beings,"[61] what I have called "formation." Probably there is some truth in all these possibilities. Certainly we can find in the *Analects* the beginning of the Confucian tradition of self-cultivation, so central in later Chinese history.[62]

What is significant from the point of view of our concern with the under-standing of the axial transformation in its several cases is how far Confucius went, or how far he and those disciples who continued his tradition went, as recounted in the *Analects,* in carrying through the essentials of that transi-tion. It is true that in the *Analects* we don't find much "second-order" thinking—that is, thinking about thinking. Formal logic never became central in Chinese thought, though as we will see, it was developed with considerable sophistication later in the Warring States period. Nevertheless, Chinese science, based on careful observation and close attention to what works and what doesn't, made striking advances—through much of history being equal to or, often, in advance of Western science, as the great work of Joseph Needham has extensively demonstrated.[63] Confucius, however, like Socrates, was interested primarily in human society, not the natural cosmos, and his contributions and those of his followers were primarily in that realm. These contributions were nonetheless major.

Critical reasoning, even though in aphoristic or dialogical form, provided explanations of why things went wrong in society and in human conduct, and suggested alternatives that might set them right. Although not all Sinol-ogists agree, I have argued, following Heiner Roetz, that the *Analects* does contain an ethics based in part on universal values. I should be clear that I do not think "universal" values exist in any culture in absolute form. They are always phrased in a particular language in a particular time and place. If we translate them as "justice," "benevolence," or the like, we are using terms in-evitably situated in a different cultural milieu and therefore approximations at best to the Chinese terms being translated. What I mean by "universal" is

an aspiration toward universality. Confucian ethics are intended to be human ethics, not Chinese ethics. Roetz has shown the remarkable lack of
ethnocentrism in early Chinese ethical thought. Although there are terms
we can adequately translate as "barbarians," these non-Chinese people are
not treated as ethically different—they may even provide instructive examples for the Chinese.[64]

Although Confucius and his followers lived in a situation that they believed exhibited moral decay, and of which they were sharply critical, we now
know that axial China, not unlike the other axial civilizations, was in a period of rapid growth, demographically, economically, and in terms of politi-
cal/military power. The ethical consequences of this "growth" stimulated
Confucian criticism. As Benjamin Schwartz has pointed out, this links China
to the other axial cases:

> I should like to say a word about Confucius' image of moral evil. In fact
> the description of these evil tendencies which impede the achievement of
> the good is strikingly similar to the diagnoses made by prophets, wise
> men, and philosophers in all the high civilizations of this period. The
> unbridled pursuit of wealth, power, fame, sensual passion, arrogance, and
> pride—these themes figure centrally as the source of "the difficulty." The
> language of the vices lends itself comparatively easily to translation into
> the vocabulary of Gautama Buddha, Plato and the Hebrew prophets.
> The material development of all the high civilizations had enormously
> increased the opportunities—at least for certain strata—for aggran-
> dizement of power, increase of luxury, and pursuit of status and pres-
> tige . . . It is precisely in the moral orientations of the creative minori-
> ties of the first millennium that we find a resounding no to certain
> characteristic modes of human self-affirmation, which had emerged
> with the progress of civilization. For them the divine no longer dwelt in
> the manifestations of power, wealth, and external glory.[65]

In trying to make sense of the response of Confucius and his followers to
these conditions, we can again turn to Schwartz when he affirms that Confucius's thought is "both sociopolitical and ethicoritual," and he finds the
two dimensions to be "inextricably intertwined." Although not uncritical of
much of Fingarette's argument, Schwartz turns to him for help in summing
up his own position: "In the end, however, there is truth in Fingarette's assertion that Confucius' vision 'is certainly not merely a political vision.' On its

most exalted level we have the vision of a society which not only enjoys harmony and welfare but a society transfigured by a life of sacred and beautiful ritual in which all classes would participate."[66]

We will see that the social conditions to which Confucius was responding, the subversion of the inherited norms of ethical and political behavior, and the rise of ever more militarized and ruthless states contending for supremacy, would only become more widespread as the Warring States period unfolded. It was to these conditions that Confucians, but also their critics, would have to continue to respond.

Mozi

Mo Di (personal name) or Mozi (Master Mo) probably was born after the death of Confucius in 479 BCE, flourished in the second half of the fifth century, perhaps surviving into the early fourth century, probably was educated by Confucians but later turned bitterly against them, and was the founder of a "school" that arose during the Warring States period and contested the dominance of Confucian teachings. Before describing his teachings and the organization of his followers, it would be well to look a bit more closely at the changes that were going on in society. Mark Lewis gives a condensed picture of changes that had begun incipiently even in the seventh and sixth centuries BCE and reached their culmination in the fourth and third centuries:

> The constant wars of the Zhou noble lineages gradually led to the creation of ever larger territorial units through the conquest of alien states and the extension of central government control into the countryside. These were called "warring states" because they devoted themselves to warfare, they were created through the progressive extension of military service, and the registration and mobilization of their populations for battle remained fundamental to their existence as states ... Whereas under the nobility the actual performance of ritually sanctioned violence had been the hallmark of authority, in the Warring States all men engaged in licit violence, while authority was associated with its manipulation and control. Instead of being a means of defending honor, sanctioned violence served to establish or reinforce the authoritarian, hierarchic bonds that constituted the new social structure. In place of the lineage as the primary unit of both politics and elite kinship, the

state secured control of military force, while the kin groups were reduced to the individual households that provided both taxes and labor
service . . . The ultimate sanction of segmentary, aristocratic rule in the
ancestral cults was replaced by forms of sanctioned violence and authority that were justified through the imitation of the "patterns of Heaven"
by a single, cosmically potent ruler. Finally, the new organization and
interpretation of violence allowed the Warring States Chinese to develop a new understanding of human society and the natural world.[67]

Whereas in Western Zhou and early Spring and Autumn China, participation in military action was limited to the aristocracy, it gradually came to
include nonaristocratic inhabitants of capital cities, but eventually the peasantry as well, so that in the mature Warring States there was something close
to universal manhood conscription. As a result the old chariot armies of the
nobility were replaced by mass infantry recruited from the lower strata of
society, eliminating the social power of the great ministerial lineages and of
the aristocracy generally. Mass infantry required far less complex skills and
was much less expensive to equip than the chariot armies of the aristocracy.
The brave aristocratic warrior engaging in single combat was replaced by the
skilled general who knew how to deploy multiple divisions of armies numbering in the thousands. As in other spheres, warfare became an art and
leadership was based on proven merit, not birth. Technological inventions
helped drive these changes in the form of warfare: the increasing use of iron
weapons, of the recently invented (or imported) crossbow, of more effective
armor, and of more effective and widely available swords. New forms of warfare, as has been true in many times and places, drove changes throughout
society, including the state, the economy, and the family.[68]

Peasant land was now "private property," in the sense that peasants were
no longer serfs bonded to noble lords, but were, as individuals and nuclear
families, subject to taxation, corvée, and conscription by centralized states.
Instead of being organized geographically into villages belonging to a noble
lineage, peasants were now organized into administrative districts under
bureaucrats appointed by the head of state. These districts combined civil
and military functions. Peasants were organized into units of five family heads,
providing the lowest-level infantry unit, and, in civil as well as military life,
were jointly responsible for each other's behavior.[69]

All this sounds very authoritarian, verging on totalitarian, and, in the theory that will later be called "Legalist," that was the intention. Nonetheless,

the Warring States period was much more fluid, even disorganized, than the above picture suggests. The constant warfare, the fall of states, the loss of status by the old aristocratic lineages, the rise of new groups of prosperous artisans and landholders, produced a society very much in flux. Members of the old elite, including its lowest level, the *shi,* were often displaced and had to seek protection and employment from rulers outside their place of birth. Even peasants were not infrequently displaced. One result of the turbulence of Warring States society was the presence of large numbers of men with various skills and abilities who had lost their ancestral roots and were available for hire by whomever wanted them. Many of these were fighters and provided troops for ambitious rulers. Others were administrators, advisors, and diplomats, some of whom developed teachings that were handed down by their disciples, but only in the Han dynasty came to be called "Legalists."

Among this large group of people who had lost their traditional places in society were itinerant scholars, often descended, as the Confucians were, from teachers of the Six Arts of the aristocratic tradition, still fashionable among the new elites. Toward the middle of the Warring States period it became a status symbol for rulers or high administrators of the larger states to attract a number of scholars of diverse backgrounds to give a kind of cultural luster to the state. We don't know much about these developments, but it does appear that the state of Qi was the first to gather such a group of scholars. Both Mencius and Xunzi may have been associated with it, though the scholars themselves were of eclectic background, as is represented by the *Guanzi,* a collective work that may consist largely of contributions of the Qi scholars.[70] The Qin state that would eventually unite the whole of China, not to be outdone by Qi, gathered a large group of scholars under the patronage of its chief minister, Lü Buwei, from which the collective work *Lüshi chunqiu* emerged.[71] Although several of the prominent Warring States thinkers, Xunzi for one, argued that their and only their views should be officially recognized, partly because they claimed to have included all that was good from the other traditions while eliminating the bad, there was no effective thought control until the Qin First Emperor tried to enforce one. A thinker who became unpopular in one place, or had annoyed a ruler of one state, could always move to another, and would often be welcomed as an addition to the local cultural capital.

Lewis sums up the situation as follows: "Apart from those that emerged from Confucius's disciples, the only full-blown school attested to in the records is the

Mohist tradition. Otherwise, each intellectual tradition is identified by the name of its putative founder and is defined entirely by a book or books that bore his name."[72] We should note that such books were handed down by disciples—we might call them scholarly lineages if we don't want to use the term "school"—who undoubtedly added to the "original" text, often difficult to distinguish from such later additions. Brooks calls this pattern "growth by accretion" and finds it present in the *Analects,* as we have noted, but in other Confucian and non-Confucian texts as well.[73] The *Mozi,* the primary text of the Mohist movement, is clearly a text of this sort. We may not know exactly how much of it goes back to Mozi himself, but it is clear that the early parts of the text are quite different from the later parts, attributed to the "Later Mohists."[74]

The Mohist movement disappeared more completely than any other major strand of Warring States thought once the country was unified, so it is hard for us to imagine that through most of the period it was the chief rival to Confucianism for intellectual dominance. We will have to consider below the cause of the movement's sudden and total demise, but we can here consider why the text itself, which did survive, attracted little interest and less devotion from Chinese scholars of imperial times. Partly the answer is that from mid-Han times Confucianism became something like an official ideology and Mohism was considered not only as opposed to Confucianism, which makes it especially interesting to us, but as having been thoroughly refuted by Confucians, something that could never quite be said of texts that were later denominated Daoist. On top of that, Mo Di does not emerge from the text as a three-dimensional figure. The portrait of Confucius in the *Analects,* however much embellished by later legend, has made an indelible impression on Chinese throughout the centuries and on Westerners as soon as they began to learn about him, but Mo Di remains a voice more than a person. Finally, the style of the book is awkward and repetitive and lacks the expressiveness of the *Mencius,* the poetry of the *Zhuangzi,* or the intellectual seriousness of the *Xunzi.* Nonetheless, as the most widespread alternative to Confucianism in the Warring States period it deserves serious consideration.

The *Analects,* as we have noted, consists largely of aphorisms and anecdotes. The axial nature of the *Analects* derives from its use of old ideas in new ways, its introduction of new terms in the moral vocabulary, and its making ideas that were previously taken for granted available for reflection, but not from the development of logical argument. However unsophisticated in its oldest levels, the *Mozi* from the beginning introduces sustained argument, often directed toward the rejection or revision of ideas attributed to Confucius. A. C. Graham argues that it is with Mozi that "rational debate in China starts." True as that may be, it is hard to see how, without the foil of Confucius, Mozi would have gotten started.

If Confucius can be understood in part because of his social situation on the border between the lowest level of the old aristocracy and commoners seeking the education that would allow them to become officials in state systems now more interested in merit than lineage, what can we say about the social situation of Mozi? We have no independent evidence for giving him a social location, but many have made inferences from the text itself, leading to the idea that he came from a somewhat lower stratum than Confucius, perhaps from the artisan class that was influential in urban settings and perhaps especially in the capitals of small states, for which Mozi seems to have been especially concerned. Michael Puett has noted the concern for craftsmanship in this text: "Indeed, metaphors of craft-building, constructing, and fashioning—are so prevalent in the Mohist writings that some scholars have argued that the Mohists were in fact a school of artisans."[75]

A. C. Graham links Mozi's status to his most distinctive teaching: "It would seem that Mozi was a man of low status, an artisan . . . and that this has something to do with his most distinctive innovation, that he judges institutions not by the tradition of Zhou but by their practical utility, by whether like the linchpin of a wheel they are beneficial to the people."[76] Puett underpins this practical emphasis of the Mohists with an argument for a basic difference with the Confucians as to the legitimacy of innovation at all. He notes that Confucius's claim to be a transmitter rather than a creator (*Analects* 7:1) can be attributed to his modesty, but when placed beside another text may have a more far-reaching meaning:

> The master said: "Great indeed was the rulership of Yao. So majestic— only Heaven is great, and only Yao patterned himself upon it. So boundless, the people were not able to find a name for it. Majestic were his achievements. Illustrious are his patterned forms [*wen zhang*]."[77]

Puett argues that the *Analects* fairly consistently emphasizes "patterning" (*wen,* "pattern," sometimes translated as "culture") rather than innovating or creating, thus giving some substance to Mozi's criticism of Confucius: "Gong Mengzi said: 'The superior man does not create [*zuo*] but only transmits.'

The master Mozi said: 'Not so . . . Desiring for goodness to increase all the more, I believe in transmitting the good things of the past and creating good things for the present.' "[78]

Puett argues that Mozi's positive evaluation of creation, not just transmission, is based on an understanding of Heaven as an active creator, not just a pattern to be imitated. Mozi writes:

> Moreover, I know from the following reason that Heaven loves the people generously: It sets forth one after another the sun and the moon, the stars and constellations to lighten and lead them; it orders the four seasons, spring, fall, winter, and summer, to regulate their lives; it sends down snow and frost, rain and dew, to nourish the five grains, hemp, and silk, so that the people may enjoy the benefit of them. It lays out the mountains and rivers, the ravines and valley streams, and makes known all affairs so as to ascertain the good or evil of the people. It establishes kings and lords to reward the worthy and punish the wicked, to gather together metal and wood, birds and beasts, and to see to the cultivation of the five grains, hemp, and silk, so that the people may have enough food and clothing. From ancient times to the present this has always been so.[79]

Although in the above passage it appears that Heaven establishes kings and lords just as primordially as the sun and the moon, there is another passage that suggests original mankind was without rulers:

> Mozi said: In ancient times, when mankind was first born and before there were any laws or government, it may be said that every man's view of things was different. One man had one view, two men had two views, ten men had ten views—the more men, the more views. Moreover, each man believed that his own views were correct and disapproved of those of others, so that people spent their time condemning one another. Within the family fathers and sons, older and younger brothers grew to hate each other and the family split up, unable to live in harmony, while throughout the world the people all resorted to water, fire, and poison in an effort to do each other injury. Those with strength to spare refused to help out others, those with surplus wealth would let it rot before they would share it, and those with beneficial doctrines to teach would keep them secret and refuse to impart them.

The world was as chaotic as though it were inhabited by birds and beasts alone.

To anyone who examined the cause, it was obvious that this chaos came about because of the absence of rulers and leaders.[80]

Here Mozi sounds almost like Hobbes, except that the source of the war of all against all is the absence of common views rather than the absence of law. But the solution is the same: rulers. Except that for Mozi the primary function of the ruler is to establish right views: "What the superior considers right all shall consider right; what the superior considers wrong, all shall consider wrong."[81] At each level, from the local to the whole world, those below are to look to those above for the right standards, standards that elsewhere Mozi tells us can be discerned by taking the will of Heaven as a compass or a carpenter's square, that is, as the model to be followed.[82] In spite of the apparently relentless authoritarianism of Mozi's view in the "Identifying with One's Superior" section, the necessity of following the judgment of those above right up to the supreme ruler, the Son of Heaven, still Mozi says:

If we examine the reason why the world was well ordered, we find that it was simply that the Son of Heaven was able to unify the standards of judgment throughout the world, and this resulted in order.

But although all the people in the world may identify themselves with the Son of Heaven, if they do not also identify themselves with Heaven itself, then calamities will never cease. The violent winds and bitter rains which sweep the world in such profusion these days—these are simply the punishments of Heaven sent down upon the people because they fail to identify themselves with Heaven.[83]

Although this may be a comment on the sad state of the times, when the judgment of the Son of Heaven (the vestigial Zhou king) was no longer in accord with Heaven, or perhaps even that there was in effect no Son of Heaven at the time, it does make clear that there was a standard other than the will of the superior, a substantive standard, the most basic idea of Mozi's teaching, in terms of which any regime would in the end have to be judged. In the passage above that recounts Heaven's creative efforts, the reason Heaven creates is stated to be because Heaven "loves the people." And for humans to identify with Heaven means that they, too, must "love the people," all the people, and without distinctions. Here we have the Mohist doctrine most commonly translated as "universal love *(jian ai)*," that Graham prefers to translate as "Concern for Everyone"[84] and David Nivison as "impartial caring."[85] A brief description of what *jian ai* means is as follows:

> Therefore Mozi said: Partiality should be replaced by universality. But how can partiality be replaced by universality? If men were to regard the states of others as they regard their own, then who would raise up his state to attack the state of another? It would be like attacking his own. If men were to regard the cities of others as they regard their own, then who would raise up his city to attack the city of another? It would be like attacking his own. If men were to regard the families of others as they regard their own, then who would raise up his family to overthrow that of another? It would be like overthrowing his own. Now when states and cities do not attack and make war on each other and families and individuals do not overthrow or injure one another, is this a harm or a benefit to the world? Surely it is a benefit.[86]

We will need to consider Mozi's justification of the doctrine of *jian ai* in terms of benefit, for that will lead us into a central issue concerning his teaching: his utilitarianism. But first we must consider another issue that the above passage raises, and certainly raised for the Confucians, the conflict between *jian ai* and filial piety *(xiao)*. The Confucians accused the Mohists of having no fathers and no older brothers, of abandoning their filial obligations altogether if they had no higher obligations to their own kin than to anyone else. In the section on the *Analects* above we concentrated on its basic moral vocabulary and did not discuss this central application of Confucian ethics, namely, to the family. Yuri Pines raises an interesting question about the history of the idea of filial piety. He argues that the term *xiao* meant primarily lineage loyalty in early Zhou thought and that it actually fell into disrepute in the Spring and Autumn period, where loyalty to insubordinate lineages threatened the viability of states. It was, he argues, only with Confucius and/or the early Confucians that filial piety *(xiao)* begins to focus on the nuclear family rather than the lineage—that is, the focus is one's obligations to one's own father or to one's own older brother—a much narrower focus than would have been the case earlier, though one in accord with social changes that were undermining extended lineages and making the nuclear family central, though never wholly abandoning concern with ancestors, and so with lineage. Brooks argues that filial piety is not prominent in the earliest level of the *Analects,* but becomes prominent only later. In any case, not only does it become prominent, but eventually it is seen as the basis of all other ethical obligations, such as loyalty to the ruler, and of the ethical virtues, even the central virtue of *ren* itself:

> Master You said: "A man who respects his parents and his elders could hardly be inclined to defy his superiors. A man who is not inclined to defy his superiors will never foment a rebellion. A gentlemen works at the root. Once the root is secured, the Way unfolds. To respect parents and elders is the root of humanity [*ren*]." (1:2, trans. Leys)

But although Confucians always believed that Mozi's teachings violated filial piety and so were to be rejected, they were not entirely immune to them. They argued that concern for one's own relatives, though a primary obligation, did not mean that one should not be concerned for nonrelatives. For example, respect for one's father, though primary, was to be complemented by respect for elders in general. And in one widely quoted passage in the *Analects,* a leading disciple of Confucius takes a view that does not seem to be wholly incompatible with that of Mozi:

> Sima Niu was grieving: "All men have brothers; I alone have none." Zixia said: "I have heard this: life and death are decreed by fate, riches and honors are allotted by Heaven. Since a gentleman behaves with reverence and diligence, treating people with deference and courtesy [*li*], all within the Four Seas are his brothers. How could a gentleman ever complain that he has no brothers?" (12:5, trans. Leys)

But what we have here, as is usual in the *Analects,* is an aphorism, pungent and to the point, an expression of moral universalism, but not a theory that can be generalized to all cases.

Graham notes that it is the relentlessness of Mozi's logic with respect to *jian ai* that sets him off not only from the Confucians, but from all other thinkers of the time:

> "Concern for Everyone" [*jian ai*] is a concern for each person irrespective of relations of kinship with oneself. It is this relentless driving of a principle to its logical conclusion which gives Mohism its appearance of being foreign, not merely to Confucian thinking, but to the whole of

Chinese civilization as in these few centuries [the Warring States period] it assumes lasting shape. No one else finds it tolerable to insist that you should be as concerned for the other man's family as for your own.[87]

I am tempted to compare Mozi, the inventor of logic in China, with Parmenides, the inventor of logic in Greece. Each in his enthusiasm with his new toy pushed the implications to an extreme. Parmenides "proved" that Being doesn't change—it just is. Change is illusory. He had pushed his metaphysical logic to a position that was at odds with any glance at the empirical world. Nonetheless he provided the impetus to later developments in logic that would be central for all Western philosophy. Mozi pushed his logic to an extreme not in metaphysics but in ethics. Although his successors, the "Later Mohists," greatly advanced his rather crude beginnings in logic, their work ceased with the general collapse of Mohism at the end of the Warring States period, and logic did not become central in later Chinese thought. Perhaps pushing logic to absurdity in the field of ethics was more dangerous than in metaphysics. It didn't take only scholars to sense that something was wrong. Indeed, later Mohists tried to moderate Mozi's argument by holding that "although concern for others should be equal, irrespective of kinship, it is to the benefit of all that each should include among his duties the care of his own kin."[88]

The problem with Mozi's relentless logic is deeper than that involved in his doctrine of *jian ai* (universal love, Concern for Everyone, impartial caring), though it includes it. It concerns his notion of benefit (*li,* a homonym but a different word from *li,* ritual) as the motive for every action, which is generally called Mozi's utilitarianism. As we have seen, Heaven has a prominent place in Mozi's teaching, having created the world as we know it out of love for human beings. As in the *Analects* it is hard to imagine translating *Tian* as Nature rather than as Heaven. And indeed, Heaven has a will that humans should obey. What Heaven wills is *yi,* right; concretely it wills that "the strong will not oppress the weak; the eminent will not lord it over the humble; the cunning will not deceive the stupid."[89] Even the Son of Heaven must obey the will of Heaven. But then, here comes the rub:

Now people in the world say: "It is perfectly obvious that the Son of Heaven is more eminent than the feudal lords and that the feudal lords are more eminent than the ministers. But we do not know that Heaven is more eminent and wise than the Son of Heaven!"

Mozi said: I know that Heaven is more eminent and wise than the Son of Heaven for this reason: If the Son of Heaven does something good, Heaven has the power to reward him, and if he does something bad, Heaven has the power to punish him.[90]

As it turns out, and we find this over and over again in the *Mozi,* Heaven does indeed desire the right and the good, but it is the infallible benefit that will result in obeying the will of Heaven and the infallible punishment that will follow disobeying that are the final reasons for obeying the will of Heaven. Even the injunction of *jian ai,* universal love, is based on the fact that if everyone acted in accordance with it we would be better off than at present when we don't. So, finally, *it is in our interest* to obey the will of Heaven and be concerned for everyone, impartially. It is this indelible utilitarianism that leads Heiner Roetz to characterize Mohism as postconventional, which is what he means by axial, though it is nevertheless postconventional at Kohlberg's stage five, "the utilitarian, relativistic, social contract orientation," and not at stage six, "the universal ethical principle orientation."[91]

Finally, if Heaven is so mechanically engaged in reward and punishment, it would seem that there is a limitation on a personal relation with Heaven. At least we cannot imagine Mozi saying, as Confucius does at *Analects* 11:9, "Heaven has abandoned me."[92] Indeed, even in distress, Mozi affirms his basic view:

Master Mozi fell ill. Die Bi came forward and inquired,

"You claim, sir, that the gods and ghosts are clear-seeing and able to bring blessings or disaster; the good they reward, the bad they punish. Now you, sir, being a sage, why have you fallen ill? Would it be that something in your doctrine is bad or that the gods and ghosts do not clearly know?"

"Even if I do fall ill," said Master Mozi, "why conclude that the gods and ghosts are not clear-seeing? There are many directions from which illness can come to a man. It can happen from heat and cold, it can happen from overwork. It is as though of a hundred doors one has shut a single one; why be surprised if thieves find a way in?"[93]

Graham sums up the essential difference from Confucianism:

The Confucian thinks of right as done for its own sake, and frees himself from the temptation to do wrong for the sake of gain by saying that wealth and poverty, long life and early death, are decreed for him by Heaven and outside his control. He can therefore act rightly with an untroubled mind, leaving the consequences to Heaven. For the Mohist on the other hand, judging all conduct in terms of benefit and harm, there can be no meaning in a morality detached from consequences.[94]

Many differences follow from this fundamental one, and some of them must rouse our admiration for the Mohists. They bitterly opposed the Confucian doctrine of "fate," of what Heaven has decreed, as an avoidance of human responsibility.[95] Similarly Mozi was indignant with Confucius's refusal to serve a lord he did not feel was worthy. For Mozi that was an expression of personal pride: any opportunity for service can be turned toward the benefit of the people. The Mohists criticized elaborate ritual, especially extensive funeral ritual, and music, meaning the elaborate musical entertainments of the elite, because of the great expense involved, money that could be used to better the lives of the people. The attack on ritual *(li)* and music, goes to the heart of the Confucian project and surely annoyed the elite of the time, as well as adding to the notion of Mohists as dour.[96]

The Mohists were against aggressive war but were not pacifists. As an organized movement, Mohists even engaged in defensive warfare, helping defend small states from the attack of large ones. Like utilitarians in later times and places, the Mohists were activists, advocates of simple living and devotion to the cause of helping others.[97] Their demise as a movement had probably more to do with their activism, and their capacity to organize for military action, than with their doctrines. Such organized activism was not at all what Qin Shihuangdi was inclined to tolerate in a newly united Chinese empire. But we have already commented on the lack of lasting appeal of Mohism as a doctrine even after the collapse of the movement. This is not at all to say Mohism had no impact. It influenced in one way or another every tendency in Warring States thought, sometimes in active opposition, sometimes in surreptitious borrowing.

The Tianxia chapter (33) of the *Zhuangzi,* written by Zhuangzi or someone later, gives an interesting assessment of Mozi that can serve as a fitting coda to this section:

Now Mozi alone refused to sing a song for the living or wear mourning for the dead . . . Teaching this to others I am afraid he was not loving to others, and practicing this in his own case most certainly he was not loving to himself. I would not slander Mozi's Way; however, if you sang he condemned you for singing, if you wept he condemned you for weeping, if you made music he condemned you for making music, was he really the same sort as the rest of us? With the living he took such pains, with the dead he was so niggardly, his way was too impoverished, he made men worry, made them pine, his code was hard to live up to, I am afraid it cannot be the Way of a sage. It went counter to the hearts of the empire, the empire would not bear it . . .

[Mozi took as a model the early king Yu, who "wore out his body for the empire."] The result was that many of the Mohists of later generations dressed in furs or coarse wool, wore clogs or hemp sandals, never rested day or night and thought of self-torment as the noblest thing of all . . .

As far as the idea of Mozi and Qin Guli [his chief disciple] is concerned, they were right; but in putting it into effect they were wrong. The result was simply that Mohists of later generations had to urge each other on to torment themselves until there was no flesh on their thighs or down on their shins. It was a superior sort of disorder, an inferior sort of order. However Mozi was truly the best man in the empire, you will not find another like him. However shriveled and worn, he would not give up. He was a man of talent, shall we say?[98]

But although Mohists pushed the idea of "benefit" to a logical extreme that placed them near the outer limit of Chinese thought, it is still well to remember that, in a more common sense way, the idea of benefit was part of the mainstream of Chinese thought. Confucians would judge rulers by whether they benefited the people—indeed, Mencius makes that the criterion of political legitimacy. Except for its fascination with logical consistency, Mohism is perhaps less eccentric relative to the Chinese tradition than at first might appear.

"Daoism" and the Turn to Private Life

We have seen Confucius and his disciples creating, on the basis of traditions of aristocratic education, a new kind of education aiming at the formation of a certain kind of character, one that could go on developing through the whole of life by means of the practice of self-cultivation. This education was intended to prepare the students for service in the newly centralizing states emerging in the Warring States period, where merit was being recognized as more important then lineage. But it was also preparing students to be a certain kind of person who could influence others by example, and lead a satisfying life whether he held office or not, supporting himself when out of office by teaching or by serving as a ritual specialist. Robert Eno believes that Confucianism was primarily a sect, oriented more to private life than to office, though the continuous concern with politics and the responsibilities of office that we find in Confucius and his successors makes this view appear one-sided.[99]

Mozi and his followers, on the other hand, seem to have been oriented primarily to public life, in service to a sympathetic lord where possible, but organizing for action when that was not possible. The quasi-military organization of the Mohists and their interest in defensive warfare, including inventing mechanical devices to foil attacking armies, suggest a degree of activism that is quite un-Confucian. Self-cultivation as such does not appear to have been a Mohist concern, though activism is itself a kind of personal formation. Though the Mohists significantly advanced logic and rational argument beyond anything we find in the *Analects,* Mohist rational discourse was always in the service of practical ends, as its relentless utilitarianism indicates.

If Confucianism appears to have attempted a balance between public and private life and Mohism veered rather strongly in the public direction, there were other tendencies, less well organized than these two, that moved in the direction of exclusive concern for private life. "Daoism," which I put in quotes because it was not in the Warring States period a coherent movement even to the extent that Confucianism and Mohism were, is a term that can be applied to several figures and/or texts that use the term *Dao* as central to their teaching, but, equally importantly, emphasize some kind of meditation technique in the process of self-development. There were, however, other tendencies emphasizing private life that cannot be called Daoist even by these loose criteria, that were also prevalent in the Warring States period. This is hardly surprising in a period of such turmoil and constant warfare.

In the face of an increasingly coherent ideology of centralized militarization and total control of the population, usually discussed under the rubric of "Legalism," it might seem that there was no "private" space to retreat to. But as I have noted before, the very disorder of the Warring States period, the fact that small states lacking strong central controls continued to exist at least for a while, suggests that there were places to which those appalled at current social conditions could retreat. Some of the centralizing states were tolerant of diverse ideological trends, even ones opposed to centralization, in their search for cultural capital and possible ideological support.

Yang Zhu and his supporters, whose ideas we will discuss shortly, were extreme in their emphasis on the individual as against society. It is significant that Mencius, representing the Confucian balance between public and private concerns, was appalled that "the words of Yang Zhu and Mozi fill the world. Yang is for selfishness, which is to have no lord; Mo is concerned for everyone, which is to have no father. To have no father nor lord is to be a bird or a beast" (Mencius 3B.9).[100] Elsewhere Mencius puts the contrast even more vividly:

> Yangzi chose selfishness; if by plucking out one hair he could benefit the world he would not do it. Mozi was concerned for everyone; if by shaving from his crown right down to his heels he could benefit the world he would do it . . . The reason for disliking those who hold to one extreme is that they cripple the Way. (Mencius 7A:26)[101]

Nonetheless, as Nivison points out, "Mencius was actually deeply influenced by both Mozi and Yang Zhu," and therefore we should not let the existence of sharp controversy lead us to overlook the fact that in the world of a "hundred schools" ideas were shared as well as contested.[102]

Yang Zhu

We have no text explicitly attributed to Yang Zhu, and even what scholars attribute to him in such texts as the *Zhuangzi* and the *Lüshi chunqiu* may be the words of his followers, as is so often the case with Warring States thinkers.[103] We have no idea of Yang's dates. If we believed that he really had dialogues with Confucius or Mozi (he could hardly have had dialogues with both) as are recounted in various texts, we would have to place him in the fifth century BCE, but it is more probable to date him some time in the fourth century. In any case he seems to represent a tendency toward radical withdrawal from society, exhibited at its extreme by those who chose to live as hermits. The *Zhuangzi* distinguishes between two types of hermits: those who withdraw to "mountain and valley," "discourse loftily and criticize vindictively," who as "condemners of the age, wither away and drown themselves"; and those who "head for the woods and moors, settle in an untroubled wilderness, angle for fish and live untroubled, interested only in Doing Nothing [*wuwei*]—such are the tastes of the recluses of the riverside and the seaside, the shunners of the age, the untroubled idlers."[104]

Yang Zhu (and, as we will see, Zhuangzi) clearly belongs to the second group. We hear of hermits in the *Analects*, but perhaps they come from a later period than that of Confucius himself, and the image of the hermit is only an extreme example of a withdrawal that could be less absolute. Graham offers some reflections that help us understand this significant tendency in Warring States thought:

> A philosophy entitling members of the ruling class to resist the overwhelming pressures to take office remained a permanent necessity in Imperial China.[105] Yangism is the earliest, to be superseded in due time by Daoism and, from the early centuries AD, by Buddhism. But Yangism differs from its successors in having nothing mystical about it. It starts from the same calculations of benefit and harm as does Mohism, but its question is not "How shall we benefit the world?" but "What is truly beneficial to man?", more specifically, "What is beneficial to myself?" Is it wealth and power, as the vulgar suppose? Or the life and health of the body and the satisfaction of the senses?[106]

Yang Zhu's teaching is easy to parody, but it is not as simple as it might seem. According to A. C. Graham, it should not be seen as a form of radical egoism, pitting the self alone against every other good, but rather as a form of selfishness, in which concern for nurturing one's own life is primary, but concern for others remains secondary, and indeed the doctrine of nurturing one's own life is seen as contributing to the general good if universally adopted.[107] As in the Mencius quote above, the idea of not giving one hair to benefit the world is a kind of trademark of Yangism. Let us look at a fuller account of this idea, as contained in a late work that Graham argues has early material embedded within it.

When a Mohist interlocutor asked Yang, "If you could help the whole world by the loss of a hair off your body, would you do it?" Yang replied that a hair wouldn't help the world. The interlocutor said, but suppose that it would? Yang was silent but a follower of his asked the interlocutor if he would give up some of his skin for a thousand in gold. The interlocutor said he would. Then the follower asked if the interlocutor would cut off a limb to obtain a state. At this point the interlocutor was silent. The follower then drove home his point: that many hairs could add up to skin; much skin could add up to a limb; starting down that road will come to a bad end; therefore how can one treat even a single hair lightly?[108]

In this interchange Yang Zhu does seem to verge on egoism. Yet consider the following, which starts out much as the above:

Yao resigned the Empire to Zizhou Qifu, who replied:

"It might not be a bad idea to make me Emperor. However, just now I have an ailment that is worrying me. I am going to have it treated, and have no time now to bother about the Empire."

The Empire is the weightiest thing of all, but he would not harm his life for the sake of it, and how much less for any other thing! Only the man who cares nothing for the empire deserves to be entrusted with the Empire.[109]

Here Zizhou's selfishness would seem to be absolute, but suddenly we are told that he above all deserves to be entrusted with the empire. Consider another Yangist passage, the opening passage of the "Making Life the Foundation" chapter of the *Lüshi chunqiu:*

Heaven is what first engenders life in things. Man is what fulfills that life by nurturing it. The person who is capable of nurturing the life that Heaven has created without doing violence to it is called the Son of Heaven. The purpose of all the son of Heaven's activity is to keep intact the life Heaven originally engendered. This is the origin of the offices of government. The purpose of establishing them was to keep life intact. The deluded lords of the present age have multiplied the offices of government and are using them to harm life—this is missing the purpose for establishing them. Consider the example of training soldiers: soldiers are trained to prepare against bandits; but if the soldiers who have been trained attack each other, then the original reason for their training has been lost.[110]

It would seem that at least some Yangists had a political teaching—one could almost say that every tendency in Warring States thought had a political teaching. Maybe one could say the same for ancient Greek thought, or axial age thought in general—that would be something to keep in mind. In the concern for the self as well as in the political conclusions drawn from it, the thought of Yang Zhou is clearly similar to that of the *Daodejing* and the *Zhuangzi*. What is missing is any concern for inner cultivation, to borrow a term from Harold Roth—that is, the practices of controlled breathing and mental concentration that were believed to lead to tranquility and insight—that is the hallmark of all strands of Daoism.[111] Even in the political teaching just quoted, the Son of Heaven is charged with "nurturing life," which could be seen as slightly more interventionist than the nonaction *(wuwei)* that is all that is required of the ideal Daoist ruler.[112] We really don't know when Yang Zhu or Zhuangzi lived or when the *Daodejing* was composed or written down, but it is reasonable to suppose that Yang was a predecessor of the Daoist thinkers, reacting strongly against the Mohists by claiming that benefit should be first of all for the sake of the individual, and only when that idea was established would all under heaven benefit. The Daoists, like the Confucians, shied away from the idea that benefit, even the benefit of a long life, was the central concern, although there remained a Yangist element in Daoism that would never be entirely lost in subsequent history.

The Farmers' School

Among the hermits of the Warring States period there was a group that developed an interesting ideology—namely, that everyone, even the rulers, should plough the fields and raise their own food. The believers in such an agrarian utopia, and we have some reason to believe that some of them practiced what they preached, revered and perhaps invented an "early king," even earlier than the Confucians' Yao and Shun, namely Shen Nong, the "Divine Farmer," who in earliest antiquity put this teaching into practice. The discovery of earlier and earlier "early kings" became more frequent as time went on, so that the principle of the earlier the king the later his appearance in historical texts was already exemplified here.

The teachings of the Farmers' School have been reconstructed from fragments embedded in the Han text, *Huainanzi:*

> Therefore the "Law of Shen Nong" says: "If in the prime of life a man does not plough, someone in the world will go hungry because of it; if in the prime of life a woman does not weave, someone in the world will be cold because of it." Therefore he himself ploughed with his own hands, and his wife wove, to give a lead to the world.
>
> In guiding the people, he did not value commodities difficult to obtain, did not treasure things without use. Consequently, any who did

not work hard at ploughing had no means to support life; any who did not work hard at weaving had nothing with which to clothe the body. Whether one had ample or less than enough was each person's own responsibility. Food and clothing were abundant, crimes and vices did not breed; they lived untroubled in security and happiness, and the world ran on an even level.[113]

The agrarian utopia of Shen Nong, needless to say, was a kind of rural anarchy, without punishments or authorities able to inflict them. Rather, all governed themselves in simple self-sufficiency. Graham notes that this ideal remained attractive long after the Warring States period, as is indicated by the many efforts to demonstrate that its principles were unworkable.[114] Although the Chinese were often enough governed by authoritarian states, there were always those who wished to withdraw from them as much as possible, and ideas that held that life could go on happily without them never completely died away. Only the Confucians developed an alternative, as we will see, and it was not a democratic one. It was, however, unlike withdrawal into private life or indulging in utopian dreams, concerned with ways to curb the worst excesses of tyranny, and, though it often failed, the degree of its success is perhaps measured by the long-term stability of the imperial Chinese political system.

Daoism

So far in this chapter we have rather blithely used such terms as "Confucianism," "Mohism," and "Daoism" as if they represented something like the doctrinal schools we are used to hearing about in Western classical philosophy—Platonism, Aristotelianism, Stoicism, Epicureanism, and so on. It is probably a mistake to reify the Greco-Roman schools any more than the Chinese ones. Each contained great diversity, conflicting student-teacher lineages that might even be called "isms," and markedly changing fortunes over time. We have already noted that in the Warring States period only Confucianism and Mohism could really be called schools. Now we must even qualify that assertion. If we think of doctrine as the primary basis for the definition of a "school," perhaps only Mohism would really count.

What we translate as Confucianism is in Chinese *Rujia,* perhaps more accurately translated as Scholarly School. There is some dispute over the meaning of *Ru*—some have imagined that it was a pre-Confucian term meaning "ritual specialists," of whom Confucius was supposedly one. Robert Eno, however, has argued convincingly that there are no pre-Confucian references to *Ru,* and that the *Rujia* was always connected to Confucius. He writes: "In sum, groups of men professionally skilled in ceremonial practice in ways similar to Confucius and his followers unquestionably existed prior to Confucius' time: however, virtually no evidence is found to suggest that the term '*ru*' was ever used to describe them. The term seems to have been an innovation originally intended to denote the new sect founded by Confucius."[115]

But the idea of the *Rujia* as the Scholarly School rather than "Confucianism" makes sense if we remember that Confucius defined himself as a transmitter rather than a creator, and that the Five Classics were at the center of the *Ru* tradition, namely, the *Odes (Shi),* the *Documents (Shu),* the three *Rites (Li)* canon, The *Changes (Yi),* and the *Spring and Autumn Annals (Chunqiu),* with the possible inclusion of a sixth classic, the lost *Music (Yue).* Note that neither the *Analects* nor the *Mencius* was among the Five Classics, though very much later, from the Song dynasty on, they became two of the Four Books that came near to replacing the Five Classics as the central texts of the Confucian tradition.[116] Although the Classics throughout Chinese history were absolutely central texts, some knowledge of which was essential to pass the examinations that were the gateway to office in imperial times, and the *Analects* was not among them, there was still a very strong relation between the Classics and Confucius, as evidenced in the words of Lu Jia at the very beginning of the Han dynasty: "The later ages declined and fell to waste. Thereupon, the later sage [i.e., Confucius] established the Five Classics and clarified the six arts to correspond to Heaven, govern Earth, and probe affairs."[117] Confucius may have been the "uncrowned king," but because he did not rule, he handed down the Five Classics to keep alive the forms of right order for a time when they could again be implemented. The Confucians were more deeply concerned with the preservation of the ancient Chinese tradition than any other school, so it is not surprising that they were known as the Scholarly School, or we might even say the Classicists. Even so, we have to remember that Confucius was always the patron saint of scholars in the classical tradition, so it is far from completely wrong to speak of the *Rujia* as Confucianism.

Harold Roth has a suggestion that will help clarify the way we should think of the various strands of Warring States thought. He holds that pre-Han schools should be defined in terms of practices or techniques (he uses these terms interchangeably) rather than doctrine. I would argue that Mohism is a partial exception, the one "school" that really was dogmatic. Roth describes these "techniques" as follows: "Broadly stated . . . for the Confucians, maintaining proper ritual in the family and the state; for the Mohists, economizing state and family expenditures to maximize the benefit of available resources; for the Legalists, establishing the rule of law and the methods of maintaining adherence to it . . . and, for the Daoists, the advocacy of mystical cultivation leading to uniting with the Way as the essential element of rulership."[118] Within the schools the primary form of organization was teacher-student lineages, leading to considerable diversity. Even the later Mohists were split into three mutually unfriendly sects. The differences between Mencius and Xunzi are only the most obvious of the many different tendencies in the Confucian school. The Daoists, who were not even called by that term until middle Han times, were always divided between followers of different teachers and the texts they took as central.

For convenience, I will organize my discussion of the major tendencies in Warring States Daoism using a typology developed by Harold Roth, even though the chronology he applies to it is contested.[119] Roth sees all strands of Daoism as being defined by mystical cultivation, but developing in three stages with respect to the social implications of their position: (1) "Individualist" because of its "virtual absence of social and political thought" (in my own view, no Chinese tradition can be called "individualist" in our sense of that term—here the meaning is that the focus is on self-cultivation without much concern for the social context); (2) "Primitivist" because of its advocacy of "a simple society and politic"; and (3) "Syncretist," because its teaching is "commended to the ruler as a technique of government, the emphasis on the precise coordination of the political and cosmic orders by the thus-enlightened ruler, and a syncretic social and political philosophy that borrows relevant ideas from the earlier Legalist and the Confucian schools."[120]

The *Neiye* Chapter of the *Guanzi*

According to Harold Roth, the *Neiye* chapter of the collective work, *Guanzi,* represents the earliest phase of what will come to be known as Daoism. Whether it is the earliest work in the Daoist tradition is disputed, but it surely represents the first of Roth's types, what he calls "Individualist," and which I would prefer to call the "Inner Cultivation" tradition, in that it contains almost no ethical or political references and is entirely concerned with the practice of self-cultivation. The text of the *Neiye* is in verse and may well represent teachings that were originally handed down orally. Roth follows

Brooks in holding that the transition from oral to literate took place approximately in the middle of the fourth century BCE, which may indicate a rough date for this text.[121] If the text is indeed this early, the technical vocabulary concerning cosmology and mystical practice may have been just developing, so that we need to be careful not to read into it later meanings of some key terms.

Without getting into too many technical details, we need to consider three important terms and their relation to the central term, *Dao,* itself. Self-cultivation is concerned with three aspects of the cosmos in which humans participate. The first is *qi,* a term so basic but so foreign to Western thought that it is usually left untranslated, which in the *Neiye* may still be understood as breath in humans and air in the natural world, but is already beginning to have the more general meaning of the "vital fluid" (sometimes translated as "ether" or "energy") out of which all things are made, but with different levels of refinement. The second term is *jing,* the "vital essence" of *qi,* which it is the purpose of meditation practices to nurture. Finally there is *shen,* originally meaning the spirits or divinities, but in the *Neiye,* according to Roth, having the more adjectival meaning of "numinous," a kind of fulfillment resulting from the cultivation of the *jing.*[122] However, all these terms are subsumed in the idea of the *Dao,* which has now become a central cosmological expression for the underlying unity of all reality. As noted above, *Dao,* literally "way," is to be found everywhere in early Chinese thought. It is generally said that in Confucian texts *Dao* points to the teachings of the school or the practices it advocates, although there are occasions where Confucian texts seem to carry cosmological meaning as well.

The *Neiye* has, according to Roth, more to say about the techniques of self-cultivation than more familiar texts such as the *Daodejing* or the *Zhuangzi.* Proper alignment of the body, involving stable sitting with limbs in order, and breathing techniques, are basic, but practices of mental concentration are also described.[123] If pursued diligently, these practices will lead to spiritual fulfillment, traditionally thought of in ancient China as becoming a sage, *"sheng,"* which Graham says is "for all the schools the ideal of the wisest man."[124]

To give an idea of the teachings of the *Neiye* I will quote what Roth considers to be the first poem in the sequence:

> The vital essence [*jing*] of all things:
> It is this that brings them to life.

It generates the five grains below
And becomes the constellated stars above.
When flowing amid the heavens [*tian*] and the earth
We call it ghostly and numinous [*shen*].
When stored within the chests of human beings,
We call them sages [*sheng*].[125]

In another poem, the fifteenth in Roth's edition, there is a pairing of the *Dao,* the Way, with the *xin,* which Roth translates as "mind," often also translated as "heart" or "heart/mind," and which he explains "is, for the early Chinese, the locus of the entire range of conscious experience, including perception, thought, emotion, desire and intuition."[126] The *xin* is where the *Dao* "happens," as it were, at least for the individual, and is an important term in subsequent Confucian as well as Daoist thought:

The Way fills the entire world.
It is everywhere that people are,
But people are unable to understand this.
When you are released by this one word [*Dao*]:
You reach up to the heavens above;
You stretch down to the earth below;
You pervade the nine inhabited regions.
What does it mean to be released by it?
The answer resides in the calmness of the mind [*xin*].[127]

Roth suggests that *Dao,* as "this one word," may have functioned as a mantra does in Indian forms of meditation—the word and the thing become fused.

The *Neiye* is concerned solely with cosmological ideas and practices of self-cultivation, but these ideas and practices are present in all other expressions of what can loosely be called the Daoist tradition, whatever else is added to them.

The *Zhuangzi*

The *Zhuangzi* is a far greater book than the *Neiye,* and, though there are significant parallels in contents, it is a very different book.[128] Like the *Neiye,* it is very much concerned with inner cultivation, but like the *Daodejing* it shows strong evidence of the Primitivist tendency. *Zhuangzi* is a book of great complexity and sophistication. It pushes the idea of the Way to an extreme and, in that it questions every aspect of given reality, it is clearly axial in its meaning. Yet in its refusal to be pinned down, its tendency to speak of the Way and then undercut the very way it speaks of the Way, it seems to be a Chinese version of negative theology. It calls in question every given reality, yet it quietly affirms the most mundane realities. To treat it adequately would transgress the limits of this chapter. What I will do instead is give a few of its many stories, allegories, parables, so that the flavor of the book may perhaps lead the reader unfamiliar with it to the text itself.

If the *Neiye* is a response to Confucianism, it is so silently, by its exclusive emphasis on inner cultivation and its lack of concern for ethics or politics. With the *Zhuangzi* (and the *Daodejing*) Confucius and his teaching are a frequent reference point, a butt of humor, or a source of error. The following story illustrates Zhuangzi's view of death and his opposition to Confucian teaching at the same time:

> The three men, Master Sanghu, Meng Zifan and Master Qinzhang, were talking together. "Which of us can be *with* where there is no being with, be *for* where there is no being for?[129] Which of us are able to climb the sky and roam the mists and go whirling into the infinite, living forgetful of each other for ever and ever?"
>
> The three men looked at each other and smiled, and none was reluctant in his heart. So they became friends.
>
> After they had been living quietly for a while Master Sanghu died. Before he was buried, Confucius heard about it and sent Zigong to assist at the funeral. One of the men was plaiting frames for silkworms, the other strumming a zither, and they sang in unison
>
> "Hey-ho, Sanghu!
> Hey-ho, Sanghu!
> You've gone back to being what one truly is,
> But we go on being human, O!"
> Zigong hurried forward and asked
> "May I inquire whether it is in accordance with the rites to sing with the corpse right there at your feet?"
> The two men exchanged glances and smiled.
> "What does he know about the meaning of the rites?"
> Zigong returned and told Confucius

"What men are these? The decencies of conduct are nothing to them, they treat the very bones of their bodies as outside them. They sing with the corpse right there at their feet, and not a change in the look on their faces. I have no words to name them. What men are these?"

"They are the sort that roam beyond the guidelines," said Confucius. "I am the sort that roams within the guidelines. Beyond and within have nothing in common, and to send you to mourn was stupid on my part."[130]

The three friends are surely among the "untroubled idlers" that Zhuangzi commended, and they shared his sense of the unity of life and death. In a similar passage Zhuangzi's friend Huishi criticized him when, after the death of his beloved wife, he was found "squatting with his knees out, drumming on a pot and singing." Zhuangzi explained that his wife was now "companion with spring and autumn, winter and summer, in the procession of the four seasons," and that she was "about to lie down and sleep in the greatest of mansions."[131] In short, for those who "roam beyond the guidelines" the formalities of mourning can be ignored. Indeed, such formalities are a limitation, a sign of a lack of understanding of the Way. In this passage Zhuangzi says that before we were born we were within the *Dao,* after we die we return to the *Dao,* and during our life, if we only knew it, we are also within the *Dao,* so what is there to worry about?

In both the *Zhuangzi* and the *Daodejing* there is a strong sense that things started out well when humans were merged with nature, but began to go downhill when culture was invented. In a variety of forms this expresses the Primitivist vision. Zhuangzi discusses the early human condition as a time of what Burton Watson translates as "Perfect Virtue." "Virtue" here translates *de,* a term discussed above in the section on Confucianism. As with the term "way" *(dao),* which in Confucianism usually referred to human beliefs and behavior, *de* (power, potency, virtue, in Confucianism) in the Daoist texts takes on a cosmological reference. Thus Zhuangzi says that in the earliest time,

the people have their constant inborn nature. To weave for their clothing, to till for their food—this is the Virtue *(de)* they share.[132] They are one in it and not partisan, and it is called the Emancipation of Heaven. Therefore in a time of Perfect Virtue the gait of men is slow and ambling; their gaze is steady and mild. In such an age mountains have no paths or trails, lakes no boats or bridges . . . In this age of Perfect Virtue men live the same as birds and beasts, group themselves side by side with the ten thousand things. Who then knows anything about "gentleman" [*junzi*] or "petty man" [*xiaoren*]? Dull and unwitting, men have no wisdom, thus their Virtue does not depart from them . . .

Then along comes the sage, huffing and puffing after benevolence [*ren*], reaching on tiptoe for righteousness [*yi*], and the world for the first time has doubts.[133]

From there it is all downhill.

Both the *Zhuangzi* and the *Daodejing* define their teachings in opposition to those of the Confucians, very much on the grounds that the latter officiously interfere with the natural functioning of life by trying to regulate people with rules and norms. Opposed to such interference, they teach *wuwei* (nonaction, or "Do Nothing," as we saw above). Actually the term *wuwei* appears in the *Analects* in a late passage cited above, and Edward Slingerland argues that the idea, as opposed to the term, is pervasive in the *Analects,* where it points, not, as in Daoism, to an original position, but to the result of long training so that one does what one ought to do "naturally," without thinking, so to speak. So nonaction is another of those terms that pervades all of early Chinese thought, though meaning different things in different contexts.[134]

In one of his vivid parables Zhuangzi makes the case for *wuwei.* The story is about Hundun, who, Hans-Georg Moeller says, "had a perfect and permanent life at the *center* of the world, but was *devoid* of personal features—he had no face."[135] The passage at the end of book 7 of the *Zhuangzi* is as follows:

> The Emperor of the South Sea was Fast, the Emperor of the North Sea was Furious, the emperor of the centre was Hundun. Fast and Furious met from time to time in the land of Hundun, who treated them very generously. Fast and Furious were discussing how to repay Hundun's generosity.
>
> "All men have seven holes through which they look, listen, eat, breathe; he alone doesn't have any. Let's try boring them."
>
> Every day they tried boring one hole. On the seventh day Hundun died.[136]

Moeller adds, "Guo Xian comments laconically on this story: *'Activism killed him.'* "[137]

The *Daodejing*

The most famous of all "Daoist" texts is surely the *Daodejing*, purportedly written by Laozi, for whom the text is also often named. It is the most often translated of Chinese texts and one of the most often translated texts in the world. It is usually paired with the *Zhuangzi* and has been so from the Han dynasty. In the Warring States period, however, it was transmitted and discussed separately from the *Zhuangzi*. In spite of their, to us, similar teachings, and their parallels with the *Neiye*, they were apparently transmitted by different lineages and not seen as parts of a single tradition until a considerably later time.[138] Formally the *Zhuangzi* is closer to the *Analects* than to the *Daodejing*: it has poetic moments but is mostly prose; it contains anecdotes and conversations similar to, though considerably more developed than, the *Analects*. Unlike the *Mozi*, with its continuity of argument, but similar to the *Analects*, each segment of the text stands alone. If it has a consistent teaching, it is built up from a variety of insights from various points of view, not by sustained argument. Like almost all early Chinese texts, with the exception of the *Mozi* and possibly the *Xunzi*, it is hazardous to try to find a "system" in thought that prefers to move from insight to insight rather than through systematic reflection.

In these respects, the *Daodejing* is similar to the *Zhuangzi*, but in other ways it is quite different. For one thing, like the *Neiye* it is entirely poetic; it could even be considered one long poem, though from early on it has been divided into two parts and 81 chapters. Rather than stories, allegories, and parables, in which the *Zhuangzi* revels, its teaching is largely expressed in a series of striking images or metaphors, metaphors that have become emblematic of "Daoism" throughout the world.

Hans-Georg Moeller makes the point that the *Daodejing* is not a "book" as we think of a book, that is, writing intended to be read silently, with a beginning, middle, and end, and remembered or forgotten as we happen to feel. Rather, even after the text was written down, and its earliest versions were probably oral, it was intended to be listened to, ultimately memorized—internalized—by those for whom it was formative. Its texture is recursive rather than linear, which means one can start anywhere and find connections with everything else in the text.[139] In most of these regards the *Daodejing* is similar to the other texts treated in this chapter, indeed to many of the texts treated in this book. But in its dense network of images and metaphors the *Daodejing* does express a power that many readers have found unique.

Within the constraints of this chapter, I can give the reader only a hint of the richness and complexity of the original.

Moeller starts his examination of the text with the short chapter 6, in part because it contains so many central images. As one of the "darker," more mysterious passages, this chapter has attracted the attention of other translators. Let us start with Moeller's translation:

> The spirit [*shen*] of the valley does not die—
>   This is called dark femininity.
> The gate of dark femininity—
>   This is called: root of heaven and earth.
> How ongoing!
>   As if it were existent.
>   In its use inexhaustible.[140]

D. C. Lau's translation is not very different, yet suggests how the use of different English words can change the overall impression:

> The spirit of the valley never dies,
> This is called the mysterious female.
> The gateway of the mysterious female
> Is called the root of heaven and earth.
> Dimly visible, it seems as if it were there,
> Yet use will never drain it.[141]

Arthur Waley translates this similarly, but uses "Doorway" instead of "gate" or "gateway," capitalizes "Heaven" and "Earth," and translates the last two lines thus:

> It [the valley spirit] is there within us all the while;
> Draw upon it as you will, it never runs dry.[142]

These examples give only a very elementary sense of how this highly condensed text can be variously read by highly knowledgeable Sinologists. In addition, Waley thinks this chapter may have circulated independently as part of "the stock of early Daoist teaching," and finds it, or passages similar to it, in other early Chinese texts.[143] Lau suggests "the remote possibility that the language used here is an echo of some primitive creation myth."[144]

Let us look at some of the individual terms that appear in this short chapter, as they provide an entry into the rich world of images and metaphors that pervade the *Daodejing*. We can briefly note that the word all three translators translate as "spirit" is the ancient word for minor divinities, *shen,* as in "ghosts and gods," *gueishen,* which we commented on in the discussion of the *Neiye.* Moeller argues that here "spirit" is impersonal and implies "a kind of virtue, strength or power, like, let's say, the 'American spirit.' "[145] That may be true, but the resonance with older ideas of divinity has survived, because the graph *shen,* even up to the present, has never lost that reference.

With the term "valley," we are already in the heart of *Daodejing* thinking. As Waley puts it, "The valleys, then, are 'nearer to *Dao*' than the hills; and in the whole of creation it is the negative, passive, 'female' element alone that has access to *Dao,* which can only be mirrored 'in a still pool.' "[146] It is the lowness of valleys to which the water comes, creating rivers that eventually run into the great water, the sea. And water itself is another central image; as chapter 8 puts it: "Highest good is like water. Because water excels in benefiting the myriad creatures without contending with them and settles where none would like to be, it comes close to the way."[147] It is the relative formlessness of the valley as compared to the mountains that makes it an effective image.

Chapter 15 links it to another whole set of related images:

Falling apart like thawing ice;
Thick like the uncarved block;
Vacant like a valley;
Murky like muddy water.
Who can be muddy and yet, settling, slowly become limpid?
Who can be at rest and yet, stirring, slowly come to life?
He who holds fast to this way
Desires not to be full.[148]

Thawing ice, uncarved wood, an empty valley, and muddy water are all apparently formless, and, in the eyes of the world, worthless, yet it is through these that the way is attained.

The metaphors of the *Daodejing* build up a complex of paradoxes in which what seems weak overcomes what seems strong. Nowhere is this more evident than in the exaltation of the feminine; chapter 61, for instance, asserts: "The female overcomes the male / by constant stillness."[149] And in chapter 28:

Know the male
But keep to the female
And be a river to the world.
If you are a river to the world
Then the constant virtue will not desert you
And you will again return to being a babe.[150]

The baby, like the woman, seems weak but is really strong. Both are closer to the source than the man or the adult, are closer to the root, another metaphor in our first example, chapter 6. The root might seem insignificant—dirty, hidden—when compared to the mature plant, but it is the source of the plant's life, it is the essential; it seems not to be doing anything, yet it does everything.

There is a debate over whether the *Daodejing* can be called "quietist," but the essential point is that in the end what prevails is quiet, not bluster and force. It is in this way that the "negativity" of the *Daodejing* is to be understood, that is, its identification of the *Dao* with "Nothing": it is from Nothing that Something comes:

Turning back is how the way moves;
Weakness is the means the way employs
The myriad creatures of the world are born from Something,
    and Something from Nothing.[151]

And it is in this context that we must understand *wuwei* in the *Daodejing.* The first line of chapter 37: "The Dao does nothing *(wuwei),* and nothing remains undone," or, more literally, "Nothing doing; nothing not done."

Michael LaFargue is the one scholar who has tried to give a social context for the teaching of the *Daodejing.* He believes that the teaching arose among a group of "*shi*-idealists," using the word *shi,* as we have seen, to designate a group that descended from the lowest rank of the nobility but had come to mean officials, or just educated people, in the Warring States period.[152] The idealists among the *shi* were those concerned with the state of society and with their own moral integrity. Under the harsh conditions of the Warring States, many of the *shi,* though they were by vocation trained for official service, were unemployed or underemployed and had become disillusioned with the current political situation. They did not turn to rebellion, but they did turn to criticism.

Whereas Confucians criticized the behavior of the ruling class and tried to convince the rulers of the day to follow the example of the ancient kings, the *Daodejing* engages in a frontal assault on contemporary cultural assumptions, such as that the high is better than the low, men are superior to women, and so on, assumptions held not only by the ancient Chinese but by most of the world's cultures. It is this assault, purveyed in vivid metaphors and images of which I have only been able to give a very few, that has appealed to readers for a long time in China and in recent years to readers all over the world.

Daoist Primitivism

As we have already seen in the *Zhuangzi*, the assault on the commonsense understanding of reality was conducive to a sense that things were better in the beginning, when humans lived "the same as birds and beasts," a horrifying idea for Confucians. This preference for simpler days, which has been called Daoist Primitivism, is nowhere better exemplified than in chapter 53 of the *Daodejing*:

> Reduce the size and population of the state. Ensure that even though the people have tools of war . . . they will not use them . . .
>
> Even when they have ships and carts, they will have no use for them; and even when they have armour and weapons, they will have no occasion to make a show of them.
>
> Bring it about that the people will return to the use of knotted rope [instead of writing],
> Will find relish in their food
> And beauty in their clothes.
> And will be content in their abode
> And happy in the way they live.
> Though adjoining states are within sight of one another, and the sound of dogs barking and cocks crowing in one state can be heard in another, yet the people of one state will grow old and die without having had any dealings with those of another.[153]

In what is almost as extreme a rejection of culture as in the *Zhuangzi* passage, it is clear that the Confucian virtues, "the huffing and puffing about benevolence and righteousness," as Zhuangzi put it, would come in for the same treatment. Indeed that is the case, as we find in chapter 38:

Therefore when the way is lost, virtue *(de)* appears; when virtue is lost, benevolence *(ren)* appears; when benevolence is lost, propriety *(yi)* appears; when propriety is lost, ritual *(li)* appears. Ritual is the husk of loyalty and trustworthiness, the way of calamity.[154]

It would seem that the Daoist rejection of conventional beliefs and complex culture includes a rejection of the normative order as well, because in the ideal Daoist society everything operates "without doing" *(wuwei)* or, like the *Dao,* "by itself" *(ziran)*. Things will "naturally" run well without the need of interference, and the ideal ruler will rule by not ruling. One might argue that there is indeed a Daoist moral order, even a feminist moral order, of gentleness and yielding in place of aggression and interference, but gentleness in the end is not recommended because it is good or right but because it "works." D. C. Lau, in his introduction to his translation of the *Daodejing,* suggests that the book is best interpreted as a "survival manual" for harsh times: one should make oneself small and scarce to stay out of trouble.[155] At best this is a teaching for "untroubled idlers" or isolated villagers, for those seeking to avoid the society that actually existed, not for its reform. Of course an almost antinomian ethic of the sort the *Daodejing* implies is perennially attractive, and only contributes to the lasting popularity of the text.

Heiner Roetz, however, offers an interesting interpretation in terms of Kohlberg's scheme with which he evaluates early Chinese thought. Though I find his interpretation in many ways problematic and at best suggestive, it is still worth considering. Roetz argues that Daoism as represented by the *Zhuangzi* and the *Daodejing* firmly rejected "conventional morality" (Kohlberg's stages 3 and 4), but did not securely reach "post-conventional morality," as represented in stages 5 and 6. Instead, it could be said to have attained a stage 4½, which he describes, following Kohlberg, as:

The stage of "anything goes," the phase of youthful protest. What is right is a question of arbitrary subjective decision. This stage is characterized by a radical rejection of the alienated conventionalism of Level B [conventional morality] and the recourse to the naïve pleasure principle of Level A [preconventional morality]. Instead of new normative rules, this stage proclaims a provocative "beyond good and evil." It is postconventional but not yet principled.[156]

In applying this idea, he says that the "Zhou Daoists"

> can be interpreted as exemplary representations of Kohlberg's Stage
> 4½. The gesture of exposing moralism, the nonconformist symbol-
> ism . . . the rejection of conventional compulsion and the emphasis on
> individual life—all this fits well with the stage of youthful protest . . .
> More than any other school, the Daoists personify the adolescent crisis
> in Chinese society . . . And even if today the unembarrassed frankness
> of the Daoists, much more than the sedate earnestness of most Confu-
> cians, appeals to us, it is probably because it evokes reminiscences of the
> naive spontaneity of childhood.[157]

Roetz does give credit to one aspect of Daoist ethics, not the least important today: "Daoist naturalism undoubtedly contains the idea of universalism. That this universalism is not discursively mediated has one advantage:
not solely the members of the linguistic community, but everything belonging to nature, also that which cannot speak, a priori falls within its range.
Ethics is macroethics from the beginning."[158] But it is the very "naturalism"
of Daoist thought, its emphasis on the *Dao* as "inactive" *(wuwei)* and nature
as everything happening "by itself" *(ziran)* that disables Daoism from telling
us how to act, even though it tells us a lot about how not to act. If in nature
everything is perfect as it is, then returning to nature is all we have to do.
Among other things there is a remarkable absence in Daoist thought of the
dark side of nature, of the fact that aggression and dominance are as natural
as their opposites. In these ways Daoism is postconventional, but offers us no
postconventional ethic.

The Politics of the Dao

The *Zhuangzi* and the *Daodejing* contain some of the most biting social criticism in any early Chinese text. Book 10 of the *Zhuangzi* says, "He who steals
a belt buckle is put to death, but he who steals a country becomes a feudal
lord."[159] The *Daodejing* says, "The people are hungry because those above eat
up too much in taxes; this is why the people are hungry."[160] Along the same
lines chapter 53 says:

> The court is resplendent;
> Yet the fields are overgrown.

The granaries are empty;
Yet some wear elegant clothes;
Fine swords dangle at their sides;
They are stuffed with food and drink;
And possess wealth in gross abundance.
This is known as taking pride in robbery.
Far is this from the Way![161]

Both the *Zhuangzi* and the *Daodejing* are well aware of the cost of warfare to ordinary people:

Where troops have encamped
There will brambles grow;
In the wake of a mighty army
Bad harvests follow without fail.[162]

Sharp as these criticisms are, they do not lead to any proposals of reform. Rather, these bad conditions are merely symptoms of how far society has fallen from its original form.

In the light of these criticisms of the rulers of the warring states, it is not only a shock but rather strange to learn that there was a relationship between Daoism and Legalism from the earliest times.[163] What could be more manipulative and domineering than the technology of tyranny that the Legalists developed? Legalism consists largely of recipes for enhancing political and military power, but without any moral foundation. At best, in a bad scene, the Legalists (Arthur Waley called them "Realists")[164] could say that tyranny is better than anarchy. Yet when the Legalists did toy with the idea of an overarching cosmology, it was always Daoism to which they were attracted. Why?

First, just a word about Legalism, to which I have referred, but which I have not defined. As usual in early Chinese thought, the term "Legalism" covers a number of thinkers and texts that differ between themselves. As Burton Watson puts it, Legalist texts belong to a genre of technical literature that is only marginally philosophical. They are instruction manuals along with "treatises on divination, medicine, agriculture, logic, military science, and so forth."[165] In terms of the axial problem, Legalism is certainly an example of a rather advanced rationalism—as Benjamin Schwartz says, "instrumental rationalism" in the Weberian sense, oriented to "the enrichment of the state and the strengthening of its military capacity," as one Legalist put it.[166]

Schwartz argues that one early legalist, Shen Buhai, developed a theory of bureaucracy, and that "the emergence of a 'theory' of bureaucracy is a most significant event in the world history of sociopolitical thought."[167] The late Warring States figure Han Fei, whose work, the *Hanfeizi,* summed up the Legalist teaching, remained, in spite of protests against his immorality, of perennial interest to later generations.[168]

The teaching that gives the school its name was its emphasis on law, on rewards and punishment, but especially punishments, as the key to effective government. This emphasis put the Legalists at odds with the Confucians, who believed that rule by punishments was a symptom of the failure of rule by virtuous example, and, one would have thought, at odds with Daoists as well. Legalist teaching was entirely oriented to the ruler and consisted largely of advice as to how a ruler could obtain and increase power. It is this narrow focus that makes Legalism marginal in this chapter, and it is the link to Daoism that explains why a discussion of it occurs only at the end of the discussion of Daoism.

No one has put more succinctly the parallels between Daoism and what he calls Realism than Arthur Waley:

> With Daoism Realism has a very real and close connection. Both doctrines reject the appeal to tradition, to the 'way of the Former Kings,' upon which the whole curriculum of the Confucians was based . . . Both condemn book learning and would have the people kept "dull and stupid," incurious of all that lies beyond their own village and home. Even the mystical doctrine of *wu-wei,* the Non-activity of the ruler by which everything is activated, finds a non-mystical counterpart in Realism. When every requirement of the ruler has been embodied in law and the penalties for disobedience have been made so heavy that no one dares to incur them, the Realist ruler can sink deep into his cushions and enjoy himself; "everything" (just as in Daoism) "will happen of its own accord."[169]

Waley goes on to point out that major Legalist/Realist texts, such as the *Hanfeizi,* often use Daoist imagery and, though very critical of other schools, especially the Confucians, seldom have anything negative to say about the Daoists. For an example of Legalist Daoism, we might look at a couple of passages from the "Wielding Power" chapter of the *Hanfeizi:*

> Do not let your power be seen; be blank and actionless. Government reaches to the four quarters, but its source is in the center. The sage

holds to the source, and the four quarters come to serve him. In emptiness he awaits them, and they come to serve him as needed.

And again:

> This is the way to listen to the words of others: Be silent as in a drunken
> stupor. Say to your self: Lips! Teeth! Do not be the first to move . . . If
> you show delight, your troubles will multiply; if you show hatred, re-
> sentment will be born. Therefore discard both delight and hatred, and
> with an empty mind become the abode of the Way.[170]

The third chapter of the *Daodejing* would seem to be all too compatible
with Legalism:

> Therefore in governing the people, the sage empties their minds but fills
> their bellies, weakens their wills but strengthens their bones. He always
> keeps them innocent of knowledge and free from desire, and ensures
> that the clever never dare to act.
>   Do that which consists in taking no action, and order will prevail.[171]

It seems that what links Daoism and Legalism is an opposition to moral-
ism; the danger is that together they reject morality. Into the vacuum of
Daoist Primitivism comes the centralized power of the Legalist state. And
the Legalists have their own explanation of why government by virtue no
longer works. In ancient times people were few and resources plentiful; today
people are many and resources few. What required little government then
requires harsh punishments today:

> Hence, when men of ancient times made light of material goods, it was
> not because they were benevolent, but because there was a surplus of
> goods; and when men quarrel and snatch today, it is not because they
> are vicious, but because goods have become scarce . . .
>   When the sage rules, he takes into consideration the quantity of things
> and deliberates on scarcity and plenty. Though his punishments may be
> light, this is not due to his compassion; though his penalties may be
> severe, this is not because he is cruel, he simply follows the custom ap-
> propriate to the time. Circumstances change according to the age, and
> ways of dealing with them change with the circumstances.[172]

It is in this way that the Legalists opposed the Confucian use of the old to criticize the present, and preferred a "Daoist" responsiveness, leavened by a little economic determinism, instead.

But the third type of Daoism, the Syncretist, mentioned early in this section, did not consist of a union of Daoism and Legalism. The rapid collapse of the Qin dynasty after its remarkable unification of the whole country, forever tainted that ideological option. Somehow a moral basis of rule was necessary after all, and though Han Syncretism included Daoism and Legalism to be sure, Confucianism now became an essential and increasingly dominant element, as is already evident in the early Han Syncretist work, *Huainanzi.*[173]

Mencius

Mencius—in Chinese, Mengzi—is one of only two Chinese thinkers whose names have been conventionally Latinized, the other being Confucius. Such is a measure of his importance. The *Mencius,* written by Mencius with additions by his disciples, belongs together with the *Analects* as a basic text in the Confucian tradition. Like the *Analects,* it consists largely of anecdotes and conversations, but the selections are considerably longer than those in the *Analects,* and, though the book is in no sense a continuous philosophical treatise, arguments are more fully developed than those in the earlier book. Although Confucius and his teachings are the indispensable starting points for him, Mencius was born close to a century after Confucius died (Mencius's dates are uncertain but are usually thought to be about 390–310 BCE), and the world of thought to which he was responding was richer and more complex than that which Confucius faced. Thus many teachings that we take for granted as Confucian were actually added by Mencius.

It is fair to say that Mencius took Confucius as his role model. Mencius too was an itinerant teacher, trying to persuade feudal lords, or quasi-illegitimately self-styled "kings," to put his teachings into practice, accompanied by a group of students as Confucius had been. But whereas Confucius still hoped for a rejuvenation of the Zhou dynasty, Mencius had given up hope for that possibility and, in accordance with the spirit of his age, began to look forward to a new dispensation, one in which Heaven would give the mandate to a new ruler who would bring about the just society for which Confucius hoped. In accordance with ideas about earlier dynasties, the new regime would unite the whole world under one ruler—a universal ruler and a universal ethic would go together. As Benjamin Schwartz puts it, Mencius shared with many of his contemporaries "an apocalyptic expectation that the time is ripe for a restoration of the *dao*."[174]

Although Mencius did not think much of the feudal lords of his day, he was always seeking one who, under his tutelage, could become virtuous enough to bring order to the world. The following account shows what Mencius was looking for.

> Mencius saw King Xiang of Liang. Coming away, he said to someone, "When I saw him at a distance he did not look like a ruler of men and when I went close to him I did not see anything that recommended respect. Abruptly he asked me, 'How can the world be settled?'
>
> 'By unification,' I said.
>
> 'Who can unite it?'
>
> 'One who is not fond of killing can unite it,' I said.
>
> 'Who can give it to him?'
>
> 'No one in the world will refuse to give it to him. Does your majesty not know about young rice plants? Should there be a drought in the seventh or eighth month, these plants will wilt. If clouds begin to gather in the sky and rain comes pouring down, then the plants will spring up again. This being the case, who can stop it? Now in the world among the shepherds of men there is not one who is not fond of killing. If there is one who is not, then the people of the world will crane their necks to watch for his coming. This being truly the case, the people will turn to him like water flowing downwards with a tremendous force. Who can stop it.?' "[175]

In this passage, with its vivid imagery, Mencius does indeed strike an apocalyptic note.

It is also clear that Mencius had an extraordinary sense of his own vocation at this critical moment in history. As we will see, he, like Confucius, felt called by Heaven, but he, also like Confucius, felt thwarted by Heaven. It was his task to accept Heaven's decrees, though not necessarily happily, as is suggested in the following passage:

> When Mencius left Qi, on the way Chongyou asked, "Master, you look somewhat unhappy. I heard from you the other day that a gentleman reproaches neither Heaven nor man."

"This is one time; that was another time. Every five hundred years a true King should arise, and in the interval there should arise one from whom an age takes its name. From Zhou to the present, it is over seven hundred years. The five hundred mark is passed; the time seems ripe. It must be that Heaven does not as yet wish to bring peace to the world. If it did, who is there in the present time other than me? Why should I be unhappy?"[176]

As Schwartz makes clear, Mencius did not think he or Confucius could actually become the Son of Heaven unless appointed by a sage king, as Shun had been chosen by Yao. But in their "exalted conception of the virtuous minister," each could have been the mentor of such a king.[177] One should note that, by Mencius's count, Confucius lived at the appropriate 500-year mark, and he himself at the overdue 700-year mark. They thus had the aura of the savior king about them, even if Heaven had decided the time was not ripe.

Although his political intent was central to his vocation, political disappointment did not deter him from the equally Confucian concern for self-cultivation. In the end, what one would achieve in the world was up to Heaven, but what kind of person one would become was up to the individual. He expresses his position succinctly as follows:

> Extensive territory and a vast population—the gentleman may desire this, but his [true] delight is not here. To stand in the center of the empire, to bring peace to the people within the four seas—the gentleman may delight in this, but what makes up his nature is not here. What the gentleman has as his true nature cannot be added to even by the greatest deed [rulership] and cannot be diminished even by dwelling in poverty. This is because he is certain about his task. What the gentleman has as his true nature—humaneness [*ren*], justice [*yi*], ritual [*li*], and wisdom [*zhi*]—is rooted in his heart [*xin*].[178]

Mencius shows a surprising blend of elitism and populism. What is "rooted in the heart" of the gentleman, the four primary virtues—humaneness *(ren)*, justice *(yi)*, ritual *(li)*, and the knowledge of good and evil *(zhi)*—have at least the beginnings, as we will see below, in everyone's heart. Human nature is fundamentally common to all:

> All palates have the same preference in taste; all ears in sound; all eyes in beauty. Should hearts prove to be an exception by possessing nothing

in common? What is common to all hearts? Reason and rightness. The
sage is simply the first man to discover this common element in my
heart.[179]

Nonetheless, the gentleman, due to self-cultivation, will, as we saw above,
maintain his virtuous heart in spite of hardship or adversity, whereas the
people "will not have constant hearts if they are without constant means."[180]
It is the responsibility of the ruler, and of the gentleman in so far as he is an
effective advisor to a ruler, to assure the people of "constant means." Thus
Mencius attacks the rapacious ruler who reduces the circumstances of the
people to misery, not only for his inhumanity, but for depriving the people of
the possibility of being virtuous.

Mencius can be as scathing in his social criticism as were the Daoists. As
he said to King Hui of Liang:

> There is fat meat in your kitchen and there are well-fed horses in your
> stables, yet the people look hungry and in the outskirts of cities men
> drop dead from starvation. This is to show animals the way to devour
> men . . . If, then, one who is the father and mother to the people, in rul-
> ing over them, cannot, in ruling over them, avoid showing animals the
> way to devour men, wherein is he father and mother of the people?[181]

Here Mencius tells King Hui rather bluntly that he is not a king.

Nothing angers Mencius more than the incessant warfare of the period in
which he lives and the reasons for it:

> In wars to gain land, the dead fill the plains; in wars to gain cities, the
> dead fill the cities. This is known as showing the land the way to devour
> human flesh. Death is too light a punishment for such men.[182]

Another time King Xuan of Qi asks Mencius, concerning Zhou, the evil last
king of the Shang dynasty killed by King Wu, whether regicide is permissi-
ble. Mencius replied:

> A man who mutilates benevolence [ren] is a mutilator, while one who
> cripples rightness [yi] is a crippler. He who is both a mutilator and a
> crippler is an "outcast." I have indeed heard of the punishment of the
> "outcast Zhou," but I have not heard of any regicide.[183]

The idea that an evil king is not a king, and so killing him is not regicide, is not unique to ancient China, but it is not an archaic idea. Mencius, however, is not preaching revolution, even though the implications of his teaching were revolutionary enough to lead some later leaders, not only in China but also in Japan, to expurgate the offending passages in his text. His advice to advisors of unjust rulers is to withdraw from service if possible, and if not, to do what they can to mitigate the ruler's evil intentions. But the populist side of Mencius makes it clear that in the long run it is the people who decide:

> The people are of supreme importance; the altars to the gods of earth and grain come next; last comes the ruler. That is why he who gains the confidence of the multitudinous people will be the Son of Heaven.[184]

In Mencius's nonviolent view, an evil ruler will simply be abandoned rather than overthrown because the people will turn to a good ruler "like water flowing downwards with a tremendous force," as we saw above.

It is Mencius's clear elevation of a moral standard above the existing political status quo that makes him exemplary of the axial turn in ancient China. Without abandoning the courtesies that political hierarchy demands, he nonetheless places the true gentleman above any ruler when it comes to virtue. Mencius recounts approvingly the response of Zisi, the grandson of Confucius and perhaps a link in his own disciple lineage, to an inquiry from Duke Mu of Lu:

> Duke Mu frequently went to see Zisi. "How did kings of states with a thousand chariots in antiquity make friends with Gentlemen?" he asked. Zisi was displeased. "What the ancients talked about," said he "was serving them, not making friends with them." The reason for Zisi's displeasure was surely this. "In point of position, you are the prince and I am your subject. How dare I be friends with you? In point of virtue, it is you who ought to serve me? How can you presume to be friends with me?"[185]

The Confucians apparently agreed with Aristotle that friendship is possible only between equals, not between superior and inferior. Here the gentleman provisionally accepts the dubious legitimacy of the ruler while insisting on the superiority of his own virtue.

Thus although Mencius believes the people have the last word—indeed, he expresses a version of *vox populi, vox dei,* as when he quotes the *Documents,* "Heaven sees with the eyes of the people. Heaven hears with the ears of the people,"[186] and is thus in some sense legitimately seen as a populist—he nonetheless believes firmly in the existence of an elite of virtue. Let us consider more closely how he can hold both beliefs.

Mencius is famous for arguing that human nature is good, particularly in contrast to Xunzi, who is said to believe that human nature is evil. This is a complex issue with a long history of argument that I need not explore at length in this chapter.[187] What is clear is that Mencius believed that everyone has the "beginnings" of virtue by nature, along with a lot of other beginnings that may not turn out to be virtuous. As A. C. Graham has pointed out, what the Chinese meant by "nature" [*xing*] is not exactly what we mean by "inborn nature," but rather the potentiality for development over the life course.[188] So here "the goodness" of human nature consists in the fact that everyone has the potentiality for the development of the primary human virtues if they are properly nurtured. In the famous passage where he describes the universal presence of moral possibilities, he begins, "No man is devoid of a heart sensitive to the sufferings of others."[189] Because "heart" *(xin)* is a key term in Mencius's moral psychology, let us examine it further, as it is the key to a better understanding of Mencius's argument.[190]

We have already seen that "heart" is a key term in the proto-Daoist *Neiye,* which is a chapter in the collective work *Guanzi* that is believed to have been produced by a group of scholars in the state of Qi in the fourth century and later. Mencius spent some time late in the fourth century at what is known as the Jixia Academy in Qi, the perhaps overly pretentious name for this group, and there is internal evidence that Mencius read the *Neiye,* because some fairly technical terms were common between them. The *Neiye,* unlike the *Zhuangzi* and the *Daodejing,* lacks any polemical attack on Confucianism. Graham speculates that the *Mencius* may, therefore, date from a period before the split between Confucianism and Daoism had become clear. In short, Mencius may have advocated methods of self-cultivation not too different from those of the progenitors of Daoism.[191]

In particular, Mencius discusses the cultivation of *qi,* the vital energy that is the source of our possibility of moral action, using a term that is almost identical with a term in the *Neiye*—namely, "floodlike" or "vast" qi *(hao ran zhi qi),* which, when properly nourished, "will fill the space between Heaven and Earth."[192] Such extraordinary *qi,* says Mencius, "is born of accumulated rightness [*yi*]," the standard of which "is set in one's heart."[193] Here we have a kind of self-cultivation that, though clearly related to that of the *Neiye,* is linked to morality in a way absent in that text. And for Mencius, the heart is the source of moral feelings, capable of discrimination if properly developed, and thus includes what we would think of as mind as well as heart, although it is moral, not primarily cognitive, intelligence that is at issue here. The point then is that, though everyone has the potentiality to develop an advanced moral consciousness, only the hard work of moral self-cultivation is likely to succeed in realizing it. Ordinary people, pressed by the needs of survival, have the moral instincts but lack the time and energy to develop them fully. Thus, if a virtuous ruler should arise and radiate his "virtue," *de,* in its archaic sense of almost physical energy, then the people can respond. Otherwise it is the gentleman, who can persist in virtue through prosperity and poverty, who is its keeper.

Throughout the discussion of central moral issues there is a recurrent reference to Heaven in Mencius. Such references are also to be found in Daoist texts, where they are often assumed to have become simply another way of referring to nature, or perhaps Nature. In Confucianism generally, but surely in Mencius, though naturalizing tendencies are not absent, a theistic element is firmly present.[194] A key passage is this:

> Mencius said, "For a man to give full realization to his heart is for him to understand his nature, and a man who knows his own nature will know Heaven. By maintaining a firm hold on his heart and nurturing his nature he serves Heaven. Whether he is going to die young or live to a ripe old age makes no difference to his steadfastness of purpose. It is through awaiting whatever is to befall him with a perfected character that he stands firm in his proper destiny."[195]

Mencius was prepared to accept the verdict of Heaven as to when a new and better age might dawn, an age where a virtuous king, or one capable of accepting the advice of virtuous advisors, would unify the realm and bring a better life, material and moral, to the people. Such was not to be the way that unification would actually come, but the ideal that Mencius stood for would never subsequently be forgotten. To sum up his teaching, I will quote what is perhaps the most famous passage in the *Mencius,* and in its finest translation, that of Arthur Waley:

> The Bull Mountain was once covered with lovely trees. But it is near the capital of a great State. People came with their axes and choppers; they

cut the woods down, and the mountain has lost its beauty. Yet even so, the day air and the night air came to it, rain and dew moistened it till here and there fresh sprouts began to grow. But soon cattle and sheep came along and browsed on them, and in the end the mountain became gaunt and bare, as it is now. And seeing it thus gaunt and bare people imagine that it was woodless from the start. Now just as the natural state of the mountain was quite different from what now appears, so too in every man (little though they may be apparent) there assuredly were once feelings of decency and kindness; and if these good feelings are no longer there, it is that they have been tampered with, hewn down with axe and bill. As each day dawns they are assailed anew. What chance then has our nature, any more than that mountain, of keeping its beauty? To us, too, comes the air of day, the air of night. Just at dawn, indeed, we have for a moment and in a certain degree a mood in which our promptings and aversions come near to being such as are proper to men. But something is sure to happen before the morning is over, by which these better feelings are ruffled or destroyed. And in the end, when they have been ruffled again and again, the night air is no longer able to preserve them, and soon our feelings are as near as may be to those of beasts and birds; so that anyone might make the same mistake about us as about the mountain, and think that there was never any good in us from the very start. Yet assuredly our present state of feeling is not what we begin with. Truly,

"If rightly tended, no creature but thrives;
If left untended, no creature but pines away."[196]

Xunzi

Xunzi is the third great Confucian thinker of the Warring States period, ranking with Confucius and Mencius, even if his reputation has suffered more ups and downs than theirs. The relatively well-preserved book that goes by his name differs from that of his great Confucian predecessors in that it is primarily a collection, not of anecdotes and dialogues, but of well-reasoned essays—covering the major issues of Warring States thought and staking out his own position in critical response to most of the other major thinkers of the period. David Nivison says that he is "the first philosopher in China who could be described as 'academic' in the modern sense," and A. C. Graham says that "no other pre-Han thinker has organized the full range of his basic ideas in such coherently reasoned essays."[197] Chronologically Xunzi brings the Warring States period to a close: one conjectural set of dates has him born in 310, possibly the year of Mencius's death, and dying in 215, six years after the Qin unification of the empire. As Mencius's life spanned most of the fourth century, Xunzi's spanned most of the third.

The social conditions that Xunzi faced in the third century were, if anything, even worse than those that Mencius faced in the fourth, and he continues the tradition of sharp social criticism. Even though his conception of social order is hierarchical, with great emphasis on the obligations of inferiors to superiors, and, like all Confucians, he cannot conceive of a good social order without monarchy and the guiding hand of an ethical elite, he, like Mencius, still takes the people as a barometer of the legitimacy of a ruler:

> The ignorant are permitted to instruct the wise; the unworthy are permitted to oversee the worthy. The life provided the people is impoverished and oppressive. Their obligatory service is toilsome and bitter. It is for this reason that the Hundred Clans [the people] consider their rulers as base as a witch and hate him as they do ghosts. Each day they hope to detect any opportunity to band together to overthrow him and ultimately to drive him into exile.[198]

It is the ruler's "insatiable and ravenous appetite constantly to desire the possessions of others" that results in oppressive taxation of the people, their impressment to build his lavish palaces and gardens, and their conscription to fight in his wars, and the consequent endangerment of his state.[199] For one who desires safety, "the best thing for him to do is to govern fairly and love the people." It is these considerations that lead Xunzi to quote an "old text," which says, "The ruler is the boat and the common people are the water. It is the water that bears the boat up, and it is the water that capsizes it."[200]

Xunzi, no more than any other early Chinese thinker, concludes from the idea that the people are basic and the ruler is legitimate only if he cares for them, that what is needed is a new institutional order in which the people would have a say in their own government. The Daoists toy with the idea of no government at all, but the only practical way of following that prescription would be to withdraw from society and become a hermit. Xunzi and other Confucians thought that the idea of the people governing themselves could only be a prescription for anarchy. For Xunzi the idea that human nature (*xing*) is evil—perhaps better translated as human nature is bad, because the idea of radical evil was absent in ancient China—arises from his sense that our nature consists primarily of numerous and insatiable desires, and that without government, something like the Hobbesian war of all against all would result as each attempted to satisfy his desires at the expense of others. Perhaps in the harsh conditions of the third century, Mencius's modest idea that human nature contained, along with numerous desires, at least the beginnings of moral impulses, seemed too optimistic to Xunzi. For him, external discipline was the secret to the development of morality, but for him, too, something internal must understand and want such discipline.

It was Xunzi's rejection of Mencius's idea that "human nature is good" that probably did more harm to his long-term reputation than anything else, and a vast literature has grown up around this issue, both in China and among Western scholars. Here I can only seek to understand Xunzi's position without entering the full complexity of the controversy.[201] The fundamental problem in understanding Xunzi's position is how, if our nature is "bad," anyone ever became virtuous in the first place. In his own terms, Mencius has the same problem, because if the moral impulses, left untended, will quickly wither away, who, then, will be motivated to tend them? The answer, in both cases, is the heart or heart/mind *(xin),* but this answer raises new questions. For Mencius the heart seems to be the source of moral intuitions that have the power to nurture the moral impulses of human nature until they produce, through self-cultivation, a genuinely moral person, a *junzi* or gentleman, who in turn can instruct others. We saw that he drew, perhaps, from the proto-Daoist *Neiye* for this idea.

A. C. Graham argues that Xunzi's idea of the heart is indebted to Zhuangzi, except that in its depth it has a moral intuition that Zhuangzi did not observe. He quotes from book 21 of the *Xunzi:*

> How does man know the Way? By the heart. How does the heart know? By being empty, unified and still. The heart never ceases to store, yet something in it is to be called empty; to be multiple, yet something in it is to be called unified; to move, yet something in it is to be called still. From birth man has knowledge, and in knowledge there is memory; "memory" is storing, yet something in it is to be called empty—not letting the already stored interfere with the about-to-be-received is called being empty. From birth the heart has knowledge, and in knowledge there is difference; of the "different" it knows each at the same time, and it knows each at the same time is multiple, yet something in

it is to be called unified—not letting one of them interfere with another is called being unified. The heart when sleeping dreams, when idling takes its own course, when employed makes plans, so never ceases to move, yet something in it is to be called still—not letting dream and play disorder knowledge is called being still.[202]

This passage could be seen as an attempt to understand the wonderful capacity of the mind, and Nivison suggests that *xin* in Xunzi "is *mind* now, not mind-heart,"[203] yet Graham still translates *xin* here as heart—maybe we can never be sure that *xin* means only one end of the heart–mind continuum.

The mind, in another metaphor with a long history, is, for Xunzi, like still water: it can reflect reality perfectly and can lead us to morality. But water is easily disturbed, so the mind is not an infallible instrument—only the properly trained mind will lead us in the right direction.[204] Xunzi exalts the Sage Kings, Yao, Shun and Yu, but particularly the "later kings," the founders of the Zhou dynasty, because we know most about them, as the ones who got things right and whose example remains true for all time. We might think, then, that the sages were some kind of extraordinary beings, different, somehow, from ordinary humans, yet Xunzi is at pains to disabuse us of that idea:

> The man in the street can become a Yu . . . If the man in the street applies himself to training and study, concentrates his mind and will, and considers and examines things carefully, continuing his efforts over a long period of time and accumulating good acts without stop, then he can achieve a godlike understanding and form a triad with Heaven and Earth. The sage is a man who has arrived where he has through the accumulation of good acts.[205]

It would seem that anyone who uses his mind properly, and doesn't rely on his inborn feelings, his nature *(xing),* as Mencius thought, would, with sufficient long-term effort, become a sage, a moral exemplar. And yet how do "godlike understanding" and "forming a triad with Heaven and Earth" suddenly get into it?

Just as there is a problem with translating *xin* as "heart" or "mind," there is a problem of translating *Tian* as "Heaven" or "Nature." In his "Discourse on Nature"[206] (book 17), Xunzi is at pains to differentiate what we would call natural events from human moral norms. That is, evil rulers do not necessarily cause earthquakes and other natural disasters; indeed, Xunzi insists that "human portents"—such as evil government that leads to untended fields and people dying by the roadside—that are the real portents of the fall of states. Here we see a rejection of what Max Weber would call magic, but not necessarily the emergence of a "secular" view of nature. The triad of Heaven, Earth, and man suggests a cosmological resonance, so that when human affairs are in order, this is in accordance with Heaven:

> When the work of Heaven has been established and its accomplishments brought to completion, when the form of man is whole and his spirit is born, then love and hate, delight and anger, sorrow and joy find lodging in him. These are called his heavenly emotions. Ears, eyes, nose, mouth, and body all have that which they perceive, but they cannot substitute for one another. They are called the heavenly faculties. The heart [xin] dwells in the center and governs the five faculties, and hence it is called the heavenly lord.[207]

It would seem that just as Heaven is Lord of the cosmos and the king is lord of the state, so the heart/mind is the (heavenly) lord of the bodily faculties. Here we have a resonance that is not magical but, in the Chinese context, is surely religious.

There are moments when Xunzi seems to think of the xin as calculating, weighing, and seeing that disorder is harmful to human beings and order beneficial; so that establishing the moral order is a way of overcoming anarchy and violence, and thus a utilitarian good. But at a deeper level Xunzi rather clearly assumes that morality is a good in itself, is the very essence of our humanity:

> Fire and water possess energy [qi] but are without life [sheng]. Grass and trees have life but no consciousness [zhi]. Birds and beasts have consciousness but no sense of duty [yi]. Man possesses energy, life, consciousness, and in addition a sense of duty. Therefore he is the noblest being on earth.[208]

For the gentleman, the moral man, there is no calculation of self-interest, only a deep commitment to doing what is right (yi):

> When justice [yi] is at stake, not to bow one's head before power and look after one's own benefit, and not to change one's convictions even if

the whole empire is offered to one, to uphold justice and not to bend oneself, though taking death seriously—this is the courageousness of the scholar and the gentleman [*shi* and *junzi*].[209]

Even without the beginnings of virtue in one's nature, one's heart has the capacity and the independence to make autonomous judgments, as securely as a Kantian:

The heart [*xin*] is the ruler of the body and the master of its godlike intelligence. It gives commands, but it does not receive any from anywhere. It prohibits and permits by itself, it decides and chooses by itself, it becomes active and stops by itself. Thus the mouth can be forced to be silent or to speak, and the body can be forced to bend or stretch itself, but the heart cannot be forced to alter its opinion. If it regards something as right, then it accepts it, and if it regards something as wrong, then it rejects it. Therefore I say: The heart is free and unobstructed in its choices. It sees all things for itself. And although its objects are complex and manifold, in its innermost essence it is undivided itself.[210]

Nonetheless, the heart when properly cultivated will not be capricious or arbitrary: what it will discern is the true Way, and the rituals *(li)* that embody it—it will not stray from the examples of the Sage Kings: "Ritual is the ridgepole of the Way of Humanity."[211]

I have not emphasized the more authoritarian side of *Xunzi,* his willingness to use punishments in an age when government by ritual alone seemed unrealistic, his willingness even to compromise with less than noble rulers if they will be better than the worst at the time. We cannot forget that two of the greatest Legalists, Han Fei and Li Si, were his students, however much they betrayed both the letter and the spirit of his teaching. And the idea that for Xunzi morality does not arise from within but can only be imposed from without, a half-truth as we have seen, is generally considered "conservative."

Nonetheless Xunzi uttered or affirmed some of the most radical ideas to be found anywhere in early Chinese thought; above all: "Follow the Dao and not the ruler, follow justice and not the father."[212] Given the heavy emphasis on obedience to rulers and fathers in imperial Confucianism, with the requirement that one remonstrate but never disobey when one differs from such superiors, this short sentence seems almost revolutionary.[213] Another hierarchical relation of central importance in the Confucian tradition is that of teacher and student. But Xunzi subjects even this relationship, and himself in it, to this firm ethical standard:

> He who criticizes me and is right is my teacher. And he who agrees with me and is right is my friend. But he who flatters me is my enemy.[214]

As we saw in connection with "the man in the street," one attains such high ethical standards neither easily nor "naturally." One has to work hard to become a moral person, and, in Xunzi's view, emphasizing a point more central in the *Analects* than in the *Mencius,* through study, through the Classics, and with the help of a worthy teacher who can spur one on and show one the way. One of Xunzi's achievements was to underline the centrality of the Classics and the necessity of constant study, something that became embedded in the tradition even when Xunzi was relatively forgotten. And among those things that had to be studied, nothing was more important than ritual *(li)* and music *(yue)*. Treatises on these subjects are among the most important in the *Xunzi.*

Xunzi's book 19 is devoted to ritual *(li)* and, as we might expect, has a great deal of detail about proper ritual, especially the sacrifices carried out by rulers at various levels and funeral rituals for rulers and others. Ritual in this sense is a continuation of the early idea of ritual contained in the "great services" discussed in the *Zuo zhuan* and referred to early in this chapter. But book 19 also contains more general discussions of the place of ritual in human life, something even close to a theory of ritual, and so it is one of the richest sources for the understanding of early Chinese thought about ritual.[215]

Xunzi begins the chapter with a discussion of human desires, which, as we have noted, are extensive and insatiable and, if not ordered, will be the source of chaos and violence. The Sage Kings, however, established ritual not in order to suppress desires but to regulate them, so that they can be fulfilled in the right way. Xunzi makes the point with the clear statement: "The meaning of ritual is to nurture."[216] Naturally, Xunzi insists that each rank of society has its own appropriate rituals, so that the ritual order reinforces the social hierarchy that all early Chinese thinkers except the Daoists took as natural.

In his description of how ritual works, Xunzi reaches an intensity that gives rise to a rhymed verse that seems to be something like a cosmological hymn to the effects of ritual:

All rites begin with coarseness, are brought to fulfillment with form, and end with pleasure and beauty. Rites reach their highest perfection when both emotion and form are fully realized . . .

Through rites, Heaven and Earth are conjoined,
the sun and moon shine brightly,
the four seasons observe their natural precedence,
the stars and planets move in ranks,
the rivers and streams flow,
and the myriad things prosper.
Through them, love and hate are tempered,
and joy and anger made to fit the occasion.[217]

As Paul Goldin indicates, "There is only one Way. The Sage Kings apprehended it, and their rituals embody it. There is no other Way, and no other constellation of rituals that conforms to the Way. It is through the Way, moreover, that Heaven plays a role in our lives."[218] Goldin compares Xunzi's idea of the Way ordained by Heaven that embodies the rituals with the Western idea of natural law ordained by God.[219]

Ritual, according to Xunzi, is not logical and so cannot be refuted by shallow theories.[220] The understanding of ritual requires an advanced stage of self-cultivation, and so only the sage fully understands it: "The sage clearly understands ritual, the scholar and gentleman find comfort in carrying it out, officials of government have as their task preserving it, and the Hundred Clans incorporate it into their customs."[221] But good customs are moral customs, and Xunzi is clear that rule by punishment makes the common people devious in the attempt to obey only the letter of the law, whereas rule by ritual will make them desire to be moral.

Book 20 is devoted to music and, as it is often paired with ritual, partakes of many of the same characteristics. It, too, is based on emotion and involves the forming of emotion. With music, however, the central emotion is joy: "Music is joy," the chapter begins.[222] It should be noted that the same graph could be read "music" or "joy" leading to occasional, perhaps sometimes intentional, ambiguities as to which word is meant. Early in the chapter Xunzi writes, "Men cannot live without music," which might also be read "Men cannot live without joy." In any case, music is essential to a fulfilled human life, and Xunzi scoffs at the Mohists for thinking otherwise. Because ritual almost always involves both music and dance, the overlap between the two is considerable, so that Xunzi's theory of ritual also applies largely to music.

With both ritual and music, learning is required to avoid the extremes of overindulgence or (particularly in the case of funerals) self-flagellation resulting in bodily injury. It is the mean that is required, and it is knowledge that helps us find the mean. For Xunzi, morality in every sphere is not "natural," but comes only with hard and unremitting learning and an understanding of the great exemplars of the past.[223] Philip Ivanhoe ends his discussion of moral self-cultivation in Xunzi with a passage from book 1:

> I once spent a whole day in *si* "reflection," but I found it of less value than a moment of *xue* "learning." I once tried standing on tiptoe and gazing into the distance, but I found I could see much farther by climbing to a high place.

Ivanhoe points out that the high place was "the edifice of culture," the climb to it took one on "the steep and rugged path of learning," but that the result "afforded a vast and incomparable view."[224]

This chapter has covered a great deal of ground, but I feel, before closing, the necessity of a cautionary note. In Chapters 6 and 7, concerned with ancient Israel and ancient Greece, we seemed to be on relatively firm ground. Educated Westerners are assumed to have some background in both these cultures. Many educated Westerners read classical Greek or Hebrew. Relatively few Westerners read classical Chinese. Even among educated East Asians, only a few read classical Chinese. A. C. Graham, one of the greatest twentieth-century scholars of early Chinese thought, in answer to the charge that classical Chinese is a "vague" language, wrote in 1961, "Most Western sinologists (including myself) read literary Chinese without being able to write it . . . None of us yet knows classical Chinese."[225] John Knoblock, in the preface to the third and final volume of his complete translation of the *Xunzi,* wrote in 1994, commenting on the fragmentary state of preservation of early Chinese texts, "The disorder of the preserved Chinese philosophy is evident to any serious student."[226] If people who have devoted their lives to the study of early Chinese thought are so uncertain, how can one as dependent on them as I be sure that I am saying anything of value?

When we try to understand the axial age, and even more what came before it, we are dealing with worlds long ago and far away. It is hard to emphasize enough how different these societies were from our own, and how tempting it is to find in them what we want to find. I have kept up with the more widely read studies in the fields of ancient Israel and ancient Greece since undergraduate days. I have the simplest knowledge of Greek, enough to allow me to see in a bilingual text what Greek term lies behind the translation, and that makes me only slightly less dependent on the translator. I have no such knowledge of Hebrew. But it is probably an illusion to think we understand Israel and Greece better than ancient China; their very familiarity may betray us, has betrayed many great scholars, to find what at the moment our culture wants to find.

Actually I am a little better prepared for the study of ancient China than I am in the other three axial cases.[227] But this is cold comfort if one thinks of the problems that Graham and Knoblock raised. More than in many fields, consensus in the study of ancient thought is fragile, central issues are contested. Those on whom I depend, and I myself, raise questions that we cannot definitively answer. I have done my best to give a coherent account, but it should be treated as an extended hypothesis, one possible interpretation, not something that anyone can be certain of.

That said, let me see what conclusions I can draw about axial-age China. I have emphasized and perhaps overly reified "Confucianism," a move not popular today when we are enjoined to look at the marginal and the peripheral. I have not ignored other tendencies in Chinese thought, even some fairly peripheral ones such as the Farmers' School, but I have focused on Confucianism, not only because it would have the greatest influence on later Chinese culture, but because it illustrates most clearly the axial transition in ancient China.[228] In the discussion of how we are to define the axial transition, some idea of "transcendence" has frequently been put forward. Benjamin Schwartz, more than anyone else, has argued that there was a transcendental breakthrough in China and that it occurred in Confucianism as well as in other Warring States schools of thought. It would be well to remember Schwartz's definition of transcendence in this context: "The word 'transcendence' is a word heavy with accumulated meanings, some of them very technical in the philosophic sense. What I refer to here is something close to the etymological meaning of the word—a kind of standing back and looking beyond—a kind of critical, reflective questioning of the actual and a new vision of what lies beyond."[229] It is true that Schwartz also argued for a more substantive kind of transcendence in China, namely a religious transcendence associated particularly with the idea of Heaven *(Tian)*, and that he was not convinced by the notion that Heaven in later Confucianism had lost all religious meaning and had become just another word for "nature." He insisted, as we have noted earlier, that the contrast between a naturalistic and a theistic interpretation of Heaven in early Chinese thought is "an antithesis which we impose on the text."[230] I have not been impressed by those like Mark Elvin who have argued the contrary view.[231] I think the treatment of the major Warring States Confucian texts in this chapter sufficiently illustrates why I think transcendence in axial-age China, in both its formal (as in Schwartz's definition above) and substantive—that is, religious—senses, can be found in Confucianism. I also have tried to show why the major non-Confucian tendencies, although in many ways meeting the definition of axial thought, failed to develop coherent axial cultural systems capable of exerting critical pressure on all subsequent Chinese society and culture to the same degree that Confucianism did.

Nonetheless one must still come to terms with Max Weber's extraordinarily brilliant and influential study of the religious ethic of China, in which he emphasized this-worldly immanence and the absence of a tension between the transcendental and mundane worlds that he thought characterized Chinese culture in general and Confucianism in particular.[232] Although Schwartz's case for transcendence in ancient China has been widely, but not universally, accepted, there has been a tendency to see ancient China, and again Confucianism in particular, as "this-worldly," in a sense bringing it closer to Greece than to the "otherworldly" cases of Israel and India.

Although I think the case for China as illustrating "this-worldly transcendentalism" is a strong one, it is one I would want to qualify somewhat, even with respect to Confucianism. The case for this-worldliness in Confucianism rests on the idea that if there is a notion of "salvation" in Confucianism, it is a political one: salvation will be realized in the political realm just as it once was realized in the political realm of the ancient Sage Kings. Certainly my discussion of the apocalyptic element in Mencius's thought, the idea that the realization of the *Dao* in the reign of a new sage king might be imminent, suggests the validity of this idea. Yet in Confucius, Mencius, and Xunzi there is an ideal of human self-cultivation leading to an identification with an ultimate moral order, with the *Dao* and the will of Heaven, that is available to individuals, however grim the social situation and however much they may seem to have "failed" to bring good order to society. This idea, too, could be seen as "this-worldly," and there was surely no emphasis on life after death or reward in any future rebirth, but it was a powerfully religious ideal that was quite independent of any worldly reward except a good conscience.

A quasi-religious faith such as Communism depended entirely on the realization of a new, ideal, political order, and it withered away when its this-worldly utopia failed to appear. If Confucianism had depended entirely on a political form of salvation, it might have met the same fate; surely its powerful personal faith in transcendent morality at whatever cost is what allowed it to survive political failure time and time again.

Nowhere was the failure more evident than at the time of the unification of the empire by the victorious armies of Qin in 221 BCE. Not the Sage King that Mencius had expected, but the exact opposite, the kind of tyrant most feared by Confucians, brought the unification about. The unifier of China, Qin Shihuangdi, was under the influence of Legalist teaching, and he ordered that Confucian books be burned and Confucian scholars buried alive.[233] As his prime minister, Li Si, who was responsible for this policy and for much else that brought the Qin to universal power, put it, "Anyone referring to the past to criticize the present should, with all the members of his family, be put to death."[234]

Li Si, as noted above, had been a student of Xunzi's, but when he chided his former teacher for relying on humaneness and righteousness when what counted was a strong army and expedient policies, Xunzi replied that such a view was shortsighted and such a regime could not last long.[235] As it turned out, Li Si was executed in 208 BCE as a result of factional conflicts after the death of the First Emperor; his execution was carried out by having him literally cut in half. Xunzi's prediction had been right: the ruthlessness of the Qin dynasty guaranteed that it would last only a few years. All succeeding Chinese dynasties, however, until the end of the Qing dynasty in 1911, were caught in the tension between an essential element of Confucian legitimation and Legalist domination, and we can hardly say that that tension is over. We might remember that Mao Zedong was a great admirer of Qin Shihuangdi!

Confucianism's lasting influence in the political realm was its ability to uphold a normative standard with which to judge existing reality, and never to compromise that standard completely. What Qin Shihuangdi (r. 221–210) tried to do, and a powerful Han emperor, Han Wudi (r. 140–87 BCE), imitated him in the attempt, was to make himself divine and immortal, with the help of *fangshi* (specialists in invoking the spirits and aiding the attainment of immortality). Michael Puett has described the process: "The Qin-Han sacrificial system involved a radically new approach. The goal was for the ruler to contact personally as many divine powers as possible in order to obtain their power . . . to become a Di [god] and to exercise direct power over the world of forms. In short, ideologically the empires under the First Emperor and Emperor Wu functioned as a celestial imperium, with the rulers as the organizing thearchs."[236] Even the Shang monarchs had not claimed to be divine, though, as ancestors, they would be worshipped after their death. The emergence of divine kingship at this point in Chinese history shows it as a structural possibility at any point in time, even though it is identified primarily with archaic civilizations. In the cases at hand, the function is clear. It involved an "end run" around the Confucians: if the emperors were divine, how could Confucians hold them up to the judgment of Heaven? By the end of Western Han (late first century BCE) the Confucians had reasserted themselves and reinstated what they understood to be the traditional sacrificial system. As Puett describes it: "In this new system, it is humans who create the center by establishing a capital and then properly aligning Heaven and Earth. This involves neither the theomorphic will to align the cosmos nor an attempt to become a spirit in accord with the patterns of the universe. Rather, it supports a hierarchy of Heaven and man; humans create the center of the cosmos, and Heaven judges man's success."[237] Never again would the systems of self-divination of Qin Shihuangdi and Han Wudi be revived. The "traditional" system would continue through all subsequent dynasties. Needless to say, it would be the Confucians who would decide the degree to which the rulers were conforming to Heaven's mandate. The axial separation between earthly rule and divine sanction was secured.

S. N. Eisenstadt has emphasized the deeper meaning of Chinese thisworldly transcendentalism and the sense in which it is always sociopolitical and personal:

> [The Chinese] mode of overcoming the tension between the transcendental and the mundane order, especially as it developed in neo-Confucianism but the roots of which exist also in the earlier, classical Confucianism, emphasized very strongly the non-traditionalistic, reflexive definition of the nature of the cosmic order and of human existence. This definition contains within itself a continuous principled awareness of the tension between the cosmic ideal and any given reality; the imperfectability of the mundane order in general and the political one in particular; its only partial legitimation in terms of the basic cosmic harmony, and the great personal tensions involved both in the attempts to maintain such harmony through proper conduct and atti-

tude, which necessitates a very stringent and reflexive self-discipline, as well as in the development of a critical attitude to the existing mundane world in general and political order in particular.[238]

Eisenstadt is, in this passage, correcting Weber's sense of Confucianism as only "adapting" to the world. Weber's notion of Confucianism was not without some basis in the ideology that was established in imperial times. Mark Csikszentmihalyi quotes the Warring States text *Guoyu (Discourses of the States)* as saying, "Serve one's lord with reverence, serve one's father with piety," a sentiment endlessly repeated down through Chinese, indeed through all East Asian, history for millennia.[239] But Xunzi's firm injunction—"Follow the Dao and not the ruler, follow justice and not the father"—was never entirely forgotten. Theodore de Bary has given examples of Confucians who followed Xunzi's injunction—particularly about questioning the ruler; it was much harder for Confucians to imagine disobeying a parent—throughout Chinese history.[240]

Simon Leys comments on Confucius's original move to reinterpret the notion of the *junzi,* literally, the lord's son, usually translated "gentleman," from the designation of a hereditary elite to the designation of a moral elite:

This view was to have revolutionary consequences: it was the single most devastating ideological blow that furthered the destruction of the feudal system and sapped the power of the hereditary aristocracy, and it led eventually to the establishment of the bureaucratic empire—the government of the scholars. For more than two thousand years, the empire was to be ruled by the intellectual elite; to gain access to political power, one had to compete successfully in the civil service examinations, which were open to all. Until modern times, this was certainly the most open, flexible, fair, and sophisticated system of government known in history (it is the very system which was to impress and inspire the European *philosophes* of the eighteenth century).[241]

Leys is already projecting well beyond the period with which this chapter is concerned, but given Weber's enormously influential analysis of China as a stagnant, traditional society, it is perhaps well to point out that such was not the heritage of the axial age to later Chinese history.

Heiner Roetz, whose work, in spite of my problems with some of it, has been enormously suggestive for me in writing this chapter, has insisted on

ethical universalism as a measure of the successful axial transition in Warring States China, and I think he is right in so doing.[242] Far from adapting
to the world, these great early Confucians stood against the currents of their
time, giving examples that would long survive them. At the end of the text of
Xunzi, in Knoblock's translation, there is a "Eulogy," whose provenance
Knoblock does not give. Nonetheless, some excerpts from this eulogy, with
its description of what it meant to be a true *junzi,* can stand as a fitting conclusion to this chapter:

> Those who offer persuasions say: Xun Qing was not the equal of Con-
> fucius. This is not so. Xun Qing was oppressed by a chaotic age and
> lived under the intimidating threat of stern punishments. On the one
> hand there were no worthy rulers, and on the other hand he faced the
> aggression of Qin. Ritual and moral principles were not observed. The
> transforming effects of teaching were not brought to completion. The
> humane were degraded and under constraint. The whole world was lost
> in darkness. Conduct that strove after completeness was ridiculed and
> derided. The feudal lords engaged in the greatest of subversions . . .
> Nonetheless, Xun Qing cherished in his heart the mind of a great
> sage, which had to be concealed under the pretense of madness and
> presented to the world as stupidity . . . This is why his fame and reputa-
> tion are not plainly evident, why his followers are not legion, and why
> his glory and brilliance are not widely known.
> Students of today can obtain the transmitted doctrines and remain-
> ing teachings of Xun Qing in sufficient detail to serve as a model and
> pattern, the paradigm and gnomon, that establish the standard of the
> whole world. His presence had the effect like that of a spirit, and wher-
> ever he passed by he produced transformation. If one closely inspects his
> good works, one could see that even Confucius did not surpass him.[243]

Moving though this tribute is, we need not decide the question of who
surpassed whom. In the end it was the teaching of Confucius, developed and
elaborated by Mencius and Xunzi, and by many more Confucians in later
years, that proved to be the most enduring and influential strand in the Chinese tradition from early times virtually to the present.

9

The Axial Age IV: Ancient India

It is with more than a little trepidation that I begin this chapter on India in the axial age. Of the four axial chapters, this is the one for which I was least prepared and had furthest to go with my research. In the case of ancient Israel, Greece, and China I had read the major primary texts in translation for most of my adult life and was aware of the major secondary literature. In preparing for those chapters I had to review much that I thought I knew and, in particular, do a lot of reading in recent secondary literature to be, so far as possible in this kind of comprehensive book, up to date with current thinking. I started each of those chapters with what one might call graduate student competence. But with respect to India I have started at the freshman level, without a knowledge of the major texts in translation or the major secondary works either.[1]

In addition to the amount of elementary work I had to do to prepare for this chapter, there were difficulties I found with respect to the Indian case relative to the three others. There are a great number of texts from first-millennium BCE India, as large as or larger than those from any of the other three cases.[2] Furthermore, the most important of them were transmitted orally and continued to be transmitted orally long after written Sanskrit appeared. In any case, evidence for writing does not date from before the third century BCE, and the first reliable dates begin with the inscriptions of Aśoka, who reigned from 273 to 232. The earliest text, the *Ṛgveda*, is variously dated from many thousands of years BCE to the late centuries of the second millennium BCE, the latter being more reasonable. But most Sanskrit texts, oral or written only in relatively recent times, can be dated only on grounds of linguistic age (and occasional internal evidence) to tell which is older than which.[3] Richard Lariviere calls this system of dating "a chronological house of cards," because if there is a mistake in the dating of one text, the whole system is in danger of collapsing.[4]

It is even problematic whether we can speak of "texts" for speech that was orally transmitted. Behind the written texts of the other three axial cases there was, to be sure, an oral tradition, and a great deal of work has been done trying to figure out exactly how it worked. Homer is the obvious example, but in Israel and China too there is evidence of oral transmission behind the texts that have come down to us. In every case, detailed arguments about the oral traditions have been contested, because, by the nature of the case, inference is all we have. Milman Parry carried out field work in Yugoslavia in the 1930s studying traditional Serbo-Croat oral poetry.[5] He argued that various techniques still in use at that time by Serbo-Croat bards, involving mnemonic devices and type phrases to fill out metrical lines, were also to be found in Homer, thus helping us understand its underlying oral basis. But one of the things Parry discovered, and in this what he found is similar to oral traditions all over the world, is that when a bard says he is "exactly repeating" a poem—even one of his that was previously recorded—he is in fact creating a new one, with structural resemblances to previous versions, but not exact verbal repetition.[6]

What makes the Indian case unique is the claim, generally believed by Indologists, that the oral transmission of these early texts is exact, word for word, even to the accents involved. What makes this believable is that the oral transmission continues to this day and seems to be accurate to the smallest detail, more accurate than the printed texts or the relatively late manuscripts that lie behind them. Thus the Indic development of what has been called hyperorality, a complex system of cross-checking for verbal accuracy, turns out to be a unique kind of oral technology that is the functional equivalent of writing. Given that in all the great traditions even written texts were often memorized and transmitted orally, with the written texts used only as prompts to memory, we must consider that we are everywhere dealing with speech as much as writing. The Indian case, however, is unique in its emphasis on orality.[7] The most sacred texts, especially the Vedas, were actually prohibited from being written—only oral transmission was considered authentic—and were probably not written until at least the middle of the first millennium CE.[8]

In addition to these "textual" problems there is a great deal of argument, one could say intense controversy, over early Indic history, particularly the role of the "Aryans" in it. We should note that the Indo-Aryan-speaking peoples who entered northwest India in the second millennium BCE did indeed call themselves *Ārya* (which originally meant "hospitable," but came to mean "noble" or "honorable," the source of our word "Aryan"); the term gained its more general and unsavory implications only in recent times. Our earliest texts are, to be sure, in an archaic form of Sanskrit, which is an Indo-Iranian language, closely related to Avestan Persian, and part of the Indo-European language family. Colonialist scholars tended to see in early India an Aryan invasion across the passes of the northwest, with hordes of chariot-riding Aryan warriors descending on and defeating the aboriginal inhabitants, whom they subordinated as a class of serfs while imposing their language and culture on them. Indian nationalism in the twentieth century created a counternarrative in which the whole Indo-European language family arose in India and then spilled out into Iran, Central Asia, and eventually Europe. Although this theory has little to recommend it, running counter to the entire known history of India, which has for millennia seen the incursion of one people after another from Afghanistan or Central Asia over the northwest passes, it has contributed to a rethinking of the "Aryan conquest" hypothesis.

Rather than a single mass descending in one body, the linguistic and other evidence from the earliest texts suggests that there were numerous, perhaps relatively small, groups that filtered into India, fighting with each other as much as with the preexisting inhabitants, and gradually acculturating to what they found. In this scenario classical Indic culture can be seen as an amalgam of the culture of the Aryan migrants and that of the indigenous inhabitants. Although this story is convincing, we cannot really know in any particular case what is Aryan and what is indigenous, because we have only Sanskrit texts, even though we can be pretty sure that what we have is some kind of mixture.[9] Some early scholars spent a great deal of time trying to separate out the two strands (or more than two, given that India was probably quite diverse at the time the Aryans arrived, nor were the Aryans necessarily homogeneous themselves), later scholars have tended to feel that we must just attend to what we have and not worry too much about what came from where. In any case the texts that we have are in various forms of older or later Sanskrit, or, in the case of early Buddhism, in Pali, a Middle Indo-Aryan dialect related to Sanskrit. Although there are words derived from Dravidian and other non-Indo-European languages, the texts in the axial period are all Indo-Aryan in one form or another.

It would be well to mention briefly the Indus Valley or Harappan civilization, which was at its zenith from roughly 2600 to 1900 BCE. I had initially wanted to discuss this Bronze Age civilization together with comparable cases in Chapter 5, which included ancient Egypt, Mesopotamia, and Shang China, but evidence of the sort that would allow me to reconstruct the religion was missing. The Harappan civilization was in many respects remarkable, covering a large territory, having a large population (perhaps a million or more) and some significant technological achievements. Much had seemed to hinge on the Harappan script, the decipherment of which was long awaited. Recently serious scholars have suggested that the Harappan signs were not writing at all and would never be deciphered.[10] Asko Parpola, a longtime researcher on the Harappan script, finds such a dismissal unconvincing, although he admits that no attempt to decipher the script so far has been successful.[11] More discouraging for my purposes, however, is his admission that, given the scantiness of the surviving texts and the likelihood that, like Mycenaean B, even if deciphered, they would contain only references to merchandise, their usefulness to understanding Harappan culture would be minimal. But even though there is not and probably will never be enough data to describe the Harappan religious system—though some inferences can be made from figurines and incised tablets—the continuity of site occupation, even at a reduced level of complexity, was sufficient to make it very likely that cultural features descended from Harappan culture were ultimately integrated into the emerging Vedic culture, even if we cannot know exactly what those elements were.[12]

In getting my footing in this new field, it was good to discover or rediscover that, as in the case of Greece with Louis Gernet and Jean-Pierre Vernant, there were good Durkheimian predecessors. (In China too there was the distinguished work of Marcel Granet, Durkheim's student, but I felt he had most to say about developments in the Han, and so later than the period with which my chapter dealt.) Of course I was long familiar with Henri Hubert and Marcel Mauss's *Sacrifice: Its Nature and Function,* and remembered the importance of Indic material in it, but it was only in rereading it that I discovered that Mauss had been a student not only of Durkheim, but of the great French Sanskritist, Sylvain Lévi, whose book, *La Doctrine du Sacrifice dans les Brahmanas,* was a fundamental source for his entire argument.[13] Also, in reading Paul Mus, who had been only a name to me before, I learned from the translator's preface to Mus's great book *Barabudur* that, not only was Mus a student of Mauss, but in lecturing at the Collège de France, Mus always carried two books, one of which was Lévi's *Doctrine du Sacrifice.*[14] And then it occurred to me that my old friend, Louis Dumont, from whom I had learned about India but also about many other things, was surely a student of Mauss, a fact confirmed by a quick look at Dumont's *Homo Hierarchicus.*[15] So, though my way was no less difficult, I felt, as a profoundly Durkheimian sociologist myself, at least in good company.

Early Vedic India

However difficult the dating of early Indic texts may be, there is general agreement that the earliest of the Vedas, the sacred texts of Indic religion, is the *Rgveda.* Michael Witzel puts it succinctly: "The Rgvedic language stands apart from the following stages in many respects, and is perhaps better characterized as the last stage of a long period of Indo-Aryan poetry than as the *beginning* of Vedic literature. Many words that occur in RV have cognates in Avesta [archaic East Iranian, which is closely related to Old Persian], while these no longer appear in post-Rgvedic texts."[16] Although the RV (to use the standard abbreviation) contains elements that could go back to the earliest days of the Aryans in India, or perhaps even to the period when they were still in Afghanistan, and thus could draw on materials from early or middle second-millennium BCE times, the hymns that make it up were, according to Witzel, probably composed in five or six generations toward the end of the period, which would probably be somewhere between 1200 and 1000 BCE.[17] Even within the RV we must make a further differentiation: the last book, book 10, and much of book 1 are considered to be later than the rest of the text and may represent a significant move beyond the world of most of the RV. In any case our first task is to understand the social and religious reality revealed in the older strata of the RV.

Because the texts as we have them are hymns used in rituals, we will start with a description of the ritual system and only gradually, using hints in the texts, some archaeology, and a great deal of inference, try to describe the kind of society in which these rituals were performed. Actually inference is there even with respect to the rituals, because the hymns used in a ritual don't describe the ritual as a whole or the varieties of rituals in which they were used. The RV hymns for the most part appear to have been used in sacrificial rituals directed toward a number of gods and asking for a variety of gifts, largely this-worldly, such as wealth in cattle, the birth of children, particularly sons, long life, and victory in battle. Stephanie Jamison and Michael Witzel have succinctly expressed the meaning of these rituals:

Perhaps the most obvious motivating idea of Vedic religion is the Roman principle of *"do ut des,"* "I give so that you will give," or in Vedic terms "give me, I give you," *dehi me dadhāmi te*—that is: reciprocity. The ritual oblations and the hymns that accompany them are not offered to the gods out of sheer celebratory exuberance. Rather, these verbal and alimentary gifts are one token in an endless cycle of exchanges—thanks for previous divine gifts, but also a trigger for such gifts and favors in the future. Most Ṛgvedic hymns contain explicit prayers for the goods of this world and for aid in particular situations, along with generalized praise of the gods' generosity.[18]

This relatively simple and straightforward pattern might remind us of Homer, and, as in Homer, sacrifices were devoted to a number of gods. The Vedic gods, however, have few cognates with Greek gods and are lacking any sense of overarching organization.[19] Although Indra is a powerful and central god, at times declared king of the gods, his capacity to control the other gods seems even less than Zeus's, and further, a number of other gods are described with his same attributes and powers. Here is a short hymn to Indra, RV 3.45, to give a sense of what the simpler hymns are like:

1. Come hither, Indra, with your bay horses that give us joy, with hair like the peacock's! May none hold you back, as trappers a bird! Go past them, as past a desert-land!
2. Devourer of Vṛtra, splitter of Vala, burster of strongholds, driver of the waters, mounter of the chariot at the neighing of his two bay horses—Indra is the shatterer of even the steadfast.
3. As the deep oceans, you increase your strength, as do cows. As cows with a good cowherd to their fodder, as irrigation ditches to a pool, they have gone.
4. Bring unto us offspring, wealth, as the share to one who makes a promise! As a man with a crook a tree bearing ripe fruit, shake down sufficient wealth, Indra!
5. You are self-sufficient, Indra, your own ruler, commanding, the more glorious by your own achievements: as such, growing in strength, O much-lauded one, do be our best listener![20]

From this hymn it is clear that Indra is a powerful warrior god. Verse 2 alludes to mythical events that need not detain us but illustrate his conquering strength. He is also, however, associated with pastoral and agricultural activities and is thus an appropriate recipient of prayers for material well-being.

The hymn just quoted might seem to be simple, but unraveling all the allusions and all the meanings of Indra's various attributes would require a great deal of exegesis. Poetically the poems are highly condensed and allusive, assuming knowledge of the myths without spelling them out. They are works of great poetic art, and the bards who composed them competed to produce the finest hymns. But as Witzel has said, trying to discern the myths, let alone the history, of the early Indo-Aryans from these hymns alone would be like trying to discern the history and religion of early Israel if we had only the Psalms as our source.[21]

Nonetheless, by mining the text of the RV carefully, Witzel has reconstructed at least a rough picture of what was happening when these texts were composed. The text tells us of some thirty tribes or peoples (we will have to consider later what we can make of their social organization) under a number of rulers (*rājan,* later translated as "kings" but here better as "chieftains"), whose lineages, as far as we can reconstruct them, cover five or six generations. As a result of the incessant fighting of the Aryan peoples not only with the *dāsa* (the indigenous, or better, culturally non-Aryan peoples) but if anything even more with each other, a group of Five Peoples centered on the Pūru gained hegemony, only to lose it to one of its late-arriving subgroups, the Bharata.

Even in RV times, the "Aryans" were no longer simply the immigrants from afar or their descendants. Chiefs with *dāsa* names were to be found among the Aryans, and many loanwords from Dravidian, Munda, and perhaps even Tibeto-Burman appear in the RV, so that "Aryan" had become a cultural, not a racial, term, referring to those who took part in the sacrifices and festivals, that is, who participated in the common culture. Further, these self-styled Aryans no longer remembered or celebrated any foreign area from which they might have come. They placed the center of the world as somewhere in northern India, and it is there that, in their own eyes, they originated. We are in a heterogeneous world genetically and culturally even though "Aryan" never lost its elite connotation.[22]

What we find amid the welter of tribes, subtribes, and lineages is a centralizing tendency that will only grow stronger at the end of the Rgvedic period. As Witzel puts it, "The Rgveda thus represents, above all, the history of two royal lineages (Pūru and Bharata) toward the middle of the Rigvedic period."[23] The result of protracted conflict was "the ultimate victory of the Bharatas over the other tribes and their settlement on the Sarasvati [River], which became the heartland of South Asia well into the Vedic period. It is here that ṚV 3.51.11 places the centre of the world, with subdued enemies in all directions."[24] Witzel attributes the earliest collection of the ṚV hymns to the centralizing tendencies of the Pūru and the Bharata, no mean feat, given that the hymns were the "sole property of a few clans of poets and priests who were not willing to part with their ancestral and (more or less) secret knowledge."[25] But willingly or unwillingly, part with them they did, and even the language of the hymns as we have them reflects that of the Purus and Bharatas and not that of some of the lineages from which they originated.[26]

The centralizing tendencies of the Purus and the Bharatas, the precursors of even stronger centralizing tendencies to come, should not lead us to imagine that they created an early state. Though they were moving in that direction, decentralizing tendencies, leading to frequent changes of leadership, were still strong. We are in the world of chiefs and paramount chiefs, not of kings and states. Witzel describes the world of the early Ṛgvedic period from which the centralizing tendencies began as one of "small, tribal, pastoral societies of the Eastern Panjab without or with only an incipient caste system, a pre-Hindu religion, a cold winter with no real monsoon, without cities, and with an economy based on cattle herding."[27] He describes the society of this early period, located in the far northwest and the Panjab, as consisting of "chieftains *(rājan)* [who] lord over fellow *rājanya/kṣatriya* (nobility) and the *viś* (the people), with the addition of the aborigines and servants/slaves *(dāsa. Dasyu. puruṣa)*."[28] Elsewhere he describes the early Ṛgvedic ritual system as consisting mainly of "a simple morning and evening fire ritual, some seasonal festivals, and the major New Year/spring Soma ritual."[29] These rituals required priests, but not necessarily a priestly class. As in ancient Greece, chiefs and heads of lineages could function as priests, though, as also in ancient Greece, there were poets'/priests' lineages, but, as yet, not a priestly class or caste.

All of this makes sense if, as George Erdosy has argued, mainly on the basis of archaeological evidence, "the reappearance of stable political structures following the collapse of Harappan urbanism, along with an eastward shift in the focus of economic and political power and the spread of a new family of (Indo-Aryan) dialects, required almost a millennium. The emergence of what may be termed simple chiefdoms, datable to c. BCE 1000, was the culmination of this process."[30] What is remarkable is that even in the four or five centuries after 1000 BCE that saw significant political and cultural change, the material culture remained remarkably simple. There were still no settlement centers large enough to be called cities, no palaces or temples, only wattle and daub houses, and there was a "general absence of luxury goods and a striking poverty of artistic expression."[31] Yet it is just in this period that, as we will see, paramount chiefdoms, even incipiently an early state, emerged together with radical social and cultural transformations.

What is striking, however, is that most of the RV was composed before 1000 BCE, and so comes out of tribal societies only beginning to develop chiefdoms, at least if Erdosy is right. But the *Rgveda* is the most sacred text of Vedic religion and, in principle, in historic Hinduism up to the present. It has been a premise of this book that "nothing is ever lost," but India exhibits that premise to a startling degree. It is true that the Homeric epics come out of, or at least depict, a society not much more complex than late second-millennium India and played a significant role in education throughout the history of classical civilization. Homer might even be called to some degree a "sacred text," but the Homeric epics never had the authority attributed to the *Rgveda*. There are parts of Genesis that are probably in their original form handed down from tribal or chiefly times, but they are not the core of the Torah. As we will see, the ideas present in the RV will become enormously elaborated in the first half of the first millennium BCE and will draw copious commentary right to the present, but an intact collection of tribal verse as the core of a religious tradition is uniquely Indic. It raises questions about the whole idea of religious evolution, with which we will have to grapple below.

We don't know enough about the ritual system in Rgvedic times to describe it in any detail, but there is evidence in the hymns to give us some idea of it. We have already described Indra, one of the most frequently mentioned gods in the RV. Though Indra and most of the gods are invisible, two of the most important, and both are important in early Iranian religion as well, are visible: Agni (fire, as anyone familiar with Latin *ignis* will note) and Soma (the Avestan cognate is Haoma, in both cases referring to a mind-altering drink about the identity of which there is ongoing debate). Ordinary fire and the soma drink participate in the major gods who bear their names and are present, and in the case of fire, indispensable, at the sacrificial ground. Maurer points out that the three most frequently mentioned gods in the RV are Indra, Agni, and Soma, but Agni is the most important:

> Every sacrifice [*yajña*], from the simplest domestic rite to the most elaborate and complex, centered around the fire, the Vedic religion hav-

ing been a fire-cult, as was its sister religion, Zoroastrianism, though the two were developed along very different lines. No sacrifice in either was possible without fire . . . One of Agni's principal roles is to serve as messenger between men and gods, in which capacity he either conveys the essence of the sacrificial meal to the gods or brings the gods themselves to the sacrificial feast, where they sit down together on the sacred grass that has been spread out for them . . . Indra, on the one hand, is the mighty warrior god, the unrelenting vanquisher not only of demons, but also of all the enemies of the Indo-Aryans and hence their staunchest protector; Agni, on the other hand, is the arch-priest, intermediary between men and gods, the great and omniscient sage, and, as the focal point of all sacrifices and provider of warmth and light in the home, closest companion to man among the gods.[32]

Soma, the third most frequently mentioned god in the RV, is the deification of the soma plant, the source of soma as a drink that played an important part in the rituals. The pressing of the stalks of the soma plant so as to release the juice, the mixing of the juice with milk, the offering of some of the soma to the gods and the drinking of the rest by the human participants, were all important aspects of the soma ritual. Maurer points out, "The hymns addressed to Soma are couched in metaphors and similes of highly imaginative character, and probably no flights of fancy have ever soared higher than those of the poets of the ninth book of the Rgveda [the ninth book consists solely of hymns devoted to Soma]."[33] The language of certain of the hymns to Soma has led some students of early India to believe that they describe drug-induced mystical experiences (RV 10.136, for example), perhaps the forerunner of later Indic mysticism.[34] In any case, soma was believed to have strong medicinal qualities and to be the drink of immortality for both gods and men. Indra was believed to be exceptionally fond of it.[35]

Although the poetry of the hymns that were recited in the rituals was complex and sophisticated, the rituals themselves were, at least in the Rgvedic period, relatively simple. There were no fixed ritual sites, no temples, but each ritual was conducted anew at a chosen spot, perhaps reflecting the frequent movement of a pastoral people. This feature, once established, continued to characterize Vedic ritual in all later times, long after pastoralism had been abandoned. The hymns are attributed by scholars to poets or bards who were not necessarily priests, and who competed for the excellence of their poems against other poets, often mentioning the reward they expected from the affluent sponsors of the ritual. They were referred to as Ṛṣis—seers who "heard" *(śruti)* the texts, though they were also said to have "seen" them, rather than composing them, and who were considered semidivine. This, however, was after the canon of the *Ṛgveda* was closed and the ancient poets had been replaced by Brahmins who were the preservers and interpreters of the old texts.[36]

The Middle Vedic Transformation

Michael Witzel has argued that there is a gap in time between the society we have tried to reconstruct from the older parts of the ṚV and the quite different society that emerges from the Brāhmaṇas. Exact dates are impossible to assign, but if we view the older parts of the ṚV as dating from the late centuries of the second millennium BCE, then perhaps the earliest Brāhmaṇas might date from a century or two into the first millennium BCE. Witzel finds some texts that represent a stage in the development of early Sanskrit that makes it likely that they come from this gap period between the two major text collections. These include mantra texts and other fragments from later collections, as well as late parts of the ṚV itself, book 10 in particular. These texts give us clues to what seem to have been major political changes that would lead to the remarkably different society and culture of the Middle Vedic period, in which the Brāhmaṇas became central.

Geographically there was a shift from the Panjab to a region further to the east, on and just beyond the divide between the Panjab and the upper Gangetic plain, a region known as Kurukṣetra. Whether this indicates a movement of population, or, just as likely, a shift in the area of cultural focus, we cannot know, but political changes were at the heart of this shift, even if we can discern them only vaguely. We have noted above that in the late ṚV first the Purus and then the Bharatas came to prominence among the thirty or more "tribes" (on the difficulties involved in the use of this term, see Chapter 3) of the Aryans, but were unable to establish any lasting rule in a constantly unstable situation. In Witzel's gap period, however, the Kurus, holding themselves to be the legitimate descendants of the Bharatas, established a stable regime that would set the pattern for all subsequent Indic political history.[37]

The Kuru leaders continued to call themselves *rājan,* which, as we have seen, should in the Ṛgvedic period be translated as "chief" rather than "king." Witzel uses both "chief" and "king" for the Kuru leaders, but at one point, in trying to pin down the Kuru polity, he refers to the leader as "great chief," and points to a paramount chiefdom, that is, a regime in which a great chief has many lesser chiefs owing allegiance to him. Witzel notes as an indicator of his new strength the capacity of the Kuru great chief not only to recycle the booty of military raids but to exact tribute *(bali)* from his subordinates, something that lesser chiefs were never able to do.[38] All of this is strongly reminiscent of the paramount chiefdoms in Hawai'i just at the time of Western contact when one of them seemed on the verge of creating an early state. My suspicion was confirmed when I found Witzel himself contrasting the later true Indic kingdoms with the Kuru regime: "Absolute power was realized only in the first great states with aspirations of empire, such as Magadha about 500 B.C. The Vedic Kuru realm still resembles that of a large Polynesian chieftainship such as that of Hawaii—and with a similar ideology."[39] But, as with Hawai'i, the Kuru realm was probably in transition to an early state, so ambiguity in terminology may reflect the social ambiguities of the time.[40]

There is both archaeological and literary evidence that Kurukṣetra was at some point in the first half of the first millennium BCE attaining a status that no Aryan society had achieved before. Erdosy, in his survey of settlements in the Indo-Gangetic divide and the Ganga valley through most of that period, found that in many places there were only two levels of settlement in terms of size, and large areas where there was only one (small) settlement level, implying that chiefdoms were the main social structure (chiefdoms would normally involve two settlement levels) beyond the still common tribal level (one settlement level would imply a tribal society). However, there was one area with a three-tiered settlement level, namely Kurukṣetra, and three levels implies paramount chieftainship at least.[41] On the basis of literary evidence Erdosy believes that perhaps by the sixth century, the term *janapada* "acquires its classical meaning of 'realm,'" and that "Kurukṣetra, home of the most famous of all Late Vedic tribes, may have been the first region to be clearly delineated [as a *janapada*]."[42]

Witzel notes that "an important, if not the chief one among the religious developments is that the new royal center in Kurukṣetra ('the land of the Kurus') gave rise to a new mythology of the region."[43] He describes the mythology that gave religious expression to this new level of political development as follows:

> Now we are able to understand the importance of Kurukṣetra. It was deliberately turned into the land of the gods, their *devayajana* [the place

where the gods sacrifice], where even the heavenly river, the Milky Way, touched down on earth and continued to flow through Kurukṣetra as the Sarasvati and Drsadvati rivers and where stood the world tree Plaksa Prasravana at the centre of the world and of heaven. While quickly becoming a peripheral area of India, this land of Kurukṣetra remained its holy land to this very day. Here the Mahabharata war was fought, here one made pilgrimages, in fact to this very day, along the banks of the sacred rivers, here one could gain immediate access to heaven, here the purest Vedic language was spoken, and from here even the medieval kings of Eastern India brought their Brahmins, the famous Sāravatas.[44]

Kurukṣetra was, of course, a region, not a city: there was no capital city, indeed no cities at all. Witzel says, "Note that the kings roam about in their territory because of their comparative lack of centralized power, in order to control the various parts of their realm."[45] The development of a unique mythology of place regarding Kurukṣetra is only one aspect of a major reorganization of religious practice that will be described below, a change intimately related to changes in social structure, as we will see.

Given that early states have emphasized hierarchy perhaps more strongly than any societies before or after, we may note that it is in the Middle Vedic period that the *varṇa* system, which divided the society into four orders, comes into view in its mature form.[46] The first full description of it is to be found in one of the latest of the Ṛgvedic hymns, 10.90. Here we find that the human hierarchy is embedded in a cosmological hierarchy, so characteristic of archaic societies, as we saw in Chapter 5. The hymn is referred to as Puruṣasūkta, "the Hymn of Man," and here *puruṣa* is the androgynous primordial man or world giant from whom the universe, the gods, and humans come. Here are some selected verses:

1. Thousand headed is Puruṣa, thousand eyed, thousand footed. He covered the earth on all sides and stood above it the space of ten fingers.
2. Puruṣa alone is all this, what has been and what is to be, and he is the lord of the immortals, who grow further by means of food.[47]
6. When with Puruṣa as oblation the gods offered sacrifice, the spring was its clarified butter, the summer the fuel, the autumn the oblation.[48]
11. When they portioned out Puruṣa, in how many ways did they distribute him? What is his mouth called, what his arms, what his thighs, what are his feet called?

12. His mouth was the Brāhmaṇa, his arms were made the Rājanya, what was his thighs was made the Vaiśya, from his feet the Śūdra was born.

13. The moon from his mind was born; from his eye the sun was born; from his mouth both Indra and Agni; from his breath the wind was born.

16. The gods sacrificed with the sacrifice to the sacrifice. These were the first rites.[49]

To give a full explication of even the verses quoted above would take the rest of this chapter, but certain things can be noted. This famous hymn has clearly moved beyond myth to mythospeculation.[50] Puruṣa, the ordinary word for (usually male) "human being," is here in transfigured form elevated above the usual gods of the *Ṛgveda* and seen as their creator, or their source, as with Indra and Agni in verse 13. Speculation has raised the question of a higher order of ultimate reality than the gods. Further, the final verse, 16, offers a new speculative idea of sacrifice. Wendy Doniger O'Flaherty explains: "The meaning is that Puruṣa was both the victim that the gods sacrificed and the divinity to whom the sacrifice was dedicated; that is, he was both the subject and the object of the sacrifice. Through a typical Vedic paradox, the sacrifice itself creates the sacrifice."[51] Typical, however, of Middle Vedic speculation, not of the older ṚV thinking as evidenced in the hymn to Indra, 3.45, quoted above. O'Flaherty also comments on "first rites" in verse 16: The word Maurer here translates as "rites," she tells us, is *dharmas,* which she translates as "ritual laws." O'Flaherty recognizes that *dharma* is a "protean word," but here designates "the archetypal patterns of behavior established during this first sacrifice to serve as models for all future sacrifices."[52]

The whole hymn is archetypal in O'Flaherty's sense, and most particularly in verses 11 and 12, which Paul Mus called "the first constitution of India," because for the first time it described the *varṇa* system, the basic structure of Indic society up to recent times. In verse 12, O'Flaherty translates *Brāhmaṇa* as "the Brahmin," *Rājanya* as "the Warrior" (also called Kṣatriya), *Vaiśya* as "the People" (which earlier translated *viś*), and *Śūdra* as "the Servants."[53] Although this is the first time a system of four orders is ranked in a cosmological context, we still need to ask if this is only the systematization of a long-standing practice and whether what we know later as the four *varṇas* is really what is being described here. In other words, what is described in ṚV 10.90 is only one moment in an evolving social system, important though that moment may be, and we must try to understand it as such.

Gregory Nagy, in an interesting effort to get at the Indo-European background of both Greek and Indic societies, has turned to the work of Georges Dumézil, particularly in connection with Dumézil's theory of the three functions that are supposed to characterize all Indo-European societies: the first function is sovereignty/priesthood, the second is the warrior class, and the third is agriculture/herding.[54] Emile Benveniste, Dumézil's follower, according to Nagy, "shows clearly that the basis of Indo-European social organization was the tribe."[55] However, most of our evidence for Indo-European societies comes from early states, where what were originally "functions" could have become more firmly differentiated and institutionalized, with the Indic *varna* system being a case in point (and with the addition of the Śūdra as the fourth *varna*, "servants," who are included but excluded in that they could not fully participate in the sacrifices and festivals that defined Aryan culture, thus indicating that they were not part of the original tripartite inheritance).

Nagy is aware of the difficulty involved in the use of the term "tribe" but he provisionally defines it, borrowing from Montgomery Watt, as "a body of people linked together by kinship, whether in the male or in the female line."[56] We have seen the term *viś* translated as "people" in contrast to "ruler" and "nobles" in early Vedic society. Nagy, drawing on Benveniste, translates *viś* as "tribe, people," and speaks of it as referring to a "social whole," again drawing on Benveniste in relating *viś*, "tribe," to *viśva*, "all."[57] He finds interesting parallels between Greek *phule*, "tribe," and Indic *viś*, in that both terms relate both to the social "all" and to a division within the all, indeed the lowest of the three Indo-European divisions:

> The semantic relationship between the name of the lowest in the order of three *phulai* [plural of *phule*], the *Pamphuloi,* and the word *phule* itself, corresponds to the semantic relationship between the name of the lowest in the order of the three leading social classes or varna-s in Indic traditions, the *vaiśya,* and the word from which it is derived, *viś* "tribe": just as the word *Pamphuloi* implies the whole community while designating the lowest of three parts, so also the word *vaiśya,* by virtue of its derivation, implies the whole community, the *viś,* while specifically designating again the lowest of three parts.[58]

What I make of all this is that there was a degree of tribal egalitarianism underlying the differentiations that were developing with the gradual emergence of an early state in Greece and India.[59] RV 10.124.8 says of the gods in relation to Indra: "Choosing him as all the people choose a king."[60] O'Flaherty here translates *viśaḥ* (plural of *viś*, and thus, literally "peoples" or "tribes") as "all the people" in this passage, but Nagy prefers to translate this late RV passage, in effect, as "Choosing him as the tribes choose an over-king [paramount chief?]."[61] Even if such a choice were largely symbolic, there was, if we can take the verse as reflecting reality, still an expression of popular consent to rulership.[62]

What we can perhaps see in RV 10.90.11–12, the earliest clear formulation of the hierarchy of the four *varṇas,* is a movement away from a loose conception of a people with chiefs and priests above and followers below, and all linked by kinship, to a society of orders, differentiated roles, that, though often inherited, in principle transcend kinship and cross tribal boundaries. Even in the Middle Vedic period, however, there was apparently more fluidity and movement between *varṇas* than there would be later. Erdosy notes a degree of mobility in that intermarriage between *varṇas* was possible and status could still be earned rather than inherited: that is, stories of youths of uncertain birth, who, through intensive study became recognized as Brahmins, and, on the other hand, the idea that one of Brahmin birth who didn't know the rituals wasn't really a Brahmin.[63] Patrick Olivelle finds in texts older than the Upaniṣads the question, "Why do you enquire about the father or the mother of a Brahmin? When you find learning in someone, that is his father, that is his grandfather."[64] And of course, all through history conquerors of whatever background could claim Kṣatriya status. As in Hawai'i, there were always those who could come up with convenient genealogies. Lineages and families remained important, as they would throughout Indic history, but the *varṇa* system brought solidarities—and antagonisms—that transcended the primary focus on kinship.

The difficulties of consolidating what had been numerous lineages of poets/priests and chiefs/subchiefs in many small chiefdoms into a relatively large paramount chiefdom were major. Even the establishment of stable chiefdoms had not been possible without conflict. Hartmut Scharfe points out that *rājan* was probably at first a temporary term, meaning a "war chief" who would function only during a campaign. In the RV Indra is frequently called *rājan* when he intervenes to fight a particular enemy, but then withdraws. "If *rājan* did not originally denote a position held in permanency, *dámpati* 'master [father?] of the house/family' and *viśpáti* 'master of the clan/settlement' surely did."[65] Hermann Kulke refers to another important term, *grāma,* which originally meant a "trek" of migrating Aryans, which later came to be used for villages, "settled treks." And whereas "the early *grāmas* were led by the *grāmaṇis* the 'trek leaders' who always belonged to the *viś* population of the *grāma,*" the settled village "witnessed the emergence of the *grāmin,* the 'village owner,' who appears to have always come from the *rājanyas* or *kṣatriyas.*"[66] Kulke suggests that the *viś* population of the *grāma* did not always take kindly to their would-be overlords, who could be thrown out, or, if worst came to worst, abandoned as the village population simply moved away. In other words, settlement and hierarchy leading to ever more centralization did not necessarily come smoothly. Strongly organized subordinate groups could resist those who sought to dominate them. Chiefdoms and paramount chiefdoms everywhere are notoriously fragile: as chiefs attempt to dominate villages, and paramount chiefs to dominate subchiefs, there is always the possibility that subordinate groups will break away. An early state develops structures and practices that make this increasingly difficult, but the state in India never quite transcended the fragility of the paramount chiefdom.

The *varṇa* system was only one effort to create larger solidarities in a society still divided by many subgroup loyalties. Lacking a powerful administrative apparatus, the Kuru rulers, with the help of a much more clearly defined Brahmin class, developed a ritual system far more complex than what had preceded it and closely related to the developing *varṇa* system. Under the direction of the Kuru king the hymns that had been created continuously for generations by many lineages in many tribes/chiefdoms were now gathered into one collection, what we know as the *Ṛgveda,* to be shared by all of the "newly formed Brāhmaṇa class," even though each hymn was still marked by the name and lineage of the original poet. Under Kuru pressure the "copyright," jealously guarded by earlier lineages, was now no longer effective as the hymns became the common resource of the newly established Brahmin priests.[67]

Most remarkably, the canon of the *Ṛgveda* was now closed. While cherishing and imitating the archaic features of the inherited material, the new priestly class was devoted to the development of a new and much more complex ritual system, one that focused on the Kuru king and his court but had other significant functions as well. In connection with this new ritual system, additional collections of texts were developed over time: the *Sāmaveda* and the *Yajurveda,* providing the ritual chants and the mantras, respectively, mostly drawn from the *Ṛgveda,* and the *Atharvaveda,* which does not supply material for the new solemn *(śrauta)* rituals but for smaller and more private rituals. The *śrauta* rituals required priests specializing in each of these four Vedas and the complex commentarial literature that developed around them.

One of the earliest of these new *śrauta* rituals has been, on linguistic grounds, dated from soon after the closing of the ṚV, and is associated with the Kuru court, possibly with the reign of the great Kuru king, Parikṣit, the Agnicayana or fire ritual.[68] Given the number of officiants required and the fact that it took nearly a year to complete the ritual, it must have been enormously expensive, such that only someone of very high status could have had it performed. Theodore Proferes writes, "The unction ceremony for the sacrificer *(abhiṣeka)* that is performed in the Agnicayana connects this rite, too, with the most powerful of leaders."[69] Proferes notes on linguistic grounds that the Aśvamedha rite, so closely linked as we will see to the institution of kingship, and the Sautrāmaṇi rite, "which, judging by its focus on the figure of Indra, may well also have been originally a royal rite," also date from this gap period and are the "Ur-liturgies" coming between the *Ṛgveda* and the earliest of the other *śrauta* texts.[70] Proferes sums up what he thinks was happening at that critical moment in Indic history: "As part of their programme to consolidate power, the Kuru kings sought to overcome the divisive tendencies inherent in the clan-based organization of their priestly elite by encouraging the development of what we might call an 'ecumenical' ritual system, one which did not rely upon or perpetuate the clan divisions characteristic of the RV-period."[71]

The extraordinary and rather sudden elaboration of a complex ritual system focusing on the Kuru *rājan,* but now with a priesthood organized to provide elaborate support to the rulers, gives evidence of a situation where political administration was rudimentary and ritual carried the brunt of providing social integration. As Erdosy points out, "We may recall that a reliance on religious sanction in preference to brute force is one of the distinguishing criteria of chiefdoms."[72] No paramount chiefdom can, however, do without force, and the Kuru king "could exert his will by a ready band of 'terrible [warriors]' *(ugra)* or henchmen. He also relied on a network of spies."[73] But much of the burden of "taming" the ambitions of chiefs and subchiefs was taken over by the new ritual system. The constant raiding and fighting among the Aryan groups, even if it amounted to little more than cattle rustling, could now be channeled into competition for ritual status. As Witzel puts it:

> A not very wealthy Vaiśya might have been content with the domestic *(gṛhya)* rituals of passage that are executed for him and his family.

However, a lower rank Kṣatriya might have attempted to go on to the next step on the socio-religious ladder and become a *dīkṣita,* that is an initiated "sacrificer" *(yajamāna),* and having learnt more of the Veda than a Vaiśya . . . After he had established the three sacred fires, he could then perform the Agnihotra, the New and Full Moon sacrifices, etc. If he wished for more, he could add the seasonal rituals and the yearly Soma ritual. If he was still not content with this and wished to impress his rivals further (who would often come to interfere with or destroy his rituals), he could go on with seven more types of soma rituals . . . What is important here is that these—only natural—rivalries were cleverly channeled in the new, Śrauta way of stratification . . .

Beyond the Kṣatriyas, the next level is that of the nobility of royal blood . . . A low rank ruler could receive the consecration as chieftain through the simple royal *abhiṣeka* . . . and finally, there was the solemn Śrauta option of the *rājasūya* [royal consecration]. Later on a revised, complicated version of the Ṛgvedic, originally even Indo-European, horse sacrifice *(aśvamedha),* was added for especially powerful supreme kings who claimed "world domination," which nevertheless only encompassed parts of (northern) India. The new Śrauta ritual thus put everyone in his proper station and at his proper place . . . There was opportunity for each and everyone to gain higher status by having the Brahmins perform more and more elaborate rituals—instead of simply raiding one's neighbors.[74]

The inner meaning of the rituals is something we must consider below, but the social function would seem to be manifest. The great *śrauta* rituals were displays of what Thorstein Veblen called "conspicuous consumption," that is, displays through elaborate and very expensive ritual of the status of the sacrificer. Some have even compared this ritual system to the potlatch of the Northwest Coast Indians. Although the Brahmin class or order comes into its own in this new system, we should not forget that the rites were created for royalty and nobility. It would be a very rich Brahmin indeed who could act as sacrificer rather than priest in the most elaborate rituals.[75]

The new society that was taking shape in the Kuru realm was headed by a king who was supposed to defend the good of all his subjects as well as the proper way of life *(dharma)* of each of them, but was in fact a sharp break with any remaining tribal egalitarianism. The four varṇas were defined by functional differentiation, but even more by rigid hierarchy. The creator of this new kind of society and its chief beneficiary was the alliance between Kṣatriyas and Brahmins *(brahmakṣatra),* who quite consciously "ate" (the term for "dominate" or "exploit") those beneath them. Our texts, composed by Brahmins, claim that they also "ate" the Kṣatriyas, but at times admitted that the opposite was true.

On the whole, this alliance, so advantageous to both its members, would persist through most of subsequent history. It is thus the whole social-ritual system with its dominant *brahmakṣatra* class alliance that Witzel points to with the term "Sanskritization," borrowed from the work of the anthropologist M. N. Srinivas, who used it to describe how castes in twentieth-century India could raise their status by imitating the practices of superior castes, copying their greater reliance on Sanskrit, the language of the sacred texts.[76] What Witzel calls "the first Sanskritization," and he notes the irony of the term when used of speakers of Vedic Sanskrit, is the fact that the Kuru realm became a model whose influence rapidly spread throughout northern India.[77] The Kuru realm was the largest and militarily strongest society of its day, but it was not primarily through conquest that its influence spread, but by example. The Kurus had created a pattern that, for all its inner conflict and apparent rigidity, could provide both social stability and resilience for generations to come.[78]

The intellectual achievement of the Middle Vedic period would be influential for later history as well, though it would be overshadowed by later developments in a way that the fundamental Kuru socioreligious pattern would not. Before considering those later intellectual developments, and the sense in which they embody an axial transition, we must first give in outline what the state of religious thinking was by the end of the Middle Vedic period. In terms of the typology of this book, Middle Vedic society as exemplified by the Kuru realm was archaic, and thus its culture and religion were most likely archaic as well. That Middle Vedic culture as exemplified in the Brāhmaṇas had the seeds of axial reflection I would concede; that it was already axial, as some have argued, I find hard to credit. But we must make an effort, however cursory, to understand this remarkable ritual system if we are to decide how to categorize it.

The Ritual System

We will take the Agnicayana sacrifice as exemplary of the whole system, not only because is it extraordinarily well documented in a 1975 performance by a film and in two enormous volumes thanks to Frits Staal and his associates, but also because it is one of the most comprehensive and important, and, as we have seen, one of the earliest of the great *śrauta* rituals.[79] It has also been proclaimed as the oldest surviving ritual in the world,[80] and "as the pinnacle of Vedic ritual, [which] occupies a special position among the *śrauta* sacrifices owing not only to its elaborateness but also to the fact that it contains many remarkable rites and ritual elements."[81] That this ritual has survived for 2,500 to 3,000 years in oral transmission and is still being accurately performed (Frits Staal found that the ritual he recorded differed only in minor details from textual descriptions that are very ancient), most recently in 2006, is something of a marvel. It is again a tribute to the fact that in India nothing is ever lost. What is remarkable about this survival, and is indeed without parallel in the world as far as I know, is that this ritual was created in a society that was just emerging from a paramount chiefdom into an early state, that is, barely archaic in terms of my typology.

In one sense this ritual and the other great *śrauta* rituals are typical of archaic societies in that they glorify the ruler and act to ensure his immortality. Though early Indic society knows no monumental architecture, no temples even of the sort that were built in Hawai'i, we can see these gigantic rituals as the functional equivalent of the pyramids of Egypt, which were also built for rulers with the intent of ensuring their immortality. There is, however, one great difference: the rituals belonged to the Brahmins, not to the rulers, and could be performed, if sufficient resources could be found, by the Brahmins themselves if they had no royal patron. That tells us something about India that really is different from all the other cases.

Jan Heesterman helps us see why this greatest of rituals focuses on fire:

Agni, fire, is the central feature of the Vedic world. We hardly need to insist on this point: all of Vedic ritual, centered as it is on the fire cult, is there to prove it. Not surprisingly, then, fire is the focus of a deeply layered, many faceted imagery. To mention only some prominent points, fire, which prepares man's food and carries offerings to the other world of gods and fathers, is both the center of the human world and the means for communicating with the ultramundane sphere. It is the pivot in the cosmic circulation of the goods of life.

Fire, then, stands for life, wealth, procreation, and the continuation of family, clan, and lineage. Hence the importance that is attached to the installation of the domestic fire and, even more to that of the separate fire for the solemn sacrifice . . . Not only are man and fire said to be father and son, but the relationship is reversible. In short, they are one, a unity that guarantees immortality. Against this background we can understand that the ritualistic concern with the fire borders on the obsessive, as appears from the elaborate casuistry regarding possible mishaps that may befall the sacrificial fire.

However, this obsessive concern seems to point to something else, too. Fire symbolizes life and immortality, but its possession is far from secure. Not only can fire be dangerous and destructive when it gets out of hand and acts in its aggressive Rudra form, it is also notoriously fickle and ephemeral.[82]

The Agnicayana (fire altar)[83] ritual illustrates many of the points Heesterman makes, not least in that its very elaboration was an effort to control the fickle and ephemeral and bring fire to its fulfillment for human destiny. I have said that in early India there were no monuments. The fire altar is the exception that proves the rule. The altar that gives the rite its name is its most outstanding—and expensive—feature: it requires more than 1,000 bricks, handmade in several sizes and shapes, to form the bird-shaped fire altar that is the focus of the ritual. But, and this is equally significant, the fire altar does not become a monument, for it is abandoned after its first use, even though it took so much time and effort to construct. Again, Heesterman explains: "Even the prestigious brick altar does not provide permanence. After its use in the Soma ritual it is considered a cadaver, Agni's dead body, as I was told by certain Nambudiris [the Brahmins who performed the 1975 ritual]."[84]

We can see in the Agnicayana many examples of the kind of thinking that characterizes Vedic thought: the correlations, homologies, similarities, and identities (the Sanskrit word is *bandhu*) that seem to provide the answers to most important questions. The ritual focuses on Agni, obviously, but Agni can, under certain circumstances, be identified with or substituted for other gods, as they can for him, and that happens in this ritual as we will see. But the fire altar itself, built of five layers of 200 bricks each, is in the shape of a bird: from above it resembles a falcon or eagle, in any case a bird of prey, with head, wings, and tail. And the bird, or the bird-shaped altar, is Agni. The adhvaryu priest, while carrying the fire from its prior location to the center of the fire altar, recites:

Agni of a thousand eyes, a hundred heads,
your exhalations hundred, inhalations a thousand,

you are lord of wealth a thousand times,
thus we worship you for strength—svāhā!
You are the bird with wings, sit on earth,
sit on the ridge of the earth;
with your glaze fill the sky,
with your light support heaven,
with your brilliance strengthen the quarters![85]

It is said that Agni is the bird because a bird first brought fire from heaven, but there are other explanations. Multiple explanations go with multiple meanings, as is the case generally with ritual thought.

Of central significance in the play of correlations is that the sacrificer (*yajamāna;* sacrifice: *yajña*), the patron and beneficiary of the whole ritual is also Agni. So if the fire altar is Agni, it is also in very complex ways the sacrificer. It is the yajamāna's size that determines the size of the bricks for the altar: measurements are taken from the tips of his fingers, with his arms raised, to the ground, from the top of his head to the ground, and from his knees to the ground.[86] These measures are divided and manipulated in ways too complex to describe here, but they provide the measurements for the several sizes and shapes of the more than 1,000 bricks that will make up the altar. This is another reason the altar can never be used again: another sacrificer will have different dimensions; the bricks will not be the same size.

Staal writes, "The main altar of the Agnicayana functions in several respects as a tomb: the golden man and five heads of sacrificial victims are buried under it."[87] He speculates that early Vedic burial mounds may lie behind this aspect of the altar. The golden man is a small gold figure of a male human. This is appropriate because the altar, among other things, is a human being. The heads are those of a horse, man, bull, ram, and he-goat, the classic species for animal sacrifice, though in practice the he-goat was usually substituted for the other species.[88] For the 1975 ceremony and probably for a long time previously, these heads were made of clay. However, there is some discussion in the early literature about how the heads, the human one in particular, were to be obtained. Some held that an actual human head, perhaps of someone who had died in battle, had to be used, but the possibility of human sacrifice cannot be ruled out. This whiff of the idea of human sacrifice, however, really indicates how very slight is the possibility that any large-scale human sacrifice, such as those in Hawai'i or Shang China, was present in early India, and we may question why this common marker of early states is missing. Could it be that the ruler, the "king," never quite achieved the ultimacy that he did in the other archaic cases because he has to share the highest rank to a significant degree with the Brahmins? Human sacrifice is the ultimate symbolization of the supremacy of the sacrificer. Perhaps the Indic king never attained that kind of supremacy.

If the fire altar is Agni, a bird, the sacrificer, and a tomb, perhaps we will not be surprised to learn that it is everything: the cosmos and its contents. The altar is composed of five levels of 200 bricks each, with the top level containing a few more. The arrangement of the bricks in each level is slightly different, but not enough to impair the basic form of a bird. But one of the meanings of the altar is that the first, third, and fifth levels represent the three worlds—earth, air, and sky—of which the universe is composed (there will be more levels of worlds added later, but three is the basic number).[89] And so the fire altar is Prajāpati, who in Middle Vedic thought has become identified with Puruṣa, the cosmic man who appeared in ṚV 10.90 above, the one from whom the whole cosmos and all that is within it are derived. And again, Prajāpati and Agni can be interchanged. Staal sums up the teaching of the Brāhmaṇas as follows:

> According to Śāṇḍilya's teaching in the Śatapatha Brāhmaṇa, the construction of the Agnicayana altar is essentially the restoration of Prajāpati, the creator god, who created the world through self-sacrifice, viz., through his own dismemberment. Since Prajāpati became the universe, his restoration is at the same time the restoration of the universe. Thus, piling up the altar means putting the world together again. Just as Prajāpati was the original sacrificer, Agni is the divine sacrificer, and the yajamāna is the human sacrificer. The designation of the fire altar as Agni indicates the identity of Agni and Prajāpati. Agni, Prajāpati, and the yajamāna are all identified with each other, with the offering altar, and with the fire installed on it.[90]

It is this kind of thinking that drove the nineteenth-century Sanskritists to the point of despair: they could make no sense of it and found it childish and even silly.[91] But more recent Indologists have succeeded in retrieving a good deal of sense in it and conveying it rather effectively. Brian K. Smith makes a good case for the Brāhmaṇas in his *Reflections on Resemblance, Ritual, and Religion*. He quotes Louis Renou as speaking of Vedic thought as "a system of equations," but asks what kind of equations and for what purpose are they constructed.[92] His answer is that Vedic thought is an effort "to correlate corresponding elements lying on three discrete planes of reality: the macrocosmos (whose contents and forces are collectively called *adhidevatā*, 'relating to the godly'), the ritual sphere (*adhiyajña*, 'relating to the sacrifice'), and the microcosmos (*adhyātman*, 'relating to the self')."[93] The correlations or equations *(bandhu)*, however, are not made just for the sake of speculation. Vedic thought is in the service of Vedic action and operates under the assumption that "reality is not given but made."[94]

The fundamental premise is that creation (or procreation, or emission—Prajāpati is not exactly a "creator god" on the model of Yahweh) is fundamentally "chaotic, disorganized and unformed." Thus it is not creation that constitutes order, but sacrifice. Smith writes:

> It is characteristic—and perhaps close to definitive—of Vedism that between mere procreation on the one hand and true cosmogony and anthropogony on the other is inserted a set of constructive rituals. Between Prajāpati's creation and the origin of the cosmos are sacrificial acts of the gods, giving form to formless nature. And between the procreation of every person and the origin of true being are also rituals, making a human out of the human in potens only. Cosmogony and anthropogony in Vedic ritualism are *actualized* only within the sacrifice and *realized* only by ritual labor or *karman*.
>
> For the Vedic priests and metaphysicians, ritual activity does not "symbolize" or "dramatize" reality; it constructs, integrates, and constitutes the real. Ritual forms the naturally formless, it connects the inherently disconnected, and it heals the ontological disease of unreconstructed nature, the state toward which all created things and beings perpetually tend.[95]

As Staal has explained the Brāhmaṇic teaching, the construction of the fire altar in the Agnicayana ritual is the reconstitution of the cosmos, because it is putting Prajāpati's body back together. And in early Vedic thought it was the entire round of sacrifices that kept the cosmos going. One of the simplest rituals, the Agnihotra, performed in the early morning and the evening, guards "the fire (as identical with the sun) overnight and its rekindling the next morning, effecting the rising of the sun."[96] We have not discussed so far, but will have to consider it further later, the analogous forming of the person as well as the cosmos, which Smith describes as "anthropogony," which is also effected by a series of rituals, life-cycle rituals that mark the development of personhood. Ritual also had to do with the individual's ultimate fate. One function of the Agnicayana was to make the sacrificer immortal, the bird form of the altar being interpreted, among other things, as the bird that will take the sacrificer to heaven, of course not at the end of the ceremony, but at the end of his life.

One aspect of the Middle Vedic ritual system that would have lasting consequences for the future was how fundamentally hierarchical it was. Smith points out that both the rituals themselves and those who participate in them are ranked hierarchically and in the same way. He cites Staal as pointing to the fundamentally hierarchical structure of Vedic ritual: "The sequence [of the ritual order] is hierarchical. There is increasing complexity. A person is in general only eligible to perform a later ritual in the sequence, if he has already performed the earlier ones. Each later ritual presupposes the former and incorporates one or more occurrences of one or more of the former rituals."[97]

Smith points out that the more complex rituals are higher because they incorporate and recapitulate simpler ones. I have noted that the Agnicayana is, among other things, a soma ritual, but have not mentioned that Soma is involved in the ritual as well as Agni, and that the day after Agni is conveyed to the brick altar, Soma together with Agni (they are sometimes combined into one god, Agnisoma), is conveyed to the altar.[98] The Agnicayana thus encompasses simpler soma rituals. But, as Smith points out, this hierarchical principle of encompassment was also central to the caste system. He cites Louis Dumont's classic work, *Homo Hierarchicus,* as showing that the higher castes "encompass" the lower ones, going on to say, "Although Dumont does not fully work this out, what seems to be implied here is an ontology of 'relative completeness,' the Brahmin being the 'more complete' instance of human being while others, relative to the Brahmin, are 'less complete.'"[99] The completeness at issue is, of course, ritual completeness. The Brahmin can participate in ritual in ways that the Kṣatriya cannot, and so on down the line. As we will see, the great rituals, such as the Agnicyana, became marginal even in the late centuries of the first millennium BCE, but the hierarchical principle remained in place.

We must now comment briefly on that marginalization and what it did to the ritual system, even though that development occurred in the period that will be considered in more detail later on. For reasons that are not entirely clear, but that perhaps have to do with the growth of a more effective state, not an "early state," but a full-scale urban (archaic?) state, the need for the complex ritual system and the competition it fostered to maintain social stability may have been lessened by more effective administrative structures and stronger capacities for royal enforcement of desired ends. But Brian Smith helps us see that this change meant, not the demise of the ritual system or its central place in religious life, but a transformation that on the surface seems to be a reversal of the hierarchical order. In this new understanding, those who could no longer celebrate the solemn *śrauta* rites could nonetheless, in their household worship (the domestic or *gṛhya* sacrifices), still keep alive the entire Vedic ritual system, now reduced to its "quintessential kernel—five 'great' sacrifices that may be performed with a piece of wood, a glass of water, some flowers and fruits, and by saying '*om*.'"[100] By maintaining the exalted status of the Brahmins and the importance of sacrifice as a validation of that status, this reduced domestic system kept the traditional understanding of the religio-social system alive and left the door open for further innovations that would open new possibilities without questioning the fundamental assumptions of Indic society.

The syllable mentioned in the previous quotation would seem to be another case of less is more. *Om* is the syllable that was believed to sum up the entire teaching of the voluminous Vedic texts in one "word." I put "word" in quotes because *om* has no meaning other than its sound: it is a mantra of the simplest kind. Nonetheless we could call it, following Frits Staal, prelinguistic language.[101] Again we are reminded of the fact that we are in an oral culture. *Om* makes sense as spoken; it is a powerful form of speech. Words, whether meaningful or not, were central to Vedic thought: words were things and had extraordinary consequences.[102] Not just words, but poetic meters could be personalized, viewed as divine, and were active in the world. In an entirely oral culture, the spoken word had consequences: one could indeed "do things with words."

Speech itself was personalized as the goddess Vāc, who in ṚV 10.125 speaks of her own greatness: "I bring forth the Father at the head of this world" (v. 7), and "Only I blow like the wind, reaching all creatures beyond the heaven, beyond the earth here—so much have I become by my greatness" (v. 8). Maurer, in his comment on this hymn, points out that it "is a glorification of this Sacred Speech of the sacrificial rite, as a creative principle and the substrate of all existing things, including the gods."[103] "Principle" and "substrate" may accurately describe what is being said in these verses unless we take them as referring to a static condition, for the very idea of the Sacred Speech, which is so essential to the sacred sacrifice, is that it is active, creative, constructive. We are still here dealing with practice more than theory.

The same can be said of two more terms that have been taken as metaphysical absolutes when their original use seems to have been linguistic and active. One of these is *ṛta,* which has been commonly translated as "cosmic order" or "cosmic harmony," but Jamison and Witzel argue it is best translated as "active, creative truth, realization of truth, *Wahrheitsverwirklichung.*" They point out that its opposite is "deceiving, cheating action," and so it is best thought of as the power of active truth, rather than "cosmic order."[104]

Even more clearly linguistic is a term that appears early but will have an enormously significant history: the neuter term *brahman,* which in its earliest uses, and often even in the Upanishads, means "formulation," particularly "the capturing in words of a significant and non-self-evident truth."[105] In its masculine form, Brahmā was a god, often the highest god, even higher than Prajāpati, but in the neuter form, the fundamental reality of the world. Actually, things were even more complicated, as the neuter form *brahman* could also be considered a god. Jan Gonda indicates that the question of whether ultimate reality is personal or impersonal was not a concern of the authors of the ancient Vedic texts, however much it is of interest to us.[106] Still, it is worth remembering that in its earliest use *brahman* is as a form of speech—creative, powerful speech.

We can now consider how to characterize Vedic thought at the stage of the Brāhmaṇas. Although they foreshadow the insights of the Upaniṣads, as both Sylvain Lévi and Paul Mus have emphasized, they remained at the level of practice, of the mimetic and narrative, of mythopoeia and mythospeculation, but not of theory.[107] They thus do not represent the axial breakthrough. The sacrificer is still embedded in the social world—status is almost everything and the purpose of the rituals was most frequently the improvement of status within a fixed hierarchy. It is only with the renouncer, who leaves the world of sacrifice and status, that we find the axial individual. Thus, Vedic thought at the level of the Brāhmaṇas remained archaic in terms of the typology of this book. There were, as in other archaic societies, forms of mythospeculation that verged on axial insights but still remained archaic. What it means that so much of later "Hindu" culture is basically continuous with the Vedic culture we have described in this section is something we will need to take into account later on.

The Late Vedic Breakthrough

It would be very helpful to know just what kind of society produced the Upaniṣads, but we are left with guesses and inferences. Late Vedic society of about the sixth century BCE, when we assume the early Upaniṣads were composed, was on the verge of urbanization or just beginning that process. Archaeologists date the first cities in the Ganga (Ganges) plain to the late sixth century or early fifth century.[108] Patrick Olivelle, the most recent translator of the Upaniṣads, tells us in his introductory remarks about the social background of the Upaniṣads that it is uncertain if "the urbanization of the Ganges valley occurred before or after the composition of the early prose Upaniṣads." There is no definite evidence of cities, "but there are very few agricultural metaphors and images in the Upaniṣads, while examples derived from crafts such as weaving, pottery, and metallurgy are numerous." Olivelle sums up by saying, "It appears to me that, by and large, their social background consists of court and crafts, rather than village and agriculture."[109] There had been a significant advance in technology over the *Ṛgveda,* and the world known to the Upaniṣads was much broader than even that of the Brāhmaṇas. Figures from the Kurukṣetra region appear in these early Upaniṣads, but the scenes are often placed in the more easterly regions of the Ganga valley, such as Videha or Kosala, where kingdoms and cities were appearing or about to appear. Witzel does not consider the date of 500 BCE as impossible for the early Upaniṣads.[110]

We can hypothesize, therefore, that the Upaniṣads represent a point where the Middle Vedic "arrested development of the state" (Romila Thapar) was giving way to new state formations. Population was growing, agricultural surpluses were increasing, extensive trade networks were developing, and the older settled village society was coming under pressure. Without being able to date either the Upaniṣads or state formation with any exactitude, we are left with speculation: namely, that the Upaniṣads suggest a response to a rapidly changing and unsettling environment. Olivelle suspects that the emergence of "new ideas and institutions, especially asceticism and celibacy," imply an urban or urbanizing environment.[111] Much more than that we cannot say.

If, as we will argue, the Upaniṣads represent the emergence of an axial breakthrough, or something very like it, we should still not overemphasize its difference from what preceded it. Jamison and Witzel speak of a "heightened continuation" of the intellectual tradition of the Brāhmaṇas.[112] One new to this literature, as I am, is struck with how much in the Upaniṣads is familiar from older texts: concern for "equations," for the proper performance of rituals, even spells for the attainment of quite worldly ends. The great speculative insights for which the Upaniṣads are famous seem to be nuggets in the midst of quite different material. Still, Jamison and Witzel point out something else new in the form as well as the content of the Upaniṣads: "The early Upaniṣads, with their dialogue form, the personal imprint of the teacher, the questioning and admissions of innocence—or claims of knowledge—from the students, seem to reintroduce some of the uncertainties of the late RV, give the sense that ideas are indeed speculation, different attempts to frame solutions to real puzzles."[113]

When Jamison and Witzel use the word "reintroduce," they refer to a long tradition of questioning and debate that goes back to the poetic contests recorded in the RV, where each poet tried to present a problem that his rival could not solve. Jan Gonda notes that riddles and contests over their solution are frequently found among tribal peoples, and have a variety of uses, often in connection with ritual.[114] So when we find such riddles in the RV, we cannot be sure whether they are a remnant of tribal practice or the beginnings of speculation that will have such remarkable development later on. The early poetic contests become developed in the Brāhmaṇic period as the *brahmodya,* which Wayne Whillier describes as "a ritualized, purely priestly extension of the poetic debates,"[115] so there was some continuity between the RV and the Upaniṣads. When Jamison and Witzel speak of "the uncertainties of the late RV," they are undoubtedly referring to hymns such as the famous *Nasadiyasūkta* (Creation hymn), RV 10.129:

1. There was neither non-existence nor existence then; there was neither the realm of space nor the sky which is beyond. What stirred? Where? In whose protection? Was there water, bottomless deep?
2. There was neither death nor immortality then. There was no distinguishing sign of night nor of day. That one breathed, windless, by its own impulse. Other than that there was nothing beyond.
3. Darkness was hidden by darkness in the beginning; with no distinguishing sign, all this was water. The life force that was covered with emptiness, that one arose through the power of heat.
4. Desire came upon that one in the beginning; that was the first seed of mind. Poets seeking in their heart with wisdom found the bond of existence in non-existence.

5. Their cord was extended across. Was there below? Was there above? There were seed-placers; there were powers. There was impulse beneath; there was giving-forth above.

6. Who really knows? Who will here proclaim it? Whence was it produced? Whence is this creation? The gods came afterwards, with the creation of this universe. Who then knows whence it has arisen?

7. Whence this creation has arisen—perhaps it formed itself, or perhaps it did not—the one who looks down on it, in the highest heaven, only he knows—or perhaps he does not know.[116]

To continue the questioning, do we have here only the challenge of a primitive poet to his competitors to see who can be silenced, having no answer, or do we have the beginning of high Vedic metaphysics? Tradition gave the latter answer, but probably both have some truth. It is worth noting that this creation hymn has echoes in other cultures: the reference to water at the beginning in Genesis 1:2, and to desire *(eros)* being there at the beginning in Hesiod's *Theogony.*

As is not unusual at times of rapid social change, the Upaniṣads depict lively discussions, not limited by caste or gender barriers that would later be harder to cross. There are so many Kṣatriyas involved in discussions that there was a theory at one time that the Upaniṣads represented a kind of *kṣatriya* alternative position to that of the Brahmins. That view has been pretty well shot down, but the fact that Kṣatriyas and Brahmins participated together in active discussion is not doubted. In some cases *kṣatriya* kings were even accepted as teachers by Brahmins. Further, there is more than one instance of women taking an active part in discussions. None of this means that everything was turned upside down—I have already stressed continuities with the earlier tradition. But even though the continuities are obvious, there were also new insights, often not entirely clear because so intertwined with older ideas, that would have the greatest importance in future developments.

Joel Brereton usefully describes some of the main themes in the Upaniṣads.[117] He draws on the *Aitareya Upaniṣad* to illustrate the theme of correlation, already evident in what we learned about the Agnicayana ritual, where the god Agni is equated with the fire on the altar, the bird that gives the altar its shape, soma, one of the major offerings, and finally with the sacrificer himself. In the *Aitareya Upaniṣad,* the cosmic man at the beginning of creation (ṚV 10.90) has become identified with the original self, the *ātman,* from whose mouth comes "speech and then fire; from its nostrils, breath and wind; from its eyes, sight and sun," and so forth. But these newly created realities fall into the sea in a state of disorganization. "They need an order, and to find it, they enter into the human form once again. Fire becomes speech and enters the mouth; wind becomes breath and enters the nostrils; the sun becomes sight and enters the eyes, and so on." Finally, "the self itself enters into the newly created human form. In this way, the self, which is the origin of all, becomes the self of each human being . . . Both physically and spiritually, therefore, the human being is a perfect microcosm."[118] Although this microcosmic/macrocosmic correlation is expressed in a number of ways in the Upaniṣads, the way that would have the greatest consequences would be phrased as the identity of *brahman,* which we noted above was rooted in the idea of powerful speech in the *Ṛgveda* but had become the term for the highest god or for ultimate reality itself, and *ātman,* the self of every person, but also the Self of the world and so identified with *brahman.*

But correlations that had worked at the level of sacrificial rites in the Brāhmaṇas, where the identity of the sacrificer with Agni could lead to the immortality of the sacrificer, were now posed as a matter of knowledge, but salvific knowledge, closely guarded and difficult to understand. Sacrificial action *(karma)* in the Brāhmaṇas becomes knowledge *(jñāna),* although these were both part of the Vedic tradition, the *karmakāṇḍa* and the *jñānakāṇḍa*—that is, the "works portion" and the "knowledge portion."[119] *Karma* will have other meanings, some of which emerge for the first time in the Upaniṣads, but the older meaning is never quite lost. But our first task is to try to understand the new emphasis on knowledge.

One of the earliest Upaniṣads puts it bluntly. In response to a question about knowing *brahman,* and *brahman* knowing the Whole, the answer is given:

> In the beginning this world was only *brahman,* and it knew only itself *(ātman)* thinking: 'I am *brahman.*' As a result, it became the Whole. Among the gods, likewise, whosoever realized this, only they became the Whole. It was the same also among the seers and among humans . . . If a man knows 'I am *Brahman*' in this way, he becomes this whole world. Not even the gods are able to prevent it, for he becomes their very self *(ātman).*

The text goes on to say that the gods then lose the sacrifices that the human who knows this would have offered, and so: "The gods, therefore, are not pleased at the prospect of men coming to understand this."[120]

Even in this rather crude form, we see at least the beginning of a move beyond mythospeculation. We are still in the world of the gods, even annoyed gods, and *brahman* seems more god than abstraction, and yet there is incipiently a level of abstraction that moves beyond narrative into conceptual thinking. In many other places even in the early *Upaniṣads* this transition has become clearer.

Although I want to argue that theory begins to emerge in the Upaniṣads, I also want to affirm that it does not do so by way of systematic reasoning, by logical deduction or empirical induction. It is revealed in metaphors, in teachings that are intentionally cryptic ("the gods love the cryptic" is a frequent Upanishadic saying, but is also found in much older texts), and its contents are in a way "secret": to be explained to those ready to understand but definitely not to be shouted from the housetops. I would argue that disciplined rational thinking begins with the Upaniṣads but only gradually reaches a mature form, such as in the grammar of Pāṇini, dated around 400 BCE.[121] For an understanding of how reason works in the Upaniṣads, let us turn to a famous dialogue in chapter 6 of the *Chāndogya Upaniṣad* in which Śvetaketu, who has been sent away at the age of 12 to learn the Vedas, returns at the age of 24, "swell-headed, thinking himself to be learned, and arrogant," to be tested by his father, Uddālaka Āruṇi.[122]

Uddālaka asks his son if he has been taught "that rule of substitution by which what has been unheard becomes heard, what has been unthought becomes thought, what has been unknown becomes known." Śvetaketu doesn't know, so his father explains, "It is like this, son. By means of just one lump of clay one would perceive everything made of clay—the transformation is a verbal handle, a name—while the reality is just this: 'It's clay'" (*Chāndogya Upaniṣad* 6.1.3–4).[123]

There has been much argument about what Uddālaka is saying, but at one level he is arguing for the existence of universals. Given the power the Upaniṣads give to names, we should not hear "the transformation is *just* a name," assuming a nominalist argument. Rather Uddālaka is saying that from this lump of clay we can understand all forms of clay, just as eventually he will show his son that once one understands the basic nature of reality, the nature of all things will be known. The example of the lump of clay is simply the first step toward what is coming:

"Bring a banyan fruit."
"Here it is, sir."
"Cut it up."

"I've cut it up, sir."

"What do you see there?"

"These quite tiny seeds, sir."

"Now, take one of them and cut it up."

"I've cut one up, sir."

"What do you see there?"

"Nothing, sir."

Then he told him: "This finest essence here, son, that you can't even see—look how on account of that finest essence this huge banyan tree stands here.

"Believe me, my child, that which is this finest essence—this whole world has that as its self. That is the real. That is the self *(ātman)*. Thus are you, Śvetaketu. *(Chāndogya Upaniṣad* 6.12)[124]

The myriad "equations" of the Brāhmaṇas have now come to a culmination: The widest external reality *(brahman)* and the deepest internal reality *(ātman)* are identical.

If the Upaniṣads mark the beginning of theoretical reflection at the level of metaphysics, where metaphors are still central but used to clarify concepts, and the argument is at the level of universal truth, then they can rightly be seen as a cognitively axial moment in the development of early Indic thought. Gananath Obeyesekere, however, has raised a question as to whether this new level of cognitive thinking involved an axial "ethicization" (his term) as well. He notes that the mid-first millennium BCE was a period "conducive to philosophical and soteriological probing and the systematization of thought (what Max Weber called the 'rationalization' of religious life)." He goes on to say, "Nevertheless, speculative and systematic thinking need not produce ethicization. The Upanishads produced a great speculative soteriology that was not concerned with ethicization."[125] Obeyesekere's point is not that there was no axial ethicization in early India, but that it occurred in the Buddhist canon, not the Vedas.

In reading Olivelle's translation of the first twelve Upaniṣads, I tried to note each instance of ethical reflection. Even stretching the definition to the limit of a mention of the word "good," and including some antinomian material as well, I found fewer than twenty such references in 290 pages of text. Perhaps the fullest ethical discussion occurs early in the *Bṛhadāraṇyaka Upaniṣad*:

Now, this self *(ātman)* is a world for all beings. So, when he makes offerings and sacrifices, he becomes thereby a world for the gods. When he recites the Vedas, he becomes thereby a world for the seers. When he offers libations to his ancestors and seeks to father offspring, he becomes thereby a world for his ancestors. When he provides food and shelter for human beings, he becomes thereby a world for human beings. When he provides fodder and water for livestock, he becomes thereby a world for livestock. When creatures, from wild animals and birds down to the very ants, find shelter in his houses, he becomes thereby a world for them. Just as a man desires the well-being of his own world, so all beings desire the well-being of anyone who knows this. (*Bṛhadāraṇyaka Upaniṣad* 1.4.16)[126]

One could argäe that *dharma* is a central ethical term in the Upaniṣads, and in a sense it is, though whether it meets Obeyesekere's criterion of ethicization is a matter we will need to consider more fully below.

If, however, it can be granted for the moment that ethics is not a central Upanishadic concern, we can ask why. One reason has to do with the private, even secret, nature of the Upanishadic teaching (the word *upaniṣad* perhaps has the basic meaning of "connection," but also carries the meaning of "secret teaching"). Transmission of the teaching is not, therefore, public, and is in some instances extremely limited. The *Chāndogya Upaniṣad* at one point restricts the teaching to the eldest son but to no one else (3.11.5) and the *Bṛhadāraṇyaka Upaniṣad* at one point restricts it to the son or the pupil (6.3.12). In other instances it is said that the teaching might be communicated to members of the twice-born—that is, the initiated, *varṇas,* the Brahmins, Kṣatriyas, and Vaiśyas—but on no account to the Śūdras.

The teaching about the identity of *brahman* and *ātman* would seem to be absolutely universal in content, and, as Brereton notes, social, not individual: "The true self is not the individual self, but rather the identity that one shares with everything else. There is no true distinction among living beings, for they all emerge from being and retreat to it. All things, both animate and inanimate, are united in being, because they are all the transformations of being."[127] Modern Hindu thinkers have drawn profound ethical consequences from these teachings, but in the early period any social and ethical consequences of these teachings remained latent: in the early texts the concern was, above all, with the possible salvation of the individual.[128] Salvation or liberation was a heroic ideal that only exceptional people could attain. Further, religious truth was of such transcendent importance that concern for the world of daily life could be seen as secondary. This assertion needs to be qualified in two directions: Vedic religion never lost its concern for everyday life, as exemplified in its emphasis on the (Brahmin) householder, particularly in the framework of caste obligations; and Buddhism had an equally transcendent idea of religious truth, but developed a significant concern for the ethical quality of everyday life.

The Upaniṣads, we should always remember, continue many of the concerns of the Brāhmaṇas, including "food, prosperity, power, fame, and a happy afterlife," as Olivelle puts it.[129] Older ideas of the afterlife, including the idea that one might simply join the gods in an everlasting happy domain not too different from life at its best on this earth, are to be found in these texts. The notion of *mokṣa*, radical salvation (Obeyesekere's term), freedom (Olivelle's term) or liberation (Halbfass's term), which will be matched by the Buddhist idea of *nirvāṇa*, is new and requires a radical reorientation of life. It is linked to ideas of karma, no longer simply ritual actions, but all forms of human action that can affect one's rebirth chances, ideas that are just emerging in the early Upaniṣads, where they are infrequent and still secret.

In one quite complex discussion of what happens after death, a king privately answers Śvetaketu's question on the subject, something he did not learn from his father, saying, "As to what you have asked me, let me tell you that before you this knowledge had never reached the Brahmins. As a result in all the worlds government has belonged exclusively to royalty [Kṣatriya]" (*Chāndogya Upaniṣad* 5.3.7).[130] This secret knowledge turns out not to be so different from the teachings of the Brāhmaṇas with respect to those who are able to escape this world and take the path leading to the gods. But for those who rely on offerings and sacrifices, "those whose behavior is pleasant can expect to enter a pleasant womb, like that of a woman of the Brahmin, Kṣatriya, or the Vaiśya class. But people of foul behavior can expect to enter a foul womb, like that of a dog, a pig, or an outcaste woman." However, there is one more possibility: "Then there are those proceeding on neither of these two paths—they become the tiny creatures revolving here ceaselessly. 'Be born! Die!'—that is the third state" (*Chāndogya Upaniṣad* 5.10.7–8).[131]

Kenneth Post makes a good deal out of the fact that it is the Kṣatriya and not the Brahmin who knows the truth about karma and rebirth, even arguing that there could not be a Vedic political philosophy because the truth of rebirth in terms of varṇa is simply a given that falls outside the teaching about the identity of *brahman* and *ātman,* so ideas of karma and rebirth, involving required and proscribed social behavior, are of more concern to rulers than to Brahmins.[132] But it would seem that Brahmins have their own reasons for being concerned with these matters. Yājñavalkya, the great Brahmin sage, secretly communicates an abbreviated version of the same teaching to one who questioned him about what happens after death, saying,

> "My friend, we cannot talk about this in public. Take my hand; let's go and discuss this in private."
>
> So they left and talked about it. And what did they talk about?—they talked about nothing but action [*karma*]. And what did they praise?—they praised nothing but action. Yājñavalkya told him: "A man turns into something good by good action and into something bad by bad action." (*Bṛhadāraṇyaka Upaniṣad* 3.2.13)[133]

Yājñavalkya, it turns out, is the first example of the renouncer *(saṃnyāsin),* who turns his back on the world to pursue the goal of religious liberation from *karma* and rebirth alike.[134] When asked to explain *brahman,* the self that is within all, Yājñavalkya replies:

> He is the one who is beyond hunger and thirst, sorrow and delusion, old age and death. It is when they come to know this self that Brahmins give up the desire for sons, the desire for wealth, and the desire for worlds, and undertake the mendicant life. The desire for sons, after all, is the same as the desire for wealth, and the desire for wealth is the same as the desire for worlds—both are simply desires. Therefore, a Brahmin should stop being a pundit and try to live like a child. When he has stopped living like a child or a pundit, he becomes a sage, And when he has stopped living like a sage or the way he was before he became a sage, he becomes a Brahmin. He remains just such a Brahmin, no matter how he may live. All besides this is grief. (*Bṛhadāraṇyaka Upaniṣad* 3.5.1)[135]

The renouncer role is one way to step entirely out of the Vedic varṇa system, as the great renouncer, the Buddha will do, but Yājñavalkya seems to link it indelibly to the Brahmin role. We will need to consider how varṇa relates to the relative lack of ethicization in the Vedic tradition.

When Yājñavalkya decided to leave his household to take up the life of a mendicant renouncer, he spoke to his two wives about making a settlement between them. One of them, Maitreyī, had taken part in philosophical discussions and asked for instruction before Yājñavalkya departed. He tries to explain, in a way that she finds confusing, the fundamental nature of a self without any kind of duality, a self that is complete without anything to perceive: "When, however, the Whole has become one's very self *(ātman)* then who is there for one to see and by what means?" He concludes:

> "About this self *(ātman)*, one can only say 'not—, not—'. He is ungraspable, for he cannot be grasped. He is undecaying, for he is not subject to decay. He has nothing sticking to him, for he does not stick to anything. He is not bound, yet he neither trembles in fear nor suffers injury.
>
> "Look—by what means can one perceive the perceiver? There, I have given you the instruction, Maitreyī. That's all there is to immortality."
>
> After saying this, Yājñavalkya went away. (*Bṛhadāraṇyaka Upaniṣad* 4.5.15)[136]

In this powerful expression of a view that might be analogous to negative theology in the West, Yājñavalkya gives evidence for the cognitively axial breakthrough in Vedic religion. We must now consider those aspects of the Vedic tradition that seem to have prevented an axial ethicization.

After giving the teaching that "in the beginning this world was only *brahman*" (*Bṛhadāraṇyaka Upaniṣad* 1.4.10, see above), the text goes on to say, using the word *brahman* with a double meaning of absolute reality and what we have been calling for convenience "Brahmin," though in Sanskrit both are *brahman*, that *brahman* had not fully developed and so "created the ruling power, a form superior to and surpassing itself." The text continues:

> Hence there is nothing higher than the ruling power. Accordingly, at a royal anointing, a Brahmin pays homage to a Kṣatriya by prostrating himself. He extends this honour only to the ruling power. Now, the priestly power *(Brahman)* is the womb of the ruling power. Therefore, even if a king should rise to the summit of power, it is to the priestly power that he returns in the end as to his own womb. (*Bṛhadāraṇyaka Upaniṣad* 1.4.11)[137]

One could hardly find a better expression of the alliance of Brahmins and Kṣatriyas *(brahmakṣatra)*. The text then goes on to say that in order to further its development, *brahman* went on to create the Vaiśya and Śūdra classes. Again we have the idea of the Brahmin varṇa "encompassing" the others—it is from its "womb" that they emerge. But then the passage concludes:

It [*brahman*] still did not become fully developed. So it created the Law
(*dharma*), a form superior to and surpassing itself. And the Law here is
the ruling power standing above the ruling power. Hence there is nothing higher than the Law . . . Now the Law is nothing but the truth.
(*Bṛhadāraṇyaka Upaniṣad* 1.4.14)[138]

Dharma is a central term in the Vedic tradition, as central in its own
sphere as *brahman* and *ātman* are in theirs, but its meanings are complex.
Contrary to what might appear from the immediately preceding quote, the
one thing Dharma is not is universal law.

In considering the etymology and development of the term, I will be heavily dependent on Wilhelm Halbfass's magisterial discussion of *dharma*.[139] It
is worth reminding the reader of one of Halbfass's major points: the textual
material we have from early India is ideological, not descriptive, and it comes
from a particular social group, the Brahmins, and undoubtedly expresses its
interests. Other groups must often have thought differently, but, until the
emergence of Buddhism and Jainism, we don't know what those differences
were. If the Kṣatriyas thought differently, as many of them probably did,
they found it politic to cooperate with the Brahmins rather than to challenge
them.

Dharma is a term similar to but not identical with *ṛta*, which was discussed above. Michael Witzel, in developing the idea that *ṛta* means something like "the force of active truth," points out that it has no equivalent in
Western languages and is perhaps similar to the equally untranslatable ancient Egyptian term *maʾat* (see Chapter 5).[140] In the typology that underlies
the argument of this book, that means that *ṛta*, like *maʾat*, is an archaic, not
an axial, term, even though we are tempted to give it axial implications.
Dharma, which is found alongside *ṛta* in the *Ṛgveda* and largely replaces it in
later texts, is subject to the same misunderstanding: though different from
ṛta, it is still an archaic term that looks axial. It becomes axial in Buddhism
and at moments, incipiently, in the Vedic tradition, yet, I will argue, remains
archaic in subsequent Indian understanding.

One key to the difference between the two terms is that whereas *ṛta* is always in the singular in the RV, *dharma* is in the plural not only in the RV but
in the Brāhmaṇas as well, and sometimes even later as in the *Mahābhārata*.
Its first use in the singular is in the *Chāndogya Upaniṣad* 2.23.1, traditionally
translated, "There are three branches of the Law,"[141] so even in the singular
its reference is plural. The term derives from the root *dhṛ*, which means "to

support," "to uphold," "to maintain" (note that *dharma,* like *ṛta,* is active, not static), and in its early uses refers almost exclusively to religious rituals.[142] The connection with the root is the belief that ritual "upholds" or "maintains" the cosmos, but *dharmas* are the many rituals that in a variety of ways do this, and not a notion of natural law, either physical or ethical. According to Vedic cosmogony, separation, holding apart, as with heaven and earth, is extraordinarily important, so the ritual action of *dharma* involves holding apart as well as upholding. It would be well to go back to the text of ṚV 10.90, which concludes that the primeval sacrifice that created the cosmos gave rise to "the first ritual laws," that is, the first *dharmas,* and to remember that in this hymn what is being held apart is not only features of the natural world, but the four varṇas.[143]

Even in the *Ṛgveda,* however, ritual is not the only meaning of *dharma:* it already has the wider sense of ethical and social "norms," "statutes," or "laws."[144] And in the later development of the Vedic tradition, while never losing an enormous variety of references, it comes to have a particular focus:

> In traditional Hinduism, *dharma* is primarily and essentially the *varṇāśramadharma,* the "order of the castes and the stages of life" which breaks down into countless specific rules and cannot at all be derived from a general principle of behavior. The *varṇāśramadharma* allocates each of the various castes and stages of life "duties" *(svadharma);* it links them to certain roles and ways of life and excludes them from the ways of life of others; it controls their access to ritual performance, to the sources of sacred knowledge, and to the means of salvation.[145]

Further, *dharma* is not a "universal lawfulness which applies to Hindu society as well as to other societies," because it does not apply at all to *mlecchas,* foreigners, non-*aryas.* One reason for this, among others, is that it can only be communicated in Sanskrit, the "correct" language for "correct" forms of behavior.[146] Thus it seems clear that *dharma* remains archaic even in historical times.

This understanding of *dharma* was not without universalistic challenges even within the Hindu tradition. There are passages in the *Mahābhārata* where *ahiṃsā,* "non-injury" or "the sparing" of living beings, is taken to be "the core and essence of *dharma.*"[147] Later *bhakti* (devotional) movements would move in the same direction. One of the most memorable examples of an ethical and universalistic concept of *dharma* is the edicts of the (Buddhist) Emperor Aśoka (third century BCE). But these tendencies never until modern times gained ascendency. One must remember that the most sacred section of the *Mahābhārata*, the *Bhagavadgītā*, teaches not *ahiṃsā*, but *svadharma*—the *dharma* appropriate to one's caste. When Arjuna quails before the task of fighting and probably killing his relatives, his charioteer and teacher, Kṛṣṇa, tells him to do his duty as a Kṣatriya—that is, as a warrior, for whom killing is part of his *dharma*—but without attachment to the results, and so without bearing the karmic consequences of his action.[148]

It is not that there was no philosophy of *dharma*. The Mīmāṃsā school of philosophy devoted a great deal of effort to defending *dharma* as absolute commandment, as a set of injunctions, while arguing that the content of the injunctions is simply given in the Veda and cannot be derived from rational reflection. Indeed, rational reflection may lead to unfortunate consequences: the idea that avoiding evil and doing good is the essence of *dharma* could lead a student to have sexual relations with his teacher's wife (one of the most severe violations of Vedic injunctions) in order to give her pleasure. Better by far to obey the injunctions as they stand without giving them rational justifications.[149] One could call the Mīmāṃsā school an axial school of philosophy (because of its sophisticated use of argument) in defense of an archaic ethical system against axial rationalization. Mīmāṃsā is by far not the only school of thought in Indian history, but it is a central and influential one, and it would be hard to argue that any other position gained a similar degree of hegemony.[150]

This discussion of *dharma* leads inevitably to the vexed problem of caste. On the whole I have avoided the use of the term "caste" because of its pejorative implications and also because there is a tradition of using "class" to translate the word *varṇa* and "caste" only to refer to the word *jāti*, a term I have not used before.[151] The four varṇas have been discussed in a variety of contexts. *Jāti* has in recent times been used for the thousands of hereditary endogamous groups, usually differentiated by occupation, and also usually classified in terms of *varṇa*, although *varṇa* assignments have been often uncertain, contested, and, possibly, changing. Halbfass, however, argues that though the two terms are not quite identical, they overlap in the early texts to a degree that they were almost the same—that is, *varṇa* was used for what we normally think of as *jāti*, and vice versa. Further, because both are endogamous hereditary groups and have grown out of the same way of classifying, the varṇa system is "the prototype for important aspects of the 'real' castes [jāti]," and so "caste" can also be used for varṇa.[152]

The central point for my argument is that caste in India has no basis in rational argument. One can talk about division of labor, and there was always a degree of relation between caste and occupation, but not a tight one. Impoverished Brahmins and Kṣatriyas as well as prosperous Śūdras (who were by no means "servants") are found throughout Indian history. The classification of varṇas is based on religious qualifications and is simply given in the Veda, beginning with RV 10.90, no more based on rational argument then the dharma that defines them. In simple terms, the Brahmins can study and teach the Veda and perform sacrifices; the Kṣatriyas can study and teach the Veda; the Vaiśyas can study the Veda; the Śūdras can neither perform sacrifices, nor teach the Veda, nor even study it; needless to say, what applies to Śūdras applies equally to those who are beyond the caste system. Even in the late Vedic period, ideas about rebirth, about *saṃsāra* and *karma,* were far from fully developed, but once they had become so ingrained as to be taken for granted, then the caste system could be seen as perfectly just, even though not rationally explicable, because everyone's position in the present life is determined by actions in previous lives, even though we can have no idea what those actions were.

It is also clear that caste is not a marginal concern in the Vedas. The revealed texts are saturated with the idea of caste, not just as a social classification, but as a way of thinking about everything in the universe. Brian K. Smith has devoted a book to a description of the many ways *varṇa* was used to make sense of the world: it was used to classify the gods, space, time, flora, fauna, and scripture, as well as society. He sums up:

> The *varṇa* system was, in sum, a totalistic ideology, by which I mean a system of ideas or categories that account for the cosmos and its parts in such a way that the interests and concerns of those who do the accounting are established, protected, and furthered . . . The exclusive concentration on the social application of *varṇa* can prevent us from grasping its real ideological persuasiveness as a universalistic classificatory system. We [have] surveyed the ways in which *varṇa* can be applied to classify the universe in many of its realms. The fact that the reach of *varṇa* is much more extensive than the social theory embedded within it should not, however, divert our attention from the powerful case that is being made for social differentiation and privilege. The *varṇa* system, a multifaceted and generalized classificatory scheme, had as its first and foremost goal to rationalize and represent an ideal form of hierarchical

social structure by projecting that form into the domains of the super-natural, the metaphysical, the natural, and the canonical.[153]

As with dharma, caste in India was never totally taken for granted, even aside from the principled criticism of the Buddhists and Jains. In the ortho-dox view, salvation was open only to those with knowledge of the Veda, and Śūdras were denied that knowledge. Not only was *mokṣa* (salvation) denied them, but their rebirth chances were impaired: knowledge of Vedic injunctions was imperative if one was to be reborn in a "pleasant womb," that is, a twice-born womb.[154] So for those at the bottom in terms of religious qualification, there was a kind of vicious circle. If they behaved well, they could be reborn in a higher group, but without the knowledge of how to behave well, that possibility was seriously diminished. There were those, particularly in the later *bhakti* movements, who went out of their way to spread the teachings to everyone, Śūdras and outcastes included. And what they taught was not the immense corpus of Vedic injunctions but reliance on the grace of god, Śiva, Viṣṇu, Kṛṣṇa, or the goddess.

In spite of resistance and variation by time and place, the caste system has remained basic to Indian social organization until recent times. The conserva-tive Mīmāṃsā position has remained hegemonic. Thus, I would argue, though Upanishadic religion was axial, and many forms of rational discourse (lin-guistics, logic, mathematics, and so on) developed, the foundation of ethics and society remained archaic. This is a position somewhat similar to one that S. N. Eisenstadt and I developed in connection with Japan, where we have argued that the basic premises of society remained non-axial even though ele-ments of axial culture have had a rich history of development.[155] The case of India is even more striking, in that one of the great religious breakthroughs of the axial age occurred there, yet the premises of society did not follow suit, except, of course, in the extremely important case of Buddhism that will be discussed below. It is also true that every axial society has had what Eric Voegelin called "an archaic mortgage."[156] Every historical post-axial society has been a combination of axial and non-axial elements, and perhaps could not otherwise have functioned. So India must be seen as an extreme case on a con-tinuum, not as unique. And we must remember that Buddhism, so much more axial ethically than the Vedic, Brahmanic, Hindu tradition, is also totally a product of Indian history, even if, in the end, it did not survive in India.[157]

I am aware that the position I am taking will make me liable to the accu-sation of Orientalism, of "essentializing" caste. If such a charge implies that

I view all "Oriental" societies as inegalitarian, that is obviously not the case: Chapter 8 describes the profound egalitarianism of classical Chinese civilization. I am convinced that Islamic societies are also profoundly egalitarian. Of course, here I speak of ideology, as I do in the case of India—in practice no society since the hunter-gatherers has been very egalitarian. And even in ideology neither Chinese nor Islamic societies were egalitarian when it came to gender.

Ronald Inden, however, in his book *Imagining India* has probably made the best case against essentializing caste, giving some substance to what he means by essentializing. He argues that those who see caste as the "essence" of Indian society deny to Indians "agency" and the capacity to change.[158] Instead of viewing human beings as actors determining their own fate, the essentializers, in his view, have given agency to institutions and/or internal ideas (culture?) and not to human beings. But like others in the sociological argument about agency and institutions, he doesn't tell us what role institutions and culture have once we recognize human agency. In this entire chapter I have been dealing with ideology, including the ideology about basic social premises, but I have never viewed ideology as exercising agency. If, as I am inclined to believe, the basic caste premises of Indian society have survived for a very long time and through many major changes, it is surely because of the vigorous agency of the Brahmin intellectuals who defended caste and of the rulers who on the whole upheld their views, in spite of many protests and other forms of resistance. Neither institutions nor ideas have any agency of their own—they must constantly be "sustained," "upheld" *(dhŗ)*, by human actors, yet no society can operate without them. As is so often the case, we cannot see ideas/institutions and agency in a zero-sum way—it is both/and, not either/or.

India has no monopoly on the history of oppression: every human society so far—except for hunter-gatherers, and even there it was better to be an adult male than a child or a woman—has been oppressive toward significant portions of its population. Democracy and slavery went together in democracy's two greatest exemplars, ancient Athens and modern America, for a long time at least, and who can say that the United States has not been one of the most oppressive societies in history in its treatment of people both within and without it. Caste is simply the form oppression takes in India.

But Inden makes a further move that I am inclined to take quite seriously. He argues that castes and other forms of association, both in the villages and in the cities, had a kind of "subject-citizenship," that is, they recognized the suzerainty of the ruler but they also claimed certain "rights" (Inden's word) to be heard and taken seriously. Local assemblies operated in a way that "disenfranchised" none but the lowest castes, and such assemblies were able to be represented at court.[159] All of this makes a great deal of sense to me. It gives effective political form to the many kinds of particularism characteristic of Indian society, of which caste is only one, though the most important one.

Inden wants to argue that reason and will were involved in the construction of Indian polities, and uses the Rashtrakuta empire of the eighth to the tenth centuries CE as an example.[160] Nonetheless, what he describes is, as far as I can see, a collection of particularistic loyalties, in the end fragile and fissile, and not a strong state by Chinese standards, for example. His description does not seriously undermine Romila Thapar's conclusion:

> Even when the lineage system [as exemplified by *jāti* and *varṇa* loyalties] was absorbed into the state, its identity was not entirely eliminated. Administration, except at the higher levels, remained a local concern and the absence of impersonal recruitment to office meant that kinship ties were still effective. Legal codes drew substantially on customary law and incorporated local practices. Legitimacy was frequently expressed through rituals pertaining to the lineage system such as the Vedic sacrifices . . . Thus it was not so much that the state was a segmentary system with a concentration of power at the centre shading off into ritual hegemony at the periphery as that the state system in itself was not a unitary, monolithic system restructuring the entire territory under its control but rather that it had a margin for flexibility in relation to peripheral areas.[161]

For me the fact that "unitary, monolithic" states (such as those constructed on the basis of Chinese legalist doctrine) were rare in India is not a "bad thing." Several features of the Indian pattern combined to limit the despotic tendencies so evident in historic societies (and not only in the "Orient"). The fact that at the top of society in the alliance between Brahmins and Kṣatriyas *(brahmakṣatra),* authority and power were divided, and that *dharma* was "the ruling power standing above the ruling power," meant that there were major restraints on arbitrary political power—despotism. The result may have been a relatively weak state—we will have to consider later the meaning of the ideal of universal rulership in the Indic tradition—but it meant that the people "on the ground," so to speak, had a variety of defenses against rationalizing tendencies that would have seriously impinged on their form of life or even their existence. Thapar mentioned the importance of customary law in India, and we should remember that *dharma* included customary law in principle as long as it did not violate Vedic injunctions, and in practice often when it did. If Inden perhaps stretches his terminology too far in speaking of "citizenship" and "rights," he is not wrong in seeing in these particularistic defenses of customary life a sort of functional equivalent to these ideas in a quite different cultural idiom. In short, as we know to our sorrow in the twentieth and twenty-first centuries, strong states are by no means an unvarnished good, even if "failed states" can be worse. In the case of traditional India we are talking about limited states, not failed states.

Before moving to a discussion of Buddhism, a brief comparative look at India and China, particularly with respect to the ethos of their dominant classes, might be instructive. In some ways Brahmins could well be compared to Confucians: both were the keepers of the normative order, *dharma* in the case of India, *li* in the case of China, and it is worth remembering that both terms originally meant sacrificial ritual, though they were broadened to include the normative order as a whole. Yet there is a striking difference in relation to the state: the Confucian saw the state as the potential embodiment of the ideal social order and so saw public office as his primary calling; the Brahmin saw a social order to a considerable extent independent of the state, though defended by it, as the ideal order, and his primary calling was as religious teacher and priest. It is this difference that has made Westerners think of China as "secular" and India as "religious," though the Chinese ideal state was supposed to embody religious values as much as the ideal Indian social order was.

But there is another matter that seems to justify what I consider a skewed Western perception: the way in which the two elites related to the highest religious order. The traditional Hindu formulation of the three "ends of life"—*dharma* (duty), *artha* (success), and *kāma* (pleasure)—held for all upper-caste householders. As Charles Malamoud has pointed out, these three ends of life do not map easily onto the varnas. The Brahmins were responsible for "*dharma* pronounced," as he puts it, the Kṣatriyas for "*dharma* protected," the Kṣatriyas also for "political *artha*," and the Vaiśas for "economic *artha*." *Kāma* "in the sense of (desire for) sensual pleasure" is common to all varnas, but has an especially strong affinity to Kṣatriyas, though it is also a dangerous temptation for them.[162] Although China did not have such a typology, the Confucians were responsible for the transmission and interpretation of the *li*. But the Indian typology was complicated by the addition of a fourth category, *mokṣa* (salvation, liberation), and although that too had a Brahmin primacy in the beginning, there was more than a little tension between the demands of *dharma* and the demands of *mokṣa,* insofar as the serious pursuit of *mokṣa* required the life of a renouncer, incompatible with the life of a householder and his primary obligation (as in China) to continue the patrilineage.[163] In the late Vedic period there was controversy over which had priority for Brahmins, householder or renouncer, as will be discussed further below, but the compromise solution that was included in the idea of *varṇāśramadharma* was that the householder and renouncer would be successive "stages of life" *(āśrama),* with the renouncer stage beginning in old age after all the obligations of the householder had been fulfilled.

If there is a term parallel to *mokṣa* in classical China, it would be one sense of *dao,* namely the Daoist sense of that with which one merges to attain "salvation." However, the Confucian meaning of *dao* was very close to the meaning of *dharma,* that is, "the Way of the ancestors." But although Daoists can be considered renouncers, in that they showed little interest in the pursuit of ordinary life, they were renouncers of a rather different type than the Indian ones, more insouciant, more aesthetic, less serious, even in a sense, less "religious." One further parallel, however, is that Confucians and Daoists were often the same persons, indicating a division of calling within the intellectual elite similar to that of India. It is just that in China one was, as the proverbial saying has it, "Confucian in office, Daoist out of office." What is interesting here is that renouncers turn up in the axial age in India and China, though with very different cultural emphasis. They are less obvious in ancient Israel and Greece, though not missing: the Nazirites in ancient Israel, the Cynics (in the technical sense of that term) in ancient Greece, though neither seems to have been as central at the moment of the axial transition as renouncers in China and India.

Buddhism

The world that becomes visible in the early Buddhist scriptures is a very different world from that of the Upaniṣads. It is a world of powerful kingdoms, large cities, extensive commerce, and great wealth. It is also a world in which "renouncers" of a variety of sorts have become common and argument between them highly developed. As we found in our effort to understand the cultural conditions in which the early Upaniṣads emerged, there is no easy answer to the question of why renouncers flourished in this later period. Clearly in the second half of the first millennium BCE, north Indian society, especially in the Ganges valley, was in rapid transition involving significant population increase, growing trade, urbanization, and stronger states. One further factor whose significance is hard to judge: India in that period experienced significant pressure in the northwest, not from the kind of "barbarians" the Chinese intermittently had to deal with, but from strong archaic and axial states, notably Achaemenid Persia and Hellenistic Greek empires. At the very least these pressures probably stimulated Indian state building.

"Renouncer" has a variety of possible meanings, but its simplest definition in the Indian context was the renunciation of the life of the "householder" for a life of asceticism, usually involving itinerant mendicancy. In the Buddhist case the choice of the life of the renouncer was called "leaving home," but that seems a good way of defining the role more generally. Certainly Yājñavalkya, the archetypal Brahmin renouncer as depicted in the *Bṛhadāraṇyaka Upaniṣad,* is shown rather dramatically as leaving home, giving instruction to one of his two wives. There is, however, a significant terminological difference between Brahmanical renouncers and non-Brahmanical renouncers. The former are called *saṃnyāsins,* whereas the latter are called *śramaṇas.* Although Brahmin renouncers were occasionally called *śramaṇas,* Buddhists and Jains were never called *saṃnyāsins.*[164] In any case, gradually there developed a sharp distinction between *brāhmaṇas* (referred to as Brahmins in this chapter) and *śramaṇas*—non-Brahmanical renouncers. The compound word *śramaṇa-brāhmaṇa* is used in the Aśokan inscriptions to represent two religious groups worthy of respect, but a century or so later the grammarian Patañjali used the same term as an example of a compound word composed of complete opposites. These terminological issues probably reflect controversy within the Brahmin community as well as conflict between Brahmins and non-Brahmanical groups.

The issue for Brahmins had to do with the status of householder versus renouncer, resolved ultimately in the *āśrama* system of four stages of the life course: studentship *(brahmacārya),* householder *(gṛhastha),* the hermit or forest-dweller *(vānaprastha),* and the renouncer *(saṃnyāsa).* It is this understanding of *āśrama* as four successive stages of the life cycle that is referred to in the fundamental term for expressing Hindu civilization, *varṇāśramadharma,* that is, the order of the four varṇas and the four stages of life. Olivelle, however, has shown that this understanding of the *āśrama* system is relatively late, perhaps only crystallizing in the first centuries CE.

The earliest description of the *āśrama* system in the Dharmasūtras, dating from the third and second centuries BCE, envision "a free choice among the *āśramas,* which were viewed as permanent and lifelong vocations": following one's studentship one could opt to become a householder, to remain with one's teacher until death, to become a hermit, or to become a renouncer.[165]

However, before the idea of the *āśrama* system had even developed, the tradition assumed the necessity of the householder status. As Olivelle puts it: "The ideal and typical religious life within vedic ideology is that of married householder. The normative character of that life is related to the two theologically central religious activities: offering sacrifices and procreating children. Only a married householder, according to that theology, was entitled and qualified to perform either of them."[166] The tension between the householder and renouncer ideals was never completely resolved. The later development of the "classical" *āśrama* system attempted to resolve it by making the renouncer role appropriate only late in life after the obligations of the householder had been fulfilled. The argument was that the householder is essential for all the *āśramas.* Without sacrifices the ancestors would not be nourished, nor would the cosmos be upheld. Without children there would be no future members of any *āśrama.* And without householders there would be no one to feed the renouncers.[167]

Medieval theologians continued to wrestle with this tension. The greatest Hindu philosopher, Śaṅkara, defended the legitimacy of the renouncer role, arguing that the texts prescribing lifelong ritual activity were "directed not at people who are detached from the world but at those who are full of desires and wish to attain a heavenly world."[168] Śaṅkara did however, unlike most later thinkers in his tradition, believe that only Brahmins could be renouncers.[169]

The importance of the renouncer role, as envisioned by such scholars as Dumont and Thapar, is that it allowed the possibility of viewing the entire tradition and the society that embodied it from the outside, so to speak. Renouncers viewed traditional society as imperfect, as not the only way life can be lived, as the quotation from Śaṅkara above suggests. Dumont sees the renouncer as a genuine individual, capable of choice, in a society dominated by ascribed roles and particularistic relationships. In these ways the renouncer role is a signal of an axial transformation, as we already noted with respect to the early Upaniṣads. In the Brahmanic tradition, however, though there is tension between the central "worldly" role of the householder and the renouncer, the fundamental worldly order itself is not called in question—that is, the renouncer may transcend dharma, but he does not reject it. In one sense, neither do the śramaṇic renouncers, including the Buddhists, but they do not accept it either. They don't attack the existing order, but in important respects they ignore it and attempt to build a society on other foundations. Romila Thapar argues that "the organized groups of renouncers of the post-Vedic period were neither negating the society to which they belonged nor trying to radically alter it: but rather they were trying to establish a parallel society."[170] She suggests that even though there was no explicit renouncer social program, there was between the renouncers and the worldly society "osmosis as a process of social change."[171]

It is worth pausing for a moment to consider that the Buddhist texts also suggest a geographical change relative to the Upaniṣads. Early Vedic texts focused on Kurukṣetra in the eastern Panjab and upper Ganges valley; the Upaniṣads place some discussions in Videha and Kosala in the middle Ganges valley. Magadha, in the lower Ganges valley, was in the early texts considered beyond the boundary of orthodox Brahmaṇic culture; but by the time of the Buddhist texts, Sanskritization, in its continuous expansion toward the east and south, had reached Magadha. Nonetheless, though Brahmins are much in evidence there, Sanskritization was relatively recent, and so it is perhaps not surprising that nonorthodox śramaṇic sects were present to contest Brahmaṇic supremacy in this important and expanding kingdom. Both Buddhist and Jain texts report a large number of such sects, each with a founder or leader and each with a doctrine to which followers were attracted. Except for the Buddhists and Jains, and even the Jain texts are quite late though they probably have early material embedded in them, none of these groups survived, so we know of them only from texts that treated them unsympathetically and probably unfairly. It is perhaps surprising that among these groups there were materialists, believing that there are no gods and no other worlds, and nihilists, believing that death is final and there is no afterlife. It is a little hard to understand how ascetic teachers, śramaṇas, could attract people to these beliefs, but perhaps for some people denial of all existing religious beliefs was a relief. Because there was continuous discussion and argument between these groups, with extensive accounts of them in Buddhist texts, the situation has been compared with the Sophistic age in ancient Greece, where there was controversy between thinkers holding extremely heterogeneous doctrines.

Here we must confine ourselves to the best-documented and historically most important of the śramaṇa groups, the Buddhists. The history of early

Buddhism is no more secure than that of any other aspect of early Indian religion, so I will be constructing an ideal type based on texts that may be of various ages and represent what later tradition thought were the Buddha's teachings more than what we can know for sure that he actually taught.

Certain things are reasonably clear: (1) the Buddha took for granted central views that had developed within the Brahmanic tradition, and (2) the Buddha transformed the tradition he received in a way that completed the axial transition in India. In Richard Gombrich's words, the Buddha "turned the Brahmin ideology upside down and ethicized the universe. I do not see how one could exaggerate the importance of the Buddha's ethicization of the world, which I regard as a turning point in the history of civilization."[172] It will be our task to try to understand both the continuities and the radical change.

One radical change that in a sense precedes all the others, but that we cannot pursue adequately within the confines of this chapter, is a double reversal of the fundamental Upanishadic soteriological equation: *ātman* (self) equals *brahman* (ultimate reality). The Buddha denied that either *ātman* or *brahman* have an essential reality, thus reducing the Upanishadic equation $1 = 1$ to the Buddhist equation $0 = 0$.[173] The doctrine of *anattā*, not-self, is expressed in the injunction not to regard anything as self: "this is not mine, this is not I, this is not myself."[174] It is the premise on which even the Four Noble Truths depend.

On the other hand the Buddha avoided getting into arguments about the ultimate reality of the self and the world, and when he was approached by monks asking such questions as "Is there (or is there not) a self" or "Is the world eternal or not," he responded with a parable, in Steven Collins's summary, "of a man pierced by an arrow, who does not want to find out the name, family, skin colour, and so on, of the man who shot it, before taking it out. In the same way, a man pierced by the arrow of suffering should aim to get rid of it before asking questions about the nature of the universe which caused such a state."[175] Both Gombrich and Collins stress that the Buddha is in this sense a physician more than a metaphysician, that his teaching is ultimately practical and therapeutic rather than didactic, though didacticism is far from absent in the Buddhist Suttas.

In spelling out what Buddhism shares with Brahmanism and almost all other Indian religious traditions, there is still a question of how much early Buddhism received and how much it contributed to the crystallization of these ideas. Nonetheless, three central Buddhist ideas existed in some form from the earlier tradition: (1) *saṃsāra*—"the round of rebirth," what is often called reincarnation, the idea that humans and other beings live through a series of lives that can take various forms in this and other worlds; (2) *karma*—"action," "moral retribution," the belief that actions have consequences for happiness or suffering in this and future lives and that happiness or suffering in this life may have been caused by actions in previous lives; and (3) *mokṣa*—"release," "liberation" (in Buddhism usually called *nirvāṇa*, Pali *nibbāna*), the state of release from the round of *saṃsāra*, the highest religious goal, though usually seen as possible only for renouncers.[176]

In each case Buddhists developed their own interpretations of these terms, often critically different from those of Brahmanism or Jainism, as will be discussed below. But in describing the Buddhist position it is surely not wrong to begin with the Four Noble Truths, believed to have been expounded in the Buddha's first sermon and serving as the basis of Buddhist teaching subsequently. These Four Noble Truths are familiar, but perhaps they deserve a bit of commentary. The First Noble Truth is that all life is suffering *(dukkha)*. The Second Noble Truth is that the cause of suffering or unsatisfactoriness is craving *(taṇha)*, desire, or attachment. The Third Noble Truth is that the way to end unsatisfactoriness is to end desire, craving, or attachment, and the Fourth Noble Truth is the way this ending can be accomplished: the "noble Eightfold Path." The path can be very demanding, but anyone can take the first steps, which are the precepts for lay followers. These basic teachings of Buddhism underlie the discussion that follows.

Although "suffering" can serve, as it has traditionally, as a translation of *dukkha* in the First Noble Truth, scholars of Buddhism have pointed out that that translation can be misunderstood: if we conclude from the First Noble Truth that Buddhism is a pessimistic, gloomy, or cold teaching, we will be making a mistake. An alternative translation that is often suggested is "unsatisfactory." The idea that life is *dukkha* does not mean that people are unhappy all the time. Ordinary suffering is everyday physical or mental pain contrasted with ordinary happiness or indifference. A deeper meaning does not claim to explain how people feel all the time, but rather how, upon reflection, serious people may come to feel: "suffering through change." This is the sense that all things are subject to impermanence and change; every happy moment will come to an end. More fundamentally it is the recognition of the vulnerability and fragility of life itself, as illustrated to the young Siddhartha when he saw what he was not supposed to see: illness, old age, and death. That knowledge, combined with the knowledge that one will be endlessly reborn and go through all this *dukkha* again and again and again, can lead the sensitive to a wish for an alternative. What the Buddha offers as the ultimate alternative, nirvana (Pali, *nibbāna*), is elusive, indescribable, but definitely deeply preferable to the round of *saṃsāra,* endlessly repeated unsatisfactory lives.[177]

Yet the Buddha was preaching to lay men and women, not only to potential religious virtuosi. He offered a way of release from *saṃsāra,* but he was also concerned with those who were not ready for the demanding task of obtaining that release. For them he described a way of life that would lead to positive future lives, and, after many rebirths, ultimately nirvana. There has been a tendency to think of this possibility as a compromise with "true" Buddhism, or a decline from its early pure form, but there are many reasons to believe it is nothing of the kind. There may be One Path, but along the way there are various routes and various lives, and following the Buddha's teaching can help in all of them. Perhaps I can borrow from a recent work of Charles Taylor, *A Secular Age,* to suggest the variety of possibilities here.

Taylor suggests the term "fullness" for those who have reached a religious realization that goes beyond the world of daily life, that gives them "something more" than the ordinary satisfactions of life. It is paired with the notion of "emptiness" or "exile," the sense that life is dark, cold, and meaningless. Often it is religious adepts who feel such emptiness most acutely, in the Christian West sometimes called "the dark night of the soul," which may be a precursor to a religious quest that ends in something like fullness, or at least a glimpse of it. But Taylor is most useful for us at this point in reminding us that there is a "middle position" in between fullness and emptiness, which some people seem happy to see as "all there is." Of the middle position (we must be careful not to confuse this with the common characterization of Buddhism as the middle way between the pursuit of sensual pleasure and self-mortification) he writes:

> This is where we have found a way to escape the forms of negation, exile, emptiness, without having reached fullness. We come to terms with the middle position, often through some stable, even routine order in life, in which we are doing things which have some meaning for us; for instance, which contribute to our ordinary happiness, or which are fulfilling in various ways, or which contribute to what we conceive of as the good. Or often, in the best scenario, all three: for instance, we strive to live happily with spouse and children, while practising a vocation

which we find fulfilling, and also which constitutes an obvious contribution to human welfare.[178]

I would suggest that it is those people who at least at times experience the
sense of emptiness, of life as dark, cold, and meaningless, who would be
most likely to embark on the difficult religious path toward nirvana, the ultimate fullness that the Buddha offered. But to those in the middle position,
what Louis Dumont called the "man-in-the-world," the Buddha also had
much to offer, a way of life based not on the Brahmanic dharma, with its
radical particularism, but on a new sense of Dharma, the teaching of the
Buddha, in which an ethical way of life in the world is a significant part. All
of this is simply to explain that "all life is *dukkha*" means, not that Buddhists
think that daily life is completely miserable, but that those who reflect seriously on life may find that it is, in spite of many rewards, ultimately unsatisfactory, and that for those not looking beyond daily life at the moment, there
is still much the Buddha has to teach.

Let us go back to the words of Gombrich, a leading scholar of early Buddhism, where he says that the Buddha "turned the Brahmin ideology upside down," and try to understand in more detail what he means. Perhaps
most fundamental is that Buddha rejected the hereditary status of the
Brahmins and of the four *varṇas* altogether. Brahmins appear rather frequently in the Buddhist scriptures, often in arguments with the Buddha
that conclude with the conversion of the Brahmin. The depiction of Brahmins is often unflattering: at the beginning of conversations they appear
rude, arrogant, and angry that the Buddha has converted other Brahmins,
but they are not treated viciously.[179] At most there is an element of satire and
humor rather than bitterness and rejection. Yet the hegemonic Brahmin ideology, starting with the status of the Brahmin, is indeed overturned. As Steven Collins puts it:

A simple example here is provided by the use to which the very word
brāhmaṇa, "brahmin," is put in Buddhist texts. Whereas for Brahmanical thought it is being born a Brahmin in social fact which gives
the highest status in religion (and indeed in everything else), for Buddhism it is the man who practices Buddhist precepts to their utmost
who has the highest status, and who is therefore the ("true" or "real")
"Brahmin." That is to say, while the particular religious content has been
changed, even reversed (from a Brahmanic social to a Buddhist ethical

emphasis), still the overall formal structure—here "being a Brahmin" as the highest value—remains the same.[180]

What one might call the "gentle rejection" of Brahmanism by the Buddhists was nonetheless seen by many Brahmin writers as a mortal threat: the Buddhists rejected the entire Vedic tradition, all the received texts, as having any authority, the very eternal texts on which Brahmanism and the dharma that it took as essential were based. Further, the Buddhists rejected sacrifice, indeed the killing of any living being, with their doctrine of *ahiṃsā,* nonviolence. The beginnings of the idea of *ahiṃsā* can be found in Vedic texts, but applied selectively, and not intended to abolish sacrifices that are prescribed in the texts.[181] We have noted the Brahmin renouncers *(saṃnyāsins)* also rejected sacrifice, internalized it so that it was expressed in thought and word, not act, but for householders, the very foundation of the Brahmanic order, sacrifice was still required. The total rejection of sacrifice could not but seem a major threat to hegemonic Brahmanism.

Gombrich has made a similar point with respect to the ritual fires, three or five depending on the circumstances, that are central to Brahmanic ritual. Again, the *saṃnyāsin* abandoned fire upon leaving the world. That is one reason why he must beg: he can't even keep a kitchen fire to cook his own food. But fire, and the fire god Agni, though marginal in the later tradition, never lost their sanctity in normative Brahmanism. Again the Buddha radicalizes the Brahmin renouncer position by using fire as such as a symbol of "the fires of passion, hatred, and delusion," which must burn out before salvation can be attained.[182]

To give an idea of the satirical but not unsympathetic way the Buddhist Suttas treated Brahmins, I will briefly recount a story concerning a certain wealthy and influential Brahmin, Soṇadaṇḍa.[183] The Buddha and some of his followers had arrived at Campā, where Soṇadaṇḍa lived in considerable comfort. Soṇadaṇḍa, a man no longer young but of irreproachable birth for seven generations on both his father's and his mother's side, learned, handsome, and the teacher of many, decides to visit the Buddha because of his great reputation. His Brahmin friends reproach him, saying that the Buddha, being younger, should visit him rather than that he should visit the Buddha, and that his reputation would suffer if he initiates the visit. However, Soṇadaṇḍa, arguing that the Buddha is fully enlightened, convinces his friends that it is right for him to make the visit. On the way, however, he begins to worry that if he asks the Buddha a question, the Buddha may say it is not a fitting question, or if the Buddha asks him a question he may not know the answer, or if he sits in silence he will look bad, and his friends will despise him. He thinks to himself, "If anyone were despised by this company, his reputation would suffer, and then his income would suffer, for our income depends on the gaining of a reputation."[184]

Soṇadaṇḍa hopes the Buddha will ask him a question from his own field of the three Vedas, and the Buddha, sensing his discomfort, does so: "By how many qualities do Brahmins recognize a Brahmin?" Soṇadaṇḍa is delighted and answers that there are five such qualities: a Brahmin is well-born for seven generations, is a scholar versed in the mantras, is handsome, virtuous, and wise.

The Buddha responds: "But if one of these five qualities were omitted, could not one be recognized as a true Brahmin, being possessed of four of these qualities?" Soṇadaṇḍa replies, "We could leave out appearance, for what does that matter?" The Buddha counters by asking if we could leave out one more quality so that only three would be enough. Soṇadaṇḍa replies, "We could leave out the mantras." Once again the Buddha asks if there were one more that could be left out, so only two qualities would be necessary, and Soṇadaṇḍa replies, "We could leave out birth." At this Soṇadaṇḍa's Brahmin friends are really upset and tell him he is giving away too much and taking the Buddha's position, not that of a Brahmin. Soṇadaṇḍa tells them to shut up and responds further to the Buddha saying that the essential qualities of a Brahmin are virtue and wisdom. The Buddha asks if one of these could be omitted, and Soṇadaṇḍa replies: "No, Gotama. For wisdom is purified by morality, and morality is purified by wisdom: where one is, the other is, the moral man has wisdom and the wise man has morality."[185] It is clear to all that Soṇadaṇḍa has given up basic elements of Brahmin belief and has in effect converted to the teachings of the Buddha, that is, Dharma in the new sense of ethics and wisdom and not *dharma* in the old sense of caste obligations.

Yet Soṇadaṇḍa asks the Buddha to forgive him if he fails to recognize him adequately in public, because if he did so, his "reputation would suffer, and if a man's reputation suffers, his income suffers."[186] According to the commentary, Soṇadaṇḍa is "represented as a convert only to a limited extent."[187] Like the rich young man in the New Testament, Soṇadaṇḍa is unwilling to give up his life of privilege, even though he has agreed with the teachings of the Buddha. Many other Brahmins described in the Suttas do become real followers of the Buddha and obtain enlightenment. But the story of this little encoun-

ter between a Brahmin and the Buddha gives a sense of the tenor of argument in the Suttas and the skeptical but not unsympathetic way in which the
Buddha was believed to have treated his interlocutors. More important for us
is that, by reducing the qualities necessary to be recognized as a Brahmin
from the traditional five to the Buddhist two, this story gives an example of
the radical ethicization involved in the Buddha's teaching.

From the point of view of axial ethicization, perhaps the most fundamental innovation of Buddhism (though shared by other non-Brahmanical renouncer sects) was the ethical necessity of making the teaching of liberation,
Dharma in the Buddhist sense, available to all people, regardless of status or
ethnicity. Obeyesekere points to a climactic moment in one of the Suttas
where the Buddha comes to realize his role as universal teacher.[188]

After his long arduous search for enlightenment, the Buddha has finally
attained Nibbāna. He thinks, "This Dhamma that I have attained is profound, hard to see and hard to understand, peaceful and sublime, unattainable by mere reasoning, subtle, to be experienced by the wise." He considers
that he lives in a generation that delights in worldliness and is unlikely to
respond to what he has to teach. Some verses come to him that sum up his
view:

> Enough with teaching the Dhamma
> That even I found hard to reach;
> For it will never be perceived
> By those who live in lust and hate.
> Those dyed in lust, wrapped in darkness
> Will never discern this abstruse Dhamma
> Which goes against the worldly stream,
> Subtle, deep, and difficult to see.

But suddenly at this point the Brahmā Sahampati appears and addresses
him:[189]

> Just as one who stands on a mountain peak
> Can see below the people all around,
> So, O wise One, All-seeing Sage,
> Ascend the palace of the Dhamma.
> Let the Sorrowless One survey this human breed.
> Engulfed in sorrow, overcome by birth and old age.

Arise, victorious hero, caravan leader,
Debtless one, and wander in the world.
Let the blessed One teach the Dhamma,
There will be those who will understand.

The Buddha listened to Brahmā's pleading, and "out of compassion for be-ings" decides to undertake the task of making his teaching available to all.[190]

Obeyesekere points out that years later, at the point of death, the Buddha reiterates his intention when Māra, "the personification of the world's evils," tells him it is time to die: "I shall not come to my final passing away, Malig-nant One, until my bhikkus and bhikkunis [monks and nuns], laymen and laywomen, have come to be true disciples—wise, well-disciplined, apt and learned, preservers of the Dhamma, living according to the Dhamma, abid-ing by the appropriate conduct, and having gleaned the Master's word, are able to expound it . . . and preach this liberating Dhamma."[191] Having reached the point where he sees that he has accomplished all this and that the Dhamma is now available to all, monastics and laypeople of every status alike, he is ready to die.

In the Suttas the Buddha is often depicted as surrounded by large num-bers of monks, and individual monks are often his conversation partners. But just as often it is laypeople, not infrequently even kings, who come to the Buddha with questions or in search of advice, with whom the Buddha speaks. Solitary renouncers are referred to, often with admiration, but the Buddha is most often shown as engaged in an active social life both with his monks and with the larger society. He is shown teaching his monastic fol-lowers the right way to conduct themselves in their quest for nirvana, but he is just as often shown teaching laypeople the right way to live—a way that will avoid the pitfalls that bad actions can produce in this and future lives, and that will instead lead to a good life here and a better life later on, ulti-mately leading to the possibility of attaining nirvana, even though for the laity that is not their immediate concern.

Thus, although Buddhism produced the earliest fully developed monas-tic system in religious history, comparable only to the later development of monasticism in Christianity, it cannot be viewed simply as a monastic reli-gion. It is also very much a religion of the laity, who are not viewed as devi-ant or "popular" Buddhists in contrast to the monks. Though further from the goal than the monks, they are equal partners in the community, and the monks are in their own way as dependent on the laity as the laity are on the monks.[192] Ilana Silber has described the core of their profound interdependence:

> Barred by *Vinaya* discipline from providing for their own food and shelter, monks were thrown into a state of dependency on the laity and hence prevented from cutting themselves off from society. This dependency is mutual, since on the laity's side the Sangha is said to form a "field of merit," in the sense that providing monks with material support through gifts *(dana)* represents the most effective (if not the only) way for the laymen to reap merit.[193]

Silber notes that this exchange should not be viewed as a magical buying of rewards, because the generous intention of the giver is essential to the efficacy of the gift. The laity are also dependent on the monks as the guardians of the canonical texts for their preaching of the Buddha's Dharma, but the monks, pledged to nonviolence as they are, are dependent on the laity to maintain order among the monks and even to discern who is a legitimate monk and who is a self-serving parasite. In short, though the Buddha and Buddhist monks have "left home" and are no longer involved in the familial, economic, and political obligations of householders, they are still very much engaged with society in the ongoing life of the Sangha.

Although a decision to "leave home" marked a sharp difference between Buddhist monk and layman, the obligations undertaken by the Buddhist laity overlap to some degree with those undertaken by novice monks. Gombrich puts the Five Precepts for the laity in a larger perspective:

> The positive values of kindness and unselfishness characterize Buddhism better than do the moral precepts for the laity which are expressed negatively. Though usually called "precepts," they are really undertakings, expressed in the first person. They are five: not to take life, steal, be unchaste (which is defined according to one's situation), lie, or take intoxicants, inasmuch as they lead to carelessness and hence to breaking the first four undertakings . . . Positively, the Buddhist's first duty is to be generous, and the primary—though by no means the only—object of his generosity is to the Sangha. Generosity, keeping the moral undertakings, cultivating one's mind: these three summarize the Buddhist path to a good rebirth and ultimately to release from all rebirth.[194]

Gombrich goes on to describe certain additional rules that the laity were encouraged to follow on certain days, the quarter days of the lunar month: "For a night and a day they undertook complete chastity, not to eat solid food after midday, not to adorn themselves or witness entertainments, not to use luxurious beds."[195] These, together with the Five Precepts, are the same as the obligations of novice monks except that in addition the monks must abstain from the use of money. Although not common, a layperson could undertake to keep these injunctions permanently. In general, then, the line between monks and laity was not as impermeable as one might think: even though the monks were expected to be concerned more with the attainment of nirvana and the laity with a better rebirth, still the latter looked forward to an eventual attainment of nirvana.

Buddhism in the West has long been viewed as a "rational" religion (often in implicit or explicit contrast to Christianity), and Buddhist religious and ethical teaching is often expressed in systematic propositional form, with premises leading to conclusions. For this reason it is easy to see Buddhism as an axial religion, if one takes the presence of "theory" as a marker of axiality. But as in the other axial cases, the "logical" aspect of Buddhist teaching is intertwined with a variety of other kinds of discourse—symbols and narratives—in ways sometimes overlooked by its Western admirers. Further, Buddhist truths are to be understood logically in terms of what the words mean (that is, semantically), but to be "really" understood they must change the hearers in their practical stance toward themselves and the world (in the linguistic sense, pragmatically).[196]

Thus even in the rather terse first sermon of the Buddha after his Awakening, the famous Deer Park Sermon, which is devoted to the exposition of the Four Noble Truths, the Buddha repeatedly stresses, after stating the truths, that he has finally "fully understood" and "realized" them so that the knowledge and vision arose in him: "Unshakeable is the liberation of my mind. This is my last birth. Now there is no more renewed existence." And it is also recounted that while he was giving the sermon, one of his followers, the Venerable Kondañña, became fully awakened to their truth: "Whatever is subject to origination is all subject to cessation."[197] Thus, understanding the words and their logical connection is only the first step; it is only when the teachings have penetrated deep into one's consciousness that they can be transforming.

Steven Collins has pointed out that, although systematic thought has always been important in Buddhist teachings, it has also always been accom-

panied by narrative and symbolic thought. In summarizing the linkages between these three kinds of thought (which can be found in all the axial
religions), Collins argues that "imagery is the bridge, the mediation" between
the systematic and the narrative:

> The two most common images of nirvana in the developed tradition
> are the quenching of fire and the city. Buddhist systematic thought
> presents a static arrangement of ideas, which are connected by logical
> not temporal relation; its narratives, whether the overall master-text or
> the stories told in actual texts, are by necessity temporally structured.
> The imagery of fire is built into the vocabulary of the systematic thought
> in which the concept of nirvana exists; but it also has a temporal di-
> mension, embodied in the verbs or verbal notions within the image: it
> is of fire *going out* or *quenched*. This temporal dimension is, in micro-
> cosm, the same as that of the larger-scale stories and histories in which
> narrative thought textualizes both time and timeless nirvana. So not
> only is the image intrinsic to the vocabulary of Buddhism (attachment-
> fuel, nirvana-quenching); it also contains—in a nutshell, or, to use a
> south Asian metaphor, in seed form—the narrative movement from
> suffering to resolution and closure in which nirvana's syntactic value is
> to be found. The city of nirvana can be a static object of textual vision;
> but in the notion of the city as the destination point of a journey, the
> terminus of the Path, which is again intrinsic to Buddhist systematic
> thought, there is also a microcosmic version of the entire Buddhist master-
> narrative. The Path to salvation is thus, in the image as in the master-
> narrative, a journey through time from the city of the transient body to
> the city of timeless and deathless nirvana: the city without fear, as one
> of the earliest texts to use the image calls it. The images set the logic of
> the concept in motion: once there is motion, there is temporal exten-
> sion, and once there is temporal extension there is narrative.[198]

Just to round out Collins's eloquent effort to capture the central concern
of Buddhist devotion, we can go to him again to explain how the word "syntactic" got into the above quotation:

> Both the concept and the imagery of nirvana eventuate, by design, in
> aporetic silence. Nirvana is the full stop (period) in the Buddhist story,
> the point at which narrative imagination must cease. But this cessation

provides the sense of an ending rather than a mere breaking-off. Nirvana is a moment within a discursive or practical dynamic, a formal element of closure in the structure of Buddhist imagination, texts and rituals. This is the sense in which I want to say that nirvana has a syntactic as well as a semantic value: it is the moment of ending which gives structure to the whole.[199]

Collins then goes on to apply his argument about the paradigmatic story of Buddhist liberation to the story of Gotama the Buddha. "For any individual, the denouement of the story of spiritual liberation—*Bildungsroman* on a cosmic scale—is both the discovery of Truth and a change in being . . . When the Saint realizes the truth, it is not that he or she has simply acquired some new knowledge, but rather that such knowledge instantiates a new existential state or condition."[200] At the central point of silence, the idea of nirvana, when all the things one can say don't seem to help, Buddhists have always turned to the Buddha in something we should hesitate to call worship because of the associations of that term in Abrahamic religions, but as an instantiation of what the whole teaching is about. As the Buddha himself said, "He who sees the Dhamma sees me, he who sees me sees the Dhamma."[201]

Thus the central Buddhist teaching, contained already in the Four Noble Truths, is the Path from suffering to nirvana, expressed in systematic and narrative thought and even in such symbols as the quenched fire. Insofar as this teaching disregards all distinctions of birth and proclaims the equality of all human beings in their capacity to follow the Path, the teaching is revolutionary relative to early Indian society with its heavy reliance on birth and lineage. But as Romila Thapar noted, the Buddha called for no revolutionary overthrow of existing institutions; rather he attempted to establish a parallel society, offering an alternative way of life, which would grow by attraction, not by conquest. Central to the establishment of this parallel society was the creation of the Sangha, the order of Buddhist monks.

Patrick Olivelle has suggested that although the Buddha surrounded himself with followers who had renounced the world, the development of the Sangha as a "formal organization," one based on the acceptance of universal rules and obligations rather than, as in most social organization of the time, on particularistic ties,[202] took place only gradually.[203] At first the call to leave home was simply to become a wandering mendicant. During the rainy season it became convenient to have the monks gather together in temporary communities for about four months, and then go their separate ways. Gradually these communities became permanent and Buddhist monasteries common, often in the vicinity of cities.

When compared to Christian monasticism, Buddhist monasticism was markedly less hierarchical. The Buddha refused to appoint a successor, saying that the Dhamma was all that the monks needed, and even within monasteries hierarchy was minimal, though the development of an elaborate set of monastic rules, the *Vinaya,* was an attempt to maintain order. Each monk was to pursue the Path on his own, but the relation between teacher and student was important and gave rise to teaching lineages; the fractures between these lineages could become the structural basis for "sectarian" splits. The Sangha was in no sense a model for society as a whole and stood deliberately at a distance from it, but the somewhat amorphous nature of Buddhist monasticism, as we have seen, necessitated a close relation between monks and lay patrons, often kings, high officials, or wealthy merchants. If there was an effort to create something like a parallel community relative to the existing social order, it consisted not of monks alone but of monks and laity together.

Buddhism, in spite of becoming one of the greatest of all missionary religions, spreading to virtually all of Southeast and East Asia, was in India, without remainder, and to some degree incomprehensibly, absorbed by Hinduism.[204] To what extent what was absorbed changed the absorbers is a matter of scholarly inquiry and argument. What is undeniable is that a degree of ethical universalism, barely foreshadowed in the Brahmanic tradition, is evident in the great theistic movements of later Hinduism.

Religion and Politics after Buddhism

The teachings of the Buddha are clearly post-Vedic, and they are but one expression of a society, and particularly a polity, that is post-Vedic as well, remembering that there is a sense in which India is never "post-Vedic." Magadha, one of the centers of early Buddhism, represents a new kind of polity—larger, more centralized, with a somewhat different conception of kingship and rule than had prevailed earlier. The Buddhist texts themselves give much evidence of significant cultural, social, and political changes, but there are other important texts that we must consider, however briefly. Perhaps most important are the great epics, the *Rāmāyaṇa* and the *Mahābhārata*—which, though they are very different from the *Iliad* and the *Odyssey,* do indeed have an epic form—but also such texts as the *Dharmaśasāstra* of Manu and the *Arthaśāstra* of Kauṭalīya. These texts are not precisely datable and probably contain material from more than one time, but in their present form they date from the last centuries BCE and the first centuries CE.

We must also consider not only the growth of centralized monarchies but the creation of what can only be called an empire: the Mauryan dynasty (321–185 BCE) founded in Magadha by Candragupta Maurya, but reaching its greatest extent under its most famous ruler, Aśoka (304–232 BCE; r. 273–232 BCE). Candragupta founded the Mauryan dynasty almost exactly a hundred years before Qin Shihuangdi founded the first imperial dynasty in China, but their futures would be very different. The Qin dynasty was succeeded, with significant breaks to be sure, by one imperial dynasty after another for more than 2,000 years, until 1911, most of them ruling over most of what we now call China. After the collapse of the Mauryan dynasty, however, India remained divided through most of its subsequent history, with no regime again reaching the size of the Mauryan empire, yet with a cultural unity that surely rivals that of China, and for which political unification was clearly not a prerequisite.

Aśoka, as we will see, was probably the most innovative ruler in Indian history, but, for reasons we will consider below, he was almost forgotten except in Buddhist texts. His inscriptions, the first examples of writing in India, extensive and full of interesting material, were written in a script and languages that made them soon after their creation unreadable until modern times. Aśoka was not as totally forgotten as Akhenaten, but given his historical importance his absence from subsequent historical memory is remarkable. Nonetheless his presence can be sensed in all the texts that give this period such a creative role in Indian religious and political thought.

We must begin our effort to understand changes in the centuries before and after the turn of the Common Era by taking a closer look at the kingdom of Magadha. In the earliest references it is described as being beyond the pale of Vedic culture, inhabited by barbarians, but the process of expansive Sanskritization had reached it by the time of the Buddha, probably the fifth century BCE, as we have noted above. Under the rule of Bimbisāra and his son Ajātaśatru, Magadha became the dominant principality in the Ganges valley and developed a polity that differed significantly from earlier times. What we can thinly discern, mainly from Buddhist and Jain sources, is a new degree of centralization and the emergence of a king with enhanced powers. We have seen a long transition from chiefdoms to paramount chiefdoms, to an uneasy early state during the first half of the first millennium BCE. We saw that the early state depended heavily on a complex ritual system, focusing on the ruling house but allowing the participation of other aristocratic lineages, and very dependent on the alliance of Kṣatriyas and Brahmins.

Sometime in the middle years of the first millennium BCE and especially clearly in Magadha, the king was able to concentrate more power in his own hands, to depend less on local notables and more on officials chosen from the royal lineage or closely dependent lineages, and to extract what have to be called taxes rather than tribute as in earlier times. The great royal rituals were still performed, but less frequently and more exclusively in the royal lineage alone. Brahmins were important and respected, but could not claim exclusive access to the sacred, with the emergence of the Buddhists, Jains, and other groups. Both kings Bimbisāra and Ajātaśatru were claimed as patrons of their religions in Buddhist and Jain texts, though in those same texts they are portrayed as having Brahmin advisors and as in no sense having "established" any one religion. Newly expansive Magadha was clearly less bound by older expectations and more inclined to experimentation in both political and religious realms than were earlier regimes. It was the seedbed of much that was to follow.[205]

Bimbisāra and Ajātaśatru, perhaps in the fifth century BCE (all dates are provisional), had greatly extended the domain of Magadha so that it included the entire lower Ganges valley and adjoining territory to the north and east. The Nanda dynasty, which followed and ruled through much of the fourth century BCE, extended the rule of Magadha significantly so that it reached the west coast, thus spanning the subcontinent from the Bay of Bengal to the Arabian Sea. But it was the next dynasty, the Mauryas, that created an empire that included most of the subcontinent, including parts of what are now Pakistan and Afghanistan, and excluding only the southernmost regions, and even they may have accepted a kind of tributary status relative to the Mauryas. The founder of the dynasty, Candragupta Maurya, overthrew the last of the Nandas in 321 BCE. According to tradition, Candragupta's takeover was masterminded by his advisor Kauṭalīya,[206] who later became his chief minister. The authorship of the important text on rulership, the *Arthaśāstra,* is attributed to Kauṭalīya. The text as we have it undoubtedly has later material, although some of it may derive from Mauryan times and even possibly from Candragupta's chief minister. Candragupta extended the territory of Magadha, as did his son Bindusāra, who completed the conquest except for the important territory to the south of Magadha, Kaliṅga. Bindusāra's son, Aśoka, succeeded his father in 278 BCE (all these dates are approximate) after an interim in which he perhaps killed one or more of his brothers in order to obtain the throne, and it was Aśoka who brought the empire to its geographical completion with the conquest of Kaliṅga a few years later.

We know far more about Aśoka than about any ruler before him and for a long time after him due to the many rock and pillar inscriptions scattered throughout his empire in which he speaks in his own voice. The inscriptions of Aśoka are the earliest surviving examples of writing in India, and some scholars believe that the earliest Indian script was invented in Aśoka's chancery. We should remember that on the northwest frontier the Indians had long been in contact with script-using peoples—the Persians, who controlled some northwestern Indian regions under the Achaemenids, and most recently the Greeks in the fourth century BCE. Alexander the Great invaded the Indus Valley in 326 BCE and was succeeded by a number of small Greek states that Candragupta Maurya conquered, but Alexander's successor in Syria and Mesopotamia, Seleucus Nicator, invaded India in 305, challenging Candragupta for control of regions that had once been under Persian control and more recently ruled by Greeks. Seleucus failed in his efforts but concluded a treaty with Candragupta in 305 BCE in which he ceded territory in return for 500 war elephants. That the Mauryan empire, the largest India had ever seen, succeeded so closely the creation of Alexander's empire, the largest Mediterranean and Middle Eastern empire up to his time, is surely significant, as were the continuing diplomatic relations of the Mauryas with the Hellenistic successor states of Alexander. The invention of writing in India could be an example of what anthropologists call stimulus diffusion: the Mauryas did not take over a foreign alphabet but invented one of their own. Another explanation, that the Indian script was developed from the Aramaic script used as a kind of lingua franca in Persia and northwest India at the time, is perhaps more persuasive.[207]

Sticking only to the most reliable sources, his own words in his inscriptions, we can say several things: that Aśoka at some point became an adherent of Buddhism, that his conquest of Kaliṅga was bloody, involving much loss of life among both combatants and noncombatants and great suffering of the civilian population, that he repented of the violence of his conquest, and that he subsequently renounced war and vowed to rule by *Dhamma,* not violence.[208] The edicts were written in Prakrit, the spoken language commonly used in north India at the time, derived from classical Sanskrit, as was Pali, the language of the early Buddhist canon, to which it was closely related. In both Prakrit and Pali, Sanskrit "dharma" had become "dhamma." It would be a mistake, however, to read Aśoka's *Dhamma* as the same as the Buddha Dhamma, as some early students of the edicts did. Although Aśoka did direct some edicts to his fellow Buddhist believers, it is clear from their contents that his own *Dhamma,* his own teaching, which the edicts were intended to communicate, was nondenominational, so to speak, addressed equally to all believers and intended to communicate values common to all the religions of the time. In particular Aśoka taught equal respect for *śramaṇas* (Buddhist monks, but also monks of other sects) and *brāhmaṇas* (Brahmins), even varying which term came first in different edicts.

Aśoka's *Dhamma* could be seen as a form of political propaganda, though with a religious quality in its content. Aśoka was surely not the inventor of political propaganda, and the rock inscriptions of Achaemenid rulers may have been the model from which those of Aśoka derived. But the difference in content is significant: for example, the Behistun Inscription of the great Achaemenid king Darius 1 (549–486 BCE), which echoes the pronouncements of many rulers before him, begins "I am Darius, the great king, king of kings, the king of Persia, the king of countries."[209] Aśoka, on the other hand, is relatively modest about himself, referring to himself most often merely as "the king Piyadassi (his personal name), the Beloved of the Gods." Darius's long inscription proceeds to recount the difficult circumstances surrounding his accession to the throne, and then at length the many conquests and particularly the violent suppression of numerous revolts and the terrible fate of the rebels, with the clear intention of warning any possible future rebels not to make the attempt. One could say that the whole inscription is drenched in blood and violence.

Virtually the only reference to warfare in Aśoka's inscriptions is his expression of remorse for his conquest of Kaliṅga, which appears in many locations, but not, significantly, in Kaliṅga itself, where the memory of the war may have left the inhabitants too scarred to hear about remorse. Aśoka's inscriptions are as devoted to peace as Darius's were to war. For example, the Sixth Major Rock Edict says:

> I consider that I must promote the welfare of the whole world, and hard work and the dispatch of business are the means of doing so. Indeed there is no better work than promoting the welfare of the whole world.

And whatever may be my great deeds, I have done them in order to discharge my debt to all beings. I work for their happiness in this life, that in the next they may gain heaven. For this purpose has this inscription of *Dhamma* been engraved.[210]

Aśoka expresses a concern for the health and well-being of his subjects and describes some of his good works, such as improving the roads by planting banyan trees for shade and providing wells and rest houses every nine miles so that humans and animals could be refreshed.[211] But he insists that the greatest gift he has to give is *Dhamma* itself:

> There is no gift comparable to the gift of *Dhamma,* the praise of *Dhamma,* the sharing of *Dhamma,* fellowship in *Dhamma.* And this is—good behaviour towards slaves and servants, obedience to mother and father, generosity towards friends, acquaintances, and relatives and toward *śramaṇas* and brahmans, and abstention from killing living beings . . . By doing so, there is gain in this world, and in the next there is infinite merit, through the gift of *Dhamma.*[212]

Although Aśoka's *Dhamma* is clearly indebted to Buddhism, it is intended as a general teaching, not a sectarian one. One of Aśoka's primary concerns is religious tolerance:

> But the Beloved of the Gods does not consider gifts of honour to be as important as the essential advancement of all sects. Its basis is the control of one's speech, so as not to extol one's own sect or disparage that of another on unsuitable occasions. On each occasion one should honour the sect of another, for by doing so one increases the influence of one's own sect and benefits that of the other, while, by doing otherwise, one diminishes the influence of one's own sect and harms the other . . . therefore concord is to be commended so that men may hear one another's principles.[213]

For example, nonviolence, *ahiṃsā,* an absolute principle in Buddhism, is frequently praised by Aśoka, but it is a moderate nonviolence, admitting of exceptions. On the whole, animals are not to be killed for food, but in a few cases it is all right. The death penalty is still enforced for certain crimes. Even with respect to warfare, though conquest is ruled out, punishment of troublesome forest tribes, for instance, is still a possibility. It should also be remembered that nonviolence was an increasingly general value, to be found in extreme form among the Jains, but widely affirmed in nascent Hinduism.

One central element in Aśoka's *Dhamma* that links it to Buddhism, though not in a sectarian way, is that it was universal. There is nothing in it about *varṇa*, about obligations arising from one's status at birth. One must respect Brahmins as one must respect ascetics of various sorts, but that did not enjoin specific caste obligations. Non-Buddhist texts that treated dharma also had general admonitions that would apply to everyone, but they were complemented by a heavy emphasis on obligations particular to various castes. It is these latter teachings that are completely missing in Aśoka's *Dhamma*. Although Aśoka's *Dhamma* cannot be called secular—it is as concerned with future lives as with this one—it is primarily political, the basis of the kind of good society that Aśoka was trying to create and that, as far as we can tell, he was at least partly successful in creating. After Kaliṅga his long reign was peaceful.

Aśoka's effort to spread *Dhamma* was not confined to inscribing admonitions. He appointed a number of officials known as *dhamma-mahāmattas,* whose duty was to spread the teaching, not only within the realm but beyond the frontiers as well, as in the missions that were sent to Hellenistic monarchs. Only a few individuals could read the inscriptions in a society where literacy was just beginning, but gatherings were held at the sites of the inscriptions, which were read to the assembled people. As with most forms of preaching in human history, it is doubtful that many people understood or acted upon what was preached, yet the influence of Aśoka's *Dhamma* was more important in subsequent Indian history than we can precisely measure.

The appointment of *dhamma-mahāmattas* is only one example of the many offices that were created under Mauryan rule. We do not, however, know how individuals were chosen for these offices and whether the criterion of merit that was so important in Chinese bureaucracy was institutionalized in any effective way. On the contrary, it would appear that the Mauryas, like Indian rulers before and after them, relied on particularistic criteria of kinship and lineage, and often delegated responsibility, especially in the areas beyond greater Magadha itself, to local notables. Thus in spite of Aśoka's attempt to unify his empire with his *Dhamma,* it remained fragile and fissile. The series of weak rulers who succeeded him saw the gradual crumbling of imperial rule, and the last of them was finally overthrown in 185 BCE by the

Śuṅga dynasty, of allegedly Brahmin lineage, who ruled over Magadha and a considerably smaller realm than the Mauryas at their height. There are some accounts that Buddhism was persecuted under the Śuṅgas, but it seems more likely that Buddhism was tolerated under an increasingly orthodox Brahmin regime.

In trying to understand the relation between religion and politics in India toward the end of the first millennium BCE, we have to take account of the Mauryas and particularly of Aśoka, because there we have evidence that is mostly missing from other polities of the day. What we know, aside from some archaeological evidence, is mainly literary, especially Aśoka's inscriptions. Our only certain knowledge of Aśoka's polity is derived from the inscriptions themselves, which are not, of course, objective descriptions, but there are some texts that are thought to be from the Mauryan period or not long after that may also shed some light. Sheldon Pollock has written that "few questions in premodern South Asian history are more unyielding to coherent and convincing answers than the nature of political power and the character of polity," noting that "not a single document from any royal archive has been preserved."[214] So what we have in the inscriptions and texts that have survived are representations of political imagination, of how those who wrote these texts wanted things to be seen to be or thought they ought to be, as opposed to how they actually were. Yet Pollock argues, rightly in my view, that such representations, as long as we do not take them as literal descriptions, still tell us a great deal of how educated Indians thought about their society, its problems and its aspirations.[215]

Even if, in trying to answer our questions, we are largely confined to language—to surviving texts from the period—we are immediately confronted by the question of what language. Aśoka's inscriptions and those of other rulers for several centuries after him "were composed not in Sanskrit but in various Middle-Indic dialects, sometimes referred to as Prakrits. While closely related to Sanskrit, these dialects were considered entirely distinct from it by premodern Indian thinkers."[216] But a number of highly important Sanskrit texts have survived that we have strong internal reasons for believing date from the centuries just before and after the turn of the Common Era. The Prakrits presumably represented the spoken languages of their day, whereas Sanskrit was an elite literary language. The Prakrit inscriptions spoke to everyone, whereas Sanskrit was the language of a special group. Some Prakrits did develop at least for a time into literary languages, and Pali,

a hybrid of several Prakrits in which the early Buddhist scriptures were written, survived for a long time in southern India and then up to the present in
Sri Lanka and Southeast Asia as the primary literary language of Theravada
Buddhism, one self-consciously *not* Sanskrit. It was, however, Sanskrit that
would come to be the "cosmopolitan language," to use Pollock's term, in the
following centuries (by the middle of the first millennium CE, even Buddhists in northern India began to write in Sanskrit), and some of the most
influential Sanskrit texts were already written in Mauryan, or, more likely,
immediately post-Mauryan times.

In trying to understand why Sanskrit was so central in the surviving texts
of our period, we can start with the fact that Sanskrit was the language of the
Vedas and so had long been the language of the Brahmanical tradition, and
the Sanskrit texts of our period were largely written by Brahmins. But there
is one fundamental difference between the language of the Vedas and the
new literary Sanskrit of post-Mauryan times: the former was oral, the latter
was written. Writing provided the possibility that had remained only incipient in the oral tradition: second-order, critical thinking, beginning with
language about language itself, in the new science of grammar.

Pāṇini's *Aṣṭādhyāyī* was a pivotal text. It was a treatise on the grammar of
the Vedas that was part of a series of texts auxiliary to the Vedas called the
vedāṅga that were developing to help students cope with a language increasingly remote from contemporary speech. As such it was part of the natural
continuation of the Vedic tradition. But it was also the first of what would
later be called *śāstras,* that is, systematic treatises concerning a particular
subject, in this case grammar. Pāṇini's capacity to think rationally about
language made his book a masterpiece in its genre—in advance of linguistic
reflection anywhere in the world when it was written and still capable of
stimulating the development of modern linguistics when it was translated
into Western languages in the nineteenth century.

Pāṇini is usually dated in the fourth century BCE—on the cusp of Indian
literacy—and there is an ongoing argument as to whether the *Aṣṭādhyāyī* was
originally oral or written. This is an argument about which I have no expert
knowledge, but it seems to me likely that, though the book is a reflection on
memorized speech, it was itself written and that writing was essential for the
reflexive character of the book, that it was a critical reflection on language. Yet
we also must remember that Pāṇini's book was not about language in general
but about Vedic Sanskrit in particular, and that he undoubtedly believed the

language he was studying was true language in itself, uniquely different from any other, which suggests the tension between the universal and the particular that exists in the Indian intellectual tradition from early on, and the special nature of Sanskrit as the "preeminent language of literature and systematic thought" long after its exclusively ritual use had been overcome.[217] It is also worth noting that Buddhists did not use Sanskrit, at least not for many centuries. The Buddha is supposed to have told his disciples to preach in whatever language the people understood, at a time when no one spoke classical Sanskrit, so the decision not to use Sanskrit was deliberate. Pali developed out of one or more spoken languages but soon became a special language itself, and almost surely a written one fairly early, surviving in the Theravada canon and southern Buddhism generally until the present, itself becoming an elite language known almost exclusively to educated monks. The split in language was an expression of the profound split in culture that was developing between Buddhism and what would be known as Hinduism.

There are *śāstras* somewhat later than Pāṇini's *Aṣṭādhyāyī* that deal with the relation of religion and politics more immediately related to our present discussion, but before considering them we may just say a little about what the term *śāstra* refers to. Pollock sometimes translates it as "science" or "systematic thought."[218] He even calls it "theory," which, unlike the other terms he uses for it, he puts in quotes. In speaking of the proliferation of *śāstras* in later centuries, he goes so far as to say that "nothing in old India was untheorized." However he makes it clear that by "theory" he mainly means "detailed inventory and taxonomy."[219] Consequently he emphasizes the empiricism of Sanskrit systematic thought, the belief that "nothing is beyond the reach of Sanskrit *śāstra*; everything, everywhere, however intimate [he is talking here about the *Kāmasūtra*], is knowable and has become known."[220] Clearly inventory and taxonomy, expressed often in *śāstras* by endless lists, are the beginning and foundation of scientific theory; but systematic thought becomes theory without quotation marks only when it reaches the level of generalizations that can be put to the test. It is interesting that the earliest *śāstra*, Pāṇini's *Aṣṭādhyāyī*, was the most scientific in this sense.

We noted above the early Indian idea of the three (or four) ends of life—*dharma* (duty), *artha* (success), and *kāma* (pleasure), also *mokṣa* (salvation, liberation)—and there were *śāstras* devoted to each of them, notably Manu's *Dharmaśāstra*, Kauṭalīya's *Arthaśāstra*, the *Kāmasūtra*, and the Yoga Sutras concerning *mokṣa*, though each of them is a composite text difficult to date precisely. The *Arthaśāstra*, a treatise on economics and politics, used by

Romila Thapar to provide some sense of what Mauryan rule was like in the absence of more direct data,[221] gives a nod to the preeminence of dharma in rulership, but is mainly devoted to the practical exigencies of rule without much sensitivity to moral or religious issues. Wendy Doniger writes, "The *Artha-shastra* is a compendium of advice for a king, and though it is often said to be Machiavellian, Kautilya makes Machiavelli look like Mother Teresa."[222] The *Arthaśāstra,* like most *śāstras,* consists largely of a list of rules, rules that can be read as descriptive but that are primarily prescriptive, so we cannot use them to tell us exactly how things were. Although at times seeming to describe a big state, the *Arthaśāstra* at other times seems to be describing a group of small states maneuvering for hegemony between enemies and allies. Undoubtedly the text, parts of which were written at different times by different authors, was concerned with both, though it is often not clear how. The great emphasis on a complex system of spies suggests precarious rule lacking in deep legitimacy. Because the *Arthaśāstra* was concerned with *artha* and not primarily with *dharma,* it is not particularly helpful with respect to the relation of religion and politics.

Manu's *Dharmaśāstra,* on the other hand, though it overlaps in part with the *Arthaśāstra,* gives much more attention to the relation of religion and politics. Written by and for Brahmins, Manu's *Dharmaśāstra* is first of all a kind of handbook for proper Brahmin behavior but secondly it is concerned with how kingship relates to dharma and more specifically to the Brahmins. It was preceded by and draws from the *Dharmasūtras,* which are classified among the *vedāṅga,* that is, works auxiliary to and explanatory of the ritual and linguistic complexities of the Vedas. As we saw in the case of Pāṇini's Grammar, these were systematizing works moving in the direction of the later *śāstras.* The four major *Dharmasūtras* are tentatively said by their translator, Patrick Olivelle, to date from the early third to the late second centuries BCE; if these dates are accurate, they may have been written texts.[223] In any case they consist largely of lists of ritual rules and rules of conduct for Brahmins through the course of the life cycle (many of these rules also apply to the other two twice-born castes), with only 6 to 12 percent of the texts devoted to statecraft.[224] Though Manu develops the same subject matter, adding a much longer treatment of rulership, his book is an organized treatise, beginning and ending with cosmological and religious reflections: it is thus a true *śāstra.*

Manu's *Dharmaśāstra* is a work of great importance, with continuing influence to the present day, because it attempted to do three things, each central to the continuity of the tradition but difficult to synthesize: (1) codify and absolutize the Vedic tradition as it was understood in the author's day; (2) affirm the new strand of Brahmanic spirituality as represented by the Upaniṣads; and (3) respond to the challenge of the ethical universalism of Buddhism and of Aśoka's *Dhamma*. With respect to the last point Olivelle writes, "The very creation of a Brahmanical genre of literature dedicated to Law *(dharma)* [of which Manu was the culmination] was possibly due to the elevation of this word to the level of imperial ideology by Aśoka."[225]

By giving the book the name of the first man and/or the first king in Indic mythology, Manu, the claim to virtual canonical status is clear. But this claim in turn is based on the status of the Vedas as uncreated scripture, on which the book of Manu claims to be based. Thus the Vedic injunctions with all their ritual and other forms of particularity are placed beyond question. Yet the renouncer tradition of the Upaniṣads, with its radical rejection of the fire sacrifice at the heart of the Vedas, is also affirmed. In fact there is much more emphasis on nonviolence and nonkilling of animals than there is on Vedic sacrifice, yet the latter is never rejected. Manu resorts to language that other religions have at times found convenient: "Killing in a sacrifice is not killing . . . The violence to those that move and those that do not move which is sanctioned by the Veda—that is known as non-violence" (*Manu* 5.39, 44).[226] Doniger points out that at a time in history when Vedic sacrifice had become "largely irrelevant and to some extent embarrassing," Manu must still defend it, even using the terms of its critics to do so.[227]

With respect to ethical universalism, Manu uses two tactics, each with its own problems. First, there are several places where Manu describes what Doniger calls general dharma as opposed to particular dharma. Doniger contrasts the particular dharma arising from caste, *svadharma,* to universal dharma, "sometimes called perpetual dharma [*sanatana dharma*] or dharma held in common [*sadharana dharma*]" that involved general moral precepts applicable to all classes and castes.[228] She cites one verse: "Nonviolence, truth, not stealing, purification, and the suppression of the sensory powers are the dharma of the four classes [varnas], in a nutshell" (10.63), and an overlapping one to the same effect (12.83–93), as well as one (6.93) somewhat different (lacking nonviolence) for the top three (twice-born) *varnas*.[229] Perhaps particularly significant because coming very near the end of the book in a discussion of the "highest good" is the list at 12:83: "The recitation of the Vedas, inner heat, knowledge, the repression of the sensory powers, non-violence and serving the guru bring about the supreme good."[230] However, Manu goes on to qualify what looks to be a rather heterogeneous list, in which only nonviolence seems to count as an ethical universal, by saying:

> One should understand that acts prescribed by the Veda are always a more effective means of securing the highest good both here and in the hereafter than the above six activities. All these activities without exception are included within the scheme of the acts prescribed by the Veda, each in proper order within the rules of a corresponding act. (12.86–87)[231]

Doniger draws the implication of such a passage when she writes, "The particular rule generally overrides the general rule; *sva-dharma* trumps general dharma."[232]

Another strategy for affirming a kind of universalism while defending particularism was Manu's portrayal of the Brahmin as being the most perfect and complete manifestation of human flourishing, the universal man. The other *varṇa*s are then defined in a kind of subtraction theory as being like the Brahmins but lacking certain of their qualities, such as the competence to perform sacrifices, ending with the Śūdras (and of course the outcastes), who cannot hear or understand the Veda. If the Brahmin ideal were a model for everyone, so that anyone who acted like a Brahmin could be considered one (an idea suggested in Buddhist scripture), it would indeed imply ethical universalism. Yet Manu relentlessly reaffirms the impossibility of this idea. In his cosmological introduction he sets down what has been and always will be:

> In the beginning through the words of the Veda alone, [the Lord] fashioned for all of them specific names and activities, also specific stations . . . As they are brought forth again and again, each creature follows on its own the very activity assigned to it in the beginning by the Lord. Violence or non-violence, gentleness or cruelty, righteousness *(dharma)* or unrighteousness *(adharma)*, truthfulness or untruthfulness—whichever he assigned to each at the time of creation, it stuck automatically to that creature. As at the change of seasons each season automatically adopts its own distinctive marks, so do embodied beings adopt their own distinctive acts. (1.21, 28–30)[233]

Doniger quotes A. K. Ramanujan commenting on Manu's "extraordinary lack of universality" in making *dharma* so "context-sensitive" that adding all the stations, classes, and stages of life to any particular ethical injunction means that "each addition is really a subtraction from any universal law. There is not much left of an absolute or common *(sādhāraṇa) dharma* which the texts speak of, if at all, as a last and not as a first resort."[234]

If *Manu* is only a collection of particular injunctions, how can we consider it to be a *śāstra,* that is, a work of "systematic thought" or "science"? Unlike the *Dharmasūtras,* Manu does not just collect particular injunctions; he writes in full awareness of the issue of universality and attempts to defend particularism theoretically, so to speak—to use universal arguments to defend particularism.[235] Only rarely do some tensions in his intellectual structure show through. Toward the end of chapter 6, which deals with the third and fourth stages of (the Brahmin's) life, the Forest Hermit and the Wandering Ascetic, which seem to be closer to the ultimate aim of life than the earlier stages, he reaffirms the superiority of the householder:

> Student, householder, forest hermit, and ascetic: these four distinct orders have their origin in the householder. All of these, when they are undertaken in their proper sequence as spelled out in the sacred texts, lead a Brahmin who acts in the prescribed manner to the highest state. Among all of them, however, according to the dictates of Vedic scripture, the householder is said to be the best, for he supports the other three. As all rivers and rivulets end up in the ocean, so do all the orders end up in the householder. (6.87–90)[236]

Yet chapter 6 ends by saying that the brahmin who has "cast off the inherent evil of rites by retiring from all ritual activities . . . erases his sins and attains the highest state" (6.95–96).[237]

Even more remarkable is a passage at the very end of the book that seems to stand alone but raises more than one question in the reader's mind:

> A man who knows the Vedic treatise is entitled to become the chief of the army, the king, the arbiter of punishment, and the ruler of the whole world. As a fire, when it has picked up strength, burns up even green trees, so a man who knows the Veda burns up his taints resulting from action. A man who knows the true meaning of the Vedic treatise, in whatever order of life he may live, becomes fit for becoming Brahman while still living in the world. (12.100–102)[238]

It is clear from the passage immediately following this one and discussions like those at the end of chapter 6 that knowing the Veda involves much more than just hearing it, that it entails ascetic and yogic practices that, according to Manu, the Veda entails. This kind of knowledge and practice characterizes the renouncer ideal of the fourth stage of life and involves a universal experience that transcends ritual and other particularistic obligations. It is for this reason that, in spite of his sense that this stage is the highest good, in chapter 6 Manu still held the householder stage to be best. But in the passage above, the renouncer ideal is wedded to the notion of rule, even world rule; this has parallels in some Buddhist teachings and is much more fully worked out in the epics. It is remarkable to find it in Manu. But what are we to make of the fact that one who truly knows the Veda "in whatever order of life he lives" can become one with Brahman in this very world? Becoming one with Brahman is equivalent to the Buddhist notion of attaining nirvana in this life. This apparently universal claim must be qualified because *śūdras* and those beneath them can have no knowledge of the Veda, but for a moment in this most particularistic book, the very standard for Hindu particularism for all succeeding time, we seem to have a glimpse of the universal.[239]

Olivelle holds that *Manu* was probably written in the period of confusion and uncertainty after the fall of the Mauryas as an effort to defend Brahmanical privilege, but, more generally, as an effort to reaffirm the Brahmanical understanding of society, while responding to the substantive challenges posed by the ascetic sects, especially Buddhism, and the teaching of Aśoka in particular.[240] He believes that the *Mahābhārata* (and I would think the *Rāmāyaṇa* as well) arose at roughly the same time and place as *Manu* and with the same concern with the reaffirmation of traditional dharma. However, though both epics are centrally concerned with dharma, both the *Mahābhārata* and the *Rāmāyaṇa* move far beyond the simple pieties of Manu in dealing with the deep tension between dharma as righteousness and the mass of particular obligations related to status that dharma means in the Brahmanic tradition. In grappling with this tension, they do not solve it, but they widen the horizon of all subsequent Indic culture, of which they can probably be said to be the formative texts. Each of these epics is immense—the *Mahābhārata* is said to be seven or eight times as long as the *Iliad* and the *Odyssey* combined— and enormously complex in both narrative and ethical reflection. Here I can only suggest why they are such formative texts, not only for the Indic imagination but for the human imagination in general.

The *Rāmāyaṇa* is both shorter and narratively clearer than its epic companion.[241] In both epics the tension between general and particular dharma comes to a head in the question of the ethical responsibility of the king, or of the kṣatriya caste, for the inevitable violence of rule in a moral world where violence is inadmissible. This, as we have seen, is the issue that most concerned Aśoka; and Sheldon Pollock, one of the most acute commentators on the epics, makes the comparison explicit. Pollock, whose comments on the epics I have found most helpful, describes Rāma, the central figure of the *Rāmāyaṇa,* who eventually became king not only of his own city of Ayodhyā but of the whole world, as uniting the political and the religious, the kṣatriya and the Brahmin ideals, by not only reaffirming dharma but by redefining it:

> Rāma resolves the contradiction [between the Brahmin and kṣatriya ideals] through a new definition of *dharma* incumbent on him as a kṣatriya. By the increment of a hieratic component, not derived from but only enriched by his temporary ascetic vocation, his code is enlarged to become simply "righteousness." It is made to intersect with and so absorb brahmanical *dharma* and its legitimizing ethics, nonviolence, and spirituality. In this way the kṣatriya becomes self-legitimizing, and the "full potential" of kingship as an integrating power can at last be activated. The political and spiritual spheres may now converge in a single locus: the king.[242]

Pollock then goes on to note the striking parallels between the teachings of Rāma and those of Aśoka:

> One is again struck by the similarity between the inscriptions [of Aśoka] and the *Ayodhyākāṇḍa* [book 2 of the *Rāmāyaṇa*]. For Aśoka, too, "the only true conquest is conquest through *dharma*": through "compassion, generosity, truthfulness, and honesty," through "reverence for Brahmans and ascetics." Glory, too, is desirable only on account of his aim that "men may [be induced] by him to practice obedience to *dharma* [in Aśoka's Prakrit, *Dhamma*], that they may conform to the duties of *dharma.*" The "drum of battle" is similarly transformed into the drum of *dharma,* and the "abiding welfare of all the world" becomes the fundamental concern.[243]

Writing his introduction to the *Ayodhyākāṇḍa* in 1986, Pollock speculates that the influence was from the *Rāmāyaṇa* to Aśoka, and even that "the *Rāmāyaṇa* may well have served as a prototype" for "the biography of the

Buddha."[244] But in 2006 in *The Language of the Gods in the World of Men,* he writes, "No convincing evidence has been offered for a pre-Ashokan date of the *Rāmāyaṇa* in its monumental form (the common denominator of all our manuscripts), let alone a date before the Buddha (c. 400 BCE)."[245] Thus, if we can speak of influence, whatever that might mean in this case, it would have to be from Buddhism and Aśoka to the *Rāmāyaṇa,* not the other way around.

Pollock sees the *Rāmāyaṇa* as, in the end, creatively ambivalent. Rāma "explicitly affirms hierarchical subordination"—many have seen this in the *Rāmāyaṇa* over the centuries—yet his "spiritual commitment that allows for his utopian rule seems implicitly to oppose it."[246] The "Golden Age" of peace and prosperity that his rule was said to inaugurate seems to be much more like Aśoka's than like Manu's. The ethical universalism that had emerged in Buddhism and the edicts of Aśoka, therefore, did not die, but lived on in tension with Brahmanic particularism in subsequent Indian history. Indeed, Aśoka's *Dhamma,* together with Buddhism, which so clearly influenced it, acted as a continuing axial challenge of ethical universalism to the archaic heritage of Brahmanic particularism, such that later Indic civilization, perhaps more than most post-axial civilizations, was an uneasy compromise between axial and archaic cultural strands.

The *Rāmāyaṇa,* in the sense that it has a happy ending, is a comedy, whereas the *Mahābhārata,* in spite of the tacked-on happy ending, is a tragedy that ends in utter catastrophe, so clearly that copies of the *Rāmāyaṇa* were often kept at home whereas copies of the *Mahābhārata* were considered too inauspicious for home use.[247] But what this shows us is that the *Rāmāyaṇa*'s happy ending comes perhaps too easily, whereas the *Mahābhārata* opens up for us the abyss between ethical practice and inevitable violence, between religious ideals and political realities, revealing tensions not only in Indian but in human society. Again Pollock is a helpful commentator: "Whatever else the *Mahābhārata* may be, it is also and preeminently a work of political theory—the single most important literary reflection on the problem of the political in southern Asian history and in some ways the deepest meditation in all antiquity on the desperate realities of political life."[248]

If, as Pollock remarks, "the *Rāmāyaṇa* is rightly said to have become a veritable language for talking about the world," the *Mahābhārata* can be seen as a kind of encyclopedia, with its vast collections of stories and teachings, that contains the whole world, yet it, like the *Rāmāyaṇa,* has a narrative core:

The [*Mahābhārata*] famously celebrates its own encyclopedism, declaring near the start that "whatever exists in the world is to be found in the *Mahābhārata* and whatever is not there does not exist." Nonetheless, the text, over the course of tens of thousands of verses, never loses sight of the narrative core—the struggle between two sets of cousin-brothers for succession to rulership in the Kuru capital, Hastināpura—or of the central problematic upon which it is so adamantly insistent, the antinomy of political power:

Man is slave to power but power is slave to no one (Mbh. 6.41.36). The dilemma of power—in the starkest terms, the need to destroy in order to preserve, to kill in order to live—becomes most poignant when those whom one must kill are one's own kin. That is why the *Mahābhārata* is the most harrowing of all premodern political narratives in the world: the *Iliad,* like the *Rāmāyaṇa,* is about a war far from home, the *Odyssey* about a post-war journey home, and the *Aeneid* about a journey for a home. The *Mahābhārata* is about a war fought at home, and in any such war, both sides must lose.[249]

Although Pollock is certainly right that the *Mahābhārata* is about the antinomy of power, that antinomy arises above all in the context of dharma: when and in what way is power consistent or not with dharma? Both epics are centrally concerned with power and dharma, though in quite different ways. Rāma, the hero of the *Rāmāyaṇa,* is the unambivalent embodiment of dharma, virtually one-dimensional, as he never wavers.[250] On the eve of his accession to the throne, in accordance with the wish of his father, the king, he is banished as a result of palace intrigue and must retire to the forest. He accepts his father's unjust decision and uses the opportunity to behave as a renouncer, though at her urgent request, taking his wife with him. When his brother charges him with not acting like a true kṣatriya, Rāma replies: "So give up this ignoble notion that is based on the code of the kshatriyas [*kśatradharma*]; be of like mind with me and base your actions on righteousness [*dharma*], not violence" (*Rāmāyaṇa* 2.18.36). Later when someone else suggests something similar, Rāma again rejects "the kshatriya's code [*kṣātraṃ dharmam*], where unrighteousness and righteousness go hand in hand [*adharmaṃ dharmasaṃhitam*], a code that only debased, vicious, covetous, and evil men observe" (2.101.20).[251] Rāma, as we have seen, takes dharma to mean general dharma, righteousness itself, and consistently rejects violence toward human beings throughout the epic. Pollock affirms the nature of Rāma as the "ideal king" by asserting that ideal characters "are imaginary solutions to problems that do not admit of real solutions."[252] But lest Rāma appear too ideal, or too close to a Buddhist renunciate, his kṣatriya aggression is allowed full sway against some animals (problematic, given the ethic of nonviolence toward animals), and especially against the Rākṣasas, demons or ogres, who may stand for human evils but who are not human. Indeed, the great war with the Rākṣasas is the dramatic climax of the *Rāmāyaṇa,* but one that does not, at least on the surface, undercut Rāma's renunciation of war, even though on occasion in later history certain human groups could all too easily be identified as Rākṣasas.[253]

In the *Mahābhārata,* however, there are no ideal characters like Rāma. On the contrary, each of the central figures, the Pāṇḍavas, the five sons of the king Pāṇḍu, is flawed in his own way, none more so than the eldest brother, Yudhiṣṭhira, the son of the god Dharma (because his human father, Pāṇḍu, could not conceive him),[254] and thus is in an important sense the embodiment of dharma itself, such that he is referred to as King Dharma. Yet the whole epic is an account of Yudhiṣṭhira's education in dharma, an education that never seems complete. The next-younger brother, Arjuna, who embodies the kṣatriya ideal, wavers at a critical moment, as any reader of the *Bhagavadgītā* knows, as to what his duty really is.

The general problem of how dharma relates to power comes to a focus in the obligation of the warrior to fight and if necessary kill for a just cause as against the ethical injunction of nonviolence and especially nonviolence toward relatives and teachers. Arjuna's charioteer, Kṛṣṇa, Arjuna's friend but also the avatar of the great God Viṣṇu, argues with Arjuna, just before the great battle with the Kauravas[255] begins, in order to dispel Arjuna's sudden unwillingness to fight at all. Kṛṣṇa's argument is the core of the *Bhagavadgītā,* and there is no necessity for me to rehearse it here, except to say that it is only with Kṛṣṇa's revelation of his true self in all his blinding glory that Arjuna finally realizes that his highest obligation is to do his caste duty, his svadharma, while renouncing any concern for the results and realizing that all is finally in the hands of God and that no one is ever definitively killed anyway as the victors will enjoy the triumph in this life and their slain opponents will be reborn in heaven. This was not Rāma's view, and as Romila Thapar put it, "Had the Buddha been the charioteer the message would have been different."[256] In any case the argument is not settled by the *Bhagavadgītā* in book 6 of the *Mahābhārata* but continues to disturb Yudhiṣṭhira in later books.

Books 6 to 9 describe the great war and end with the final triumph of the Pāṇḍavas after the near-total annihilation of their rivals, the Kauravas. Book 10, the *Sauptikaparvan,* or "The Massacre at Night," however, describes how three surviving Kaurava leaders steal into the Pāṇḍava camp at night and murder all the children and grandchildren of the Pāṇḍavas, the five brothers themselves having been drawn away from the scene by Kṛṣṇa and thus surviving.[257] After the near-universal slaughter on both sides, Yudhiṣṭhira expresses the wish to refuse the kingship that is now his right and retire into the forest, because he cannot imagine perpetrating any more violence than has already taken place. It falls to Arjuna to argue the case as to why this would be wrong and why he must accede to the throne, the country needing a just ruler at last. At this critical moment Arjuna moves beyond the argument from svadharma, one's "own" dharma, which in practice means the inherited dharma of one's caste, and which is, in the case of kṣatriyas, to kill. They are not alone. Arjuna argues that we are all killers and comes up with quite a list:

> I see no being that lives in the world without violence. Creatures exist at one another's expense; the stronger consume the weaker. The mongoose eats mice, just as the cat eats the mongoose; the dog devours the cat, your majesty, and wild beasts eat the dog . . . People honor most the gods who are killers. Rudra is a killer, and so are Skanda, Agni, Varuna, Yama. I don't see anyone living in the world with nonviolence *(ahimsa).* Even ascetics *(tapasas)* cannot stay alive without killing. (*Mahābhārata* 12.15)[258]

Though Yudhiṣṭhira had said, "I am determined not to be cruel," thus affirming the value of noncruelty *(ānṛśaṃsya),* he allows himself to be convinced that it is his duty to become king and orders a horse sacrifice *(aśvamedha),* one of the great sacrificial rituals of kingship, to be held. Alf Hiltebeitel describes nonviolence *(ahiṃsā)* and noncruelty *(ānṛśaṃsya)* as two values central to the *Mahābhārata,* which, more than once, calls each of them the "highest dharma." However, Hiltebeitel has discovered 54 references in the epic to something as "the highest dharma," of which there are 8 for noncruelty and 4 for nonviolence, among the most frequently mentioned (although truth at 5 slightly surpasses nonviolence). Actually a very wide assortment of virtues and spiritual practices are described as the highest dharma, leading Hiltebeitel to the following definition of the "highest dharma" in the *Mahābhārata:* "The highest dharma seems to be knowing the highest dharma for whatever particular situation one is in, and recognizing that situation within an ontology that admits virtually endless variation and deferral in matters of formulating and approaching 'the highest.'"[259]

All that may be true and has surely served the tradition well, yet the *Mahābhārata* itself leaves us in some doubt as to how well it satisfied Yudhiṣṭhira. As for the great Horse Sacrifice, it was apparently successfully concluded, though not without an incident where Arjuna's son "killed" his father, who was nonetheless successfully revived.[260] "But," comments Doniger, "the success of the sacrifice is undermined by a story told right after it ends and the guests depart. A mongoose came out of his hole there and declared in a human voice, 'This whole sacrifice is not equal to one of the grains of barley that were given by a Brahmin who lived by observing the vow of gleaning.'"[261] The mongoose is expressing the typical renouncer view that sacrifice is as nothing compared to a simple act of charity. Certainly the great Rājasūya sacrifice early in the *Mahābhārata,* symbolizing Yudhiṣṭhira's rule as a *cakravartin,* "wheel-turning emperor," had disastrous consequences in that it led to the fatal gambling episode from which arose the trouble with the Kauravas and all the catastrophes that followed.[262] Here, too, we have the featuring of one of the great Vedic rituals with a very ambiguous outcome.

As Pollock puts it, by the end of the story, although the "Pāṇḍavas political power has been confirmed, both the war and the new meaner Kali Age it has inaugurated have sapped their strength and will," so that Yudhiṣṭhira can exclaim, "Cursed be the law of power that has left us dead in life" (*Mahābhārata* 15.46.8).[263] Pollock sums up one reading of the epic as chiefly addressing "the collapse of social value" by quoting a ninth-century thinker who believes that "[the *Mahābhārata's*] purpose as a whole is the production of despair with social life." Pollock goes on to say that "this is an interpretation of epic not as social fullness but as social abyss, of power not as perfected but as unperfectable since, as Vyāsa [the reputed author] says, it is 'slave to no man.'"[264] In the end, the *Mahābhārata* leaves us in the dark as to what exactly its central term, *dharma,* means. It would seem that only God knows and that, as Hiltebeitel puts it, "the *Mahābhārata* is an argument with God."[265]

Just to complete our discussion of epic as a mode of dealing with central ethical and religious issues in the Indic tradition, I would like to refer briefly to the *Vessantara Jātaka,* which has been called "A Buddhist Epic."[266] The Jātakas are tales of the Buddha's previous births and are of various and unknown dates, though clearly on the whole later than the Suttas, and many of them probably do come from the same period before and after the turn of the Common Era from which the Hindu epics come.[267] The importance of the *Vessantara Jātaka* is underlined by Richard Gombrich in the introduction to Margaret Cone's English translation:

> The selfless generosity of Vessantara, who gave away everything, even his children and his wife, is the most famous story in the Buddhist world. It has been retold in every Buddhist language, in elegant literature and in popular piety; it has been represented in the art of every Buddhist country; it has formed the theme of countless sermons, dramas, dances, and ceremonies. In the Theravada Buddhist countries, Ceylon and South-East Asia, it is still learnt by every child; even the biography of the Buddha is not better known.[268]

Although not nearly as long as the Hindu epics, the *Vessantara Jātaka* is an epic in that it recounts the deeds and sufferings of a great hero. It is also the case that in its longest and most literate version it is tightly organized and well written. It rivals the Hindu epics in its capacity to express central concerns of the religious tradition in a compelling and influential way to broad audiences, both educated and popular, for centuries.

Collins shows that the *Vessantara Jātaka* is far closer in spirit to the *Rāmāyaṇa* than to the *Mahābhārata,* in that Vessantara, like Rāma, is a prince of perfect virtue, chosen by his father to rule as regent, but then is banished to the forest where he lives as a renouncer, only to return in the end to rule as an "ideal king." Vessantara gets in trouble with the public because of his extreme generosity, especially when he gives away the state elephant, with magical rain-making capacities, when some Brahmins from another country suffering from a drought ask him for it. This gives rise to a popular demand that Vessantara be banished. He, his wife, and his two children go to a forest retreat that is in many ways idyllic until a disgruntled Brahmin comes and demands Vessantara's children, and the ever-generous Vessantara accedes, much to his wife's distress. Indra, the king of the gods, comes to Vessantara in disguise asking for his wife in order to forestall the evil Brahmin from asking for her too. Indra then reveals his true self and returns Vessantara's wife, who now cannot be given away again, as a gift returned is inviolable. Much of the pathos of the tale is in the misery of the wife at the loss of her children. These events make it clear that the life of perfect renunciation, which implies perfect generosity, is the cause of extreme pain on the level of normal human relationships. What does not happen in the *Vessantara Jātaka* is any war against the offending Brahmin, so the parallel with the *Rāmāyaṇa* fails at that point. Vessantara is incapable of violence against anyone, even a demon, which surely the Brahmin in his unmitigated evil truly is. Nonetheless the behavior of the Brahmin comes to light, and Vessantara is not only reunited with his family but thereafter becomes the perfect king and rules happily ever after. (The evil Brahmin, by the way, is actually given a ransom for the children and set up in a palace, but he promptly eats himself to death, thus bringing about his own punishment.) Collins's overall interpretation of the story is as follows:

> It is, *inter alia,* a painfully honest confrontation of the difficulties of renunciation, showing that real human goods must, ultimately, be abandoned in the ascetic search for ultimate felicity; and it is the most subtle and successful attempt in Pali literature to infuse ascetic values into an ordinary, productive and reproductive society. This society is only glimpsed at the end of the story, inevitably, since sustained narrative description would falter on the contradictions and paradoxes [inherent in such a society]: just as the fabled *Rāma-rājya,* the utopia that follows Rāma's victory over Rāvana and his consecration as king, occupies only nine verses at the end of Book 6 of the *Rāmāyaṇa.*[269]

Collins points out that the Buddhist absolute commitment to nonviolence, without either the relativism of the *Mahābhārata* or the allowance of violence toward nonhumans in the *Rāmāyaṇa,* although well expressed in the *Vessantara Jātaka,* is not quite as simple a contrast with the Hindu epics as it might seem. He argues that in practice in Buddhist societies Dhamma has two modes: "Mode 1, grounded in the principle of reciprocity, which requires and legitimates violence, when it repays bad with bad in the form of punishment for crime and in self-defense; and Mode 2, where values, including that of nonviolence, are absolute."[270] The power of the *Vessantara Jātaka* is its recognition of the presence of both modes and their costs. That Buddhists have always seen it as a joyous story and not a tragedy has much to do with the fact that it points beyond itself: "Often known simply as *Mahājātaka,* the 'Great Birth Story,' it tells of events in the penultimate human birth in the sequence which was to become Gotama Buddha, when he brought to perfection the virtue of giving; thereafter he was reborn as a god in the Tusita heaven, before his last and final birth as Siddhattha Gotama."[271] It is to the Buddha and to his nirvana that the story points.

It is worth thinking about the fact that the three epics we have been discussing raise the question of violence and its evils, of the good king and the good society, in ways far more explicit than do the *Iliad,* the *Odyssey,* or the *Aeneid.* In part this is because the Greek epics arose at a time when the warrior societies they describe were recent (and Virgil's Latin epic takes the Greek epics as a model too closely to break the mold), but the parallel Indian warrior societies were but a distant memory when our versions of the epics were composed. In the Indic epics it is the capacity of narrative to take insights from systematic thought and show their complexities and inner contradictions unflinchingly that is most impressive. Without their narrative depth, we would have a truncated view of how the tradition would play itself out in subsequent history.

10

Conclusion

Pascal in one of his fragments says something that applies to this book: "The last thing one discovers when writing a work is what one should put first."[1] After having written Chapters 1 through 9, and in the course of completely rewriting Chapter 2, "Religion and Evolution," I discovered the importance of play among mammals and the extraordinary way in which play in animals provided the background for the development of play, ritual, and culture among humans.[2] So play, though discovered last, did get in quite early in this book, but then is largely ignored through the whole trek from tribal to axial religions. Play was there all the time, just below the surface, though I didn't point it out. Because, having been at work for thirteen years, I can't imagine rewriting the whole book to give adequate attention to play, I will here in the Conclusion try briefly to make up for that deficiency by discussing the importance of play and those things that endanger play in human life.

Schiller

I will begin by alluding to an important classical discussion of play that I overlooked in Chapter 2, namely Friedrich Schiller's *On the Aesthetic Education of Man*.[3] Schiller picks up on a brief analogy in Kant, who remarked that art is to handicraft as play is to work,[4] but he develops his conception of play far beyond anything in Kant. Schiller already guessed at the nature of animal play, which Gordon Burghardt has so brilliantly analyzed in his remarkable book *The Genesis of Animal Play*—namely, that play is a realm of freedom relative to the pressures of the struggle for existence: it can occur only in what Burghardt calls a "relaxed field."[5] As Schiller puts it:

Certainly nature has given even to the creatures without reason more than the bare necessities of life, and cast a gleam of freedom over the darkness of animal existence. When the lion is not gnawed by hunger and no beast is challenging him to battle, his idle energy creates for itself an object; he fills the echoing desert with his high-spirited roaring, and his exuberant power enjoys itself in purposeless display . . . The animal *works* when deprivation is the mainspring of its activity, and it *plays* when the fullness of its strength is the mainspring, when superabundant life is its own stimulus to activity.

Schiller contrasts "the sanction of need, or *physical seriousness*" with the "sanction of superfluity, or *physical play*," but suggests that human play, though also beginning in physical play, can move to the level of aesthetic play in which the full spiritual and cultural capacities of humans can be given free reign.[6] Schiller was a poet of major stature and a philosophical amateur, so some of his reasoning is not easy to follow. What he seems to be arguing is that human life is riven by a series of dichotomies that play overcomes: matter and form, sense and intellect, actuality and necessity, and so forth. He opposes the reduction of play to "a mere game" when he writes, "But why call it a *mere* game, when we consider that in every condition of humanity it is precisely play, and play alone, that makes man complete and displays at once his twofold nature." He culminates this line of reflection with a remarkable assertion: "For, to declare it once and for all, Man plays only when he is in the full sense of the word a man, and *he is only wholly Man when he is playing*."[7]

One other point, among the many interesting things that Schiller says, has to do with play and time:

The sense impulse requires variation, requires time to have a content; the form impulse requires the extinction of time, and no variation. Therefore the impulse in which both are combined (allow me to call it provisionally the *play impulse*), this play impulse would aim at the extinction of time *in time* and the reconciliation of becoming with absolute being, of variation with identity.[8]

Schiller here seems to be saying that taking place in "time out of time," which Lévi-Strauss, as we noted in Chapter 1, saw as characteristic of music and myth, is perhaps primordially characteristic of play.[9] The "extinction of time in time" would seem to be what happens in a relaxed field, in a form of life not subject to the struggle for existence, and play, as the first such form, reaches far back in biological time.

I think Schiller helps us move from the description of animal play in Chapter 2 to the description of tribal ritual in Chapter 3. In all three tribal examples we see how ritual takes place in a relaxed field, and that it takes considerable effort to create such a field. Among the Kalapalo, a major ritual requires weeks, if not months, of preparation. Some of this involves rehearsal and the construction of the ritual paraphernalia that will be used during the performance, but there is also an intensification of economic effort to provide the surplus food that will be given out to the participants and attendees at a major ritual. Having to forage in the midst of a ritual would surely break the spell. Indeed, it would seem that the capacity for a significant degree of food storage would be a prerequisite for rituals involving more than one's immediate group, if they are to be held at all. We can see similar preparations among the Australian Aborigines and the Navajo. One can imagine that in pre-state times one would want to hold a ritual at a time and place relatively safe from outside aggressors as well. So human ritual requires work to prepare a relaxed field; animal play requires that the players be fed and safe, but no special or extended preparation is necessary. That human play and work are not only opposites but in various ways interdependent is an insight we will need to consider further below.

The descriptions of tribal rituals themselves usually exhibit features that we could characterize as play: such ritual is very much embodied as in singing, dancing, feasting, and general hilarity, but there is also a powerful element of pretend play that can have serious meanings. We can cite a relevant description of Kalapalo ritual:

> Musical performance is associated with powerful beings and is a means of communicating with them although it is not directly addressed to them . . . Communication may be said to occur not by singing *to* a powerful being but by singing it *into being*. Highly focused mental images of the powerful being are created in the minds of the performers by means of the performance . . . There is a consequent merging of the self with what is sung about; just as in myth powerful beings participate in human speech, so in ritual humans participate in *itseke* [powerful being] musicality and thereby temporarily achieve some of their transformative power. In public ritual, this is power of community.[10]

We can also turn to Ellen Basso's description of the sense of moral equality that the ritual generates, which we already saw as foreshadowed in the egalitarian rules of animal play: "Economically, it means that everyone is obligated to participate, but everyone receives regardless of contribution. *Ifutisu,* the most basic value of Kalapalo life (subsuming the notions of generosity, modesty, flexibility, and equanimity in facing social difficulties, and respect for others) is extended beyond the domain of family to all people in the community."[11]

But although animal play takes place in a society organized in a more or less harsh dominance hierarchy, hunter-gatherer and some horticultural societies, such as those described in Chapter 3, are relatively egalitarian. One must wonder if the egalitarianism that is endemic in play and ritual has somehow been generalized outside the ritual context in such societies. Perhaps hunter-gatherer egalitarianism can be explained entirely on economic grounds as some have tried to do, but a cultural push from the domain of play and ritual might also be involved. I have argued in Chapter 4 that the continual reassertion of equality in the ritual context probably helped such societies cope with the ever-present threat of the domineering upstart.

Play, Ritual, and the Early State

What happens when, with the spread of agriculture, village settlements, and increase of population, dominance hierarchies reappear, at first modestly and then—in the early state—with a vengeance? We noted a ritual bifurcation: some rituals are reserved for the dominant elite and take place out of sight or at a distance from the rest of the population, although communal rituals of various sorts continue among the non-elite population. In the Tikopia—an example of a "traditional" Polynesian chiefdom where the chief had little coercive power and was still seen as the head of an extended lineage that included the whole group, but was treated with a reverence unknown to hunter-gatherers—the beginnings of something we can call worship appeared. It is the chief and only the chief who offers sacrifices, in this case of food and drink, to powerful beings who can now be called gods, as requests for their protection and assistance are central elements in the ritual that only chiefs can perform. However, after observing these sacred rituals from a distance, the words of which are secret and spoken so softly that the commoners cannot hear them, there is a general festival involving singing, dancing, and feasting that reminds us of the communal rituals of tribal societies.

Even in Hawai'i, which was an early state or very close to becoming one at the time of Western discovery, there was an annual alternation of rituals. During the period of the year belonging to Kū, the war god, rituals took place in walled temples where the general populace could not enter. There the priests undertook sacrifices, most significantly human sacrifices, to magnify the power and prestige of the paramount chiefs on the verge of becoming kings. But for the rest of the year, the Makahiki season, especially beginning with the New Year rituals, a very different kind of ritual prevailed. Significantly, in this period the gates of the temples of Kū were closed. As we saw in Chapter 4, no one worked during the four days and nights that follow the *hi'uwai* rite. People of all classes devote themselves to feasting, mockery, obscene and satirical singing, and, above all, to dancing., Laughter overcomes *kapu* [tabu], and sexual advances during the dancing cannot be refused. Valeri writes that "these marvelously coordinated dances" realize "a perfect fellowship" that reconstitutes society itself. All of this takes place in an atmosphere of "hierarchical undifferentiation."[12] For a while at least, the old egalitarianism reappeared.

Even in strongly hierarchical societies, rituals of reversal—which involve the violation of ordinary rules, such as rules involving gender identity, for example, but also rules of deference to superiors—can be found all over the world. Generally these have been interpreted as "letting off steam" and so ultimately reinforcing the status quo, yet to some degree they may allow the expression of real feelings even if under carefully controlled conditions. In these rituals the play element is particularly obvious.

In modern totalitarian societies, where the most sacred rituals occur in the Central Committee or the Party Congress, great public rituals, sometimes involving hundreds of thousands of people and broadcast to all parts of the realm, reaffirm the solidarity of all with the now quite remote leadership. And democratic societies, where leadership is supposed to be "transparent," though it is seldom entirely so, regularly hold great public rituals, such as the inauguration of a newly elected president. But however much public participation in ritual survives in class-divided state societies, the central myths and ideologies reinforce the legitimacy of the dominant ruling group, though, from the axial age on, not without challenge.

We have noted that although the official ideology usually emphasizes the crushing dominance of the ruler, as in the case of the Behistun inscriptions of the great Persian Achaemenid king, Darius I, it also usually contains some expression of nurturance. Yet even here the frequent reference to the ruler as father or shepherd of the people, though more benign than the symbolism of ruthless power, does emphasize that the rulers are adults and the ruled are children. In archaic societies and in varying degrees even in axial societies, the ruler is related to the divine in a way different from that of ordinary people, so that religious or ideological sanction of the existing regime reinforces the existing power structure.

But there is another feature of class-divided state societies that involves play: in most monarchical early states, and for many such states throughout historic time, it is hard work to become a king—there are brothers, cousins, powerful provincial governors who also have their eyes on the throne. And once attained, kingship often requires hard work to maintain. Yet the elite classes in such societies, what we might call the aristocrats, the extended families of relatives or close allies of monarchs, enjoy a uniquely exalted state. In Hawai'i, as we saw, they were considered quasi-divine. Needless to say, they had little work to do in the ordinary sense of the word, as they were waited on hand and foot by social inferiors. What characterizes them is that they play. They hunt and engage in military exercises that can have serious consequences when put to use in war but are often playful competitions in the meantime. They learn to dance and sing with sophisticated elegance. They sometimes write poetry or engage bards to do so, so that they listen to epic lays or exchange lyric poems with their lovers. We find such aristocracies not only in ancient Greece, where many of us are most familiar with them in the Homeric poems, but also in ancient China, Japan, India, Africa, and Polynesia.[13]

One more feature of play that has developed, particularly among aristocrats, is the appearance of competition, of *agon,* to use the Greek word, which may be present in tribal play and ritual but is not prominent there. Rousseau thought that even in simple societies, like those I have called tribal, some element of competition was already present but was not emphasized.[14] But in aristocratic societies, competitive sporting events, perhaps deriving from military training, became common, and involved racing, wrestling, and many other "sports"—sports that survive to this day. It may be that competitive games involving team play have the same origin. We find such developments among aristocratic classes in many societies, clearly in Polynesia, for example, but again the case that comes first to mind for those familiar with Western history is Greece. Here agonistic sports and games were highly developed, and often in connection with ritual—one thinks of the games organized by Achilles for the funeral of Patroclus in the *Iliad*—but the most obvious example, because it lives on in rather different form among us, is the Olympic Games, only one of several Panhellenic athletic events. What is striking here, and so different from our own Olympic Games, is that they took place in the context of a great festival, dedicated to Zeus, of which the games were only a part.

What I want to point out about the emergence of agonistic, competitive play is that, though still taking place in a relaxed field—during the games a truce was called between all warring Greek cities so that athletes could gather without fear, and, significantly, losers were defeated but not killed— the competitions do bring an element of the struggle for existence into the play situation itself. The standard maxim has always been "It's not who wins or loses but how you play the game," and clearly that has had more than a negligible influence, but the Greeks were very concerned to win. Though it was noble to compete, it was godlike to win. Perhaps no society until modern America ever emphasized winning more. But when winning becomes obsessive, play can become negative, something like an addiction, and, as Rousseau supposed, may bring inequality to the fore in a basically egalitarian arena.[15]

Renouncers and the Legitimation Crisis of the Early State

But here play takes on still another meaning: while some work, others play.[16] It is not that those who work have no play, but that for them play is constricted in time and quality because of the heavy burdens they carry just to make a living. Here play may be egalitarian among the players, but it is not equally shared in the whole society. Ideologists have often promised that modernity would democratize "leisure," a word closely related to play, but today even the "leisured classes" don't have much leisure and for the rest a couple of hours of television a day is mainly what is on offer.

We saw, however, even in an early state like Hawai'i, the emergence of what can be called moral upstarts—prophet-like figures who, at great peril to themselves, held the existing power structures to a moral standard that they clearly did not meet. The axial age—the middle of the first millennium BCE—was the time when such challenges to the dominant cultural order become widely apparent. It is part of the definition of the axial age that it was then that a universally egalitarian ethic first appeared. How can we think about that momentous time today?

Here I would turn to Jürgen Habermas's essay "Toward a Reconstruction of Historical Materialism" as a point of departure. In speaking of the transition from tribal societies organized by kinship to the emergence of the early state, he writes:

> Social integration accomplished via kinship relations . . . belongs, from a developmental-logical point of view, to a lower stage than social integration accomplished via relations of domination . . . Despite this progress, the exploitation and oppression *necessarily* practiced in political class societies has to be considered retrogressive in comparison with the less significant social inequalities *permitted* by the kinship system. Because of this, class societies are structurally unable to satisfy the need for legitimation that they themselves generate.[17]

It is true that the early state and its accompanying class system emerged in what I have called archaic societies well before the axial age and generated a degree of popular unhappiness that can be discerned in the texts we have from such societies, but the legitimation crisis of which Habermas speaks arises with particular acuteness in the axial age, when mechanisms of social domination increased significantly relative to archaic societies and when coherent protest for the first time became possible. It would surely be far too simple to interpret the axial transitions as forms of class struggle, but it cannot be denied that they all involved social criticism and harsh judgments on existing social and political conditions.

In answer to the question of where this criticism was coming from, there has been a tendency to speak of "intellectuals," though what that term means in reference to the first millennium BCE is not obvious. Scribal and priestly classes come to mind, but we can assume that most of them were too tied in to the existing power systems to be very critical. Even though the kind of state that existed then tried to override, and in some important ways succeeded in overriding, kinship relations, various kinds of particularistic and ascriptive associations were widespread. It is not easy to imagine the social space for criticism in such societies. It is in this context that we have to consider the role of the "renouncer," to take a term most often used for ancient India.

There were renouncers already in late Vedic India; perhaps the first of whom we have an account is Yajnyavalkya, who appears in the Brhadaranyaka *Upanishad*. What the renouncer renounces is the role of the householder and all of the social and political entanglements that go with it. Buddhism provided a radical form of the renouncer, whose initial act is to "leave home" and who thereafter remains permanently homeless. If the renouncer is "nowhere," then he, and sometimes she, can look at established society from the outside, so to speak. It is not hard to see the Hebrew prophets as, in a sense, renouncers, though I have also called them denouncers. They too stood outside the centers of power, attempting to follow the commandments of God, whatever the consequences. Even in opposition, they were more oriented to power than were Buddhist monastics, to be sure, but, as we will see, the Buddhist monks also had a radical critique of worldly power. It is easy to see the Daoists who appear in Warring States China as renouncers, and they too have a critique of power, though perhaps more satirical than ethical. But there is a sense in which the Confucians, especially the greatest ones, who never held office or held only lowly ones briefly and were in principle opposed to serving an unethical lord, were renouncers, criticizing power from the outside. And finally I will argue that Socrates and Plato were, in different ways, also renouncers, who were in but not of the city and also criticized it from the outside.[18]

For all the differences in what can in most cases only loosely be called renouncers in the several axial cultures, the one thing such renouncers shared was that they were teachers, and founders of schools or orders, thus more or less, and often less, securely institutionalizing a tradition of criticism. Ultimately their power was exercised through the extent to which they influenced or even controlled elite education, as, to some degree paradoxically, many of them ultimately did.[19] And inevitably their survival depended on what they charged for their services or were freely given.

By pointing out the significance of renouncers, we in a sense return to our original question. How did renouncers garner the support that allowed them to survive in their outsider position? It seems apparent that some degree of unease about the state of the world must have been relatively widespread, even among the elite, to provide the support without which renouncers would simply have faded away into the wilderness. But the sociological basis for the culture of renunciation was the establishment of some kind of relaxed field within which the followers of the new spiritual virtuosi, as Weber called them, formed groups for religious practice. In one sense what the renouncers renounced was "work," and what they pursued instead was "play," often a very serious kind of play but having its joyous moments. Shared ritual was almost everywhere central to their practice, but almost all of them also took responsibility for the education of outside sympathizers. Traditions survived and were elaborated only when they gained the toleration, even the respect, though sometimes the hostility, of elite political groups. Much of the history of such groups arising in the axial age has to do with their complex and ambivalent relation to political power.

If Habermas is right about the legitimation crisis of the axial-age state, brought on by the dissonance between the developmental-logical advance and the moral-practical regression, as I think he is, I would like to illustrate the response to this legitimation crisis by referring to the utopian projections of a good society that the various kinds of renouncers offered in criticism of the existing order. These utopian projections took quite different forms in the four cases, but each one of them was harshly critical of existing social-political conditions. One thing being criticized was the harsh conditions of work, and almost all axial-age utopias had a large element of play.

Axial-Age Utopias

In ancient Israel the prophets sharply criticized the behavior of foreign states, but also conditions within the kingdoms of Israel and Judah. According to Amos, the rich and the rulers "trample the head of the poor into the dust of the earth, and turn aside the way of the afflicted" (Amos 2:6–7). In contrast the prophets look forward to the Day of the Lord when judgment will come to the earth and justice will "roll down like the waters, and righteousness like an ever-flowing stream" (Amos 5:24). The prophets admonish rulers and people alike to change their ways, but look forward to a divine intervention that will finally put things right.

In ancient China, Mencius, for example, but many Confucians before and after him, bemoaned the sad state of society, the corruption of the rulers, and the oppression of the peasantry, and offered an alternative form of government: rule by moral example, by conformity with the *li*, the normative order, and not by punishment. The Confucian hope for an ethical ruler who would follow Confucian injunctions did not involve any idea of divine intervention, except a vague notion that Heaven would eventually punish behavior that was too outrageous, but it was in its own way as utopian as the prophetic hope of ancient Israel.

Plato, in the *Gorgias* and in the first book of the *Republic,* is a critic of a politics where the strong could inflict harm on the weak with impunity: for him despotism was always the worst form of government. In the *Republic* he depicted a good society in contrast to the one he criticized, but which he knew was a "city in words," or a "city in heaven," and not likely to be realized on this earth.

The Hindu epic, the *Ramayana,* can be seen as a critique of existing society, offering a different ideal of kingship. The early Buddhist canon describes an ideal society so different from existing reality as to be perhaps the most radical utopia of all, the most drastic criticism of society as it is.

In each axial case, what I am calling social criticism is combined with religious criticism, and the form and content of the axial symbolization take shape in the process of criticism. I will take the Greek case as exemplary because their term "theoria" was the source of our term "theory," which I, following Merlin Donald, take as diagnostic of the axial transition, there. I argued in Chapter 7 that Plato completed the axial transition: it is therefore not surprising that it was Plato who transmuted the traditional term for ritual *theoria* into philosophical *theoria,* which, as I will attempt to show, is not the same as what we mean by theory, but is its lineal predecessor, and we can also see the beginning of the transition to what we mean by the term in Aristotle, Plato's pupil.

My discussion of theory in Plato would not be possible except for the remarkable book by Andrea Nightingale, *Spectacles of Truth in Classical Greek Philosophy:* Theoria *in Its Cultural Context,* from which I will draw extensively. Nightingale describes *theoria* before Plato as "a venerable cultural practice characterized by a journey abroad for the sake of witnessing an event or spectacle." It took several forms, but the one that Plato took as the analogy for philosophical *theoria,* most extensively in the Parable of the Cave in books 5–7 of the *Republic,* was the civic form where the *theoros* (viewer, spectator) was sent as an official representative of his city to view a religious festival in another city and then return to give a full report to his fellow citizens. Nightingale notes that by its very nature *theoria* in this sense was "international," Panhellenic, and that Athens itself attracted many *theoroi* from other cities to view its great festivals, the Panathenaia and the city Dionysia.[20] She notes that Plato himself begins and ends the *Republic* with examples of traditional *theoria.* The dialogue begins with Socrates going to the Piraeus, the port of Athens, to attend the festival of the Thracian goddess, Bendis, suggesting that the festival was more "international" than the short distance to the Piraeus might indicate, especially in view of Socrates's remark that the Thracian procession was as fine as the Athenian one, expressing a Panhellenic viewpoint. And the *Republic* ends with the Myth of Er, which turns out to be a most remarkable *theoria,* because Er, who had been killed in battle and was about to be cremated, awoke and told his fellow countrymen about a journey he had made to the land of the dead and the festival he had attended there.[21]

Nightingale notes that in the *Republic,* books 5–7, Plato for the first time has Socrates give an account of what he meant by "philosophy," a term that confused his interlocutors, who knew it only in its previous sense of broad intellectual cultivation, but which is now to be understood in the context of a new meaning of "*theoria*' as the quintessential activity of the true philosopher."[22] The traditional *theoros* was a lover of spectacles, particularly of religious rituals and festivals, whereas the philosophical *theoros* "loves the spectacle of truth."[23] Plato puts great emphasis on vision, on seeing the truth more than hearing it; it is also a special kind of seeing, seeing with "the eye of the soul." This kind of seeing is possible only after a protracted philosophical education that prepares one for it, but it ends with the "*theoria* [the "seeing"] of all time and being" (*Republic* 486d).

Thinking of this kind of vision from an Indian or Chinese perspective, one might imagine that the way to attain it would be through some form of meditation, probably involving breath control. Although Socrates is portrayed twice in the *Symposium* as being in some kind of trance, it is not meditation that Plato finds to be the way to philosophical vision. The education that ends with "seeing reality," or "seeing Being," begins with number and calculation, which "enables the mind to 'view' the great and the small in themselves, abstracted from their concrete manifestations."[24] Geometry and astronomy follow, each of which involves "seeing" higher truths. What Plato meant by astronomy is not so much stargazing as "the mathematical principles that govern the motions of the heavenly bodies," which one "sees" when "gazing with the mind and not the eyes." Finally comes "dialectic," which Socrates never plainly defines but uses metaphors to describe, speaking of the "journey of dialectic" toward the contemplation of "true being."[25] What is involved is not "implanting vision in the soul," but turning the vision in a new direction, "away from the world of becoming and toward true being"[26] (*Republic* 521d).

At the critical moment, then, Plato turns to narrative, what Nightingale calls the Analogy of the Cave—which is not simply an allegory that can be translated into propositional language, but a kind of myth that reveals truth on its own terms, and that I would rather call the Parable of the Cave. The Buddha too uses stories, often referred to as "similes" in the secondary literature, to make a point, as in the famous Parable of the Blind Men and the Elephant. It seems that at the very point when thought was emerging from myth to theory, narrative still had to function as the midwife.

I cannot here give an account of the beauty and complexity of the Parable of the Cave, but only allude to those aspects of it that relate to my argument.

The Parable begins with a person who is "at home," though home in the *Republic* is more apt to be the *polis,* the city, than the *oikos,* the household. Home, however, turns out to be a dark cave that is in fact a prison where one is in bonds, so that one is forced to look at shadows on the wall cast by people (ideologists?) behind one's back projecting images by holding various objects in front of fires. Still, those shadowy images are what one is used to, so that in a situation where one is freed from one's bonds and, in Plato's words, "compelled to suddenly stand up and to turn [one's] head and to walk and turn upward toward the light" (515c), one will be confused, in a state of *aporia,* profound uncertainty, the opposite of *poria,* certainty. One will have entered, in Nightingale's words, "a sort of existential and epistemic no-man's-land," being no longer able to recognize the old familiar shadows nor yet to see anything in the blinding light above, so that one would be tempted to flee from the whole journey and return to the old familiar prison.[27]

Yet the would-be philosopher does not flee back, even becomes accustomed in some degree to the condition of uncertainty, *aporia,* which Nightingale describes as "(among other things) a state of homelessness." She goes on to describe the new condition as basically similar to the renouncer position in other cultures:

> In addition to the state of *aporia,* the philosopher's departure from home leads to a permanent state of *atopia* [no place, nowhere]. For the person who has detached himself from society and gone on the journey of philosophic *theoria,* will never be fully "at home" in the world. *Theoria* uproots the soul, sending it to a metaphysical region where it can never truly dwell and from which it will inevitably have to return. As a *theoros,* the Platonic philosopher must journey to "see" truth (in various degrees of fullness) and bring his vision back to the human world.[28]

In a good city he will be given civic office and expected to serve, even though he would rather spend his time in contemplation, yet even in office he is still a kind of foreigner in his own city. But if he returns to a bad city, his report of what he has seen will be mocked as foolish and nonsensical: he will be abused, he may even be killed. Nightingale sums up: "When he returns to the human world, then, he is *atopos,* not fully at home: he has become a stranger to his own kind."[29]

We still need to understand, as best we can, what philosophical *theoria* itself is; the ritual *theoros* sees the festival; what does the philosophic *theoros* see? Here we need to discount the caricature of classical theory, which assumes that the philosopher is a disengaged spectator, viewing at a distance what is an object different from himself as a subject, a kind of premature Descartes. Plato does not help us understand what the philosopher sees—that is, the "forms," *eide,* and in particular the "form of the good," *agathon,* which seems to be truth and reality itself—because he stays in the myth to talk about them. In the myth Plato compares the form of the good to the source of all light, something like the sun to the eye of the soul. But if we gazed at the sun very long with our physical eye, we would go blind, whereas the soul who gazes at the form of the good sees all things as they really are.

Nightingale shows us that the forms are not abstractions, but are, to the eye of the soul, ontological presences, "beings" or "substances." Further, the vision of the forms is not disengaged, but involves participation, for part of ourselves, our *nous,* inadequately translated as "rational soul," is akin to the forms. The vision is genuinely interactive: as Nightingale puts it, the vision is "granted to us as a gift."[30] Furthermore, it is anything but cool and detached: it is affective and emotional, it brings intense pleasure and happiness, it is erotic, even sexual. The soul, says Plato, "draws near to and has intercourse with (makes love to) reality" (490b) Furthermore, the experience of the vision is utterly transformative; one becomes a different person as a result.[31] One could speak of the soul as "enlightened," but if, as in translating *nirvana* or *moksha,* one wanted to avoid eighteenth-century terminology, one could speak of the soul as "awakened," or even "released," for hasn't the transformed soul been released from the prison of the cave in order to participate in the really real?

Plato then goes on to describe the good city to which the fortunate philosophic *theoros* returns. To discuss that in detail would take us too far afield, but I want to allude to a couple of aspects of the good city. The good city, as we noted, is ruled by the philosophically liberated, even though they would rather be doing something else. Why then do they take on political responsibility? Nightingale provides an interesting discussion of this issue:

> *If* there is an ideal city—and it is by no means clear that Plato believed in its possibility—then it can and must be ruled by philosophers. In this case alone, the philosopher must live a double life (as it were): he will practice philosophy and serve as a ruler. To qualify for this position, an individual must possess theoretical wisdom and practical virtue; in addition, he or she must not want to rule or lead a political life

(347c–d, 521a–b). A person who does want to rule is, by definition, not a true philosopher and thus disqualified from ruling. The philosopher in the ideal city, however, will agree to rule, in spite of his disinclination, to do so. Since he is a "just" person responding to a "just command," the philosopher is "willing" to return and rule the city (520d–e).[32]

This is all the more odd because, as Nightingale notes, the philosopher remains a foreigner in his own city, a "non-mercenary mercenary," who is supported but not paid, can own nothing, and can never touch gold or silver. Many scholars have been puzzled by this situation, but Nightingale, drawing on the work of Christopher Gill, points out that simply because they are "'just men obeying just commands,' they are eager to pay back their city for the education and rearing that has been granted them."[33] And remember that it had been the obligation of the ritual *theoros* to return and give an account of what he had seen to his fellow citizens.

The rulers, or, as they are often called, the "guardians," are an ascetic lot, and have been compared to a monastic order. Not only are they committed to a life of poverty (they live on what the city gives them, not on anything of their own, and can be considered in a way to be beggars), but their sexual life is so regulated that, though they have children, they have no family life, no personal household: the children are raised in common. They embody the virtue of wisdom, but they preside over a city that is characterized by the virtues of justice and moderation, and, not insignificantly, where there are no slaves. A democracy the ideal city is not, and I'm sure we wouldn't want to live in it, and perhaps even Plato would have had his doubts. In any case there are no examples of the ideal city ever existing.

In books 8 and 9 of the *Republic* Plato describes a steady decline from a mythical first regime that is a version of his ideal city, a decline that begins because some of the guardians go astray, desiring personal enrichment, even though that involves, for the first time, the enslavement of fellow citizens. This produces timocracy, the rule of honor, with Sparta as an actual example. But unchecked desires lead to a further downward spiral, first to oligarchy and then democracy. Although Plato's argument compels him to say that democracy is the worst regime short of tyranny, he also says it is the freest of regimes, and the freedom of democracy is what makes it the only regime where philosophy is possible. Within the multicolored variety of democratic ways of life, the philosophical life can be pursued, at least until the democratic lack of self-control leads to tyranny, the worst of all possible regimes.

Outside the rigid logic of decline, it would seem that Plato has more sympathy with democracy than he admits. In any case, in the greatest of the few dialogues where someone else takes the part of Socrates, the *Laws,* the central character is an Athenian philosopher, not a Spartan, that is, someone from what in the scheme of decline should have been a better city than Athens. But then, there were no philosophers in Sparta, and besides, no Spartan could ever have talked as much as the Athenian in the *Laws.*

Compared to the cities of his day, Plato was holding up an ideal. It has often been called an aristocratic ideal, but aristocrats on the whole favored oligarchy, which Plato despised, and Nightingale argues that Plato used aristocratic ideals against the aristocrats, who were not "real" aristocrats in his eyes, just as the Buddha criticized the Brahmins for not being "real" Brahmins.

Which takes us to the Buddhist case, where religious reform and political criticism also went hand in hand. I have been presenting a more Buddhist Plato than usual before turning to the Buddha himself. There are some interesting parallels between them: recent revisions of the dates of the Buddha bring him into the fourth century BCE, and make the Buddha and Plato possible contemporaries. One striking parallel is the degree to which each one threw out his respective inherited tradition and attempted to replace it with an entirely new one. I noted in Chapter 7 that Plato composed a huge corpus intended to replace the entire poetic, dramatic, and wisdom traditions that preceded him. Fortunately he did not succeed in eliminating his forbears, but start a new tradition he did, as the famous quip of Alfred North Whitehead indicates (the European philosophical tradition is a series of footnotes to Plato). The Buddha similarly threw out the entire Vedic tradition, from the Rig Veda to the Upanishads, and in its place left us with a collection of sermons and dialogues, the Buddhist canon, which is several times bigger than Plato's complete works. We can be relatively sure that all that is attributed to the Buddha is not his, that successive generations added to the tradition in his name. It is not improbable that the Platonic corpus is similarly layered. But here we are interested in the degree to which both men succeeded in starting something quite new.

Of course, the Buddha, like Plato, owed a great deal to his predecessors and is inconceivable without them. But as Richard Gombrich has pointed out, those who see Buddhism simply as a later school of Brahmanism and those who see it as a totally new conception are equally mistaken: Buddhism is a reformulation of Brahmanism so radical that it began a new and enormously influential tradition, even though it did not survive in India. Both men could be seen as in some ways visionaries; both also as great rationalists, adept in argument, superb in dialogue; and both were before all else teachers, and—though we often fail to see this side of Plato, because of the quite artificial distinction we make between philosophy and religion, or that we project back into premodern times—both were teachers of salvation.

The Buddhist version of the Myth of the Cave is in an important sense the whole elaborate story of the Buddha's life as the tradition handed it down. Just as the philosopher had to leave his *oikos* and his *polis*, so the Buddha had to leave his *oikos* and his *polis*, or rather his kingdom, the rule of which should have come to him. But seeing sickness, old age, and death, the Buddha wanted to leave that cave, and spent years of suffering and deprivation trying to do so. In the end, however, he found a middle way between the sensual indulgence of the world and the harsh austerities of the renouncers who preceded him, a way in which serene meditation could lead him to the truth and to the release he sought.

It was during his meditation under the Bodhi tree that he famously attained his vision of the truth and his release from the wheel of samsara, the endless cycle of birth and rebirth. Sometime later when he was considering what to do next, he almost concluded that there was no use in trying to teach what he had learned to a world filled with lust and hate. But just then he was approached by the deity Sahampati, who implored him to return to the world after all, as we saw in Chapter 9:

> Let the Sorrowless One survey this human breed,
> Engulfed in sorrow, overcome by birth and old age.
> Arise, victorious hero, caravan leader,
> Debtless one, and wander in the world.
> Let the blessed One teach the Dhamma,
> There will be those who will understand.

And so the Buddha undertook, out of compassion for all sentient beings, forty-five years of itinerant preaching to make sure that the truth he had seen would not be lost to the world.[34]

Followers of the Buddha, like those of Plato, knew a lot about the legitimation crisis of axial-age society, as is evident in many texts. Following Steven Collins, we can take a particularly vivid example from one of the Jataka stories (stories of the Buddha's previous lives, one of the most widely known genres of the Buddhist canon), a story that is long and fascinating, which I will all too briefly summarize.[35] "Once upon a time there was a king of Benares who ruled justly *(dhammena)*. He had sixteen thousand women, but did not obtain a son or daughter from any of them."[36] Indra, the king of the gods, took pity on him and sent the future Buddha to be born as a son to his chief queen. The child was named Temiya, and his father was delighted with him. When he was a month old he was dressed up and brought to his father, who was so pleased with him that he held him in his lap as he held court. Just then four criminals were brought in, and the king sentenced one of them to be imprisoned, two to be lashed or struck with swords, and one to be impaled on a stake. Temiya was extremely upset and worried that his father would go to hell for his terrible deeds. The next day Temiya remembered his previous births, including that in the past he had been king of this very city and that, as a result of his actions, he subsequently spent 80,000 years in an especially terrible hell, where he had been cooked on hot metal in excruciating pain the whole time. He determined that this would not happen again, so he pretended to be lame, deaf, and dumb, so that he could not succeed to the kingship.

Because he was beautiful and had a perfectly formed body, people found it hard to believe in his defects, but because he was a future Buddha, he was able to resist all temptations to give himself away, whether with loud noises, terrifying snakes, or beautiful girls. When he was 16 the soothsayers told the king that he would bring bad luck to the royal house and should be killed. His mother begged him to save himself by showing that he was without defect, but knowing what his fate would be if he succeeded to the kingship, he refused. Temiya was sent in his chariot to the charnel ground, where he was to be killed, but the gods saw to it that the charioteer took him to the forest instead. At that point Temiya revealed his true self, showing himself strong and fit. His charioteer offered to take him back to the city so he could claim his succession to the throne, but Temiya explained to him the dreadful fate in hell that awaited him if he did so and declared his intention to become an ascetic instead. At that point, "the chariot-driver, seeing that Temiya had cast kingship aside 'as if it were a dead body,' wanted to become an ascetic also."[37] Temiya ordered him instead to return to the city and tell his parents what had happened.

When Temiya's parents received the news, they rushed to the forest where he was, and overwhelmed with his new self, proceeded to renounce the world themselves. Soon the whole city had come out to the forest and everyone became a renouncer. They left gold and jewels in the streets of the city as of no more use. Soon a neighboring king, hearing what had happened, decided to annex Benares and scoop up the gold and jewels, but once in the city he felt an overwhelming impulse to find the ascetic prince and his parents. Upon finding them, he, too, and his subjects following him, became renouncers. Another king followed his example. Soon it was clear that Temiya was, after all, a *cakravartin,* a universal ruler, though his rule was renunciation.

Collins sums up by saying, "It is difficult to imagine a more explicit condemnation of kingship: despite the narrative voice's assertion in the first sentence that Temiya's father ruled justly, or 'in accordance with what is right' *(dhammena).*"[38] Collins points out that *dhamma* is used in two senses, worldly *dhamma* and *buddhadhamma,* and that it is the former that the kingdom embodied and the latter that it drastically violated. Temiya's father's kingdom represented what Peter Brown, the great historian of late classical antiquity, described as "the more predictable, but no less overbearing 'gentle violence' of a stable social order."[39] In a class society, even if those who serve and are never served are not beaten or hungry, as in fact they often are, they are always at the whim of those they serve; they have no control over their own lives. If it is unlikely that Plato ever imagined that his ideal city could be realized, it is very clear that in this Buddhist story Temiya's universal empire of renunciation could never be realized on this earth: it would involve not only the absence of violence; it would involve the absence of sex. Nonetheless, as with all the great axial utopias, it stands as a measure of just how short life in this world falls compared to what it ought to be.

Axial Utopias and Play

It may not be easy to bring the thought of the great axial thinkers into the realm of play, but it is worth considering. Plato, as noted near the end of Chapter 2, took play very seriously as a way in which men and gods interact. For him the freedom of play was linked to another realm where necessity does not reign. The Parable of the Cave has an element of play in that it involves a release from its starting point, life in the cave, which is a realm of coercion: its inhabitants are chained. When the protagonist is released from his chains and turns around, leaves the cave, and finds himself in the open air with the sun above, he is at first anxious. He is free and he doesn't know what to do with his freedom—it has been a long time since he experienced the world of play, if he ever had—so he is even half inclined to return to the cave. But what he actually does is ascend to the vision of the form of the good, a joyous, overwhelming experience of being and meaning. Is that so far from play at its best? Can we not see a play element at the climax of Plato's central narrative? And though, at least in the texts I have read, the Buddha doesn't talk about play, is there not a wonderful atmosphere of play at the climax of the story of Temiya? When Temiya's parents, the king and queen of Benares, are so overwhelmed with joy that they too become renouncers and then the citizens of Benares and of the neighboring kingdoms too are all swept away in this joyous transformation, is there not something like play going on? Have we not seen that play is possible only in a relaxed field where the pressures of the struggle for existence are in abeyance, and is this not what we find in these two great narratives?

It would even be possible to press the analogy one step further. Aren't all utopias a kind of pretend play where one can imagine a world that is itself a relaxed field where the ordinary pressures of life are suspended? If we can imagine a world of Buddhist renouncers, it would be a world of sheer joy, where the sufferings and desires of this world have been left behind, where there is no coercion of any kind, interior or exterior. There is a marvelous description of something surprisingly similar in Second Isaiah. After a fairly bloody description of what will happen to sinners, there is a picture of the end of times that is a relaxed field indeed:

> For behold, I create new heavens and a new earth;
> and the former things shall not be remembered
>   or come into mind.
> But be glad and rejoice for ever in that which I create;
> for behold, I create Jerusalem a rejoicing,
>   and her people a joy.
> I will rejoice in Jerusalem,
>   and be glad in my people;
> no more shall be heard in it the sound of weeping
>   and the cry of distress.
> They shall build houses and inhabit them;
>   they shall plant vineyards and eat their fruit.
> They shall not build and another inhabit;
>   they shall not plant and another eat;
> for like the days of a tree shall the days of my people be,
>   and my chosen shall long enjoy the work of their hands.

The wolf and the lamb shall feed together,
>   the lion shall eat straw like the ox;
>   and dust shall be the serpent's food.
They shall not hurt or destroy in all my holy mountain,
>   says the Lord. (Isaiah 65:17–19, 21–22, 25, RSV)

What we see here is a world of absolute nonviolence, but also of social justice: the rich and powerful will not take away the houses or the harvests of the poor, but ordinary people shall long enjoy the work of their hands. This utopia even seems to be vegetarian, given the diet of the lion; and the serpent, though still accursed with bad food, is not to be killed. Above all it is a world of rejoicing where the sound of weeping and the cry of distress will no longer be heard. The legitimation crisis of the axial age is solved, even if only at the end of times.

Plato's *Republic* (and even more the city described in the *Laws*) is more "realistic" than the Buddhist utopia—life in the real polis had too strong a hold on Plato for it to be otherwise. The basic idea is a society created by educational play and moral example, but hierarchy and coercion enter because some prove immune to such teaching. So even violence is necessary, at least at first before the ethical life has been fully internalized by the population. The hallmark of Confucian utopianism was the rule of virtue by ritual and example, which would ultimately replace the rule of war and punishment, though, as in the case of Plato, the Confucians recognized that punishment might have to be phased out gradually.

Ritual is central in each of these examples. In the Buddhist utopia it would take the form of meditation.[40] The Confucian utopia would be above all the expression of ritual, *li,* though a form of ritual expanded beyond the ancient form to include the whole of humanity. In Plato one could see the vision of the good itself as a kind of ritual, and there are ritual aspects to Plato's thought in many dialogues. And even in the end time we can imagine that the ritual prescriptions of the Torah would still be binding. But if we think of any of these utopias realistically, as their authors usually did, we can see that they would never work. We live in a world where the struggle for existence still dominates and is not about to transform itself completely into a relaxed field.

Overlapping Fields

Yet the presence of relaxed fields is not without its influence on the world of the struggle for existence. In life and clearly in human culture there are no impenetrable boundaries and no fields that aren't overlapping. Indeed, play can be sucked into the world of daily life, can become part of the struggle for existence. I mentioned above the relation between play and practice for battle in aristocratic societies. In the modern military we have things called "war games," and the term is not without meaning. We have leaders of nation-states enmeshed in their own fantasy games of what will happen if, say, they invade Iraq—play fantasies that prove impervious to all the advice they receive about what will really happen.[41] And where does play end and work begin in the world of professional sports, so pervasive in much of the modern world? The players are indeed hired, sometimes at exorbitant salaries, though we should not forget those who are paid less, work only a few years, and sometimes suffer debilitating injuries while "at work." On the other hand, as I pointed out in Chapter 1, even in professional sports, participation in the game can become an end in itself, a player can be "in the zone," fully at one with what he or she is doing.

But if play can get sucked into the world of daily life, work, in the sense of overcoming deficiency, can sometimes be transformed into forms of play. Art, which is linked to play, also involves a kind of work. Kant, in his description of art as play that stimulated Schiller's complex reflections, noted that art involves work as well. He says that though the spirit of art must be free, there is something compulsory that is always required, without which the art "would have no body at all and would entirely evaporate," and he gives the example of "correctness and richness of diction as well as prosody and meter" in the art of poetry.[42] We surely know that practice, which we noticed was going on in preparation for the great rituals among the Kalapalo, is often very hard work, as every dancer and musician knows, and this work makes the freedom of art, the play element, possible.

But I think we need to take these examples one step further and ask when ordinary work (that is, not work that is a professionalized form of play or work that is an inevitable part of art) can become play or have an aspect of play. Let us back up a minute to remember Burghardt's *Genesis of Animal Play*. Burghardt notes that although the primary function of play is the sheer joyous expression of play itself, the play will be ruined if the players don't follow the rules governing the game. Those rules are at least incipiently ethical because they involve the protection of equality between the players, what we now refer to as "fair play" or "a level playing field." But play, according to Burghardt, can also take on secondary and tertiary functions. Hans Joas, in his book *The Creativity of Action*, which has a great deal to say about play in

its many forms, reminds us of some of the ways in which play has the secondary function of pulling children out of their early fusion of subjectivity
and objectivity into an increasingly differentiated view of the world. He cites
the interesting work of the psychoanalyst Donald Winnicott on transitional
objects in infancy, things like security blankets, that combine features of
selfhood and otherness but allow exploration of the world without loss of the
security of the mother.[43] George Herbert Mead, one of the great writers on
play, particularly the role of play in the ethical development of the child,
analyzed the capacity of children, when playing team sports, to imagine
themselves in every role in the game, not only their own, and thus to "take the
role of the other," a crucial capacity in human understanding.[44] Joas quotes
John Dewey, another major American pragmatist along with Mead, as saying that work and play are "equally free and intrinsically motivated, apart
from false economic conditions which tend to make play into idle excitement
for the well to do, and work into uncongenial labor for the poor."[45] But here
Dewey was engaging in social criticism, because he knew well that what he
called "false economic conditions" were the norm for his own society and
historic societies in general. As in the axial age, the overlapping of fields has
ethical implications.

Dewey in *Art as Experience* develops further his understanding of the relation of play and work. He emphasizes that the play of children at first has no
more purpose than the play of a kitten, but that as play becomes more complex, it takes on an intention and a goal. He gives the example of a child
playing with blocks, building a house or a tower. Here play involves the fulfillment of a preconceived idea. "Play as an event is still immediate. But its
content consists of the mediation of present materials by ideas drawn from
past experiences . . . This transition effects a transformation of play into
work, provided work is not identical with toil or labor. For any activity becomes work when it is directed by accomplishment of a definite material result, and it is labor only as the activities are onerous, undergone as *mere*
means by which to secure a result. The product of artistic activity is significantly called the *work* of art."[46] He then goes on to say, "Play remains as an
attitude of freedom from subordination to an end imposed by external necessity, as opposed, that is, to labor; but it is transformed into work in that
activity is subordinated to *production* of an objective result."[47] Perhaps Dewey
in a good American way pushes too quickly beyond play or work as an end
in itself into the realm of production, but surely he is raising the question of
what in other theoretical traditions is called alienated labor or alienated

work, and offering the possibility that all work could be unalienated, perhaps another utopian idea that puts pressure on the world of daily life.

It is worth noting that the psychologist Mihaly Csikszentmihalyi, in his study of what he calls flow—which he defines as a kind of optimal experience of full engagement with the world and full realization of one's own potentialities, as we noted in Chapter 1—has found that, contrary to expectations, and to a degree contrary sometimes to the subjects' beliefs, many American do experience flow at work.[48] The sociologist Arlie Hochschild has even worried that some of the people she studied get more satisfaction at work than they do at home, though she focuses more on time pressure than on the intrinsic satisfaction of work.[49] Perhaps this possible increase in the intrinsic satisfaction of work has to do with the changes in a modern economy where fewer jobs involve heavy manual labor, although desk jobs are widely viewed as often meaningless. We can be reasonably sure that we have a way to go before everyone's job has the same quality as play, art, or flow.

Theoria and Types of Consciousness

Flow goes all the way back, because it is found in animal play, in ritual, in art, and in work that is intrinsically meaningful, but there is another related but different kind of experience that is at least equally ancient. The psychologist Alison Gopnik has interestingly contrasted flow, which she equates with what she calls "spotlight consciousness," which we have "when our attention is completely focused on a single object or activity, and we lose ourselves in that activity," with what she calls "lantern consciousness." Flow involves concentration in a single direction, thus the spotlight metaphor: "In flow we enjoy a peculiarly pleasurable kind of unconsciousness. When we're completely absorbed in a task we lose sight of the outside world and even lose consciousness of each particular action we must take. The plan just seems to execute itself."[50]

Lantern consciousness, which Gopnik sees as common in infants and attainable by adults usually only with certain forms of meditation, is not oriented to one particular direction but is open to the whole undifferentiated world.[51] "Lantern consciousness leads to a very different kind of happiness [than does flow]. There is a similar feeling that we have lost our sense of self, but we lose ourselves by becoming part of the world."[52] Both spotlight consciousness and lantern consciousness would seem to be part of what Maslow called B-cognition, as described in Chapter 1, because neither is oriented to deficiency, Maslow's D-cognition. Yet there is a significant difference: flow is active, lantern consciousness is receptive. With these modern psychological categories in mind, let us return to the question of *theoria* and theory in the axial age.

Theoria is accurately translated as "contemplation," a state that is not active but is not passive either, for it is open to the whole of reality and receptive of what is given in that experience of openness. This seems to be similar to what Gopnik is describing with her idea of lantern consciousness, where everything is illuminated, and her notion that in that state we "become part of the world." Lantern consciousness is similar to the unitive event that was the first of our stages of religious experience as described in Chapter 1. Both the vision of the idea of the Good in Plato's *Republic* and the Buddha's experience of release under the Bodhi tree seem to have this quality. Parallels in ancient China are easy to find in Daoism, but less obvious in Confucianism, though the idea of the original state of Bull Mountain in Mencius's parable of that name contains such a vision. There are more than a few visions in the Hebrew scriptures. The great vision of Isaiah, chapter 6, in which the temple in Jerusalem is seen as identical with the whole cosmos, is a good example, but so is the vision of the end time in Isaiah 65 quoted above.

Experiences of *theoria,* if we can use Plato's word for them—they are usually visual, and *theoria* is a kind of seeing, though they can involve hearing, as was often the case in ancient Israel—provide an insight into reality so deep that the whole empirical world is called into question. Such experiences can remain private, but when they are taken as the focus for subsequent reflection they can lead to a radical questioning of the way things are, that is, the world is relativized in the light of an all-encompassing truth.

Josef Pieper in his *Leisure, the Basis of Culture* provides Latin contrast terms from medieval scholasticism that seem to be getting at a relevant contrast: *intellectus* is receptive contemplation; *ratio* is active reason.[53] The Greek terms that lie behind this much later distinction are not easy to specify: *nous* in some uses could be behind *intellectus,* and *logos* could be behind *ratio,* but both *nous* and *logos* have many meanings. In any case, when Donald and I, following him, use "theory" as a way of characterizing a new cultural capacity in the axial age, it is theory or reason in the active sense, not *theoria* as contemplation that we are primarily thinking of. However, I want to argue that there is a relation between these two senses of the term. If Gopnik is right that what she calls lantern consciousness is characteristic of all young children (and probably many animals as well), we can hardly argue that it is something new in the axial age.[54] It is, however, something that doesn't come readily to adults, who may have to "work" to attain it. And in the cultural context of the axial age it can, for intellectually and spiritually attuned adults, take on a significance not given to such experiences earlier. What I want to argue is that *theoria* as contemplation may open up the possibility of theory in the active sense, related to Gopnik's spotlight consciousness, but not quite identical.

Gopnik emphasizes the relation of spotlight consciousness and flow: the task takes over and pulls us along, sometimes without our even being conscious that it is happening, but in talking about active reason I want to emphasize the conscious side of spotlight consciousness. Those engaged in demanding intellectual work, scientists and scholars, often have the experience of flow when all is going well in their work. But there are occasions when all does not go well, when facts turn up that don't fit one's expectations, contradictions appear in arguments that had seemed coherent. Then one must stop the flow and think about what is going on. It is then, I would argue, that we engage in "second-order thinking," thinking about thinking, to try to clarify our problems and find a way to deal with them. It is here that "theory," which is related in origin to both lantern consciousness and flow, comes into its own as active reason, as involving a higher level of abstraction and methods of investigation that may be required to solve problems. Here we find the beginnings of science, cognitive speculation, and the universalization of ethics, all of which were beginning to appear in the axial age, though still in relation to embodied practice and story, mimetic and mythic culture.

When the experience of radical truth—which is given, not achieved, which is the original meaning of philosophical *theoria*—is reflected on after the experience itself has passed, the door may be opened to this new kind of thinking about the world and particularly society, which is now "demystified," in that the shadows in the cave are revealed as fake, as not reality but a manipulated simulacrum of reality. This new kind of theory in axial religion led to two major consequences that worked themselves out in various ways in the four axial cases. One is that the person who experienced theoria as "seeing truth" was driven to imagine the kind of society in which that truth could transform the world of daily life. The second consequence of thinking through the vision of the Good coming from a true experience of *theoria* was—because changing the whole society proved impossibly utopian—to consider limited kinds of utopia within the world, forms of group organization that would protect the vision and provide a relaxed field, at least for its devotees. Both kinds of response to the experience of *theoria* would continue to work themselves out over the subsequent millennia right up to the present, though a consideration of those later developments is not our present concern. Both projects are utopian, but the first is a big, almost fantastic, utopia, whereas the second is a more modest, even practical, one.

Two Kinds of Theory in Two Kinds of Utopia

Plato's big utopia took its model, as noted above, from the polis, though a very new kind of polis. After the vision of the Good in the Parable of the Cave, which is *theoria* in the classic sense, Plato turns to theory in the active sense, a way of thinking about the world to determine how it could be different. Active theory or active reason requires Plato to think about the practical realities of the world of daily life, the world of the struggle for existence. In order to show citizens who had not shared his transcendent experience that the city he is proposing is good, he invented the "noble lie" to convince the various orders in the city to accept their stations as "natural." And in the *Laws* Plato justifies punishments, even including the death penalty, for those whose souls have not been improved by the enlightened "musical" education laid out for them, though in time such punishments would no longer be necessary. Confucians would come to a similar position when they admitted that the city of virtue under a moral king could not abandon harsh punishments at once, even though that was the goal. The renouncer, then, sees the world with new eyes: as Plato says of the ones who have returned to the cave, they see the shadows for what they are, not naively as do those who have never left. One could say that the ideological illusion is gone. One gazes at a distance, objectively, so to speak.

Once disengaged vision, what I am calling active theory, becomes possible, then theory can take another turn: it can abandon any moral stance at all and look simply at what will be useful, what can make the powerful and exploitative even more so. One thinks of the Legalists in China, and of Kautilya's Arthashastra in India. Although the Hebrew prophets saw and condemned the self-serving manipulations of the rich and powerful, we can find in the Bible no example of someone arguing for such behavior in principle. Except possibly for some of the Sophists, whose surviving writings are fragmentary, we have nothing quite like Han Fei or Kautilya in Greece. Or do we?

Aristotle was not an amoralist; he was one of the greatest moral theorists who ever lived. Yet in Aristotle we can see the possibility of a split between knowledge and ethics that will, when it is fully recognized, have enormous consequences in later history, a split that was already foreshadowed in Plato's "noble lie," as we have seen. Pierre Hadot argues that Plato's school, for all its concern for mathematics and dialectic, had an essentially political aim: philosophers in principle should be rulers. Aristotle's school, however, is specifically for philosophers, those who do not participate actively in the life of the city, in a way a school for renouncers.[55] But in distinguishing the philosophical life from the political life so clearly, Aristotle threatens the link between wisdom *(sophia)* and moral judgment *(phronesis),* in which he still clearly believed. Most of his surviving texts were notes for lectures within the school and express aspects of the philosophical life, though the *Ethics* and the *Politics* were intended for a larger audience of active citizens. The link between the two realms is not direct but appears in the fact that both are oriented to good forms of life, one toward knowledge for its own sake, the other toward the creation of a good city.

Although the highest form of *theoria* is contemplation of the divine, and through it the philosopher, however briefly and partially, actually participates in the divine, *theoria* includes the search for knowledge of all things, including the transient ones. Pierre Hadot, however, argues that Aristotle's massive research project is not quite what it seems to modern minds: "It is thus indisputable that for Aristotle the life of the mind consists to a large degree, in observing, doing research, and reflecting on one's observations. Yet this activity is carried out in a certain spirit, which we might go so far as to describe as an almost religious passion for reality in all its aspects, be they humble or sublime, for we find traces of the divine in all things."[56] And he goes on to quote a passage in which Aristotle says, "In all natural things there is something wonderful."[57] It is as though *theoria* in its highest form is close to what Gopnik calls "lantern consciousness," the apprehension of reality as a whole, but in its lesser forms it becomes various kinds of "spotlight consciousness," focusing on each aspect of reality, however humble, in an effort to understand it and what causes it.

So one possible split apparent in Aristotle is between his metaphysics, where he describes the ultimate source of all knowledge, and the many particular fields of inquiry that he had so much to do with founding. But the second possible split is between *theoria,* contemplation, in all its various levels, as the best life for human beings, and the life of the city, of politics and ethics. *Theoria,* in his words, is useless. It is a good internal to itself, but it has no consequences for the world.

But perhaps we miss Aristotle's point if we ask what the theoretical life is good for. Being the best kind of life, and good in itself, then the question is what kind of person and what kind of society could make this life possible. The *Ethics* and *Politics* describe the conditions under which the theoretical life could be pursued. But unlike Plato's *Republic,* Aristotle's *Politics* is no utopia, but an empirical and analytical description of actual Greek society, containing ethical judgments between better and worse, but objective, distant, as an analysis of the second-best kind of life, one that has its final value in making possible the first kind of life. Aristotle was the founder of sociology, which Durkheim recognized when he assigned the *Politics* as the basic textbook for his students when he first began to teach at the University of Bordeaux. All I am suggesting is that the distinctions between two kinds of *theoria,* pure contemplation and various fields of inquiry, and two kinds of ethical life, the intellectual and the practical, made possible, if the unity of Aristotle's thought was broken, separate developments that could lead to autonomous sciences and utilitarian ethics in the long run.

Aristotle was really a stranger in his own city, if Athens was his own city: he was not a citizen. He had to set up his school, the Lyceum, in a public building, because, as an alien, he could not own land in Athens and so could not buy land for his school. And when things turned grim, he, unlike Socrates, had no compunction about getting out in time, so that Athens would not commit the same crime a second time. He was a teacher, one of the greatest who ever lived, but one of his (not very apt) pupils was Alexander, the greatest conqueror of the ancient world. Aristotle on the whole used the word *theoria* in Plato's sense, but he also used it from time to time for "investigation," or "inquiry," that is, for the study of all things in the world, natural and cultural, to see how they work and what they are for.

The beginnings of science, of a critical view of the world, of knowledge for its own sake, can be found in all the axial cases, though in Israel, as in the case of Philo (20 BCE–50 CE) or Josephus (37–ca. 100 CE), for example, creative thinkers often wrote in Greek and were profoundly influenced by Greek thought, which dominated most of the Middle East for centuries. Talcott Parsons spoke of ancient Israel and Greece as "seedbed" societies because their heritages, even when they lost political independence, continued to germinate in subsequent history.[58] In reality, all the axial societies were seedbed societies, and one of the things we would need to consider if we were to follow up this metaphor, is that they cross-pollinated in a variety of ways. Just as Jewish and Greek traditions interpenetrated, Buddhism had a powerful effect on

China, and Indian mathematics on the West. The axial transitions themselves were probably not simply parallel, though the connections between them are hard to determine, but in subsequent history they all deeply influenced each other.

My point is that the axial age gave us "theory" in two senses, and neither of them has been unproblematic ever since. The great utopian visions have motivated some of the noblest achievements of mankind; they have also motivated some of the worst actions of human beings. Theory in the sense of disengaged knowing, inquiry for the sake of understanding, with or without moral evaluation, has brought its own kind of astounding achievements but also has given humans the power to destroy their environment and themselves. Both kinds of theory have criticized but also justified the class society that first came into conscious view in the axial age. They have provided the intellectual tools for efforts to reform and efforts to repress. But the legitimation crisis of the axial age remains unresolved to this day. One must wonder what kind of transformation state societies would have to undergo, what kind of cosmopolitan institutions would have to limit and partly replace them, for that resolution to become imaginable.

As I already suggested in mentioning Aristotle's Lyceum, which was modeled in part on Plato's Academy, the second great consequence of the axial-age breakthroughs was the creation of institutions that would keep the traditions alive and shelter their adherents from the surrounding world, relaxed fields within the "gentle violence" of established social orders and sometimes the not so gentle violence in times of political turmoil. In India the hereditary caste of the Brahmins carried the tradition, or important parts of it, though later adherents of Vishnu or Shiva founded their own associations. The Buddhists created a new kind of institution, the monastic order, which may well have influenced the emergence of Christian monasticism in the West some centuries later. Educational institutions were important in all the cases, and we refer to "schools" that carried distinct traditions particularly in the classical Greek and Roman world, the Stoics and the Epicureans, for example, and in China, the Confucians, Mohists, and Daoists, though, perhaps under the influence of Buddhism, the Daoists later established religious institutions somewhat different from schools.[59]

Israel is a particularly interesting case because of its later history as a diaspora rather than an empire. In a sense, Judaism came closest to being a realized utopia, though under the most difficult of conditions. As an often-persecuted minority, Jews were deprived of independent political power, though in both

Christian and Muslim societies they often had significant ties to power holders. Under the best circumstances, however, Jews were able to establish their own self-governing communities under the protection of the ruling powers; these communities lacked state power, particularly military power, but had their own judiciary bodies to maintain order within the communities. The strongest sanction tended to be expulsion from the community, because violence was in the hands of the surrounding political order, though expulsion was a grave sanction indeed.[60] When I liken these communities to axial utopias, because within them life was guided by the Torah, however problematic external relations might be, I mean to say they had some similarities to Buddhist and Christian monastic communities, in that in these communities too the religious life and ordinary life were more closely identified than in most historic societies. It is perhaps ironic that as a result of the great emancipation of the Jews in modern times, the immemorial hope of return to the promised land could be combined with modern nationalism to create the state of Israel, which is no more utopian than any other modern nation—indeed, which faces all the tensions between ethical ideals and practical exigencies that are endemic to state organization.

To trace the great network of religious institutions that grew out of the axial traditions in later centuries, the Christian church, the Islamic Ummah, the Buddhist Sangha, and their related educational institutions, including the Islamic madrasas and the Christian universities, using their relatively relaxed fields for great cultural creativity, would take us well beyond the scope of this volume. But all of them, in one way or another, kept the religious utopian idea alive within their not always entirely relaxed boundaries.

Metanarratives Again

Let us return to an issue I raised in the Preface: How can we undertake, as I have done, a metanarrative, even an evolutionary metanarrative, when such narratives have most frequently in the past been used to justify the winners and vilify the losers in history viewed as the struggle for existence. Thomas McCarthy, in his recent book *Race, Empire, and the Idea of Human Development,* has raised these issues sharply, yet has affirmed, even in the face of great difficulties, the value, even the inescapability, of what he, following Kant, calls universal history.[61] In responding to him I hope to clarify where I stand. There are three great defects with most attempts at this genre, coming, as they largely do, from Europe and America.

1. There is a strong tendency, even in Kant, the most universalistic of early modern philosophers, to deal with humanity in terms of a radical dichotomy: us (Europe, later Europe plus America) versus them, and divided not only culturally, but alas, even by Kant, racially.[62] The white race is taken to be superior, even biologically superior, to all the others, though the other races can sometimes be seen as capable of learning to be more like Westerners. Even when the distinction between human groups is seen culturally rather than racially, dichotomy is still the primary way of categorizing: civilization versus barbarism. When distinctions between the less civilized were made, the distinctions between them were still minimal: "Orientals" may be superior to primitives, but they are still categorized as sharing a single, static, and, in particular, despotic culture: thus Oriental despotism. One needs look no further than Edward Said's *Orientalism* to see how recently such a dichotomy has dominated Western thought.[63]

2. This basic dichotomy can be put into time, sometimes evolutionary time, as a distinction between earlier and later, with the later, namely us, distinguishing ourselves from the others by a higher degree of progress. All existing societies can be arranged in terms of stages of progress, with Europe or Euro-America at the apex. Imperialism was justified as educational, bringing the possibility of liberty, after a suitable (long) period of tutelage, to those without it. Again we are disappointed to find John Stuart Mill, who most of his adult life worked for the East India Company, as did his father, James, giving eloquent expression to such views, and in his great essay *On Liberty,* no less. Freedom, we find, is "meant to apply to human beings in the maturity of their faculties," whereas "despotism is a legitimate mode of government in dealing with barbarians, provided the end be their improvement and the means justified by actually effecting that end." British rule in India is, in Mill's words, "good despotism." After all, "the greater part of the world has, properly speaking, no history, because the despotism of custom is complete. This is the case over the whole East."[64]

3. Past or present horrors can be justified as necessary preconditions for a better (democratic? socialist?) future. McCarthy notes that Walter Benjamin was particularly eloquent in finding unbearable "the thought of history's countless victims being nothing more than stepping stones along the path of development."[65] McCarthy notes that both Kant and Mill said repeatedly that no act that infringes on the dignity, much less

the existence, of another human being is ever morally justified. Yet each of them, and countless others less schooled in moral philosophy, found ways of justifying the unjustifiable. This part of our (Western) heritage, in McCarthy's view, calls not only for apology, but for reparation for those who are still suffering from the results of what we have done.[66]

Yet in spite of this crushing indictment of most existing metanarratives, McCarthy still believes that the very idea of developmental change is inevitable and irrepressible in the light of the fact that human capacities really have grown dramatically over historical time and that, like it or not, we are all moderns now, though in practice cultural differences will always remain. Furthermore, "it has proven dangerous to leave this field to those who misuse it."[67] And McCarthy gives us a recipe for the kind of metanarrative that we still very much need:

Kant's understanding of grand metanarrative—universal history from a cosmopolitan point of view—as the object neither of theoretical knowledge nor of practical reason, but of "reflective judgment," was closer to the mark. On his view, while such metanarratives must take account of, and be compatible with, known empirical data and causal connections they always go beyond what is known in aspiring to a unity of history. And that can best be done from a point of view oriented to practice: grand metanarratives give us an idea of the kinds of more humane future for which we may hope, but only if we are prepared to engage ourselves in bringing them about.[68]

In measuring this book against McCarthy's standards, let me try to show how in several ways I have tried to meet them. There is no dichotomy in my book. Although the book is inevitably written from the point of view of a particular present, its narrative stops 2,000 years ago. It does not deal with culture wars (except, incidentally in Chapter 2, the culture war between some kinds of religion and some kinds of science) or the "clash of civilizations"—for one thing, Christianity and Islam are not even discussed, as they are outside the temporal parameters of this book. Nor, indeed, do I treat modernity, though perhaps much about it is implied. It is not that I have nothing to say on these matters—I hope to say more about them—just that in this book "modernization" is not an issue. If "we" means Westerners, and Israel and Greece are "our" predecessors, I have certainly not favored them. They get less space than China and India, I have tried to treat all four axial cases with equal respect and value them for their remarkable achievements. And if for Mill the "whole East" has no history, I have tried to show just what a vivid and dramatic history China and India, and their predecessors throughout the world, natural and cultural, have had.

As for homogenizing the "Other," again I have everywhere tried to avoid doing that. I have shown great inner diversity even in two of my tribal societies, the Australian Aborigines and the Navajo, and certainly in the archaic and axial societies, where deep inner tensions are what fuel the emergence of new insights and creative novelty. Nor have I treated the past, again biologically or culturally, triumphally. Throughout Chapter 2, I tried to show that the distinction between "higher" and "lower" is always relative, that the bacteria, for example, could be seen as the most successful of all forms of life, and that we have no grounds for sneering at the dinosaurs. And though I gave most space to the axial age, whose leading figures are still present in the lives of any educated person, I did not disparage pre-axial cultures, but tried to show the inner value and meaning of each of them.

Finally I did attempt a universal history (though only 4 billion less 2,000 years long) that shared Thomas McCarthy's criteria of the kind of history we need. I did not shy away from the fact that natural selection is the primary mechanism of evolution, biological and cultural, but I was concerned with the emergence of "relaxed fields" in animal play and human culture, where the struggle for existence or the survival of the fittest did not have full sway, where ethical standards and free creativity could arise, forms that in many cases did turn out to be selected, as they had survival value, though they arose in contexts where the good was internal to the practice, not for any external end. Nor did I claim that all was for the good or deny that history is full of horrors. I showed that the good guys often lose and the bad guys often triumph.

The Practical Intent

As for the "practical intent" of this book, which McCarthy takes as the only justification for universal history, I have tried to show that the evolution of life and culture gives no ground for any kind of triumphalism. I do believe we need to speak of evolution, which is the only shared metanarrative among educated people of all cultures that we have, but in a way that shows the dangers as well as the successes in evolution and that is not afraid to make distinctions between good and evil.

So let me turn to a startling example of what deep history can show us about the moral situation humans are in today and about the changes we need to make. There have been at least five major extinction events—defined as events that involve the extinction of at least 50 percent of all animal species—as evidenced in the fossil record of the last 540 million years. The most recent, the Cretaceous-Tertiary extinction event of 65 million years ago, is the best known, as it was then that all the dinosaurs except the birds died out. The greatest extinction event was the Permian-Triassic event of 245 million years ago, when about 96 percent of all marine species and an estimated 70 percent or more of land species, including vertebrates, insects, and plants, died out. It is called the "Great Dying" because of its enormous evolutionary consequences.

As some of us know, and all of us should know, we are in the midst of the sixth great extinction event at this very moment—indeed, we have been in it for a considerable time. The paleontologist Niles Eldredge describes this event as one that "threatens to rival the five great mass extinctions of the geological past."[69] He points out that all previous extinction events have had physical causes, including collisions with extraterrestrial objects, great volcanic explosions, or dramatic changes in plate tectonics, but this one has a different cause: "It is the first recorded global extinction event that has a biotic, rather than a physical, cause."[70] That cause is us.

Eldredge argues that this extinction event began at least 100,000 years ago when humans developed hunting techniques that allowed them to overhunt game species, including, but not exclusively, the megafauna like mammoths and mastodons. Such extinctions occurred whenever humans occupied new territories—as in Australia about 40,000 years ago and in the Americas about 12,500 years ago. Much more recently, when humans arrived in Polynesia they wiped out all the large land bird species.[71]

But the impact of human agriculture on the environment beginning about 10,000 years ago was much worse. According to Eldredge, "Agriculture represents the single most profound ecological change in the entire 3.5 billion-year history of life." This was because humans no longer depended on other species in their natural state, but could manipulate them for their own needs, thus allowing humans to overpopulate beyond any natural ecological carrying capacity. The development of agriculture was "essentially to declare war on ecosystems—converting land to produce one or two food crops, with other native plant species now classified as unwanted 'weeds'—and all but a few domesticated species of animals now considered pests."[72] The enormous increase in population, which has now reached 6 billion and continues to increase logarithmically, has reached the point where in many places soil erosion is massive, water is in short supply, the oceans are polluted and fish depleted, and the atmospheric changes have led to rapid global warming. Eldredge concludes his article by saying: "Only 10% of the world's species survived the third mass extinction. Will any survive this one?"[73]

Of course we may well blow each other up with atomic weapons before we wipe out all species of life, including our own, by more gradual means. Massive inequalities between rich and poor nations and the diminishing supplies of energy and water could bring on such a fatal conflict. In my Preface I pointed out that our rate of adaptation has increased so greatly that we are having difficulty adapting to our adaptations. All of this should make it clear that, though I do believe in evolution in the sense of increasing capacities, and in stages of evolution going far back in biological time resulting from those new capacities, I have never argued that more is better, that we are the apex of life, or that there is any certainty that we will not sooner rather than later end our own existence and that of most other species, leaving the earth to the bacteria, who, as in Chapter 2 I quoted Stephen Jay Gould as saying, are "the organisms that were in the beginning, are now, and probably ever shall be (until the sun runs out of fuel) the dominant creatures on earth by any standard evolutionary criterion."[74] If there is one primary practical intent in a work like this that deals with the broadest sweep of biological and cultural evolution, it is that the hour is late: it is imperative that humans wake up to what is happening and take the necessarily dramatic steps that are so clearly needed but also at present so clearly ignored by the powers of this earth.

But I would like to close by discussing another practical intent of my work, one less apocalyptic than our ecological crisis, yet one of great importance. That is the possibility we have of understanding our deepest cultural differences, including our religious differences, in a dramatically different way than most humans have ever done before. Ethnocentrism can be found everywhere, so we should not be surprised to find it among our ancestors.

Great as the major figures of the axial age were, and universalistic as their ethics tended to be, we cannot forget that each of them considered his own teaching to be the only truth or the highest truth, even such a figure as the Buddha, who never denounced his rivals but only subtly satirized them. Plato, Confucius, Second Isaiah, all thought that it was they and they alone who had found the final truth. This we can understand as an inevitable feature of a world so long ago.

But it is painfully relevant for a book dealing with religious evolution to remember that even the best of early modern thinkers normally assumed the superiority of Christianity to all other religions. For Kant and Hegel, perhaps the most influential of all modern philosophers, it wasn't just Christianity that was superior, it was Protestant Christianity in particular, a view widespread until just yesterday.

It is poignant to remember that for Max Weber it was not just Protestant Christianity, but what he called "ascetic Protestantism," by which he meant mainly Calvinism, that set the standard for stimulating rationalization, particularly but by no means exclusively, in the economic sphere, and against which all other religions were to be measured and found more or less wanting, beginning with Catholicism, but then going on to the religions of China and India. It is true that Weber didn't really like ascetic Protestantism, which he called "a religion of universal unbrotherliness," and which was not compatible with the figures he took as representing religion at its best: Jesus, Francis, and the Buddha. Still it was ascetic Protestantism that did most to further the spread of rationalization throughout human life, a process about which he had many doubts (the "iron cage") but that he thought was inevitable and, on the whole, for the best.[75]

Yet the twentieth century began to see the emergence of a new point of view, one that could understand and appreciate all religions on their own terms and that was not driven to set up one as the apex, either because it was the best, or because it was the most historically progressive. I am not thinking here primarily of "new age" consciousness, which proclaimed that "all religions are different paths to the same God," though the appearance of such opinions was indicative of a new cultural situation. Weber satirized the cultural elite of his day for "decorating their souls with antiques drawn from all the world's religions," and much of what was happening was indeed foolish, especially the inevitable tendency to read what one wanted to find into other religions rather than to try to understand them in their own terms. Nor am I thinking primarily of inter-religious dialogue, important though that is, in which we recognize each other's right to existence, and to defense if under persecution, although we may still continue to believe that our own religion is the best one—though surely such dialogue is a great advance against earlier tendencies.

What I am thinking of now is the increasing number of serious students of religion who can accept religious pluralism as our destiny without making a claim to the superiority of one tradition. In the middle of the twentieth century a great step forward in this respect came in Karl Jaspers's *The Meaning and Goal of History,* where he used the phrase "axial age" to apply to several great traditions that emerged in the first millennium BCE, taking the Christian idea of Jesus Christ as the "axis" of history and generalizing it to include the other great traditions of that early period.[76]

The person who taught me most about the acceptance of other religions is Wilfred Cantwell Smith, both in his scholarship and in his person, expressed in his lifelong work with Muslims. Smith, in his own idiosyncratic way, believed that all religions are historically related but that "essentializing" them as a series of "isms" fails to appreciate their enormous variety, within as well as between the traditions we distinguish. So it is our task, right down to the individual believers who are never exactly the same as any other believer even in their own faith, to try to understand such believers in what they share and do not share but above all in their terms, not ours. In the book where he spells out his own position most fully, *Toward a World Theology,* he uses the term "God" as the basic reference of all religions, though recognizing the difficulties in so doing. But his use of the word "God" in this context is not Christian in any exclusive sense and does not require a belief in Christ or the Trinity, though Smith identified himself as a Christian. Smith wants to include the whole of human religiosity in his perspective without privileging any one tradition or any kind of tradition.[77]

I have also been influenced by Charles Taylor in his work on multiculturalism, but particularly by his treatment of other religions, sometimes only incidentally, in *A Secular Age,* where he uniformly takes them seriously in their own terms.[78] Herbert Fingarette has spelled out as well as anyone the position I am trying to describe:

> It is the special fate of modern man that he has a "choice" of spiritual visions. The paradox is that although each requires complete commitment for complete validity, we can today generate a context in which we see that no one of them is the sole vision. Thus we must learn to be naive but undogmatic. That is, we must take the vision as it comes and trust ourselves to it, naively, as reality. Yet we must retain an openness to experience such that the dark shadows deep within one vision are the mute, stubborn messengers waiting to lead us to a new light and a new vision . . .
>
> We must not ignore the fact that in this last analysis, commitment to a specific orientation outweighs catholicity of imagery. One may be a

sensitive and seasoned traveler, at ease in many places, but one must have a home. Still, we can be intimate with those we visit, and while we may be only travelers and guests in some domains, there are our hosts who are truly at home. Home is always home for someone; but there is no Absolute Home in general.[79]

Perhaps this last claim, that there is no Absolute Home in general, would be the most unsettling to many believers and will rouse the cry of relativism about Fingarette, but also about the others I have mentioned. But the relativism charge is really inapt in every case. One can make judgments of better and worse with respect to any religion, but they are more likely to be on point if one has seriously tried to understand them in their own terms.

I am far from believing that such an attitude toward the religions of mankind is very widespread. Gross prejudice is not in good repute, to be sure, and many people are able to combine the belief that their own religion is best with the belief that the followers of other religions can also be saved. Nor is the view I am proposing necessarily widespread among religious intellectuals, where there is still a widespread belief that one can give convincing reasons why one religious or philosophical position is better than all the others.

There are two related reasons why the very idea of a best position must, in my opinion, fail. One is that the variety of differences in the "argument" that must be won or lost are at the level of theory as I have been using it in this chapter. But dealing with other people's theories means that one has to disembed them from the mix that historical theories are always part of, in particular their relation to embodied practices and stories, Donald's mimetic and mythic forms of culture, which are reorganized by theoretical innovations but not abandoned.

Having made this mistake it is almost inevitable that one will make the next one: one will treat the theories of others as if they were answers to questions in our own theoretical tradition. Wilfred Smith taught me, among other important things, that religions don't differ so much in giving different answers to the same questions as in asking different questions. But if we think the other traditions are answering our questions, then it is only a matter of circular logic that those traditions will turn out to answer those questions less well than our own, which was, after all, designed to answer those questions.

It is not, then, an argument for relativism to note that universal categories, important though they are in each tradition, come bound up with particularities that give them different emphases. Thomas McCarthy puts it well: "The conceptual point is this: *by their very nature,* the universal cannot be actual without the particular, nor the formal without the substantive, the abstract without the concrete, structure without content."[80] And thus it follows that "from our present perspective, it is clear that the irreducible variety of hermeneutic standpoints and practical orientations informing interpretive endeavors, however well informed, will typically issue in a 'conflict of interpretations' and thus call for dialogue across differences."[81]

So the final lesson of this chapter and this book for our present situation in a world of multiple traditions is that theory that has come loose from its cultural context can assume a superiority that can lead to crushing mistakes. The theoretical breakthrough in each axial case led to the possibility of universal ethics, the reassertion of fundamental human equality, and the necessity of respect for all humans, indeed for all sentient beings. And yet in each case these assertions came out of living communities whose religious practices defined who they were and whose stories were essential to their identities. To assume that "we," particularly if we mean by that the modern West, have universal truths based on revelation, philosophy, or science that we can enforce on others, is the ideological aspect of racism, imperialism, and colonialism. If we could see that we are all in this, with our theories, yes, but with our practices and stories, together, even though we must contend through mutual discussion with abiding differences, we might make just a bit more likely the actualization of Kant's dream of a world civil society that could at last restrain the violence of state-organized societies toward each other and the environment.

Notes

Index

Notes

Preface

1. Thomas Mann, *Joseph and His Brothers* (New York: Knopf, 1958), 32–33.

2. Although I thought I knew the *Mencius* well, it was only when Yang Xiao called this passage to my attention that I saw that it belonged with the first two epigraphs I long had in mind. See Yang Xiao, "How Confucius Does Things with Words: Two Hermeneutic Paradigms in the *Analects* and Its Exegeses," *Journal of Asian Studies* 66 (2007): 513.

3. Eric Hobsbawm, *The Age of Extremes: The Short Twentieth Century, 1914–1991* (London: Weidenfeld and Nicolson, 1994), 15, as cited in David Christian, *Maps of Time: An Introduction to Big History* (Berkeley: University of California Press, 2004).

4. Christian, *Maps of Time;* Daniel Lord Smail, *On Deep History and the Brain* (Berkeley: University of California Press, 2008).

5. An early trenchant argument for this coevolution is Clifford Geertz's "The Growth of Culture and the Evolution of Mind," in *The Interpretation of Cultures* (New York: Basic Books, 1973 [1962]), 55–83. I am sorry to say that biologists, writing about biological/cultural coevolution based on much more recent work, uniformly fail to cite this important paper.

6. Richard Dawkins, *The Selfish Gene* (New York: Oxford University Press, 1989), v, 2.

7. See, for example, Stephen Jay Gould, *The Structure of Evolutionary Theory* (Cambridge, Mass.: Harvard University Press, 2002), 618–619, 638–641. Mary Midgley, in *Evolution as a Religion* (New York: Routledge, 2006 [1985]), argues that the use of an ethical term like "selfish" to describe biological entities such as genes is a category mistake of the first order. See also Joan Roughgarden, *The Genial Gene: Deconstructing Darwinian Selfishness* (Berkeley: University of California Press, 2009).

8. Actually, in *The Extended Phenotype* (New York: Oxford University Press, 1982), the book he wrote following *The Selfish Gene,* Dawkins himself noted that whether you take genes or organisms as the basic unit of evolution is a matter of interpretation, not fact, each being valid in its own right.

9. Mary Jane West-Eberhard, "Developmental Plasticity and the Origin of Species Differences," *Proceedings of the National Academy of Sciences USA* 102, suppl. 1 (2005): 6547. See

also Eva Jablonka and Marion J. Lamb, *Evolution in Four Dimensions: Genetic, Epigenetic, Behavioral, and Symbolic Variation in the History of Life* (Cambridge, Mass.: MIT Press, 2005).

10. Marc Kirschner and John Gerhart, *The Plausibility of Life: Resolving Darwin's Dilemma* (New Haven: Yale University Press, 2005), 252–253.

11. One line of thought within evolutionary psychology has argued that several features of religion are genetic, involving "modules" for such things as "supernatural beings." But many students of psychological and cultural evolution remain unconvinced. That there is a "religion gene" or a "God gene" is most unlikely.

12. Derek Bickerton, *Roots of Language* (Ann Arbor: Karoma, 1981), 216. For a fuller development of this idea, see Bickerton's *Language and Species* (Chicago: Chicago University Press, 1990), esp. chap. 4, "The Origins of Representational Systems."

13. F. John Odling-Smee, Keven N. Laland, and Marcus W. Feldman, *Niche Construction: The Neglected Process in Evolution* (Princeton: Princeton University Press, 2003), 186; also see table 4.1 on p. 176, which compares natural selection and niche construction. Terrence W. Deacon, in his work in progress, *Mind from Matter: The Emergent Dynamics of Life,* stresses the inevitability of teleological thinking where organisms are concerned.

14. Odling-Smee, Laland, and Feldman, *Niche Construction,* 365–366; see also 21, 243.

15. For an accessible discussion of these capacities, see Marc Bekoff and Jessica Pierce, *Wild Justice: The Moral Lives of Animals* (Chicago: University of Chicago Press, 2009). See also Frans de Waal, *The Age of Empathy: Nature's Lessons for a Kinder Society* (New York: Harmony House, 2009).

16. Richard Dawkins, *River out of Eden* (New York: Basic Books, 1995), 133. I found this and one of the previous quotes from *Selfish Gene* in Roughgarden, *The Genial Gene,* but without page citations. I got the books (and several others by Dawkins that she refers to) in order to find the page numbers and ended up reading them. I came to have considerable respect for Dawkins but also to believe that too often he allows his rhetoric to get away from him. I have also learned that biology is a contentious field, more like social science than I had imagined, and that Dawkins's views cannot be taken as representative of the present state of the field.

17. Clifford Geertz, especially in his essay on religion as a cultural system, hovers over most of the rest of this Preface in ways that I did not expect he would until I reread that essay in preparation for writing this Preface. I cannot quite forgive Cliff for dying at the age of 80 and thus not being able to read and respond to what I have written.

18. Geertz's full definition is this: "Religion is (1) a system of symbols which acts to (2) establish powerful, pervasive, and long-lasting moods and motivations in men by (3) formulating conceptions of a general order of existence and (4) clothing these conceptions with such an aura of factuality that (5) the moods and motivations seem uniquely realistic." Geertz, "Religion as a Cultural System," in *The Interpretation of Cultures* (New York: Basic Books, 1973 [1966]), 90.

19. I had originally thought I would remain silent about Talal Asad's essay on Geertz and his conception of religion, with my silence speaking for itself. Asad's essay was first published as "Anthropological Conceptions of Religion: Reflections on Geertz," *Man,* n.s., 18 (1983): 237–259, and reprinted in revised and somewhat more moderate form in his *Genealogies of*

Religion: Discipline and Reasons of Power in Christianity and Islam (Baltimore: Johns Hopkins University Press, 1993), 27–54. But early readers of this Preface pointed out to me that Asad's essay has shaped a whole generation's thinking about Geertz. Although I have read the essay carefully and more than once, I cannot here take the time to refute Asad's assertions one by one. I can only recommend to serious readers that they read Geertz himself to see whether Asad's charges apply. Also they might have a look at the references to Geertz in Edward Said's *Orientalism* (New York: Pantheon Books, 1978) for the difference between Said's view and Asad's.

20. Geertz, "Religion," 119, citing Alfred Schutz, "On Multiple Realities," in Schutz's *Collected* Papers, vol. 1, *The Problem of Social Reality* (The Hague: Martinus Nijhoff, 1967), 226–228.

21. Geertz, "Religion," 111, citing Schutz, "On Multiple Realities," 208–209.

22. Schutz, "On Multiple Realities," 229.

23. Stephen Jay Gould was probably getting at something similar to Geertz's notion of cultural spheres when he spoke of science and religion as "non-overlapping magisteria," non-overlapping because they are doing different things, one dealing with fact and the explanation of facts, and the other with ultimate meaning and moral value. See Gould, *Rocks of Ages: Science and Religion in the Fullness of Life* (New York: Ballantine Books, 2002). Whether cultural spheres can ever fail entirely to overlap as they impinge on the world of daily life is open to question.

24. Geertz, "Religion," 111.

25. Ibid., 112–114.

26. Ibid., 118. Mary Midgley, without mentioning Geertz, succinctly summarizes his point when she says that a religion has "the power to make sense of a threatening and chaotic world by dramatizing it." Mary Midgely, *Evolution as a Religion* (New York: Routledge, 2006 [1985]), 18.

27. Geertz, "Religion," 119.

28. Merlin Donald, *Origins of the Modern Mind: Three Stages in the Evolution of Culture and Cognition* (Cambridge, Mass.: Harvard University Press, 1991). He has developed his argument further in *A Mind So Rare: The Evolution of Human Consciousness* (New York: Norton, 1999).

29. The term comes from Karl Jaspers, *The Origin and Goal of History* (London: Routledge and Kegan Paul, 1953 [1949]), and will be discussed further at the start of Chapter 6.

30. Mark Strand, "On Becoming a Poet," in *The Making of a Poem: A Norton Anthology of Poetic Forms,* ed. Mark Strand and Eaven Boland (New York: Norton, 2000), xxii, xxiii, xxiv.

31. Johan Huizinga, *Homo Ludens: A Study of the Play-Element in Culture* (Boston: Beacon Press, 1955 [1938]). The English title replicates a usage that Huizinga himself did not approve of. He says he resisted every effort to replace "The Play Element of Culture" with "The Play Element in Culture" in English translation because "it was not my object to define the place of play among all other manifestations of culture, but rather to ascertain how far culture itself bears the character of play" (foreword, unnumbered page). Could we interpret Huizinga as arguing that "culture" is offline? Every serious book on the biology of play that I consulted cited Huizinga with great respect, viewing his argument as evolutionary.

32. Derek Bickerton, *Adam's Tongue: How Humans Made Language, How Language Made Humans* (New York: Hill and Wang, 2009), 194.

33. Gordon M. Burghardt, *The Genesis of Animal Play: Testing the Limits* (Cambridge, Mass.: MIT Press, 2005), 118–121.

34. When I first gave an oral presentation at the University of Chicago of what became my 1964 article "Religious Evolution," Geertz was in the audience. After I finished, he came up to me and said, "I loved your talk even though I disagree with it entirely." The talk was published as Robert N. Bellah, "Religious Evolution," *American Sociological Review* 29 (1964): 358–374; reprinted most recently in *The Robert Bellah Reader,* ed. Robert N. Bellah and Steven M. Tipton (Durham, N.C.: Duke University Press, 2006), 23–50.

35. Stephen Jay Gould, *Full House: The Spread of Excellence from Plato to Darwin* (New York: Harmony Books, 1996).

36. Leszek Kolakowski, *Modernity on Endless Trial* (Chicago: University of Chicago Press, 1997).

1. Religion and Reality

1. Émile Durkheim, *The Elementary Forms of Religious Life,* trans. Karen E. Fields (New York: Free Press, 1995 [1912]), 44. Durkheim's full definition reads as follows: "A religion is a unified system of beliefs and practices relative to sacred things, that is to say, things set apart and forbidden *(séparées, interdites)*—beliefs and practices which unite into one single moral community called a Church, all those who adhere to them." In the original the entire definition is in italics. See Émile Durkheim, *Les formes élémentaires de la vie religieuse* (Paris: Presse Universitaires de France, 1968), 65.

2. Alfred Schutz, "Multiple Realities" (1945), in *Collected Papers,* vol. 1, *The Problem of Social Reality* (The Hague: Martinus Nijhoff, 1967), 207–259.

3. Weber contrasted the extraordinary to the everyday, and argued for a special relation between the extraordinary and "charisma," a key term in his sociology, especially his sociology of religion. Weber's is one influential version of a contrast we will observe repeatedly in this chapter. See Weber, "Charisma and Its Transformations," in *Economy and Society,* ed. G. Roth and C. Wittich (Berkeley: University of California Press, 1978 [1921]), 2:1111–12.

4. Alfred Schutz, "Multiple Realities," 229.

5. *The Complete Works of Chuang Tzu,* trans. Burton Watson (New York: Columbia University Press, 1968) [hereafter cited as *Chuang Tzu*], 49.

6. Freud pointed out this difference when he saw dreams as operating with what he called primary process, quite different from the secondary process that governs our world of daily life. See Freud, *The Interpretation of Dreams* (London: Allen and Unwin, 1954 [1900]), chap. 7, sec. E, "The Primary and Secondary Processes—Regression," 588–609.

7. William James, *The Principles of Psychology* (Cambridge, Mass.: Harvard University Press, 1983 [1890]), 929. This reference is to chapter 21, "The Perception of Reality," where James speaks of multiple "realities" and "worlds" interchangeably. Schutz, at the beginning of his famous essay "Multiple Realities," acknowledges James as the source of his terminology. For James, however, realities are subjective, whereas in Schutz's phenomenological approach they are intersubjective. James is concerned with mental realities, Schutz with reali-

ties that are also cultural. In general, however, James's insistence on "pluralism" was as much ontological as it was psychological.

8. *Chuang Tzu*, 47–48.

9. Abraham Maslow, *Toward a Psychology of Being* (Princeton: Van Nostrand, 1962). Maslow is particularly interested in what he calls peak experiences, which may or may not be explicitly religious.

10. Michael Murphy, in *The Future of the Body* (Los Angeles: Tarcher/Perigree, 1993), 444, writes that in sports, "concentration can produce a state of mind graced by extraordinary clarity and focus. British golfer Tony Jacklin said, for example: 'When I'm in this state, this cocoon of concentration, I'm fully in the present, not moving out of it. I'm aware of every half inch of my swing . . . I'm absolutely engaged, involved in what I'm doing at that particular moment. That's the important thing. That's the difficult state to arrive at. It comes and it goes, and the pure fact that you go out on the first tee of a tournament and say, "I must concentrate today," is no good. It won't work. It has to already be there.' Many sportspeople have described 'the zone,' a condition beyond their normal functioning. Describing such a condition to me, quarterback John Brodie said: 'Often in the heat and excitement of a game, a player's perception and coordination will improve dramatically. At times, and with increasing frequency now, I experience a kind of clarity that I've never seen adequately described in a football story.' As they try to describe such experience, athletes sometimes begin to use metaphors similar to those used in religious writing. Listening to such accounts, I have come to believe that athletic feats can mirror contemplative graces."

11. Herbert Richardson, *Toward an American Theology* (New York: Harper and Row, 1967), 57.

12. Ibid., 60, quoting Edwards, "Memoirs," in *The Works of Jonathan Edwards,* vol. 1 (New York, 1881), 16.

13. Václav Havel, *Letters to Olga* (New York: Knopf, 1988 [1984]), 331–332.

14. Wallace Stevens, from "Notes toward a Supreme Fiction," in *The Collected Poems of Wallace Stevens* (New York: Knopf, 1955), 386.

15. Alfred Schutz, "Symbol, Reality, Society" (1955), in *Collected Papers,* 1:287–356.

16. Kenneth Burke, *Language as Symbolic Action* (Berkeley: University of California Press, 1966), 298–299. Burke proposes a new English verb, "to beyond," which would mean to see something in terms of something beyond it. Burke argues that Aristotle's theory of tragedy involves a kind of beyonding when catharsis transcends pity and fear. He gives as an example Sophocles's *Oedipus at Colonus:* "We feel pity and fear at his [Oedipus's] death precisely when he is transcending the miseries of this world—that is, *going beyond* them, and becoming a *tutelary deity*" (299, Burke's italics).

17. Alasdair MacIntyre, *After Virtue* (South Bend, Ind.: Notre Dame University Press, 1981), 174–183.

18. Mihaly Csikszentmihalyi, *Flow: The Psychology of Optimal Experience* (New York: Harper and Row, 1990), chap. 7.

19. Victor Turner, "Liminal to Liminoid in Play, Flow, and Ritual: An Essay in Comparative Symbology," *Rice University Studies* 60, no. 3 (1974): 53–92. Ritual in the pejorative sense, as, for example, in Robert Merton's notion of ritualism, means meaningless or obsessive repetition. See Robert K. Merton, *Social Structure and Social Theory* (Glencoe, Ill.: Free Press, 1957), 150, 184.

20. George Lindbeck, *The Nature of Doctrine* (Philadelphia: Westminster, 1984), 16, 31–41.

21. Jean Piaget and Barbel Inhelder, *The Psychology of the Child* (New York: Basic Books, 1969), 22. On the basis of recent research, Piaget's notion of adualism must be qualified, or even, perhaps, applied only to the period before birth. George Butterworth has argued that "a boundary exists in infant perception between infant and the world such that the absolute 'adualism' assumed by Piaget is not supported." But he adds, "On the other hand, it is clear that the very young infant has no objective, reflective self-awareness." George Butterworth, "Some Benefits of Egocentrism," in *Making Sense: The Child's Construction of the World,* ed. Jerome Bruner and Helen Haste (London: Methuen, 1987), 70–71.

For a discussion of the relation between psychological regression and mystical union, see Herbert Fingarette, *The Self in Transformation: Psychoanalysis, Philosophy, and the Life of the Spirit* (New York: Basic Books, 1963), chap. 7, "The Consummatory Phase: Mystic Selfishness."

22. Jerome Bruner, *Studies in Cognitive Growth* (New York: Wiley, 1966), 12–21. Although "enactive" is the only term I have taken directly from Bruner, his typology of representations in the opening chapters, "On Cognitive Growth," is the source of my three major modes of religious representation. But where Bruner calls his second type iconic (sometimes spelled *ikonic*) and his third symbolic, I call the second type symbolic (with iconic being a subtype of symbolic) and the third type conceptual. Bruner's typology explicitly owes much to Piaget. The clearest exposition of Piaget's three categories that are cognate with Bruner's, and so with mine, can be found in Jean Piaget, *Play, Dreams and Imitation in Childhood* (New York: Norton, 1962), a book whose original title, *La formation du symbole,* is more accurately descriptive. There Piaget speaks of "sensory-motor activity," "egocentric representative activity," and "operational activity." Piaget uses the term "symbol" to characterize what he calls egocentric representational activity, for reasons that will be explained below. My use of the term "symbolic representation" is thus closer to Piaget's original usage. Because there is no agreement about terminology in this area, one can only try to be clear about what one means by particular terms.

23. The *Somnium Scipionis* is found in book 6 of Cicero's *De Re Publica,* in Cicero, *De Re Publica, De Legibus,* Loeb Classical Library (Cambridge, Mass.: Harvard University Press, 1923), 260–283.

24. Robert N. Bellah, *Tokugawa Religion* (New York: Free Press, 1957), 201–202.

25. Émile Durkheim, *Elementary Forms,* 218.

26. Bruner, *Studies in Cognitive Growth,* 16. Bruner notes the priority of "looking behavior" to sensorimotor manipulation in early childhood learning, which is a modification of Piaget's view, but Bruner still affirms Piaget's insight. On how much the very young child can "know" just by looking, see Michael Tomasello, *The Cultural Origins of Human Cognition* (Cambridge, Mass.: Harvard University Press, 1999), 57–58.

27. Bruner, *Studies in Cognitive Growth,* 17, quoting from Jean Piaget, *The Construction of Reality in the Child* (New York: Basic Books, 1954).

28. Bruner, *Studies in Cognitive Growth,* 11. Bruner notes that in a personal communication Piaget "doubts whether what we have been calling enactive representation ought to be called representation at all, for it is questionable whether action 'stands for' or represents anything beyond itself" (10).

29. Ibid., 6–8. Bruner's distinction is similar to the distinction between models of and models for in Clifford Geertz's "Religion as a Cultural System" [1966], in *The Interpretation of Cultures* (New York: Basic Books, 1973), 93–94.

30. Bruner, *Studies in Cognitive Growth,* 8. The reference is to A. R. Luria, *The Role of Speech in the Regulation of Normal and Abnormal Behavior* (New York: Pergamon, 1961).

31. Bruner, *Studies in Cognitive Growth,* 19.

32. Ibid., 21.

33. George Herbert Mead, *Mind, Self and Society,* ed. Charles W. Morris (Chicago: University of Chicago Press, 1934), 42–43. See also "Social Consciousness and the Consciousness of Meaning" (1910), in Mead, *Selected Writings,* ed. Andrew J. Reck (Chicago: University of Chicago Press, 1964), 123–124.

34. Dogen (1200–1253) in the "Bendowa" section of the *Shobogenzo* said: "The view that practice [*zazen,* sitting *zen*] and enlightenment are not one is heretical. In the Buddhadharma they are one. Inasmuch as practice is based on enlightenment, the practice of a beginner is all of original enlightenment. Therefore, in giving the instruction for practice, a Zen master advises his disciples not to seek enlightenment beyond practice, for practice itself is original enlightenment. Because it is already enlightenment of practice, there is no end to enlightenment; because it is already practice of enlightenment, there is no beginning to practice." Hee-Jin Kim, *Dogen Kigen—Mystical Realist* (Tucson: University of Arizona Press, 1975), 79. For another translation, see Masao Abe and Norman Waddell, trans., "Dogen's Bendowa," in *The Eastern Buddhist* 4 (1971): 144.

35. R. R. Marett, *The Threshold of Religion,* 2nd ed. (London: Methuen, 1914), xxxi. Marett's contrast is inaccurate to the degree that enactive representation is also a kind of thinking—thinking with the body. As Piaget says, "language is not enough to explain thought, because the structures that characterize thought have their roots in action and in sensorimotor mechanisms that are deeper than linguistics." Jean Piaget, *Six Psychological Studies* (New York: Random House, 1967), 98. If, however, Marett is arguing that religion is not simply a matter of conceptual belief, as many of his contemporaries thought, his oft-quoted remark still has a point.

36. Richard Ellmann, *Yeats: The Man and the Masks* (New York: Macmillan, 1948), 285.

37. Piaget and Inhelder, *Psychology of the Child,* 57–63. In Piaget's theoretical vocabulary, assimilation involves the transformation of reality to suit the preexisting schemas of the child, whereas accommodation involves the alteration of those schemas in order to adapt to reality. Thus there is something "subjective" about assimilation.

38. Exercise play involves, for example, banging. When the child learns to bang, it will bang any object within reach for the sheer pleasure of exercising this new capacity. Ibid., 59.

39. Jean Piaget, *The Child's Conception of the World* (Paterson: Littlefield, Adams, 1960), 169–251. The qualifications about Piaget's notion of adualism also apply to his idea of egocentrism.

40. Piaget and Inhelder, *Psychology of the Child,* 60.

41. Jerome Bruner, *Child's Talk: Learning to Use Language* (New York: Norton, 1983), 46.

42. Jerome S. Bruner, "Nature and Uses of Immaturity," in *The Growth of Competence,* ed. Kevin Connolly and Jerome Bruner (London: Academic Press, 1974), 32.

43. Sigmund Freud, "Mourning and Melancholia," in *Collected Papers,* vol. 4 (London: Hogarth, 1956 [1917]), 152–170.

44. Paul Ricoeur, *The Symbolism of Evil* (New York: Harper and Row, 1967), 12–13. In speaking of hierophanies Ricoeur is drawing on the work of Mircea Eliade, *Patterns in Comparative Religion* (New York: Sheed and Ward, 1958 [1949]).

45. Bruner, *Studies in Cognitive Growth,* xv. Just because images or symbols "have muscles," we must add to Paul Ricoeur's dictum that "the symbol gives rise to thought" the notion that the symbol gives rise to acts. Ricoeur, *The Symbolism of Evil,* 347–355.

46. Rhoda Kellogg and Scott O'Dell, *The Psychology of Children's Art* (New York: CRM–Random House, 1967), 19–25. The joy of this book is in the reproductions of children's paintings, so full of life, particularly before they become literal.

47. Ibid., 27–34.

48. Ibid., 35–41.

49. Ibid., 53–63. See also Jose and Miriam Arguelles, *Mandala* (Berkeley: Shambala, 1972); and Carl G. Jung et. al., *Man and His Symbols* (Garden City: Doubleday, 1964). Jung treats mandala forms primarily as expressions of "individuation," thus perhaps unduly psychologizing them.

50. Susanne K. Langer, *Philosophy in a New Key* (New York: Penguin, 1948 [1942]), 198. Chapter 8, "On Significance in Music," is an excellent review of the older modern literature on symbolism in music.

51. Alfred Schutz, "Making Music Together," in *Collected Papers,* vol. 2 (The Hague: Martinus Nijhoff, 1964 [1951]), 173.

52. Ibid., 175.

53. Patricia Cox Miller, "In Praise of Nonsense," in *Classical Mediterranean Spirituality,* ed. A. H. Armstrong (New York: Crossroad, 1989), 498.

54. Ibid., 499.

55. Allan Bloom, *The Closing of the American Mind* (New York: Simon and Schuster, 1987). Bloom writes: "My concern here is not with the moral effects of this music—whether it leads to sex, violence or drugs. The issue here is the effect on education, and I believe it ruins the imagination of young people and makes it very difficult for them to have a passionate relationship to the art and thought that are the substance of liberal education. The first sensuous experiences are decisive in determining the taste for the whole of life, and they are the link between the animal and the spiritual in us. The period of nascent sensuality has always been used for sublimation, in the sense of making sublime, for attaching youthful inclinations and longings to music, pictures and stories that provide the transition to the fulfillment of the human duties and the enjoyment of the human pleasures . . . Rock music encourages passions and provides models that have no relation to any life the young people who go to universities can possibly lead, or to the kind of admiration encouraged by liberal studies. Without the cooperation of the sentiments, anything other than technical education is a dead letter" (79–80).

56. Arthur Waley, *The Analects of Confucius* (London: Allen and Unwin, 1938), 68.

57. Confucius, *The Analects,* trans. D. C. Lau (New York: Penguin, 1979), 133–134.

58. *Analects,* trans. Lau, 87.

59. Eric Voegelin, *Order and History,* vol. 3, *Plato and Aristotle* (Baton Rouge: Louisiana State University Press, 1957), 268.

60. Langer, *Philosophy in a New Key,* chap. 4, "Discursive and Presentational Forms."

61. Piaget, *Child's Conception of the World,* 69–70.

62. From "An Ordinary Evening in New Haven," in *Collected Poems,* 473. Or again, from "Man Carrying Thing" (1947), in *Collected Poems,* 350: "The poem must resist the intelligence / Almost successfully."

63. Schutz, "Making Music Together," 173.

64. Langer, *Philosophy in a New Key,* 212.

65. John L. Austin, *How to Do Things with Words* (Cambridge, Mass.: Harvard University Press, 1962).

66. Helen Vendler, "Shakespeare's Sonnets: Reading for Difference," *Bulletin of the American Academy of Arts and Sciences* 47 (1994): 37–41.

67. Mons Teig, "Liturgy as Fusion of Horizons: A Hermeneutical Approach Based on Hans-Georg Gadamer's Theory of Application" (Ph.D. diss., Graduate Theological Union, Berkeley, California, 1991), 295–296.

68. Bruner, "Immaturity," 34–35.

69. Bruner, *Child's Talk,* 129, 131.

70. Basil Bernstein, *Class, Codes and Control* (London: Routledge and Kegan Paul, 1971).

71. Mary Douglas, *Natural Symbols: Explorations in Cosmology* (New York: Pantheon Books, 1982 [1970]), 10–11, 21.

72. Benedict Anderson, *Imagined Communities* (London: Verso, 1991 [1983]), 145, 147.

73. Wallace Stevens, from "Owl's Clover" (1936), in *Opus Posthumous* (New York: Knopf, 1989 [1936]), 85. Adelaide Kirby Morris, in her *Wallace Stevens: Imagination and Faith* (Princeton: Princeton University Press, 1974), has explored the background and implications of Stevens's relation to religion. She examined the sense in which the imagination, for Stevens, transcends the individual (114–115).

74. Wallace Stevens, from "Final Soliloquy of the Interior Paramour," in *Collected Poems,* 524. In a 1955 letter Stevens wrote, "In spite of its solemnity, Easter is the most sparkling of all fetes since it brings back *not only the sun but all the works of the sun,* including those works of the spirit that are specifically what might be called Spring-works: the renewed force of the desire to live and to be part of life." *Letters of Wallace Stevens,* ed. Holly Stevens (New York: Knopf, 1966), 879, italics added.

75. Langer, *Philosophy in a New Key,* 78.

76. Richardson, *Toward an American Theology,* 66. Jerome Bruner, in *Acts of Meaning* (Cambridge, Mass.: Harvard University Press, 1990), 121, says the same thing about the "spontaneous autobiographies" that he collected: "As stories of development, these 'spontaneous autobiographies' were constituted of smaller stories (of events, happenings, projects), each of which achieved its significance by virtue of being part of a larger-scale 'life.' In this respect they shared a universal feature of all narratives. The larger overall narratives were told in easily recognizable genres—the tale of a victim, a *Bildungsroman,* antihero forms, *Wanderung* stories, black comedy, and so on. The storied events that they comprised made sense only in terms of the larger picture."

77. Claude Lévi-Strauss, *The Raw and the Cooked* (New York: Harper and Row, 1969), 15–16.

78. Bruner, *Acts of Meaning,* 83.

79. Ibid., 89. This study is reported in Katherine Nelson, ed., *Narratives from the Crib* (Cambridge, Mass.: Harvard University Press, 1989).

80. Bruner, *Acts of Meaning,* 111–113. The Roy Schafer quotation occurs on p. 111. Herbert Fingarette made essentially the same argument in *The Self in Transformation,* esp. chap. 1.

81. Bruner, *Acts of Meaning,* 114.

82. Erving Goffman, *The Presentation of Self in Everyday Life* (Garden City, N.Y.: Doubleday, 1959 [1956]).

83. Anderson, *Imagined Communities,* 197–206. Eric Hobsbawm and Terence Ranger have edited a valuable book about this process: *The Invention of Tradition* (Cambridge: Cambridge University Press, 1983).

84. Bruner, *Acts of Meaning,* 50. Bruner is drawing from Kenneth Burke, *A Grammar of Motives* (New York: Prentice-Hall, 1945), but with some changes of terminology: Goal instead of Purpose, Instrument instead of Agency. Although Trouble is an appropriately Burkean term, I could not find it in *A Grammar of Motives.*

85. W. E. H. Stanner, *On Aboriginal Religion,* Oceania Monograph 11 (Sydney: University of Sydney, 1966 [1959–1963]), 40. Narrative continues to be central even in the most sophisticated religious discourse. See Stanley Hauerwas and L. Gregory Jones, eds., *Why Narrative? Readings in Narrative Theology* (Grand Rapids, Mich.: Eerdmans, 1989).

86. Anderson, *Imagined Communities,* 205–206.

87. Bruner, *Acts of Meaning,* 80.

88. Kenneth Burke, *The Rhetoric of Religion* (Boston: Beacon Press, 1961), chap. 3, "The First Three Chapters of Genesis," 172–272.

89. Piaget, *The Child's Conception of the World,* 227.

90. Piaget, *Play, Dreams and Imitation,* 288. In *Cultural Origins* Tomasello argues, on the basis of much new research, that children learn to understand the intentions of others at a much earlier age than Piaget believed (140–145). Nevertheless, it probably takes some time for that understanding to be fully appreciated.

91. Thomas Hobbes, *De Corpore* (1655), in Hobbes, *Body, Man, and Citizen,* ed. Richard S. Peters (New York: Collier, 1962), 3.7.48.

92. Thomas Hobbes, *Leviathan,* ed. C. B. MacPherson (Harmondsworth: Penguin, 1968 [1651]), 102, 147, 160.

93. Eugen Rosenstock-Huessy, *Out of Revolution* (Windsor, Vt.: Argo, 1969), 754, 756. The passage of Descartes on which Rosenstock-Huessy is elaborating is: "And because we have all to pass through a state of infancy to manhood, and have been of necessity, for a length of time, governed by our desires and our preceptors (whose dictates were frequently conflicting, while neither perhaps always counselled us for the best), I further concluded that it is almost impossible that our judgments can be so correct or solid as they would have been, had our Reason been mature from the moment of our birth, and had we always been guided by it alone." René Descartes, *Discourse on Method,* trans. John Veitch (LaSalle, Ill.: Open Court, 1946 [1637]),13. Earlier in part 2 Descartes speaks (metaphorically!) of ancient cities in which over time the streets have become crooked and the buildings jumbled and of ill-fitting sizes and styles, comparing them unfavorably to cities newly, and rationally, laid out with buildings of harmonious size and style. The books and ideas of the ages are like the

streets and buildings of old cities: it would be better to start afresh with reason alone. Yet Descartes admits that "it is not customary to pull down all the buildings of a town with the single design of rebuilding them differently." *Discourse on Method,* 11–13.

94. Ernest Gellner, *Postmodernism, Reason and Religion* (London: Routledge, 1992), 51. Gellner is affirming a term criticized by Clifford Geertz in "Anti Anti-Relativism" (*American Anthropologist* 86 [1984]: 276 n. 2), which Gellner first used in *Spectacles and Predicaments* (Cambridge: Cambridge University Press, 1979), 146. Herbert Fingarette in *The Self in Transformation,* 233–234, describes some of the costs of being on our side of the Big Ditch: "It is unfortunate that our slavery to the physical-causal mode of thought is so great that many attempts to assign 'ontological primacy' to the human, the dramatic realities, are beset by charges of mystification, obscurantist irrationalism, even—ironically— antihumanism. It is ironic that the directly graspable world of human beings in dramatic conflict, the world that has been familiar to humankind since the beginnings of the race— all this we now find dark, obstreperous, esoteric, even silly or boring. The *human* world in the West has become peripheral and surreptitious, an 'underground' world."

95. Stanley Tambiah, *Magic, Science, Religion, and the Scope of Rationality* (New York: Cambridge University Press, 1990), 89, quoting from Lucien Febvre, *The Problem of Unbelief in the Sixteenth Century: The Religion of Rabelais,* trans. Beatrice Gottlieb (Cambridge, Mass.: Harvard University Press, 1982), 356–357.

96. Michael Polanyi, *Personal Knowledge: Towards a Post-Critical Philosophy* (Chicago: University of Chicago Press, 1958), chap. 6.

97. Jerome Bruner, *Possible Worlds, Actual Minds* (Cambridge, Mass.: Harvard University Press, 1986). Bruner writes: "[Science] rides from time to time on wild metaphors . . . The history of science is full of them. They are crutches to help us get up the abstract mountain. Once up, we throw them away (even hide them) in favor of a formal, logically consistent theory that (with luck) can be stated in mathematical or near-mathematical terms. The formal models that emerge are shared, carefully guarded against attack, and prescribe ways of life for their users. The metaphors that aided in this achievement are usually forgotten or, if the ascent turns out to be important, are made not part of science but part of the history of science" (48). On falsification, see Karl Popper, *Objective Knowledge: An Evolutionary Approach* (Oxford: Clarendon Press, 1972.)

98. Cited in Stanley Tambiah, *Magic, Science, Religion, and the Scope of Rationality* (Cambridge: Cambridge University Press, 1990), 17.

99. Cited in Polanyi, *Personal Knowledge,* 7.

100. Burke, *A Grammar of Motives,* 503–504.

101. Thomas Kuhn, *The Structure of Scientific Revolutions,* 2nd ed. (Chicago: University of Chicago Press, 1970 [1962]).

102. Ernest Gellner, *Postmodernism, Reason and Religion,* 58–60.

103. From "Science" (1925), in Robinson Jeffers, *Selected Poems* (New York: Vintage, 1965), 39.

104. Cited in Polanyi, *Personal Knowledge,* 199, quoting from Russell's *Mysticism and Logic* (New York: Norton 1929 [1910]), 62.

2. Religion and Evolution

1. David Christian, *Maps of Time: An Introduction to Big History* (Berkeley: University of California Press, 2004), 6. Italics in original.

2. Eric J. Chaisson, *Cosmic Evolution: The Rise of Complexity in Nature* (Cambridge, Mass.: Harvard University Press, 2001), 211–213.

3. Mary Midgley, *Evolution as a Religion* (New York: Routledge, 2006 [1985]), 8.

4. Ibid., 5.

5. Ibid., 2, quoting Jacques Monod, *Chance and Necessity* (London: Fontana, 1974 [1970]), 160.

6. Oliver Sacks: "Darwin and the Meaning of Flowers," *New York Review of Books* 55 (2008): 67.

7. It is sometimes noted that Hindu and Buddhist measures of time are even larger than those of modern cosmology; the kalpa, for example, comes in many lengths, but the largest is the mahakalpa or great kalpa, which is 1.28 trillion years long, whereas the universe of scientific cosmology is a mere 13.5 billion years. However, the great kalpa is made up of smaller kalpas, and kalpas of still smaller units, in a continual repetition, with each smaller unit having a particular characteristic, such as a decline in morality, though it is really a cycle of the world as we know it, until the world ends and a new cycle begins. Thus, though the units are immense, they are intelligible in human terms in a way that scientific cosmological time isn't, or isn't readily.

8. Here I, like the scientists I have quoted, am getting into the act with a statement that will have to be qualified as we go along.

9. Steven Weinberg, *The First Three Minutes* (New York: Basic Books, 1993 [1977]), 140.

10. "K" stands for Kelvin, a temperature scale that is based, not like Celsius on the melting point of ice, but on absolute zero—that is, no heat at all.

11. Weinberg, *The First Three Minutes,* 146.

12. Steven Weinberg, at the beginning of *The First Three Minutes,* quotes a Norse creation myth to show how many questions it leaves unanswered, apparently unaware of the irony that his own narrative raises many as yet unanswered questions, as science always does, which is not to say that it isn't an improvement on the Norse narrative, insofar as we understand that myth as quasi-scientific explanation.

13. Christian, *Maps of Time,* 502–503.

14. For cosmic history I am relying mainly on Weinberg, *The First Three Minutes;* Christian, *Maps of Time;* and Chaisson, *Cosmic Evolution.* I have also checked a few websites to see whether what these books say has been superseded. Most of cosmic history is so staggering in terms of time, size, speed, and heat as to tax my imagination, so I can only recount what I barely understand.

15. Christian, *Maps of Time,* 40.

16. Ibid., 62.

17. Ibid., 63.

18. Weinberg, *The First Three Minutes,* 154.

19. Midgley, *Evolution,* 96, 157.

20. For Weinberg's atheism, see his essay "Without God," *New York Review of Books,* September 25, 2008, 73–76. In this essay he discusses several features of religion that are

leading to what he believes to be the decline and probable extinction of religious belief. At the time I wrote a letter to the *NYRB* suggesting that Weinberg had as much standing to discuss religion as I do to discuss theoretical physics. They decided not to publish my letter. Upon reading Weinberg's essay again in preparation for this chapter, I think they were right. The essay is a personal memoir, not a scholarly discussion, and from a man of his distinction, appropriate for the *NYRB*. As to the universe, his view in 2008 was much the same as in 1977. He writes, "The worldview of science is rather chilling" as we don't "find any point to life laid out to us in nature." Thus he lives his life "on a knife-edge, between wishful thinking on the one hand and, on the other, despair." But he has his consolations: not only in the joy of his work as a physicist, but in the New England countryside in the spring and in the poetry of Shakespeare. Yet he concludes with a kind of hard stoicism: "There is a certain honor, or perhaps just a grim satisfaction, in facing up to our condition without despair and without wishful thinking—with good humor, but without God" (76).

21. Weinberg, *The First Three Minutes,* 154–155.

22. Midgley quotes Marcus Aurelius as expressing a somewhat more grown-up relation to the universe: "Whether the world subsists by a fortuitous concourse of atoms, or an intelligent Nature presides over it, let this be laid down as a maxim, that I am part of a whole, governed by its own nature . . . I shall never be displeased by what is allotted to me by that whole . . . Let us then properly employ this moment of time allotted to us by fate, and leave the world contentedly, like a ripe olive dropping from its stalk, speaking well of the soil that produced it, and of the tree that bore it." *Meditations* 10.6 and 4.39. Quoted in Midgley, *Evolution,* 106. We should remember that in Marcus's Stoicism there was the belief that the world goes through cycles, ending in general conflagrations before beginning again. I might also note that Marcus's comments are a rebuke to my earlier comment on the cheerlessness of the cosmic metanarrative.

23. Richard Dawkins, *The God Delusion* (Boston: Houghton Mifflin, 2006), 406–407.

24. Ibid., 408.

25. Ibid., 162.

26. Ibid., 169–170.

27. Ibid., 162.

28. Although I am in no position to judge, the idea of emergence as opposed to sheer chance is appealing to me. Among those who have pursued the idea of emergence are Stuart Kauffman, *At Home in the Universe: The Search for the Laws of Self-Organization and Complexity* (New York: Oxford University Press, 1995); Harold J. Morowitz, *The Emergence of Everything: How the World Became Complex* (New York: Oxford University Press, 2002); and Terrence Deacon, "Emergence: The Hole at the Wheel's Hub," in *The Re-Emergence of Emergence,* ed. Philip Clayton and Paul Davies (New York: Oxford University Press, 2006), 111–150. Deacon's forthcoming book develops these ideas more fully. See Terrence W. Deacon, *Mind from Matter: The Emergent Dynamics of Life.* At an earlier period when emergence first became an issue, George Herbert Mead, one of the founders of sociology, strongly advocated it. See Mead, *Selected Writings* (Chicago: University of Chicago Press, 1964), esp. 277 and 345.

29. Stephen Jay Gould, *The Structure of Evolutionary Theory* (Cambridge, Mass.: Harvard University Press, 2002), 898; see the chart of the three domains, with the three tiny twigs on the far right, 899. Archaea are the third kind of monocellular organisms that were discovered relatively recently and that for my purposes can safely be ignored. For a fuller treatment of

the remarkable characteristics of bacteria and why we still live in "the age of bacteria," see Stephen Jay Gould, *Full House: The Spread of Excellence from Plato to Darwin* (New York: Harmony House, 1996), esp. 167–216.

30. Gould, *Full House.*

31. Christian, *Maps of Time,* 113, quoting Lynn Margulis and Dorion Sagan, *Microcosmos: Four Billion Years of Microbial Evolution* (New York: Summit Books, 1986), 114.

32. John Maynard Smith and Eörs Szathmáry, *The Major Transitions in Evolution* (Oxford: W. H. Freeman, 1995).

33. Marc W. Kirschner and John C. Gerhart, *The Plausibility of Life: Resolving Darwin's Dilemma* (New Haven: Yale University Press, 2005).

34. Ibid., 256.

35. Ibid., 47.

36. Ibid., 253.

37. Ibid., 255.

38. Ibid., 51–55, 255.

39. Ibid., 55–57, 255–256.

40. Ibid., 57–58.

41. Gould, *Full House,* 175–176.

42. Kirschner and Gerhart, *The Plausibility of Life,* 62.

43. Ibid., 68–69.

44. Richard Dawkins, *The Selfish Gene* (New York: Oxford University Press, 1989), v.

45. Kirschner and Gerhart, *The Plausibility of Life,* 252–253. Another evolutionary biologist whose work complements that of Kirschner and Gerhart is Mary Jane West-Eberhard. Like them she emphasizes the role of the organism (phenotype) in its own evolution: "I consider genes followers, not leaders, in adaptive evolution. A very large body of evidence shows that phenotype novelty is largely reorganizational rather than a product of innovative genes. Even if reorganization was initiated by a mutation, a gene of major effect on regulation, selection would lead to genetic accommodation, that is, genetic change that follows, and is directed by, the reorganized condition of the phenotype. Some authors have expressed this pattern as 'phenotype precedes genotype.'" West-Eberhard, "Developmental Plasticity and the Origin of Species Differences," in *Proceedings of the National Academy of Sciences USA* 102, suppl. 1 (2005): 6547. See also her book *Developmental Plasticity and Evolution* (New York: Oxford University Press, 2003).

46. Kirschner and Gerhart, *The Plausibility of Life,* 264.

47. Merlin Donald, *Origins of the Modern Mind: Three Stages in the Evolution of Culture and Cognition* (Cambridge, Mass.: Harvard University Press, 1991).

48. Kirschner and Gerhart, *The Plausibility of Life,* 1–5.

49. Ibid., 271–273.

50. Charles Darwin, *On the Origin of Species: A Facsimile of the First Edition,* annotated by James T. Costa (Cambridge, Mass.: Belknap Press of Harvard University Press, 2009 [1859]), 345. The relevant sentence is: "The inhabitants of each successive period in the world's history have beaten their predecessors in the race for life, and are, in so far, higher in the scale of nature; and this may account for that vague yet ill-defined sentiment, felt by many palaeontologists, that organization on the whole has progressed."

51. Gould's most extensive discussion of Darwin's ambiguous, ambivalent attitude toward progress is in *Structure of Evolutionary Theory*, 475–479.

52. Gould points out that the Cretaceous-Tertiary extinction event "drove several groups to extinction through no adaptive failure of their own, while imparting fortuitous exaptive success to creatures that had lived throughout the long reign of dinosaurs, and never made any headway toward replacement, or even toward shared dominion with one of the most successful vertebrate groups in the history of life." Ibid., 1332.

53. Sarah Blaffer Hrdy, *Mothers and Others: The Evolutionary Origins of Mutual Understanding* (Cambridge, Mass.: Harvard University Press, 2009).

54. Frans de Waal, *The Age of Empathy: Nature's Lessons for a Kinder Society* (New York: Harmony House, 2009), 123.

55. Ibid., 139.

56. Ibid., 67.

57. Hrdy, *Mothers and Others*, 38–39.

58. De Waal, *The Age of Empathy*, 131.

59. Gordon Burghardt suggests that this common view of reptiles is inaccurate and that reptiles too "may form bonds, have extensive parental care, have long-term mates, live in extended kin groups, and so on." Personal communication.

60. Irenäus Eibl-Eibesfeldt, *Love and Hate: The Natural History of Behavior Patterns* (New York: Aldine, 1996 [1971]), 128.

61. Ibid., 127.

62. Ibid., 111.

63. Freud, using a broad definition of sexuality, would see parental care itself as sexual, as the importance of the mammary glands so clearly indicates. But whereas sexual reproduction goes back to the eukaryotes, parental care is much more recent. They overlap, but because their origins are so different, conflict between sexuality and love is a recurrent problem, obviously among humans.

64. Eibl-Eibesfeldt, *Love and Hate*, 122.

65. Ibid., 65–66. It is worth remembering that premodern human warfare, though often costly in lives, was also often moderated by ritualized rules of combat. To give an ancient Chinese example: it would not be fair to attack an invading army while they are crossing a river, as they would be too vulnerable. "Total war" is a modern invention.

66. Hrdy, *Mothers and Others*, 67.

67. De Waal, *The Age of Empathy*, 208.

68. Ibid., 48.

69. Ibid., 77.

70. Ibid., 75. Although Michael Tomasello on the whole argues for the uniqueness of human capacities relative to our primate relatives, in contrast to de Waal, who sees strong similarities (probably each is right from his own perspective), interestingly he shares de Waal's skepticism about the argument over altruism, talking about "mutualism," which seems similar to de Waal's "merging." He writes: "I will certainly not solve the evolution-of-altruism problem here. But that is okay because I do not believe it is the central process anyway; that is, I do not believe altruism is the process primarily responsible for human cooperation in the larger sense of humans' tendency and ability to live and operate together in institution-based

groups. In this story altruism is only a bit player. The star is mutualism, in which we all benefit from our cooperation, but only if we work together, what we may call collaboration." Michael Tomasello, *Why We Cooperate* (Cambridge, Mass.: MIT Press, 2009).

71. De Waal, *The Age of Empathy,* 65.

72. Ibid., 74. Gordon Burghardt points out that, for example, reptiles, snakes, and iguanas are quite responsive to human behavior and that snake handlers who are confident and not antagonistic seldom get bitten. Personal communication.

73. "Cold perspective-taking" may be limited, but it is essential for many human activities—science, for instance.

74. Ibid., 100,

75. Just a few of Frans de Waal's books are *Chimpanzee Politics: Power and Sex among Apes* (Baltimore: Johns Hopkins University Press, 2007 [1982]); *Good Natured: The Origins of Right and Wrong* (Cambridge, Mass.: Harvard University Press, 1996); and *Primates and Philosophers: How Morality Evolved* (Princeton: Princeton University Press, 2006).

76. Gordon Burghardt, personal communication.

77. I learned of this early work of Maslow from Frans de Waal's *Good Natured,* 99, 126–127.

78. Ibid., 113.

79. Ibid., 123–124.

80. Ibid., 103.

81. Ibid., 131. As a background for my discussion of dominance hierarchies, see ibid., chap. 3, "Rank and Order," 89–132.

82. Ibid., 91–92.

83. Johan Huizinga, *Homo Ludens: A Study of the Play Element in Culture* (Boston: Beacon Press, 1950 [1938]).

84. Gordon M. Burghardt, *The Genesis of Animal Play: Testing the Limits* (Cambridge, Mass.: MIT Press, 2005), 81. I also found very helpful Robert Fagan's book *Animal Play Behavior* (New York: Oxford University Press, 1981). Because Burghardt includes research done since 1981, I have found it best to cite mainly him. I was also happy to learn from his acknowledgments that work on his book went on "over a more than 15-year period" (xvi), which is even longer than mine has taken, but not much longer.

85. Burghardt, *Genesis of Animal Play,* 71. Huizinga says that play is "different from 'ordinary' life." *Homo Ludens,* 4.

86. Darwin took the phrase "struggle for existence" from Thomas Malthus and used it as the title of chapter 3 of *On the Origin of Species.* Herbert Spencer coined the phrase "survival of the fittest" and first used it in his *Principles of Biology* (N.p., 1864), 444. In the fifth edition of *Origin* (1869), Darwin himself adopted the phrase. When discussing "the struggle for existence," he wrote, "The expression often used by Mr. Herbert Spencer of the Survival of the Fittest is more accurate, and is sometimes equally convenient." For Darwin both phrases pointed to fitness for reproduction, and the struggle could be with the environment as well as other organisms. But Darwin uses such phrases as a species "beating" its competitors or "gaining victory" over them often enough that the popular meaning often seems implied. Biologists today use neither phrase but speak only of natural selection.

87. Burghardt, *Genesis of Animal Play,* 73. Huizinga says, "First and foremost, then, play is a voluntary activity. Play to order is no longer play" (*Homo Ludens,* 7).

88. Burghardt, *Genesis of Animal Play,* 74.

89. Ibid., 75.

90. Ibid., 77–78.

91. Ibid., 84.

92. Ibid., 87. See 83–89 for his discussion of types of play.

93. All quotations in the last three paragraphs are from ibid., 119.

94. Ibid., 129.

95. Ibid., 172.

96. Ibid., 151–156, discusses various theories of the relation of energy and play and warns that the relation is complex and multidimensional. My discussion is necessarily simplified.

97. Marc Bekoff and Jessica Pierce, *Wild Justice: The Moral Lives of Animals* (Chicago: Chicago University Press, 2009), 121.

98. Burghardt, *Genesis of Animal Play,* 89.

99. Ibid., 90.

100. Ibid.

101. De Waal, *Good Natured,* 47.

102. Ibid., 48.

103. Burghardt, *Genesis of Animal Play,* 90–98.

104. Gregory Bateson, in his essay "A Theory of Play and Fantasy," in *Steps to an Ecology of Mind* (New York: Ballantine Books, 1972), writes, "It appears that play is a phenomenon in which the actions of 'play' are related to, or denote, other actions of 'not play.' We therefore meet in play an instance of signals standing for other events, and it appears, therefore, that the evolution of play may have been an important step in the evolution of communication" (181). On 179 he refers to the exchange of signals meaning "this is play" as "metacommunication."

105. For a chart of chimpanzee gestures, several of which are used to initiate play, see Michael Tomasello, *Origins of Human Communication* (Cambridge, Mass.: MIT Press, 2008), 24.

106. Martin Buber, *I and Thou* (New York: Simon and Schuster, 1996 [1923]). Walter Kaufmann was the translator for this, the second translation of Buber's *Ich und Du;* though Kaufmann kept the English title from the original 1937 translation, he consistently translates the German phrase *Ich und Du* as "I and You." The first translation, which gave the now-indelible title to the book, uses "Thou" instead of "You" because *Du* in German is second-person singular, as is "Thou" in English. But, as Kaufmann points out, *Du* in German is used to address lovers and intimate friends today, whereas, for centuries now, one would not use "Thou" for such persons in English. "Thou" has an archaic and slightly pious connotation entirely missing in the German usage of *"Du,"* for which "You" is a more accurate translation.

107. Darwin himself, when speaking of insects, where the power of instinct seems almost total, wrote, "A little dose, as Pierre Huber expresses it, of judgment or reason, often comes into play, even in animals very low in the scale of nature" (*Origin,* 208).

108. Annotation by James T. Costa, on p. 488 of Darwin, *Origin.* It is far from clear when the "earliest appearance" of *Homo sapiens* really was, in a process of speciation that was gradual.

109. Derek Bickerton develops the argument for protolanguage among *Homo erectus* in *Adam's Tongue: How Humans Made Language, How Language Made Humans* (New York: Hill and Wang, 2009). Richard Wrangham, in his *Catching Fire: How Cooking Made Us Human* (New York: Basic Books, 2009), argues that cooking originated with *Homo erectus,* with important consequences for human physiology and behavior.

110. Peter J. Richerson and Robert Boyd, *Not by Genes Alone: How Culture Transformed Human Evolution* (Chicago: Chicago University Press, 2005), 126.

111. Gordon Burghardt points out that there are other species more altricial than humans, "born without hair or feathers, senses undeveloped, especially vision (mice, rats, cats, dogs, bears, etc. cannot see at all)." Personal communication.

112. Sue Taylor Parker and Michael L. McKinney argue strongly against neoteny or juvenilization in their *Origins of Animal Intelligence* (Baltimore: Johns Hopkins University Press, 1999), 336–355.

113. Melvin Konner, *The Evolution of Childhood: Relationships, Emotion, Mind* (Cambridge, Mass.: Harvard University Press, 2010), 139.

114. John E. Pfeiffer, *The Emergence of Man,* 3rd ed. (New York: Harper and Row, 1978), 254–255.

115. Hrdy, *Mothers and Others,* 282. Michael Tomasello, in *The Cultural Origins of Human Cognition* (Cambridge, Mass.: Harvard University Press, 1999), argues that what Hrdy calls emotional modernity, the capacity to understand and sympathize with the intentions of others, probably appeared with *Homo sapiens* in the Pleistocene, 250,000 or so years ago, whereas Hrdy thinks it appeared among earlier members of the genus *Homo,* even as long as 2 million years ago. The whole question of dating is vexed.

116. Hrdy, *Mothers and Others,* 204–206.

117. Terrence Deacon, *The Symbolic Species: The Co-evolution of Language and the Brain* (New York: Norton, 1997), 23. Of course, Deacon was pointing to language, which in some simpler form could have been in existence before *Homo sapiens.*

118. Kathleen R. Gibson, "Putting It All Together: A Constructionist Approach to the Evolution of Human Mental Capacities," in *Rethinking the Human Revolution,* ed. Paul Mellars et al. (Cambridge: McDonald Institute for Archaeological Research, 2007), 70.

119. Terrence Deacon, "Relaxed Selection and the Role of Epigenesis in the Evolution of Language," in *Handbook of Developmental Behavioral Neuroscience,* ed. M. Blumberg et al. (New York: Oxford University Press, 2009), 750.

120. Ibid., 731.

121. Deacon tells me that the "relaxed field" that Burghardt takes as one element of the definition of animal play is analogous to what he means by "relaxed selection" but not identical to it. Personal communication.

122. Such an argument goes back to the nineteenth century but was forcefully argued by Arnold Gehlen in the mid-twentieth century. See his *Man: His Nature and Place in the World* (New York: Columbia University Press, 1988 [1950]). While I cannot accept Gehlen's radical dichotomy between humans and all other animals, I have found much that is valuable in his book. It was Lenny Moss who called my attention to Gehlen's work. For Moss's development of some of these ideas, see his "Detachment, Genomics and the Nature of Being Human," in *New Visions of Nature,* ed. M. Drenthen et al. (New York: Springer, 2009), 103–115.

123. This argument has been reviewed extensively in many chapters of Mellars, *Rethinking the Human Revolution*.

124. See Sally McBrearty, "Down with the Revolution," in ibid., 133–151, and her exhaustive discussion of the evidence in Sally McBrearty and Alison S. Brooks, "The Revolution That Wasn't: A New Interpretation of Modern Human Behavior," *Journal of Human Evolution* 39 (2000): 453–563.

125. Alison Gopnik, *The Philosophical Baby: What Children's Minds Tell Us about Truth, Love, and the Meaning of Life* (New York: Farrar, Straus and Giroux, 2009).

126. Ibid., 14. George Herbert Mead stressed the importance of play in child development in *Mind, Self, and Society* (Chicago: University of Chicago Press, 1934).

127. Gopnik, *The Philosophical Baby*, 15.

128. Ibid., 19.

129. Ibid., 71.

130. Huizinga argues that "play" as a term has a primary force that all the terms for "not-play" lack. "Play is a thing by itself. The play-concept as such is of a higher order than is seriousness. For seriousness seeks to exclude play, whereas play can very well include seriousness." *Homo Ludens*, 45.

131. Gopnik, *The Philosophical Baby*, 14.

132. Quoted in Burghardt, *Genesis of Animal Play*, xiv. With respect to the question of Freud's understanding of "reality," we might ponder the remark he is supposed to have made—"There is only one God, and we don't believe in him"—a remark with more than a little ambiguity.

133. Alasdair MacIntyre, in *After Virtue* (South Bend, Ind.: University of Notre Dame Press, 1981), 175, defines a practice as follows: "By a 'practice' I am going to mean any coherent and complex form of established cooperative human activity through which goods internal to that activity are realised in the course of trying to achieve those standards of excellence which are appropriate to, and partially definitive of, that form of activity, with the result that human powers to achieve excellence and human conceptions of the ends and goods involved, are systematically extended." He gives football as an example and uses chess to describe what he means, so games are included, but he also includes arts, sciences, and politics in the Aristotelian sense, but not ritual. It would be hard to argue, however, that ritual doesn't meet the criteria. MacIntyre includes some forms of play as practices, but does not see play as the prime source of such practices, as I do, but then he is not trying to explain the origin of practices.

134. Michael Tomasello, *Cultural Origins*, 31–33, 62–66; and Tomasello, *Origins of Human Communication*, 20–34, 60–71.

135. De Waal, *Good Natured*, 151–152, emphasis in the original; see also 174, 176, and 205. De Waal mentions neither Durkheim nor Victor Turner, though his description may call them to mind. It is interesting, though, that de Waal's "celebration" would seem to reverse Turner's ritual sequence, in that the effervescent phase expresses "structure" but is followed by something that looks like "communitas." See Victor W. Turner, *The Ritual Process* (Chicago: Aldine, 1969).

136. Shared intention is central to Tomasello's argument in all the books of his cited above, but he is also concerned with shared attention. He even sees "attention as a kind of

intentional perception" (*Cultural Origins,* 68), as what will be attended to is in part determined by one's intention. Merlin Donald discusses attention and intention; he focuses particularly on attention in *Origins of the Modern Mind,* but on both attention and intention in *A Mind So Rare* (New York: Norton, 2001).

137. Huizinga, *Homo Ludens,* 17–18.

138. Ibid., 5.

139. The idea that we have in our brains a "module for supernatural beings" seems to me one of the most obvious absurdities of one form of evolutionary psychology.

140. Barbara Herrnstein Smith, in *Natural Reflections: Human Cognition at the Nexus of Science and Religion* (New Haven: Yale University Press, 2009), writes, "Anthropologist Maurice Bloch notes that among many peoples who worship supposedly supernatural ancestors, attitudes toward such ancestors are not very different from attitudes and behaviors toward living elders: 'The motivations, emotions, and understanding of elders and ancestors are assumed to be the same. Ancestors are simply more difficult to communicate with. Thus, when rural Malagasy, in perfectly ordinary contexts, want to be overheard by the dead, they speak more loudly, something they often also do when they want elders to take notice, since these are often deaf . . . The ancestors are not as close as living parents or grandparents, but they are not all that distant' " (91–92).

141. One could add two more parallel examples: what Wittgenstein called "language games," though these precede language as a cultural form, and what Pierre Bourdieu called "fields."

142. Graham Greene, in the last chapter of his *Monsignor Quixote* (New York: Penguin, 2008), 192–193, reflects on the distinction between fact and fiction, a distinction the Trappist monk, Father Leopoldo, finds hard to make but the American, Professor Pilbeam, does not doubt. The issue comes to a head when Monsignor Quixote performs a Latin mass in a dreamlike state just before his death. Quixote places an invisible wafer in the mouth of his friend Sancho, which Father Leopoldo thinks is "really" there, but which Professor Pilbeam is equally sure really isn't. Actually the whole novel is about how problematic this distinction is.

143. Pierre Hadot, *Philosophy as a Way of Life* (Oxford: Blackwell, 1995 [1987]).

144. The term "scientist" dates to only the early nineteenth century. In the seventeenth century, what we call scientists were referred to as "natural philosophers," and philosophers—Descartes and Leibniz, for example—were scientists and mathematicians as well.

145. Stephen Jay Gould, *Rocks of Ages: Science and Religion in the Fullness of Life* (New York: Ballantine Books, 2002).

146. Kirschner and Gerhart, *The Plausibility of Life,* 271–273.

147. Morowitz, *The Emergence of Everything,* 196.

148. Ibid., 200. Some Christians say, in blessing the bread that is shared with the homeless: "Christ has now on earth no body but ours; no hands but ours, no feet but ours. Ours are the hands by which the whole earth is blessed." They would not, however, I think, claim to be the mind of God, though in his own way Meister Eckhart came close to that.

149. Kauffman, *At Home in the Universe: The Search for the Laws of Self-Organization and Complexity* (New York: Oxford University Press, 1995), 302–304.

150. Stuart Kauffman, *Reinventing the Sacred: A New View of Science, Reason, and Religion* (New York: Basic Books), 2008.

151. Ibid., 6.

152. Ibid., 285–286.

153. Ibid., 288, 273.

154. I have found particularly unhelpful those who think of the mind as composed of modules and of religion as explained by a module for supernatural beings. Representative works in this genre are Pascal Boyer, *Religion Explained: The Evolutionary Origins of Religious Thought* (New York: Basic Books, 2001)—the reference to thought and not to practice in his title is indicative of the weakness of this approach; and Scott Atran, *In Gods We Trust: The Evolutionary Landscape of Religion* (New York: Oxford University Press, 2002). B. H. Smith, in *Natural Reflections,* though giving an appreciative reading of these books that would have been hard for me, has described at length their tendency toward speculative theorizing and their lack of insight into religion as actually lived. But the reader will note how much I depend on other kinds of evolutionary psychology, as represented by such scholars as Merlin Donald and Michael Tomasello, though their work deals only incidentally, if at all, with religion.

155. Robert Wright, *The Evolution of God* (Boston: Little, Brown, 2009); Nicholas Wade, *The Faith Instinct: How Religion Evolves and Why It Endures* (New York: Penguin, 2009); David Sloan Wilson, *Darwin's Cathedral: Evolution, Religion, and the Nature of Society* (Chicago: Chicago University Press, 2003).

156. Ursula Goodenough and Terrence W. Deacon, "The Sacred Emergence of Nature," in *The Oxford Handbook of Religion and Science,* ed. Philip Clayton (New York: Oxford University Press, 2006), 865. When I got hold of this very large book with contributions from many distinguished thinkers, I hoped that it would help me with my project. I was almost completely disappointed. By viewing science and religion primarily as theories and not as practices, they ended up comparing apples and oranges, interesting as examples of how educated people think today but not helpful in understanding the different ways in which science and religion work.

157. Goodenough and Deacon, "Sacred Emergence," 867.

158. Terrence Deacon and Tyrone Cashman, "The Role of Symbolic Capacity in the Origin of Religion," *Journal for the Study of Religion, Nature and Culture* 3 (2009): 490–517. Here Deacon and Cashman move toward the explanation of religion as a practice in a way that the earlier article and most of the others in the *Oxford Handbook of Religion and Science* do not.

159. Gopnik, *The Philosophical Baby,* 138–140.

160. Deacon and Cashman, "Role of Symbolic Capacity," 9.

161. Gananath Obeyesekere, *Imagining Karma: Ethical Transformation in Amerindian, Buddhist, and Greek Rebirth* (Berkeley: University of California Press, 2002), 19–71.

162. Deacon and Cashman, "Role of Symbolic Capacity," 10.

163. Huizinga, *Homo Ludens,* 28–45.

164. Deacon and Cashman, "Role of Symbolic Capacity," 13.

165. Huizinga discusses personification in *Homo Ludens* in the chapter titled "The Elements of Mythopoiesis," where he writes of myth: "As soon as the effect of a metaphor consists in describing things or events in terms of life and movement, we are on the road to personification . . . Personification arises as soon as we feel the need to communicate our

perceptions to others. Conceptions are thus born as acts of the imagination. Are we justified in calling this innate habit of mind, the tendency to create an imaginary world of living beings, a playing of the mind, a mental game?" (136).

166. Buber, *I and Thou,* 85.

167. Ibid., 59.

168. Ibid., 57, 144–146.

169. Ibid., 172,

170. Ibid., 173. Buber is willing to include not just trees, but "this huge sphere that reaches from the stones to the stars."

171. Ibid., 150.

172. Ibid., 124.

173. Blaise Pascal, *Pensées,* rev. ed., trans. A. J. Krailsheimer (London: Penguin, 1995 [1670]), 285.

174. Ibid., 127. Passage numberings in two editions are Blaise Pascal, *Pénsees,* ed. Louis Lafuma (Paris: Editions du Seuil, 1962), 423 (hereafter cited as Lafuma), and Blaise Pascal, *Pensées et Opuscules,* ed. Leon Brunschvicg (Paris: Hachette, 1920), 277 (hereafter cited as Brunschvicg).

175. Ibid., 56. Lafuma 185, Brunschvicg 265.

176. Ibid., 28–29. Lafuma 110, Brunschvicg 282. This passage as a whole is particularly helpful for Pascal's view of the heart.

177. Ibid., 57. Lafuma 190, Brunschvicg 543.

178. Ibid., 60. Lafuma 199, Brunschvicg 72.

179. Ibid., 66. Lafuma 200, Brunschvicg 347.

180. Plato, *Laws,* 2.653, in *The Laws of Plato,* trans. Thomas Pangle (New York: Basic Books, 1980), 32–33, with help from A. E. Taylor's translation in *Plato: The Collected Dialogues,* ed. Edith Hamilton and Huntington Cairns (New York: Pantheon Books, 1961), 1250–51. We will see in Chapter 3 that Plato was right about rhythm and harmony: only humans can "keep together in time."

181. Plato, *Laws,* 7.796, in Huizinga, *Homo Ludens,* 18–19.

182. Huizinga, *Homo Ludens,* 143.

183. Plato, *Statesman,* 268d. I have drawn on J. B. Skemp's translation in Hamilton and Cairns, *Complete Dialogues,* 1033, and C. J. Rowe's translation in *Plato: Complete Works,* ed. John M. Cooper (Indianapolis: Hackett, 1997), 310.

184. Huizinga, *Homo Ludens,* 149–150, citing Aristotle, *Poetics,* 1447B.

185. Plato, *Symposium* 223d, trans. Michael Joyce, in Hamilton and Cairns, *Collected Dialogues,* 547.

186. Smith, *Natural Reflections,* 140–146.

187. Ibid., 33.

188. Ibid., 27.

189. Ibid., 135.

190. Ibid., 132.

191. Ibid., 89–94.

192. Ibid., 31–32.

3. Tribal Religion

1. Merlin Donald, *Origins of the Modern Mind: Three Stages in the Evolution of Culture and Cognition* (Cambridge, Mass.: Harvard University Press, 1991). Donald has developed his argument further in *A Mind So Rare: The Evolution of Human Consciousness* (New York: Norton, 2001).

2. Donald, Origins of the Modern Mind, 149.

3. John H. Crook, "The Experiential Context of Intellect," in *Machiavellian Intelligence: Social Expertise and the Evolution of Intellect in Monkeys, Apes, and Humans,* ed. Richard W. Byrne and Andrew Whiten (Oxford: Clarendon Press, 1988), 359–360.

4. The last chapter of Robert N. Bellah, Richard Madsen, William M. Sullivan, Ann Swidler, and Steven M. Tipton, *The Good Society* (New York: Knopf, 1991), is entitled "Democracy Means Paying Attention."

5. Our knowledge of *Homo habilis,* the first of our genus, who flourished between 2.3 million years ago and the emergence of *H. erectus* 1.8 million years ago, is too fragmentary to hazard a guess about their capacities.

6. Johanna Nichols, "The Origin and Dispersal of Languages: Linguistic Evidence," in *The Origin and Diversification of Language,* ed. Nina G. Jablonski and Leslie C. Aiello (San Francisco: California Academy of Sciences, 1998), 127–170.

7. Jared M. Diamond, *The Third Chimpanzee: The Evolution and Future of the Human Animal* (New York: Harper Trade, 1992).

8. Derek E. Wildman, Lawrence I. Grossman, and Morris Goodman, "Functional DNA in Humans and Chimpanzees Shows They Are More Similar to Each Other than Either Is to Other Apes," in *Probing Human Origins,* ed. Morris Goodman and Anne Simon Moffat (Cambridge, Mass.: American Academy of Arts and Sciences, 2002), 2.

9. Ibid., 1.

10. Ian Tattersall, *Becoming Human: Evolution and Human Uniqueness* (New York: Harcourt Brace, 1998), 121. Tattersall does allow himself one line of speculation: In quadrupedal monkeys, the newborn emerges from the birth canal facing the mother, who can assist in the final emergence. "In humans, on the other hand, the baby has to twist to face away from the mother, who therefore cannot provide such assistance for fear of breaking the baby's back. Neither can the mother attend by herself, as monkeys can, to clearing mucus from the baby's nose and mouth to allow it to breathe or to unwinding the umbilical cord from around the baby's neck. All these attentions are frequently necessary, which is why midwifery is virtually universal in human societies. It has been suggested that the involvement of females other than the mother in the birth process goes right back to the origins of bipedalism; and if so, this implies a level of cooperation and coordination among early hominid females that goes far beyond that involved in the occasional infant care by 'aunts' seen in other primates" (121–122).

11. Robin Dunbar, *Grooming, Gossip, and the Evolution of Language* (Cambridge, Mass.: Harvard University Press, 1996), 130.

12. Ibid., 62–66.

13. Ibid., 77.

14. Ibid., 78.

15. It is beyond my competence to resolve this issue. The idea of a language module has originated among followers of Noam Chomsky and is described at length in Stephen Pinker, *The Language Instinct* (New York: William Morrow, 1994). Merlin Donald argues, convincingly to me, that there is no such thing as a language module. See *A Mind So Rare,* esp. 36–39.

16. Donald, *A Mind So Rare,* 279–285.

17. Tattersall, *Becoming Human,* 128.

18. See the diagram in Colin Renfrew, "The Origins of World Linguistic Diversity: An Archaeological Perspective," in Jablonski and Aiello, *Origin and Diversification,* 178.

19. Donald, *A Mind So Rare,* 263–265.

20. My twin granddaughters were playing quietly when one of them said rather loudly, "mama." My daughter responded and was told "not you!" It was the other granddaughter who, in their play, was at the moment the mama.

21. Donald, *A Mind So Rare,* 264.

22. Tattersall, *Becoming Human,* 138.

23. Donald, *Origins of the Modern Mind,* 179.

24. Tattersall, *Becoming Human,* 139.

25. Donald, *A Mind So Rare,* 264.

26. Ibid.

27. Ibid., 205.

28. Ibid., 266.

29. Linguists have discovered that in all cultures parents speak to infants in something they call "motherese," a kind of simplified, highly repetitive, singsong, partly nonsense, kind of language, one that communicates feeling rather than information. Each language has its own version of motherese, to be sure, but the basic characteristics seem to be quite universal. Because motherese is made up largely of singsong nonsense syllables, it is easy to imagine that it had a prelinguistic mimetic precursor. On motherese, see Pinker, *The Language Instinct,* 39–40.

30. See William H. McNeill, *Keeping Together in Time: Dance and Drill in Human History* (Cambridge, Mass.: Harvard University Press, 1995).

31. Donald, *Origins of the Modern Mind,* 182.

32. Leslie C. Aiello, "The Foundations of Human Language," in Jablonski and Aiello, *Origin and Diversification,* 23.

33. Dunbar, *Grooming,* 78.

34. Though we tend to think of language in terms of abstract meanings, heavily influenced as we are by our constant exposure to written language, it is well to remember that speech is gestural, bodily enacted, and involves subtle muscular training, just as other forms of gesture do.

35. Dunbar, *Grooming,* 140.

36. Steven Brown, "The 'Musilanguage' Model of Music Evolution," in Nils L. Wallin, Björn Merker, and Steven Brown, *The Origins of Music* (Cambridge, Mass.: MIT Press, 2000), 275.

37. Ibid., 277.

38. Dunbar, *Grooming,* 146.

39. See Lawrence H. Keeley, *War before Civilization: The Myth of the Peaceful Savage* (New York: Oxford University Press, 1996). Donald makes a telling point: "It is surely no coincidence that only one subspecies of the entire hominid line has survived; most other species of mammals have at least several co-existing subspecies, each occupying a special niche. But not humans. Apparently only one hominid can occupy the human niche for any substantial length of time." Donald, *Origins of the Modern Mind,* 209.

40. Donald, *Origins of the Modern Mind,* 197–198.

41. Since the publication of Donald's *Origins of the Modern Mind* in 1991, which is summarized here, the work of scholars like de Waal and Tomasello, as discussed in Chapter 2, has shown a considerable degree of shared consciousness among the great apes.

42. Ibid., 198.

43. Ibid., 200.

44. Donald, *A Mind So Rare,* 36–39.

45. Donald, *Origins of the Modern Mind,* 283, citing Jerome Bruner, *Possible Worlds, Actual Minds* (Cambridge, Mass.: Harvard University Press, 1986).

46. Terrence Deacon, *The Symbolic Species: The Co-evolution of Language and the Brain* (New York: Norton, 1997).

47. Ibid., 402–403.

48. Donald, *A Mind So Rare,* 282.

49. Ibid., 283, citing George Lakoff and Mark Johnson, *Metaphors We Live By* (Chicago: University of Chicago Press, 1980). See also Lakoff and Johnson, *Philosophy in the Flesh: The Embodied Mind and Its Challenge to Western Thought* (New York: Basic Books, 1999).

50. Donald, *A Mind So Rare,* 283–284.

51. Donald, *Origins of the Modern Mind,* 215.

52. Ibid., 214.

53. Claude Lévi-Strauss, *Myth and Meaning* (New York: Schocken Books, 1979), 17. Italics in the original.

54. It is worth remembering that in his later writings Durkheim identified "society" not with its existing reality but with the ideals that gave it coherence and purpose.

55. James McClenon, in *Wondrous Healing: Shamanism, Human Evolution, and the Origin of Religion* (Dekalb: Northern Illinois University Press, 2002), argues on neo-Darwinist grounds that shamanistic healing is the "origin" of religion. Though interesting, his argument seems much too simple to me.

56. Jonathan Z. Smith, *Imagining Religion: From Babylon to Jamestown* (Chicago: University of Chicago Press, 1982), 63. Italics in the original.

57. Morris Berman, *Wandering God: A Study in Nomadic Spirituality* (Albany: SUNY Press, 2000), 83.

58. Roy A. Rappaport, *Ritual and Religion in the Making of Humanity* (Cambridge: Cambridge University Press, 1999), 24. Keith Hart in his preface to this posthumously published book invokes Émile Durkheim's *Elementary Forms of the Religious Life* and holds that Rappaport's book is "comparable in scope to his great predecessor's work" (xiv), a judgment with which I agree.

59. Bruce Richman, "How Music Fixed 'Nonsense' into Significant Formulas: On Rhythm, Repetition, and Meaning," in Wallin, Merker, and Brown, *The Origins of Music,* 304.

60. This is the central thesis of Morris Berman's *Wandering God.* Berman believes that "religion" begins only with agriculture and is therefore quite recent in human evolution. Allen Johnson and Timothy Earle, in *The Evolution of Human Societies* (Stanford: Stanford University Press, 1987), argue for very small early human groups that are "naturally" individualistic.

61. Mary Douglas, *Natural Symbols: Explorations in Cosmology* (New York: Pantheon Books, 1982 [1970]), 99.

62. Ibid., xi–xii, quoting Fredrik Barth, *Nomads of South Persia: The Basseri Tribe of the Khamseh Confederacy* (London: Allen and Unwin, 1964), 21.

63. In *War before Civilization,* Keeley argues that most of the few examples of societies without war are, in fact, "defeated refugees," too traumatized and exhausted to think of mounting offensive action.

64. Alan Barnard has made an interesting contrast between the Bushman and the Australian models of hunter-gatherer societies, concluding that the former are more likely to be closer to early *Homo sapiens* society for two reasons: (1) Australian models are unique to Australia, and (2) Australian models are too elaborate to be the basis of early culture. See his "Modern Hunter-Gatherers and Early Symbolic Culture," in *The Evolution of Culture,* ed. Robin Dunbar et al. (New Brunswick: Rutgers University Press, 1999), 50–68. I have already dealt with the issue of cultural elaboration. David H. Turner, in *Life before Genesis: A Conclusion* (Toronto: Peter Lang, 1985), has argued for tendencies toward the Australian type in North America, and for the Australian type as a logical possibility everywhere.

65. Ellen B. Basso, *The Kalapalo Indians of Central Brazil* (New York: Holt, Rinehart and Winston, 1973); and Basso, *A Musical View of the Universe: Kalapalo Myth and Ritual Performances* (Philadelphia: University of Pennsylvania Press, 1985).

66. Basso, *Kalapalo,* 1–3. During the period of Basso's second visit (1978–1980) the Kalapalo still held to their traditional culture. The protection provided by the park "made possible their continued survival in the face of increasingly disastrous demographic, social, and economic pressures which on several occasions have threatened the integrity of the reserve," making them, though "with fearful tenuousness," virtually unique among native peoples of Latin America. Basso, *Musical View,* xi–xii.

67. Ibid., 5.

68. Basso, *Musical View,* 65. It is worth noting that in her first book Basso refers to *itseke* (powerful beings) only as "monsters," having been more impressed by the dangers associated with them than anything else. Basso, *Kalapalo,* 21–23. The fieldwork for *Musical View* concentrated on mythology and ritual and led her to a much deeper understanding of powerful beings.

69. Basso, *Musical View,* 69.

70. Ibid., 68.

71. Basso indicates that the powerful beings can be localized: "Certain landmarks—trees, areas of a river, regions of a particularly deep forest, and so forth—are supposed to be the homes pf particular monsters [*itseke*]. While passing by these places, one is expected to be silent in order not to attract the creatures" (*Kalapalo,* 116). In *Musical View,* as we will see, Basso says the powerful beings live in a "sky village."

72. Basso, *Musical View,* 243.

73. Ibid., 253. Italics in the original.

74. We will see something like this in other tribal and archaic societies.

75. Basso, *Musical View,* 256–257.

76. Jan Vansina notes that in oral cultures chronology is inevitably shallow: "Beyond a certain time depth chronology can no longer be kept. Accounts fuse and are thrown back into the period of origin—typically under a cultural hero—or are forgotten. The shortest such time depth I know of is that of the Aka of Lobaye (Central African Republic), where it does not exceed one generation of adults. Historical consciousness works on only two registers: time of origin and recent times. Because the limit one reaches in time reckoning moves with the passage of generations, I have called the gap a floating gap." Vansina, *Oral Tradition as History* (University of Wisconsin Press, 1985), 24. Later he notes how a historical memory could be swept into a creation myth after some length of time: "a major personage in Lugbara [Congo/Uganda] creation is a British District Officer from the turn of the century" (177).

77. Basso, *Musical View,* 254, quoting Victor Zuckerkandl, *Man the Musician,* 2nd ed. (Princeton: Princeton University Press, 1976), 374.

78. Basso, *Musical View,* 37–39.

79. Ibid., 170.

80. Basso, *Kalapalo,* 113–119; Basso, *Musical View,* 71, 106–107.

81. On witchcraft see Basso, *Kalapalo,* 124–131.

82. Basso, *Musical View,* 91–140.

83. Ibid., 308–309.

84. Ibid., 310–311.

85. Ibid., 11ff.

86. Rappaport, *Ritual and Religion,* 27.

87. Ibid., 37.

88. Victor Turner has usefully emphasized the relation between ritual and dramatic performance, and the boundary between them is indeed fuzzy. See particularly part 2 of his *On the Edge of the Bush: Anthropology as Experience* (Tucson: University of Arizona Press, 1985).

89. Arnold van Gennep, *The Rites of Passage,* trans. Monika B. Vizedom and Gabrielle L. Caffee (Chicago: University of Chicago Press, 1960 [1908]).

90. Rappaport, *Ritual and Religion,* 107.

91. My main sources, M. J. Meggitt and Nancy D. Munn, call this group the Walbiri, and so I will follow their usage, though more recent publications use a slightly different orthography and call the same group the Warlpiri.

92. "As all outsiders were from agricultural traditions and came by sea to coastal areas, it follows that the desert interiors of Australia would be the last places to have their old order disturbed. (Thus studies from the Central and Western Deserts written in the second half of this [twentieth] century can sometimes be legitimately said to describe Aborigines having minimal contact with the non-Aboriginal world.)" Tony Swain, *A Place for Strangers: Towards a History of Australian Aboriginal Being* (New York: Cambridge University Press, 1973), 7.

93. Ibid., 277.

94. W. E. H. Stanner, *On Aboriginal Religion,* Oceania Monograph 11 (Sydney: University of Sydney, 1966), chaps. 4 and 5.

95. Nancy D. Munn, *Walbiri Iconography: Graphic Representations and Cultural Symbolism in a Central Australian Society* (Ithaca: Cornell University Press, 1973), 23–24.

96. Ibid., 24.

97. Swain, *A Place for Strangers,* 22. Swain's italics.

98. Ibid., 4, 49.

99. W. E. H. Stanner, "The Dreaming," in *Cultures of the Pacific,* ed. Thomas G. Harding and Ben J. Wallace (New York: Free Press, 1970 [1956]), 305. Christian Aborigines who have not been fully acculturated to biblical ideas of time imagine that Adam, Moses, and Jesus were all contemporary, all part of the Christian Dreaming. The idea of *Heilsgeschichte,* salvation history, has not penetrated their accustomed way of thinking.

100. Nancy D. Munn, "The Spatial Presentation of Cosmic Order in Walbiri Iconography," in *Primitive Art and Society,* ed. Anthony Forge (New York: Oxford University Press, 1973), 214–215.

101. Fred R. Myers, *Pintupi Country, Pintupi Self: Sentiment, Place, and Politics among Western Desert Aborigines* (Washington, D.C.: Smithsonian Institution Press, 1986), 54.

102. Munn, *Walbiri Iconography,* 77–78.

103. Munn, "Spatial Presentation," 197; Swain, *A Place for Strangers,* 32.

104. Swain, *A Place for Strangers,* 33.

105. Swain describes how, among one Aboriginal group, "the newborn child is immediately placed in a small earthy depression from which it is then 'born'—an act surely stating unambiguously that the child comes not from a mother but from a location." Ibid., 44.

106. See Nancy Munn's description in *Walbiri Iconography,* 27–31; also Swain's discussion of kinship and place in *A Place for Strangers,* 36–49.

107. Both "Dreaming" and "Law" are English words now widely used by Aborigines. It is interesting that they do not use the word "religion" to refer to their deepest beliefs.

108. Quoted in Frank Brennan, "Land Rights: The Religious Factor," in *Religious Business: Essays on Australian Aboriginal Spirituality,* ed. Max Charlesworth (Cambridge: Cambridge University Press, 1998), 169.

109. We will find the metaphor of the Way used in many cultures with similar connotations.

110. M. J. Meggitt, *Desert People: A Study of the Walbiri Aborigines of Central Australia* (Chicago: University of Chicago Press, 1962), 251–252.

111. Munn, *Walbiri Iconography,* 44.

112. The best short treatment of Australian totemism is W. E. H. Stanner, "Religion, Totemism and Symbolism," in Ronald M. Berndt and Catherine H. Berndt, *Aboriginal Man in Australia* (Sydney: Angus and Robertson, 1965), 207–237.

113. Meggitt, *Desert People,* 221.

114. T. G. H. Strehlow suggests the truth of "totemism" in the very subtitle of his short book, *Central Australian Religion: Personal Monototemism in a Polytotemic Community* (Bedford Park, S.A.: Australian Association for the Study of Religion, 1978).

115. Munn, *Walbiri Iconography,* 208.

116. Swain, *A Place for Strangers,* 69.

117. Paul Ricoeur, *Time and Narrative,* vol. 1 (Chicago: University of Chicago Press, 1984), 31–51.

118. Stanner, "The Dreaming," 307.

119. Ibid., 313.

120. Ibid., 309.

121. Ibid., 306.

122. Ibid., 313.

123. Mircea Eliade, *Australian Religions: An Introduction* (Ithaca: Cornell University Press, 1973), chap. 1; Wilhelm Schmidt, *Ursprung der Gottesidee,* vol. 1, 2nd ed. (Münster: Aschendorf, 1926).

124. Jonathan Z. Smith, *To Take Place: Toward Theory in Ritual* (Chicago: University of Chicago Press, 1987), 10.

125. Swain, *A Place for Strangers,* chap. 3.

126. Ibid., 119.

127. Ibid., 127–140.

128. Tocqueville comments on the "instinctive love of country" that held the American Indians to their land: "'We will not sell the spot which contains the bones of our fathers'—that is the first answer they always make to anybody proposing to buy their land." Alexis de Tocqueville, *Democracy in America,* trans. George Lawrence (Garden City, N.Y.: Doubleday, 1969), 323. This passage occurs in volume 1, in the famous chapter 10, "The Three Races That Inhabit the Territory of the United States."

129. In this discussion I am relying on Swain, *A Place for Strangers,* chap. 4.

130. Ibid., 183–184.

131. M. J. Meggitt, *Gadjari among the Walbiri Aborigines of Central Australia,* Oceania Monographs 14 (Sydney: University of Sydney, 1966).

132. Stanner, *On Aboriginal Religion,* 40–42, 80.

133. Ibid., 43.

134. Ibid., 170.

135. Ibid., 53.

136. David H. Turner, "Australian Aboriginal Religion as 'World Religion,'" *Studies in Religion* 20 (1991).

137. David H. Turner, *Life before Genesis;* Turner, *Return to Eden: A Journey through the Aboriginal Promised Landscape of Amagalyuagba* (Toronto: Peter Lang, 1996); and Turner, *Afterlife before Genesis: An Introduction—Accessing the Eternal through Australian Aboriginal Music* (Toronto: Peter Lang, 1997).

138. Deborah Bird Rose, *Dingo Makes Us Human: Life and Land in an Aboriginal Australian Culture* (Cambridge: Cambridge University Press, 1992).

139. See A. P. Elkin, *Aboriginal Men of High Degree* (New York: St. Martin's Press, 1978).

140. Stanner, *On Aboriginal Religion,* 20.

141. Munn, *Walbiri Iconography,* 16, 147.

142. Swain in Tony Swain and Garry Trompf, *The Religions of Oceania* (New York: Routledge, 1995), 109.

143. Stanner, "Religion, Totemism and Symbolism," in Berndt and Berndt, *Aboriginal Man in Australia,* 218.

144. Robert N. Bellah, *Apache Kinship Systems* (Cambridge, Mass.: Harvard University Press, 1957).

145. Marshall Tome, "The Navajo Nation Today," in *Handbook of North American Indians,* vol. 9, *Southwest,* ed. Alfonso Ortiz (Washington D.C.: Smithsonian Institution, 1983), 679–683.

146. For the most traumatic events in Navajo history, as well as for the capacity of the people to deal with these events, see Robert Roessel, "Navajo History, 1850–1923," and Mary Shepardson, "Development of Navajo Tribal government," both in Ortiz, *Southwest,* 506–523, 624–635.

147. The term comes from the work of Anthony F. C. Wallace. See his *Religion: An Anthropological View* (New York: Random House, 1966), 30–39, 157–166.

148. David M. Brugge, *Navajo Pottery and Ethnohistory,* Navajoland Publications ser. 2, Navajo Tribal Museum, Window Rock, 1963; and Brugge, "Navajo Prehistory and History to 1850," in Ortiz, *Southwest,* 489–501. Brugge suggests that Blessingway was "new" in its structure and function, not that all its elements were new.

149. What was then called the New Mexico Territory, which included the present states of Arizona and New Mexico, was formally ceded to the United States by Mexico in 1848.

150. An added difficulty is that there are several levels of ritual knowledge and the student trying to understand Navajo religion may not know what level the informant feels it is appropriate to reveal. Maureen Schwarz describes twelve levels of knowledge, each appropriate to particular persons of different age and status. See Maureen Trudelle Schwarz, *Molded in the Image of Changing Woman: Navajo Views on the Human Body and Personhood* (Tucson: University of Arizona Press, 1997), 24–33.

151. Notable among these efforts are Karl W. Luckert, *The Navajo Hunter Tradition* (Tucson: University of Arizona Press, 1975); Guy H. Cooper, *Development and Stress in Navajo Religion* (Stockholm: Almqvist and Wiksell International, 1984); and, most recently, Jerrold E. Levy, *In the Beginning: The Navajo Genesis* (Berkeley: University of California Press, 1998).

152. Luckert, *Navajo Hunter,* 133–142. As an example of Luckert's "pre-human flux" among the Navajo, Maureen Schwarz reports that in the First (underground) World, the male and female beings were not in their "present form" but would later become First Man and First Woman. "The other beings dwelling in this world were thought of as Air-Spirit or Mist Beings. They had no definite form or shape but were to change in subsequent worlds into humans, animals, birds, reptiles, and other creatures." Maureen Trudelle Schwarz, *Navajo Lifeways: Contemporary Issues, Ancient Knowledge* (Norman: University of Oklahoma Press, 2001), 12–13.

153. Luckert, *Navajo Hunter,* 142–148.

154. Ruth Fulton Benedict, *The Concept of the Guardian Spirit in North America* (Menasha, Wis.: American Anthropological Association, 1923).

155. Although the Navajo do not believe they are born from the land in quite the way the Aborigines do, they have an intense attachment to place. The heroes in the curing ceremonials visit many named places in Navajo country, and some features of the environment are said to be the bodies of monsters slain by Monster Slayer. Keith Basso gives an excellent account of the importance of place among the Western Apache, the Apache group closest in culture to the Navajo, most of which probably applies equally well to the Navajo. See Keith H. Basso, *Wisdom Sits in Places* (Albuquerque: University of New Mexico Press, 1996).

156. For a helpful comparative analysis of Pueblo and Navajo ceremonialism, see Louise Lamphere, "Southwestern Ceremonialism," in Ortiz, *Southwest,* 743–763. I made some

comparisons between the Navajo and Zuni Pueblo in my contribution to the Harvard Values Study volume. See Robert N. Bellah, "Religious Systems," in *People of Rimrock: A Study of Values in Five Cultures,* ed. Evon Z. Vogt and Ethel M. Albert (Cambridge, Mass.: Harvard University Press, 1966), 227–264.

157. Sam D. Gill, *Sacred Words: A Study of Navajo Religion and Prayer* (Westport, Conn.: Greenwood Press, 1981), 84.

158. Gladys A. Reichard, *Navajo Religion: A Study of Symbolism* (New York: Pantheon Books, 1950), 289.

159. Gary Witherspoon, *Language and Art in the Navajo Universe* (Ann Arbor: University of Michigan Press, 1977), 152.

160. Reichard, *Navajo Religion,* 289–291.

161. John R. Farella, *The Main Stalk: A Synthesis of Navajo Philosophy* (Tucson: University of Arizona Press, 1984), 20.

162. One might better say "absent among the Navajo in the past." With the establishment of Navajo Community College in 1969 in Tsaile, Arizona, with a branch at Shiprock, and its development of a Navajo Studies Program, with the extensive use of materials written in Navajo, but also in English, the institutional basis for the development of Navajo philosophy and theology in a theoretic direction has been established. It seems to me that although Witherspoon and Farella both recognize the fundamental importance of narrative, their work represents a degree of systematization that reflects the inevitable rationalizing process when Navajo culture becomes conceptually "bilingual." The work of James McNeley, cited below, can also be cited in this connection. See Gloria J. Emerson, "Navajo Education," in Ortiz, *Southwest,* 669–670.

163. Schwarz, *Navajo Lifeways,* 10, quoting Rik Pinxton and Claire Farrerr, "On Learning a Comparative View," *Cultural Dynamics* 3 (1990): 249.

164. I will greatly condense the narrative for Blessingway, relying largely on material from Leland C. Wyman, *Blessingway* (Tucson: University of Arizona Press, 1970).

165. Ibid., 11–112.

166. Schwarz, *Navajo Lifeways,* 19.

167. Levy, *In the Beginning,* 73. The Navajo understanding of the positive social function of delousing suggests a vestigial survival of primate grooming among *Homo sapiens.*

168. Witchcraft beliefs are widespread among the Navajo, as they are among the Kalapalo and the Aborigines. The basic work on this subject is Clyde Kluckhohn, *Navajo Witchcraft* (Cambridge, Mass.: Peabody Museum, Harvard University, 1944; repr., Boston: Beacon Press, 1967).

169. Schwarz, *Navajo Lifeways,* 20.

170. Witherspoon, *Language and Art,* 17; Wyman, *Blessingway,* 398.

171. Witherspoon gives a close linguistic analysis of the phrase *sa'ah naaghaii bik'eh hozho* in *Language and Art,* 17–27. Farella offers what might be called a metaphysical analysis of it in *The Main Stalk,* 153–187.

172. Farella, *The Main Stalk,* 66–68.

173. On completeness, ibid., 181; on wind, James Kale McNeley, *Holy Wind in Navajo Philosophy* (Tucson: University of Arizona Press, 1981); on kin, Witherspoon, *Language and Art,* 88, where he speaks of "the Navajo ideal of relating to everyone as a kinsman."

174. Schwarz, *Molded in the Image,* 235.

175. Wyman, *Blessingway,* 8.

176. Gill, *Sacred Words,* 56, citing Katherine Spencer, *Mythology and Values: An Analysis of Navaho Chantway Myths* (Philadelphia: American Folklore Society, 1967). See also her *Reflection of Social Life in the Navaho Origin Myth,* University of Arizona Publications in Anthropology 3 (1947).

177. Schwarz, *Navajo Lifeways,* particularly chap. 3, "The Holy Visit of 1996." Schwarz gives voice to some of the more somber warnings in her brief conclusion, chap. 7, "Final Thoughts."

178. The most extensive work on Navajo Peyote has been done by David F. Aberle. He estimates that 40 to 60 percent of Navajos were adherents of the Peyote religion in 1972. See his "Peyote Religion among the Navajo" in Ortiz, *Southwest,* 558. The fullest treatment of the subject is Aberle's *The Peyote Religion among the Navajo,* Viking Fund Publications in Anthropology 42 (New York, 1966).

179. It should be remembered that the Navajo, the Walbiri, and perhaps by now the Kalapalo, live in a symbiotic relation with societies with an advanced theoretic culture. For example, in the case of the Navajo and the Aborigines, a working relation has developed between medical doctors and native curers so that each refers to the other cases they feel they cannot treat. Modern education, to which tribal peoples are increasingly exposed, is also a conduit for theoretic culture. In the case of the Navajo the emphasis on bilingual education helps keep the traditional culture alive, but the inevitable dominance of a theoretic approach, particularly at the community college level, even in the Navajo Studies Program, suggests that there is no way to preserve mythic culture in a watertight compartment.

4. From Tribal to Archaic Religion

1. Frans B. M. de Waal, "Apes from Venus: Bonobos and Human Evolution," in *Tree of Origin: What Primate Behavior Can Tell Us about Human Evolution,* ed. de Waal (Cambridge, Mass.: Harvard University Press, 2002), 62.

2. Christopher Boehm, *Hierarchy in the Forest: The Evolution of Egalitarian Behavior* (Cambridge, Mass.: Harvard University Press, 1999).

3. Ibid., 147, 163.

4. Ibid., 10–11.

5. Ibid., 60.

6. Whether modernity represents still another turn (this time a downward turn in the degree of despotism) is a matter we can postpone until a later chapter.

7. There has long been an argument over whether *Herrschaft,* as Weber uses the term, should be translated as "legitimate authority" or "domination." In terms of my argument, depending on context, either translation could be appropriate. Further, though we usually use the term "domination" for the rule of the stronger, it does derive from the Latin word *dominus,* "lord," often used for "the Lord God," just as God in German is termed *Herr Gott.* Domination and legitimate authority are indeed hard to separate empirically.

8. It is possible that both are found even among the primates. There is a debate over whether the alpha male chimpanzee, for example, provides any services useful to the group as a whole, or is only enhancing his own procreative chances. To the extent that the alpha

male provides some leadership in the hunt and in conflict with other chimpanzee bands or breaks up fights between lower-ranking chimps, he can be seen as providing services to the group.

9. Fred R. Myers, *Pintupi Country, Pintupi Self* (Washington D.C.: Smithsonian Institution Press, 1986), 22–23.

10. Ibid., 224.

11. Ibid., 240.

12. Ibid., 255.

13. Ibid., 246.

14. Ellen B. Basso, *A Musical View of the Universe: Kalapalo Myth and Ritual Performances* (Philadelphia: University of Pennsylvania Press, 1985), 255. For more on the *anetaū,* see Ellen B. Basso, *The Kalapalo Indians of Central Brazil* (New York: Holt, Rinehart and Winston, 1973), 132–153.

15. Basso, *The Kalapalo,* 132.

16. Basso, *Musical View,* 256.

17. Basso, *The Kalapalo,* 132.

18. A good place to begin if one wanted to consider these issues among the Pueblos would be Peter M. Whitely, *Deliberate Acts: Changing Hopi Culture through the Oraibi Split* (Tucson: University of Arizona Press, 1988). Whitely finds that, in spite of previous ethnographic emphasis on Hopi egalitarianism, it is a rank society, divided between elite and commoners, the elite being defined by religious knowledge and ritual leadership. The highest ritual leader functioned as the village chief (similar to Tikopia below), but had no coercive power and made decisions in consultation with other clan and ritual leaders. As among the Kalapalo (and Tikopia), the differentiation into an elite and a commoner class, according to Whitely, was "unmarked by economic differences" (70).

19. Patrick V. Kirch and Roger C. Green, *Hawaiki, Ancestral Polynesia: An Essay in Historical Anthropology* (New York: Cambridge University Press, 2001).

20. Firth had the good fortune to live in Tikopia for two years (1928–1929) when the traditional culture, and particularly the traditional religion, was still functioning. Tikopia is thus arguably the best ethnographically documented of any Polynesian society. Firth's most famous book is *We the Tikopia: A Sociological Study of Kinship in Primitive Polynesia* (New York: American Book Company, 1936), but several other books of his will be cited below. We have the further good fortune that Tikopia has been the subject of an excellent archaeological study, Patrick V. Kirch and Douglas E. Yen, *Tikopia: The Prehistory and Ecology of a Polynesian Outlier* (Honolulu: Bernice P. Bishop Museum, 1982).

21. One might take the Pueblos as a baseline case of simple chiefdoms in the American Southwest before moving on to the Aztecs in the Valley of Mexico as an example of early state formation. However, the relation between these two cultures is highly problematic: it is possible that the Anasazi, the ancestors of the Pueblos, had been hunter-gatherers who began to develop new social forms under the indirect influence of the culture of the Valley of Mexico, but the lack of information about intermediate forms means that it is only with difficulty that the Anasazi could be seen as analogous to an early stage of the civilization of the Valley of Mexico.

22. Firth, *We the Tikopia,* 409.

23. Raymond Firth, *Rank and Religion in Tikopia: A Study in Polynesian Paganism and Conversion to Christianity* (London: Allen and Unwin, 1970), 42. Firth goes on to add: "In a very real sense, then, his *tapu* was created by them as a symbol of their collective action; it represented in a kind of practical Durkheimianism the values of their assembly and their society."

24. Ibid., 35.

25. Raymond Firth, *History and Traditions of Tikopia* (Wellington: Polynesian Society, 1961), 53.

26. Morton H. Fried, *The Evolution of Political Society: An Essay in Political Anthropology* (New York: Random House, 1967), 133, quoting from Raymond Firth, *Primitive Polynesian Society* (London: Routledge, 1939).

27. The classic treatment of the Big Man is Marshall Sahlins, "Poor Man, Rich Man, Big Man, Chief: Political Types in Melanesia and Polynesia," *Comparative Studies in Society and History* 5 (1963): 285–303. On how "secular" the Big Man is, see Tony Swain and Gary Trompf, *The Religions of Oceania* (London: Routledge, 1995), 142.

28. Firth, *History and Traditions,* 17.

29. Both *tapu* and *mana* have entered the vocabulary of comparative religion, though their application to non-Polynesian societies has been challenged. They are, nonetheless, central terms in all Polynesian societies and probably have even deeper roots. Kirch and Green have reconstructed the terms in Proto Oceanic, and *tapu* even in Proto Eastern Maylayo Polynesian as well. See Kirch and Green, *Hawaiki,* 239–240.

30. Firth, *Rank and Religion,* 46.

31. Ibid., 23.

32. Irving Goldman, *Ancient Polynesian Society* (Chicago: University of Chicago Press, 1970), 354.

33. Firth, *Rank and Religion,* 25

34. Ibid., 29.

35. Ibid., 90–91.

36. Ibid., 111–112.

37. Ibid., 297.

38. Firth, *History and Traditions,* 122.

39. Ibid., 128–143. Who exactly the Nga Ravenga and the Nga Faea were is open to speculation. Human occupation of Tikopia goes back to about 900 BCE, well before the origin of Polynesian culture in the area of Samoa and Tonga in about 500 BCE. The Polynesian "outliers," of which Tikopia is one, were settled by Polynesians from the east probably sometime in the first millennium CE. Thus the Nga Ravenga and the Nga Faea could have been pre-Polynesians or simply an earlier group of Polynesian settlers. Kirch has discovered through archaeology that Tikopia suffered a geological change due to tectonic uplift in the period just preceding the expulsions, a change that turned an ocean bay into a brackish lake, making the area of the ancestors of present Tikopia much less productive and creating a need for territory occupied by others. Finally, whether the departure of the Nga Faea was a suicide mission or an effort to find new land to colonize (as had happened frequently in Polynesian history) remains an open question. On all these issues, see Patrick Kirch, *The Evolution of Polynesian Chiefdoms* (New York: Cambridge University Press, 1984), 80, 125, 202.

40. Goldman, *Ancient Polynesian Society,* xviii.

41. Ibid., 17.

42. And aggression may be more strongly linked to males. See de Waal, "Apes from Venus."

43. For examples, see Frans de Waal, *Good Natured: The Origins of Right and Wrong in Humans and Other Animals* (Cambridge, Mass.: Harvard University Press, 1996).

44. Marcel Mauss, *The Gift: Forms and Functions of Exchange in Archaic Societies* (Glencoe, Ill.: Free Press, 1954), 72. Irving Goldman brought this passage to my attention in *Ancient Polynesian Society,* 18.

45. Goldman describes Tikopia as an example of a "traditional status system" in his typology of status systems. Goldman, *Ancient Polynesian Society,* 20–28. He describes Hawai'i in its Early Period (CE 124–1100) as "traditional" (212).

46. Marshall Sahlins, *Stone Age Economics* (Chicago: Aldine-Atherton, 1972), 101.

47. Sahlins, in his essay "The Original Affluent Society," chap. 1 of *Stone Age Economics,* describes the "underproduction" of the many hunter-gatherer societies, whose members appear satisfied with meeting immediate needs. Agriculturalists are necessarily deprived of this kind of affluence.

48. Ibid., 140.

49. Timothy Earle, *How Chiefs Come to Power: The Political Economy of Prehistory* (Stanford: Stanford University Press, 1997), 76–77. But Earle also indicates that the officials of complex chiefdoms in Hawai'i did organize work to intensify irrigation agriculture and thus increase surplus that could be appropriated (78–79).

50. Lawrence H. Keeley, in *War before Civilization: The Myth of the Peaceful Savage* (New York: Oxford University Press, 1996), argues that war is coterminous with human society. Raymond C. Kelly, in *Warless Societies and the Origin of War* (Ann Arbor: University of Michigan Press, 2000), takes issue with Keeley by defining war as I have done in the preceding paragraph.

51. Goldman, *Ancient Polynesian Society,* 41.

52. "Despite the sizable population of North Island in late prehistory, the Maori never amalgamated into large polities, nor did they undergo a socio-political transformation from a simple chiefdom level of organization to a complex, hierarchical social formation, as seen in Hawai'i or the Society Islands." Patrick V. Kirch, *On the Road of the Winds: An Archeological History of the Pacific Islands before European Contact* (Berkeley: University of California Press, 2000), 283.

53. Ibid., 205.

54. Goldman, *Ancient Polynesian Society,* 86.

55. Kirch, *Evolution of Polynesian Chiefdoms,* 206; Kirch, *On the Road,* 255.

56. "Charisma," in Weber's sense, is one possible translation of *mana.*

57. Kirch, *On the Road,* 257. It would seem that a possible relation between religion and terror goes way back, though perhaps not, contrary to Rene Girard in his *Violence and the Sacred* (Baltimore: Johns Hopkins Press, 1977), all the way back.

58. Kirch quotes an earlier authority on late precontact Rapa Nui as saying, "The various communities scattered over the island became more and more like predatory bands, and much of the older, more ordered way of life gradually vanished" (Kirch, *Evolution of Polynesian*

Chiefdoms, 277). Kirch himself adds that the Dutch explorer Roggeveen found on Easter Day, 1722, a "war-torn, debilitated society" (278). Mangaia and Rapa Nui are by far not the only societies that have malfunctioned or maladapted. For a general survey of such cases, see Robert B. Edgerton, *Sick Societies: Challenging the Myth of Primitive Harmony* (New York: Free Press, 1992). What makes Mangaia and Rapa Nui especially interesting is that their breakdown was due entirely to endogenous causes, not to any external pressure. Such cases do not negate the value of "functional" analysis. Indeed, if societies never malfunctioned, functionalism would be tautologous.

59. Kirch, *On the Road,* 290, 312, 351 n. 49.

60. Kirch, *Evolution of Polynesian Chiefdoms,* 98; Kirch, *On the Road,* 248.

61. Earle, *How Chiefs,* 86.

62. Matthew Spriggs suggests that there may have been Tahitian influence on Hawaiian development in the period when voyages between the two were reported in traditional accounts, by modern reckoning, between 1100 and 1400 CE: "In traditional histories this is the 'migration period' when two-way voyaging took place between Tahiti and Hawaii bringing new chiefs and new ideas, in particular a new religious system involving human sacrifice and ceremonies in walled temples from which the common people were excluded. There is a greater stress on distinctions of rank and attendant *kapu* separating chiefs and commoners. Several of the major *luakini heiau* (temples of human sacrifice) were said to have been constructed at this time." See Spriggs, "The Hawaiian Transformation of Ancestral Polynesian Society: Conceptualizing Chiefly States," in *State and Society: The Emergence and Development of Social Hierarchy and Political Centralization,* ed. John Gledhill et al. (London: Unwin Hyman, 1988), 60. Archaeological evidence for such a connection is slight, and other scholars doubt the accuracy of the traditional account concerning Tahitian influence.

63. Earle, *How Chiefs,* 36, 45.

64. David Malo, *Hawaiian Antiquities* (Honolulu: Bernice P. Bishop Museum, 1951 [1898]), 57–58.

65. Valerio Valeri, *Kingship and Sacrifice: Ritual and Society in Ancient Hawaii* (Chicago: University of Chicago Press, 1985), 164.

66. Goldman, *Ancient Polynesian Society,* 218.

67. Valeri, *Kingship and Sacrifice,* 36.

68. Ibid., 15.

69. Ibid., 200–233.

70. Ibid., 177–178.

71. Valeri writes "king," but I wish to reserve the discussion of the legitimacy of that terminology until later.

72. Valeri, *Kingship and Sacrifice,* 219.

73. Ibid., 206, 380 n. 10.

74. Ibid., 218–219.

75. Ibid., 211–213.

76. Goldman, *Ancient Polynesian Society,* 206.

77. See Valeri's detailed description in *Kingship and Sacrifice,* 234–339. It is worth noting that although the Makahiki Festival and the Work of the Gods in Tikopia are clearly vari-

ants of a general Polynesian first-fruits ceremonial, there is no equivalent in Tikopia to the *luakini* temple ritual.

78. See, for example, the dispute between the anthropologist Gananath Obeyesekere and Marshall Sahlins over whether the Hawaiians thought Captain Cook and their own chiefs were gods. The essential documents are Obeyesekere, *The Apotheosis of Captain Cook: European Mythmaking in the Pacific* (Princeton: Princeton University Press, 1992); and Sahlins, *How "Natives" Think: About Captain Cook, for Example* (Chicago: Chicago University Press, 1995).

79. Valeri, *Kingship and Sacrifice,* 151.

80. Ibid., 140. Valeri adds, "He is, in sum, the point of connection between the social whole and the concept that justifies it" (142). Valeri's debt to Durkheim and Mauss is obvious throughout his excellent book.

81. Ibid., 140, citing S. M. Kamakau.

82. A claim made by political leaders from time immemorial. Even in "egalitarian" America, George Washington is "the father of his country."

83. Valeri, *Kingship and Sacrifice,* 151.

84. Ibid., 370 n. 36.

85. Ibid., 165.

86. Ibid., 277–278.

87. Ibid., 157.

88. This reminds one of the words attributed to Han Gaodi, the first emperor of the Han dynasty after the collapse of the quintessential upstart Qin dynasty, that "one can conquer an empire on horseback but one cannot rule an empire on horseback."

89. Valeri, *Kingship and Sacrifice,* xxiv.

90. Malo, *Hawaiian Antiquities,* 60–61.

91. The fact that Malo wavers between the terms "chief" and "king" suggests just the ambiguity that I will deal with below. However, in this case Kamehameha I was a king by any definition.

92. Malo, *Hawaiian Antiquities,* 58.

93. Ibid., 195.

94. Ibid., 190.

95. Valeri, *Kingship and Sacrifice,* 220.

96. Periods of disorder after the death of a ruler are not unknown in other societies. Those who lived through the three days after the assassination of John F. Kennedy in November 1963 will remember that, although social order did not collapse, there was a widely shared sense of psychic collapse.

97. Kirch and Green, *Hawaiki,* 246.

98. Malo, *Hawaiian Antiquities,* 114.

99. Ibid., 115. The biblical overtones of this passage might cause doubts as to its authenticity. One might remember that the early Hebrew prophets, *nabi,* lived in a society not entirely different from late precontact Hawai'i. It is worth noting that *kāula* was the term used for "prophet" in the Hawaiian translation of the bible. Compare Jeremiah 1:9–10: "Then the Lord put out his hand and touched my mouth; and the Lord said to me, 'Now I have put my words in your mouth. See, today I appoint you over nations and over kingdoms, to pluck up and to pull down, to destroy and to overthrow, to build and to plant.'"

100. Valeri, *Kingship and Sacrifice,* 139. Malo, *Hawaiian Antiquities,* 251–254, recounts a legend of a struggle to the death between a king and a woman prophet.

101. Valeri, *Kingship and Sacrifice,* 139.

102. Eli Sagan's *At the Dawn of Tyranny: The Origins of Individualism, Political Oppression, and the State* (New York: Knopf, 1985) includes an extensive analysis of this phenomenon. Sagan also discusses the extent to which the people identified with the extraordinary power of the ruler.

103. Malo, *Hawaiian Antiquities,* 57.

104. The power of life and death over its subjects or citizens, through capital punishment or mobilization for war, gives every state, however apparently secular, an element of the sacred. See my discussion of the religio-political problem in the introduction to Robert N. Bellah and Philip E. Hammond, *Varieties of Civil Religion* (New York: Harper and Row, 1980), vii–xv.

105. Sahlins, *Stone Age Economics,* 148.

106. Kirch, *Evolution of Polynesian Chiefdoms,* 263. Italics in original.

107. Kirch, *On the Road,* 300. Eli Sagan in *Dawn of Tyranny* also argues that the break with kinship is the defining feature of what he calls advanced complex societies; in his view, Hawai'i was one of those societies that had made that break. In 2010 a new book by Kirch was published, unfortunately too late to be taken into account in this chapter. We may only note here that not only does this book confirm Kirch's belief that what he calls an archaic state and I have called an early state emerged in Hawai'i before Western contact, but he dates the transition as beginning already in the late seventeenth century. See Patrick Vinton Kirch, *How Chiefs Became Kings: Divine Kingship and the Rise of Archaic States in Ancient Hawai'i* (Berkeley, Calif.: University of California Press, 2010).

108. Lawrence Krader, *Formation of the State* (Englewood Cliffs, N.J.: Prentice-Hall, 1968), 28. Italics in original.

5. Archaic Religion

1. Bruce G. Trigger, *Understanding Early Civilizations* (Cambridge: Cambridge University Press, 2003), 28.

2. The Indus Valley civilization flourished from approximately 2500 to 2000 BCE. It had well-built cities with good water systems, as well as some irrigation agriculture, but not much in the way of public buildings. With nothing that can be clearly described as temples or palaces, neither the religious nor the political system is at all clear. For a recent treatment, see Jane R. McIntosh, *A Peaceful Realm: The Rise and Fall of the Indus Civilization* (Boulder, Colo.: Westview Press, 2002).

3. Claessen and Skalník speak of "inconspicuous processes" that slowly produce institutions that only in retrospect can be recognized as characteristic of the state. Henri J. M. Claessen and Peter Skalník, eds., *The Early State* (The Hague: Mouton, 1978), 620–621.

4. Trigger, *Understanding Early Civilizations,* 44–45.

5. Ibid., 46.

6. Ibid., 48.

7. Ibid., 79–87.

8. Ibid., 88–89.

9. Ibid., 92–119.

10. Timothy Earle, *How Chiefs Come to Power: The Political Economy of Prehistory* (Stanford: Stanford University Press, 1997), 177.

11. Trigger, *Understanding Early Civilizations,* 639, 684.

12. Hans J. Nissen suggests that around the middle of the fourth millennium BCE, climatic changes occurred in Mesopotamia involving a decrease in rainfall. Heavy rainfall earlier would have sent such intense flooding into the alluvial plain that agriculture would have been impossible, but more moderate rainfall allowed its fruitful cultivation. See Nissen, *The Early History of the Ancient Near East, 9000–2000 B.C.* (Chicago: University of Chicago Press, 1988), 55.

13. Andrew Sherratt, "Plough and Pastoralism: Aspects of the Secondary Products Revolution," in Ian Hodder, Glynn Isaac, and Norman Hammond, *Pattern of the Past: Studies in Honour of David Clarke* (Cambridge: Cambridge University Press, 1981), 261–305.

14. Ibid., 287.

15. Ibid., 284.

16. Susan Pollack, *Ancient Mesopotamia* (Cambridge: Cambridge University Press, 1999), 5–6.

17. Nissen, *Early History,* 72.

18. Pollack, *Ancient Mesopotamia,* 118; A. Leo Oppenheim, *Ancient Mesopotamia: Portrait of a Dead Civilization* (Chicago: University of Chicago Press, 1977 [1964]), 95–109.

19. Thorkild Jacobsen, "Mesopotamia," in *Before Philosophy: The Intellectual Adventure of Ancient Man,* ed. Henri Frankfort, Mrs. Henri Frankfort, John A. Wilson, and Thorkild Jacobsen (Harmondsworth: Pelican, 1949 [1946]), 141–142. Oppenheim, in *Ancient Mesopotamia,* 111–114, discusses the evidence for the existence of a city "assembly," consisting of local notables not directly connected to temple or palace.

20. On heterarchy, see Peter Bogucki, *The Origins of Human Society* (Malden, Mass.: Blackwell, 1999), 256–257.

21. Thorkild Jacobsen, *Treasures of Darkness: The History of Mesopotamian Religion* (New Haven: Yale University Press, 1976), 114.

22. Also spelled *Hammurabi.*

23. Oppenheim, *Ancient Mesopotamia,* 98. The "awe-inspiring luminosity" of Assyrian kings is reminiscent of the "raging blazes" that were said to characterize the Hawaiian *ali'i.*

24. Amélie Kuhrt, *The Ancient Near East, c. 3000–330 BC* (London: Routledge, 1995).

25. For a description of the major gods, see Jacobsen, *Treasures of Darkness,* 93–143 (if I had to recommend one book on ancient Mesopotamian religion, this would be it); and Jean Bottéro, *Religion in Ancient Mesopotamia* (Chicago: University of Chicago Press, 2001 [1998]), 44–58.

26. Bottéro, *Religion in Ancient Mesopotamia,* 138–139.

27. Jacobsen, *Treasures of Darkness,* 12.

28. Can we hear an echo of the Work of the Gods in Tikopia, or of the Makahiki festival in Hawai'i?

29. On the "service to the gods," see Jean Bottéro, *Mesopotamia: Writing, Reasoning, and the Gods* (Chicago: University of Chicago Press, 1992 [1987]), 1–2; on the "care and feeding of the gods," see Oppenheim, *Ancient Mesopotamia,* 183–298.

30. For a full account of the story, see Jacobsen, *Treasures of Darkness,* 116–121.

31. Ibid., 117.

32. Except for the retainer burials in Early Dynasty Ur, this kind of mythical reference is as close as we get to human sacrifice in ancient Mesopotamia, although war captives were frequently slaughtered on the field of battle.

33. Jacobsen, *Treasures of Darkness,* 121. The foreshadowing in the Story of Atraḥasīs of both the creation story and the Noah story in Genesis has long been observed.

34. Ibid., 95, 98.

35. Jacobsen, "Mesopotamia," 157. Here the wild Enlil reminds us of the Hawaiian wild Kū. The figure of the third-millennium Sumerian Enlil, with all his ambiguity, is in the early second millennium transformed into the Babylonian Marduk, and in the late second millennium and first millennium into the Assyrian Assur.

36. Kuhrt, *Ancient Near East,* 1:39.

37. Nissen, *Early History,* 186.

38. Kuhrt, *Ancient Near East,* 1:77.

39. Bottéro, *Mesopotamia,* 168. It should be noted that the "shepherd" motif was a commonplace for kings in both Mesopotamia and Egypt. Samuel Noah Kramer translated a Sumerian hymn to the high god Enlil in which the god is addressed as "shepherd." Kramer, *History Begins at Sumer* (Philadelphia: University of Pennsylvania Press, 1984 [1956]), 91–92.

40. Bottéro, *Mesopotamia,* 183. Italics in original.

41. Ibid., 182.

42. Bottéro, *Religion in Ancient Mesopotamia,* 220.

43. Kuhrt, *Ancient Near East,* 1:105. According to Oppenheim, prophets were found mainly in the north (Assyria) and northwest. Ecstatic and shamanistic concepts were largely missing in the Mesopotamian heartland. *Ancient Mesopotamia,* 221–222.

44. "The Babylonian Theodicy," in *The Ancient Near East: A New Anthology of Texts and Pictures,* ed. James B. Pritchard (Princeton: Princeton University Press, 1975), 162.

45. Jacobsen, *Treasures of Darkness,* 162.

46. The Gilgamesh epic entered world literature quite early. It was by far the most widely circulated piece of Mesopotamian literature, being known all over the ancient Near East—fragments of translations into Hurrian and Hittite have been found. It arguably influenced both the *Iliad* and the *Odyssey.* See M. L. West, *The East Face of Helicon: West Asiatic Elements in Greek Poetry and Myth* (Oxford: Oxford University Press, 1997), 65, 336–347, 403–417.

47. Jacobsen, "Mesopotamia," 137.

48. The strangeness of Mesopotamian religion led Oppenheim, famously, to argue "why a 'Mesopotamian Religion' should not be written." Thus: "Western man seems to be both unable and, ultimately, unwilling to understand such [higher polytheistic] religions except from the distorting angle of antiquarian interest and apologetic pretenses. For nearly a century he has tried to fathom these alien dimensions with the yardsticks of animistic theories,

nature worship, stellar mythologies, vegetation cycles, pre-logical thought, and kindred panaceas, to conjure them by means of the abracadabra of mana, taboo, and orenda. And the results have been, at best, lifeless and bookish syntheses and smoothly written system-atizations decked out in a mass of all-too-ingenious comparisons and parallels obtained by zigzagging over the globe and through the known history of man." *Ancient Mesopotamia,* 172, 183. Leaving aside the fact that Oppenheim, even in the book from which this passage comes, himself made major contributions to the understanding of Mesopotamian religion, it is still a question whether the present effort has avoided his strictures.

49. Nissen, *Early History,* 3.

50. Oppenheim notes that the taking of interest on loans became common practice in Mesopotamia, though "usury" was viewed with horror by most other Near Eastern societies. See *Ancient Mesopotamia,* 88ff.

51. "Mesopotamia . . . represents perhaps the most stubbornly bureaucratic use of writing known from any ancient civilization. For 600 years after the introduction of true writing it was used exclusively by administrators. And from one period of some 75 years at the very end of the third millennium, the so-called 'Ur III period', we have hundreds of thousands of such administrative procedures. Single documents could regulate transactions involving tens of thousand of persons, and at the same time the loss of half a pound (0.25 kg) of wool from a warehouse would be discovered and accounted for with a frightening inevitability. So it seems fair to say that the potential of this technology for its use as a controlling device was realized to the full in Mesopotamia." Mogens Trolle Larsen, "Introduction: Literacy and Social Complexity," in *State and Society: The Emergence and Development of Social Hierarchy and Political Centralization,* ed. John Gledhill et al. (London: Unwin Hyman, 1988), 173–191.

52. Oppenheim, on the basis of some written sources, says "there exists meager, but unquestionable, evidence of a rich and productive oral literary tradition in Mesopotamia." *Ancient Mesopotamia,* 22.

53. Jan Assmann, *Moses the Egyptian: The Memory of Egypt in Western Monotheism* (Cambridge, Mass.: Harvard University Press, 1997).

54. Michael Walzer, *Exodus and Revolution* (New York: Basic Books, 1985).

55. Barry J. Kemp, *Ancient Egypt: Anatomy of a Civilization* (London: Routledge, 1989), 3.

56. Assmann, *Moses the Egyptian,* 14.

57. William H. McNeill, *Mythistory and Other Essays* (Chicago: Chicago University Press, 1986).

58. Assmann, *Moses the Egyptian,* 14–15.

59. Erik Hornung, *Conceptions of God in Ancient Egypt: The One and the Many* (Ithaca: Cornell University Press, 1982), 251. Italics in the original.

60. For northerners like Europeans and North Americans, it seems odd that "upper" means "southern" from the point of view of Egypt, because the Nile flows from south to north. Conversely, the Egyptians found Mesopotamia odd because from their point of view the Tigris and the Euphrates flow "backward."

61. Kemp, *Ancient Egypt,* 34–44.

62. Toby A. H. Wilkinson, *Early Dynastic Egypt* (London: Routledge, 1999). Wilkinson argues that from as early as 3500 BCE at least three Upper Egyptian "kingdoms" had come

into existence, as indicated by the towns and adjacent burial grounds of Hierakonpolis, Nakada, and This. He describes the use of the term "Dynasty 0" as applying to several kings not long before 3000 BCE, one or more of whom may have ruled over a united Egypt. See 52–58.

63. Michael A. Hoffman, *Egypt before the Pharaohs: The Prehistoric Foundations of Egyptian Civilization* (New York: Knopf, 1979), 336.

64. Kemp, *Ancient Egypt,* 37.

65. Henri Frankfort, *Kingship and the Gods: A Study of Ancient Near Eastern Religion as the Integration of Society and Nature* (Chicago: University of Chicago Press, 1948).

66. Georges Posener, *De la divinité du pharaon* (Paris: Cahiers de la Société Asiatique, 1960).

67. Jan Assmann, *The Search for God in Ancient Egypt* (Ithaca: Cornell University Press, 2001 [1984]), 49. Italics in original.

68. Ibid., 89.

69. Jan Assmann, *The Mind of Egypt: History and Meaning in the Time of the Pharaohs,* trans. Andrew Jenkins (Cambridge, Mass.: Harvard University Press, 2003 [1996]), 300.

70. Eric Voegelin, *Order and History,* 5 vols. (Baton Rouge: Louisiana State University Press, 1956–1987).

71. Hornung, *Conceptions of God,* 172–185.

72. Ibid., 180.

73. Ibid., 181.

74. Ibid., 182.

75. John Baines, "Society, Morality, and Religious Practice," in *Religion in Ancient Egypt: Gods, Myths, and Personal Practice,* ed. Byron E. Shafer (Ithaca: Cornell University Press, 1991), 132.

76. Hoffman calls retainer burial *sati* in *Egypt before the Pharaohs,* 275–279. Wilkinson, in *Early Dynastic,* describes retainer sacrifice but also other forms of ritual human sacrifice in late predynastic and early dynastic times (265–267).

77. Assmann, *The Mind of Egypt,* 62. Barry Kemp phrases the process only slightly differently: "The 4th Dynasty and later pyramids convey a new image of kingship. Gone is the raw power of the supreme territorial ruler. The king is now sublimated into a manifestation of the sun-god. Architecture conveyed this fundamental reappraisal to the greatest possible effect." *Ancient Egypt,* 62.

78. Assmann, *The Mind of Egypt,* 125, 127.

79. Ibid., 84.

80. Egypt was divided into some twenty odd "nomes" or provinces, so that a ruler of a nome was called a nomarch. Ankhtifi had united three nomes under his rule.

81. Miriam Lichtheim, *The Old and Middle Kingdoms,* vol. 1 of *Ancient Egyptian Literature* (Berkeley: University of California Press, 1973), 86.

82. Assmann, *The Mind of Egypt,* 100.

83. Ibid., 103.

84. Ibid., 104.

85. Ibid., 127.

86. Eric Voegelin, *Israel and Revelation,* vol. 1 of *Order and History* (Baton Rouge: Louisiana State University Press, 1956), 79.

87. Assmann, *The Mind of Egypt,* 127–128.

88. Ibid., 184.

89. Ibid., 193.

90. Ibid., 131.

91. Assmann, *The Search for God,* 9.

92. In *The Ecumenic Age,* vol. 4 of *Order and History* (Baton Rouge: Louisiana State University Press, 1974), Voegelin speaks of "mytho-speculation," which becomes in vol. 5, *In Search of Order* (Baton Rouge: Louisiana State University Press, 1987), "mythospeculation," without the hyphen. What he means by the term, in his own phraseology, is as follows: "The dimension of reason in the symbolism [of mythospeculation] does not reflect the light of a fully differentiated noetic consciousness; as far as their relevance is concerned, the pragmatic materials are illuminated rather by a speculation that remains subordinate to the cosmological myth. Mythopoesis and noesis combine into a formative unit that holds an intermediate position between cosmological compactness and noetic differentiation. It will suitably be called mytho-speculation, *i.e.,* a speculation within the medium of the myth." *The Ecumenic Age,* 64.

93. Assmann, *The Search for God,* 152.

94. Ibid., 149.

95. Assmann, *Moses the Egyptian,* 45.

96. On the centrality of kingship in Egyptian culture and belief, see David O'Connor and David P. Silverman, eds., *Ancient Egyptian Kingship* (Leiden: Brill, 1995), especially the two essays by John Baines: "Kingship, Definition of Culture, and Legitimation" and "Origins of Egyptian Kingship."

97. Assmann, *The Search for God,* 17.

98. Ibid., 159.

99. Plutarch, *De Iside et Osiride,* in *Moralia* V, Loeb Classical Library (Cambridge, Mass.: Harvard University Press, 1936), 1–191.

100. Hornung, *Conceptions of God.* The very term "monotheism" is highly problematic, as will be apparent as we go along.

101. "The Instruction Addressed to King Merikare," in Lichtheim, *Old and Middle Kingdoms,* 106. For another translation and commentary, see Assmann, *The Mind of Egypt,* 189–191. See also Assmann, *The Search for God,* 171–174.

102. Assmann, *The Search for God,* 171. For a complete translation, see Lichtheim, *Old and Middle Kingdoms,* 149–163.

103. Assmann, *The Search for God,* 174–175; and commentary, 174–177. For a complete translation of the text, see Lichtheim, *Old and Middle Kingdoms,* 131–133.

104. See Walter Brueggemann, *Theology of the Old Testament: Testimony, Dispute, Advocacy* (Minneapolis: Fortress Press, 1997).

105. See especially Jan Assmann, *Egyptian Religion in the New Kingdom: Re, Amun and the Crisis of Polytheism* (London: Kegan Paul International, 1995 [1983]). The "crisis of polytheism" points especially to the Amarna religion, to be discussed below.

106. Ptah is the creator god in the so-called Memphite Theology, known from a basalt block inscribed during the reign of King Shabaka in the eighth century BCE. The inscription claims to be a copy of an Old Kingdom text, but scholars have come to believe it was actually

composed in the eighth century, though written in an archaic style. In any case it undoubtedly draws on material from the New Kingdom and even possibly the Middle Kingdom. Ptah is the god of Memphis, and Shabaka was trying to reassert the primacy of Memphis as the capital of Egypt. It should be remembered that even gods for whom universal claims were made had a local habitation. Thus Re is the god of Heliopolis, an ancient cult center near Memphis, Amun the god of Thebes, and Ptah the god of Memphis. It is the Memphite Theology that contains the famous doctrine of creation by the Word (of Ptah), though Assmann argues that it is the written word, the hieroglyph, not the spoken word, that has creative power. For a complete translation, see Lichtheim, *Old and Middle Kingdoms,* 51–57. For a commentary, see Assmann, *The Mind of Egypt,* 345–358.

107. Assmann, *The Search for God,* 223.

108. Ibid., 225.

109. Ibid., 235

110. Jan Assmann, *Egyptian Solar Religion in the New Kingdom: Re, Amun and the Crisis of Polytheism* (London: Kegan Paul International, 1995), 75.

111. Ibid., 87. Assmann notes that it was through Plotinus and ultimately Plato that Goethe got this "Egyptian" idea.

112. Erik Hornung, *Akhenaten and the Religion of Light* (Ithaca: Cornell University Press, 1999 [1995]).

113. On the indigenous development of the early state in China, see especially Li Liu, "Settlement Patterns, Chiefdom Variability, and the Development of Early States in North China," *Journal of Anthropological Archaeology* 15 (1996): 237–288. Also relevant are the many publications of Kwang-chih Chang, most conveniently his summary of the Chinese Neolithic in "China on the Eve of the Historical Period," in *The Cambridge History of Ancient China,* ed. Michael Loewe and Edward L. Shaughnessy (Cambridge: Cambridge University Press, 1999), 37–73.

114. It is, of course, true that the Shang oracle bones were lost until unearthed by modern excavations. Still, if Chinese scholars had discovered them in imperial times, they would have perhaps had some difficulty deciphering them, but they would have needed no Rosetta stone, for they would have been able to discover many links to later graphs and words.

115. Chang, "China on the Eve," 59.

116. David N. Keightley, "The Shang: China's First Historical Dynasty," in Loewe and Shaughnessy, *Ancient China,* 232.

117. Edward L. Shaughnessy, "Western Zhou History," in Loewe and Shaughnessy, *Ancient China,* 351.

118. David N. Keightley, "The Religious Commitment: Shang Theology and the Genesis of Chinese Political Culture," *History of Religions* 17, nos. 3–4 (1978): 212. I am deeply indebted to David Keightley, one of the world's leading experts on the Shang, not only for his writings but for his advice in the writing of this section.

119. A convenient summary, with judicious comments about dating, can be found in Derk Bodde, "Myths of Ancient China," in *Mythologies of the Ancient World,* ed. Samuel Noah Kramer (New York: Doubleday Anchor, 1961), 367–408. Also helpful is Sarah Allan, *The Shape of the Turtle: Myth, Art, and Cosmos in Early China* (Albany: SUNY Press, 1991).

120. David N. Keightley, "The Making of the Ancestors: Late Shang Religion and Its Legacy," in *Chinese Religion and Society: The Transformation of a Field,* vol. 1, ed. John Lagerwey (Hong Kong: University of Hong Kong Press, 2004), 13–14.

121. Perhaps we are unwise to use the term "capital." Anyang was surely a significant ritual center, but the king was not necessarily a permanent resident. Arthur Waley has the following to say of possible capitals in the early Zhou dynasty, considerations that would surely apply to the Shang: "We do not know at what date the later conception of a 'capital' began. When we discuss where the earliest kings had their 'capital,' we are perhaps committing an anachronism. Possibly in early times the center of government was where the king was at the moment." *The Book of Songs,* trans. Arthur Waley, ed. Joseph R. Allen (New York: Grove Press, 1996), 210. We have noted for other archaic territorial empires that rulers were peripatetic.

122. Paul Wheatley, *The Pivot of the Four Quarters: A Preliminary Enquiry into the Origins of the Ancient Chinese City* (Chicago: Aldine, 1971), 52–61. Wheatley's application of the idea of patrimonialism to the Shang case is particularly nuanced.

123. Trigger, *Understanding Early Civilizations,* 421–426.

124. Technically speaking, divination did not involve questions, but charges—that is, assertions that could be affirmed or denied. Thus, "[the Shang diviners] did not ask, 'Today, will it rain?' They stated, 'Today, it /may//will not/rain.' Divination was a way of telling the Powers what man wanted, and of seeking reassurance from the fact that the Powers had been informed." David N. Keightley, "Divination and Kingship in Late Shang China" (unpublished, 1991), 368.

125. Wheatley, *Pivot,* 55–56.

126. Keightley, "Making of the Ancestors," 34.

127. Ibid., 203–204.

128. Ibid., 208.

129. Ibid., 209.

130. David N. Keightley, "Spirituality in China: the Neolithic Origins" (unpublished).

131. David N. Keightley, "Shamanism, Death, and the Ancestors: Religious Mediation in Neolithic and Shang China (ca. 5000–1000 BCE)," *Asiatische Studien/Études Asiatiques* 52, no. 3 (1998): 795.

132. Herrlee G. Creel, *The Origins of Statecraft in China,* vol. 1, *The Western Chou Empire* (Chicago: University of Chicago Press, 1970), 495–500. David Keightley (personal communication) indicates that subsequent research confirms Creel's view that there is no Shang evidence for the use of *Tian* in the Zhou sense.

133. *Book of Songs,* trans. Waley, nos. 255, 261. The Allen edition of Waley's translation uses the traditional Mao numbers and, by providing new translations of the few entries untranslated by Waley, gives a complete translation of the traditional book.

134. Wheatley, *Pivot,* 118–122.

135. Creel, *Origins of Statecraft,* 320.

136. Ibid., 168–170, 381–382, 387–416. I have not been able to find any discussion by either Creel or Wheatley of the other's views. Creel's book was published in 1970 and Wheatley's in 1971, so it is quite possible that neither was aware of the other's argument.

137. Ibid., 419.

138. As does Edward L. Shaughnessy for his own purposes in his *Before Confucius: Studies in the Creation of the Chinese Classics* (Albany: SUNY Press, 1997).

139. Shaughnessy, in *Before Confucius,* reviews the arguments for the dating of the earliest chapters of the *Shu,* indicating that Herlee Creel believed that some of them date from the time of the Duke of Zhou himself, whereas David Keightley held that they were probably composed toward the end of the Western Zhou period. Shaughnessy himself holds that although the critical chapters cannot be exactly dated, "there can be no doubt that they long predate the hagiographical traditions that, by about the time of Confucius, developed around the Duke of Zhou; they thus almost certainly reflect historiographical concerns of the Western Zhou period" (130–131). Shaughnessy also discusses the dating of various chapters of the *Shu* in his *"Shang shu,"* in *Early Chinese Texts: A Bibliographical Guide,* ed. Michael Loewe (Berkeley: Society for the Study of Early China, Institute of East Asian Studies, University of California, Berkeley, 1993), 377–380.

140. Shaughnessy, *Before Confucius,* 115. See Bernhard Karlgren's translation of the *"Shao gao"* in his *The Book of Documents,* Museum of Far Eastern Antiquities, Bulletin 22 (Stockholm, 1950): 48–51.

141. See especially Shaughnessy, "Western Zhou History," 317, but also more generally 313–317 of that article; and *Before Confucius,* 101–164.

142. Cho-yun Hsu and Katheryn M. Linduff, *Western Chou Civilization* (New Haven: Yale University Press, 1988), 111. By "Jaspersian breakthrough" the authors mean the axial breakthrough, as the term "axial age" was first put into general use by Karl Jaspers in *The Origin and Goal of History* (London: Routledge and Kegan Paul, 1953 [1949]).

143. Translation from Creel, *Origins of Statecraft,* 98. The words within the square brackets are Creel's. Cf. Karlgren, *The Book of Documents,* 59.

144. Translation from Creel, *Origins of Statecraft,* 99.

145. Karlgren, *The Book of Documents,* 46.

146. *Book of Songs,* trans. Waley, nos. 172, 146.

147. Ibid., nos. 253, 256. Here "middle kingdom" does not yet mean China but the central Zhou domain.

148. Ibid., nos. 113, 88.

149. Ibid., nos. 288, 302.

150. Ibid., nos. 204, 188.

151. Ibid., nos. 209, 195.

152. Ibid., nos. 194, 172.

153. Ibid., nos. 193, 172.

154. *Analects* 3:14. See *The Analects of Confucius,* trans. Arthur Waley (London: Allen and Unwin, 1938), 97. Chinese words have been rendered here in Pinyin. For discussion of this system, see Chapter 8, note 1.

155. When I said that China was the one case of unbroken continuity from the Neolithic to the present, I was only partly right. Japan also shows such continuity. I have, however, argued that although Japan moved from the Neolithic to the archaic, it never, to this day, has become an axial civilization. This may appear an odd assertion, as Japan has absorbed several major axial traditions: Confucianism, Buddhism, Christianity, and the Western

Enlightenment, including its successors such as Marxism. Thus, clearly, Japan is not pre-axial, as all other archaic cases have been; yet, I would argue, it is non-axial, because it has used, with great brilliance and success, axial culture to defend its archaic presuppositions. I have made this argument elsewhere at length, so it does not require repetition here. See "Introduction: The Japanese Difference," in Robert N. Bellah, *Imagining Japan: The Japanese Tradition and Its Modern Interpretation* (Berkeley: University of California Press, 2003), 1–62. S. N. Eisenstadt has made a similar argument in his *Japanese Civilization* (Chicago: University of Chicago Press, 1997).

156. Kramer (*History Begins at Sumer,* 123) sums it up with a laconic Sumerian proverb:

You go and carry off the enemy's land;

The enemy comes and carries off your land.

157. Lewis Mumford, *The Myth of the Machine: Technics and Human Development* (New York: Harcourt, Brace, 1967), 164.

158. Jacobsen, "Mesopotamia," 147.

159. We should not forget Paul Radin's *Primitive Man as Philosopher* (New York: Dover, 1957 [1927]), though some of the speculation reported there seems to me to have been stimulated by missionary interrogation and would not likely have been produced in precontact times.

160. Voegelin, *Israel and Revelation,* 8.

161. Jacobsen, "Mesopotamia," 217.

162. Mumford, *Myth,* 186.

6. The Axial Age I

1. An earlier version of the introduction to this chapter appeared as the essay "What Is Axial about the Axial Age," *Archives Européennes de Sociologie* 46, no. 1 (2005): 69–89, Cambridge University Press. Copyright © 2005 Archives Européennes de Sociology. Reprinted with permission of the publisher.

2. Thorkild Jacobsen, "The Cosmos as a State," in *Before Philosophy: The Intellectual Adventure of Ancient Man*, ed. Henri Frankfort, Mrs. Henri Frankfort, John A. Wilson, and Thorkild Jacobsen (Harmondsworth: Pelican, 1949 [1946]), 137–199.

3. Marcel Gauchet, in *The Disenchantment of the World: A Political History of Religion* (Princeton: Princeton University Press, 1997 [1985]), makes the point that the emergence of the state focusing on a divine or quasi-divine king destabilizes the equilibrium of what he calls "primeval religion," which he describes as both egalitarian and immobile. Though his notion of pre-state religion as "the reign of the absolute past" is hardly adequate, failing as it does to catch the openness and diversity of such religions, his emphasis on the emergence of the archaic state as the essential precondition for the axial age is surely correct. See esp. chaps. 1 and 2, and pp. 23–46.

4. Christianity and Islam fall outside the axial age chronologically, but they are historically intelligible only as developments of Israel's axial breakthrough.

5. Eric Voegelin, *Israel and Revelation,* vol. 1 of *Order and History* (Baton Rouge: Louisiana State University Press, 1956), 164.

6. Arnaldo Momigliano, *Alien Wisdom: The Limits of Hellenization* (Cambridge: Cambridge University Press, 1975), 8–9.

7. Karl Jaspers, *The Origin and Goal of History* (London: Routledge and Kegan Paul, 1953 [1949]), 1.

8. Ibid., 4.

9. Ibid., 6.

10. Susan and Andrew Sherratt, in "The Growth of the Mediterranean Economy in the Early First Millennium BCE," *World Archaeology* 24 (1993): 361–378, describe the remarkable economic growth of the first half of the first millennium in the Near East and the Mediterranean: "In 1000 BCE most of the Mediterranean was effectively prehistoric; by 500 BCE it formed a series of well differentiated zones within a world-system." There was not only a significant growth of trade, but an increase in manufacturing, urbanization, and literacy throughout the Mediterranean basin. The Sherratts attribute the driving force of this change to Phoenicia, under Assyrian pressure, especially from the tenth through the eighth centuries. Only from the seventh century do the Greeks begin to rival the Phoenicians in trade and colonization. Similar developments, though perhaps a few centuries later, have been observed in northern India and northern China.

11. "Neo-Assyrian" to distinguish it from the Old Assyrian state (ca. 1900–ca. 1830 BCE) and the Middle Assyrian state (ca. 1400–ca. 1050).

12. See Momigliano, *Alien Wisdom,* chap. 6, "Iranians and Greeks," 123–150, on the disappointing quality of the surviving Greek observations of the Persian Empire, as well as the severe limitations of all other forms of documentation.

13. Max Weber, *Economy and Society,* ed. Guenther Roth and Claus Wittich (Berkeley: University of California Press, 1978 [1921–1922]), 441–442, 447.

14. Eric Voegelin, *Order and History,* 5 vols. (Baton Rouge: Louisiana State University Press, 1956–1987).

15. Eric Voegelin, *The World of the Polis,* vol. 2 of *Order and History* (1957), 19–23. In vol. 4, *The Ecumenic Age* (1974), 2–6, Voegelin abandons the idea that leaps in being can be located at any specific period in history, while admitting his earlier debt to Jaspers.

16. S. N. Eisenstadt, "Introduction: The Axial Age Breakthroughs—Their Characteristics and Origins," in *The Origins and Diversity of the Axial Age,* ed. S. N. Eisenstadt (Albany: SUNY Press, 1986), 1. Eisenstadt recognizes the contributions of Jaspers and Voegelin, and also of the Daedalus conference on the axial age organized by Benjamin Schwartz and published as *Wisdom, Revelation, and Doubt: Perspectives on the First Millennium* B.C., special issue, *Daedalus* 104, no. 2 (Spring 1975). In particular, Eisenstadt noted the emphasis on "the strain toward transcendence" in the axial age in Schwartz's essay "The Age of Transcendence" in the *Daedalus* volume. See also S. N. Eisenstadt, *Comparative Civilizations and Multiple Modernities,* 2 vols. (Leiden: Brill, 2003), especially the essays in vol. 1, pt. 2, "Axial Civilizations." The most recent collection of work on the axial age in which Eisenstadt has been engaged is *Axial Civilizations and World History,* ed. Johann P. Arnason, S. N. Eisenstadt, and Björn Wittrock (Leiden: Brill, 2005).

17. For doubts about China, see Mark Elvin, "Was There a Transcendental Breakthrough in China?" in Eisenstadt, *Origins and Diversity,* 325–359. Similar arguments have been made with respect to Greece.

18. Johann Arnason, "The Axial Age and Its Interpreters: Reopening a Debate," in Arnason, Eisenstadt, and Wittrock, *Axial Civilizations,* 31–32. He refers to a passage in Jaspers, *Origin and Goal,* 2.

19. Merlin Donald, *Origins of the Modern Mind: Three Stages in the Evolution of Culture and Cognition* (Cambridge, Mass.: Harvard University Press, 1991), 214.

20. Ibid., 269.

21. Ibid., 272.

22. Ibid., 312.

23. Ibid., 273.

24. Jerome Bruner, *Actual Minds, Possible Worlds* (Cambridge, Mass.: Harvard University Press, 1986), xiii. I discovered the source of the James quotation in "Brute and Human Intelligence," in William James, *Writings, 1878–1899* (New York: Library of America, 1992 [1878]), 911.

25. Lucien Lévy-Bruhl, *La mentalité primitive* (Paris: Librairie Felix Alcan, 1922); translated into English as *Primitive Mentality* (London: George Allen and Unwin, 1923). A careful reading of Lévy-Bruhl will disclose that he was not as ridiculous as he has been made out to be.

26. Donald, *Origins of the Modern Mind,* 339–340.

27. Ibid., 341.

28. Yehuda Elkana, "The Emergence of Second-Order Thinking in Classical Greece," in Eisenstadt, *Origins and Diversity,* 40–64. Eisenstadt frequently uses the phrase "second-order thinking" as a synonym for his term "reflexivity."

29. Momigliano, *Alien Wisdom,* 9.

30. Elkana, "Emergence," 64.

31. See David Hume, *The Natural History of Religion,* chap. 9, "Comparison of these Religions [polytheism and monotheism], with regard to Persecution and Toleration," where Hume compares polytheistic toleration with monotheistic "zeal and rancour, the most furious and implacable of all human passions." *Hume on Religion,* ed. Richard Wollheim (New York: Meridian, 1964 [1757]), 65.

32. Jan Assmann, *Moses the Egyptian: The Memory of Egypt in Western Monotheism* (Cambridge, Mass.: Harvard University Press, 1997), 25. See also Erik Hornung, *Akhenaten and the Religion of Light* (Ithaca: Cornell University Press, 1999 [1995]).

33. "The Great Hymn to the Aten," Miriam Lichtheim, in *Ancient Egyptian Literature,* vol. 2, *The New Kingdom* (Berkeley: University of California Press, 1976), 96–100.

34. James P. Allen, "The Natural Philosophy of Akhenaten," in *Religion and Philosophy in Ancient Egypt,* ed. W. K. Simpson, *Yale Egyptological Studies* 3 (1989): 89–101. See also Jan Assmann, "Akhanyati's Theology of Light and Time," *Proceedings of the Israel Academy of Sciences and Humanities* 7, no. 4 (1992): 143–175; and Assmann, *The Mind of Egypt: History and Meaning in the Time of the Pharaohs* (Cambridge, Mass.: Harvard University Press, 2003 [1996]), 214–228.

35. Arnaldo Momigliano, "Religion in Athens, Rome, and Jerusalem in the First Century B.C.," in *On Pagans, Jews, and Christians* (Middletown, Conn.: Wesleyan University Press, 1987), 76–77. How far back the handshake goes, we do not know, though Momigliano reports it for the Persians and the Celts as well as the Greeks and Romans.

36. Randall Collins, *Interaction Ritual Chains* (Princeton: Princeton University Press, 2004), 53–54. He also argues, convincingly to me, that genuine learning requires the physical presence of teachers and students, so that "distance learning" is ersatz at best.

37. Hubert L. Dreyfus and Stuart E. Dreyfus, *Mind over Machine: The Power of Human Intuition and Expertise in the Age of the Computer* (New York: Simon and Schuster, 1986).

38. Jerome Bruner, *Acts of Meaning* (Cambridge, Mass.: Harvard University Press, 1990), 111.

39. Walter J. Ong, *Orality and Literacy* (London: Methuen, 1982), 66–67. This is not the place to pursue the important issue of the relation between orality and literacy, but Walter Ong in several books besides the one cited has made important contributions, as have Eric Havelock and Jack Goody.

40. Eric Weil, "What Is a Breakthrough in History?" *Daedalus* 104, no. 2 (Spring 1975): 21–36.

41. Ibid., 26.

42. Jaspers, *Origin and Goal,* 20.

43. Weil, "What Is a Breakthrough," 22.

44. Niels Peter Lemche, in *Prelude to Israel's Past: Background and Beginnings of Israelite History and Identity* (Peabody, Mass.: Hendrickson, 1998), 222–225, considers possible dates and tends to believe, though there are valid arguments for a variety of dates, that the Persian or Hellenistic periods are the most likely.

45. Moshe Weinfeld argues for a number of parallels between Greco-Roman migration/foundation stories and Israelite ones. He cites, in particular, a number of structural parallels between the *Aeneid* and the Abraham stories in Genesis. He also calls attention to parallels with the Exodus/Moses narrative. See Weinfeld, *The Promise of the Land: The Inheritance of the Land of Canaan by the Israelites* (Berkeley: University of California Press, 1993), 1–21.

46. Mark S. Smith, *The Memoirs of God: History, Memory, and the Experience of the Divine in Ancient Israel* (Minneapolis: Fortress Press, 2004), 24. Some have suggested that Exodus 15, Genesis 49, and Deuteronomy 33 may be premonarchical; others date them to the early monarchy.

47. For a summary of these arguments, see Norman K. Gottwald, *The Politics of Ancient Israel* (Louisville, Ky.: Westminster John Knox Press, 2001), 158–162.

48. One might note that the pharaoh claims to have utterly destroyed the Israelites—but then victory inscriptions were famously exaggerated.

49. Donald B. Redford, *Egypt, Canaan, and Israel in Ancient Times* (Princeton: Princeton University Press, 1992), 208–209.

50. Alexander H. Joffe, "The Rise of Secondary States in the Iron Age Levant," *Journal of the Economic and Social History of the Orient* 45, no. 4 (2002): 437.

51. Ibid., 440.

52. On the Edomite origin of Yahweh and the close relation between early Israel and early Edom, see Smith, *The Memoirs of God,* 27, 153–154, 170–171.

53. On the folk etymology of the name Israel as "God rules," see Stephen A. Geller, *Sacred Enigmas: Literary Religion in the Hebrew Bible* (London: Routledge, 1996), 22. On Isra-el vs. Isra-yahu, see Smith, *The Memoirs of God,* 26.

54. Karel van der Toorn, *Family Religion in Babylonia, Syria and Israel: Continuity and Change in the Forms of Religious Life* (Leiden: Brill, 1996), 254–255.

55. See especially Frank M. Cross Jr., *Canaanite Myth and Hebrew Epic: Essays in the History of the Religion of Israel* (Cambridge, Mass.: Harvard University Press, 1970). See also Mark S. Smith, *The Origins of Biblical Monotheism: Israel's Polytheistic Background and the Ugaritic Texts* (New York: Oxford University Press, 2001).

56. Rainer Albertz, *A History of Israelite Religion in the Old Testament Period*, vol. 1, *From the Beginnings to the End of the Monarchy* (Louisville, Ky.: Westminster John Knox Press, 1994 [1992]), 32.

57. The evidence for a number of gods in early Israel is overwhelming. Ziony Zevit signals this new consensus in his use of the plural in the title of his book, *The Religions of Ancient Israel: A Synthesis of Parallactic Approaches* (London: Continuum, 2001). Mark S. Smith has meticulously examined the evidence in several books: *The Early History of God: Yahweh and the Other Deities in Ancient Israel* (San Francisco: Harper San Francisco, 1990; 2nd ed., Grand Rapids, Mich.: Eerdmans, 2002); *The Origins of Biblical Monotheism*; and *The Memoirs of God*. The use of the word "polytheism" is purely descriptive. The suffix *-ism* in this case does not refer to any theory nor, certainly, does it refer to any contrast with "monotheism."

58. Albertz, *History of Israelite Religion*, 1:32.

59. Joffe, "Rise of Secondary States," 425.

60. Ibid., 445.

61. See the discussion of Gideon and Abimelech in Gottwald, *Politics of Ancient Israel*, 42–43.

62. Frank Cross, in his *Canaanite Myth*, writes, "The institution of prophecy appeared simultaneously with kingship in Israel and fell with kingship. This is no coincidence:. . . the charismatic principle of leadership which obtained in the era of the Judges survived in its liveliest form in the office of the prophet" (223). Cross argues that Samuel was paradigmatic in that he designated the one chosen by Yahweh to be king; he judged the acts of the king and could take away the designation; and he could declare holy war (223–224).

63. The term for prophet came to be used for figures earlier than Samuel, above all for Moses, the superprophet, but that is a later development, probably late- or postmonarchical. On Moses as superprophet, see Geller, *Sacred Enigmas*, 192.

64. Even more strangely, it was God who incited David to make the census out of anger at Israel. 2 Samuel 24:1.

65. Albertz, *History of Israelite Religion*, 1:140–143. Mark Smith has discussed the possibility that the original God of the Exodus was El, not Yahweh. See his *Origins of Biblical Monotheism*, 146–148.

66. "Divine sons" follows the Greek text. The Masoretic Hebrew text says "children of Israel," but this is thought to be an alteration to avoid just the implications described below.

67. On the transition from general Western Semitic ideas of the pantheon to that of early Israel, see the much richer and more detailed account in Smith, *The Memoirs of God*, 101–119; and also Smith, *Origins of Biblical Monotheism*, 142ff.

68. Mark Smith notes that history has seen a shift from "a world theology relating [Israel's] god to the gods of other nations" to "a cosmic theology of a single deity," to a common version

of world theology today in which the world's religions "pursue different paths toward reality and truth." See his *Memoirs of God,* 171.

69. For the process of convergence and differentiation, see Mark Smith, *Early History of God,* 7–9.

70. Van der Toorn, *Family Religion,* 277–281.

71. Steven W. Holloway, *Aššur Is King! Aššur Is King! Religion in the Exercise of Power in the Neo-Assyrian Empire* (Leiden: Brill, 2002), 260.

72. The narrative tradition can be seen in part as a qualification of the liturgical elevation of David to near-divinity. The David narrative (esp. 2 Samuel 9:1 to 20:26) is a literary masterpiece on a par, in the entire Hebrew Bible, only with the Joseph story in Genesis. It is a depiction of David as very human, experiencing great triumphs but also terrible loss, and suffering the decline of extreme old age. But the narrative text also contains the Lord's promise that David's house will stand forever—it comes to David through the words of the prophet Samuel, which echo the similar passage in Psalm 89. See 2 Samuel 7:12–16.

73. Smith, *Origins of Biblical Monotheism,* 160, discusses the arguments about whether David is really addressed as "God" in this text. Many have attempted to read it otherwise.

74. For commentary on these passages, see Albertz, *History of Israelite Religion,* 1:116–122. Note the New Testament resonance of these terms.

75. Holloway, *Aššur Is King!,* 189.

76. The dating of Psalm 89 and of various passages in it is not a matter on which I have any competence to speak, but verses 30 to 33 sound very much like Deuteronomy, a late monarchical text, and could well have been added later to qualify the extravagance of the early text.

77. Jon D. Levenson, *Sinai and Zion: An Entry into the Jewish Bible* (Minneapolis: Seabury, 1985), 108–109.

78. For a discussion of these issues, see Albertz, *History of Israelite Religion,* 1:122–138.

79. Levenson, *Sinai and Zion,* 94.

80. Note that Clifford Geertz, in *Negara: The Theatre State in Nineteenth-Century Bali* (Princeton: Princeton University Press, 1980), describes a situation where each of several rulers, dividing between them the small island of Bali, claimed to be ruler of the universe.

81. But we must remember that Israel has never abandoned Zion, has always held Sinai and Zion somehow together. For a superb analysis of how this was possible, see Levenson, *Sinai and Zion.*

82. For an extensive discussion of the Yahweh-alone movement, see Morton Smith, *Palestinian Parties and Politics That Shaped the Old Testament* (New York: Columbia University Press, 1971). "Yahweh alone" is ambiguous from a theoretical point of view: it could mean the obligation to worship only Yahweh although other gods exist, or it could mean only Yahweh exists. Using Greek roots, the first option is called monolatry and the second monotheism. "Yahweh alone" translates Hebrew words and is preferable to language with built-in Greek preconceptions.

83. Geller, *Sacred Enigmas,* 193.

84. Albertz, *History of Israelite Religion,* 1:159–170.

85. Compare van der Toorn, *Family Religion.*

86. Robert R. Wilson, in his *Prophecy and Society in Ancient Israel* (Philadelphia: Fortress Press, 1980), gives a valuable summary of information about prophecy in comparative perspective, as well as in Israel.

87. On Isaiah, see Abraham J. Heschel, *The Prophets: An Introduction* (New York: Harper, 1969), 61–97; and Wilson, *Prophecy and Society,* 270–274. Wilson suggests that the account of the political situation involving Isaiah to be found in 2 Kings 18:17–19:9a, 36–37, describes him as a prophet in the northern tradition, though what he views as a later addition, 2 Kings 19:9b–35, shows him as a spokesman for the Jerusalemite royal theology (*Prophecy and Society,* 213–219).

88. Zevit, *Religions of Ancient Israel,* 653.

89. Geller, *Sacred Enigmas,* 176.

90. See George Mendenhall, "Law and Covenant in Israel and the Ancient Near East," *Biblical Archaeologist* 17 (1954): 49–76.

91. Moshe Weinfeld, *Deuteronomy and the Deuteronomic School* (London: Oxford University Press, 1972). Eckart Otto, in "Political Theology in Judah and Assyria: The Beginning of the Hebrew Bible as Literature," *Svensk exegetisk arsbok* 65 (2000): 59–76, has extended the Assyrian model to Exodus and the Moses narrative.

92. Geller, *Sacred Enigmas,* 182–183.

93. Holloway has this to say, in *Aššur Is King!:* "The vassal treaties of Esarhaddon yield important and explicit data on the manner in which vassals were expected to comport themselves in the presence of their overlords' pantheon. The vassal is commanded to 'fear *(lipluḫū)*' Aššur, 'your god *(ilkunu)*'; he is enjoined to guard the image *(ṣalmu)* of 'Aššur, king of the gods and the great gods, my lords,' the images of the king, the crown prince, and the seals of Aššur and the king which are presumably meant to refer to those on the vassal treaty tablets themselves" (61).

94. William L. Moran has written the classic article on this point: "The Ancient Near Eastern Background to the Love of God in Deuteronomy," *Catholic Biblical Quarterly* 25 (1963): 77–87.

95. See especially Weinfeld, *Deuteronomy,* pt. 1, chap. 2, 59–158.

96. Ibid., 77–78.

97. Ibid., 117–118, citing Deuteronomy 28.

98. Baruch Halpern, "Jerusalem and the Lineages in the Seventh Century BCE: Kinship and the Rise of Individual Moral Liability," in *Law and Ideology in Monarchic Israel,* ed. Baruch Halpern and Deborah W. Hobson (Sheffield: JSOT Press, 1991), 11–107.

99. Halpern argues that the shift from collective moral responsibility to individual responsibility to be found in the texts of Deuteronomy, Jeremiah, and Ezekiel can be understood as reflecting these social conditions: "Traditional Judahite culture was gone for good, swept away in the scheme of Assyrian deportations," which "loosened the ties between the fates of individuals and those of their ancestors and collaterals" ("Jerusalem," 79).

100. Otto, "Political Theology," 73–74. Otto points out that the story was Neo-Assyrian in origin but attributed to Sargon of Akkad, who reigned in the third millennium BCE and was thus part of an archaizing movement with parallels in Egypt (where the late "Memphite Theology" was attributed to the Old Kingdom). Thus the elevation of the archaic figure of Moses to centrality was the Israelite parallel of tendencies general in the Near East at the

time. Otto finds that other details of the Moses epic, however, were derived from contemporary Assyrian royal ideology.

101. Ibid., 75. If the vassal treaty of Esarhaddon was the model for many of the stipulations in Deuteronomy, it is hard to see how they would still have been available to provide a model for writers in exilic or postexilic times.

102. Michael Walzer, *Exodus and Revolution* (New York: Basic Books, 1985), 66.

103. David Malo, *Hawaiian Antiquities* (Honolulu: Bernice P. Bishop Museum, 1951 [1898]), 57.

104. Walzer, *Exodus and Revolution,* 66–68.

105. Ibid., 126.

106. Machiavelli, calling Moses a "prophet armed," went on to say that "all armed prophets win, and unarmed ones fall" because people are variable and the prophet must be ready "to make them believe by force." *The Prince,* chap. 6, in Niccolò Machiavelli, *The Chief Works and Others,* vol. 1, trans. Allan Gilbert (Durham, N.C.: Duke University Press, 1965), 26. (Machiavelli is silent about the ways in which unarmed prophets may also "win.") In *The Discourses,* 3.30.4, Machiavelli discusses the passage from Exodus 32 cited above and writes, "He who reads the Bible with discernment will see that, before Moses set about making laws and institutions, he had to kill a very great number of men who, out of envy and nothing else, were opposed to his plans." *The Discourses of Niccolò Machiavelli,* vol. 1, trans. Leslie J. Walker (London: Routledge and Kegan Paul, 1975), 547. It is also of interest that Machiavelli insists that if a new commonwealth is to be formed or an old one thoroughly reformed, there must be one sole authority. He writes in *The Discourses,* 1.9.2, in a context where Moses is mentioned as an example, "One should take it as a general rule that rarely, if ever, does it happen that a state, whether a republic or a kingdom, is either well-ordered at the outset or radically transformed vis-à-vis its old institutions unless this be done by one person. It is likewise essential that there should be but one person upon whose mind and method depends any similar process of organization." *Discourses of Niccolò Machiavelli,* trans. Walker, 1:234. This observation might be helpful in understanding the overwhelming emphasis on the single ruler in all the early states.

107. Marc Zvi Brettler, in his *God as King: Understanding an Israelite Metaphor,* JSOT Supplement Series 76 (Sheffield: Sheffield Academic Press, 1989), holds that God as king "is the predominant relational metaphor used of God in the Bible, appearing much more frequently than metaphors such as 'God as lover/husband' or 'God as a father'" (160).

108. Geller, *Sacred Enigmas,* 192.

109. Ibid., 31.

110. Ibid., 50.

111. According to Otto, "Political Theology," 65, "Even the Deuteronomic revision of the Covenant Code according to the aspect of cult-centralization in Deuteronomy was guided by an anti-Assyrian impulse. If YHWH was to compete with the Assyrian God Aššur and Jerusalem with the capital of Aššur, which housed the only Aššur temple in the Assyrian empire, then YHWH's worship was not to be dispersed to several sanctuaries in Judean villages and towns."

112. See Mary Douglas, *Leviticus as Literature* (Oxford: Oxford University Press, 1999); and, especially, Douglas, *Jacob's Tears: The Priestly Work of Reconciliation* (Oxford: Oxford University Press, 2004).

113. See Geller's valuable interpretation of the Priestly work in chap. 4 of *Sacred Enigmas*, 62–86. For the later influence of this tradition, see esp. 85–86. Geller also interestingly notes that P offers a New Cult, by no means identical with the old royal cult, for P "amputated the role of the king completely" (82).

114. Stephen A. Geller, "The God of the Covenant," in *One God or Many? Concepts of Divinity in the Ancient World*, ed. Barbara Nevling Porter, *Transactions of the Casco Bay Assyriological Institute* 1 (2000): 286.

115. Jürgen Habermas, who finds the very germ of reason in the first commandment, has this to say: "From a philosophical point of view, the first commandment expresses that 'leap forward' on the cognitive level which granted man freedom of reflection, the strength to detach himself from vacillating immediacy, to emancipate himself from his generational shackles and the whims of mythical powers." Quoted in Sandro Magister, "The Church Is under Siege, but Habermas, the Atheist, Is Coming to Its Defense," www.chiesa.repubblica.it.

116. Geller, "God of the Covenant," 293, but see the whole discussion, 290–296. I have added the rest of verse 5, which Geller doesn't quote here, together with the Hebrew for the key terms, which he does discuss. In the same essay Geller discusses the relation between God's transcendence and his availability to humans in relation to the question of his name. When Moses asks God for his name, God replies, "I am what I am" (or "shall be what I shall be") (Exodus 3:13–14, Geller's translation). Given the ancient Near Eastern idea that one's name is one's power, God is reticent in answering Moses's question. In two other passages God (or an angel) refuses to give his name: Genesis 32, Judges 13. Yet God tells Moses that Yahweh, "he is," the form the name "I am" naturally takes in the third person (Exodus 15, Geller's translation), is "my name forever." Geller comments: "In such an ancient, and biblical, context it is clear that God has refused to reveal his true name to Moses, and to Israel. He replies, 'I am whatever I am,' and that will suffice. It is, in fact, a mild rebuke. But in terms of the immediate context of rescue, and the future one of covenant, 'I am / shall be' is a totally meaningful name, because it takes up the promise earlier in the story that 'I shall be with you.' In other words, on a cosmic level God remains unknown and unknowable, but in relation to Israel, he is to be forever accessible." Geller, "God of the Covenant," 307.

117. Ibid., 295–296.

118. Timothy Polk, *The Prophetic Persona: Jeremiah and the Language of the Self*, JSOT Supplement Series 32 (Sheffield: Sheffield Academic Press, 1984). Polk makes it clear that he is analyzing the Jeremiah of the text as we have it, and is not trying to discover the "real" Jeremiah of history, a quest that may not be hopeless but is not essential for his purpose.

119. Polk, *The Prophetic Persona*, 44.

120. Ibid., 149–150.

121. Ibid., 148.

122. See the remarkable essay by Jochanan Muffs, "Who Will Stand in the Breach? A Study of Prophetic Intercession," in *Love and Joy: Law, Language and Religion in Ancient Israel* (Cambridge, Mass.: Harvard University Press, 1992), 9–48.

123. Smith, *Origins of Biblical Monotheism*, 179. Smith's analysis of "Second Isaiah," which I have found most helpful, says that the use of quotation marks reminds us that we do not know if the author or authors of this text ever intended it to be read as a separate work.

124. Ibid., 179. The criticism of idolatry, though understandable in terms of the emphasis on Yahweh as the one God, was quite unfair. The Babylonians, for example, had great affection for Marduk's temple and his image contained therein, but they did not believe his image "was" Marduk, only that he was on occasion present there. Marduk was a great cosmic God of storm and empire and could never be wholly identified with any image. See Jon Levenson, "Is There a Counterpart in the Hebrew Bible to New Testament Antisemitism?" *Journal of Ecumenical Studies* 22 (1985): 242–260.

125. Axel Honneth, *The Struggle for Recognition: The Moral Grammar of Social Conflicts* (Cambridge, Mass.: MIT Press, 1996). Honneth has worked out his three phases of recognition in the context of modern history and believes that they are not so clearly distinguished in premodern times. I will argue that recognition as love and recognition as justice are explicit in the Hebrew scriptures, but recognition as creator of value remains largely implicit.

126. Peter Machinist has surveyed the biblical passages that insist on Israel's distinctiveness from other peoples and has found that they concentrate on two issues: the uniqueness of Israel's God and the uniqueness of Israel as a people. Machinist, "The Question of Distinctiveness in Ancient Israel: An Essay," in *Ah, Assyria . . . : Studies in Assyrian History and Ancient Near Eastern Historiography Presented to Hayim Tadmor,* ed. Mordechai Cogan and Israel Eph'al (Jerusalem: Magnes Press, Hebrew University, 1991), 196–212.

127. Geller, *Sacred Enigmas,* 181.

128. Walter Brueggemann, *Theology of the Old Testament: Testimony, Dispute, Advocacy* (Minneapolis: Fortress Press, 1997).

129. An insight that Hegel came to see in his late lectures on the philosophy of religion, after having initially thought of the Jews as living in bondage to the law. Georg Wilhelm Friedrich Hegel, *Lectures on the Philosophy of Religion,* vol. 2 (Berkeley: University of California Press, 1987 [1827]), 679.

130. See Jon D. Levenson, *Creation and the Persistence of Evil: The Jewish Drama of Divine Omnipotence* (Princeton: Princeton University Press, 1988).

131. Ibid., 86.

7. The Axial Age II

1. Louis Gernet (1882–1962) was the student of Durkheim who specialized in ancient Greece; he was one year ahead of Marcel Granet, the Durkheimian who specialized in ancient China. Gernet spent thirty years, from 1918 until 1948, teaching Greek composition at the University of Algiers. Although he continued to publish, he worked in comparative isolation during these years when the Durkheim school was in disarray. But in 1948, at the age of 66, he returned to Paris to teach at the École Pratique des Hautes Études, and it was only then that he built up a following among younger classicists. On his career, see S. C. Humphreys, "The Work of Louis Gernet," in her *Anthropology and the Greeks* (London: Routledge and Kegan Paul, 1978), 76–106. Paul Cartledge makes note of the remarkable revival of work influenced by Durkheim in postwar France when he writes: "In terms of intellectual vitality and influence there is only one possible rival within the domain of the 'Sciences Humaines' in France to the so-called 'Annales School' of sociologically minded historians inspired by Marc Bloch and Lucien Febvre, and that is the 'Paris School' of cul-

tural historians of ancient Greece and especially ancient Greek religion and mythology dominated for the past three decades by J.-P. Vernant. It is no accident (as they say) that both 'Schools' were crucially influenced in their origins by the work of the sociohistorical psychologist Émile Durkheim." Translator's introduction in Louise Bruit Zaidman and Pauline Schmitt Pantel, *Religion in the Ancient Greek City* (Cambridge: Cambridge University Press, 1989), xv–xvi.

2. Louis Gernet, "Ancient Feasts" (1955), in *The Anthropology of Ancient Greece* (Baltimore: Johns Hopkins University Press, 1981 [1968]), 35. The *agapai* with which this passage closes were "love feasts" in which gods and men participated together.

3. Hugh Lloyd-Jones, *The Justice of Zeus* (Berkeley: University of California Press, 1971), 3, citing *Iliad* 2:462f. and 17:446–447.

4. Ibid., 3–4.

5. Although there is no evidence that the Greeks ever considered themselves chosen as such, it is possible, as we will see below, that the Athenians felt chosen by Athena.

6. To a Greek audience it may be that Hector did not seem as admirable, particularly in comparison to Achilles, as he does to us.

7. E. R. Dodds in *The Greeks and the Irrational* (Berkeley: University of California Press, 1951), 35, 54, citing Aristotle's *Magna Moralia* 1208B.30 and *Nicomachean Ethics* 1159A.5. But Dodds also points out that "we can hardly doubt that the Athenians loved their goddess" (54).

8. The term *anax* was also used for Priam and a few other leaders.

9. Eric Havelock has a useful discussion of the terminology of *anax* and *basileus* in Homer in *The Greek Concept of Justice: From the Shadow in Homer to the Substance in Plato* (Cambridge, Mass.: Harvard University Press, 1978), 94–99.

10. In Chapter 6 we saw that the opposite is true in the Hebrew scriptures, where Yahweh is more often referred to as king than as father, even though, on the whole, Yahweh is more "fatherly" to the Israelites than Zeus is to the Greeks.

11. My research assistant, Timothy Doran, did a comprehensive search for me of all the uses of *anax* and *basileus* in Homer, Hesiod, and the Homeric hymns. Also, his findings on Zeus as *pater* were most helpful.

12. See Jonathan M. Hall, *Ethnic Identity in Greek Antiquity* (Cambridge: Cambridge University Press, 1997), for a discussion of the reasons for doubting that though Dorian is indeed a dialect of Greek, "the Dorians" can be viewed as a cultural or military group in Mycenaean or archaic times. See also Hall's *Hellenicity: Between Ethnicity and Culture* (Chicago: Chicago University Press, 2002).

13. Ian Morris, *Archaeology as Cultural History: Words and Things in Iron Age Greece* (Malden, Mass.: Blackwell, 2000), 202, 203, 206–207.

14. Oscillations between hierarchy and egalitarianism in the ancient Near East have been documented from the earliest times. On the Natufians in the Levant, see Ofer Bar-Yoseph, "From Sedentary Foragers to Village Hierarchies: The Emergence of Social Institutions," in *The Origins of Human Social Institutions*, ed. W. G. Runciman (New York: Oxford University Press, 2001), 1–38.

15. Walter Donlan, "Chief and Followers in Pre-State Greece," in *The Aristocratic Ideal and Selected Papers* (Wauconda, Ill.: Bolchazi-Carducci, 1999), 355. The books of the *Odyssey*

in question are those that recount the adventures of "Odysseus and his followers (*hetairoi* = 'companions,' 'comrades') on their return from the Trojan War" (348).

16. Donlan, *The Aristocratic Ideal,* 19, citing, for *aristoi, Iliad* 2.577–578, 5.780, 12.89, 12.197, 13.128; and for heroes, *Iliad* 2.110, 12.165, 15.230, 19.34.

17. *Iliad* 12.310–321, trans. Richmond Lattimore (Chicago: University of Chicago Press, 1951). Though Sarpedon and Glaukos were Lykian allies of Troy and so technically non-Greek, they expressed Greek sentiments in the passage above.

18. *Odyssey* 19.108–114, trans. Richmond Lattimore (New York: Harper and Row, 1967).

19. Hesiod, *Works and Days,* in *Hesiod,* trans. Apostolos N. Athanassakis (Baltimore: Johns Hopkins University Press, 2004), 225–247. M. L. West, in *The East Face of Helicon: West Asiatic Elements in Greek Poetry and Myth* (Oxford: Oxford University Press, 1997), 321–323, gives a number of Near Eastern, especially Assyrian, analogous passages (136), but he especially stresses analogies with the Hebrew scriptures, e.g., Leviticus 26, Deuteronomy 28, Amos 9, and a number of Psalms.

20. Hesiod, *Theogony,* in *Hesiod,* trans. Athanassakis, 81–92.

21. We might note the relation of the two archetypal Israelite kings, David and Solomon, to poetry and wisdom. David is a "singer and lyre player," to whom the Psalms are attributed, and Solomon is famous for his wisdom, with several books of wisdom attributed to him (though in the narrative, he is not so wise, sowing the seeds of the division of the kingdom). In early Greece the relation of poetry, wisdom, and politics is, if anything, even clearer.

22. W. G. Runciman, "Origin of States: The Case of Archaic Greece," *Comparative Studies in Society and History* 24 (1982): 354.

23. Robin Hägg, ed., *The Greek Renaissance of the Eighth Century B.C.: Tradition and Innovation–Proceedings of the Second International Symposium at the Swedish Institute in Athens, 1–5 June, 1981* (Stockholm: Svenska Institutet i Athen, 1983).

24. Jonathan Hall in *Hellenicity,* 53ff., doubts that the "Akhaioi" in Homer, though the commonest word for those we call the Greeks, were really identical with the Hellenes. He sees Hellenic identity as emerging quite late, "in the elite environment of the Olympic Games during the course of the sixth century" (227), and as being consolidated in opposition to the early fifth-century Persian invasion.

25. One could think of the autonomous polis as an element in the Panhellenic culture much as the nation-state is an element in contemporary international culture. John Meyer and his associates have argued persuasively for this latter relationship. See John W. Meyer and Michael T. Hannon, eds., *National Development and the World System* (Chicago: University of Chicago Press, 1979); Connie L. McNeely and D. A. Chekki, eds., *Constructing the Nation-State* (Santa Barbara: Greenwood, 1995); and Frank Lechner and John Boli, *World Culture: Origins and Consequences* (Malden, Mass.: Blackwell, 2005).

26. See particularly the work of Ian Morris, such as *Archaeology as Cultural History.*

27. The most succinct treatment of the Greek nobility is Louis Gernet, "The Nobility in Ancient Greece," in Gernet, *Anthropology of Ancient Greece,* 279–288.

28. Panhellenic culture would seem to count as what is commonly called a "civilization," that is, a multistate culture area, where all the constituent entities share with one another beliefs and practices that differentiate them all from neighboring "civilizations." Norman

Yoffee, referring to early Mesopotamian civilization in Sumeria (discussed in Chapter 5 of this book), emphasizes that the "civilizational" ideology includes notions about what each constituent "state" should be like. See his *Myths of the Archaic State: Evolution of the Earliest Cities, State, and Civilizations* (Cambridge: Cambridge University Press, 2005), 17. In the case of Greece, the polis as a political form, including a strong belief in its autonomy and the lack of even a lingering notion that, as was believed in Sumeria, centralization was desirable, was part of Panhellenic civilization. Yoffee also notes that civilizations are often constituted in significant part by the long-distance trading and gift exchange of elites, as would seem to have been the case in Greece.

29. Orlando Patterson, *Slavery and Social Death: A Comparative Study* (Cambridge, Mass.: Harvard University Press, 1982); and Patterson, *Freedom*, vol. 1: *Freedom in the Making of Western Culture* (New York: Basic Books, 1991).

30. Robert Parker, in his *Athenian Religion: A History* (Oxford: Oxford University Press, 1996), speaks of Greek women enjoying "cultic citizenship" (80). He also says that "though lacking most political rights, [Athenian] women are citizens" when it comes to religion (4). Several important festivals were restricted to women participants.

31. M. R. Popham and L. H. Sackett, *Lefkandi I, the Iron Age: The Settlement and the Cemeteries* (London: Thames and Hudson, 1979), supp. vol. 11 (British School of Archaeology at Athens).

32. Quoted by Nicholas Purcell in "Mobility and the *Polis*," in *The Greek City: From Homer to Alexander,* ed. Oswyn Murry and Simon Price (Oxford: Oxford University Press, 1990), 38.

33. One effort (which has not gone uncontested) to characterize the economic basis of the eighth-century transformation is David W. Tandy's *Warriors into Traders: The Power of the Market in Early Greece* (Berkeley: California University Press, 1997). The paucity of evidence from the eighth century leaves open a variety of interpretations.

34. Herodotus, admittedly at a much later period and in the context of the Athenian resistance to the Persian invasion, defines Greek cultural identity as follows: "and then there is our common Greekness: we are one in blood and one in language; those shrines of the gods belong to us all in common, and the sacrifices in common, and there are our habits, bred of a common upbringing." Herodotus, *The History* 8.144, David Grene translation (Chicago: University of Chicago Press, 1987). Notably absent is a common polity.

35. See Walter Burkert, *The Orientalizing Revolution: Near Eastern Influence on Greek Culture in the Early Archaic Age* (Cambridge, Mass.: Harvard University Press, 1992); and Burkert, *Babylon, Memphis, Persepolis: Eastern Contexts of Greek Culture* (Cambridge, Mass.: Harvard University Press, 2004). Of course, the common cultural world did not disappear after the archaic period: Greece continued to learn from societies to its east, as they, in turn, did from Greece.

36. Richard P. Martin, *The Language of Heroes: Speech and Performance in the Iliad* (Ithaca: Cornell University Press, 1989).

37. Peter W. Rose, *Sons of the Gods, Children of the Earth: Ideology and Literary Form in Ancient Greece* (Ithaca: Cornell University Press, 1992).

38. For a person like me who has spent much of his life studying Japan, the absence of an emphasis on loyalty between leader and follower in a warrior culture is quite shocking.

39. An extensive treatment of the *mesoi* and their importance in early Greek society is given by Victor Davis Hanson in *The Other Greeks: The Family Farm and the Agrarian Roots of Western Civilization* (Berkeley: University of California Press, 1995). Hanson has a principled objection to the term "peasant," which he sees as indicating a degree of dependence and subservience missing among those he prefers to call "farmers." See also: Ian Morris, "The Strong Principle of Equality and the Archaic Origins of Greek Democracy," in *Dēmokratia: A Conversation on Democracies, Ancient and Modern,* ed. Josiah Ober and Charles Hedrick (Princeton: Princeton University Press, 1996), 19–48. Morris has discussed the ongoing conflict between "middling ideology" and "elitist ideology" in *Archaeology as Cultural History: Words and Things in Iron Age Greece* (Malden, Mass.: Blackwell, 2000), chap. 5, "Antithetical Cultures," 155–191. He believes that by about 500 BCE, elitist ideology had pretty much evaporated and middling ideology became hegemonic. The emergence of a "conservative" criticism of Greek democracy in the fourth century was based in large part on principles that had originally been part of middling ideology.

40. Josiah Ober uses the term "dignity" to characterize the citizens of Athenian democracy; see Josiah Ober, *The Athenian Revolution: Essays on Ancient Greek Democracy and Political Theory* (Princeton: Princeton University Press, 1996), 87. He borrows his sense of the term from Charles Taylor, "The Politics of Recognition," in Charles Taylor et al., *Multiculturalism: Examining the Politics of Recognition* (Princeton: Princeton University Press, 1994), 25–73.

41. Ian Morris, *Burial and Ancient Society* (Cambridge: Cambridge University Press, 1987), 2–3. Italics in original.

42. W. G. Runciman, "Doomed to Extinction: The *Polis* as an Evolutionary Dead-End," in Murray and Price, *The Greek City,* 347.

43. Paul Cartledge, "Comparatively Equal," in Ober and Hedrick, *Dēmokratia,* 182.

44. Christian Meier, *The Greek Discovery of Politics* (Cambridge, Mass.: Harvard University Press, 1990 [1980]), 21; see also 144: "The city was grounded in its citizens, not in an autonomous state apparatus. The citizens constituted the state."

45. Warrior assemblies and city assemblies are known from many parts of the world: see, for example, Yoffee, *Myths,* under *assemblies* in the index. There is a question whether the polis assemblies had been originally warrior assemblies and only later assemblies of all (adult male) citizens. Jean-Pierre Vernant has argued for the priority of warrior assemblies that were then transformed into citizen assemblies. His chapter "City-State Warfare" in his *Myth and Society in Ancient Greece* (New York: Zone Books, 1988 [1974]), ends with the statement, "On the one hand the army is nothing if not the city itself; on the other, the city is nothing but a troop of warriors" (53). Homeric evidence is mixed: there are warrior assemblies in the *Iliad* and a citizen assembly in Ithaca in the *Odyssey.* Morris in the several works cited above seems to think that the eighth century saw and responded to a greater demand for inclusion by non-noble citizens, without reference to warrior status. Although assemblies, particularly in chiefdoms and early states, are not rare in history, there is no case known, other than Greece, where they actually replaced monarchy as a primary form of governance.

46. Morris, *Archaeology as Cultural History,* esp. chap. 4.

47. Rosalind Thomas in her *Literacy and Orality in Ancient Greece* (Cambridge: Cambridge University Press, 1992), writes of Homer "singing his poetry aloud to an audience" (4). Later she writes that the performance of the Homeric rhapsode, though without musical

accompaniment, "is better described as 'chanting' than simply reciting," and goes on to cite Plato's *Ion* 535b–e as indicating that the rhapsode not only uses costume and gesture but is so overcome with emotion at critical moments in the narrative that he is as one possessed, and moves the audience to similar emotion (118). This suggests a powerfully mimetic aspect in Homeric performance.

48. Walter Burkert, *History in Greek Mythology and Ritual* (Berkeley: University of California Press, 1979), 23. Italics in the original.

49. For the argument that "history" and "myth" inevitably overlap, see William McNeill, *Mythistory and Other Essays* (Chicago: University of Chicago Press, 1986).

50. Lines 26–28, trans. Athanassakis.[0]

51. Marcel Detienne, *The Masters of Truth in Ancient Greece* (New York: Zone Books, 1996 [1967]), 52, where he speaks of "performative truth," and 89–106.

52. Eric A. Havelock, *Preface to Plato* (Cambridge, Mass.: Harvard University Press, 1963), 61–86. See also, Eric A. Havelock, *The Greek Concept of Justice: From Its Shadow in Homer to Its Substance in Plato* (Cambridge, Mass.: Harvard University Press, 1978), 106–122.

53. Jenny Strauss Clay, *The Wrath of Athena: Gods and Men in the Odyssey* (Princeton: Princeton University Press, 1983), 244. Her quote is from Gregory Nagy, *The Best of the Achaeans: Concepts of the Hero in Archaic Greek Poetry* (Baltimore: Johns Hopkins University Press, 1979), 18. Clay's work has been instructive for my purposes. Although she is not interested in the social context and confines herself to close readings, her concern for early Greek theology in each text she studies has been helpful. In addition to her work on Homer, cited above, she has written on the Homeric Hymns in *The Politics of Olympus: Form and Meaning in the Homeric Hymns* (Princeton: Princeton University Press, 1989), and on Hesiod in *Hesiod's Cosmos* (Cambridge: Cambridge University Press, 2003).

54. Havelock, *Preface*, 62. It is worth remembering that the title of Plato's last great work in political philosophy, *Laws,* is, in Greek, *Nomoi.*

55. Although the verb from the same root, *nemein,* is present and will, as we shall see below, turn out to be significant.

56. Whether these texts are any more "critical" than some texts to be found in many pre-axial societies is an open question. Kurt A. Raaflaub has gone so far as to argue that in Homer the axial transition had already occurred in Greece: see his "Polis, 'the Political,' and Political Thought: New Departures in Ancient Greece, c. 800–500 BCE," in *Axial Civilizations and World History,* ed. Johann P. Arnason et. al. (Leiden: Brill, 2005), 253–283. But Raaflaub has confused political thought with political theory, which emerges only in the late fifth / early fourth centuries, the time of the axial transition in Greece, as we will see. Raaflaub develops his views of early Greek political thought further in his "Poets, Lawgivers, and the Beginnings of Political Reflection in Archaic Greece," in *The Cambridge History of Greek and Roman Political Thought,* ed. Christopher Rowe and Malcolm Schofield (Cambridge: Cambridge University Press, 2000), 23–59.

57. Richard Seaford in his *Money and the Early Greek Mind: Homer, Philosophy, Tragedy* (Cambridge: Cambridge University Press, 2004), 52, points out, however, that the Greek sacrifice, though always dedicated to a god, was a communal event, with the meat shared among the participants and with only the bones and the fat burned for the god, as against

the more normal Mesopotamian case where the sacrifice was dedicated primarily to the god and only the king or priests could partake.

58. Ibid., 53.

59. Ibid., 49, italics added. Because this was still true in Greek cities under Rome, it is clear why Christian refusal to participate in civic sacrifices or eat sacrificial meat (Christians had their own sacrifice) placed them outside the bounds of the civic community.

60. Ibid., 49–50. Italics in original. Seaford's discussion in *Money and the Early Greek Mind* sums up and expands the rich treatment of these issues in his *Reciprocity and Ritual: Homer and Tragedy in the Developing City-State* (Oxford: Oxford University Press, 1994).

61. Walter Burkert, *Greek Religion* (Cambridge, Mass.: Harvard University Press, 1985), 95. Burkert writes "almost without priests" because there were a few vestigial hereditary priesthoods, perhaps the most significant of which was the priesthood at Eleusis.

62. Zaidman and Pantel, *Religion in the Ancient Greek City*, 49.

63. On the procession, see Burkert, *Greek Religion*, 99–101.

64. See article "Festivals" in *The Oxford Classical Dictionary*, 3rd rev. ed., ed. Simon Hornblower and Antony Spawforth (Oxford: Oxford University Press, 2003), 593.

65. Meier, *Greek Discovery of Politics*, 44–45.

66. I am indebted to an unpublished paper by Timothy Doran, "*Ate*, Antisocial Behavior, and Polis Building in Solon's Political and Poetical Efforts" (2005), for my understanding of this aspect of Solon's teaching.

67. Seaford, *Reciprocity and Ritual*, 74–114.

68. See Parker, *Athenian Religion*, 43–55.

69. Christian Meier, *Athens: A Portrait of the City in Its Golden Age* (New York: Holt, 1998 [1993]), 71; Meier goes on to say, "Although he demanded more from himself than from others, he expected nothing more for himself in return, and he did not seek to be superior to the common man." Eric Voegelin, *The World of the Polis*, vol. 2 of *Order and History* (Baton Rouge: Louisiana State University Press, 1957), 199; Voegelin goes on to say, "[Solon] created the type of the lawgiver, the *nomothetes*, in the classical sense, not for Hellas only, but as a model for mankind . . . The Eunomia he created in the polis was the Eunomia of his soul. In his person came to life the prototype of the spiritual statesman."

70. Rebecca H. Sinos, "Divine Selection: Epiphany and Politics in Archaic Greece," in *Cultural Poetics in Archaic Greece: Cult, Performance, Politics,* ed. Carol Dougherty and Leslie Kurke (New York: Oxford University Press, 1998), 73–91. Parker, in *Athenian Religion,* 83–84, finds this a plausible account.

71. W. Robert Connor, "Civil Society, Dionysiac Festival, and the Athenian Democracy," in Ober and Hedrick, *Dēmokratia*, 217–226. For a fuller discussion of Cleisthenes's reforms, see Meier, *Greek Discovery of Politics*, 49–81.

72. It is worth remembering that in Plato's *Laws* Dionysus shares honors with Apollo as the bringer of festivals for the relief of human suffering (2.653d) and that in the choral singing and dancing that are central in the education of children, but which continue in the ideal city throughout the life cycle, it is to Apollo and Dionysus that the hymns are sung (2.665b). Nietzsche in *The Birth of Tragedy* not only saw Apollo and Dionysus as complementary, but also described Dionysiac rituals as leading to a sense of communion and community. For Nietzsche, music was essential to the effects produced by Dionysiac ritual. It was

to the power of music that he ascribes the following consequences: "Now the slave emerges as a freeman; all the rigid, hostile walls which either necessity or despotism has erected between men are shattered. Now that the gospel of universal harmony is sounded, each individual becomes not only reconciled to his fellow but actually at one with him—as though the veil of Maya had been torn apart and there remained only shreds floating before the vision of mystical Oneness. Man now expresses himself through song and dance as the member of a higher community; he has forgotten how to walk, how to speak, and is on the brink of taking wing as he dances." Friedrich Nietzsche, *The Birth of Tragedy and the Genealogy of Morals,* trans. Frances Golffing (Garden City, N.Y.: Doubleday Anchor, 1956), 23.

73. Connor, "Civil Society," 222.

74. Ibid., 223.

75. Ibid., 224.

76. Parker, *Athenian Religion,* 69, 75, notes the uncertainty of the dates of the founding of the City Dionysia, holding that it could have been founded under the Pisistratids, but could also have been founded around the time of Cleisthenes's reforms, the data being uncertain. Christiane Sourvinou-Inwood in her *Tragedy and Athenian Religion* (Lanham: Rowman and Littlefield, 2003), 103–104, challenges Connor's dating and argues for the period 540–520 for the founding of the City Dionysia, although she accepts the idea of a major reorganization of the festival around the time of Cleisthenes.

77. Connor, "Civil Society," 224.

78. Meier, *Athens,* is the best account of fifth-century Athens that I know of. It combines political, social, and cultural history in an integral way, and it uses tragedy to illuminate its argument at many points. Meier shows Athens at its wisest and most foolish, at its truly ethical and its disgracefully unethical, and all with an even hand, never forgetting the greatness he is recounting or apologizing for the terrible lapses; he is a model for historians.

79. Finley argued that though most Greek cities from the middle of the sixth century increased the participation of the poor, they did so through "compromise systems" that allowed the rich "greater weight in decision-making. Athens eventually shifted that weight, and the only variable that was unique in Athens was the empire, an empire for which the navy was indispensable, and that meant the lower classes who provided the manpower for the navy. That is why I hold the empire to have been a necessary condition for the Athenian type of democracy. Then, when the empire was forcibly dissolved at the end of the fifth century BCE, the system was so deeply entrenched that no one dared attempt to replace it, difficult as it was in the fourth century to provide the necessary financial underpinning." M. I. Finley, *Democracy Ancient and Modern* (New Brunswick, N.J.: Rutgers University Press, 1973), 49–50. Josiah Ober holds that the continued vitality of Athenian democracy in the fourth century creates more problems for Finley's argument than he admits, but goes on to say, "Perhaps there never would have been a full-blown 'radical' democracy at Athens without the empire to buffer the financial strains of its development." Josiah Ober, *Mass and Elite in Democratic Athens: Rhetoric, Ideology, and the Power of the People* (Princeton: Princeton University Press, 1989), 24. There is a parallel argument as to whether slavery was a necessary prerequisite for radical democracy, the argument being that the kind of direct democracy in Athens requires so much of the time and energy of the citizens that only if they had slaves to attend to day-to-day business would they have been able to sustain their high rate of

participation. Ober argues against this view as well, indicating that many citizens were not slaveholders. See Ober, *Mass and Elite,* 24–27. Of course, a similar argument could be made about women—without them to run the *oikos* the men would not have had time to be citizens.

80. Because my analysis focuses on the cultural level, and then on the religious and political institutions that underlie it, I have necessarily neglected the economic structure of ancient Greece, about which so much has been written. Let me say just a word here about matters I cannot consider in this chapter. The classic Marxist characterization of the ancient economy as a slave economy has been pretty well abandoned, even though the importance of slavery is not denied. A good treatment of the relatively marginal importance of slavery in the lives of the peasant-citizens of ancient Athens is given by Ellen Meiksins Wood in her *Peasant-Citizen and Slave* (London: Verso, 1988). Mohammad Nafissi sums up the evidence for a relatively modern market economy in ancient Athens in his article "Class, Embeddedness and the Modernity of Ancient Athens," *Comparative Studies in Society and History* 29, no. 2 (2000): 207–238. For a full discussion of the argument over the nature of the ancient economy, see Mohammad Nafissi, *Ancient Athens and Modern Ideology: Value, Theory and Evidence in Historical Sciences, Max Weber, Karl Polanyi and Moses Finley* (London: Institute of Classical Studies, 2005).

81. Simon Goldhill, *Love, Sex and Tragedy: How the Ancient World Shapes Our Lives* (Chicago: University of Chicago Press, 2004), 223.

82. Ibid., 224–226. The Isocrates quotation is from 226.

83. Ibid., 227.

84. Jean-Pierre Vernant, *Myth and Tragedy in Ancient Greece* (New York: Zone Books, 1988 [1972]), 185. Sourvinou-Inwood, *Tragedy and Athenian Religion,* 50–53, argues that the chorus, out of which tragedy perhaps initially evolved and which was never absent in any tragedy, represented the people of Athens worshipping Dionysus in the present, as well as whatever role they had within the drama. If she is right, the chorus linked play and audience in a way no modern play can do. Nietzsche in *The Birth of Tragedy* interestingly anticipated this view: "What must be kept in mind in these investigations is that the audience of an Attic tragedy discovered *itself* in the chorus of the orchestra. Audience and chorus were never fundamentally set over against each other: all was one grand chorus of singing, dancing, satyrs, and those who let themselves be represented by them . . . An audience of spectators, such as we know it, was unknown to the Greeks" (54; italics in the original).

85. Vernant, *Myth and Tragedy,* 187–188. For Aristotle on poetry as more philosophical than history, see *Poetics* 1451bff. Nietzsche holds that "Dionysos *remains* the sole dramatic protagonist . . . all the famous characters of the Greek stage, Prometheus, Oedipus, etc., are only masks of that original hero." *Birth of Tragedy,* 66, italics in original.

86. Vernant, *Myth and Tragedy,* 43. Goldhill gives a remarkable example of how a Greek tragedy can speak to a contemporary audience. He describes a performance of Sophocles's *Electra* in Derry, Northern Ireland, in 1990, during a week in which eight people had been killed in sectarian violence, that was so stunning that the audience refused to leave the theater after the end of the play without discussing the traumas that the passion for revenge creates. Goldhill, *Love, Sex and Tragedy,* 215.

87. Voegelin, *The World of the Polis,* 251: "The leap in being does not assume the form of an Israelite revelation of God, but of the Dionysiac descent into man, to the depth where Dike [Justice] is to be found."

88. Sourvinou-Inwood, *Tragedy and Greek Religion,* 197–200.

89. Ibid., 153.

90. Ibid.

91. Ibid., 291.

92. I was privileged to attend a splendid performance of the *Persians* at the Aurora Theater in Berkeley, California, in 2005. The play was necessarily somewhat "adapted," but the writers carefully avoided obvious references to the American invasion of Iraq, which could be seen as a kind of reverse West invades East to Aeschylus's East invades West. The Auora auditorium is so small that the audience is virtually inside the play, and I think we all felt, quite powerfully, that the play was about us.

93. Christian Meier, *The Political Art of Greek Tragedy* (Baltimore: Johns Hopkins University Press, 1993 [1988]), 78.

94. Sourvinou-Inwood, *Tragedy and Greek Religion,* 226.

95. Near the end of the Peloponnesian War, at a moment when defeat had become palpable, the island of Samos demanded and received Athenian citizenship, an example of what was desired but denied earlier, and which came too late by then.

96. Lyric poetry from the seventh century on was of no small importance in Greek cultural history, but the highly condensed nature of the present treatment precludes giving it serious attention.

97. On these early developments, see especially Detienne, *Masters of Truth.*

98. I have found Richard P. Martin's article "The Seven Sages as Performers of Wisdom," in Dougherty and Kurke, *Cultural Poetics,* 108–128, especially helpful and will rely on it for much of the following discussion of the sages.

99. Ibid., 113.

100. Ibid., 113–115.

101. Ibid., 115–116.

102. Ibid., 117.

103. Ibid., 118. The Jakobson quote is from Roman Jakobson, *Selected Writings,* vol. 4, *Slavic Epic Studies* (The Hague: Mouton, 1966), 673.

104. Martin, "The Seven Sages," 122.

105. Sourvinou-Inwood, *Tragedy and Greek Religion,* 154ff. Sourvinou-Inwood goes on to suggest that the poet, as the original "actor," impersonated Dionysus.

106. See Sitta von Reden and Simon Goldhill, "Plato and the Performance of Dialogue," in *Performance Culture and Athenian Democracy,* ed. Simon Goldhill and Robin Osborne (Cambridge: Cambridge University Press, 1999), 257–289. Von Reden and Goldhill choose passages from the *Charmides,* the *Laches,* and the *Lysis,* not only to show the subtlety of Plato's dramatic depiction, but to illustrate moments where Socrates himself is "performing" before an audience, often largely of boys, in the gymnasium.

107. For the centrality of the dialogue form in Plato's thought, see especially Charles H. Kahn, *Plato and the Socratic Dialogue: The Philosophical Use of a Literary Form* (Cambridge:

Cambridge University Press, 1996). See also the chapter on dialogue in Paul Friedländer, *Plato: An Introduction* (New York: Pantheon Books, 1958 [1954]), 154–170.

108. This point was suggested to me by Bernard Williams in his "Plato: The Inventor of Philosophy," reprinted in *The Sense of the Past: Essays in the History of Philosophy* (Princeton: Princeton University Press, 2006 [1998]), 150–151. The translation is Williams's. For Plato, "image" means a copy rather than an original—second best, that is.

109. Merlin Donald, *Origins of the Modern Mind: Three Stages in the Evolution of Culture and Consciousness* (Cambridge, Mass.: Harvard University Press, 1991); for "hybrid system," 368ff.

110. Ibid., 335. By "external memory sources" Donald means, primarily, written texts.

111. Stephen White, after critically examining the oral traditions upon which our knowledge of Thales is based, concludes that he was "a pioneer in the very pragmatic realms of commerce and politics, both regional and international, as well as engineering, surveying, and navigation." In sum, "Thales it seems pioneered the quantitative treatment of empirical data. Call him a philosopher or not, he fully deserves credit as the founder of Greek astronomy." Stephen White, "Thales and the Stars," in *Presocratic Philosophy: Essays in Honor of Alexander Mourelatos,* ed. Victor Caston and Daniel W. Graham (Aldershot: Ashgate, 2002), 3.

112. On this point see the chapter titled "Tradition and Innovation" in G. E. R. Lloyd's *The Revolutions of Wisdom: Studies in the Claims and Practice of Ancient Greek Science* (Berkeley: University of California Press, 1987), 50–108.

113. M. L. West, in his *Early Greek Philosophy and the Orient* (Oxford: Oxford University Press, 1971), gives numerous Mesopotamian and Persian parallels, particularly to Anaximander, Anaximenes, and Heraclitus.

114. Francis M. Cornford, *From Religion to Philosophy: A Study in the Origins of Western Speculation* (New York: Harper Torchbook, 1957 [1912]), 66. In his *Principium Sapientiae: The Origins of Greek Philosophical Thought* (Cambridge: Cambridge University Press, 1952), 187–201, Cornford gives a more nuanced picture of the background of Ionian cosmogony, tracing the continuities with Hesiod while recognizing the significant abandonment of mythological beings as actors in the story. See also West, *Early Greek Philosophy,* on the Mesopotamian and Persian influences on the Ionian "philosophers."

115. Because our knowledge of Thales's thought is both sparse and questionable, it is not clear that he really did argue for water as the primal element, but if he did, he was not far from several Middle Eastern creation myths that saw the world beginning with water—Genesis 1:2, for example.

116. G. E. R. Lloyd, *Magic, Reason and Experience: Studies in the Origin and Development of Greek Science* (Cambridge: Cambridge University Press, 1979); on Anaximander's contribution to astronomy, see 170; on the Milesian cosmogonies as being primarily contributions to a "new or 'reformed theology,'" see 11. In general Lloyd is skeptical about the sources for the thought of the Milesian philosophers.

117. Charles H. Kahn, *Anaximander and the Origins of Greek Cosmology* (Indianapolis: Hackett, 1994 [1960]), 7.

118. Ibid., 234.

119. Ibid., 133.

120. Ibid., 199. The presentation of natural science as a kind of epic poem is still very much alive today, as we saw in Chapter 2.

121. Ibid., 238–239.

122. The quote is from Plato's *Laws* 899b.9, where it is thought to be attributed to Thales.

123. G. S. Kirk, J. E. Raven and M. Schofield, *The Presocratic Philosophers,* 2nd ed. (Cambridge: Cambridge University Press, 1983), 145.

124. Kahn, *Anaximander,* 201–202. Italics in original.

125. Paul Ricoeur, *The Rule of Metaphor: Multi-Disciplinary Studies of the Creation of Meaning in Language* (Toronto: University of Toronto Press, 1977 [1975]), 42–43. Ricoeur also expresses doubts as to whether "imitation" is a good translation of *mimesis,* but that is an issue beyond our present concern.

126. The ambiguity of "nature" is not entirely lacking in English: the "nature" of natural science is not quite the "nature" of the mountain climber.

127. For the influence of Greek political life on the development of early Greek thought, see, among others, Jean-Pierre Vernant, *The Origins of Greek Thought* (Ithaca: Cornell University Press, 1982 [1962]); and Lloyd, *Magic, Reason and Experience,* esp. chap. 4. For the influence of Greek legal practice, see Michael Gagarin, "Greek Law and the Presocratics," in Caston and Graham, *Presocratic Philosophy,* 19–24. Gagarin notes that Havelock, in *The Greek Concept of Justice,* had some time ago noted the importance of the argumentative nature of Greek legal procedure for the development of Greek thought.

128. Eric Havelock was the most vigorous proponent of the importance of literacy in the development of Greek thought, although he never slighted the continuing importance of orality. See in particular his *Preface to Plato* and *The Literate Revolution in Greece and Its Cultural Consequences* (Princeton: Princeton University Press, 1982).

129. For a full discussion, see Seaford, *Money and the Early Greek Mind,* chap. 8, "The Features of Money," 147–172.

130. Ibid., 93.

131. Ibid., 94.

132. Robert Hahn, *Anaximander and the Architects: The Contribution of Egyptian and Greek Architectural Technologies to the Origins of Greek Philosophy* (Albany: SUNY Press, 2001).

133. Ibid., 69ff.

134. On the shape of the earth, see Kahn, *Anaximander,* 55–56; and Hahn, *Anaximander,* 177ff. On Plato's cosmic axis, see *Republic* 10.616bff.

135. On the basis of scant and problematic evidence, Hahn argues that the monumental Ionian temples were meant to symbolize oligarchical or tyrannical government, and only inadvertently came to symbolize the solidarity of the whole community, an argument that I find doubtful. See his *Anaximander,* 219–240.

136. Charles H. Kahn, *Pythagoras and the Pythagoreans: A Brief History* (Indianapolis: Hackett, 2001), which draws on and to some degree improves the fundamental work on Pythagoreanism, Walter Burkert's *Lore and Science in Ancient Pythagoreanism* (Cambridge, Mass.: Harvard University Press, 1972 [1962]).

137. Kahn speculates that in the absence of definite information to the contrary, the basic Pythagorean mathematical conception of the cosmos may well have been Pythagoras's own.

He writes, "The notion of cosmic harmony expressed in numerical ratios and conceived as astral music is one of those ideas of genius that has remained amazingly fruitful over the centuries," and concludes that because there was no other Pythagorean of comparable stature, the idea may well go back to Pythagoras himself. *Pythagoras,* 38.

138. Michael L. Morgan, *Platonic Piety: Philosophy and Ritual in Fourth-Century Athens* (New Haven: Yale University Press, 1990), 15. It is worth remembering that in Athens, at least, Dionysiac religion, through the City Dionysia and the performance of tragedy, was integrated into the polis religion, which was not therefore exclusively Delphic, in Morgan's sense. Also the cult at Eleusis was very much part of Athenian life. Initiation into the cult was open to any Greek speaker who could pay the fee, but Athens considered the cult an ornament to its own preeminence among the poleis.

139. G. E. R. Lloyd, *Adversaries and Authorities: Investigations into Ancient Greek and Chinese Science* (Cambridge: Cambridge University Press, 1996), 21, 24. Italics in the original.

140. For a translation of the hymn, see A. A. Long and D. N. Sedley, *The Hellenistic Philosophers,* vol. 1 (Cambridge: Cambridge University Press, 1987), 326–327. For Cleanthes, Zeus, though "omnipotent" and "prime mover of nature," is only "the most majestic of immortals," nor does Cleanthes's devotion to Zeus become central for all later Stoics.

141. Kirk, Raven, and Schofield, *The Presocratic Philosophers,* 168. See also the respectful treatment of Xenophanes in Werner Jaeger, *The Theology of the Early Greek Philosophers* (Oxford: Oxford University Press, 1947), 38–54.

142. Kirk, Raven, and Schofield, *The Presocratic Philosophers,* 168.

143. Ibid., 169.

144. Ibid., 169–170.

145. Jaeger, *Theology,* 42.

146. For the argument that Heraclitus and Parmenides were essentially doing the same thing with different means, see particularly Alexander Nehamas, "Parmenidean Being / Heraclitean Fire," in Caston and Graham, *Presocratic Philosophy,* 45–64. Hegel has an interesting take on these two. Parmenides, he says, "began philosophy proper. A man now constitutes himself free from all ideas and opinions, denies their truth, and says necessity alone, Being, is the truth. This beginning is certainly still dim and indefinite, and we cannot say much of what it involves; but to take up this position certainly is to develop Philosophy proper, which has not hitherto existed." Of Heraclitus he writes, "The advance requisite and made by Heraclitus is the progression from Being as the first immediate thought, to the category of Becoming as the second. This is the first concrete, the Absolute, as in it is the unity of opposites. Thus with Heraclitus the philosophic Idea is to be met with in its speculative form . . . Here we see land; there is no proposition of Heraclitus which I have not adopted in my Logic." G. W. F. Hegel, *Lectures on the History of Philosophy,* vol. 1, trans. E. S. Haldane and Frances H. Simson (Atlantic Highlands, N.J.: Humanities Press, 1974), 254, 279. Hegel does not argue that Heraclitus was later than Parmenides; his connection between them is logical, not chronological.

147. Friedrich Nietzsche, *Philosophy in the Tragic Age of the Greeks,* trans. Marianne Cowan (Chicago: Regnery, 1962), 50ff. This book was left unfinished at Nietzsche's death; his notes and fragments were published posthumously.

148. Charles H. Kahn provides an excellent introduction in *The Art and Thought of Heraclitus: An Edition of the Fragments with Translation and Commentary* (Cambridge: Cambridge University Press, 1979). Heraclitus seems to dare his reader to not just read what he says, but to "perform" it, in that the riddle-like quality of his sayings require a very active response if one is to make any sense of them.

149. Havelock, *Literate Revolution,* 240–246.

150. Ibid., 245.

151. Ibid., 246. Havelock does not give this honor to Anaximander, whether because he doesn't consider him to have been writing philosophical prose, or because we have only one sentence of the prose he was said to have written.

152. Kahn, *Art and Thought,* 88–89.

153. Heraclitus, D.41, in Kahn, *Art and Thought,* 55.

154. Ibid., 172.

155. Heraclitus, D.32, in Kahn, *Art and Thought,* 83. Heraclitus puns in Ionic dialect, so that "the name of Zeus" can also mean "the name of life" (267).

156. Edward Hussey, "Heraclitus," in *The Cambridge Companion to Early Greek Philosophy,* ed. A. A. Long (Cambridge: Cambridge University Press, 1999), 88–112; the quotation is on 108.

157. Heraclitus, D.1, in Kahn, *Art and Thought,* 29. Anthony Long treats *logos,* which he leaves untranslated, as perhaps the key term in Heraclitus. Long also notes two important innovations in the thought of Heraclitus: "Heraclitus is the earliest Greek thinker to postulate an everlasting world, and he is also the earliest to apply the term *kosmos* (meaning a beautiful structure) to the World." A. A. Long, "Heraclitus" in *Routledge Encyclopedia of Philosophy,* vol. 4 (New York: Routledge, 1998), 368.

158. Heraclitus, D.34, in Kahn, *Art and Thought,* 29.

159. Voegelin, *The World of the Polis,* 209.

160. Ibid., 211.

161. Nietzsche, *Philosophy in the Tragic Age,* 77. Nietzsche describes the "moment" in Parmenides's life when he discovered Being as a turning point not only in his own life but in the history of early Greek thought: "Once in his life Parmenides, perhaps at a fairly advanced age, had a moment of purest absolutely bloodless abstraction, unclouded by any reality. This moment—un-Greek as no other in the two centuries of the Tragic Age—whose product is the doctrine of Being—became for Parmenides' own life the boundary stone that separates two periods. At the same time however, this moment divides Presocratic thinking into two halves. The first might be called the Anaximandrian period, the second the Parmenidean proper" (69).

162. There is a wide consensus that Parmenides represents a significant break in the history of Greek thought. Detienne's *Masters of Truth* is described in the foreword by Pierre Vidal-Naquet as "a prehistory of Parmenides' poem" (8). Detienne, after pointing out that the whole setting of the poem "refers back to the attitudes of the diviner, the poet, and the magus," that the form of the poem owes more than a little to Hesiod, and that the prologue "resorts to the religious vocabulary of the sects and brotherhoods," holds that it nonetheless represents something radically new: "Parmenides' *Alētheia,* truth pronounced by a man connected in some way with the masters of truth, is also the first kind of truth in ancient Greece

that is open to rational challenge. It is the first version of objective truth, a truth established in and through dialogue" (130–134). Lloyd, in *Magic, Reason and Experience,* describes what the new kind of truth is: in the "rigorous deductive form of its argument" it is "revolutionary" (70). But he also points out that "what we may broadly call empirical methods and evidence are not merely not used: they are ruled out" (71).

163. Alexander Mourelatos, *The Route of Parmenides: A Study of Word, Image and Argument in the Fragments* (New Haven: Yale University Press, 1970), 36–37.

164. Ibid., 160–161

165. Ibid., 177.

166. Michael Frede, "The Philosopher," in *Greek Thought: A Guide to Classical Knowledge,* ed. Jacques Brunschwig and Geoffrey E. R. Lloyd (Cambridge, Mass.: Harvard University Press, 2000), 8, 10. Frede develops further his characterization of the difference between classical and modern conceptions of rationality in the introduction to Michael Frede and Gisela Striker, eds., *Rationality in Greek Thought* (Oxford: Oxford University Press, 1996), 1–28. On the "practical" aspect of classical thought, see Pierre Hadot, *Philosophy as a Way of Life: Spiritual Exercises from Socrates to Foucault,* ed. Arnold Davidson, trans. Michael Chase (Oxford: Blackwell, 1995).

167. Paul Woodruff, "Rhetoric and Relativism: Protagoras and Gorgias," in Long, *Early Greek Philosophy,* 305.

168. Fernanda Decleva Caizzi, "Protagoras and Antiphon: Sophistic Debates on Justice," in Long, *Early Greek Philosophy,* 322.

169. Ibid., 324–325.

170. Werner Jaeger, *Paideia: The Ideals of Greek Culture* (Oxford: Oxford University Press, 1945), esp. vol. 1, bk. 2, "The Sophists," 286–381. See also Hegel, *History of Philosophy,* 1:355: "Indeed, the sophists are the teachers of Greece through whom culture first came into existence in Greece, and thus they took the place of poets and rhapsodists, who before this were the ordinary instructors."

171. Jaeger, *Paideia,* 1:316.

172. But if the sophists can be considered the forerunners of reductionist and positivistic social science, it was surely Plato and Aristotle who invented humanistic social science. When Durkheim first began to teach, he assigned Aristotle's *Politics* to his graduate students as their basic text.

173. On the sophists in general and Protagoras in particular as progressive democrats, see particularly Eric Havelock's *The Liberal Temper in Greek Politics* (New Haven: Yale University Press, 1957).

174. Caizzi, "Protagoras and Antiphon," 331.

175. Kahn, in his very large book on the verb "to be" in ancient Greek thought, a book originally undertaken to "get behind," as it were, the concept of Being in Parmenides, confirms Hegel's idea of "objective reason" when he writes of Parmenides, but also of much later Greek thought, that there was "a virtual non-existence of the concept of the self or subject in classical Greek metaphysics" as a "consequence of the great positive achievement in this field: the serenely objective concerns with the concepts of predication, existence, and truth in their general form." Charles H. Kahn, *The Verb "Be" in Ancient Greek* (Indianapolis: Hackett, 2003 [1973]), 418.

176. Hegel, *History of Philosophy,* 1:368–371. There is a subjective element in Heraclitus when he wrote (D.101) "I went in search of myself" (or "I searched into myself"), but it is hardly central in his work.

177. Eric Voegelin, *Plato and Aristotle,* vol. 3 of *Order and History* (Baton Rouge: Louisiana State Press, 1957), 8. Socrates's *daemon* had no positive teaching and was heard only when it wished to restrain Socrates from something.

178. It has been tempting for translators of the *Apology* to use the word "God," because of the feeling that Socrates, as early Christians believed, was so close to the Christian usage, but it is much safer to translate *theos* as "god" or "the god," though it would be equally unwise to identify this unspecific term with Apollo or any particular Greek god.

179. *Apology* 29d–e, 30a, trans. G. M. A. Grube, in Plato, *Complete Works,* ed. John M. Cooper (Indianapolis: Hackett, 1997), 27–28.

180. Eli Sagan, *The Honey and the Hemlock: Democracy and Paranoia in Ancient Athens and Modern America* (New York: Basic Books, 1991).

181. Jaeger, *Paideia,* 2:13.

182. Hegel, *History of Philosophy,* 425–448.

183. Jaeger, *Paideia,* 2:27.

184. Ibid., 75.

185. Voegelin, *Plato and Aristotle,* 13.

186. Gabriela Roxana Carone, *Plato's Cosmology and Its Ethical Dimensions* (Cambridge: Cambridge University Press, 2005).

187. Kahn, *Plato and the Socratic Dialogue.*

188. Terry Penner, "Socrates," in Rowe and Schofield, *Greek and Roman Political Thought,* 164–189.

189. Bernard Williams makes the point when he writes, "Plato invented the subject of philosophy as we know it . . . Western Philosophy not only started with Plato, but has spent most of its life in his company." *The Sense of the Past,* 148.

190. Malcolm Schofield, "Approaching the *Republic,*" in Rowe and Schofield, *Greek and Roman Political Thought,* 202. He says this in specific refutation of views like those of Popper and Strauss.

191. Simon Goldhill, *Who Needs Greek? Contexts in the Cultural History of Hellenism* (Cambridge: Cambridge University Press, 2002), 63.

192. Ibid., 61.

193. Those states described as totalitarian in modern times have uniformly been presided over by tyrants: Hitler, Stalin, Mao, Pol Pot, Ceausescu, and so on.

194. *Republic,* trans. Paul Shorey, Loeb Classical Library (Cambridge, Mass.: Harvard University Press, 1935), 417 (592b).

195. Marcel Detienne in *The Creation of Mythology* shows that early on, in Hesiod, for example, *muthos* and *logos* are virtually synonymous, both meaning story or account, but that in Pindar and Herodotus *muthos* appears rarely and is largely pejorative—rather most of what we (and Plato) would call myth is referred to as *logos.* Thucydides firmly banishes both *mythos* and *logos* insofar as they apply to early unknowable events. Detienne's view of *muthos* in Plato differs from Brisson's but in the end does not contradict Brisson's claim that it was Plato who first made the distinction that we assume is natural.

196. Luc Brisson, *Plato the Myth Maker,* trans. and ed. Gerard Naddaf (Chicago: Chicago University Press, 1998 [1994]), 90.

197. Brisson suggests that Plato's ambivalence about writing is in part due to his historical situation, a moment when oral culture was still vital but writing was becoming ever more important: "Plato's testimony on myth is thus balanced on a razor's edge. At the turning point between two civilizations, one founded on orality and the other on writing. Plato in fact describes the twilight of myths. In other words, Plato describes that moment when, in ancient Greece in general and at Athens in particular, memory changes; if not in its nature, then at least in its means of functioning. A memory shared by all the members of a community is now opposed by a memory which is the privilege of a more limited number of people: those for whom the use of writing is a matter of everyday habit." *Plato the Myth Maker,* 38–39.

198. Hans-Georg Gadamer, "Plato and the Poets," in *Dialogue and Dialectic: Eight Hermeneutical Studies on Plato* (New Haven: Yale University Press, 1980 [1934]), 46.

199. Kahn, *Plato and the Socratic Dialogue,* xiii–xiv. Bernard Williams says something similar: "The resonance of [Plato's] images and the imaginative power of his style, the most beautiful ever devised for the expression of abstract thought, implicitly affirm the reality of the world of the senses even when the content denies it." *The Sense of the Past,* 24.

200. *Laws* 654a–b, trans. Trevor J. Saunders, in Cooper, *Works,* 1345.

201. Ibid., 653c–d.

202. Kathryn A. Morgan, in her *Myth and Philosophy from the Presocratics to Plato* (Cambridge: Cambridge University Press, 2000), gives a valuable reading of Plato's myths. Carone also appreciates the myths in Plato's later dialogues, which she says supplement the arguments and carry a degree of their own truth. She argues, however, that in cases where a myth used to supplement an argument seems to contradict it, the argument has to be given priority. See *Plato's Cosmology,* 14–16. Neither Morgan nor Carone discusses myth in Plato outside of what he himself designates as myth.

203. David K. O'Connor, "Rewriting the Poets in Plato's Characters," in *The Cambridge Companion to Plato's Republic,* ed. G. R. F. Ferrari (Cambridge: Cambridge University Press, forthcoming). O'Connor points out that it was Leo Strauss who first developed the argument about the use of Hesiod's races of metal in the *Republic* in Strauss's "On Plato's Republic" in *The City and Man* (Chicago: Rand McNally, 1964), 50–138.

204. My inclusion of the *Laws* among the great literary dialogues might need some defense. See the particularly appreciative essay on the *Laws* by André Laks in Rowe and Schofield, *Greek and Roman Political Thought,* 258–292; and, of course, Voegelin's great chapter on the *Laws,* in *Plato and Aristotle,* 215–268, which ends, "Plato died at the age of eighty-one. On the evening of his death he had a Thracian girl play the flute to him. The girl could not find the beat of the nomos. With a movement of his finger, Plato indicated to her the Measure."

205. Bernard Williams makes my point in his own way: "Plato did think that if you devoted your life to theory, this could change your life. He did think, at least at one period, that pure studies could lead to a transforming vision. But he never thought that the materials or conditions of such a transformation could be set down in a theory, or that a theory would, at some suitable advanced level, explain the vital thing you needed to know . . . Rather, Plato seems to have thought that the final significance of philosophy for one's life does not lie in anything that could be embodied in its findings, but emerges, rather, in its activities." *The*

Sense of the Past, 179. Charles Kahn says something similar: "For Plato philosophy is essentially a form of life and not a set of doctrines." *Plato and the Socratic Dialogue,* 383.

206. Again, Williams's insight is helpful: "Not everything asserted in a dialogue, even by Socrates, has been asserted by Plato: Socrates asserting may be Plato suggesting. Because Plato is an immensely serious philosopher, who indeed set philosophy on the path of claiming to address our deepest concerns by means of argument, orderly inquiry, and intellectual imagination . . . we may well underestimate the extent to which he could combine intensity, pessimism, and even a certain religious solemnity, with an ironical gaiety and an incapacity to take all his ideas equally seriously." *The Sense of the Past,* 149–150.

207. Plato in the *Phaedrus* had this insight but never developed it as Aristotle did in his *Rhetoric.*

208. Could we say that Plato suffered the birth pangs of philosophy, but Aristotle found it already a healthy young person? Parmenides had put rigorous argument on the agenda of Greek thought, though his rigor was as much intimidating as appealing. Plato developed argument as a rich and subtle resource, but although he returned over and over again to a few central questions, he provided a series of not always compatible ways to answer them, rather than a single coherent system. (Kahn and Williams, among others, agree with this point.) Aristotle was the first to create something like a systematic philosophy, though not yet as modern philosophers would attempt to do, given the priority of practical concerns in Aristotle's thought.

209. Hadot in his *Philosophy as a Way of Life* shows that Aristotle and his followers were as devoted to a way of life as were the followers of Plato or any other philosophic school.

210. See Luc Brisson, *How Philosophers Saved Myths: Allegorical Interpretation and Classical Mythology* (Chicago: University of Chicago Press, 2004 [1996]).

211. Paul Veyne, *Bread and Circuses: Historical Sociology and Political Pluralism* (London: Penguin, 1990 [1976]).

212. Runciman, "Doomed to Extinction," 348–367. Runciman very succinctly sums up his argument as to why no Greek polis was able to go the way of Rome or Venice: "the *poleis* were all, without exception, far too democratic" (364).

213. W. G. Runciman, "The Exception That Proves the Rule? Rome in the Axial Age," in *Comparing Modernities: Pluralism versus Homogen[e]ity,* ed. Eliezer Ben-Rafael and Yitzhak Sternberg (Leiden: Brill, 2005), 125–140. He says that "in selectionist evolutionary theory" there is "a universal underlying process of heritable but interacting levels of biological, cultural, and social evolution. Distinctive species, cultures, and societies are all the outcome of the distinctive *path dependent* sequences in which selective pressure comes to bear on the extended phenotypic effects of information transmitted either genetically (by strings of DNA passed from parents to offspring), culturally (by imitation or learning), or socially (by imposition of institutional inducements and sanctions)" (139).

8. The Axial Age III

1. Following current standard practice, I have used the pinyin system of Romanization throughout, and, even in direct quotations, have changed other systems to pinyin. For someone of my age, raised on the Wade-Giles system, this has not been easy. For the

non-Sinological reader, pinyin has advantages and disadvantages. "Zhou" in this sentence is closer to the actual pronunciation than "Chou" in the Wade-Giles system. *Daodejing* is closer than *Tao Te Ching*. On the other hand, x and q may be challenging. X as in *xin* becomes clearer when we remember that it is "hsin" in Wade-Giles, and q as in *qi* becomes clearer when we remember that it is "ch'i" in Wade-Giles.

2. It is important to remember that at the time of Confucius, and through most of the pre-imperial period, even though written texts of various sorts existed, teaching was primarily oral. The *Odes,* in particular, were memorized, but so were some of the *Documents.* The written texts we have are not necessarily the same as what is referred to in the *Analects* of Confucius. The books we know as the *Odes* and the *Documents* almost certainly include material that was written well after the time of Confucius, and perhaps lack some of what was available to him. For an extreme view that there were no references at all to the documents and the odes in the earliest stratum of the *Analects* and that the books that came to be known by these names may not even have been written, but certainly were not compiled, until well after Confucius's death, see E. Bruce Brooks and A. Taeko Brooks, *The Original Analects: Sayings of Confucius and His Successors* (New York: Columbia University Press, 1998), 255.

3. Edward L. Shaughnessy, "Western Zhou History," in Michael Loewe and Edward L. Shaughnessy, *The Cambridge History of Ancient China* (Cambridge: Cambridge University Press, 1999), 292–351.

4. Mark Edward Lewis, *Sanctioned Violence in Early China* (Albany: SUNY Press, 1990).

5. Ibid., 17.

6. Ibid., 17. Translation is Lewis's. Compare James Legge, *The Ch'un Ts'ew with the Tso Chuen*, vol. 5 of *The Chinese Classics* (Hong Kong: Hong Kong University Press, 1960 [1895]), 382. Burton Watson has translated a volume of selections from the *Zuo* that is much easier to use than Legge and gives the flavor of the text, but is only a small portion of the whole. See his *The Tso Chuan: Selections from China's Oldest Narrative History* (New York: Columbia University Press, 1989).

7. Lothar von Falkenhausen, *Chinese Society in the Age of Confucius (1000–250 BC)*: The Archaeological Evidence (Los Angeles: Cotsen Institute of Archaeology, UCLA, 2006), 156.

8. Ibid., 12.

9. Lewis, *Sanctioned Violence*, 22.

10. Ibid., 25.

11. Ibid., 38.

12. As Falkenhausen puts it, "In China the notion of a centrally administered bounded territory was an Eastern Zhou innovation. In the early Bronze Age, and still for much of the time documented by the *Zuo zhuan* [that is, the Spring and Autumn period], political authority radiated outward from a polity's capital *(guo),* petering out fairly quickly as distance from the capital increased . . . By Warring States times, by contrast, the principal meaning of *guo* had become 'state' rather than 'capital,' and the exact delimitation of each state's territory became a matter of major importance." *Chinese Society,* 406.

13. Yuri Pines, *Foundations of Confucian Thought: Intellectual Life in the Chunquiu Period, 722–453 BCE* (Honolulu: University of Hawai'i Press, 2002), 89.

14. Falkenhausen, *Chinese Society,* 326–399.

15. Ibid., 370.

16. Ibid., 366.

17. Ibid., 365.

18. Ibid., 28.

19. Ibid., 32.

20. For a discussion of the historical reliability of the *Zuo,* see Pines, *Foundations of Confucian Thought,* 26–39. Mark Lewis, in *Sanctioned Violence* (1990), relies heavily on the *Zuo* for his portrait of Chunqiu society, but in *Writing and Authority in Early China* (Albany: SUNY Press, 1999), he expresses doubts as to its reliability. Falkenhausen lends considerable support to the reliability of the *Zuo* by finding numerous archaeological confirmations: Falkenhausen, *Chinese Society,* under *Zuo zhuan* in index.

21. On the changing meaning of *junzi,* see Pines, *Foundations of Confucian Thought,* 165–171. A third terminological shift paralleled those of *shi* and *junzi:* during Western Zhou, *baixing* (one hundred clans/surnames) referred to the ranked aristocracy, but by late Chunqiu times it came to mean "the people" *(min)* when "increasing numbers of commoners acquired surnames *(xing)*." Ibid., 44.

22. Lewis, *Sanctioned Violence,* 48, and footnotes citing passages in the *Zuo.*

23. See *Analects* 7:1, where Confucius speaks of himself as "transmitting but not creating."

24. Pines, *Foundations of Confucian Thought,* 205–206.

25. Benjamin Schwartz, *The World of Thought in Ancient China* (Cambridge, Mass.: Harvard University Press, 1983), 60. Italics in the original.

26. See Brooks and Brooks, *The Original Analects,* Appendix 1, The Accretion Theory of the Analects, 201–248.

27. Michael Nylan, *The Five "Confucian" Classics* (New Haven: Yale University Press, 2001), 20.

28. Arthur Waley, *The Analects of Confucius* (London: Allen and Unwin, 1938).

29. Translation from Brooks and Brooks, *The Original Analects,* 14. I have replaced the Brookses' idiosyncratic Romanization with *pinyin.*

30. Translation from Roger T. Ames and Henry Rosemont Jr., *The Analects of Confucius: A Philosophical Translation* (New York: Ballantine Books, 1998), 119. I have dropped Ames's translation of *ren* as "authoritative person," as I wish for the moment to leave open the issue of translating the term.

31. Translation from Waley, *Analects of Confucius,* 129. In Waley's numbering this is 7:29. I have replaced Waley's translation of *ren* as "goodness" for the reason stated in the previous note.

32. A. C. Graham, *Disputers of the Tao: Philosophical Argument in Ancient China* (La Salle: Open Court, 1989), 112–113.

33. Ames and Rosemont, *The Analects of Confucius,* 49.

34. Heiner Roetz, *Confucian Ethics of the Axial Age* (Albany: SUNY Press, 1993 [1992]), 123, quoting the *Lüshi chunqiu:* "Confucius regards *ren* the highest."

35. Here I part company with Ames, who believes that because *ren* is indelibly relational, it must also be particularistic. See Ames and Rosemont, *The Analects of Confucius,* 20ff. And I agree with Roetz as to the universalism of *ren.* See Roetz, *Confucian Ethics,* 119ff.

36. Herbert Fingarette, *Confucius: The Secular as Sacred* (New York: Harper Torchbooks, 1972), 77.

37. Graham, *Disputers of the Tao,* 13.

38. *Dao* here, however much its usual Confucian use is social and political, would seem to carry a transmundane meaning. Or could we say that Confucius's ideal society, the Way of the ancients, is itself something sacred?

39. Fingarette, *Confucius,* 19–20.

40. In other translations, this is often included in 10:12.

41. Simon Leys, *The Analects of Confucius* (New York: Norton, 1997), 192.

42. Graham, *Disputers of the Tao,* 15.

43. Fingarette, *Confucius,* 65, 67–68.

44. Ibid., 68–69. He goes on to say: "The vision of emerging unity among men was thus not merely a political vision—though even as such this Confucian vision was one of the most grandiose—and successful—of any political vision in recorded history. But it was a philosophical vision, even a religious one. It revealed humanity, sacred and marvelous, as residing in community, community as rooted in the inherited forms of life" (69).

45. See William McNeill, *Mythistory and Other Essays* (Chicago: Chicago University Press, 1986). A. C. Graham comments as follows on the central role of Confucianism in the transmission of the historical tradition: "The strength of the Confucians was that as preservers of the Zhou tradition they were the guardians of Chinese civilization as such. It was never quite possible to treat them as just another of the competing schools unless, like the First Emperor beginning history with himself, or Mao Zedong during the Cultural Revolution, you could contemplate razing it to the foundations to make a wholly new start. One may add that since Confucianism roots all its general ideas in the minute study of existing custom, arts and historical precedent, it alone held the promise of the full integration of the individual into his culture, community, and cosmos which must be part of the secret of China's social immortality." *Disputers of the Tao,* 33.

46. Roetz, *Confucian Ethics,* 122. I have substituted the original terms for Roetz's translations and slightly revised the passage in light of other translations. It is worth noting that Yan Yuan, often referred to as Yan Hui, in earlier passages of the *Analects* seems to understand *ren* better than anyone, perhaps better than Confucius himself, so here it is a bit odd that he seems unclear about it. It is also worth noting that, probably because of his closeness to *ren,* Yan Yuan is treated by Confucius in these earlier passages as "the beloved disciple," the most promising of his disciples, though he died young.

47. Again I have substituted the original Chinese terms for Waley's translation of them.

48. Kwong-Loi Shun has an interesting article in which he discusses both of these passages, together with various efforts to prove that one of them takes precedence over the other, and comes up with a way of reconciling them. See his "*Ren* and *Li* in the *Analects,*" in *Confucius and the* Analects: *New Essays,* ed. Bryan W. Van Norden (New York: Oxford University Press, 2002), 53–72.

49. Fingarette, *Confucius,* 53–54. Fingarette leaves the key terms untranslated.

50. For Roetz's version of the Kohlberg scheme, see his *Confucian Ethics,* 26–27. Roetz may well have been influenced by Jürgen Habermas, who has used the Kohlberg scheme in a number of publications.

51. Ibid., 111–118. Shun also pairs *yi* with *ren* in contrast to *li*. See Shun, *"Ren and Li,"* 68–69. Brooks and Brooks, as in the passages quoted above, translate *yi* as "right." Shun translates it as "rightness." Leys, like Roetz, translates it as "justice."

52. Translation from Ames and Rosemont, *The Analects of Confucius,* omitting the translation of *ren.*

53. Roetz, *Confucian Ethics,* 133.

54. Ibid., 142, transcribed exactly.

55. Ibid., 135.

56. See Wilfred Cantwell Smith, *The Meaning and End of Religion* (New York: Macmillan, 1962).

57. Graham, *Disputers of the Tao,* 17.

58. Ibid., 17. The best treatment of the idea of Heaven in the *Analects* that I know of is in Schwartz, *World of Thought,* 122–127.

59. See *Analects* 5:13.

60. Graham, *Disputers of the Tao,* 18.

61. Robert Eno, *The Confucian Creation of Heaven: Philosophy and the Defense of Ritual Mastery* (Albany: SUNY Press, 1990), 41.

62. See Philip J. Ivanhoe, *Confucian Moral Self Cultivation,* 2nd ed. (Indianapolis: Hackett, 2000). The first chapter, on Kongzi (Confucius), gives a much richer account of the subject than I can give here.

63. Joseph Needham, *Science and Civilization in China,* vol. 1 (Cambridge: Cambridge University Press, 1954), and many subsequent volumes.

64. See the discussion of "The Concept of Man" in Roetz, *Confucian Ethics,* 123–126. Confucian philosophical anthropology, he argues, is not particularistic but "denies any natural distinction between men" (125).

65. Schwartz, *World of Thought,* 83.

66. Ibid., 117. The Fingarette quote is from *Confucius,* 69.

67. Lewis, *Sanctioned Violence,* 53–54.

68. Ibid., 60ff.

69. For these developments, besides his *Sanctioned Violence,* see also Mark Edward Lewis, "Warring States Political History," in Loewe and Shaughnessy, *Ancient China,* 587–650

70. W. Allyn Rickett, *Guanzi: Political, Economic, and Philosophical Essays from Early China,* vols. 1 and 2 (Princeton: Princeton University Press, 1985, 1998).

71. John Knoblock and Jeffrey Riegel, *The Annals of Lu Buwei,* a translation and commentary (Stanford: Stanford University Press, 2000.

72. Lewis, "Warring States," 641.

73. Brooks and Brooks, *The Original Analects,* 4–5, 201ff. The Brookses make the case for accretion, especially with respect to the *Daodejing* and the *Mencius.* A. C. Graham has made the case relative to the *Zhuangzi.* See his *Chuang Tzu: The Seven Inner Chapters and Other Writings from the Chuang Tzu* (London: Allen and Unwin, 1981).

74. A. C. Graham, *Later Mohist Logic, Ethics and Science* (Hong Kong: Chinese University Press, 1978).

75. Michael Puett, *The Ambivalence of Creation: Debates concerning Innovation and Artifice in Early China* (Stanford: Stanford University Press, 2001), 51. In a footnote Puett

warns against using the metaphors and analogies in a text to prove the social origin of the authors. Socrates frequently uses examples from the crafts, but then he was a stonemason.

76. Graham, *Disputers of the Tao,* 34.

77. Translation from Puett, *The Ambivalence of Creation,* 47. It should be noted that in the *Analects,* Yao was the first of the "ancient kings."

78. Ibid., 43.

79. Burton Watson, *Mo Tzu: Basic Writings* (New York: Columbia University Press, 1963), 88.

80. Ibid., 34.

81. Ibid., 35.

82. Ibid., 83.

83. Ibid., 37.

84. Graham considers the phrase "universal love" to be misleading because "it is both too vague (*jian* implies 'for each' rather than 'for all') and too warm (the Mohist *ai* is an unemotional will to benefit people and dislike of harming them). The Mohists were rather dour people whose ears were open to the demands of justice rather than to the appeal of love." *Disputers of the Tao,* 41.

85. David S. Nivison, "The Classical Philosophical Writings," in Loewe and Shaughnessy, *Ancient China,* 763.

86. Watson, *Mo Tzu,* 40.

87. Graham, *Disputers of the Tao,* 42–43.

88. Ibid., 43.

89. Watson, *Mo Tzu,* 82.

90. Ibid., 84.

91. Roetz, *Confucian Ethics,* 27, 243. It should be clear that Mozi's utilitarianism was theoretical; indeed, he seemed to believe it was the only completely convincing theoretical basis for his moral concerns. But he and most of his followers were not utilitarian in the sense of making one's own self-interest primary. They were "selfless" in their activism, largely in defense of the weak. The same point could perhaps be made with respect to philosophical utilitarianism in eighteenth- and nineteenth-century Britain.

92. Of Mozi's "theism" Benjamin Schwartz writes, "the subtle mysterious dialectic of the interplay between divine plan and human action which we find in the Hebrew Bible cannot be found here." *World of Thought,* 162.

93. Graham, *Disputers of the Tao,* 49. Mozi affirms the existence of "gods and ghosts" along with Heaven and gives them the same function.

94. Ibid., 50.

95. Watson, *Mo Tzu,* "Against Fatalism," 117–123.

96. Ibid., "Moderation in Funerals," 65–77; "Against Music," 110–116.

97. Ibid., "Moderation in Expenditure," 62–64.

98. A. C. Graham, *Chuang Tzu,* 276–277.

99. Eno, *Confucian Creation,* 50–52.

100. Translation from Schwartz, *World of Thought,* 259, and Graham, *Disputers of the Tao,* 54.

101. Translation from Graham, *Disputers of the Tao,* 54; D. C. Lau, trans., *Mencius* (Harmondsworth: Penguin, 1970), 188.

102. Nivison, "The Classical Philosophical Writings," 768.

103. Graham, *Disputers of the Tao,* 55, attributes chaps. 28–31 of the *Zhuangzi* and chaps. 1:2, 1:3, 2:2, 2:3, and 21:4 of the *Lüshi chunqiu* to the Yangist tradition.

104. Graham, *Chuang Tzu,* 264–265.

105. Graham points out that in the Warring States period, many came to "prefer the comforts of private life to the burdens and perils of the increasingly murderous struggle for power and possessions." *Disputers of the Tao,* 53.

106. Ibid., 56.

107. Ibid., 59–64.

108. *The Book of Lieh-tzu,* trans. A. C. Graham (London: John Murray, 1960), 148f.

109. *Lüshi chunqiu* 2/2.2, "Valuing Life" chapter. Translation from Graham, *Disputers of the Tao,* 58.

110. *Lüshi chunqiu* 1/2.1, translation from Knoblock and Riegel, *Annals of Lu Buwei,* 64.

111. Harold D. Roth, *Original Tao: Inward Training* (Nei-yeh) *and the Foundations of Taoist Mysticism* (New York: Columbia University Press, 1999).

112. "Therefore if the gentleman is left with no choice but to preside over the world, his best policy is Doing Nothing." *Zhuangzi,* 11, translation from Graham, *Chuang Tzu,* 12.

113. Graham, *Disputers of the Tao,* 66–67.

114. Ibid., 72–74.

115. Eno, *Confucian Creation,* 191–192. Eno goes on to say that there is no convincing etymology of the term *"ru"* (192–197).

116. It was the Song dynasty philosopher Zhu Xi (1130–1200) who "elevated the Four Books over the Five Classics." Nylan, *The Five "Confucian" Classics,* 56.

117. Cited in Michael J. Puett, *To Become a God: Cosmology, Sacrifice, and Self-Divinization in Early China* (Cambridge, Mass.: Harvard University Press, 2002), 253.

118. Roth, *Original Tao,* 180.

119. Edward Slingerland argues that the *Laozi* is older than the *Neiye* (*Inner Training,* or as Roth translates, *Inward Training*), whereas Roth holds that the *Neiye* is the oldest Daoist text. See Slingerland's *Effortless Action: Wu-wei as Conceptual Metaphor and Spiritual Ideal in Early China* (New York: Oxford University Press, 2003), 280–282.

120. Roth, *Original Tao,* 7–8; see also 195ff.

121. Ibid., 25, 213, citing Brooks and Brooks, *The Original Analects,* 156.

122. Roth, *Original Tao,* 107. In the same place, Roth considers whether the use of *shen,* originally "spirit," as in "ancestral spirit," could involve a generalization of the earlier shamanistic practice of invoking the *shen* at the ancestral sacrifices. Michael Puett strongly opposes that idea, also put forth by A. C. Graham, *Disputers of the Tao,* 100ff., and argues that the *Neiye* represents a rejection of traditional ritual practice and a claim for individual self-divinization, an idea not entirely convincing to me. See Puett, *To Become a God,* 109ff.

123. Roth, *Original Tao,* 109–115.

124. Graham, *Disputers of the Tao,* 494.

125. Roth, *Original Tao,* 46.

126. Ibid., 42.

127. Ibid., 72.

128. Ibid., 153–161, cites numerous passages on inner cultivation in the *Zhuangzi* that closely parallel the *Neiye.*

129. Eske Mollgaard translates this passage as a moral imperative: "Do for others in not doing for others." He finds a resonance with Kant's categorical imperative that overcomes the limitations of the golden rule. His argument is interesting, if not entirely convincing. See his "Zhuangzi's Religious Ethics," *Journal of the American Academy of Religion* 71, no. 2 (2003).

130. Graham, *The Chuang Tzu,* 89.

131. Ibid., 123–124.

132. Here there is perhaps a resonance with the Farmers' School.

133. Burton Watson, *The Complete Works of Chuang Tzu* (New York: Columbia University Press, 1968), 105.

134. On *wuwei* in the Analects, see Slingerland, *Effortless Action,* 43–76. Slingerland's book is concerned with *wuwei* in early Chinese thought, with the exception of Legalism, where he finds the use of the term to be "completely divorced" from its use in other strands of thought (288).

135. Hans-Georg Moeller, *Daoism Explained: From the Dream of the Butterfly to the Fishnet Allegory* (Chicago: Open Court, 2004), 35. Italics in original.

136. Graham, *Chuang Tzu,* 98.

137. Moeller, *Daoism Explained,* 35. Italics in original.

138. Roth cites the parallels between the *Neiye* and the *Daodejing* in *Original Tao,* 144–153.

139. Han-Georg Moeller, *The Philosophy of the Daodejing* (New York: Columbia University Press, 2006), chap. 1, "How to Read the *Daodejing,*" 1–20. Moeller's example of the "hypertext" of a website as a parallel for reading the *Daodejing* is suggestive in that, like the *Daodejing,* the hypertext is recursive rather than linear, assumes a lot of background knowledge that it doesn't make explicit, suggests many connections with what has gone before, and is more a "recipe" for action than an argument (5–7). There is, however, one fundamental difference: the Web hypertext is eminently disposable; the *Daodejing* is to be internalized.

140. Ibid., 7.

141. D. C. Lau, trans., *Tao Te Ching* (New York: Penguin, 1963), 62.

142. Arthur Waley, *The Way and Its Power* (London: Allen and Unwin, 1934), 149.

143. Ibid., 56–57.

144. Lau, *Tao Te Ching,* 44.

145. Moeller, *Philosophy of the Daodejing,* 7.

146. Waley, *The Way,* 57.

147. Lau, *Tao Te Ching,* 64.

148. Ibid., 71.

149. Moeller, *Philosophy of the Daodejing,* 22.

150. Lau, *Tao Te Ching,* 85. I have altered lines 3 and 4 in accordance with Moeller's translation in *Philosophy of the Daodejing,* 21.

151. Lau, *Tao Te Ching,* chap. 40, p. 101.

152. Michael LaFargue, *Tao and Method: A Reasoned Approach to the Daodejing* (Albany: SUNY Press, 1994), 118–122.

153. Lau, *Tao Te Ching*, 142.

154. Pines translation, *Foundations of Confucian Thought*, 89.

155. Lau, *Tao Te Ching*, esp. 29–30, 41–42.

156. Roetz, *Confucian Ethics*, 27.

157. Ibid., 257. I have found the work of Hans-Georg Moeller, both his *Daoism Explained* and his *Philosophy of the Daodejing*, to be extraordinarily helpful: no one that I have read has opened up the depths of the images in these texts and the rich network of meanings between them as well as he has. But when, at the end of *The Philosophy of the Daodejing*, he develops, with the help of Michel Foucault, a nonhumanist or post-humanist philosophy as a counterpart to his interpretation of Daoism as a prehumanist philosophy, it seems to me he merely ends up in Kohlberg's stage 4½.

158. Ibid., 255.

159. Translation from Roetz, *Confucian Ethics*, 253.

160. Chap. 75, in Philip J. Ivanhoe, trans., *The Daodejing of Laozi* (New York: Seven Bridges Press, 2002), 78.

161. Ibid., 30.

162. Chap. 30, Lau, *Tao Te Ching*, 88.

163. It is interesting that, in his magisterial overview of early Chinese philosophy, David Nivison devotes one section to "Han Feizi, Laozi, Legalism, and Daoism." Nivison, "The Classical Philosophical Writings," 799–808.

164. Arthur Waley, *Three Ways of Thought in Ancient China* (London: Allen and Unwin, 1939), 199ff.

165. Burton Watson, *Han Fei Tzu: Basic Writings* (New York: Columbia University Press, 1964), 14.

166. Schwartz, *World of Thought*, 328.

167. Ibid., 336.

168. See Burton Watson's translation of selections from the *Hanfeizi*, containing a brief biography of this interesting and tragic figure. *Han Fei Tzu*, 2–3.

169. Waley, *Three Ways*, 202–203.

170. These passages are as modified by Nivison in "The Classical Philosophical Writings," 801, from Watson's *Han Fei Tzu*, 35, 38.

171. Lau, *Tao Te Ching*, 59.

172. Watson, *Han Fei Tzu*, 98–99.

173. See the translation of the *Huainanzi* chapter on rulership in Roger Ames, *The Art of Rulership: A Study in Ancient Chinese Political Thought* (Honolulu: University of Hawai'i Press, 1983). Paul Goldin argues that the Huainanzi was not syncretist in the sense usually assumed, but borrowed from various schools to support a singularly authoritarian form of government that was certainly not Confucian. See Paul R. Goldin, "Insidious Syncretism in the Political Philosophy of *Huainanzi*," in *After Confucius: Studies in Early Chinese Philosophy* (Honolulu: University of Hawai'i Press, 2005), 90–111.

174. Schwartz, *World of Thought*, 285.

175. Lau, *Mencius*, 1A6, 53–54, modified with the help of Schwartz's translation of part of this passage, *World of Thought*, 282.

176. Lau, *Mencius*, 2B13, 94, as modified.

177. Schwartz, *World of Thought,* 284.

178. 7A21, translation from Roetz, *Confucian Ethics,* 86, as modified.

179. Lau, *Mencius,* 6A7, 164.

180. Ibid., 1A7, 58.

181. Lau, *Mencius,* 1A4, 52.

182. Ibid., 4A14, 124.

183. Ibid., 1B8, 68.

184. Ibid., 7B14, 196, as modified.

185. Ibid., 5B7, 157. Brooks and Brooks, in *The Original Analects,* 285, argue that Zisi could not have been Confucius's grandson, though he was a successor in his family line.

186. Lau, *Mencius,* 5A5, 144.

187. For an excellent discussion of human nature in Mencius, see A. C. Graham, "The Background of the Mencian Theory of Human Nature," in *Studies in Chinese Philosophy* (Albany: SUNY Press, 1990), 7–66. See also Kwong-Loi Shun, *Mencius and Early Chinese Thought* (Stanford: Stanford University Press, 1997), 180–231.

188. Graham, *Disputers of the Tao,* 123ff. For those interested in the controversy over human nature, this would be a good place to begin.

189. Lau, *Mencius,* 2A6, 82.

190. I. A. Richards, in his *Mencius on the Mind: Experiments in Multiple Definition* (London: Kegan Paul, 1932), 80, notes, "We have reason to suppose that Mencius' pronouncements ought probably to be read more as injunctions than as statements," thus pointing out their performative intent, without necessarily denying them theoretical validity.

191. There is a short passage, *Mencius* 4B12, in Lau, *Mencius,* 130, that reads: "Mencius said, 'A great man is one who retains the heart of a new-born babe.'" Here Mencius uses the common Daoist symbol of the baby, but perhaps with the emphasis on the moral potential of the baby rather than its premoral power.

192. D. C. Lau argues that Mencius is "more truly a mystic" than Laozi or Zhuangzi because "not only does he believe that a man can attain oneness with the universe by perfecting his own moral nature, but he has absolute faith in the moral purpose of the universe." *Mencius,* 46.

193. Ibid., 2A2, 77–78.

194. Benjamin Schwartz reminds us that this very contrast between a naturalistic and a theistic interpretation of Heaven is "an antithesis which we impose on the text." *World of Thought,* 289. In general Schwartz's discussion of the religious dimension of early Chinese thought is particularly judicious.

195. Lau, *Mencius,* 7A1, 182, as modified.

196. Waley, *Three Ways,* 116–117. This passage was read at Waley's funeral.

197. Nivison, "The Classical Philosophical Writings," 791; Graham, *Disputers of the Tao,* 237. John Knoblock goes so far as to say, "The domain of knowledge traversed by Xunzi's thought exceeds that of any other ancient Chinese thinker and bears comparison only with Aristotle in the West." Knoblock, *Xunzi: A Translation and Study of the Complete Works,* vol. 3 (Stanford: Stanford University Press, 1994), vii.

198. John Knoblock, *Xunzi: A Translation and Study of the Complete Works,* vol. 2 (Stanford: Stanford University Press, 1990), 168.

199. Ibid., 168.

200. Burton Watson, *Hsün Tzu: Basic Writings* (New York: Columbia University Press, 1963), 37.

201. The best treatment of this issue in Xunzi that I have come across is Paul Rakita Goldin, *Rituals of the Way* (Chicago: Open Court, 1999), 1–13, 72–81.

202. Graham, *Disputers of the Tao*, 253.

203. Nivison, "The Classical Philosophical Writings," 792. Italics in original.

204. Knoblock, *Xunzi*, bk. 21, 3:107; Watson, *Hsün Tzu*, 131–132.

205. Knoblock, *Xunzi*, bk. 23, 3:166–167.

206. Knoblock's translation, *Xunzi*, 3:14–22. Watson translates the title as "A Discussion of Heaven."

207. *Xunzi*, bk. 17; Watson, trans. *Hsün Tzu*, 80–81. Robert Eno, in *The Confucian Creation of Heaven*, has a judicious discussion of the various meanings of *Tian* in Xunzi, and insists that they span the gamut between naturalism and theism. See chap. 6, "Ritual as a Natural Art: The Role of T'ien in the *Hsun Tzu*," 131–169.

208. *Xunzi*, bk. 9, translation from Nivison, "The Classical Philosophical Writings," 796, adapted from Watson, *Hsün Tzu*, 45.

209. *Xunzi*, bk. 4, translation from Roetz, *Confucian Ethics*, 173.

210. Ibid., bk. 21, 159–160, as modified with the help of Watson, *Hsün Tzu*, 129.

211. Translation from Goldin, *Rituals*, 73. Compare *Xunzi*, bk. 19, in Knoblock, *Xunzi*, 3:61.

212. *Xunzi*, bk. 29, translation from Roetz, *Confucian Ethics*, 64–65. Compare Knoblock, *Xunzi*, 3:251–252. Knoblock translates the title of book 29 as "On the Way of Sons." The whole of this short book is remarkable. Some have held that this book and other late ones were appended by disciples, but Knoblock believes they were teaching texts of Confucian traditions that Xunzi used with his own students.

213. One can imagine Yamazaki Ansai's hair standing on end if he ever read this statement. Ansai was the founder of absolutist Confucianism in Tokugawa Japan, and, according to Herman Ooms, "erased" any notion in the Confucian tradition that a superior could be disobeyed. See Herman Ooms, *Tokugawa Ideology: Early Constructs, 1570–1680* (Princeton: Princeton University Press, 1985), 247.

214. *Xunzi*, bk. 2, translation from Roetz, *Confucian Ethics*, 223, modified with the help of Watson, *Hsün Tzu*, 24. Compare Knoblock, *Xunzi: A Translation and Study of the Complete Works*, vol. 1 (Stanford: Stanford University Press, 1988), 151. Roetz points out the parallel with Aristotle's statement that he loves his teacher (Plato) but he loves truth more.

215. Robert F. Campany compares Xunzi's theory of ritual with that of Durkheim, finding it equally sophisticated, and with many parallels. See his "Xunzi and Durkheim as Theorists of Ritual," in *Discourse and Practice*, ed. Frank Reynolds and David Tracy (Albany: SUNY Press, 1992), 197–231.

216. Xunzi, bk. 19, in Knoblock, *Xunzi*, 3:55.

217. Knoblock, *Xunzi*, 3:60.

218. Goldin, *Rituals of the Way*, 73.

219. Ibid., 105.

220. Knoblock, *Xunzi*, 3:61.

221. Ibid., 3:72.

222. Ibid., bk. 20, 3:80.

223. Heiner Roetz argues that Xunzi's rejection of our nature as the source of our better feelings is more a rejection of the Daoists than of Mencius. "To make nature a norm not only destroys morality. It is treason to man himself, who is thrown back into the animal kingdom where he, contrary to the assertion of the Daoist utopia, cannot survive." *Confucian Ethics,* 223.

224. Ivanhoe, *Confucian Moral Self Cultivation,* 37. Compare Knoblock, *Xunzi,* 1:136.

225. A. C. Graham, "Being in Western Philosophy Compared with *shih/fei* and *yu/wu* in Chinese Philosophy," *Asia Major* 8, no. 2 (1961), as reprinted in Graham, *Studies in Chinese Philosophy,* 359.

226. Knoblock, *Xunzi,* 3:viii.

227. In the early 1950s I began a Ph.D. program specially created for me in sociology and what was then called at Harvard "Far Eastern Languages." Even though I was intending to specialize in the study of Japan, I was required to study Chinese, and I took a semester of classical Chinese in which I read selections of the original texts of the *Analects* and the *Mencius.* In my dissertation on religion in the Tokugawa period I took as a case study an eighteenth-century Japanese religious-ethical movement called Shingaku (Ch. *Xinxue,* "heart learning"), and translated as an appendix a short work, the *Ishida Sensei Jiseki,* put together by the disciples of the founder of the movement, Ishida Baigan, composed of short anecdotes and brief dialogues with his students, obviously following the pattern of the *Analects.* (See Robert N. Bellah, *Tokugawa Religion* [Glencoe, Ill.: Free Press, 1957], appendix 1, "A Memoir of Our Teacher, Ishida," 199–216. When, in 2000, I was invited by the remaining followers of Shingaku to speak in Kyoto at a commemoration of the founding of the movement, they asked me if they could translate the appendix. But, I said, it is in Japanese. However, they replied, we cannot read it, but we can read your English translation. Premodern Japanese, even as late as the eighteenth century, cannot be read by educated Japanese unless they are specialists.) Baigan was, among other things, a Confucian, and a great admirer of Mencius along with several neo-Confucian thinkers. I had to work hard at translating his many references to Chinese thought. I might also note that Benjamin Schwartz was one of my teachers and Weiming Tu was one of my first graduate students, and later a colleague at Berkeley. None of this makes me a specialist in ancient Chinese thought. It does, however, make it easier for me to follow translations when I have the Chinese text in hand.

228. I do want to avoid "essentialism" with respect to either Chinese culture or Confucianism. Chinese culture, like all cultures, is complex and diverse; we could well speak of Confucianisms rather than of Confucianism—I have tried to suggest the differences between even the major figures who have most powerfully shaped the tradition. Mark Csikszentmihalyi has reminded us that Confucianism refers to a number of related phenomena: for purposes of this chapter, the school, or rather schools, who transmitted the Classics, that is Ruists, with an interpretation deriving from Confucius but different depending on different teacher-student lineages, is most important, but the term also has been used to denote a variety of political ideologies, bureaucratic status ethics, and familial practices. See Mark Csikszentmihalyi, "Confucianism," in *God's Rule: The Politics of the World Religions,* ed. Jacob Neusner (Washington, D.C.: Georgetown University Press, 2003), 213–214. But even in denoting the range of meanings of Confucianism, one is struck by how many of them apply

to central tendencies of premodern Chinese culture generally, including the many tensions and conflicts within it.

229. Benjamin Schwartz, "The Age of Transcendence," in *Wisdom, Revelation, and Doubt: Perspectives on the First Millennium* B.C., special issue, *Daedalus* 104, no. 2 (Spring 1975): 3.

230. Schwartz, *World of Thought*, 289.

231. See his singularly obtuse essay "Was There a Transcendental Breakthrough in China?" in *The Origin and Diversity of Axial Age Civilizations*, ed. S. N. Eisenstadt (Albany: SUNY Press, 1986), 325–359. I admire Elvin's work on Chinese economic and ecological history, which is his primary interest.

232. Max Weber, "Konfuzianismus und Taoismus," in *Gesammelte Aufsätze zur Religionssoziologie* (Tübingen: J. C. B. Mohr, 1921), 1:276–536. Translated into English by Hans Gerth as *The Religion of China* (Glencoe, Ill.: Free Press, 1951).

233. Because what we know of the Qin dynasty comes from writers in the following Han dynasty who had a strong motive to blacken its reputation, we don't really know how many books were burned or scholars killed, if any. That Qin Shihuangdi, under the influence of Li Si, attempted to suppress critical thought seems, however, to be certain.

234. Graham, *Disputers of the Tao*, 372.

235. Schwartz, *World of Thought*, 320.

236. Puett, *To Become a God*, 245. Paul Goldin has given a similar description of the regime of Qin Shihuangdi as Li Si saw it: "Any institution whose authority did not derive directly from the emperor inherently challenged the foundations of the empire and had to be destroyed. Philosophers and teachers, who routinely appealed to traditions, scriptures, and august precedents, would have constituted a conspicuous example of what Li Si feared most. The Qin empire was not merely an empire; it was a unified cosmos with a proper cosmology. The ruler of the cosmos, similarly, was not merely an emperor or great king; he was the center of the cosmos, the prime mover of all order and logic." See "Li Si Chancellor of the Universe," in Goldin's *After Confucius*, 71.

237. Puett, *To Become a God*, 312–313.

238. S. N. Eisenstadt, "This Worldly Transcendentalism and the Structuring of the World—Weber's 'Religion of China' and the Format of Chinese History and Civilization" (unpublished, 1980), 51. This paper was published in German as "Innerweltliche Transzendenz und die Strukturierung der Welt: Max Webers Studie über China und die Gestalt der Chinesischen Zivilisation," in *Max Webers Studie über Konfuzianismus und Taoismus: Interpretation und Kritik*, ed. Wolfgang Schluchter (Frankfurt am Main: Suhrkamp, 1983). A shortened version was published in *Journal of Developing Societies* 1, no. 2 (1985): 168–186.

239. Csikszentmihalyi, "Confucianism," 122.

240. To give just one example where a number of sharply critical Confucians are discussed, see Wm. Theodore de Bary, *The Trouble with Confucianism* (Cambridge, Mass.: Harvard University Press, 1991).

241. Leys, *Analects*, xxvii. I am sure Leys is aware of the dark side of Chinese history when the government of "the intellectual elite" was unable to control the horrors of despotism. Here I take him to be emphasizing only the relative benevolence of Chinese rule, given the prevalence of the horrors of despotism in all human history, not least in the modern world.

242. Roetz puts aside the question of religion in defining what he means by the axial transition in early China (*Confucian Ethics,* 19–22), something I see no reason to do, and turns to what he calls "a universal heuristic of enlightenment," which in practice is an adaptation of Kohlberg's scheme of moral development (26–32). Although I have reservations about Kohlberg as well, Roetz uses his scheme effectively.

243. Knoblock, *Xunzi,* 3:269. According to a personal communication from Jeffrey Riegel, the text that Knoblock translated as the "Eulogy" is attached to the end of book 32, "The Questions of Yao," in the original Chinese text. That is, there is no separation between the "Eulogy" and book 32. Because the former, however, was clearly not written by Xunzi and is quite different in content from the remainder of book 32, and given its content, Knoblock separated the two. There is precedent in Qing discussion of the text for doing so. Although the Qing authorities and Knoblock believed that the text of the "Eulogy" was written quite early—perhaps by an immediate disciple—there is insufficient evidence to establish with certainty the date and authorship of the "Eulogy." It is assumed that it was included in the original Liu Xiang edition of the text, so it can be no later than the first century BCE.

9. The Axial Age IV

1. As a novice, in this chapter I am even more dependent on scholars in the field than I am in the other three axial chapters. Without Michael Witzel's work on Vedic India and Steven Collins's work on Theravada Buddhism, this chapter would have been virtually impossible for me to write. Each of them combines philological scholarship of the highest level with sociological imagination, not something to be lightly assumed. In addition I am grateful to Witzel for detailed comments and corrections on the first two-thirds of the chapter.

2. "Indian Philosophy is a mighty ocean which is difficult to navigate. No people on earth has a philosophical and religious literature which can compare with Indian Literature in the size, richness and manifoldness of its contents." Erich Frauwallner, *History of Indian Philosophy,* vol. 1, trans. V. M. Bedekar (Delhi: Motilal Banarsidass, 1973 [1953], 3.

3. "The division into historical periods is especially difficult in India where it is almost impossible to determine with any precision or certitude the dates of most major historical events, whether they be the reign of kings, the birth of leaders, or the writing of texts." Patrick Olivelle, *The Āśrama System* (New York: Oxford University Press, 1993), 129.

4. Lariviere quote cited by Patrick Olivelle, trans. and ed., *Dharmasūtras: The Law Codes of Ancient India* (Oxford: Oxford University Press, 1999), xxxii.

5. Milman Parry, *The Making of Homeric Verse: The Collected Papers of Milman Parry,* ed. Adam Parry (Oxford: Clarendon Press, 1971). Albert Lord further developed Parry's ideas after his early death. See Albert Bates Lord, *The Singer of Tales* (Cambridge, Mass.: Harvard University Press, 1964).

6. Interestingly, Lord, Parry's successor, felt that oral poetry was basically free improvisation and that, therefore, the Vedic hymns "could not be *oral* in any except the most literal sense" (*The Singer of Tales,* 280). Perhaps Lord already sensed that the Vedic tradition, in differing from most oral cultures, had the functional equivalent of literacy.

7. See William A. Graham, *Beyond the Written Word: Oral Aspects of Scripture in the History of Religion* (Cambridge: Cambridge University Press, 1987). Graham discusses what we have called the hyperorality of the Vedic texts (67–75) but makes the point that in all the

great religious traditions, scripture as spoken and heard has priority over scripture as written, even when the latter is greatly respected.

8. Hartmut Scharfe, in trying to explain the ban on writing, says, "Sāyana wrote in the introduction to his Ṛgveda commentary that 'the text of the Veda is to be learned by the method of learning it from the lips of the teacher and not from a manuscript.'" Hartmut Scharfe, *Education in Ancient India* (Leiden: Brill, 2002), 8. Oral transmission was thus deeply embedded in the personal relation between teacher and student.

9. Michael Witzel suggests that non-Sanskrit "loanwords in the ṚV show that village life, music and dance, and low level religion (Small Tradition) are indigenous, thus not Indo-Aryan." Personal communication.

10. Steve Farmer et al., "The Collapse of the Indus-Script Thesis: The Myth of a Literate Harappan Civilization," *Electronic Journal of Vedic Studies* 11, no. 2 (2004): 1–39.

11. Asko Parpola, "Study of the Indus Script," *Transactions of the International Conference of Eastern Studies* 50 (2005): 28–66.

12. R. A E. Coningham argues that, though much was lost after the high point of Harappan culture, including the signs that may have been a script, the decline during the second millennium BCE was not as extreme as often imagined. He concludes that "the foundations for the emergence of the Early Historic [mid-first millennium BCE] city were already being laid during the second millennium BC." See Coningham, "Dark Age or Continuum? An Archeological Analysis of the Second Emergence of Urbanism in South Asia," in *The Archaeology of Early Historic South Asia: The Emergence of Cities and States,* ed. F. R. Allchin (Cambridge: Cambridge University Press, 1995), 72.

13. Henri Hubert and Marcel Mauss, *Sacrifice,* trans. W. D. Halls (Chicago: University of Chicago Press, 1964 [1898]); Sylvain Lévi, *La doctrine du sacrifice dans les Brahmanas* (Paris: Presses Universitaires de France, 1966 [1898]).

14. Paul Mus, *Barabudur: Sketch of a History of Buddhism Based on Archaeological Criticism of the Texts,* trans. Alexander W. Macdonald (New Delhi: Indira Gandhi National Centre for the Arts, Sterling Publishers, 1998 [1935]), xxiii. The other book was Emile Senart's edition and translation of the *Bṛhad-āraṇyaka Upaniṣad.*

15. I also found a charming anecdote about a fellow student of Dumont that reveals the teaching not only of Mauss, but of the whole Durkheimian school: "Toward the end of the year in which he was to take his diploma in ethnology, a fellow student told me that a strange thing had happened to him. He said something like this: 'The other day, while I was standing on the platform of a bus, I suddenly realized that I was not looking at my fellow passengers in the manner I was used to; something had changed in my relation to them. There was no longer "myself and the others"; I was one of them. For a while I was wondering what was the reason for this strange and sudden transformation. All at once I realized: it was Mauss' teaching.' The individual of yesterday had become aware of himself as a social being; he had perceived his personality as tied to his language, attitudes and gestures whose images were reflected by his neighbors. This is the essential humanist aspect of the teaching of anthropology." Louis Dumont, *Homo Hierarchicus: The Caste System and Its Implications* (Chicago: University of Chicago Press, 1980 [1966]), 7–8.

16. Michael Witzel, "Tracing the Vedic Dialects," in *Dialectes dans les littératures Indo-Aryennes,* ed. Colette Caillat (Paris: Collège de France, Institut de Civilisation Indienne: Depositaire exclusive: Édition-diffusion de Boccard, 1989), 124.

17. Michael Witzel, "The Development of the Vedic Canon and Its Schools: The Social and Political Milieu," in *Inside the Texts beyond the Texts: New Approaches to the Study of the Vedas,* ed. Michael Witzel (Cambridge, Mass.: Department of Sanskrit and Indian Studies, Harvard University, 1997), 263.

18. Stephanie W. Jamison and Michael Witzel, "Vedic Hinduism," in *The Study of Hinduism,* ed. Arvind Sharma (Columbia: University of South Carolina Press, 2003), 65–113; this article was written in 1992/95, and a long version (1992) is available at www.people.fas.harvard .edu/~witzel/vedica.pdf. Long version, p. 63, slightly edited, removing references and such. This almost book-length essay is the best general introduction to Vedic religion that I have come across.

19. Ibid., 53.

20. Walter H. Maurer, *Pinnacles of India's Past: Selections from the Ṛgveda,* vol. 2 (Philadelphia: John Benjamins / University of Pennsylvania Studies on South Asia, 1986), 67. Jamison and Witzel recommend this and Wendy Doniger O'Flaherty's *The Rig Veda: An Anthology* (London: Penguin 1981) as two useful translations of selected hymns in the absence of a modern scholarly translation of the entire text. But Joel Brereton and Stephanie Jamison will bring out such a complete translation in the near future.

21. Michael Witzel, "Early Indian History: Linguistic and Textual Parameters," in *The Indo-Aryans of Ancient South Asia: Language, Material Culture and Ethnicity,* ed. George Erdosy (Berlin: de Gruyter, 1995), 93.

22. Ibid., 109.

23. Michael Witzel, "Ṛgvedic History: Poets, Chieftains and Politics," in Erdosy, *Indo-Aryans,* 339.

24. Ibid.

25. Ibid., 337.

26. Ibid., 338.

27. Michael Witzel, "How to Enter the Vedic Mind? Strategies in Translating a *Brāhmaṇa* Text," in *Translating, Translations, Translators: From India to the West,* trans. Enrica Garzilli, Harvard Oriental Series, Opera Minora, vol. 1 (Cambridge, Mass.: Department of Sanskrit and Indian Studies, Harvard University, 1996), 5.

28. Michael Witzel, "Early Sanskritization: Origins and Development of the Kuru State," in *Recht, Staat und Verwaltung im klassische Indien* [The State, the Law, and Administration in Classical India], ed. Bernhard Kölver (Munich: Oldenbourg, 1997), 30.

29. Michael Witzel, "The Realm of the Kurus: Origins and Development of the First State in India," *Nihon Minami Ajia Gakkai Zenoku Taikai, Hokohu Yoshi* [Summaries of the Congress of the Japanese Association for South Asian Studies] (Kyoto, 1989), 2. The Soma ritual will be discussed further below.

30. George Erdosy, "City States of North India and Pakistan at the Time of the Buddha," in Allchin, *Archaeology,* 99. This statement summarizes his discussion in the previous chapter of the same book, "The Prelude to Urbanization: Ethnicity and the Rise of Late Vedic Chiefdoms," 75–98.

31. Erdosy, "The Prelude," 82–83.

32. Maurer, *Pinnacles of India's Past,* 10–11.

33. Ibid., 76.

34. Frits Staal, *Exploring Mysticism: A Methodological Essay* (Berkeley: University of California Press, 1975).

35. Maurer, *Pinnacles of India's Past,* 76.

36. *Brahman* is a term that can apply to a god, to absolute reality, to a class of scriptures, and to the priestly class. I follow the usage of some but not all Indologists in calling the latter group Brahmins to avoid terminological confusion.

37. It is interesting to note that in the Indian constitution the name of the country is given as "India" or "Bharat." This choice of "Bharat" as a name for the country probably reflects the prestige of the great Indian epic, the *Mahābhārata,* which looks back to this early period but was composed considerably later.

38. Witzel, "Early Sanskritization," 46.

39. Ibid., 47. The last section of chapter 4 of this book deals at length with the political and ritual situation in Hawai'i.

40. Claessen and Skalnik say that it is almost impossible to "pinpoint the precise moment of the birth of the state," and speak of "inconspicuous processes" that slowly produce institutions that only in retrospect can be recognized as characteristic of the state. Henri J. M. Claessen and Peter Skalník, eds., *The Early State* (The Hague: Mouton, 1978), 620–621. This was the case in Hawai'i and probably in Middle Vedic Kurukṣetra as well.

41. Erdosy, "The Prelude," 80.

42. Ibid., 86.

43. Witzel, "Early Sanskritization," 42–43.

44. Witzel, "Realm of the Kurus," 4.

45. Witzel, "Early Sanskritization," 45. Such "roaming" was also the case in Hawai'i, where too there were no cities. The same may have been true in very early Egypt. Bruce Trigger has divided early states into two types: territorial and city-states. In territorial states it was the court, not the city, that provided the center, and the court was often peripatetic. See Bruce G. Trigger, *Understanding Early Civilizations* (Cambridge: Cambridge University Press, 2003), 92–119.

46. Probably "order" or "class" is the best translation of *varṇa* in the early period, though later "caste" is not entirely wrong.

47. Jan Gonda explains the beginning of this verse as follows: "It is the first expression of the idea that the creation of the universe is the self-limitation of the transcendent Person (Puruṣa), 'who is this All,' manifesting himself in the realm of our experience." Gonda, *Vedic Literature* (Weisbaden: Otto Harrassowitz, 1975), 137. Maurer explains the end of the verse as indicating that the gods (the immortals), who derive from Puruṣa, are in need of (sacrificial) food, whereas Puruṣa is "quite independent of the need of any sustenance at all." *Pinnacles of India's Past,* 273. Or, as we will see, he is his own sustenance.

48. Maurer comments on this verse that this is the "evolved Puruṣa" now being sacrificed by his creatures, the gods, to the primeval Puruṣa. *Pinnacles of India's Past,* 274.

49. Ibid., 271–272.

50. See Chapter 5, note 92, where Eric Voegelin is quoted as defining mythospeculation as "speculation within the medium of the myth."

51. O'Flaherty, *The Rig Veda,* 32.

52. Ibid., 31–32.

53. Ibid., 31.

54. Georges Dumézil, *Les dieux souverains des indo-européens* (Paris: Gallimard, 1977). Nagy also draws from the work of Emile Benveniste, *Indo-European Language and Society* (Coral Gables: University of Miami Press, 1973 [1969]).

55. Gregory Nagy, *Greek Mythology and Poetics* (Ithaca: Cornell University Press, 1990), 276.

56. W. Montgomery Watt, "The Tribal Basis of the Early Islamic State," *Accademia Nazionale dei Lincei* 359, no. 54 (1962): 153.

57. Nagy, *Greek Mythology and Poetics,* 277.

58. Ibid., 281.

59. The development of early states took different directions in the two cases, with the Greeks developing a polis (city-state?) that in some respects reverted to tribal egalitarianism at a more complex level, whereas the Vedic Aryans moved in the direction of stronger emphasis on hierarchy, as was almost always the case in early states. See ibid., 279.

60. O'Flaherty, *Rig Veda,* 111.

61. Nagy, *Greek Mythology and Poetics,* 277 n. 9. This version of the RV verse is my construction of how it would have gone following Nagy's argument in this note.

62. Romila Thapar notes that the early Vedic literature indicates that *rājanya* and *viś* were originally senior and junior lineages in the same kinship group, that the *kṣatra* and the *viś* "should eat from the same vessel," and that "the *kṣatra* is created out of the *viś.*" It is therefore clear that originally the two were "superior and inferior statuses in the same species." See Thapar, *From Lineage to State: Social Formations in the Mid-First Millennium B.C. in the Ganga Valley* (Delhi: Oxford University Press, 1984), 31.

63. Erdosy, "The Prelude," 89.

64. Patrick Olivelle, trans., *Upaniṣads* (Oxford: Oxford University Press, 1996), 341 n. 4.5.

65. Hartmut Scharfe, "Sacred Kingship, Warlords, and Nobility," in *Ritual, State and History in South Asia: Essays in Honour of J. C. Heesterman,* ed. A. W. van den Hoek, D. H. A. Kolff, and M. S. Oort (Leiden: Brill, 1992), 311–312.

66. Hermann Kulke, "The Rājasūya: A Paradigm of Early State Formation?" in van den Hoek, Kolff, and Oort, *Ritual, State and History,* 188–199.

67. Witzel, "Early Sanskritization," 40–41.

68. Theodore Proferes gives an argument for the dating of the original rite in his "Kuru Kings, Tura Kāvaṣeya, and the *–tváya* Gerund," *Bulletin of the School of Oriental and African Studies* 66, no. 2 (2003): 212–214. This rite survived among certain groups of South Indian Brahmins until virtually the present. In 1975 Frits Staal recorded a complete performance of the ritual. See his *Agni, the Vedic Ritual of the Fire Altar,* 2 vols. (Delhi: Motilal Banarsidass, 1984).

69. Proferes, "Kuru Kings," 217.

70. Ibid., 216–217.

71. Ibid., 217.

72. Erdosy, "The Prelude," 87. Romila Thapar, however, points out that the socially stabilizing influence of the ritual system was not without its costs. The resources devoted to ritual could not be utilized for state building, and the relative autonomy of the subchiefs limited

the sovereignty of the "king" (paramount chief) to the extent that Thapar describes as "an arrested development of the state." *From Lineage to State,* 67.

73. Witzel, "Early Sanskritization," 47.

74. Ibid., 39–40. A unified system of ritual appropriate to each status level would be an outcome similar to the processes of ritual reform that we noted in China before the Warring States period.

75. Hubert and Mauss in their book *Sacrifice* avoid the ambiguity in the Vedic sacrificial system between the person for whom the sacrifice is performed and the priest performing the sacrifice by calling the former the "sacrifier" and the latter the "sacrificer," but this usage has not been followed by later authors.

76. Mysore Narasimhachar Srinivas, *Religion and Society among the Coorgs of South India* (Oxford: Oxford University Press, 1952); and Srinivas, *The Cohesive Role of Sanskritization* (Delhi: Oxford University Press, 1989).

77. Witzel, "Early Sanskritization," 51.

78. "We are, I believe, entitled to call the Kuru realm the first state in India. To quote W. Rau, who has described the social and political conditions of the YV Saṃhitā and Brāhmaṇa period in such detail: 'The Indians of the Brāhmaṇa period lived in political organizations which, with good reasons, can be called states.'" Ibid., 51–52. In his work on early India, Witzel frequently cites Wilhelm Rau, *Staat und Gesellschaft im alten Indien, nach den Brahmana-Texten dargestellt* (Wiesbaden: Otto Harrassowitz, 1957).

79. See the great two-volume work of Frits Staal, ed., *Agni, the Vedic Ritual of the Fire Altar* (Delhi: Motilal Banarsidass, 1984). It is worth noting that the 1975 performance took twelve days, whereas in the Middle Vedic period it would have taken a year: in this case one day for one month.

80. Staal does not actually make this claim, but it can be found on the Web in connection with the performance he recorded.

81. Tsuji Naoshiro, "The Agnicayana Section of the Maitrāyaṇi-Saṃhitā with Special Reference to the Mānava Śrautasūtra," in Staal, *Agni,* 2:135.

82. Jan Heesterman, "Other Folk's Fire," in Staal, *Agni,* 2:76–77.

83. Agni is of course fire, and cayana is the "piling up" of the bricks that will make the altar.

84. Ibid., 78.

85. Staal, *Agni,* 1:558.

86. Ibid., 196.

87. Ibid., 128.

88. Ibid., 306–307.

89. Ibid., 65. It is worth noting that every brick is not only a part of Prajāpati's body, but a verse of the Veda.

90. Ibid., 65. Staal, it should be noted, puts no stock in this kind of Brāhmaṇic speculation, finding it completely unhelpful in understanding the ritual, and noting that the Nambudiri Brahmins who performed the 1975 ritual gave no such explanations, just saying this is the way they have always done it. For Staal it is the rules that count, a kind of ritual syntax, not the meaning, which is ephemeral and largely irrelevant. But it all depends on what one is looking for.

91. Wendy Doniger O'Flaherty, in a brief review of early Western views, which she entitles "The Western Scorn for the Brāhmaṇas," quotes Max Müller, one of the nineteenth-century founders of the study of early Indic religion, as writing in 1900: "However interesting the Brāhmaṇas may be to students of Indian literature, they are of small interest to the general reader. The greater portion of them is simply twaddle, and what is worse, theological twaddle." Some years earlier Müller had even called the Brāhmaṇas "the twaddle of idiots and the ravings of madmen." For this and similar quotations, see her *Tales of Sex and Violence: Folklore, Sacrifice, and Danger in the* Jaiminīya Brāhmaṇa (Chicago: University of Chicago Press, 1985), 3–6.

92. Brian K. Smith, *Reflections on Resemblance, Ritual, and Religion* (Oxford: Oxford University Press, 1989), 31. It is worth remembering that "equations" are common in ritual thought: for many Christians the bread and the wine in the (sacrificial) ritual of the Eucharist *are* the body and blood of Christ. And in John 14, when Jesus says, "I am the way, and the truth, and the life," Christians have understood that as more than metaphorical.

93. Ibid., 46.

94. Ibid., 50.

95. Ibid., 50–51. Smith's description of the natural state is reminiscent of the second law of thermodynamics. However, what Hermann Oldenberg meant by his term "pre-scientific science" was not exactly this, but rather the immense effort to correlate and classify, which does indeed lie behind what we would call real science. See Hermann Oldenberg, *Vorwissenschaftliche Wissenschaft: Die Weltanschauung der Brāhmaṇa-Texte* (Göttingen: Vandenhoek and Ruprecht, 1919).

96. Jamison and Witzel, "Vedic Hinduism," 38.

97. Frits Staal, *Rules without Meaning: Ritual, Mantras, and the Human Sciences* (New York: P. Lang, 1989), 101.

98. Staal, *Agni,* 1:590ff.

99. Smith, *Reflections,* 48.

100. Ibid., 199.

101. Actually Staal says that because ritual is older than language, probably by hundreds of thousands of years (see chapter 3 of *Rules without Meaning*), "mantras occupy a domain that is situated between ritual and language." He notes that there are "mantra like sound structures among animals." Staal, *Rules without Meaning,* 261.

102. "From the perspective of later Hindu thought, the entire Veda is sometimes associated with the idea of a protosemantic presence of 'words' and 'sounds.' In this view, the Veda is 'primarily word' *(śabdapradhāna)* and thus distinguished from the Purāṇas, which are said to be *arthapradhāna,* that is texts in which 'meaning' and 'information' predominate." Wilhelm Halbfass, *Tradition and Reflection: Explorations in Indian Thought* (Albany: SUNY Press, 1991), 6.

103. Maurer, *Pinnacles of India's Past,* 280–281.

104. Jamison and Witzel, "Vedic Hinduism," 67.

105. Ibid., 66.

106. Jan Gonda, *Notes on Brahman* (Utrecht: J. L. Beyers, 1950), 62–63.

107. Both Lévi (in *La doctrine du sacrifice,* see esp. 10–11) and Mus (in *Barabudur*) point out the structural parallel between the sacrificer who, through the ritual, becomes identified

with the divine, and the renouncer who, through austerities and meditation, finds that his Self *(ātman)* is identical with the Absolute *(brahman)*. Yet I think they both see that what I call theory was present in the case of the renouncer but not in the case of the Vedic sacrificer. Mus, if I understand him correctly, finds Upanishadic thought so theoretical that it cannot offer salvation and must be replaced later in Hinduism by *bhakti* (devotional) religion, whereas Buddhism managed to combine the Upanishadic breakthrough with the Brāhmanic emphasis on practice.

108. See Erdosy, "City States"; and Erdosy, *Urbanisation in Early Historic India* (Oxford: British Archaeological Reports, International Series, 1988).

109. Olivelle, *Upaniṣads,* xxix.

110. Witzel, "Tracing the Vedic Dialects," 245.

111. Olivelle, *Upaniṣads,* xxix.

112. Jamison and Witzel, "Vedic Hinduism," 75.

113. Ibid., 75–76.

114. Jan Gonda, *Brahman,* 58–61.

115. Wayne Whillier, "Truth, Teaching, and Tradition," in *Hindu Spirituality: Vedas through Vedanta,* ed. Krishna Sivaraman (New York: Crossroad, 1989), 48.

116. O'Flaherty, *Rig Veda,* 25–26. Note that this hymn, like ṚV 10.90, is quite late, anywhere between 1000 and 600 BCE.

117. Joel Brereton, "The Upanishads," in *Eastern Canons: Approaches to the Asian Classics,* ed. William Theodore de Bary and Irene Bloom (New York: Columbia University Press, 1990), 115–135. I am also indebted to Hermann Oldenberg, *The Doctrine of the Upaniṣads and Early Buddhism,* trans. Shridor B. Shrotri (Delhi: Motilal Banarsidass, 1991 [1923]), chap. 1, "The Older Upaniṣads," for many helpful suggestions.

118. Brereton, "Upanishads," 121.

119. Halbfass, *Tradition and Reflection,* 40.

120. *Bṛhadāraṇyaka Upaniṣad* 1.4.10, in Olivelle, *Upaniṣads,* 15.

121. Paṇini's Sanskrit grammar (ca. 400 BCE) is generally accepted as the beginning of scientific linguistics and the stimulus for modern Western developments in that field. Staal argues that Pāṇini's linguistics developed out of a "science of ritual" and was related to the need to understand what was by then archaic Vedic language (*Rules without Meaning,* 33–60).

122. I will be using the translations of Olivelle, *Upaniṣads,* 148, and Brereton, "The Upaniṣads," 122. The *Chāndogya Upaniṣad* is the most important early Upaniṣad besides the *Bṛhadāraṇyaka Upaniṣad.*

123. Olivelle, *Upaniṣads,* 148.

124. Ibid., 154, except for the last paragraph, which is from Brereton, "The Upaniṣads," 124. Olivelle, for reasons that he explains in his notes, translates the famous last sentence, *tat tvam asi,* as "And that's how you are, Śvetaketu," whereas Brereton is closer to traditional translations. Edgerton, for example, translates the phrase "That art thou, Śvetaketu." Franklin Edgerton, *The Beginnings of Indian Philosophy* (London: George Allen and Unwin, 1965), 176.

125. Gananath Obeyesekere, *Imagining Karma: Ethical Transformation in Amerindian, Buddhist, and Greek Rebirth* (Berkeley: University of California Press, 2002), 111. Obeyesekere

is one of the few scholars of early India who have explicitly discussed the axial-age question, citing Jaspers and Eisenstadt.

126. Olivelle, *Upaniṣads,* 17.

127. Brereton, "The Upaniṣads," 124.

128. For the modern thinkers, see Wilhelm Halbfass, *India and Europe: An Essay in Understanding* (Albany: SUNY Press, 1988).

129. Olivelle, *Upaniṣads,* lvi.

130. Ibid., 140.

131. Ibid., 142. A somewhat different version of this dialogue appears in the *Bṛhadāraṇyaka Upaniṣad* 6.2, Olivelle, *Upaniṣads,* 81–84. "Pleasant" and "foul" appear to describe behavior appropriate to caste status rather than conforming to universal ethical norms.

132. Kenneth H. Post, "Spiritual Foundations of Caste," in Sivaraman, *Hindu Spirituality,* 101.

133. Olivelle, *Upaniṣads,* 38.

134. Witzel has an interesting discussion of Yājñavalkya as "one of the few *lively* people in the oldest strata of Indian literature" [italics in original], the others being Vasiṣṭha and the Buddha. Vasiṣṭha appears briefly but vividly in the *Ṛgveda,* bk. 7, but is the only such figure to stand out until late Vedic times when Yājñavalkya appears. Because Yājñavalkya is the very embodiment of the Upanishadic axial transition, and axial transitions often produce striking individuals, whereas archaic societies produce vivid gods but individuals largely defined by status, not personality, his very existence confirms the axial turn, as does, of course, the Buddha. See Michael Witzel, "Yājñavalkya as Ritualist and Philosopher, and His Personal Language," in *Paitimāna: Essays in Iranian, Indo-European, and Indian Studies in Honor of Hanns-Peter Schmidt,* ed. Siamak Adhami (Costa Mesa, Calif.: Mazda, 2003), 104–105.

135. Olivelle, *Upaniṣads,* 39–40.

136. Ibid., 71.

137. Ibid., 16.

138. Ibid.

139. Halbfass, *India and Europe,* chap. 17, "*Dharma* in the Self-Understanding of Traditional Hinduism," 310–333.

140. Witzel, "How to Enter the Vedic Mind?" 12.

141. Olivelle, *Upaniṣads,* 334.

142. Halbfass, *"Dharma,"* 314, 317.

143. Ibid., 317–318.

144. Ibid., 318.

145. Ibid., 320–321.

146. Ibid., 320.

147. Ibid., 316–317.

148. *Bhagavadgītā* 24[2]ff., in J. A. B. van Buitenen, *The* Bhagavadgītā *in the* Mahābhārata (Chicago: University of Chicago Press, 1981), 73ff.

149. Halbfass, *"Dharma,"* 326, 329.

150. Ibid., 333.

151. See, for example, A. L. Basham, *The Wonder That Was India* (New York: Grove, 1959), 148.

152. Halbfass, *Tradition and Reflection,* chap. 10, "Homo Hierarchicus: The Conceptualization of the Varṇa System in Indian Thought," 352. Halbfass says that he is not defending Dumont's famous book in this chapter, but that he does agree with what Dumont called "the main idea" of his book, that is, "the idea of hierarchy separated from power" (350).

153. Brian K. Smith, *Classifying the Universe: The Ancient Indian Varṇa System and the Origins of Caste* (New York: Oxford University Press, 1994), 82.

154. It might be thought that the great philosophers of later centuries would have rejected these exclusions of Śūdras, but such is not the case. Both Śaṅkara and Rāmānuja agreed with the exclusion of Śūdras from the study of the Vedas. Śaṅkara even approved the rule that Śūdras who listened to Vedic texts should have their ears filled with molten metal. Halbfass, *Tradition and Reflection,* 380–381.

155. S. N. Eisenstadt, *Japanese Civilization: A Comparative View* (Chicago: Chicago University Press, 1996); and Robert N. Bellah, *Imagining Japan: The Japanese Tradition and Its Modern Interpretation* (Berkeley: University of California Press, 2003).

156. Eric Voegelin, *Israel and Revelation,* vol. 1 of *Order and History* (Baton Rouge: Louisiana State University Press, 1956), 164.

157. Alexander von Rospatt reminds me that classic Indian Buddhism did survive to the present in one traditionally Indian area: Nepal, particularly the Kathmandu Valley. It is only there that Sanskrit Buddhism can be found today, I am grateful for this and other suggestions that he gave me.

158. Ronald B. Inden, *Imagining India* (Cambridge: Blackwell, 1990), 73–74.

159. Ibid., 217ff.

160. Ibid., 212–262.

161. Thapar, *From Lineage to State,* 171–172. S. N. Eisenstadt and Harriet Hartman, "Cultural Traditions, Conceptions of Sovereignty and State Formation in India and Europe," in van den Hoek, Kolff, and Oort, *Ritual, State and History,* 493–506, discuss Indian society in a way that supports and extends Thapar's analysis. They write, "Indian politics developed predominantly patrimonial characteristics, the rulers relying mostly on personal loyalty" (499). Society they see as composed of rather complex networks of ascriptive and particularistic groups that were by no means similar to geographically limited "tribal" solidarities, but could be extended to wide areas. Caste solidarities were particularistic yet could provide some functional equivalents to more universalistic solidarities because of their capacity to transcend local geography.

162. Charles Malamoud, "Semantics and Rhetoric in the Hindu Hierarchy of the 'Aims of Man,'" in his *Cooking the World: Ritual and Thought in Ancient India,* trans. David White (Delhi: Oxford University Press, 1996 [1989]), 125, 128. Malamoud translates the ends as "Order *(dharma),* Interest *(artha),* and Desire *(kāma)*" (113).

163. Whillier, "Truth, Teaching, and Tradition," 53.

164. Olivelle, in *The Āśrama System,* cites a number of places in the epics where "the term *śramaṇa* is used for a variety of Brāmaṇical ascetics" (15 n. 34).

165. Patrick Olivelle, "The Renouncer Tradition," in *The Blackwell Companion to Hinduism,* ed. Gavin Flood (Oxford: Blackwell, 2003), 277. For a fuller description, see Olivelle, *The Āśrama System;* and Olivelle, *Dharmasutras.*

166. Olivelle, *The Āśrama System,* 36.

167. Olivelle quotes from dharma texts to show how strongly the householder order was upheld: "All orders *(āśramas)* subsist by receiving support from the householder," and "As all rivers, both great and small, find a resting-place in the ocean, even so men of all orders find protection with householders," from *Manu;* "there is one *āśrama* only, because the others do not beget offspring," from the *Baudriliya Dharmasutra.* See also Patrick Olivelle, *The Origin and Early Development of Buddhist Monachism* (Colombo: Gunasena, 1974), 5.

168. Olivelle, *The Āśrama System,* 242.

169. Ibid., 227.

170. Romila Thapar, "Renunciation: The Making of a Counter-Culture?" in *Ancient Indian Social History: Some Interpretations* (Bashir Bagh: Orient Longman, 1978 [1976]), 63. This is one of four papers that are particularly helpful in understanding the role of renouncers in Indian history. The others are Louis Dumont, "World Renunciation in Indian Religions," in *Religion/Politics and History in India: Collected Papers in Indian Sociology* (The Hague: Mouton, 1970 [1960]); Jan Heesterman, "Brahmin, Ritual, and Renouncer," in *The Inner Conflict of Tradition: Essays in Indian Ritual, Kingship, and Society* (Chicago: University of Chicago Press, 1985 [1964]), 26–44; and Charles Malamoud, "Village and Forest in the Ideology of Brahmanic India," in *Cooking the World,* 74–91. Heesterman and Malamoud deal largely with the early period; Thapar and Dumont deal with Indian history as a whole.

171. Thapar, "Renunciation," 63.

172. Richard Gombrich, *How Buddhism Began: The Conditioned Genesis of the Early Teachings* (London: Athlone, 1996), 51.

173. Gombrich, *How Buddhism Began,* 33.

174. See Steven Collins, *Selfless Persons: Imagery and Thought in Theravāda Buddhism* (Cambridge: Cambridge University Press, 1982), 125; Collins in this book presents the fullest account of *anattā* available in English.

175. Ibid., 136–137, referring to *Majjhima Nikāya* 63.5.

176. My description of these three fundamental categories is a condensation of Collins's exposition of them in his *Selfless Persons,* 29. A recent book by Johannes Bronkhorst, *Greater Magadha: Studies in the Culture of Early India* (Leiden: Brill, 2007), offers a radical alternative view of the origin of these three ideas, suggesting that their origin is not in the Vedic tradition but in the rather different culture of "Greater Magadha" that developed outside the Vedic orbit and was only gradually assimilated to the Vedic tradition. I am in no position to evaluate this argument, which runs counter to other sources I have used. The specialists will have to decide these issues, but, as I have learned from scholarship on the Hebrew scriptures, arguments about chronology can go on interminably when there is little or no basis outside the texts for dating them before or after other texts.

177. I am very indebted to Collins, *Selfless Persons,* esp. 191–193, for his illuminating discussion of *dukkha.*

178. Charles Taylor, *A Secular Age* (Cambridge, Mass.: Harvard University Press, 2007), 6–7.

179. Maurice Walshe, in the introduction to his translation of the *Digha Nikaya,* says that in the treatment of the Brahmins in the Buddhist texts "one is insistently reminded of the New Testament picture of the Pharisees, though in both cases the picture as presented is, to

say the least, one-sided." Maurice Walshe, trans., *The Long Discourses of the Buddha: A Translation of the Dīgha Nikāya* (Boston: Wisdom), 22.

180. Collins, *Selfless Persons,* 32–33.

181. This teaching was shared with and even conceivably borrowed from the Jains, who took it to lengths to which Buddhism usually did not go.

182. Gombrich, *How Buddhism Began,* 68–69. Gombrich notes that the Mahāyāna tradition gave expression to this basic idea "in one of the most famous passages in the whole of Mahāyāna literature, the allegory of the [world as a] burning house in the *Lotus Sūtra* (chapter 3)" (69).

183. *Soṇadaṇḍa Sutta, Dīgha Nikāya* 4, in Walshe, *The Long Discourses,* 125–132.

184. Ibid., 128.

185. Ibid., 129–131.

186. Ibid., 132.

187. Ibid., 550 n. 169.

188. Obeyesekere, *Imagining Karma,* 114.

189. Although *Brahman* in the singular, either as the highest god or as the absolute, is not to be found in the Suttas, Brahmas, in the plural, are among the many gods that continued to be recognized by Buddhists. Having a Brahma request that the Buddha take on the lifelong arduous task of teacher to the world is one of the ironies that the Suttas delight in. Not least of the ironies is that Vedic orthodoxy limited the teaching of liberating truth to a few, whereas here Brahma urges the Buddha to make it available to all.

190. *Ariyapariyesanā Sutta* 19–21, in Bikkhu Bodhi, trans., *The Middle Discourses of the Buddha: A Translation of the Majjhima Nikāya* (Boston: Wisdom, 1995), 260–262.

191. Obeyesekere, *Imagining Karma,* 114–115. The passage is from the *Mahāparinibbāna Sutta* (The Buddha's Last Days) 3.7–8. For another translation, see Walshe, *Long Discourses,* 246–247.

192. For an excellent discussion of the relation of Buddhist monasticism to the laity, see Ilana Friedrich Silber, *Virtuosity, Charisma, and Social Order: A Comparative Sociological Study of Monasticism in Theravada Buddhism and Medieval Catholicism* (New York: Cambridge University Press, 1995). It is in this book that Silber argues for Buddhism and Christianity as the only religions where true monasticism developed.

193. Ibid., 67.

194. Richard F. Gombrich, *Theravada Buddhism: A Social History from Ancient Benares to Modern Colombo,* 2nd ed. (London: Routledge, 2007), 66.

195. Ibid., 78.

196. Here I am drawing from Steven Collins's discussion in his *Nirvana and Other Buddhist Felicities* (New York: Cambridge University Press, 1998), 282–285.

197. Bikkhu Bodhi, *The Connected Discourses of the Buddha: A Translation of the* Saṃyutta Nikāya (Boston: Wisdom, 2000), 1846. The Deer Park Sermon is to be found in the *Saṃyutta Nikāya* 56.11.

198. Collins, *Nirvana,* 284. For Collins's idea of nirvana as, in the linguistic sense, syntactic as well as semantic and pragmatic, see below. Kenneth Burke has written an essay that moves in the opposite direction from Collins but makes the same point: the interchangeability of systematic and narrative thought, with the remaining significant difference

that one is atemporal and the other necessarily temporal. For Burke, the first three chapters of Genesis, the Garden of Eden story, though narrative in form, can be reformulated in "philosophical," that is, timeless propositional form, as the logical consequences that necessarily follow the postulation of the idea of order. See Burke, "The First Three Chapters of Genesis" in *The Rhetoric of Religion: Studies in Logology* (Boston: Beacon Press, 1961), 172–272.

199. Collins, *Nirvana,* 243.

200. Ibid., 243–244. My whole discussion of the "knowledge" the gaining of which is so central to the Buddhist Path as not only cognitive but also affective and behavioral draws largely from Collins's book. For a summary discussion of Buddhist knowledge as the gaining of skill rather than fact alone, see Collins's summary, *Nirvana,* 153.

201. Ibid., 245.

202. On this Weberian characterization of the Sangha, see Collins, *Nirvana,* 558.

203. Patrick Olivelle, *The Origin,* pt. 2, "The Growth of Buddhist Cenobitical Life," 35–77.

204. With the exception of Sanskrti Buddhism in Nepal, pointed out above.

205. For a good brief summary of this history, see Hartmut Scharfe, *The State in Indian Tradition* (Leiden: Brill, 1989), chap. 6, "A Synthetic View of the Development of the State in India."

206. I use the spelling of Kauṭalīya preferred by Romila Thapar in her important book *Aśoka and the Decline of the Mauryas,* rev. ed. with new afterword (Delhi: Oxford University Press, 1997). The new afterword discusses research between the first edition of 1961 and the publication of the revised edition. Other authors prefer the spelling Kauṭilīya.

207. Romila Thapar, *Early India: From the Origins to AD 1300* (Berkeley: University of California Press, 2004), 162–163. For Aśoka's *Dhamma,* I will use italics to distinguish it from Buddhist Dhamma.

208. My account of Aśoka and his teaching relies largely on Thapar's book, *Aśoka,* including her translations of the edicts in appendix 5. In addition to the afterword in that book, which takes account of research up until 1997, her treatment of Aśoka in *Early India,* though abbreviated, gives her views as of 2002 when it was first published.

209. See on the Web the Wikipedia article "Full Translation of the Behistun Inscription."

210. Translated by Thapar, *Aśoka,* 253.

211. From Pillar Edict 7, translated in ibid., 265.

212. From the 11th Major Rock Edict, translated in ibid., 254–255.

213. From the 12th Major Rock Edict, translated in ibid., 255.

214. Sheldon Pollock, *The Language of the Gods in the World of Men: Sanskrit, Culture, and Power in Premodern India* (Berkeley: University of California Press, 2006), 5, 7.

215. Ibid., 2–10.

216. Ibid., 60.

217. Ibid., 50.

218. Ibid., 3, 76.

219. Ibid., 300.

220. Ibid., 198.

221. Thapar, *Aśoka,* and especially her appendix 1, "The Date of the *Arthaśāstra,"* 218–225.

222. Wendy Doniger, *The Hindus: An Alternative History* (New York: Penguin, 2009), 202.

223. Olivelle, *Dharmasūtras,* xxxiv.

224. Patrick Olivelle, *The Law Code of Manu* (New York: Oxford University Press, 2004), xix. Wendy Doniger has also translated Manu, in *The Laws of Manu* (New York: Penguin, 1991). Both are worth consulting. Olivelle is translating a critical edition of the text and has a useful introduction. Doniger is translating the traditional version and also has a useful introduction.

225. Olivelle, *Law Code of Manu,* xliii.

226. Doniger, *The Laws of Manu,* xlii.

227. Ibid., xliii.

228. Doniger, *The Hindus,* 209; but see her discussion of the ends of life in chap. 8.

229. Ibid., 210.

230. Doniger, *The Laws of Manu,* 286.

231. Olivelle's translation is clearer in this passage. See his *Law Code of Manu,* 217.

232. Doniger, *The Hindus,* 211.

233. Olivelle, *Law Code of Manu,* 14–15. For Doniger's translation of this passage, see *The Hindus,* 210. This sounds remarkably like Calvinist double predestination if one can make such a remote comparison.

234. Doniger, *The Laws of Manu,* xlvi.

235. In so doing, Manu illustrates a possibility that under quite other circumstances was often a feature of Japanese thought. See the introduction to Bellah, *Imagining Japan.*

236. Olivelle, *Law Code of Manu,* 105.

237. Ibid.

238. Ibid., 218.

239. It would seem that Manu understood the position of universal ethics and consciously rejected it. Instead he opted for moral/political regression, with unhappy consequences for as long as his text was influential.

240. Olivelle, *Law Code of Manu,* xli–xlv.

241. The standard English translation of the *Rāmāyaṇa* is *The Rāmāyaṇa of Vālmīki: An Epic of Ancient India,* vol. 1: *Bālarāmāyaṇa,* trans. Robert P. Goldman (Princeton: Princeton University Press, 1984). Five further volumes had been published by 2009, each volume containing one book of the epic, with one more volume to go.

242. *The Rāmāyaṇa of Vālmīki: An Epic of Ancient India,* vol. 2, *Ayodhyākāṇda,* trans. Sheldon I. Pollock (Princeton: Princeton University Press, 1986), 70.

243. Ibid., n. 12, 70–71. Pollock cites the inscriptions of Aśoka that parallel passages in the *Ayodhyākāṇda.*

244. Ibid., 70.

245. Pollock, *Language of the Gods,* 81.

246. Pollock, *Rāmāyaṇa,* 2:72.

247. One might want to qualify the idea of the *Rāmāyaṇa* as a comedy if one seriously considered the second most important character in the epic, Rāma's wife Sītā, whose tribulations

and ultimate fate, and whose treatment by Rāma, are problematic indeed. The standard English translation of the *Mahābhārata* is that published by the University of Chicago Press: *The Mahābhārata*. Vol. 1, bk. 1, *The Book of the Beginning*, trans. and ed. J. A. B. van Buuitenen, was published in 1973. Three more volumes have been published subsequently: vol. 2, containing books 2 and 3; vol. 3, containing books 4 and 5; and vol. 7, containing book 11 and part 1 of book 12. There are eighteen books in all.

248. Pollock, *Language of the Gods,* 17–18.

249. Ibid., 225.

250. Pollock, *Rāmāyana,* 2:48–52.

251. Ibid., 67–68.

252. Ibid., 51.

253. On this point see Sheldon Pollock, "*Rāmāyana* and Political Imagination in India," *Journal of Asian Studies* 52, no. 2 (1993): 261–297.

254. To explain the double parentage of the Pāndavas would take far more space than I have, this being an example of plot complexities defying brief description that characterize the whole epic.

255. The cousin-brothers of the Pāndavas.

256. Thapar, *Early India,* 178.

257. A translation of book 10 can be found in W. J. Johnson, trans., *The Sauptikaparvan of the Mahābhārata: The Massacre at Night* (New York: Oxford University Press, 1998). In his interesting introduction, Johnson points out the cosmological level of the concept of dharma, which is only one of several such levels treated in the vast epic. I have stayed with the ethical/ political level, which has implications for other levels of meaning, but is complex enough for my brief treatment.

258. Doniger, *The Hindus,* 266, 270.

259. Alf Hiltebeitel, *Rethinking the Mahābhārata: A Reader's Guide to the Education of the Dharma King* (Chicago: University of Chicago Press, 2001), 208. See his general discussion of these issues, 202–214.

260. It would take us too far afield to discuss this incident in detail, but Gananath Obeyesekere, in *The Work of Culture* (Chicago: University of Chicago Press, 1990), 80–81, notes that it is the only Hindu example of Freud's classic Oedipus complex, and a highly ambiguous one, whereas examples of the classic Oedipus complex are frequent in Buddhist literature. See the whole discussion of the Hindu case, 75–88.

261. Doniger, *The Hindus,* 274–275.

262. Pollock refers to the Rājasūya as a "consecration [of Yudhisthira] as a *cakravrtin*" (*Language of the Gods,* 226), the universal ruler. The term seems to have dropped out of later Hinduism, though it continued to be important in Theravada Buddhism. Pollock is particularly interested in the conquest of the four directions by Yudhisthira's four brothers in preparation for the consecration, and in the fact that the description of the conquest geographically includes the known world of Indic culture. The description of the world occurs three times again in the *Mahābhārata* and helped define the political geography of subsequent Indic civilization, and also the political trope that a truly good king is a world ruler (e.g., Rāma or the ruler described near the end of Manu above), regardless of the size of his actual

kingdom. Here the example of Aśoka has a continuing afterlife. See Pollock, *Language of the Gods*, 226–237.

263. Ibid., 227.

264. Ibid., 554.

265. Hiltebeitel, *Rethinking the Mahābhārata*, 214.

266. Margaret Cone and Richard F. Gombrich, *The Perfect Generosity of Prince Vessantara: A Buddhist Epic* (Oxford: Clarendon Press, 1977). For a recent collection of Jātaka stories, see *The Jātakas: Birth Stories of the Bodhisatta*, trans. Sarah Shaw (New Delhi: Penguin, 2006), which contains the interesting *Temiya Jātaka*, somewhat parallel to the *Vessantara Jātaka*.

267. Although there is no way of dating exactly the most comprehensive Pali text from which the other versions seem to derive, we know that the story goes back to the second and first centuries BCE because episodes from it are to be found in relief carvings of that period in northern India. Cone and Gombrich, *Vessantara*, xxxv.

268. Ibid., xv.

269. Collins, *Nirvana*, 501. In connection with his discussion of Buddhist utopian thought in this book, Collins cites the very interesting article by Northrop Frye, "Varieties of Literary Utopias," in *The Stubborn Structure: Essays on Criticism and Society* (Ithaca: Cornell University Press, 1970), 109–134. (This essay was originally published in *Daedalus* 99, no. 2 [1965]: 323–347.) Frye makes a powerful defense of literary utopias against their contemporary detractors.

270. Collins, *Nirvana*, 522.

271. Ibid., 333.

10. Conclusion

1. Blaise Pascal, *Pensées*, rev. ed., trans. A. J. Krailsheimer (London: Penguin, 1995 [1670]), 323. There is another passage in Pascal relevant to this book: "As we cannot be universal by knowing everything there is to be known about everything, we must know a little about everything, because it is much better to know something about everything than everything about something." Pascal, *Pensées*, 58. Here Pascal rejects overspecialization, but, even trying to follow his injunction, all I could do is know a little about a lot of things, not even a little about everything. Pascal is sarcastic about philosophers who claim to know everything about everything.

2. As indicated in Chapter 2, I owe a great debt to Gordon Burghardt for his work on animal play and to Johann Huizinga for his work on play as the basis of human culture. Perhaps just a word about why Chapter 2 was the only substantive chapter to be rewritten after the others were completed (I did write a new Preface in the fall of 2009 to replace one that had been written at the beginning before I had an adequate sense of where the book was going). Although it is true that the understanding of biological evolution had changed dramatically in the decade or so since the first draft was completed, to a lesser degree that is true of the subject matter in each substantive chapter and alone would not have justified a rewriting. The main reason is that, though I still believe that religion in any intelligible sense does not

precede our own species and so arose in the Paleolithic period, I had come to see that the deep background that made that origin possible was also of such importance that it needed extensive discussion.

3. Friedrich Schiller, *On the Aesthetic Education of Man,* trans. Reginald Snell (New York: Dover, 2004 [1801]).

4. Immanuel Kant, *Critique of the Power of Judgment,* ed. and trans. Paul Guyer (Cambridge: Cambridge University Press, 2000 [1790]), sec. 43, 183.

5. Gordon M. Burghardt, *The Genesis of Animal Play: Testing the Limits* (Cambridge, Mass.: MIT Press, 2005), 77–78. Upon inspection I found that Burghardt not only refers to Schiller in his book, but actually quotes a passage that partly overlaps the following quote from Schiller on p. 28 of his book, a reference that I failed to follow up on first reading. It was Burghardt more than anyone else who opened my eyes to the enormous importance of animal play in evolutionary history.

6. Schiller, *Aesthetic Education,* letter 27, pp. 133–134. Italics in original. One might perhaps see in Schiller the distinction we found in Abraham Maslow in Chapter 1 between Deficiency cognition (D-cognition) and Being cognition (B-cognition). Abraham Maslow, *Toward a Psychology of Being* (Princeton: Van Nostrand, 1962).

7. Schiller, *Aesthetic Education,* letter 15, pp. 78–80. Italics in original.

8. Ibid., letter 14, p. 74. Italics in original.

9. Claude Lévi-Strauss, *The Raw and the Cooked* (New York: Harper and Row, 1969), 15–16, where he says, "It is as if music and mythology needed time only in order to deny it."

10. Ellen B. Basso, *A Musical View of the Universe: Kalapalo Myth and Ritual Performances* (Philadelphia: University of Pennsylvania Press, 1985), 253. Italics in original.

11. Ibid., 256–257.

12. Valerio Valeri, *Kingship and Sacrifice: Ritual and Society in Ancient Hawaii* (Chicago: University of Chicago Press, 1985), 218–219.

13. On aristocratic play in early state societies, see particularly Eli Sagan, *At the Dawn of Tyranny: The Origins of Individualism, Political Oppression, and the State* (New York: Knopf, 1985), esp. 166–183.

14. Of this situation Rousseau wrote: "They now began to assemble round a great tree: singing and dancing, the genuine offspring of love and leisure, became the amusement or rather the occupation of the men and women, free from care, thus gathered together. Everyone began to notice the rest, and wished to be noticed himself; and public esteem acquired a value. He who sang or danced best; the handsomest, the strongest, the most dexterous, or the most eloquent, came to be the most respected: this was the first step toward inequality, and at the same time toward vice." J.-J. Rousseau, *Discourse on the Origin of Inequality,* in *The First and Second* Discourses, trans. Roger D. Masters (New York: St. Martin's Press, 1964 [1755]), 149.

15. On the negative side of play, including play as an addiction (gambling would be an example), see Gordon Burghardt, *Genesis of Animal Play,* 385–393.

16. Although play in humans can occur throughout life, it is characteristic particularly of childhood. The consequences of "some work, others play" in Brazil is vividly pointed out by David F. Lancey, *The Anthropology of Childhood: Cherubs, Chattel, Changelings* (Cambridge: Cambridge University Press, 2008): "in Brazil childhood is a privilege of the rich and practically nonexistent for the poor" (1).

17. Jürgen Habermas, "Toward a Reconstruction of Historical Materialism," in *Communication and the Evolution of Society* (Boston: Beacon Press, 1979 [1976]), 163. Italics in the original.

18. Perhaps it would be best to call only Plato a renouncer. Andrea Nightingale argues with Simon Goldhill, who called Socrates a "performer in exile" because he did not display his wisdom in the assembly or other political gatherings (except on one important occasion). She holds that in his exchanges with his fellow citizens Socrates remained intimately tied to the city. See Andrea Nightingale, *Spectacles of Truth in Classical Greek Philosophy:* Theoria *in Its Cultural Context* (Cambridge: Cambridge University Press, 2004), 73 n. 2. Can we call Socrates a "dissident," who, like Václav Havel, criticized his city but refused to leave it at whatever cost? Fortunately Havel only had to serve four years in prison.

19. Of course, as in many legitimation struggles, what began as a tradition of criticism could become a tradition of legitimation.

20. Nightingale, *Spectacles,* 40–41.

21. Ibid., 74–77.

22. Ibid., 78.

23. Ibid., 98.

24. Ibid., 80.

25. Ibid., 81.

26. Ibid., 80

27. Ibid., 105–106.

28. Ibid., 106.

29. Ibid., 106–107.

30. Ibid., 111.

31. Ibid., 110–116.

32. Ibid., 134. Italics in original.

33. Ibid., 135.

34. On the Buddha's visions in his "meditative trance" on the night of his "Awakening," see Gananath Obyeyeskere, *Imagining Karma* (Berkeley: University of California Press, 2002), 158. For the words of the Brahman, see *Ariyapariyesanā Sutta* 19–21, in *The Middle Discourses of the Buddha: A Translation of the Majjhima Nikāya,* trans. Bikkhu Bodhi (Boston: Wisdom, 1995), 261.

35. This is the well-known "Birth Story of the Dumb Cripple" (*Mugapakkha Jataka,* Ja.6.1ff., no. 538) as recounted and partly translated in Steven Collins, *Nirvana and Other Buddhist Felicities: Utopias of the Pali Imaginaire* (Cambridge: Cambridge University Press, 1998), 425–433. For a complete translation, see "The Story of Temiya, the Dumb Cripple," in *The Jatakas: Birth Stories of the Bodhisatta,* trans. Sarah Shaw (New Delhi: Penguin, 2006), 179–221.

36. Collins, *Nirvana,* 426.

37. Ibid., 430.

38. Ibid., 233–234.

39. Ibid., 417. The quote is from Peter Brown, *Authority and the Sacred: Aspects of the Christianisation of the Roman World* (Cambridge: Cambridge University Press, 1995), 53. It is worth noting that the "gentle violence" of which Brown speaks was inflicted by an empire that had become "Christian," just as "Buddhist" empires would do the same.

40. I know that there are those who don't consider meditation to be ritual and that the Buddha dismissed Vedic ritual as unhelpful. But in my terms, even private meditation, and surely communal meditation, is ritual. Anyone who has ever been in a Zendo would see that.

41. See Burghardt, *Genesis of Animal Play*, 393, on war as "the ultimate form of play" for many of the world's leaders.

42. Kant, *Power of Judgment*, sec. 43, 183.

43. Hans Joas, *The Creativity of Action* (Chicago: University of Chicago Press, 1996), 164–167, citing Donald W. Winnicott, *Playing and Reality* (Harmondsworth: Penguin, 1974).

44. George Herbert Mead, *Mind, Self, and Society* (Chicago: University of Chicago Press, 1934).

45. Joas, *The Creativity of Action*, 155.

46. John Dewey, *Art as Experience* (1934), in *John Dewey: The Late Works, 1925–1953*, vol. 10 (Carbondale: Southern Illinois University Press, 1987), 283.

47. Ibid., 284.

48. Mihaly Csikszentmihalyi, *Flow: The Psychology of Optimal Experience* (New York: Harper and Row, 1990), chap. 7.

49. Arlie Russell Hochschild, *The Time Bind: When Work Becomes Home and Home Becomes Work* (New York: Metropolitan Books, 1997).

50. Alison Gopnik, *The Philosophical Baby: What Children's Minds Tell Us about Truth, Love, and the Meaning of Life* (New York: Farrar, Straus and Giroux, 2009), 129.

51. Gopnik notes that flow is something unique to adults, whereas lantern consciousness is fundamental for babies but attainable under certain circumstances by adults. She gives the example of "open awareness" meditation by Zen monks who consciously seek to prevent spotlight consciousness so that they can be open to the whole undifferentiated world. Gopnik, *The Philosophical Baby*, 127–128. Interestingly Pierre Hadot has described similar practices among ancient Greek philosophers who tried to focus on the present moment alone, without any concern for past or future. The practice was common to Stoics and Epicureans, who otherwise differed on almost everything. He notes that for these thinkers, "The instant is our only point of contact with reality, yet it offers us the whole of reality," and he quotes Seneca describing that instant by saying, "For Seneca, the sage plunges himself into the whole of the universe *(toti se inserens mundo)*." Pierre Hadot, *Philosophy as a Way of Life* (Oxford: Blackwell, 1995), 229–230.

52. Gopnik, *The Philosophical Baby*, 130.

53. Josef Pieper, *Leisure, the Basis of Culture* (New York: Pantheon Books, 1964), 11. Because leisure, as Pieper uses the term, is the quintessential relaxed field, it clearly overlaps with the meaning of play. In fact Pieper's whole book could be seen as a meditation on play as discussed in this concluding chapter.

54. It could be that it is related to episodic consciousness in Donald's terms, which in Chapter 3 I have related to unitive consciousness.

55. Pierre Hadot, *What Is Ancient Philosophy?* (Cambridge, Mass.: Harvard University Press, 2002 [1995]), 78. My discussion of Aristotle draws heavily from Hadot's chapter on Aristotle in this book, 77–90.

56. Hadot, *What Is Ancient Philosophy?*, 82.

57. Aristotle, *De Partibus Animalium I and De Generatione Animalium,* trans. I. D. M. Balm (Oxford: Oxford University Press, 1972), 18, 645a.

58. Talcott Parsons, *Societies: Evolutionary and Comparative Perspectives* (Englewood Cliffs, N.J.: Prentice-Hall, 1966), chap. 6, 95–108.

59. The word "school," which has meant educational institutions through most of history, has taken on the secondary meaning of traditions of teaching, though in Plato's Academy and Aristotle's Lyceum the two meanings came together. Josef Pieper, however, in *Leisure,* chap. 4, reminds us that the root meaning of school, that is, *skole* in Greek or *scola* in Latin, is leisure. Leisure points to education as taking place in a relaxed field, as having an element of play. In our society, "school" has become the site of intense and sometimes cutthroat competition, so we may have difficulty in seeing it as "leisure." However, in most historical societies only a small minority went to "school"; the others went to work as soon as they were physically able. So education as leisure made sense. Even when it is democratized it still makes sense that education should take place in an atmosphere of leisure if its true purpose, human flourishing, is to be its result.

60. Probably Spinoza is the most famous of those expelled from the synagogue. He survived only because he had supporters in the non-Jewish community.

61. Thomas McCarthy, *Race, Empire, and the Idea of Human Development* (Cambridge: Cambridge University Press, 2009).

62. See McCarthy, *Race, Empire,* chap. 2, "Kant on Race and Development," 42–68.

63. Edward Said, *Orientalism* (New York: Pantheon Books, 1978).

64. Quotations from Mill, *On Liberty,* in McCarthy, *Race, Empire,* 168, 172, 180.

65. Ibid., 153.

66. See particularly ibid., the final chapter, 230–243.

67. Ibid., 241–242.

68. Ibid., 224–225. McCarthy has written a strikingly original book that is an extremely valuable resource for thinking about our current problems. But besides his indebtedness to Kant, of whom he is hardly uncritical, he draws significantly from Jürgen Habermas's discourse ethics, as he acknowledges.

69. Niles Eldredge, "The Sixth Extinction," actionbioscience.org/newfrontiers/eldredge2 .html, 1.

70. Ibid., 2.

71. Ibid., 3–4.

72. Ibid., 4–5.

73. Ibid., 5.

74. Stephen Jay Gould, *The Structure of Evolutionary Theory* (Cambridge, Mass.: Harvard University Press, 2002), 898.

75. For a fuller discussion of Weber's views on religion, see Robert N. Bellah, "Max Weber and World-Denying Love," in *The Robert Bellah Reader,* ed. Robert N. Bellah and Steven M. Tipton (Durham, N.C.: Duke University Press, 2007), 123–149.

76. Karl Jaspers, *The Origin and Goal of History* (London: Routledge and Kegan Paul, 1953 [1949]). For a recent, very useful interpretation of the axial age and its relevance to modernity, see Steven G. Smith, *Appeal and Attitude: Prospects for Ultimate Meaning* (Bloomington: Indiana University Press, 2005).

77. Wilfred Cantwell Smith, *Toward a World Theology* (Philadelphia: Westminster, 1981).

78. Charles Taylor, *A Secular Age* (Cambridge, Mass.: Harvard University Press, 2007).

79. Herbert Fingarette, *The Self in Transformation: Psychoanalysis, Philosophy, and the Life of the Spirit* (New York: Basic Books, 1963), 236–237. Can we see a special kind of "renouncer" in Fingarette?

80. McCarthy, *Race, Empire,* 223. Italics in the original.

81. Ibid., 187.

Index